WRITE SOURCE

A BOOK FOR WRITING, THINKING, AND LEARNING

Written and Compiled by

**Dave Kemper, Patrick Sebranek,
and Verne Meyer**

Illustrated by

Chris Krenzke

WRITE SOURCE®

GREAT SOURCE EDUCATION GROUP

a division of Houghton Mifflin Company
Wilmington, Massachusetts

Reviewers

Technology Connection for *Write Source*

Visit our Web site for additional student models, writing prompts, updates for citing sources, multimedia reports, information about submitting your writing, and more.

The Write Source Web site . . . . **www.thewritesource.com**

Printed in the United States of America

International Standard Book Number: 978-0-669-53134-3 (hardcover)
International Standard Book Number: 0-669-53134-0 (hardcover)

1 2 3 4 5 6 7 8 9 10 -DOC- 11 10 09 08 07 06

International Standard Book Number: 978-0-669-53138-1 (softcover)
International Standard Book Number: 0-669-53138-3 (softcover)

1 2 3 4 5 6 7 8 9 10 -DOC- 11 10 09 08 07 06

Using *Write Source*

Your **Write Source** book is loaded with information to help you learn about writing. One section that will be especially helpful is the "Proofreader's Guide" at the back of the book. This section covers the rules for language and grammar.

The book also includes four main units covering the types of writing that you may have to complete on district or state writing tests. In addition, a special section provides samples and tips for writing in science, social studies, math, the applied sciences, and the arts.

Write Source will help you with other learning skills, too—test taking, note taking, and making oral presentations. This makes *Write Source* a valuable writing and learning guide in all of your classes. (The **Quick Tour** on the next two pages highlights many of the key features in the book.)

Your *Write Source* guide . . .

With practice, you will be able to find information in this book quickly using the guides explained below.

- The **Table of Contents** (starting on page **vi**) lists the six major sections in the book and the chapters found in each section.
- The **Index** (starting on page **765**) lists the topics covered in the book in alphabetical order. Use the index when you are interested in a specific topic.
- The **Color Coding** used for "A Writer's Resource" (green), and the "Proofreader's Guide" (yellow) make these important sections easy to find. Colorful side tabs also provide a handy reference.
- **Page References** in the book tell you where to turn for additional information about a specific topic. *Example:* (See page **74**.)

If, at first, you're not sure how to find something in *Write Source*, ask your teacher for help. With a little practice, you will find everything quickly and easily.

A Quick Tour of *Write Source*

Write Source contains many key features that will help you improve your writing and language skills. Once you become familiar with this book, you will begin to understand how helpful these features can be.

Writing guidelines help you, step-by-step, to complete different forms of writings.

Checklists serve as effective revising and editing guides within the writing units.

Rubrics help you evaluate your finished pieces of writing. They also help to keep you on track during your writing.

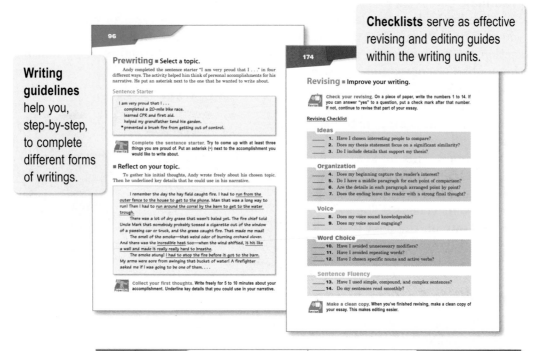

Analyzing a Theme 259

Response Essay

Gary Soto's short story, "The No-Guitar Blues," tells about a boy trying to collect enough money to buy a guitar. The response essay below analyzes the story's plot and character development to reveal the main theme.

260

Beginning
The beginning names the story and author and focuses on the theme (underlined).

Fausto's Guilt

In Gary Soto's short story, "The No-Guitar Blues," the main character, a teenage boy named Fausto, takes advantage of some rich folks. As a result, he is consumed by guilt. The story shows that deep down, people want to do the right thing.

The story begins with Fausto wanting to play guitar in his own band. He wonders how he can get a guitar. Soto uses idioms to illustrate that Fausto's family does not have a lot of money. For example, Fausto worries that if he asks for a guitar, his parents will say, "Money doesn't grow on trees," or "What do you think we are, bankers?" (56). When he does ask for a guitar, his mother replies, "Honey, a guitar costs a lot of money . . . but we'll see" (57).

Middle
Each middle paragraph explains a different stage in the development of the theme.

But Fausto is determined. He hops on a bike and rides north, away from his home near the vacant lot on Olive Street. In the nicer section of Fresno, he goes door-to-door searching for work, hoping to be paid enough to buy a guitar. The author says that Fausto only earns a "grimy, dirt-caked quarter" (58) and one juicy orange. Little does Fausto know that this orange will lead him straight into a lie.

As Fausto sits eating the orange, a sad-eyed dog comes along. Fausto begins feeding it orange slices. Fausto has an idea: "At that moment, a light came on inside Fausto's head" (59). He notices that the dog looks healthy and well fed. He spots a collar and tag, and he realizes that "Roger" probably belongs to rich people. The address is only six blocks away. This is when Fausto decides to tell a lie. He will say that he found Roger near the freeway, and maybe the owners will give him a reward big enough to buy a guitar.

Fausto feels guilty at the thought of lying. The guilt steadily builds. It increases as he stands on the porch knocking on the door. It gets worse as the man and woman

Middle
The last middle paragraph focuses on decisions that cause the main character to change.

of the house are nice and offer him turnovers to eat. The guilt is unbearable when the woman stuffs a $20 bill into Fausto's shirt pocket, a reward for rescuing Roger. Because of his guilt, Fausto tries to give the money back, but the couple insists that he take it. The man says, "You have to. You deserve it, believe me" (60). Fausto takes it. He starts up the street "like a zombie," saying under his breath, "Oh man, I shouldn't have lied" (60).

Now, Fausto has a choice to make; he can use the money for a guitar and continue to feel guilty, or he can find a way to get rid of his guilt. He thinks about going to confession, but confession hours are over. Instead, he goes to mass at Saint Theresa's Church. Fausto kneels, prays, and says some Hail Marys, but the guilt stays with him. He cannot stop thinking about lying to the folks who were so nice to him. Finally, when the wicker basket comes his way, Fausto drops the $20 bill inside. Almost immediately, he feels better. The guilt leaves him, and he concentrates on forgetting about the guitar.

Ending
The ending paragraph analyzes the theme.

Fausto has changed. He realizes now that it is wrong to act selfishly after something he wants, not caring about how it might affect others. As he thinks about the kindness of the man and woman and the guilt he felt, Fausto understands that it feels good to do the right thing. In the end, he gets his guitar. His mother gives him an old bass guitarron (an oversized guitar used in Mexican bands) that belonged to his grandfather. It is one of the happiest days of Fausto's life.

Respond to the reading. Answer the following questions about the sample response essay.

Ideas (1) How does the main character change by the end of the story? (2) Which detail in the analysis clearly reveals this theme?
Organization (3) How is the middle part of the response essay organized?
Voice & Word Choice (4) Does the writer sound knowledgeable about the story? Explain.

> The **writing samples** will stimulate you to write your own effective essays.

> **Graphic organizers** show you how to organize your ideas for writing.

Personal Narrative 97

Prewriting ■ Gather different types of details.

An effective personal narrative contains three types of details: *actions, sensory details,* and *personal thoughts.* Andy completed a chart to gather details for his narrative.

■ **Actions** relate what you (and others) did in a situation.
■ **Sensory details** show what you saw, smelled, heard, tasted, or touched.
■ **Personal thoughts** reveal what you thought during your experience.

Details Chart

Actions	Sensations	Thoughts
Checking fences	Smelled smoke; saw flames	Get help!
Spotted fire; ran to house to call 911	Tired legs	The fire could spread to the barn!
Called Uncle Mark	Listened to voice mail	I'm all alone!
Ran to corral/barn	Hard breathing; couldn't see in smoke	That hose won't reach far enough.
Grabbed water bucket; threw water on grass	Horses snorting; felt wall of heat from fire	This is scary!
Firefighters arrived	Sirens, flashing lights, aching arms	Relieved

Create a details chart. Refer to your freewriting on page 96 for the main details of your experience. Then fill in a chart like the one above with specific details about what you did, sensed, and thought.

■ **Focus on the traits.**

> **Ideas** Action is the skeleton of a narrative, but sensory details and thoughts are the muscles that keep it moving. Include all three types of details in your writing.

574

Comparison and Contrast

Organizing by comparison shows the similarities or differences between two subjects. To compare dairy farming of the past with that of today, one student used a Venn diagram. After organizing her details, she found that the two styles were more different than alike. Those differences are explained in her paragraph.

Venn Diagram

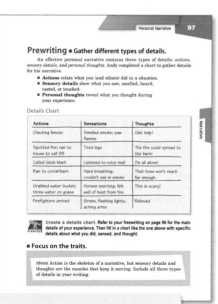

Topic Sentence / Body / Closing Sentence

Farming Then and Now

The family farm of the '50s had little in common with the modern dairy farm. Of course, dairy farms have always held sanitary conditions as a top priority, and farmers have always been at the mercy of both the weather and milk prices. The family farm gave way to farms owned by corporations and run by accountants. On the family farm, cows grazed rich pastures between milkings, while on modern farms, every inch of land is utilized for crops. That means many herds spend their lives in large barns or drylots (pens with no grass) with no room to roam. All feed and supplements were natural in the past, but today, hormones might be administered to promote milking three times a day rather than twice. Old-time farmers used individual milking machines: rubber cups suctioned the milk into a steel container. The machines were then emptied into a larger milk can, which was placed in a cooler until the milk truck came to pick it up. Today, the suction cups lead to sterile pipelines that run the milk directly into a large tank, which is then pumped into huge tanker trucks. Farming today is less of a personal relationship between farmer and animal and more of an efficient business.

> **Links to the traits** help you appreciate the importance of different traits at different points in the writing process.

contents

The Writing Process

The Forms of Writing

NARRATIVE WRITING

contents

EXPOSITORY WRITING

PERSUASIVE WRITING

contents

RESPONSE TO LITERATURE

CREATIVE WRITING

contents

RESEARCH WRITING

WRITING ACROSS THE CURRICULUM

contents

Tools of Learning

contents

Basic Elements of Writing

A Writer's Resource

contents

Proofreader's Guide

Why Write?

Have you ever seen pictures of primitive cave drawings? These drawings suggest that since the earliest times, human beings have felt the need to record their experiences, to describe their lives, and to show what is important to them.

Perhaps you have felt the same need to record your thoughts, feelings, and experiences. Today, though, instead of crawling into a cave with a hunk of charcoal, you can stay right where you are. All you need is a pencil, a piece of paper, and the endless thoughts that tumble through your head.

This chapter addresses the question "Why write?" It also explores other basic questions you may have about writing and provides many answers. Maybe your own personal answer to the question "Why write?" will be like that of writer Anne Lamott: "The act of writing turns out to be its own reward."

- **Reasons to Write**
- **Getting Started**
- **Using a Writer's Notebook**

"Writing is not apart from living. Writing is a kind of double living."
—Catherine Drinker Bowen

Reasons to Write

In his book *Writing Reminders*, writing teacher Jim Burke says, "In the act of composing, writers learn about themselves and their world and communicate their insights to others." In one sentence, Mr. Burke has answered the question "Why write?" in many ways. The rest of this page helps analyze the ideas in that one sentence.

Writing helps you . . .

Learn more about yourself.

Writing lets you look deep within yourself, sometimes with surprising results. When you keep a writer's notebook of your thoughts and feelings, you may, as you read your entries later, see yourself in a whole new light.

Learn more about your world.

By recording observations of the world around you (what you hear and see and sense), you can learn from the events that shape you. Your observations also serve as a fascinating record of your time in history. Finally, writing about your classes helps you remember and make sense of what you are learning.

Share your ideas and insights.

Sometimes writing is the best way to share your thoughts with others. Unlike conversation, writing gives you time to decide exactly what you want to say before anyone else "hears" it.

Express what you know.

Writing actually helps you become a better thinker. It lets you review what you already know, reflect on it, and add new thoughts. Think of writing as exercise for your mind.

Tip

Remember, writing is a skill. As with all other skills, the more you practice, the better you will become.

Write to learn. Think of the most important piece of writing you have ever completed. Write freely for 5 minutes about this piece, exploring why it was important to you.

Getting Started

Think of writing as a skill. Just as you set aside time to improve your musical or athletic skills, do the same with writing. Exercise your mind as well as your body. Keep sharp as well as in shape. Improvement will come if you make an honest effort.

Where should I write?

Write in school. Here are ways you can write throughout your school day:

- Take classroom notes.
- Keep a learning log in each of your classes.
- Complete writing assignments and papers.

Write at home. Writing in your spare time can help you gain fluency—the ability to write quickly and easily. Here are ways to write at home:

- Write e-mail messages and letters.
- Keep a writer's notebook. (See pages **4–5**.)
- Create short stories and poems.

Write wherever you are. Write in a car, on the bus, or on the subway. In her book *Writing Down the Bones*, Natalie Goldberg suggests that you write wherever you feel comfortable.

What should I write about?

You can write about anything and everything. The more you write, the more you learn. Here are just a few things you can write about:

- **Observations:** What is happening around you right now? What do you think about what is happening?
- **Memories:** What was the best moment of your day? Your week? Your year? What was the worst moment?
- **Hopes and dreams:** What do you want in life? What do you wish for your future?
- **People:** What person means the most to you? What person do you admire? What sort of person do you not understand?
- **Places:** Where are you right now? Where do you wish you were? Where do you never want to be again?
- **Things:** What is your favorite possession? Your least favorite? What one invention would you like to outlaw, and why?

 Write freely for 5 to 10 minutes using one of the ideas listed above as a starting point. Then read what you have written and circle at least two ideas that interest you or surprise you.

Using a Writer's Notebook

Your most powerful writing tool can be a notebook reserved exclusively for daily writing. A **writer's notebook** (also called a *journal*) is a place to record your thoughts on any topic. As you write regularly in your notebook, you will make countless discoveries about your world.

In his book *Breathing In, Breathing Out: Keeping a Writer's Notebook*, Ralph Fletcher compares a writer's notebook to a compost heap. Over time, all the cuttings and leftovers that a gardener composts turn into rich fertilizer. In the same way, all the thoughts and feelings that you record can turn into useful starting points for your future writing.

■ Ensure success.

To make sure that your writer's notebook is a success, consider the quantity, quality, and variety of your entries. Also follow the rules at the bottom of the page.

- **Quantity:** Teachers often require a certain number of pages or entries per grading period. Know your teacher's expectations for your notebook.
- **Quality:** Approach each entry with a high level of enthusiasm and interest. Develop your ideas fully with sensory, memory, and reflective details.
- **Variety:** Write some of your entries from different points of view. For example, after an argument with a friend, write about it from your friend's point of view, or from the perspective of someone who overheard the argument.

Rules for a Writer's Notebook

- **Date each entry.** The date on an entry helps you find it later and puts it in perspective with other entries.
- **Write freely.** Don't worry about producing perfect copy. Just get your ideas on paper.
- **Write regularly.** Develop the habit of writing daily.
- **Reflect on your work.** Reread your entries to consider the discoveries you have made and to look for writing ideas.

Process

■ Take it personally.

Here is a page, from a student writer's notebook, that focuses on both the writer's past and on a favorite pair of shoes. This entry does a lot of important things. It . . .

- ■ captures a moment in time,
- ■ describes something that is important to the writer,
- ■ starts with a "seed idea" (a worn-out pair of shoes), and
- ■ reflects on the writer's life.

Sample Notebook Entry

February 6, 2006

While cleaning out my closet, I came across my favorite pair of sneakers from seventh grade. They seemed out of place among my heels, cross-trainers, and boots. They look awful, old and cracked, and the laces are done for. But they bring back so many memories.

I remember opening the box they came in. I was so excited to have cool new shoes. I wanted to go to school so that I could show them off.

I remember wearing them as I ran to the bus, late as usual, thinking that my new shoes helped me run faster. I also remember wearing them when I waded through the icy water in a tunnel that ran under the road. I didn't think my feet would ever feel warm again! I put those shoes through a lot.

I'm sad to throw them away. It's like saying good-bye to an old friend. I'll never forget them or the person I was when I wore them. Hmm. I wonder what adventures I'll remember when my new cross-trainers look like these old friends.

Remember: Keeping a writer's notebook lets you look at ordinary things in new ways, describe your feelings, choose good descriptive words, and practice writing until you feel confident.

Write a quick reflection. Think about an object that was once very important to you. Write freely for 5 to 10 minutes about that object and what it meant—and still means—to you.

6

Using the Writing Process

Understanding the Writing Process

Skilled athletes work very hard to perform at a high level. They train individually, practice with their teams, compete, assess their performances, and consult with their peers and coaches. To do their best, athletes must repeat this process again and again.

Skilled writers also follow a process. For specific projects, they gather and organize their thoughts (prewriting), connect their ideas on paper (writing), make changes as needed (revising and editing), and assess and share their finished copy (publishing). To do their best work, writers must address these steps for each piece they develop.

This chapter will help you learn the writing process and build some valuable writing habits at the same time.

- **Building Good Writing Habits**
- **Understanding the Writing Process**
- **The Process in Action**
- **Focusing on the Traits**

"What is written without effort is in general read without pleasure."
—Dr. Samuel Johnson

Building Good Writing Habits

Writing success begins with good writing habits. Follow the tips below and you will see real improvement in your writing.

When to Write

Set aside time each day to write. Regular writing will help you develop fluency—the ability to write quickly and easily.

"When I am working on a book or a story, I write every morning as soon after the first light as possible."

—Ernest Hemingway

Where to Write

Write in school and at home. Write on the bus or in a coffee shop. Just keep writing wherever you can.

"I type in one place, but I write all over the house."

—Toni Morrison

What to Write

Write about anything and everything that interests you—personal experiences, current events, music, books, or sports.

"Most of the basic material a writer works with is acquired before the age of fifteen."

—Willa Cather

How to Write

Relax and let the words flow. Share your true feelings and, before long, your distinctive writing voice will develop.

"Any writer overwhelmingly honest about pleasing himself is almost sure to please others."

—Marianne Moore

 Write about your day. Think about something that has happened to you today. Write nonstop for 5 to 10 minutes about this experience. Let the words flow freely! Afterward, underline any thoughts or ideas that surprise you.

Understanding the Writing Process

Before a piece of writing is ready to share, it should have gone through a series of steps called the *writing process*. This page contains brief descriptions of these steps.

The Steps in the Writing Process

Prewriting

The first step in the writing process involves selecting a specific topic, gathering details about it, and organizing those details into a writing plan.

Writing

During this step, the writer completes the first draft using the prewriting plan as a guide. This draft is a writer's *first* chance to get everything on paper.

Revising

During revising, the writer first reviews the draft for five key traits: ***ideas, organization, voice, word choice,*** and ***sentence fluency.*** After deciding what changes to make, the writer deletes, moves, adds to, and rewrites parts of the text.

Editing

Then the writer edits the revised draft for the ***conventions*** of punctuation, capitalization, spelling, and grammar. A writer should also proofread the final copy before sharing it.

Publishing

This is the final step in the writing process. Publishing is the writer's opportunity to share his or her work with others.

Analyze your process. Which step in the writing process is easiest for you? Which step is hardest, and why? Explain one way to make that step easier for yourself.

The Process in Action

The next two pages give a detailed description of each step in the writing process. The graphic below reminds you that, at any time, you can move back and forth between the steps in the writing process. Be aware that if you put more effort and care into the early stages of the process, you'll move through the later stages more easily.

Prewriting ▪ Select a topic.

- ▪ Search for topics that meet the requirements of the assignment.
- ▪ Select a specific topic that appeals to you.

▪ Gather and organize details.

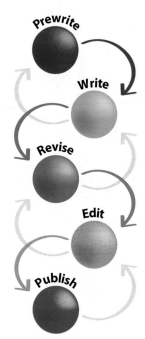

- ▪ Gather as many ideas and details as you can about the topic.
- ▪ With the purpose of the assignment in mind, find one point to emphasize about the topic—either an interesting part or your personal feeling about it. This will be the focus, or thesis, of your writing.
- ▪ Decide which details to include in your writing.
- ▪ Organize your details into a writing plan, perhaps using an outline or a chart.

Writing ▪ Develop the first draft.

- ▪ When writing the first draft, concentrate on getting your ideas on paper. Don't try to produce a perfect piece of writing.
- ▪ Use the details you collected and your prewriting plan as a guide, but feel free to add new ideas and details as you go along.
- ▪ Make sure your writing has a beginning, a middle, and an ending.

Tip

Write on every *other* line and on only *one* side of the paper when using pen or pencil and paper. Double-space on a computer. This will give you room for revising, the next step in the process.

Process

Revising ■ Improve your writing.

- Set aside your first draft for a while so you can return to it with a fresh perspective.
- Read your first draft slowly and critically.
- Use these questions as a revising guide:
  - Is my topic interesting for the reader?
  - Does the beginning catch the reader's attention?
  - Are the ideas in order and easy to understand?
  - Have I included enough details to support my central idea?
  - Does the ending leave the reader with something to think about?
  - Do I sound interested in, and knowledgeable about, the topic?
  - Are the nouns specific and the verbs active?
  - Are the modifiers (adjectives and adverbs) clear and descriptive?
  - Does the whole piece read smoothly?
- Ask at least one other person to review your writing and give suggestions.
- Make as many changes as necessary to improve your writing.

Editing ■ Check for conventions.

- Check for errors in punctuation, capitalization, spelling, and grammar.
- Have at least one other person check your writing for errors.
- Prepare a neat final copy.
- Proofread the final copy before publishing it.

Publishing ■ Share your writing.

- Share your writing with friends, classmates, and family.
- Consider submitting your writing to a newspaper or other publication.
- Also consider including the writing in your portfolio.

Tip

For assignments, save all your work. Refer to your original writing and to the teacher's comments on the graded piece for ideas and inspiration for future writing projects.

 Consider the process. Think about a recent writing assignment. Did you go through a process like the one explained on these two pages? Write about the differences between the process you followed and this one.

Focusing on the Traits

Writing is complicated, so you can't focus on everything at once. For example, you can't check punctuation and the effectiveness of your beginning and ending paragraphs at the same time. The writing process lets you focus on the different traits of good writing at different times. (See pages **39–54**.)

Connect the traits to the writing process.

Prewrite

Ideas	What topic should I write about? What part of the topic should I focus on? What details should I include?
Organization	How should I organize my details? Which graphic organizer should I use for my planning?
Voice	What is my attitude about the topic?

Write

Ideas	What do I want to say?
Organization	How do I want to arrange my ideas?
Voice	How do I want to sound?

Revise

Ideas	Are my ideas clear and complete?
Organization	Do my beginning, middle, and ending work well?
Voice	Did I create an appropriate tone?
Word Choice	Have I chosen specific nouns and active verbs?
Sentence Fluency	Are my sentences varied? Do they read smoothly?

Edit

Conventions	Have I used correct punctuation, capitalization, spelling, and grammar?

Publish

Ideas, Organization, Voice, Word Choice, Sentence Fluency, Conventions What do you think of my work?

Try It!

Reflect on the traits. Answer the following questions:

1. Which trait is it easiest for you to work with? Explain.
2. Which trait is it hardest for you to work with? Explain.

One Writer's Process

Every writer approaches writing differently, but the best writers have this in common: They approach writing as a process. Step-by-step, they show that they care not only about their topic but also about the writing itself.

This chapter shows how student writer Dario Ramirez used the steps in the writing process to develop an expository essay about computer graphics (CG) used in films. As you follow his work, you'll see how he shaped his initial ideas into an effective piece of writing.

- **Previewing the Goals**
- **Prewriting**
- **Writing**
- **Revising**
- **Editing**
- **Publishing**
- **Assessing the Final Copy**
- **Reflecting on Your Writing**

"Easy writing makes hard reading, but hard writing makes easy reading."

—Florence King

Previewing the Goals

Before Dario Ramirez began writing his essay, he previewed the goals for expository writing, which are shown below. Dario also looked over the rubric for expository writing on pages 180–181. Both of these activities helped him get started.

TRAITS OF EXPOSITORY WRITING

- **Ideas**
  Select a specific topic that captures your interest. Create and support a thesis statement that explores an important part of the topic.

- **Organization**
  Organize your essay's ideas into three main parts—beginning, middle, and ending—and connect them smoothly.

- **Voice**
  Use words and details that fit the audience and the purpose of your writing.

- **Word Choice**
  Choose precise words that clearly explain your topic.

- **Sentence Fluency**
  Use a variety of sentences that connect your ideas smoothly.

- **Conventions**
  Use punctuation, mechanics, and grammar properly.

Try It!

Answer the following questions about the goals of Dario's assignment:

1. What must Dario remember when selecting a topic?
2. What should the thesis statement do?
3. What must Dario remember about voice?

Prewriting ■ Select a topic.

Dario's teacher wrote this expository writing prompt on the board.

> ### Explain how technology affects...
>
> | | | | |
> |---|---|---|---|
> | Publishing | Movies | Live Drama | TV |
> | Periodicals | Music | Comic Books | Art |

Dario wrote down several of the suggested subjects and listed ways that technology had affected each one. When he found the specific topic that interested him, he underlined it.

> Publishing (e-books, books on CD)   Music (P2P file sharing, videos)
>
> TV (VCR/DVD, DVD collections)   Movies (digital filming, CG)

■ Reflect on the topic.

Dario did some freewriting in his journal to think about his topic.

> I want to write about movies. My cousin Luis is studying film and CG animation, and he takes me to the movies whenever he visits. When we see a movie on DVD, Luis tells me about moviemaking techniques while we watch it. Now I even watch for those special features on my own.
>
> With CG, movies have much better-looking aliens, ghosts, and special effects than they used to. Luis told me that Gladiator had a lot of CG to make the buildings. He also said the last Spider-Man movie we saw had a huge amount of CG action. I loved the dinosaurs in the Jurassic Park movies—they were incredibly realistic.

Try It!

Freewrite for 10 minutes on one of the other topics above. Write about why the topic interests you and how you would write about it.

Prewriting ■ Gather details.

Dario went to the library and looked for details about computer graphics (CG) in books, in magazines, and on the Internet. He used search engines and keywords like "CG," "CGI," and "special effects."

Sources of Information

To keep track of his research, Dario recorded complete source information on note cards.

> Richard Rickitt. Special Effects: The History & Technique. Watson-Guptill. New York, 2000.

> Anne Thompson. "F/X Gods: The 10 Visual-Effects Wizards Who Rule Hollywood." WIRED. February 2005. Pages 8-15. Visited online April 20, 2005. http://wired-vig.wired.com/wired/archive/13.02/fxgods_pr.html

Quotations and Paraphrases

During his research, Dario recorded quotations and paraphrases. Dario's teacher asked students to use quotations or paraphrases from at least two sources.

Quotation

> "People didn't go to The Day After Tomorrow because of the acting, directing, and writing," says Scott Ross of Digital Domain. "They went to see New York flooded and L.A. ripped apart by a twister."
> Source: Thompson, "F/X Gods," p.10.

Paraphrase

> Lucasfilm made the first CGI character—a knight made of stained glass—for Young Sherlock Holmes in 1985.
> Source: Carlson, "CGI Historical Time Line," http://accad.osu.edu/~waynec/history/timeline.html

Try It!

What keywords would you use to locate information about the topic that you explored on page 15? Find one book and one magazine that contain information on the topic.

■ Form a thesis statement.

Once Dario had enough information, he was ready to write a *thesis statement* for his essay. (A thesis statement identifies the focus of the writing.) An effective thesis statement consists of two parts: a specific topic plus a particular feeling or opinion about it. Dario used the formula below to write his thesis.

A specific topic + a particular feeling = **an effective thesis statement.**

Dario's thesis statement

> CG (specific topic) **allows filmmakers to show things in the movies that people could only imagine before** (particular feeling).

■ Organize the essay.

Next, Dario wrote a topic outline for the body of his essay. This step organized the details that supported his thesis.

Dario's Outline

Thesis statement: CG allows filmmakers to show things in the movies that people could only imagine before.

  I. Creates totally imaginary characters
    A. Stained-glass knight, Young Sherlock Holmes
    B. Dinosaurs in Jurassic Park
    C. Gollum (Andy Serkis), The Two Towers
    D. Aliens, Attack of the Clones
 II. Creates totally imaginary settings
    A. Ancient Rome & coliseum in Gladiator
    B. Looking down at rocket in Apollo 13
    C. Seeing inside and around tornadoes in Twister
III. Creates dangerous effects
    A. Tidal waves—Deep Impact
    B. Fire & lava effects—Dante's Peak
    C. Entire armies using just a few people—Return of the King
 IV. Can overwhelm a film
    A. Too much CG doesn't help story—Ross quote
    B. Spielberg quote about Jaws and CG shark

Writing ■ Develop your first draft.

Dario referred to his outline as he wrote his first draft. At this point, he needed to get all his ideas on paper and not worry about getting everything just right.

■ Dario's First Draft

The first paragraph introduces the topic and ends with the thesis statement.

Each middle paragraph covers one part of the topic.

Sources of information are given in parentheses.

The Sky's Not the Limit

I would always laugh at the older stuff they used for special effects on film. They used model buildings. They used hand-drawn cartoons. They used stop-motion animation. Still, the effects never seem real enough. In the last twenty years, however CG has made it possible to create special effects in movies. CG allows filmmakers to show things in the movies that people could only imagine before.

CG can create totally imaginary characters that look real. An early example is a knight coming through a stained-glass window in Young Sherlock Holmes. Later on, CG showed us the amazing dinosaurs of Jurassic Park. Motion-capture suits allow actors to help animate a CG character. The voice and acting of Andy Serkis combined with CG to create the incredible character of Gollum (The Two Towers). Today, CG often replaces older special effects. Yoda, a mere puppet in the original, is an example of this. Now, even the most fantastic creatures in science fiction can seem real in the movies.

CG also allows film makers to tell the stories they want. CG animaters can rebuild old cities the way they were long ago. They made the coliseum of ancient Rome in Gladiator. Computers even let film makers look at stuff in new ways, like watching a rocket blast off from overhead (Apollo 13). Film makers can change little things in a setting to add interest, like creating laser bolts and light sabers.

In addition, CG lets film makers create dangerous effects such as an erupting volcano or a tidal wave. Nobody gets hurt and nothing gets damaged, since it's all in the computer. CG can even create an awesome army on the battlefield from only a few figures. They save millions of dollars by not hiring tons of actors. CG can show stuff too dangerous to shoot before.

CG makes movies better, usually. But it can easily overwhelm a film. Scott Ross of Digital Domain says they saw The Day After Tomorrow "to see New York flooded and L.A. ripped apart by a twister" (Thompson 84). In fact, some of the best movies use your mind to complete what you don't see. In the movie Jaws, the excitement comes from not seeing the shark. Director Steven Spielberg admits "The shark would be fully CG" today and it wouldn't be a better movie" (Westbrook 8). CG leaves nothing to the imagination, and that can ruin a movie. CG can't make a movie alone.

Computers let directors make movies with imaginary people, places, and effects. The only limits with CG now are the filmmakers' imaginations. Most directors balance CG effects with stories. Steven Spielberg states, "We must rescue ourselves from indulging in the technology we now have. . . . CG is just another tool—a means to an end. It shouldn't be an end itself" (Westbrook 8). CG can't replace a story, but it can help make it great.

Direct quotations are used.

The ending paragraph sums up the topic and provides one last thought.

Try It!

Look through Dario's outline and first draft. Then answer these questions. Does Dario's first draft contain all the details from his outline (page **17**)? Does he add any new details? If so, what are they? What other movies could Dario have included in his discussion? Try to name at least one.

Revising ■ Improve the writing.

After Dario completed his first draft, he set aside his essay for a day. Then he rechecked the goals on page **14** before reviewing his first draft. Dario's thoughts below reveal the changes he planned to make.

Ideas

Select a specific topic that captures your interest. Create and support a thesis statement that explores an important part of the topic.

"I've included my basic ideas, but some of them don't fit my thesis statement. I also need more details to support my main points."

Organization

Organize your essay's ideas into three main parts—beginning, middle, and ending—and connect them smoothly.

"My middle is weak. I need more examples to illustrate my ideas. I also need more transitions."

Voice

Use words and details that fit the audience and the purpose of your writing.

"I need to use third person (he/she/they) instead of first person (I/we) to sound more objective. I need a stronger opening statement to sound more confident about my topic."

Try It!

Choose a classmate to be your partner. Together, review the changes in Dario's first revision on page **21**. What other changes in ideas, organization, or voice would you make to Dario's essay? Try to name two.

■ Dario's First Revision

Here are the revisions that Dario made in the first part of his essay.

The voice in the opening sentence is made more formal. A technical abbreviation is defined.

Ever since people began making movies, filmmakers
~~I would always laugh at the older stuff they used for~~
have tried to put imaginary things
~~special effects~~ on film. They used model buildings. They used hand-drawn cartoons. They used stop-motion animation.

Still, the effects never seem real enough. In the last twenty
    computer graphics (CG)
years, however, ~~CG~~ has made it possible to create special effects in movies. CG allows filmmakers to show things in the movies that people could only imagine before.

CG can create totally imaginary characters that look real. An early example is a knight coming through a stained-glass window in <u>Young Sherlock Holmes</u>. Later on, CG showed

Unnecessary details that do not support the topic sentence are deleted.

us the amazing dinosaurs of <u>Jurassic Park</u>. ~~Motion-capture suits allow actors to help animate a CG character.~~ The voice and acting of Andy Serkis combined with CG to create the incredible character of Gollum (<u>The Two Towers</u>). Today, CG often replaces older special effects. Yoda, a mere puppet
    The Empire Strikes Back
in ~~the original~~, is an example of this. Now, even the most fantastic creatures in science fiction can seem real in the movies.

Details that show the writer's knowledge of the subject are added.

CG also allows film makers to tell the stories they want. CG animaters can rebuild old cities the way they were long
                    look very authentic   the movie
ago. They made the coliseum of ancient Rome in Gladiator. Computers even let film makers look at stuff in new ways, like
        or seeing inside a tornado (Twister)
watching a rocket blast off from overhead (<u>Apollo 13</u>).

Revising ■ Use a peer response sheet.

Christine evaluated Dario's essay using a rubric like the one on pages 180–181. Her suggestions on the response sheet below showed Dario where he could make additional improvements.

Peer Response Sheet

Writer: Dario Ramirez   Responder: Christine Whitney

Title: The Sky's Not the Limit

What I liked about your writing:

• You chose an interesting topic.

• You show that you really know a lot about movies and CG.

• You cover your topic well, from characters to settings to story actions.

Changes I would suggest:

• I don't know all the movies you mentioned in the second paragraph. Could you add dates to show us when these movies were made?

• Could you come up with a more specific topic sentence in the third paragraph? What keeps filmmakers from telling their stories?

Try It!

Review Christine's suggestions for improvement above. Which suggestion seems to be the most important? Explain why. Add at least one new suggestion to improve Dario's writing. Look at the explanations of ideas, organization, and voice on page **20** to help you make that suggestion.

Process

■ Dario's Revision Using a Peer Response

Using Christine's comments, Dario revised his essay again. The changes that he made in three middle paragraphs are shown here.

> Dates of the movies are added for clarity.

CG can create totally imaginary characters that look real. An early example is a knight coming through a stained-glass window in Young Sherlock Holmes (1985). Later on, CG showed us the amazing dinosaurs of Jurassic Park (1993). The voice and acting of Andy Serkis combined with CG to create the incredible character of Gollum (The Two Towers) 2002. Today, CG often replaces older special effects. Yoda, a mere puppet in The Empire Strikes Back (1980) ~~is an example of this~~ is CG in the new movies of a series. Now, even the most fantastic creatures in science fiction can seem real in the movies.

> The topic sentence is improved.

CG also allows film makers to tell ~~the~~ stories wherever and however they want. CG animaters can rebuild old cities the way they were long ago. They made the coliseum of ancient Rome look very authentic in the movie Gladiator (2000). ~~Computers even let~~ film makers use CG to look at stuff in new ways, like watching a rocket blast off from overhead (Apollo 13) 1995 or seeing what it looks like inside a tornado (Twister) 1996. Film makers can change little things in a setting to add interest, like creating laser bolts and light sabers (Attack of the Clones) 2002.

> Ideas are made more specific and clear.

> Specific details are added.

In addition, CG lets film makers create dangerous effects such as a rampaging forest fire, an erupting volcano or even a tidal wave swallowing New York City (Deep Impact, 1998). Nobody gets hurt and nothing gets damaged. CG can even create an awesome army on the . . .

Revising ■ Focus on style.

Dario also reviewed his writing for its flow and style. His thoughts below tell you what changes he planned to make.

Word Choice

Choose precise words that clearly explain your topic.

"I should use more technical terms to improve the level of language. I also want to add more exciting verbs and modifiers."

Sentence Fluency

Use a variety of sentences that connect your ideas smoothly.

"I need to combine some of my choppy sentences in order to create a better flow in the text."

Try It!

Review Dario's improved essay on page **23**. What other changes in word choice could he make? Name one or two. What other changes could he make to improve the sentence fluency? Name one.

■ Dario's Improvements in Style

Dario next reviewed the style and sound of his writing. He focused on improving his word choice and sentence structure.

Combining sentences improves sentence fluency.

Ever since people began making movies, filmmakers have tried to put imaginary things on film. They used model buildings. ~~They used~~ hand-drawn cartoons. *and* ~~They used~~ stop-motion animation. Still, the effects never seem real enough. In the last twenty years, however computer graphics (CG) has made it possible to create *realistic* special effects in movies. CG allows filmmakers to show things ~~in the movies~~ *on-screen* that people could only imagine before.

Word choice is improved.

CG can create totally imaginary characters that look real. An early example is a knight ~~coming~~ *crashing* through a stained-glass window in Young Sherlock Holmes (1985). Later on, CG showed us ~~the amazing~~ dinosaurs ~~of~~ *in* Jurassic Park (1993). *More recently,* The voice and acting of Andy Serkis combined with CG to create the incredible character of Gollum (The Two Towers, 2002). Today, CG ~~often~~ *even* replaces older special effects *technologies* in new movies of a series. Yoda, a mere puppet in The Empire Strikes Back (1980), is CG in the new movies. Now, even the most fantastic creatures *from folklore to* ~~in~~ science fiction can seem real *on-screen.* ~~in the movies.~~

Transitions make the sentences flow more smoothly.

CG also allows film makers to tell stories wherever and however they want. *For instance,* CG animaters can rebuild old cities the way they were long ago. They made the coliseum of ancient Rome look very authentic in the movie Gladiator (2000). *In addition,* Film . . .

Editing ■ Check for conventions.

Finally, Dario was ready to edit his essay. He checked his work for punctuation, capitalization, spelling, and grammar errors.

Editing Checklist

Conventions

Use punctuation, mechanics, and grammar properly.

"I'll look carefully at my essay for punctuation, capitalization, spelling, and grammar errors."

For help with conventions, Dario used the "Proofreader's Guide" in the back of his *Write Source* textbook and the checklist below.

PUNCTUATION

_____ **1.** Do I use end punctuation correctly?

_____ **2.** Do I use commas correctly?

_____ **3.** Do I correctly italicize or use quotation marks for titles?

_____ **4.** Do I use apostrophes correctly?

MECHANICS (Capitalization and Spelling)

_____ **5.** Have I capitalized all the proper nouns and adjectives?

_____ **6.** Have I spelled words correctly?

_____ **7.** Have I used the spell-checker on my computer?

_____ **8.** Have I double-checked words my spell-checker may have missed?

GRAMMAR

_____ **9.** Do I use the proper tense and voice for my verbs?

_____ **10.** Do my subjects and verbs agree in number?

_____ **11.** Do my pronouns clearly agree with their antecedents?

DOCUMENTATION

_____ **12.** Are sources properly presented and documented?

Try It!

Find three or four errors in Dario's revised draft on page **25**. Did you find the same errors as Dario found (on page **27**)?

Dario's Editing

Here is Dario's editing for the first part of his essay. (See the inside back cover of this textbook for common editing and proofreading marks.)

A verb-tense error, a number, and a punctuation error are corrected.

Ever since people began making movies, filmmakers have tried to put imaginary things on film. They used model buildings, hand-drawn cartoons, and stop-motion animation. Still, the effects never ~~seem~~ *seemed* real enough. In the last ~~twenty~~ *20* years, however, computer graphics (CG) has made it possible to create realistic special effects in movies. CG allows filmmakers to show things on-screen that people could only imagine before.

CG can create totally imaginary characters that look real. An early example is a knight crashing through a stained-glass window in Young Sherlock Holmes (1985). Later on,

A spelling error and a punctuation error are corrected.

CG showed us ~~believeable~~ *believable* dinosaurs in Jurassic Park (1993). More recently, the voice and acting of Andy Serkis combined with CG to create the incredible character of Gollum (The Two Towers, 2002). Today, CG even replaces older special effects technologies in new movies of a series. Yoda, a mere puppet in The Empire Strikes Back (1980), is CG in the new movies. Now, even the most fantastic creatures from folklore to science fiction can seem real on-screen.

Additional spelling errors are corrected.

CG also allows film makers to tell stories wherever and however they want. For instance, CG ~~animaters~~ *animators* can rebuild old cities the way they were long ago. They made the ~~coliseum~~ *Colosseum* of ancient Rome look very authentic in the movie . . .

Publishing ▪ Share your writing.

Dario used the information below to produce a clean and effective copy of his final essay.

Tips for Handwritten Copies

- Use blue or black ink and write clearly.
- Write your name according to your teacher's instructions.
- Skip a line and center your title on the first page; skip another line and begin your essay.
- Indent each paragraph and leave a one-inch margin on all four sides.

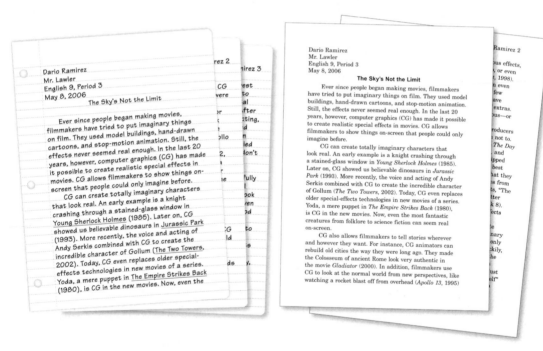

Tips for Computer Copies

- Use an easy-to-read font set at a 10- or 12-point type size.
- Double-space the text and set your margins so that you have a one-inch space around the outside of each page.
- For more tips on using a computer, see pages **33–38**.

■ Dario's Final Copy

Dario proudly presented a printed copy of his essay to Mr. Lawler and volunteered to share his writing about movies with the class.

Dario Ramirez
Mr. Lawler
English 9, Period 3
May 8, 2006

The Sky's Not the Limit

Ever since people began making movies, filmmakers have tried to put imaginary things on film. They used model buildings, hand-drawn cartoons, and stop-motion animation. Still, the effects never seemed real enough. In the last 20 years, however, computer graphics (CG) has made it possible to create realistic special effects in movies. CG allows filmmakers to show things on-screen that people could only imagine before.

CG can create totally imaginary characters that look real. An early example is a knight crashing through a stained-glass window in *Young Sherlock Holmes* (1985). Later on, CG showed us believable dinosaurs in *Jurassic Park* (1993). More recently, the voice and acting of Andy Serkis combined with CG to create the incredible character of Gollum (*The Two Towers,* 2002). Today, CG even replaces older special-effects technologies in new movies of a series. Yoda, a mere puppet in *The Empire Strikes Back* (1980), is CG in the new movies. Now, even the most fantastic creatures from folklore to science fiction can seem real on-screen.

CG also allows filmmakers to tell stories wherever and however they want. For instance, CG animators can rebuild old cities the way they were long ago. They made the Colosseum of ancient Rome look very authentic in the movie *Gladiator* (2000). In addition, filmmakers use CG to look at the normal world from new perspectives, like watching a rocket blast off from overhead (*Apollo 13,* 1995) or seeing what it looks like inside a tornado (*Twister,* 1996). Filmmakers can change little things in a setting to add interest, too, like creating laser bolts and light sabers (*Attack of the Clones,* 2002).

In addition, CG lets filmmakers create dangerous effects, such as a rampaging forest fire, an erupting volcano, or even a tidal wave swallowing New York City (*Deep Impact,* 1998). Nobody gets hurt, and nothing gets damaged. CG can even create a realistic army on the battlefield from only a few figures (*The Return of the King,* 2003). Filmmakers save millions of dollars by not having to hire thousands of extras. With CG, people can see stories that were too dangerous—or impossible—to shoot before.

CG definitely enhances many movies. The best producers and directors, though, know when to use it—and when not to. Scott Ross of Digital Domain says, "People didn't go to *The Day After Tomorrow* [2004] because of the acting, directing, and writing. They went to see New York flooded and L.A. ripped apart by a twister" (Thompson 84). In fact, some of the best movies have relied on the viewers' minds to complete what they don't see. In the movie *Jaws* (1975), the excitement comes from rarely seeing the shark. Director Steven Spielberg admits, "The shark would be fully CG" today, and "it wouldn't be a better movie. I would have used the shark too much" (Westbrook 8). Fortunately, most audiences realize that even cool CG effects can't tell a story or make a good movie by themselves.

Computers provide new tools for filmmakers to create movies they never could attempt before. CG creates imaginary people, places, and effects that seem totally realistic. The only limits with CG now are the filmmakers' imaginations. Luckily, most directors know they should balance CG effects with the stories. Steven Spielberg states, "We must rescue ourselves from indulging in the technology we now have. . . . CG is just another tool—a means to an end. It shouldn't be an end itself" (Westbrook 8). CG can never replace a story, but it sure can help make it great.

Assessing the Final Copy

Dario's teacher used a rubric like the one found on pages **180–181** to assess his final copy. A **6** is the very best score that a writer can receive for each trait. The teacher also included comments under each trait.

6 Ideas

Your topic is interesting. I learned a lot about CG special effects. The quotations are very effective. Your essay convinced me to see some movies I've never wanted to watch.

5 Organization

Your writing is well organized and very clear. The beginning, middle, and ending paragraphs all work well together.

5 Voice

You obviously have a great deal of interest in your topic. Your voice conveys a sense of confidence about your topic.

4 Word Choice

You miss a few opportunities to teach new words to your readers. You also overuse these words: <u>filmmakers</u>, <u>imaginary</u>, <u>real</u>, <u>realistic</u>.

5 Sentence Fluency

You use a wide variety of sentences. Your sentences all read smoothly from one idea to another.

6 Conventions

Your writing is free of careless errors.

Review the Assessment. Do you agree with the scores and comments made by Dario's teacher? Why or why not? In a brief paragraph, discuss your own reaction to Dario's essay and how you would grade it.

Reflecting on Your Writing

After the whole process was finished, Dario filled out a reflection sheet. This helped him think about the assignment and plan for future writing. (Complete a reflection sheet like this right after you finish your writing.)

Dario Ramirez
Mr. Lawler
English 9, Period 3
May 8, 2006

Expository Essay: The Sky's Not the Limit

1. **The best part of my essay is . . .**
   my conclusion. It covers the entire topic and uses quotations to show good points and bad points.

2. **The part that still needs work is . . .**
   my word choice. I need to make sure that I don't overuse certain words.

3. **The most important part of my prewriting and planning was . . .**
   exploring the history of CG special effects and the people who used them. That gave me the details I needed to explain my topic.

4. **During revising, I spent a lot of time dealing with . . .**
   adding more details from my notes to support my main points.

5. **What I've learned about this type of essay is . . .**
   that it's important to find a variety of details. Telling about the misuse of CG gives the end of my essay energy and surprises my readers.

6. **Here is one question I still have . . .**
   Are there other ways to note sources in a paper without using the parentheses?

Writing with a Computer

A computer is more than just an alternative to writing with pen and paper. It's a valuable writing tool. Computers can aid writers at every step in the writing process, helping them produce effective essays, articles, and reports.

In this chapter, you will learn strategies for planning and writing with a computer. As you will see, there is no better tool for gathering and organizing information, creating a first draft, and improving a draft through revisions. The computer also takes a lot of the guesswork out of editing and proofreading. And once all the changes are made, a computer makes publishing the writing an easy process.

- **Understanding the Basics**
- **Prewriting**
- **Writing**
- **Revising**
- **Editing**
- **Publishing**

"I work on a word processor for the first draft, but for revisions I always print out a copy and do my corrections by hand."

—Betsy Byars

Understanding the Basics

Basically, a computer is a machine that receives information (*input*), *processes* it, and *outputs* the results. Here is a quick overview of how a computer works as a writing tool.

Input: You'll most often provide input by using a keyboard or mouse. For tablet and pocket computers, a stylus is commonly used. (Pocket computers are often called PDA's–Personal Data Assistants.)

- **Keyboard:** A keyboard contains letters, numbers, and other characters. It allows users to type faster than they can write longhand.
- **Mouse:** The mouse allows users to select items with an arrow, position the cursor, or highlight areas of text.
- **Stylus:** A stylus is like a pencil for writing on an electronic drawing pad or a touch-sensitive computer screen. It can also point and select like a mouse.

Process: Input is processed by a program loaded into the computer's memory from storage. Knowing the difference between memory and storage can save you a lot of trouble.

- **Memory:** Often called RAM, computer memory operates only when the power is on. If you shut down your computer before you save your work, that work is lost—so save often.
- **Storage:** Most computers have a built-in hard drive for permanent storage. Data saved on the hard drive is kept when the computer shuts down. Removable storage includes magnetic disks (floppies), CD's, DVD's, and flash memory devices. (Pocket computers use internal flash memory instead of a hard drive.)
- **Program:** Often called software, programs are instructions a computer uses to recognize input, process it, store it, and output it.

Output: After information has been processed, the computer must output it to the user.

- **Monitor:** Often referred to as a computer screen, a monitor shows the user immediate results of his or her input.
- **Printer:** A printer allows a computer to output text and graphics on paper. This printout is commonly called hard copy.

Tip

Most computer programs have built-in help files. Look for "Help" in the program's menu. You can browse those files to learn more about the program.

Prewriting

For some prewriting strategies, pencil and paper may work well. For others, a computer can speed up the process. This page discusses ways a computer can help during prewriting.

■ Select a topic.

- **Journaling:** Use a computer to keep a personal journal or learning log. Review your entries when you need ideas for essays or stories. Then copy and paste material into a new file, and start writing!

- **Freewriting:** Use a computer to write freely to discover possible writing ideas. Simply let your thoughts flow. It's helpful to begin with a focus in mind—one that is related to your assignment.

■ Gather and organize details.

- **Creating Graphic Organizers:** Use the table function on your word processor to create T-charts, sensory charts, 5 W's charts, time lines, and gathering grids. The table automatically expands to include as much information as you add.

T-Chart

Cause	Effect

Sensory Chart

See	Hear	Smell	Taste	Touch

Time Line

First	
Next	
Then	
After	

- **Researching:** Use your computer and its Internet connection to conduct research. Search for relevant Web sites and print out pages that seem to be helpful. Be sure to keep track of useful Web sites as *favorites*.

- **Listing and Outlining:** Use the computer to list main points and details. Then rearrange the details in logical outline order. Activate the outline function of your computer so that it automatically labels each new line of your outline with the correct letter or number.

Try It!

Create graphic organizers. Use your word processor's table function to create a T-chart, a sensory chart, or a time line.

Writing

Once you know how to type or keyboard, writing a first draft on a computer is much easier than writing a draft longhand. Here are some helpful writing tips.

■ Get started.

- **Start a new document.** Always begin a new document for each project. In this way, you will keep your outline or organizer intact in the file.
- **Let your ideas flow.** Refer to your outline as you write, but feel free to include new ideas as they come to mind. For now, don't worry about getting every word or sentence just right.

Tip

If you can't resist the temptation to make a lot of changes during first drafts, turn down the resolution on your monitor. This should help you maintain a free flow of ideas, because you won't see what you're writing.

■ Keep it going.

- **Stay with your writing.** Using a computer will help you to thoroughly develop a piece of writing. If you are having trouble with one part, fill it in with placeholder text, or just write a note to yourself.
- **Save often.** Learn the shortcut key to save your text (often pressing "Control" or "Alt" and "S"). By saving often, you will avoid unexpectedly losing your work to a cranky computer or a power outage. Also consider setting your computer's "auto-save" feature to save your work every few minutes.
- **Share your work.** Writing on a computer makes it easier for you to share early drafts. You can simply print out a copy for others to read. By sharing your work, you become more aware of a real audience.

Try It!

Find out how often your computer is set up to save your work. Check the main toolbar for "Help" and click on it. In the help screen, type "save options" or "auto save." Then check your help file to find out how to retrieve "last save" versions of your file.

Process

Revising

On handwritten copy, making revisions can be messy. There will be crossed-out sentences, words written in the margins, and circled ideas. When writing on a computer, the text automatically reflows with every change, so there's no mess. The tips below can help you get the most out of revising on a computer.

■ Manage your document.

- **Start with a printout.** Begin by reading a printed copy of your first draft. Then make changes on this copy before you make changes on the computer. (It's easier to make quick notes and experiment on a printed copy of your work.)
- **Save each round of revisions.** Save a printed copy of each set of revisions; also save each set separately on the computer (*revision 1, revision 2,* and so on). If you work in this way, you will have an accurate history of the changes you have made.
- **Save major deletions.** Dump large chunks of deleted text in a separate file so that you can easily review them if necessary.
- **Use the windows features.** For example, you can keep two files open when you need to move text from one file to another.

FYI

Using a computer during revising makes it easier to conduct group-advising sessions because everyone can have a clean printout to read and respond to.

■ Employ the features.

- **Use "Cut," "Copy," and "Paste."** Use these features to delete, add, or rearrange words, phrases, sentences, and paragraphs.
- **Learn to drag text.** This feature allows you to move text: You highlight the part you want to move; click on it again, holding down the button; and drag it to a new spot.
- **Try out "Track Changes."** Your computer may allow you to keep track of the changes you make. (See your help file.)
- **Learn about other revising features.** Look for features such as *search and replace, word count,* and *dictionary functions.*

Try It!

Take a toolbar tour. Click on each item on your main toolbar and check each drop-down menu. Explore some of these features.

Editing

Most word-processing programs offer two main tools to help with editing and proofreading: the grammar checker and the spell-checker.

■ Understand your grammar checker.

■ **Watch for agreement errors.** Pay attention to underlined subject-predicate pairs. The underlining means that the grammar checker has identified an agreement problem. Select the best change suggested by the checker.

■ **Watch for passive sentences.** Note when a whole sentence is underlined. Typically this means it is passive in construction. Consider reworking the sentence in the active voice. (See page **722.1**.)

■ **Keep a critical eye.** Be aware that grammar checkers can be wrong in what they flag as a problem. When in doubt, check the "Proofreader's Guide" in this book before following a suggestion.

■ Use your spell-checker.

■ **Set the spell-check option to "Auto-Correct."** This feature corrects misspellings when they are first typed in.

■ **Watch for underlined words as you type.** Correct errors yourself or let the checker suggest replacements.

■ **Spell-check the final document.** When you finish editing, run the spell-checker on the whole document. The checker flags any word that isn't in its database. Carefully monitor the changes your checker makes. Always proofread a printout of the final copy. A spell-checker won't catch a homophone (*their, there, they're*) or a word that is spelled correctly that is not the word you want.

Try It!

Explore the options available on your grammar and spell-checkers. Enable and disable different features by clicking on them. Decide which settings work best for you.

Publishing

Before you share your final copy, be sure that the document itself is well designed. See pages **76–78** for information about designing your writing with a computer.

Understanding the Traits of Writing

At times, jazz musicians stay with the beat, playing within a specific rhythm or pattern; at other times, they improvise, suddenly breaking out of the basic structure to create a whole new sound. Good writers often work in a similar way. They start with a basic plan, but as they go along, new ideas may come to mind, taking them in more interesting directions.

You will do your best writing if you keep an open mind, always expecting to take a few side trips that reveal new ways of thinking about your topic. Writing that isn't forced, that is formed "partly though accident," will likely display the **traits** found in all good writing—*stimulating ideas, engaging voice, original word choice,* and so on. This chapter will introduce you to all the traits of writing.

- Introducing the Traits
- Understanding the Traits
- Guide for Effective Writing

"Good writing is formed partly through plan and partly through accident."
—Ken Macrorie

"The idea is to write so that people hear it, and it slides through the brain and goes straight to the heart."

—Maya Angelou

Introducing the Traits

The chart below identifies the main features of effective writing. If you write with these traits in mind, you will be pleased with the results.

TRAITS OF WRITING

- **Ideas**

  Strong writing presents a clear focus, or message. The writing contains specific ideas and details that support the focus.

- **Organization**

  Effective writing creates a meaningful whole—with interesting beginning, middle, and ending parts. The supporting details are arranged in the best order.

- **Voice**

  Writing that has voice reflects the writer's personality. It is engaging and appropriate for the audience.

- **Word Choice**

  Good writing contains strong words, including specific nouns, verbs, and modifiers. Word choice helps deliver a clear message.

- **Sentence Fluency**

  Effective writing flows smoothly from sentence to sentence. None of the sentences cause the reader to stumble or become confused.

- **Conventions**

  Strong writing follows the rules for punctuation, capitalization, spelling, and grammar. It is carefully edited to be error free.

FYI

Also consider the trait of presentation. An effective final copy looks neat and follows the guidelines for margins, indenting, spacing, and so on. The writing's appearance affects the reader's overall impression of it. (See pages **76–78**.)

Process

The Traits in Action

The following excerpt from a personal narrative by Latrisha Jones displays the effective use of the traits of writing.

Ramadan Feast

The narrative starts with an interesting topic.	The sun was setting behind me as I walked into the Islamic Center. I'd never been in a mosque, but now I was going to a feast to celebrate the holiest month of the Islamic year: Ramadan.
The details are arranged chronologically.	I wondered what to expect. Would I see veils, pillows, and incense burners, like in the old movies? No. Instead, I saw linoleum floors, painted cinder blocks, and ceiling tiles. On the walls hung kids' drawings that celebrated Ramadan, posters with the words of the prophet Mohammed, and handwritten essays about being Muslim in America.
The writer's personal voice comes through.	"Latrisha!" called a voice. I turned to see my friend Helah hurrying toward me. She wore a hooded caftan, a silk robe that reached to her ankles, and she was beaming. "Helah," I said as I took her hands. "I'm so nervous!" I touched the Kente hat I'd worn, knowing girls were supposed to cover their heads.
Specific nouns and verbs create clear images.	Helah smiled, "I like the hat, but you didn't have to cover your head. We know you're not Muslim. We just want you to celebrate with us." She led me into the gym, decked out like the Student Council banquet, with round tables and folding chairs and a buffet that steamed with Persian food. Helah took a deep breath. "I can't wait to taste the lamb."
Varied sentences engage the reader.	"Me, too," I said, my stomach rumbling. I'd fasted all day—no food or drink since sunup. "You do this every day for the whole month of Ramadan? I've never fasted before." "You fasted today?" Helah asked, and she gave me a hug. "Muslims fast because it's one of the Five Pillars, or duties to honor Allah." She looked slyly at me. "But you fasted because you're my friend."
Correct punctuation makes the writing easy to read.	I nodded as we took our seats among the others. There were dates on a plate in the middle of the table. "So, friend, when do we eat?"

Respond to the reading. Which two traits stand out in this narrative? Explain.

Understanding Ideas

Quality ideas drive good writing, making it possible to develop strong essays, research papers, articles, and stories. No other trait is even remotely as important. As writer Joyce Carol Oates says, "As soon as you connect with your true subject [your ideas], you will write."

■ Select effective ideas.

If you start out with effective ideas, there's a good chance that the rest of your writing will go smoothly. Follow these tips.

1. Begin with a specific topic. (Make sure that it genuinely interests you and meets the requirements of the assignment.)
2. Focus on an interesting or important part of the topic. (This will help you develop a more unified paper.)
3. Collect specific details that support the topic.

Sample Paragraph

Carefully read the following paragraph, paying close attention to the topic, the focus, and the specific details.

A Man with Imagination

You know Leonardo da Vinci (1452–1519) as a famous painter, but did you know that he was a famous inventor, too? The National Museum of Science and Technology in Milan, Italy, has more than 6,000 sketchbook pages of da Vinci's invention ideas. Included in the collection are sketches of military weapons and factory equipment. In addition, ideas for bizarre flying machines show da Vinci's incredible imagination. One of the most famous machines is called the aerial screw. It features a flattened spiral of fabric winding around a central pole. In theory, spinning the fabric "propeller" would lift the machine. Although such a machine couldn't actually work, the idea inspired other inventors. Some experts say that it may have inspired the early designs of the helicopter. Da Vinci will always be known for famous paintings like the *Mona Lisa*, but don't forget his contributions in other areas.

 Respond to the reading. What part of the topic does the paragraph focus on? What supporting details seem especially important? Name two.

Process

■ Find important details.

Details are the information that supports the focus of your writing. When the details are clear and complete, the writing has impact. Consider using the four types of details listed below. (See pages **569–570** for other types of details.)

Types of Details

- **Facts** are details that can be proven.
- **Statistics** present numerical information.
- **Examples** illustrate a main point.
- **Quotations** are statements from other people.

Sample Paragraph

Read the following paragraph, paying close attention to the types of details that it includes.

Up in Smoke

Smoking continues to be a health problem in the United States, despite the accompanying risks. According to the American Heart Association, more than 20 percent of women and 25 percent of men in the United States are smokers. The American Lung Association states that in 2003, 4.5 million of those smokers were teens. Smokers suffer from yellow stains on their teeth and hands, increased colds, insomnia, nervousness, and high blood pressure. They are more prone to arthritis, heart disease, and lung disease, among other ailments. The death of ABC newscaster Peter Jennings is an example of how dangerous smoking can be. Even 20 years after quitting smoking, Jennings developed lung cancer—a deadly form of the disease. Upon Jennings' death, Barbara Walters said, "If you have kids who are smoking, for heaven's sake, tell them that we lost Peter." Smoking is one habit that all people should avoid at all costs.

 Respond to the reading. Name one fact included in the paragraph. Name one example. Name one statistic. What does the quotation add to the writing?

Try It!

Write a paragraph about a topic of your choice. Include three or four types of details listed above.

Understanding Organization

Writer Donald Murray states that strong writing stems from "the solid construction of thoughts." A clear plan of organization gives writing unity, which makes it easy to follow from one point to the next.

At a basic level, writing can be organized **deductively** or **inductively**. Most scientific and informative writing requires deductive organization, making complicated material easier to understand. Personal and some types of informational writing use inductive organization.

■ Work deductively.

You are working deductively when you start with a topic sentence or thesis statement and follow with supporting details. The informational paragraph below opens with a main point about global warming and follows with supporting details.

Sample Paragraph

A Critical Meltdown

Global warming is changing the face of our world, and evidence suggests it will soon become an even bigger problem. Its effects can be seen in this country in Montana's Glacier National Park, where the number of glaciers in the park has shrunk from 150 in 1850 to just 35 today. Some experts suggest that by the year 2030, all the remaining glaciers there will have melted. Elsewhere, the glaciers of Antarctica are melting and crashing into the ocean, causing an ecological nightmare for the animals living on that continent. The resulting rising sea levels will eventually impact many aspects of life as we know it. For example, if global warming continues at its current rate, it could affect the coastal areas of the earth's continents, flooding some cities and causing incalculable damage. Unfortunately, it may be too late to address this impending crisis.

Respond to the reading. Which sentence contains both the topic and focus of this paragraph? Which supporting details seem the most critical?

Try It!

Write an informational paragraph that follows the deductive pattern of organization. Use the sample paragraph above as a guide.

"Work hard to master these tools of writing. Simplify, prune, and strive for order."

—William Zinsser

■ Work inductively.

You are working inductively when you start with specific details and lead up to an important summary statement. In the sample personal paragraph below, the final sentence is a summary topic sentence. When you write inductively, you hold the reader's interest because he or she must read to the end to discover the specific topic. Details that are organized inductively build in suspense or lead to a logical conclusion.

Sample Paragraph

Read the following paragraph, paying close attention to the way specific details are used to lead up to a summary or key point.

Building in Force

The day had been muggy, the heat relentless as the hazy sun baked the ground. As the morning progressed, the haze turned to clouds, at first too thin to hide the sun, but growing thicker as they inched their way to the east. Then the sun was completely covered, and a low growl rumbled from the black western sky, accompanied by quick snake-tongues of lightning. The muggy air began to stir, and little dust clouds spun across the driveway. Thunder rolled across the darkening sky. A large drop of rain hit my cheek, followed by another and another. Then, with a crash, the sky parted, and the rain poured down in pulsing sheets. The predicted thunderstorm had arrived.

Respond to the reading. **What is the topic of this paragraph? Which sentence states the specific topic? What is the role of the other sentences?**

Try It!

Write a paragraph that follows the inductive pattern of organization. (Your topic can be informational or personal.) Use the sample paragraph above as a guide.

Understanding Voice

Voice is the special quality that attracts a reader to your writing. Novelist Kurt Vonnegut says that a writer whose unique voice comes through in his or her work serves as a "good date" for the reader.

■ Know your reader.

Writing with an appealing voice will help you connect with your reader. Your writing will always have voice if you . . .

- keep your purpose in mind,
- show respect for your reader,
- engage your reader's interest, and
- anticipate and address your reader's questions.

Sample Paragraph

Carefully read the following paragraph, paying attention to its voice.

To the Principal:

On behalf of the Student Council Spirit Committee, I would like to request that you consider creating a student lounge. Such a room would be designated for students who have shown through good grades and behavior that they deserve such a privilege. Students with a 2.5 average and no disciplinary problems for a full term would be issued a pass to use the lounge during their study halls. The student council could locate donated furniture for the room and decorate it. As for space, the large storage room off the cafeteria would be the perfect place. It is basically unused, and the few supplies kept there could easily be stored in the supply room by the kitchen. I hope you will consider this proposal. Offering a student lounge would encourage students to work hard.

Respond to the reading. Who is the intended reader or audience? How does the writer engage the reader? Identify any two appropriate and/or appealing words, phrases, or ideas.

Try It!

Write a paragraph, either to your principal or to your classmates, addressing a school-related topic. Make sure to connect with your reader.

Process

"By the time I reach the fifth version, [my writing] begins to have its own voice."

—Ashley Bryan

■ Sound interested.

Your writing voice will be heard loud and clear if you are enthusiastic and interested in your topic. Of course, to sound interested, you ought to know a lot about your topic. In the following sample, the writer's enthusiasm is evident.

Sample Paragraph

Programmed Pets

The pet world has just expanded, thanks to the world of robotics. An impressive range of robotic pets is available, including dogs, cats, parrots, and even frogs. Adorable robo-dogs are programmed to be affectionate and do a variety of tricks, while charming robo-cats purr when they are petted. Designed to look futuristic but friendly, the pets are made out of plastic that is either brightly colored or shimmering with a metallic finish. Robotic pets are a good option for people with allergies and for people with hectic schedules. While these toys won't replace golden retrievers or Siamese cats, they do appeal to techno fanatics. Instead of feeding the dog, the next generation of pet owners will simply recharge a battery.

Respond to the reading. How does the writer's enthusiasm come through? What interesting information does the writer include? Name two details. How does the closing sentence add appeal?

Try It!

Write freely for 5 to 10 minutes about a topic that truly interests you. When you finish, underline three or four phrases or ideas that show your enthusiasm.

Understanding Word Choice

Writer Dorothy Parker once said, "I can't find five words but that I change seven." Like all experienced writers, Parker appreciated the importance of word choice. She knew that her message would be delivered only with strong words.

■ Choose words carefully.

Since your words will communicate your message, you should choose them carefully. As you read the following sample, pay careful attention to the clear, colorful word choice.

Sample Paragraph

Peekaboo!

When I was little, Mom always played hide-and-seek with me at home, so I never thought that it would be a problem playing it at the store. While Mom was examining new bath mats, I snuck across the aisle to a circular dress rack. I slipped between the silky dresses where I waited, knowing at any moment Mom would thrust her smiling face inside the cave and yell, "Peekaboo!" But she didn't. Instead, I heard her ask someone to help her look for me. By this time, I realized I had done something wrong. For some reason, I held still as the seconds crawled by. What if Mom never found me? Tears formed and started rolling down my cheeks. My nose began to drip, and I started sobbing. Then the dresses parted and a strange lady peeked in at me. She shouted to my mother, who pulled me out and enveloped me in a hug. After that, I saved my games for home.

Respond to the reading. What is the topic of this paragraph? Which verbs communicate specific actions? Name two or three. Which modifiers create clear or colorful images? Name two or three.

Try It!

Write freely for 5 to 10 minutes about a recent experience. Afterward, circle four words in your writing that seem especially colorful and clear, and underline three words that could be improved. Then substitute better choices for your underlined words.

▪ Watch out for adjective overload.

Mark Twain once gave this piece of advice, "When you catch an adjective, kill it." He knew from experience that using too many adjectives can sound forced and unnatural. (See pages **540–541** for more information.)

Too Many Adjectives

A tall, shocking **column of** thick, yellow **smoke marked the** exact **spot.**

Adjectives Used Selectively

A **column of** thick, yellow **smoke marked the spot.**

Sample Paragraph

As you read the following paragraph, pay careful attention to the adjectives; they are used selectively.

Treasure Hunt

Whenever I feel down, I head straight to my tall dresser where I keep my memory bowl. It's just a plain red ceramic bowl with blue flowers painted around the outside, but it holds my most treasured possessions. There's the crystal geode my older brother and I found by the river. He split it open and gave me half when he left for college. He kept the other half, telling me that meant we would always be connected. Also in my bowl is my grandfather's prized fishing lure. The colorful feathers remind me of the fun we have fishing when he comes to visit. At the bottom of the bowl rests a scuffed baseball with fraying stitches. It is the game ball from last year when we won the conference championship. When I look at it, I remember the fun we had, and I look forward to next year's season. Looking at the things in my memory bowl always cheers me up.

Respond to the reading. Which adjectives seem especially effective? Name two. Which verbs communicate specific actions? Name two.

Try It!

In a brief paragraph, describe the inside of your locker. Then underline the adjectives that you have used.

Understanding Sentence Fluency

Strong writing is seamless—meaning that the sentences are easy to follow from start to finish. To ensure this seamless style, William Zinsser says that he writes "entirely by ear, reading everything aloud before letting it go out into the world."

■ Check for variety.

In effective writing, the sentences are not predictable. They vary in the way they begin, in length, and in verb choice. Use the following strategy to ensure sentence variety in your writing.

1. In one column on a piece of paper, list each sentence's opening word. (Decide if you need to vary some sentence beginnings.)
2. In another column, write the number of words in each sentence. (Decide if you need to change the length of some sentences.)
3. In a third column, list the verbs in each sentence. (Decide if you need to change any general verbs—*is, are, look,* and so on.)

Sample Paragraph

Read the following brief paragraph, paying careful attention to the flow of the sentences.

Bold Buildup

The lights dimmed in the amphitheater. Multicolored spotlights danced overhead, bouncing off the ceiling. Bold sounds grew in intensity. At first, the sounds thundered in the distance, but soon they roared in our heads. People all around stamped their feet and clapped their hands. Blasts from a bass guitar drowned out the fans. Behind a blinding flash of light, the band appeared on stage. At last, the concert began.

 Respond to the reading. On your own paper, use the three-step strategy above to test the sentences in the sample paragraph.

Try It!

Write freely for 5 to 10 minutes about a concert or sporting event you have attended. Then test your sentence variety using the strategy above.

■ Add style to your sentences.

You can learn about sentence style by examining the sentences in professional essays, articles, and stories. Experienced writers often use *loose* and *cumulative* sentences.

- ■ A **loose sentence** expresses the main idea near the beginning (in blue below) and adds details as needed.

   The regimental flags led, **men trailing out behind each flag in a V-shaped mass, struggling over rocks and logs.**

   —"Missionary Ridge," Bruce Catton

- ■ A **cumulative sentence** places the main idea in the middle (in blue below) with modifiers coming before and after it.

   Each afternoon during the wonderful spring, I had to stay in, **two hours a day for six weeks, working long division.**

   —*Good Old Boy*, Willie Morris

Try It!

Write sentences modeled after each example below. (You do not have to follow the examples exactly.) One sentence has been modeled for you.

Wil nodded to himself and slipped away, **softly as a mouse, toward the back of the house where the tourists were never taken.**

—"A Room Full of Leaves," Joan Aiken

   Student Version: *Josie smiled to herself and jogged along,* **gracefully as a deer,** *toward the pond in the park where many ducks were always feeding.*

He was born around 1840, **by the Belle Fourche River, near Bear Butte, in what is now South Dakota.**

—*Crazy Horse*, Larry McMurtry

I spent hours in the bedroom playing with the set, **studying the directions, and working one experiment after another.**

—*Gifted Hands*, Ben Carson

Born in 1927, my mother, Johnny Florence Gooch, was her mother's right hand, **just as I am to her.**

—*An American Story,* Debra J. Dickerson

Creeping through her bones, the pain had become insistent, **nearly without letup.**

—*A Tidewater Morning*, William Styron

Understanding Conventions

Effective writing is easy to read because, among other things, it follows the conventions for punctuation, capitalization, spelling, and grammar. Writer and editor Patricia T. O'Conner summarizes the importance of punctuation in this way: "When you write, punctuation marks are the road signs that guide the reader, and you wouldn't be understood without them."

■ Know the basic rules.

The English language is always growing; it includes more words than any other "living" language. It stands to reason that there are a lot of rules for using English. The checklist below can guide you as you check your writing for conventions. Also see the "Proofreader's Guide" (pages **604–763**).

Conventions

PUNCTUATION

_____ 1. Do I use end punctuation after all my sentences?

_____ 2. Do I use commas and semicolons correctly?

_____ 3. Do I use apostrophes to show possession (*that boy's keys* and *those boys' keys*)?

_____ 4. Do I use quotation marks and italics correctly?

CAPITALIZATION

_____ 5. Do I start each sentence with a capital letter?

_____ 6. Do I capitalize the proper names of people and places?

SPELLING

_____ 7. Have I checked my spelling using a spell-checker?

_____ 8. Have I also checked the spelling with a dictionary?

GRAMMAR

_____ 9. Do I use correct forms of verbs (*had eaten*, not *had ate*)?

_____ 10. Do my subjects and verbs agree in number (*the dog barks* and *the dogs bark*)?

_____ 11. Do I use the correct word (*their, there,* or *they're*)?

"Cut out all those exclamation marks. An exclamation mark is like laughing at your own joke."

—F. Scott Fitzgerald

■ Create a smooth-reading rhythm.

Carefully selected punctuation can help the reader follow the ideas in your writing. For example, if you use commas and semicolons especially well, they can give your writing an effective rhythm.

Sample Paragraph

Read the following paragraph to see how the punctuation controls the flow of ideas.

Flying Solo

Amelia Earhart never flew in an airplane until 1920, but by 1922, she had already set the women's altitude record at 14,000 feet. In 1932, Earhart became the second person to fly solo across the Atlantic, exactly five years after Charles Lindbergh's historic flight. Two years later, Earhart accepted her greatest challenge, flying around the world. She flew more than 22,000 miles—from California to Florida; across South America, Africa, and Asia; and then out across the Pacific. She departed from New Guinea on July 2. A few hours later, after a last cryptic radio message, Earhart and her airplane disappeared.

Respond to the reading. How many of the sentences contain commas? How many contain semicolons? Which sentence seems especially rhythmic? Write it on your paper and explain your choice. Does any sentence contain punctuation that you don't normally use? Explain.

Try It!

Write a brief paragraph about someone you know and admire. Include a few sentences that require commas and one sentence that uses a semicolon.

GUIDE FOR EFFECTIVE WRITING

If a piece of writing meets the following standards, it exhibits the traits of effective writing. Check your work using these standards.

- **Ideas**

  The writing . . .

  _____ maintains a clear, specific focus or purpose.

  _____ presents interesting details that support the focus.

  _____ holds the reader's attention (and answers his or her questions about the topic).

- **Organization**

  _____ includes a clear beginning, middle, and ending.

  _____ arranges the details in the best order.

  _____ contains transitions to connect ideas.

- **Voice**

  _____ speaks in a sincere, natural way.

  _____ shows that the writer is knowledgeable about and interested in the topic.

  _____ effectively addresses the reader (audience).

- **Word Choice**

  _____ contains specific, clear nouns and verbs.

  _____ presents an appropriate level of formality or informality.

- **Sentence Fluency**

  _____ flows smoothly from sentence to sentence.

  _____ includes sentences that vary in beginning, length, and style.

- **Conventions**

  _____ adheres to the rules of punctuation, spelling, and grammar.

  _____ follows established guidelines for presentation.

Peer Responding

If you're like most students, you're reluctant to make changes after working hard to write a first draft. But as you know, first drafts seldom, if ever, turn out clear and convincing. Unless you continue to work with it, your writing will never be as good as it could be.

Participating in peer-response sessions can help you stay with your writing. Classmates can point out what works well in your writing and what may need improving. At first, you may find it hard to share your writing. However, once you see how helpful peer responses can be, you'll come to appreciate them. Think of yourself and your responders as teammates who share the same goal: to make your writing the best it can be.

- **Peer-Responding Guidelines**
- **Using the Traits to Respond**

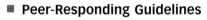

"Listen to good criticism, but pick your critics carefully."

—Paula Danziger

Peer-Responding Guidelines

The guidelines below will help you conduct effective response sessions. (If you're just starting out, work in small groups of two or three classmates.)

The Author's Role

Come prepared with a meaningful piece of writing. Make a copy for each responder. Also come to the session with an open mind. If you are defensive about your work, you may not "hear" all the comments. Follow these tips.

- **Introduce your writing.** Briefly explain what your writing is about, but don't go into too much detail.
- **Read your writing out loud.** You may, instead, ask the group members to read your writing silently.
- **Ask for comments.** Listen carefully. You don't have to make every change that is suggested, but keep an open mind.
- **Take notes.** Write comments on your copy as the session progresses, so you can remember exactly where changes need to be made.
- **Answer questions.** It's okay to say, "I don't know. I'll have to look into that," if you are unsure.
- **Ask for help.** If you are having trouble with something in your writing, ask for advice.

Asking for Constructive Criticism

To get constructive criticism, ask for it in the right way:

First ask . . .

"What do you think works best in my writing? Why?"

Then ask . . .

"What parts do you think could be improved? How?"

By asking for comments in this way, you create a cooperative relationship with responders. The answers to "Why?" and "How?" will help you to significantly improve your writing.

The Responder's Role

Respond honestly but be sensitive to the author's feelings. Express your comments politely; be sure that they are constructive and helpful. Follow these tips.

- **Listen carefully.** You owe it to the author to pay close attention.
- **Take notes.** Mark places in the margins of your copy so that you can show the author exactly where revisions may be needed.
- **Start with what is good.** Find something positive to say about the author's writing. Be specific about what you liked.
- **Ask questions.** If you are not sure about something, ask for clarification.
- **Make suggestions.** Even when you are pointing out a problem, be positive and constructive. (See below.)

Giving Constructive Criticism	
Don't give commands . . . "Change the beginning so that it grabs my attention."	**Do give suggestions . . .** "The beginning would be stronger if it grabbed my attention right away."
Don't focus on the writer . . . "You jumbled up the middle paragraphs."	**Do focus on the writing . . .** "The argument would be clearer if the details came in a different order."
Don't focus on the problem . . . "There aren't enough details to support your focus."	**Do focus on the solution . . .** "More details would make your essay even more informative."
Don't give general comments . . . "Your sentences are boring."	**Do give specific advice . . .** "You could try changing some of the passive verbs to active verbs."

Try It!

Rewrite the unhelpful comments below to make them more constructive.

1. You didn't use any transition words or phrases to connect your ideas.
2. The last paragraph doesn't leave me with any kind of final thought.
3. Cut out the sentence that compares highways to arteries.
4. You sound really unsure of yourself.

Using the Traits to Respond

As a responder, your goal is to help an author rethink, refocus, and revise her or his writing. You may find it helpful to base your responses on the traits of writing. Early in the process, focus on these three traits: *ideas, organization,* and *voice.*

■ Address ideas, organization, and voice.

Ideas: Help the author focus on the ideas.

- How would you state the main idea of your writing?
- It seems to me that you're trying to say . . . Is that right?
- Are these points the main ideas in your writing?
- The most convincing details include . . .
- A few more details like . . . may strengthen your work.
- Details like . . . may distract from your main idea.
- Your writing left me thinking . . . Is that what you intended?

Organization: Help the author focus on the organization.

- You got my attention in the beginning by . . .
- This sentence seems to state your focus. Is that correct?
- Are the middle paragraphs organized according to . . . ?
- Why did you place the information about . . . in the fourth paragraph?
- Is the purpose of your ending to . . . ?
- I wonder if a transition is needed between the second and third paragraphs.

Voice: Help the author focus on the voice.

- The sentences that most clearly show your personality are . . .
- I would describe your attitude about this topic as . . .
- What audience do you want to reach with your writing?
- In this paragraph, your writing sounds too formal/informal.
- The overall feeling I get from this writing is . . .
- Are you too subjective in the middle part of your essay?

Try It!

Why are these three traits important early in the revising process? Explain.

■ Address word choice and sentence fluency.

Later in the process, you may respond to the author's word choice and sentence fluency.

Word Choice: **Help the author focus on the nouns, verbs, and modifiers.**

- ■ The strongest verbs in the writing are . . .
- ■ I found these general nouns: . . . What specific nouns could you use instead?
- ■ Do you think all the modifiers in the second paragraph are necessary?
- ■ What does . . . mean? Could you define it in your writing?
- ■ The words . . . seem to have the wrong feeling. Could you replace them with words that are more . . . ?
- ■ Have you used . . . too often in the first part of your writing?

Sentence Fluency: **Help the author focus on the sentences.**

- ■ I like the flow of the sentences in the beginning paragraph.
- ■ Do too many sentences in the middle paragraphs begin the same way?
- ■ How could you vary the sentences in the closing paragraph?
- ■ Could some of the sentences in the second paragraph be combined?
- ■ For the most part, your sentences have a nice rhythm.

Tip

Listen carefully to your peers' comments, but don't think that you have to act on all of them. Peer responders offer their opinions, but you should weigh the value of each comment and proceed accordingly. The following tips will help you get the most out of response sessions.

- ■ Trust your own judgment about your writing.
- ■ Determine which issues are the most important.
- ■ Pay attention to comments made by more than one responder.
- ■ Get another opinion if you are not sure about something.
- ■ Be patient. Focus on one problem area at a time.

Try It!

Why are word choice and sentence fluency important in the revising process? Share your comments with your classmates.

Sample Peer Response Sheet

Use a response sheet like the one below to make comments about one of
your classmate's essays. (Sample responses are included.)

Peer Response Sheet

Writer: Riley Carruthers Responder: Thea Karas

Title: Buckling Up Is Not Enough

What I liked about your writing:
- You made a topic that I never thought about (Formula One racing) very interesting.
- You obviously know a lot about safety issues with racing.
- I like the little story in the beginning paragraph.
- You clearly explain complicated concepts like the Head-and-Neck Support system.

Changes I would suggest:
- Many of your sentences seem to be the same length. Could you make some long and some short?
- Would the thoughts and feelings of an actual driver make your paper even more interesting?
- You use a few terms—"external circuit breakers" and "faceplates"—that need more explanation.

Try It!

Exchange a recent piece of writing with a classmate.

1. Read the paper once to get an overall feel for it.
2. Read the paper again, paying careful attention to its strengths and weaknesses.
3. Fill out a response sheet like the one above.

Using a Rubric

How can you assess your writing? Most word-processing programs can count the number of words in an essay, and even find errors in grammar, but they can't begin to assess the ideas, organization, and voice in your writing. With a rubric in hand, though, you can evaluate your work and the work of others.

Rubrics aren't just for final assessment, either. They can help you get started on a project, guide your early writing, and provide specific suggestions for making improvements. In fact, by using a rubric throughout the process, you can expect to produce a final draft that you can be proud of. In this chapter, you will learn about all of these uses of a rubric—and more.

- **Understanding Rubrics**
- **Reading a Rubric**
- **Getting Started with a Rubric**
- **Revising and Editing with a Rubric**
- **Assessing with a Rubric**
- **Assessing in Action**
- **Assessing an Expository Essay**

"I have kind of an internal monitor. . . . I'm trying to make the story suitable for me."
—Christopher Paul Curtis

Understanding Rubrics

A **rubric** is simply a rating scale. Have you ever rated the popularity of something on a scale of 1 (terrible) to 10 (fantastic)? With rubrics, you can rate your writing—in this case on a scale of 6 (amazing) to 1 (incomplete).

The quality of any piece of writing can be rated on the basis of six traits: *ideas, organization, voice, word choice, sentence fluency,* and *conventions.* (For an introduction to these traits, see pages **39–54**.) A single essay might be well organized (score of 5) but have repetitive, general word choice (score of 3).

Rating Guide

Here's a brief description of the rating scale.

A **6** means that the writing is **amazing**.
It far exceeds expectations for a certain trait.

A **5** means that the writing is very **strong**.
It clearly meets the requirements for a trait.

A **4** means that the writing is **good**.
It meets most of the requirements for a trait.

A **3** means that the writing is **okay**.
It needs work to meet the main requirements for a trait.

A **2** means that the writing is **poor**.
It needs a lot of work to meet the requirements of a trait.

A **1** means that the writing is **incomplete**.
The writing is not yet ready to be assessed for a trait.

Process

Reading a Rubric

Rubrics in this book are color coded according to the trait. *Ideas* appear in a green strip, *organization* in a pink strip, and so forth. There is a description for each rating to help you assess your writing for a particular trait.

Rubric for Expository Writing

6 Ideas	**5**	**4**
The topic, thesis, and details make the essay unforgettable.	The essay is informative with a clear thesis and specific details.	The essay is informative with a clear thesis. More specific details are needed.

Organization		
The organization and transitions make the essay crystal clear and compelling.	The beginning interests the reader. The middle supports the focus. The ending works well. Transitions are used.	The essay is divided into a beginning, a middle, and an ending. Some transitions are used.

Voice		
The writer's voice has the confident, knowledgeable, sound of a professional writer.	The writer's voice sounds knowledgeable and confident. It fits the audience.	The writer's voice sounds knowledgeable most of the time and fits the audience.

■ Guide your writing.

A rubric helps you . . .

- **plan your work**—knowing what is expected,
- **create a strong first draft**—focusing on *ideas, organization,* and *voice,*
- **revise and edit your work**—considering each trait, and
- **assess your final draft**—rating the traits throughout the whole piece of writing.

Think about the rubric. Read the level-5 descriptions above and consider what they have to say about ideas, organization, and voice. What should the essay include? What should each part of the writing do? How should a writer's voice sound?

Getting Started with a Rubric

Each of the writing units in this book includes a page like the one below. This page, which is arranged according to the traits of writing, explains the main requirements for developing the essay in the unit. Studying the "goals" page will help you get started with your planning.

148

Understanding Your Goal

Your goal in this chapter is to write a well-organized expository essay that compares two famous people. The traits listed in the chart below will help you plan and write your essay.

TRAITS OF A COMPARISON ESSAY

- **Ideas**
  Select two famous people to compare. Develop your essay by providing key similarities between these two people.

- **Organization**
  Include a strong beginning and ending. In the middle, set up your points of comparison chronologically—early life, beginning career, middle career, and late career.

- **Voice**
  Engage the reader by using a voice that sounds knowledgeable.

- **Word Choice**
  Select precise words and avoid repetition and unneeded modifiers.

- **Sentence Fluency**
  Write a variety of sentences that smoothly connect your ideas.

- **Conventions**
  Use correct punctuation, capitalization, spelling, and grammar.

 Get the big picture. Review the rubric on pages 180–181 before you begin your writing. Use this rubric as a guide to develop your essay and as a tool to assess your completed writing.

> "If you would not be forgotten as soon as you are gone, either write things worth reading or do things worth writing."
> —Benjamin Franklin

Process

A Closer Look at Understanding Your Goal

The following steps will help you get an overview of the assignment in each writing unit.

1. **Read through the traits chart** to familiarize yourself with the unit's goals.
2. **Focus on *ideas, organization,* and *voice*** at the start of the project, when you are prewriting and writing. These traits form the foundation of good writing.
3. **Identify specific requirements** for each trait (such as using "a point-by-point organizational pattern" and "a knowledgeable-sounding voice").
4. **Ask questions** if you aren't sure about any part of the assignment.

A Special Note About the Traits

Different traits are important at different stages of the writing process. The following chart shows when the specific traits are important.

> During **prewriting** and **writing**, focus on the *ideas, organization,* and *voice* in your work.
>
> During **revising**, focus on *ideas, organization, voice, word choice,* and *sentence fluency*. (For some assignments, your teacher may ask you to pay particular attention to one or two of these traits.)
>
> During **editing** and proofreading, concentrate on *conventions*—spelling, punctuation, capitalization, and grammar.
>
> When you are **assessing** your final copy, consider all six traits. (For some assignments, your teacher may ask you to assess the writing for just a few of the traits.)

Exercise

Write a paragraph. Review the goals on page **64**. Then write an expository paragraph comparing two people, places, or things. Keep the traits in mind as you write.

Revising and Editing with a Rubric

 6 My essay shows strong similarities between the two people and is full of surprising contrasts.

 5 My essay shows the similarities and differences between the two people.

 4 My essay shows how the two people are similar, but it could use more details showing differences.

In this book, the pages that deal with revising and editing begin with a rubric strip. Each strip focuses on one trait of writing and will help you improve your first draft. The strip on these two pages focuses on the *ideas* for an expository comparison essay.

How can rubric strips help me assess my writing?

A rubric strip can help you look objectively at your writing. Follow these steps as you use the rubric strip to consider each trait:

1. Begin by reading over the number 5 description (a rating of strong).
2. Decide if your writing rates a 5 for that trait.
3. If not, check the 6 or 4 descriptions.
4. Continue until you find the rating that most closely matches your writing.
5. Notice how levels 4, 3, 2, and 1 offer suggestions on how you can improve your writing.

George H. W. Bush and George W. Bush have a lot in common beyond family and presidential ties. Both men followed two-term presidents into office, and both confronted Saddam Hussein. Each president waged a war in the Middle East. The outcome of their work was quite different. While the first President Bush presided over a brief war, the second President Bush captured Hussein but had to deal with a much more extended fight afterward. That's one other great difference between the two men.

 Try It!

Review the expository paragraph above. Then rate it for ideas using the strip at the top of these two pages as a guide. Give reasons for your rating.

Process

3 I need more details that show the similarities and differences between the two people.

2 I need to address the similarities and differences between the two people.

1 I need to understand how to compare and contrast two people.

How can rubric strips help me revise and edit?

Once you have rated your writing for a given trait, you will see ways to improve your score. The writer of the paragraph on page **66** gave his ideas a score of 4, meaning that the writing meets *most* of the requirements for the trait. The score description told him just what he needed to do to improve his work: include "more details showing differences." (Scores of 4 or lower offer suggestions for improving your writing.)

In the main writing units, each rubric strip is followed by brief lessons that will help you revise or edit your writing to improve that trait. There are separate rubric strips and lessons for each trait—ideas, organization, voice, word choice, sentence fluency, and conventions.

Make changes.

The writer decided to add another detail and a surprising contrast to finish in a more dramatic way. He made the following changes.

Additional details help make the contrast clearer.	. . . The outcome of their work **, though,** was quite different. While the first President Bush presided over a brief war **that failed to capture Hussein**, the
A new closing sentence strengthens the impact of the paragraph.	second President Bush captured Hussein but had to deal with a much more extended fight afterward. That's one other great difference between the two men. **The legacy of H. W. is clear, but the legacy of W. is still being written.**

 Revise your paragraph for ideas. Revise the paragraph you wrote on page 65, using the strip on these two pages as a guide.

Assessing with a Rubric

Follow these four steps when you use a rubric (see pages **70–71**) to assess a piece of writing.

1. **Create an assessment sheet.** On your own paper, write each of the key traits from the rubric, preceded by a short line. Under each trait, leave two or three lines to allow for comments.

2. **Read the final copy.** First, get an overall feeling for the writing. Then read more carefully, paying attention to each trait.

3. **Assess the writing.** Use the rubric to rate each trait. First, check the level-5 rubric description and then go up or down the scale until you find the correct rating. Write the score next to the trait on your assessment sheet.

Assessment Sheet   Title: _____

_____ Ideas

_____ Organization

_____ Voice

_____ Word Choice

_____ Sentence Fluency

_____ Conventions

Evaluator: _____

4. **Provide comments.** Under each trait, make whatever comments would be helpful for improving the writing.

Exercise

Assess your expository paragraph. Make an assessment sheet like the one above. Evaluate your paragraph using the rubric on pages **180–181**. For each trait, write a comment about something you did well and something you'd like to improve. (See the sample on page **71**.)

180

Rubric for Expository Writing

Use this rubric to guide and assess your expository writing. Refer to it to improve your writing using the six traits.

Comparison Essay 181

Expository

6 Ideas	**5**	**4**	**1**
The topic, thesis, and details make the essay unforgettable.	The essay is informative with a clear thesis and specific details.	The essay is informative with a clear thesis. More specific details are needed.	The writer should select a new topic.
Organization			
The organization and transitions make the essay crystal clear and compelling.	The beginning interests the reader. The middle supports the focus. The ending works well. Transitions are used.	The essay is divided into a beginning, a middle, and an ending. Some transitions are used.	The essay should be reorganized.
Voice			
The writer's voice has the confident, knowledgeable sound of a professional writer.	The writer's voice sounds knowledgeable and confident. It fits the audience.	The writer's voice sounds knowledgeable most of the time and fits the audience.	The writer needs to learn about voice.
Word Choice			
The word choice is precise, with just the right nouns, verbs, and modifiers.	Specific nouns and action verbs make the essay clear and informative.	Some nouns and verbs could be more specific.	Too many general words are used. Specific nouns and verbs are needed.
Sentence Fluency			
The sentences have flair and flavor, and the reader will enjoy them.	The sentences read smoothly.	Most of the sentences read smoothly, but some are short and choppy.	Many short, choppy sentences need to be rewritten to make the essay read smoothly.
Conventions			
The essay is error free.	The essay has a few minor errors in punctuation, spelling, or grammar.	The essay has some errors in punctuation, spelling, or grammar.	Several errors confuse the reader.

Each rubric addresses all six traits of writing.

The rubrics provide a scale in which 6 is the highest rating and 1 is the lowest.

General or missing words make this essay difficult to understand.

The writer needs help finding specific words.

Many sentences are choppy or incomplete and need to be rewritten.

Most sentences need to be rewritten.

Many errors make the essay difficult to read.

Help is needed to make corrections.

Assessing in Action

In the following expository essay, the writer shares information about a type of technology. Read the essay, paying attention to its strengths and weaknesses. Then read the student self-assessment on the following page. **(The essay contains some errors.)**

A Shrinking Dream

Can you imagine a computer that is no bigger than a wristwatch? What if heart surgery could be performed by a tiny device that travels a patient's bloodstream and operates from within? These are just two possibilities opened up by the world of nanotechnology, a world brilliantly initiated by Richard P. Feynman in 1959 (*Engineering & Science*, Feb 1960).

Feynman was speaking to physicists at the California Institute of Technology (Caltech), and he put a challenge of historical proportions to them. He had one simple question, and asked: "Why can't we write the entire 24 volumes of the *Encyclopaedia Britannica* on the head of a pin?" Then he outlined a world where wires might be only ten atoms in diameter, where a letter could be encoded on a metal cube measuring five by five by five atoms!

The resulting research has lead to the field of nanotechnology. The design and manufacture of machines that are measured in atoms and molecules rather than millimeters and inches. The term *nanotechnology* was first coined by Norio Taniguchi in 1974 (nanodot.org), but in all the years since the historic speech, scientists have been working to bring Feynman's dream into reality.

In 1993, the Foresight Institute began offering the Feynman Prizes in Nanotechnology. Two prizes, one for theoretical work and one for actual experimentation, are awarded every year to the scientists who have made the greatest progress. Millions of dollars have been awarded to date.

Feynman's question about nanotechnology is no longer "Is it possible?" Now, we are wondering when his goals will be attained. The title of Feynman's seminal speech is: "There is plenty of room at the bottom." New advances, some too small to see with the human eye, are occurring every day! And there is plenty of room to keep on shrinking.

Sample Self-Assessment

The student who wrote "A Shrinking Dream" created the following assessment sheet to evaluate her essay. She used the expository rubric on pages 180–181 as her assessment guide. Under each trait, she wrote comments about the strengths and weaknesses of her writing.

Assessment Sheet　　　Title: A Shrinking Dream

4　Ideas
　　The topic seems interesting.
　　A clearly stated thesis is needed.

3　Organization
　　My essay follows my plan.
　　The middle part needs much more development.

4　Voice
　　I sound interested.
　　I could have learned more about the topic.

4　Word Choice
　　My words are accurate.
　　I could have used more specific verbs.

4　Sentence Fluency
　　I used different sentence structures.
　　Some of my sentences are too long, and there
　　is one fragment.

5　Conventions
　　I caught many errors.
　　I used "lead" instead of "led" in one sentence.

Evaluator: Katrina

Exercise

Review the assessment. On your own paper, explain why you agree with the responses above (or why you don't). Consider each trait carefully.

Assessing an Expository Essay

Read the essay below, focusing on its strengths and weaknesses. Then follow the directions at the bottom of the page. **(The essay contains errors.)**

H. G. Wells: A Science Fiction Original

Herbert George Wells was born in 1866. His books are still read today. Although he wrote many books between 1895 and 1946, he is best remembered for four science fiction novels he wrote during the late 1890s. (*Britannica*, v12, 574).

The Time Machine was published in 1895. The novel was an imaginative story about a man who wished to travel to the past, but instead went nearly a million years into the future! He found a peaceful society but learned that there was still evil and suffering. Like all of Wells works, the book makes a statement about his world, as well as his imaginary world.

The Island of Dr. Moreau in 1896 was also popular. Wells wrote about a mad scientist trying to make creatures better than humans. It is a classic story of a man trying to play God and failing.

Next, in 1897, came *The Invisible Man*. It is Wells' "scientific romance" about a scientist who discovers a potion that makes him disappear. He uses it to terrify the people of Sussex, England.

Wells' preceding books were overshadowed in 1898 with *The War of the Worlds*. It was the first popular story about an alien invasion of Earth. The book is full of action and horror, though it ends with hope. It has left a storytelling legacy that continues up to the modern day, as well as a genre of "little green men" alien invasion stories (*War*, xii).

After witnessing two world wars and many personal difficulties, Herbert George Wells became pessimistic about the future of humankind. But these four books are still popular, and his stories are still being retold. It is a legacy that any author would be proud to enjoy.

Exercise

Use an expository rubric. Assess this expository essay, using the rubric on pages **180–181** as your guide. To get started, create an assessment sheet like the one on page **68**. *Remember:* After each trait, try to write one comment about a strength and one about a weakness.

Publishing Your Writing

When you first learn to play an instrument, you're not ready for an audience. You're unsure of yourself and make too many mistakes. However, once you become more skilled, you'll be ready to share your talent with others.

The same is true of writing. Some of it is not ready for an audience, especially your personal writing. However, the essays and stories that you develop are meant to be shared. Publishing makes all that hard work worth the effort.

Publishing your writing can be as simple as reading it to a friend or classmate or as complex as submitting it to a literary magazine. In any form, publishing is a very important step in the writing process. It helps you see how well you are doing. The purpose of this chapter is to help you with all of your publishing needs—from preparing a piece for publication to launching your own Web site.

- **Preparing to Publish**
- **Publishing Ideas**
- **Designing Your Writing**
- **Publishing Online**
- **Creating Your Own Web Site**
- **Finding Places to Publish**

"You learn ways to improve your writing by seeing its effect on others."

—Tom Liner

Preparing to Publish

Your writing is not ready to share until you have taken it through all the steps in the writing process. The tips below will help you prepare your writing for publication.

Follow these publishing tips.

- **Take advantage of peer response sessions.**
  Make sure that you have addressed the important concerns identified by your classmates.
- **Check for the traits of writing.** (See pages **39–54**.)
  The ideas, organization, voice, word choice, sentence fluency, and conventions in your writing are all important.
- **Put forth your best effort.**
  Continue working until you feel good about your writing from start to finish.
- **Save all drafts for each writing project.**
  Then you will be able to double-check the changes you have made.
- **Seek editing help.**
  Ask at least one trusted editor to check your work for conventions. Another person may spot errors that you miss.
- **Prepare a neat final copy.**
  Use a pen (blue or black ink) and one side of the paper if you are writing by hand. Select a typestyle that is easy to read if you are using a computer. (Always use a computer when you submit your writing to outside publishers.)
- **Consider different publishing options.**
  There are many ways to publish writing. (See page **75**.)
- **Follow all publishing guidelines.**
  Each publisher has certain requirements for publishing. Be sure to follow their directions exactly.

Try It!

Prepare to publish. Select a piece of writing that you would like to publish. Review the tips listed above. Is there anything more to do before the writing is truly ready to publish?

> "I tend to do as much revising as editors will let me do."
> —Tom Wolfe

Publishing Ideas

The simplest way to publish your writing is to share it with a friend or classmate. Other publishing ideas, such as entering a writing contest, take more time and effort. Try a number of these publishing ideas during the school year. All of them will help you grow as a writer.

Self-Publishing

- Newsletter
- Greeting Cards
- Personal Book
- Web Site
- Web Log

Performing

- Sharing with Classmates
- Reading to Other Audiences
- Multimedia Presentation
- Open-Mike Night

Sharing in School

- Literary Magazine
- Writing Portfolio
- Classroom Collection
- School Newspaper/Yearbook

Sending It Out

- Local Newspaper
- Magazines
- Web Sites or E-zines
- Writing Contests
- Young Writers' Conferences

Posting

- Bulletin Boards
- Display Cases
- Business Windows
- Literary/Art Fairs

Plan your publishing. What types of publishing have you tried in the past? In what way would you like to publish the piece of writing that you identified on page 74? Why? How else would you like to publish? Explain.

Designing Your Writing

Always focus first on the content of your writing. Then consider its design, or appearance. For most types of publishing, you'll want to use a computer for your final copy. These guidelines will help you to design your writing.

■ Select an appropriate font.

- **Choose an easy-to-read font.** In most cases, a serif typestyle is best for the text, and a sans serif style works for any headings.

    The letters of **serif** fonts have "tails"—as in this sentence.

    The letters of **sans serif** fonts are plain, without tails—as in this sentence.

- **Include a title and headings.** Use the title to introduce your paper and use headings to guide the reader through the text. Headings break a long report into readable parts.

■ Use consistent spacing and margins.

- **Set clear margins.** Use a one-inch margin (top, bottom, left, and right).
- **Indent paragraphs.** Use a half-inch indent.
- **Use one space after every period.** This will improve the readability of your paper.
- **Avoid awkward breaks.** Don't leave a heading or the first line of a paragraph at the bottom of a page or a column. Never split a hyphenated word between pages or columns.

■ Include graphic elements.

- **Use lists if appropriate.** Use numbered lists if your points have a clear number order. Otherwise, use bulleted lists (like the ones on this page).
- **Include graphics.** Use tables, charts, or illustrations to help make a point. Keep graphics small within the text. If a graphic needs to be large, display it on its own page.

Try It!

Working with a partner, compare the design features of articles from two different magazines. How are the design features the same? How are they different? Decide which design is the most effective, based on the magazine's audience and purpose.

Effective Design in Action

The following two pages show a well-designed student essay. The side notes explain the design features.

Ilse Haraldson
Ms. Serapio
General Science
January 31, 2006

Secrets of the Moon Illusion

Have you noticed that the moon looks larger on the horizon than overhead? People have wondered why for thousands of years. Scholars from Greece and China posed the question as early as the 7th century B.C.E. Aristotle wrote about it in 350 B.C.E, and the Arab scientist Ibn Alhazan studied the problem around 1000 C.E. Many explanations have been offered for this "moon illusion," but none have yet proved true.

Refraction Hypothesis

The earth's atmosphere distorts light and makes the day sky look blue and the night stars seem to twinkle. When the moon is low on the horizon, its color is darkened and it seems flattened. Does the atmosphere swell the moon's image? No. Measure the moon's image with a bent paperclip held at arm's length. Try it when the moon is low and high, and you'll see that its image remains the same size.

Context Cues Hypothesis

Another explanation for the moon illusion involves context. When the moon is overhead, there is nothing for comparison; but when it is on the horizon, buildings and trees make it seem larger. However, pilots in flight, with no context cues, see the moon illusion. If you bend over and look with your head upside down, the moon on the horizon no longer looks bigger. So context cues don't explain this.

Flattened-Sky-Dome Hypothesis

Some scholars think that the moon illusion happens because people view the sky as a flattened dome. (See diagram.) They say this makes the moon seem closer overhead, so the brain adjusts to make it look smaller. This seems logical in a diagram, but it doesn't make sense. If the moon seems closer overhead, it should look bigger—not smaller.

Complex Human Vision

Experts who study vision say many things could contribute to the moon illusion:

- **Focal distance:** Depth of focus changes the apparent size of objects. When the moon is on the horizon, people focus at maximum stereoscopic distance (50–100 feet); when it is overhead, they focus at resting distance (3–6 feet).

- **Linear and angular size:** Seen through a window, a mountain looks both bigger (linear size) and smaller (angular size) than the window. The eyes and brain together decipher these two perspectives and judge size and distance of that mountain—and of the moon.

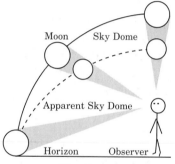

Moon Sky Dome

Apparent Sky Dome

Horizon Observer

Sky Dome

- **Visual orientation:** People see things better up close and on the same level than far away and high or low. People's sense of balance affects their vision, which is why the moon illusion disappears when looking upside down.

- **Age:** The moon illusion decreases with age, as the brain acquires more experience in judging size and distance.

Obviously, the reasons for the moon illusion are not simple. This subject continues to fascinate scholars and probably will for years to come.

A graphic helps to clarify an idea and adds visual appeal.

A bulleted list helps the reader digest related information.

Try It!

Design a page. Create an effective design for an essay or a report you've written. Then share that design with a classmate. Does the design appeal to the reader's eye? Is it clear and easy to follow? Does it distract the reader in any way?

Publishing Online

The Internet offers many publishing opportunities, including online magazines and writing contests. The information below will help you submit your writing for publication on the Net. (At home, always get a parent's approval first. In school, follow all guidelines established by the administration.)

■ Check local sites.

Ask your teacher whether your school has a Web site where students can post work. Also check with local student organizations to see if any of them have Web sites that accept submissions.

■ Find other sites.

Use a search engine to find sites that publish student work. Pay special attention to online magazines for young adults. Also refer to the Write Source Web site—*www.thewritesource.com*—and click on the "Publish It" link for publishing ideas. If you don't have any luck with getting published, consider creating your own Web site. (See pages **80–81**.)

■ Submit your work.

Once you find online sites where you would like to submit your work, carefully follow these tips.

- **Understand the publishing guidelines for each site.** Be sure to share this information with your teacher and your parents.
- **Send your writing in the correct form.** Some sites have online forms. Others will ask you to send your writing by mail or e-mail. Always explain why you are sending your writing.
- **Provide contact information.** Don't give your home address or any other personal information unless your parents approve.
- **Be patient.** Within a week or so of your submission, you should receive a note from the publisher verifying that your work has been received. However, it may take many weeks for the publisher to make a decision about publishing it.

Try It!

Surf the Net. Look for Web sites that accept student submissions for publication. List two or three possibilities. Print out the submissions guidelines for each one.

Creating Your Own Web Site

To create a Web site on your home computer, check with your Internet service provider to find out how to get started. If you are using a school computer, ask your teacher for help. Then follow these steps.

■ Plan your site.

Begin by answering the following questions:
■ What will be the purpose of this Web site?
■ How are my favorite sites set up?
■ How many pages will I include?
■ How will my pages be linked together?

■ Create the pages.

First plan your pages by sketching them out. Then create each page as a text file. Most word-processing programs let you save a file as a Web page. If yours doesn't, you will have to add hypertext markup language (HTML) codes to format the text and make links to graphics and other pages. You can find instructions about HTML on the Net. (See "Web Design" on the Write Source Web site—*www.thewritesource.com*—for help.)

■ Test your pages.

Use your browser to open your first page. Then follow any links to make sure they work correctly. Finally, be sure that all the pages look the way that you want them to look.

■ Upload the site.

Ask your Internet provider how to upload your finished pages. (If you're working at home, make sure to get your parents' approval first. If you're using school equipment, work with a teacher.) When you complete this step, visit your site to make sure it still works.

■ Publicize the site.

Once your site is up, e-mail your friends and tell them to visit it. Ask visitors to your site to spread the word to other people they know.

Try It!

If you're interested in creating a personal Web site, plan your site. Then sketch out your pages.

Sample Home Page

This home page includes links to the student's art, his blog site, and his best writing. It also gives information about one of his favorite hobbies—skateboarding.

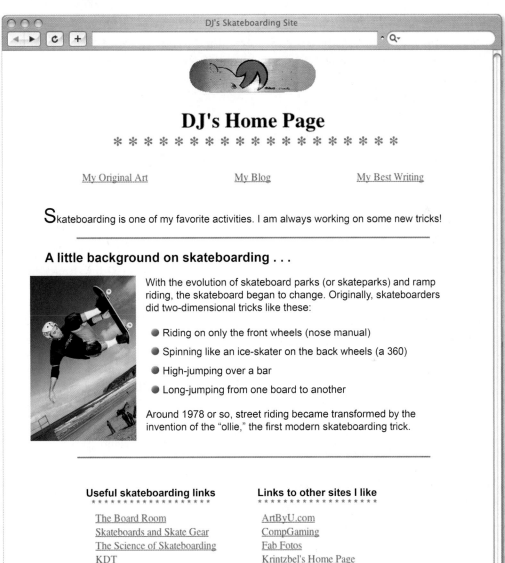

Finding Places to Publish

Here are publications that accept student submissions, and the facts about three writing contests. (Refer to *Writer's Market*—found in most libraries—for more places to publish.) Be sure you understand the publishing conditions for a publication or a contest and share this information with your parents.

Publications

Kids Byline: A Magazine for Kids by Kids (Grades 2–12)
FORMS: Fiction, nonfiction, poetry
SEND TO:
P.O. Box 1838
Frederick, MD 21702

Teen Ink (Grades 6–12)
FORMS: Articles, art, photos, reviews, poems, fiction
SEND TO:
P.O. Box 30
Newton, MA 02461

The High School Writer (Grades 9–12)
FORMS: Fiction, poetry, nonfiction
SEND TO:
Senior High Edition
P.O. Box 718
Grand Rapids, MN 55744

Skipping Stones: A Multicultural Children's Magazine (Ages 8–16)
FORMS: Art, stories, photos, and articles in any language
SEND TO:
P.O. Box 3939
Eugene, OR 97403

Writing Contests

Read Writing Contests (Grades 9–12)
FORMS: Short stories, personal essays
SEND TO:
Read Writing and Art Awards
Weekly Reader Corporation
200 First Stamford Place
P.O. Box 120023
Stamford, CT 06912-0023

The American Library of Poetry: Student Poetry Contest
(Grades 8–9 and 10–12)
FORMS: One poem (20-line limit) on any subject, and in any form
SEND TO:
Student Poetry Contest
P.O. Box 978
Holuton, ME 04730

Scholastic Writing Awards
(Grades 9–12)
FORMS: Short story, essay, poetry, dramatic script, humor, science fiction, fantasy, writing portfolio
SEND TO:
The Scholastic Art and Writing Awards
557 Broadway
New York, NY 10012

Try It!

To which magazine or contest on this page would you most like to submit your writing? Why? Which piece of your writing would you submit? Why?

Creating a Portfolio

A **writing portfolio** is a collection of your work that shows your skill as a writer. In most cases, you will be asked to compile a *showcase portfolio*—a collection of your best writing for a school term. Compiling a portfolio gets you involved in the assessment process. You decide which writing to include; you decide how to present your work; and you reflect on your writing progress. In short, compiling a portfolio puts you in control.

A writing portfolio is like a photo album. Instead of showing just one picture of you as a writer, a portfolio shows a series of pictures at different points in your development as a writer. An album of your writing gives a very clear picture of your writing abilities.

- **Understanding Portfolios**
- **Parts of a Portfolio**
- **Creating a Cover Sheet**
- **Completing an Evaluation Checklist**

"It's not what a piece of writing is about, but how it's written, that makes good writing good."

—Katie Wood Ray

Understanding Portfolios

There are four basic types of writing portfolios: a *showcase portfolio*, a *growth portfolio*, a *personal portfolio*, and an *electronic portfolio*.

A **growth portfolio** shows your progress as a writer. It contains writing assignments that show how your skills are developing.

A **showcase portfolio** presents the best writing you have done during a term. This type of portfolio is used for evaluation.

An **electronic portfolio** is any type of portfolio available online or on a disc. It often includes writing, graphics, video, and sound.

A **personal portfolio** contains writing you want to keep and share with others. Many writers and artists keep personal portfolios arranged according to themes, styles of writing, and so on.

■ Create a portfolio.

Use these tips as a guide when you develop a writing portfolio. Also make sure to follow your teacher's instructions.

Tip

- **Know what is expected of you.** Make sure that you understand all of the requirements for your portfolio.
- **Keep track of all your work.** Save all your prewriting notes, rough drafts, and revisions for each writing project. Then you will have everything you need when compiling your portfolio.
- **Store your papers in a safe place.** Reserve a special folder to keep all of your work.
- **Set a reasonable schedule for creating your portfolio.** You can't put together an effective portfolio by waiting until the last minute.
- **Take pride in your work.** Make sure that your portfolio shows you at your best.

Parts of a Portfolio

Most showcase portfolios contain the following parts. (Before creating your portfolio, though, make sure to check with your teacher for specific requirements.)

- A **table of contents** lists the material included in your portfolio.
- A **brief essay** or **letter** introduces your portfolio, telling how you put it together, how you feel about it, and what it means to you.
- A **collection of writing samples** presents your best work. (Your teacher may require that you include all of your planning, drafting, and revising for one or more of your writings.)
- A **cover sheet** for each sample explains why you selected it.
- **Evaluations, reflections,** or **checklists** identify the skills you have mastered, as well as the skills that you still need to work on.

■ Write your opening pages.

The first two pages of a showcase portfolio are shown here.

Table of Contents

Showcase Portfolio
Justine Grady

Table of Contents

Opening Letter

Dear Ms. Keller,

    I was surprised at how much I wrote this semester. My goal for this class was to keep up with my assignments, and I met that goal. I enjoyed choosing my own topics. It was easier to get to work on my writing and not put it off like I did before. I'm glad I took this class, and I've chosen my best work for my showcase portfolio.

    My first piece is my personal narrative about sledding when I was little. I usually don't like to write personal narratives, but I honestly liked this one. All the prewriting helped for that assignment. (I included my life map and list of memories from early childhood with my rough draft.) Comparing my rough draft to my final copy, I can see that I added a lot of sensory details about the snow and how my breath came out in little crystal puffs. I think I finally understand what "show, don't tell" means.

    I also included my persuasive essay because I have a definite opinion about whether or not only athletes should earn letters. I could tell that it was a good topic because it sparked so much "discussion" in our writing workshop.

    My favorite piece in this portfolio is the expository essay I wrote comparing and contrasting Sylvia Plath and Virginia Woolf. When I started writing, I didn't know much about these writers except that they were women. As I found out more about them, though, I got excited about being a writer myself. I found out I wasn't just comparing them to each other, but comparing them to me.

    In the future, I'd like to focus on my word choice and vocabulary. I'll be reading my favorite authors this summer to inspire me.

    Have a great summer, and I'll see you next year.

Sincerely,
Justine Grady

Try It!

Imagine that you are putting together a showcase portfolio. Think of two pieces of writing that you would include in it. In a brief paragraph, explain the reasons for your choices.

Creating a Cover Sheet

For a showcase portfolio, it's common to attach a cover sheet to each writing project in your portfolio. (See the cover sheet below written for a student essay comparing Sylvia Plath and Virginia Woolf.) Your cover sheet should do one or more of the following things:

- Explain why you chose the piece for your portfolio.
- Tell about the process of writing you used, including any problems that you faced.
- Describe the strong points and the weak points in the writing.
- Reflect on the writing's importance to you.

Sample Cover Sheet

Our assignment was to compare two writers. I read short biographies of several writers, and was surprised by the similarities between Sylvia Plath and Virginia Woolf. They were interesting, and I thought it would be fun to see just how much they were alike.

When I began, I thought it would be easy to compare the two. But I found it was a lot tougher to come up with important ways they were different. I also had some trouble setting up the paper. I actually wrote two first drafts, setting up the information in two different ways, before I could decide what the final format should be.

I think my strongest point in this paper is my voice. As I did my research, I found that both writers were really brilliant but sad people, and I felt really sorry for them. I think my feelings showed in my writing, and that helped make the subjects seem more real, both to me and to the reader. My weakest point was probably my organization. Sometimes my details seemed out of place, even after I rearranged them.

I always thought that a writer was a writer, and gender didn't matter, so I was really surprised to learn how hard it used to be for a woman to be a writer. I also learned how hard it was just to be a writer, period.

Try It!

Write a sample cover sheet for a piece of writing that you would like to include in a portfolio.

Completing an Evaluation Checklist

In a portfolio, it's also common to include a final evaluation checklist in which you review your strengths, weaknesses, and progress as a writer.

Sample Evaluation

The evaluation checklist below covers one student's progress as a writer.

Evaluation

Writer: __Justine Grady__   Class & Term: __English/2__

Skills Mastered:
1. I finally figured out how to use a cluster to find a topic.
2. I now write a first draft without making it perfect right away. My writing sounds more like me from the start!
3. I learned to read my writing backward, one sentence at a time, to edit for spelling and punctuation.

Skills to Work On:
1. I have to be careful when I'm collecting my details. I still tend to put too much information in my writing.
2. My introductions and conclusions are still too short. I have to work more on making them interesting.
3. I still have some trouble with transitions. I don't always use the best words to connect my ideas.
4. I don't always use proofreading marks. I should learn them.

Goals:
1. I would like to make my thoughts flow more smoothly.
2. I also want to learn to build longer, more interesting sentences.

Final Thoughts:
1. I think my writing has really improved. I organize my thoughts more effectively.
2. I'm a more careful editor with punctuation.

Try It!

Create a checklist like the one above on your own paper. Then fill it out to evaluate your own progress as a writer.

Narrative Writing

Narrative Writing

Writing a Personal Narrative

A personal narrative re-creates a specific experience or event in your life. This kind of writing invites the reader to experience what you've experienced. So if a reader says, "It all seems so real to me," you'll know you succeeded.

To write an effective narrative, select an experience that you feel strongly about. For this chapter, you will write about a personal accomplishment—making a team, overcoming a fear, volunteering for a good cause. If you include plenty of action, sensory details, and dialogue, your personal story is sure to connect with the reader.

Writing Guidelines

Subject: A personal accomplishment
Form: Personal narrative
Purpose: To share an important experience
Audience: Classmates

"All writers who have produced anything have done it out of their specific experience."

— Gloria Naylor

Narrative Writing Warm-Up: Be selective.

When you write a personal narrative, it's important to include specific details. However, a reader doesn't need to know every little thing—like the color of the shoes you wore to a band concert. You need to be selective, choosing those details that are key to appreciating the experience.

A writer compiled the list of details below for a narrative paragraph. After reading through his ideas, he crossed out those that weren't important enough to include.

Sample Details List

Climbing Mount Chocorua

— climbed the mountain last summer
— in New Hampshire
— ~~not the highest peak in White Mountains~~
— ~~drove up Mount Washington first~~
— did it on a dare by my brother
— ~~he also dared me to do other things~~
— took a few energy bars and bottled water
— trail started easy
— saw waterfalls, rivers, and jutting rocks
— path steeper above tree line
— ~~no trees above a certain point~~
— had to climb a rocky wall
— brother determined to continue
— ~~no rest stations~~
— saw a dog and other people at top
— missed the easier path at one point
— gorgeous view

Note: This final list of details guided the writer as he wrote a paragraph about his experience. (See the next page.)

Try It!

Think of an exciting experience in your life. List key details related to this experience. Afterward, review your list and cross out any details that are really not that important.

Writing a Narrative Paragraph

A personal narrative paragraph shares a specific experience. The paragraph has three parts:

- The **topic sentence** introduces the experience.
- The **body sentences** share details that re-create the experience.
- The **closing sentence** reflects on the experience.

Sample Narrative Paragraph

In the following narrative paragraph, the writer shares a challenging personal experience—climbing a mountain.

The **topic sentence** introduces the experience.

The **body sentences** share the important details in chronological order.

The **closing sentence** reflects on the experience.

A Gorgeous Dare

Last summer, I climbed a huge mountain, Mount Chocorua in New Hampshire. I wasn't sure that I could make it, but my brother Travis dared me to join him. At first, the rocky trail seemed easy enough. Crystal clear rivers ran along the path, and we stopped in different places to admire a waterfall and fantastic rock formations. After a while, the trail got steeper, and we found ourselves hiking up sharply angled rock faces. After a few hours, we were above the tree line. It was hotter now without any shade and harder to climb, harder to breathe, and the path seemed to disappear. We picked out what we thought was the path, but it led us to a steep rocky wall. Determined not to turn back, my brother began climbing the wall hand over hand, holding on to rocky ledges and cracks. I followed behind, trying to make the same moves that Travis made. Finally, we reached the top, and to our surprise, we were greeted by a dog! A little farther along, there were a lot of people, admiring the view. We discovered that the path that had "disappeared" came up around the other side, and made a much easier, safer climb. We laughed at ourselves as we ate our energy bars. Looking around at the gorgeous scenery, we were glad that we had kept going. **Rough or not, our climb had been worth it.**

Write your narrative paragraph. Review the three parts of a paragraph (top of page) and what they do. Then use your details list from page 90 to write a narrative paragraph about *your* experience.

Understanding Your Goal

Your goal in this chapter is to write a narrative essay about a personal accomplishment or victory in your life. The traits in the following chart can help you do your planning and writing.

TRAITS OF NARRATIVE WRITING

- **Ideas**

  Choose an important accomplishment in your life. Re-create the experience with plenty of specific details.

- **Organization**

  Present the experience in chronological order. Include a strong beginning, middle, and ending.

- **Voice**

  Sound natural, believable, and interested. Use dialogue to make the experience seem real and to reveal the people in your essay.

- **Word Choice**

  Choose specific words with the appropriate connotation, or feeling.

- **Sentence Fluency**

  Use sentences that flow smoothly from one idea to the next.

- **Conventions**

  Be sure that your punctuation, capitalization, spelling, and grammar are correct.

Get the big picture. On pages 124–125 you will find a rubric for narrative writing that will guide you through your writing. Your goal is to write an engaging essay about a personal accomplishment.

"No tears in the writer, no tears in the reader. No surprise for the writer, no surprise for the reader."
—Robert Frost

Personal Narrative

In this personal narrative, the student writer tells about his participation in a fund-raiser. The side notes help explain key parts of the essay.

Walking for Life

Beginning
The writer starts in the middle of the action and introduces the experience.

"Please, Max! You'll have a great time!" Kendra gave me her puppy-dog eyes, and I hesitated.

"Sure, okay, I'll do this Hope thing," I sighed, and she shoved a pledge sheet into my hand. I was supposed to get people to sponsor me for an overnight walk to raise money for cancer research. I hated fund-raisers, I hated asking people for money, and I hated the thought of walking around the high school track for 24 hours. I scribbled my own name down on the sheet and pledged 10 dollars. There. That was enough.

Friday afternoon I arrived at the track. Kendra waved me over to where our team was "camping." Her dad had put up a tent for when we weren't walking—each team had to have at least one member walking at all times.

"Thanks, Max, this means a lot to me." Kendra smiled. As she took my form, a frail-looking woman wearing a bright bandana around her head came up to us.

"Kendra, don't forget to register," the woman said. Kendra hugged her, and I suddenly realized who she was.

"Thanks, Mom, I'll go now. Come on, Max." We started toward the registration booth.

Middle
Dialogue helps move the story along.

"I didn't know—" I mumbled.

"It's okay. She's going to beat it." Kendra pulled out her pledge sheet. It was covered with pledges, front and back.

"You can hand in your pledge sheet now, if you want," she said. Suddenly I looked at my empty sheet. That's how I was feeling inside, empty.

"Uh, no, not yet," I said.

"Walkers, we're ready to start!" Mayor Harris called through a bullhorn, and people started moving toward the starting line.

"Do you want to take the first shift?" Kendra asked.

"No, you go first. I still have a few people to call," I said, pulling out my cell phone.

Middle
Specific details help the reader "see" the experience.

I called everyone I knew—every relative, every friend. I begged, I promised—and I nearly filled my pledge sheet. When it was my turn to walk with the others, I felt as though I belonged with them.

At dusk, the mood became solemn as plain brown paper bags were placed around the perimeter of the track and workers walked along, lighting the candles inside. Each bag had the name of someone's friend or relative who had faced cancer. As the darkness deepened, the field lights were shut off, leaving us in the glow of hundreds of candles. Everyone moved into the bleachers, and Mayor Harris began to speak.

"This disease has touched everyone," she said. "We've come so far, and now more and more people are surviving. Yet there still is no absolute cure. Your participation here will fund research, so that more people can be labeled survivors.

Then the survivors took to the track for the first lap by candlelight. As they walked, the mayor read the names of local people who had died from the disease. Kendra's mother walked by, and I felt a lump in my throat as she waved at us. After the first lap, without a word, everyone left the bleachers to join in, but the only sound was the mayor's voice reading the list of names.

Ending
The writer shares the importance of the experience.

As the crowd moved onto the track, I thought of the money I was raising, of how it would be used, and I knew that I was accomplishing something important. I closed my eyes and listened as the last names were read. Then I took Kendra's hand, and we silently headed to the track to join the other walkers.

Respond to the reading. Answer the following questions about the narrative you just read.

Ideas (1) What is the writer's topic? (2) What two specific details stand out?

Organization (3) How does the writer start his narrative? (4) How is the narrative organized?

Voice & Word Choice (5) How can you tell that the writer is interested in his topic?

Prewriting

Your personal narrative will be about an accomplishment in your life. In your prewriting, you will choose a specific topic, gather your details, and organize your thoughts.

Keys to Effective Prewriting

1. Think about personal successes and accomplishments you could share.

2. Choose one special accomplishment to be your topic.

3. Gather specific details about the experience.

4. Identify the key sensory details related to this time.

5. Organize your ideas chronologically.

6. Use dialogue to add personality to your writing.

Prewriting ■ Select a topic.

Andy completed the sentence starter "I am very proud that I . . . " in four different ways. The activity helped him think of personal accomplishments for his narrative. He put an asterisk next to the one that he wanted to write about.

Sentence Starter

I am very proud that I . . .

    completed a 20-mile bike race.

    learned CPR and first aid.

    helped my grandfather tend his garden.

* prevented a brush fire from getting out of control.

Complete the sentence starter. **Try to come up with at least three things you are proud of. Put an asterisk (*) next to the accomplishment you would like to write about.**

Prewrite

■ Reflect on your topic.

To gather his initial thoughts, Andy wrote freely about his chosen topic. Then he underlined key details that he could use in his narrative.

> I remember the day the hay field caught fire. I had to <u>run from the outer fence to the house to get to the phone</u>. Man that was a long way to run! Then I had to <u>run around the corral by the barn to get to the water trough</u>.
>
> There was a lot of dry grass that wasn't baled yet. The fire chief told Uncle Mark that somebody probably tossed a cigarette out of the window of a passing car or truck, and the grass caught fire. That made me mad!
>
> The smell of the smoke—that weird odor of burning orchard clover. And there was the <u>incredible heat too</u>—when the wind shifted, <u>it hit like a wall and made it really really hard to breathe</u>.
>
> The smoke stung! <u>I had to stop the fire before it got to the barn.</u> My arms were sore from swinging that bucket of water! A firefighter asked me if I was going to be one of them. . . .

Collect your first thoughts. **Write freely for 5 to 10 minutes about your accomplishment. Underline key details that you could use in your narrative.**

Prewrite

Narrative

Prewriting ■ Gather different types of details.

An effective personal narrative contains three types of details: *actions, sensory details,* and *personal thoughts.* Andy completed a chart to gather details for his narrative.

- **Actions** relate what you (and others) did in a situation.
- **Sensory details** show what you saw, smelled, heard, tasted, or touched.
- **Personal thoughts** reveal what you thought during your experience.

Details Chart

Actions	Sensory details	Thoughts
Checking fences	Smelled smoke; saw flames	Get help!
Spotted fire; ran to house to call 911	Tired legs	The fire could spread to the barn!
Called Uncle Mark	Listened to voice mail	I'm all alone!
Ran to corral/barn	Hard breathing; couldn't see in smoke	That hose won't reach far enough.
Grabbed water bucket; threw water on grass	Horses snorting; felt wall of heat from fire	This is scary!
Firefighters arrived	Sirens, flashing lights, aching arms	Relieved

Prewrite

Create a details chart. Refer to your freewriting on page 96 for the main details of your experience. Then fill in a chart like the one above with specific details about what you did, sensed, and thought.

■ Focus on the traits.

Ideas Action is the skeleton of a narrative, but sensory details and thoughts are the muscles that keep it moving. Include all three types of details in your writing.

Prewriting ▪ Build narrative suspense.

Memorable narratives are suspenseful; they make the reader want to know what happens next. Here's how to build suspense into your narrative:

Start with a problem (conflict)—some type of physical or mental obstacle in your way. The problem in Andy's narrative is a brush fire that he has to deal with.

Work in actions that respond to the problem. Andy does a series of things—calls the fire department and his uncle, throws water on the fire, and so on. Each of these actions builds suspense into the story.

Build toward the climax or high point. This is the most exciting part of the narrative, in which the writer does or does not overcome the challenge. Andy's narrative builds to the point when the firefighters finally arrive and control the fire. This part should happen near the end of the narrative.

▪ Focus on the traits.

> **Organization** Narratives follow the classic shape of a plot line. The beginning grabs the reader's attention by identifying the problem. Then rising action builds suspense. (Include at least two or three key actions.) The climax brings the writer face-to-face with the problem. The falling action quickly leads to the resolution. The resolution tells how the person is changed.

Plot Line

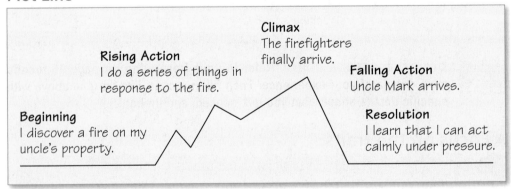

Climax
The firefighters finally arrive.

Rising Action
I do a series of things in response to the fire.

Falling Action
Uncle Mark arrives.

Beginning
I discover a fire on my uncle's property.

Resolution
I learn that I can act calmly under pressure.

Prewrite

Create a story line. Plot out the main actions of your narrative in a story line like the one above. Be sure that you include details that build suspense into your writing. Use your details chart from page 97.

Narrative

Prewriting ■ Add dialogue.

Dialogue makes a personal narrative come alive with added information about the experience. It reveals the speakers' personalities and keeps the action moving. The chart below shows how a writer can express the same idea with or without dialogue. (The dialogue examples are taken from the model on pages 93–94.)

	Without Dialogue	With Dialogue
Show a speaker's personality	I reluctantly got involved with a fund-raiser.	"Sure, okay, I'll do this Hope thing," I sighed, . . .
Keep the action moving	Kendra said that I could turn in my pledge sheet, which was totally empty of pledges.	"You can hand in your pledge sheet now, if you want," she said. Suddenly I looked at my empty sheet. That's how I was feeling inside, empty.
Add information	I discovered that Kendra's mom was battling cancer.	"I didn't know—" I mumbled. "It's okay. She's going to beat it." Kendra pulled out her pledge sheet.

Prewrite

Consider dialogue for your narrative. For practice, write some dialogue that would be appropriate near the beginning of your narrative. (See page 120 for information about punctuating dialogue.)

Prewriting ■ Review features of a narrative.

Remember, memorable personal narratives include action, sensory details, dialogue, and personal thoughts. Look for these features as you read "Fore!"

"Fore!"

I looked at the sea of faces and felt like I was drowning. Why did we have to take a public speaking class anyway? I figured I'd never have to make a speech once I was out of school! Yet there I stood, my eyes watering, my knees shaking, and my stomach flip-flopping.

"Brendan, you may begin whenever you're ready," Ms. Dailey said from the back of the room. What was I going to do? I had to begin, but my mind was frozen.

"Take a deep breath," Ms. Dailey said. "Focus on what you want to say." I didn't want to say anything, but I breathed deeply. It seemed to help. I grasped the pale wood of the podium. Glancing at my first note card, I saw the words "Golf is life." I tried to imagine being on a golf course, the sun warming my face.

"Golf is life. At least that is the way that I look at it," I said. As I continued talking, the words started to flow. "When I make a perfect swing, I know that life is good." I felt good as long as I talked about my game. I lost it in a couple of spots, until I checked my note cards.

"So, anytime you want a little fresh air and exercise, as well as a mental challenge, I suggest you head for the nearest golf course."

I was done! Chelsea gave me a thumbs-up, and Ms. Daily said, "Thank you, Brendan."

I eased into my seat and sighed. One speech down, six more to go. And who knows? Maybe someday I'll win the Masters, and then I will have to give a speech! Now I'll be ready.

On your own paper, identify at least one example of each narrative feature—*action, sensory details, dialogue,* and *personal thoughts*—in the sample above. Then make sure to include these elements in your own personal narrative.

"You want the reader to feel swept along, as if on a kind of trip, from sentence to sentence."

—Russell Freedman

Writing

Now that you have planned your narrative, you're ready to write your first draft.

Keys to Effective Writing

1. Tell the complete story—the beginning, the middle, and the ending.

2. Grab the reader's interest in the beginning, build suspense in the middle part, and, in the ending, tell how you were changed by your experience.

3. Use the details you gathered and organized as a general guide. Feel free to add new ideas as they come to mind.

4. Include dialogue whenever it makes sense to do so.

5. Write on every other line, leaving space for additions and changes later on.

Writing ■ Get the big picture.

The chart below shows how the parts of a personal narrative fit together. (The examples shown are from the essay on pages **103–106**.) As you begin your first draft, be sure you have

- collected plenty of details about your personal accomplishment,
- decided how you will build narrative suspense, and
- considered using dialogue.

BEGINNING

The **beginning** identifies the problem and grabs the reader's attention.

Opening Sentences
Late last summer, I was checking fences on my uncle's property when I smelled smoke. I looked up to see the hay field was on fire!

MIDDLE

The **middle** paragraphs use a variety of details to show what happened. Dialogue keeps the narrative moving.

"There's a brush fire just east of where Highway 9 crosses the White River!"

I hung up the phone and ran outside. I knew I had to do something on my own.

I coughed as smoke filled my lungs.

ENDING

The **ending** explains how the experience changed the writer.

Closing Sentences
I had been scared, but I learned that I could handle emergencies and not panic when things got tough. Learning that about myself was just a bonus on top of helping to save the barn that day.

Tip

How you shape your narrative depends on what you want your story to do. If you want to keep readers in suspense, leave out anything that blows the ending. If you want to make the readers laugh, you'll have to surprise them. Make them expect one outcome but show them another.

Writing ■ Start your personal narrative.

Once you've planned the main parts of your narrative, you're ready to write your first draft. An effective opening paragraph will

■ **grab your reader's attention,**
■ **start in the middle of the action,**
■ **introduce the main problem, and**
■ **include important background information about the experience.**

Beginning Paragraph

> The writer introduces the problem and gains the reader's attention.

    Late last summer, I was checking fences on my uncle's property when I smelled smoke. I looked up to see the hay field was on fire! Since I was the only one there, I had to do something. First, I hopped the split-rail fence and ran to the house. When I got there, I grabbed the phone in the kitchen and dialed 911.

■ Use transitions.

Transitions move the reader smoothly through your writing by signaling time shifts. Choose natural-sounding transitions from the chart below to express the passage of time. For additional choices, see pages **592–593**.

Transition Words and Phrases					
about	besides	later	second	today	when
after	but	meanwhile	so far	tomorrow	whenever
as soon as	during	next	soon	until	while
at	finally	now	then	until now	yesterday
before	first	recently	this time	usually	

Write your beginning. On your own paper, write the first paragraph of your personal narrative. Use transitions to connect your ideas. Afterward, circle any transitions that you have used.

Writing ■ Develop the middle part.

The middle part of your narrative shares the important information related to your experience. *Remember:* Your goal is to tell a good story and hold the reader's interest. Use the tips below as a guide when you develop this part of your writing.

- **Include the key actions,** showing how you reacted to your problem. (See page **97** for help.)
- **Add sensory details** to create effective images (word pictures).
- **Work in your personal thoughts** and feelings whenever they add interest to your narrative.
- **Maintain suspense!** (See page **98**.)

Middle Paragraphs

The writer shows his personality through the dialogue.

> "911. What's the nature of your emergency?"
>
> "There's a brush fire just east of where Highway 9 crosses the White River!"
>
> "Your name and address, sir?"
>
> "I'm Andy Summers at 47113 Hammer Lane. This is Greenwood Stables. When will you guys get here?"
>
> "It'll take at least 10 minutes to get out to you. What I need you to do now—"
>
> "Oh man! The barn could be on fire by then!"
>
> "Stay calm, sir. I need you to—"

Each new action builds the suspense.

> I hung up and called my uncle's cell phone. The phone rang four times before he picked up. "This is Mark—"
>
> "Uncle Mark! There's a fire—" I yelled, but his voice kept going.
>
> "—Greenwood Stables. Please leave me a voice-mail message after the beep and let me know where and when to call you back. Thanks."

Narrative

After the beep, I said, "Uncle Mark! There's a fire in the hay field! I called 911 already, but get home quick!"

I hung up the phone and ran outside. I knew I had to do something on my own. If the tall grass around the stables caught fire, we could lose the barn, the stables, and even the house!

The fire didn't have roaring flames, but it spread fast in the dry grass. Uncle Mark and I had mowed the hay field a few days before, but we had only baled half of the cut grass. Just then, the smoke blew in thick and made the horses run and snort in the corral. I felt scared when smoke surrounded me as I ran between the corral and the barn. Suddenly I hit a wall of heat, and I could hardly breathe or see. I kept running toward the water trough on the other side of the hay field fence, hoping I could slow the fire down.

By now, the fire was about 100 feet away from the horses and me. I knew the hose on the side of the barn wouldn't reach the fire. I grabbed a bucket by the water trough and started throwing buckets of water on the grass between the barn and the fire. I knew I couldn't stop the blaze, but I thought I could slow it down if I soaked the grass enough. I coughed as smoke filled my lungs. I was really scared. Then I heard the distant sirens of the fire trucks growing louder as they approached.

The writer includes his personal thoughts and feelings.

Sensory details create effective images.

Another key action builds to the climax.

Write

Write your middle paragraphs. Use your prewriting notes to guide your writing. Keep the following drafting tips in mind.

Tip

- Remember that your purpose is to tell about a personal accomplishment or victory.
- Write freely. Relax and let your ideas flow. Don't worry about having everything correct in a first draft.
- Add important ideas that occur to you along the way.

Writing ■ End your personal narrative.

The ending of your personal narrative shows how you overcame your problem and accomplished something. It is your chance to reflect on the experience and tell what you learned about yourself.

Ending Paragraphs

> The writer builds suspense up to this point.

> Through the smoke, I saw the flashing lights of the fire engines. A tanker truck on the highway began to spray water on the eastern side of the fire. Another tanker truck pulled into the driveway behind me. Firefighters started to spray around the barn. I was relieved when Uncle Mark's truck skidded to a stop at the barn.
>
> Uncle Mark yelled, "Andy? You okay?"
>
> I smiled at him and said, "I guess so." I had been scared, but I learned that I could handle emergencies and not panic when things got tough. Learning that about myself was just a bonus on top of helping to save the barn that day.

> The conclusion tells what the writer learned.

Write

Write your ending and form a complete first draft. Complete your essay by sharing the climax of your personal accomplishment and telling what you learned from the experience. Then write a final copy of your narrative, double-spacing so you have room to revise your writing.

Tips

- If you are having difficulty with the ending, put your writing aside for a while. Stepping away from your work for a time will make it easier to reflect on the importance of the experience.

- Consider these suggestions if you're finding it hard to write your ending:

  - Think in terms of *before* and *after*. What were you like before the experience, and how were you different after it?

  - What one word describes how you felt after the experience (*proud, mature, happy*)? Why did you feel that way?

  - Consider the *good* and the *bad*. What did you do well during this experience, and what could you have done better?

Revising

Your first draft is your first look at a developing narrative. During the revising step, you improve your first draft by adding to, rewriting, or reorganizing different parts. Focus on these traits when you revise: *ideas, organization, voice, word choice,* and *sentence fluency.*

Keys to Effective Revising

1. Set aside your first draft for a day or two, if possible, before you review your writing.

2. Be sure each main part—the beginning, the middle, and the ending—works well.

3. Revise any parts that seem confusing or incomplete.

4. Pay special attention to your writing voice. Do you sound truly interested in the experience?

5. Use specific words that reflect your feelings about the experience.

6. Be sure your sentences read smoothly.

Revising ■ for Ideas

 6 My writing tells about one experience. My ideas and details totally engage the reader.

 5 My narrative "shows" my ideas with details that hold my reader's interest.

 4 I have enough details, but my narrative should "show" more ideas, not "tell" them.

When you revise for *ideas*, be sure your narrative "shows" your experience and doesn't just "tell" it. Be sure you have included enough details to make the narrative clear. The rubric above will help guide you as you revise and improve your ideas.

■ Do I *show* rather than *tell* in my narrative?

Your narrative *shows* if sentences contain action, sensory details, dialogue, and your personal thoughts and feelings. Writing that shows makes a personal narrative come alive for the reader. Review the sentences that follow to see the difference between showing and telling in writing.

Telling: It looked like rain.

Showing: Dark gray clouds loomed overhead and thunder rumbled in the distance.
(Sensory details create a strong image.)

 ## Exercise

Decide whether each of the following sentences *shows* or *tells*.

1. Grace had never seen the aurora borealis.
2. We saw many neat things in the desert.
3. Marcus staggered across the finish line, nearly doubled over in pain.
4. The sky was black with birds, all racing to the south.
5. Jeff told me that the sound system wasn't working.
6. Under the boardwalk, a few homeless people hang up sheets, lay out old clothes, and stack up full plastic bags.
7. I knew I was in for a bumpy ride when Dad said, "Let's use the old pickup."

Revise

Review your sentences. Be sure that your narrative contains enough action, details, and dialogue to show rather than tell.

Narrative

3 I should focus on one experience and use more sensory details.

2 I should focus on one experience and use more details.

1 I should include more details about my topic or choose a different experience.

■ Have I included enough details?

You have included enough details if the reader has a complete picture of your experience. Use the 5 W's and H—*who? what? when? where? why?* and *how?*—to learn whether you have covered the experience thoroughly enough.

Exercise

Read the following paragraph about a personal experience. Then, on your own paper, list the 5 W's and H for the experience.

> To complete pull-ups in Mr. Brown's gym class is a major accomplishment. I found that out last week when we had fitness tests in the gym. We had to start a pull-up by hanging from the bar with our arms straight. Our palms had to face toward the bar. As we raised ourselves, our bodies had to remain straight. Mr. Brown tapped our stomachs with a yardstick if we started to bend or wiggle. Our chins had to rest on the bar. I wasn't sure how I would do because I hadn't worked out too much. . . .

Revise

Check your details. Review the first draft of your personal narrative to be sure that it answers the 5 W's and H. If it does not answer one or more of these questions, add the necessary details.

Ideas
A variety of details are added to help show the experience.

Just then, the smoke blew in thick and made the horses
I felt scared when smoke surrounded me as
run and snort in the corral. I ran between the corral and the
and I could hardly breathe or see.
barn. Suddenly I hit a wall of heat, but I kept running toward

the water trough on the other side of the hay field fence.
hoping
I just hoped I could slow the fire down.

Revising ■ for Organization

 6 The organization makes my narrative very enjoyable to read.

 5 My narrative has a clear beginning, middle, and ending. My transitions are effective.

 4 My narrative is clearly organized. My beginning or ending could be stronger. I use transitions.

When you revise for *organization*, be sure all parts of your narrative work smoothly together. Use the rubric above to guide you.

■ Does my beginning grab the reader's attention?

Your beginning grabs the reader's attention if it does one of these things: (1) starts in the middle of the action, (2) creates a clear image with sensory details, or (3) opens with a personal thought.

- ■ Start in the middle of the action.

  Number 44 kicked the ball. It soared high above our heads as the teams charged down the field.

- ■ Create an image with sensory details.

  The rain hit my helmet, like a soft tapping on a door. I pulled my chin strap tighter and snapped it on the other side.

- ■ Give a personal thought.

  Fourth down in overtime . . . this is the stuff dreams are made of.

Exercise

Decide whether each opening starts in the middle of the action, creates an image, or gives a personal thought.

1. I guess all kids go through a pretending stage. Why dressing up was so important to me, though, I don't know.
2. The train screeched to a halt, just far enough up the hill for me to see a waterfall cascading into a deep ravine.
3. "Jermaine, get into the game for Eddie," Coach Lee said. "On defense, switch with Terrell. I want you to guard Adams, and don't let him get to the basket."

Revise

Reread your beginning. If your beginning seems a little flat, improve it by trying one of the strategies above.

3 My beginning or ending is weak. Some details are out of order. I need more transitions.

2 I need clearer beginning, middle, and ending parts. I should use transitions.

1 My narrative is very confusing. I should organize my writing chronologically.

■ Does my ending work well?

You know you have created an effective ending if you can answer *yes* to these four questions.

1. Does my essay build to my personal victory or accomplishment?
2. Does my personal narrative end soon after the most intense or most important moment?
3. Will my reader know why this event is important to me?
4. Are all my reader's questions answered?

If any of these questions leads to a *no* answer, revise your ending to make it solid and satisfying.

Revise

Check your ending. Answer the questions above in order to improve your essay's ending.

Organization
The writer adds details about what he learned.

Uncle Mark yelled, "Andy? You okay?"

I smiled at him and said, "I guess so." I had been
                                        and not panic when things got tough
scared, but I learned that I could handle emergencies.
Learning that
~~What I learned~~ about myself was just a bonus. ~~What really~~
on top of helping to save the barn that day.
~~mattered was that the fire didn't wreck anything.~~

Tip

To conclude a speech, speakers often say, "In closing, I would like to leave you with this . . . " To end your narrative, make sure to leave the reader with a thought that truly puts your experience in perspective.

Revising ■ for Voice

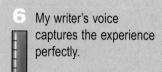
6 My writer's voice captures the experience perfectly.

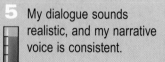
5 My dialogue sounds realistic, and my narrative voice is consistent.

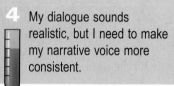
4 My dialogue sounds realistic, but I need to make my narrative voice more consistent.

When you revise for *voice*, be sure your dialogue sounds realistic and your narrative voice is consistent. The rubric above can guide your revision.

■ Does my dialogue sound realistic?

Your dialogue sounds realistic if it reveals the speaker's personality. Here are some adjectives that can describe both the words and personality of a speaker.

eager	bubbly	suspicious	hopeful	bold	elegant
angry	cautious	awkward	bored	confused	worried

Flat Dialogue

"I just heard that I was chosen for the debate team." (flat voice)

Dialogue That Shows Personality

"This rocks! I made the debate team!" (eager)

"How did this happen? I never tried out for the debate team . . . " (suspicious)

Exercise

Read the dialogue below and write an adjective that best describes each speaker's personality.

1. "I'm no good at talking in public."
2. "Nobody can beat me in an argument."
3. "The key to winning any debate is to conduct careful research."
4. "I think the other debate team is up to something."

Revise

Check your dialogue. Think of an adjective to describe the personality of each speaker in your narrative. Does that adjective also describe the words of that person? Rework your dialogue until it sounds realistic.

Narrative

3 My dialogue needs to sound more natural, and my narrative voice needs to be more consistent.

2 My dialogue sounds unnatural, and I don't have a narrative voice.

1 My writer's voice needs work. It is inconsistent, sounds unnatural, and lacks dialogue.

■ Have I created a consistent narrative voice?

You have created a consistent narrative voice if your writing sounds like you throughout the piece. Any parts of your writing that sound unnatural will distract the reader.

Exercise

Read the following paragraph. Identify two sentences that sound unnatural. Rewrite them to fit the predominant narrative voice.

> When I was little, my dad decided that I should learn about farm animals. So he took me to the petting zoo in the city park. His initial action was to deposit me in the goat containment. The wobbly little goats just quietly stared at me—until the keeper set a milk bottle in my hand. Suddenly, the spindly mob charged me, bleating and fighting for food. I held the bottle higher, which made the animals start to climb me! My father quickly rescued me after I started sobbing. I did not hold these animals in high regard, but over time, I learned to enjoy them. I just always left the feeding to the caretaker.

Revise

Check your narrative voice. Read your narrative aloud and listen for sentences that introduce an unnatural voice. Rework them.

Voice
The dialogue is made more realistic, and the voice is made consistent.

"911. What's the nature of your emergency?"

~~"I have~~ There's a brush fire ~~at the junction~~ just east of Highway 9 where ~~and the~~ White River ~~!"~~ crosses

"Your name and address, sir?"

~~"Where you at, kid?"~~

Revising ■ for Word Choice

6 My word choice captures the experience and relates it vividly.

5 My word choice is specific and conveys the right feeling.

4 Most of my words have the right feeling, but they aren't always specific enough.

When you revise for *word choice*, be sure to use specific verbs and words with the right connotation, or feeling. Use the rubric strip above as a guide.

■ Have I used specific verbs?

You know you have used specific verbs when your sentences share clear actions. General verbs do not create a clear picture.

General Verbs	Specific Verbs	
move	shift	amble
	wobble	dawdle
	dart	sneak
look	gaze	study
	stare	peek
	gawk	view

Exercise

In the following sentences, replace the underlined words with specific verbs. Use a thesaurus if you need help.

1. The yapping dachshund <u>moves</u> across the sidewalk.
2. I <u>say</u>, "Watch out! It sounds mean!"
3. Jill and I <u>walk</u> away, but the dachshund <u>comes</u> after us.
4. Suddenly a boy <u>says</u> the dog's name and whistles.
5. The dachshund turns and starts <u>moving</u> its tail.

Revise

Check for specific verbs. Make sure that your verbs give a clear idea of what is happening in your narrative. If you need to replace a general verb, check a thesaurus.

3 I need to use more specific words and words with the appropriate feeling.

2 My words are very general. I need to find words with the right feeling.

1 I need help finding the right words. My words do not express my feelings.

■ Do my verbs have the right connotation?

Your verbs have the right connotation when they create the feeling you want. *Connotation* is the suggested meaning or feeling of a word. Notice the different feeling in each set of verbs below.

yell	call	bellow
laugh	giggle	jeer
smile	grin	sneer
discuss	debate	argue

Exercise

For each verb below, write one synonym that has a different connotation. Use a thesaurus if you need help.

1. watch   **4.** repeat   **7.** laugh
2. change   **5.** say   **8.** go
3. walk   **6.** look   **9.** take

Revise

Check connotations. Read through your narrative and watch for verbs with the wrong feeling. Replace them to create the tone or the feeling that fits your story.

Word Choice
Specific words with the right feeling create a stronger tone.

The fire didn't have ~~big~~ roaring flames, but it spread fast in the dry grass. Uncle Mark and I had mowed the hay field a few days before, but we had only ~~gathered~~ baled up half the cut grass.

Revising ■ for Sentence Fluency

 6 My sentences are skillfully written and hold the reader's interest throughout.

 5 I have a variety of sentences that flow smoothly.

 4 Most sentences flow smoothly, but I could use some longer sentences.

When you revise for *sentence fluency*, check to see if you have used a variety of long and short sentences. Use the rubric above as a guide.

■ When should I use long sentences?

Long sentences work best to express complex ideas. In the following example, notice how each long sentence (in blue) expresses several ideas and creates a thoughtful tone.

> That morning, I woke up in Aunt Chante's spare bedroom, the one where she grew up and where she still kept her "Lionel Richie Shrine." Lionel Richie was a singer when Aunt Chante was my age, and she still had all her posters of him on the walls and a couple of Commodores album covers thumbtacked to the paisley wallpaper. **I smiled.** Even though Chante was almost 40, at heart she was a teenager like me—funny and crazy with an I-don't-care-what-you-think-of-me attitude. **It was going to be a good day.**

Exercise

Choose one of the long sentences above and write your own sentence that models it. Replace each phrase with a similar phrase about your own topic. Here is an example modeled after the second sentence:

> John Wayne was an actor before I was born, but I still like watching the Westerns he made in the '50s and reading biographies about his career.

Check your sentence style. Do you use long sentences to express complex or reflective ideas? Add long sentences or combine short sentences into longer sentences as needed.

3 Too many sentences are the same. I should use some long and some short sentences.

 2 My sentences are choppy or incomplete, making them hard to read and understand.

 1 Most of my sentences should be rewritten.

■ When should I use short sentences?

Short sentences work well to deliver especially important ideas. Use them like an exclamation point to give a powerful punch. The short sentence in the following example (in blue) makes the reader sit up and take notice.

> **Chante took me to Trinity Church where she sang in a choir with more than 300 people, all of them in Kente cloth and all of them swaying as they belted out Gospel music.** Chante sang a solo.

A series of short sentences can quicken the pace, like a heart beating faster and faster.

> She sang *Amazing Grace*, low and smooth. Then the key changed. Chante took the song up a few steps. The choir sang faster and louder. Chante overtopped them all. They all reached the final chord. What a chord it was! **I suddenly wished that Lionel Richie could see Chante now, wished that I were up there singing with her, too.**

Revise

Check your sentence style. Watch for places in your narrative where a single short sentence could deliver an important idea to the reader. Watch for places where a series of short sentences could speed up the pace. Consider adding or changing sentences.

Sentence Fluency
Combine short sentences to convey complex ideas.

> I grabbed a bucket by the water trough, ∧ started throwing ^and^
>
> buckets of water on the grass between the barn and the
>
> fire. I knew I couldn't stop the blaze, ∧ I thought I could slow it ^, but^
>
> down if I soaked the grass enough. . . .

Revising ■ Improve your writing.

Check your revising. On your own paper, write the numbers 1 to 12. Put a check by the number if you can answer "yes" to that question. If not, continue revising that part of your personal narrative.

Revising Checklist

Ideas

_____ **1.** Do I focus on one personal accomplishment?
_____ **2.** Do I include action, sensory details, and personal thoughts?
_____ **3.** Do I *show* more than *tell*?

Organization

_____ **4.** Are my beginning, middle, and ending parts effective?
_____ **5.** Do the actions in the middle part create suspense?
_____ **6.** Are the actions and details organized chronologically?

Voice

_____ **7.** Does my dialogue sound realistic?
_____ **8.** Do I have a consistent narrative voice?

Word Choice

_____ **9.** Do I use specific nouns and verbs and explain technical terms?
_____ **10.** Do I use verbs with the right connotation?

Sentence Fluency

_____ **11.** Do I use some long sentences to express complex thoughts?
_____ **12.** Do I use short sentences to pick up the pace or deliver an important idea?

Make a clean copy. When you've finished revising your essay, make a clean copy to edit.

Editing

Once you've made your revisions, you can edit your writing for conventions: punctuation, capitalization, spelling, and grammar.

Keys to Effective Editing

1. Use a dictionary, a thesaurus, and the "Proofreader's Guide" on pages 604–763 in this book to guide your corrections.

2. Check for any words or phrases that may be confusing to the reader.

3. Check your narrative for correct use of punctuation, capitalization, spelling, and grammar.

4. Edit on a printed computer copy and then enter your changes on the computer.

5. Use the editing and proofreading marks on the inside back cover of this book to note your changes.

Editing ■ for Conventions

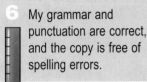
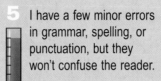
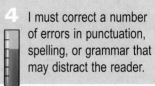
When you edit for *conventions*, you check punctuation, capitalization, spelling, and grammar. Use the rubric strip above to help you edit your writing for conventions.

■ Have I punctuated dialogue correctly?

You have punctuated dialogue correctly if you have followed the three rules shown below.

- ■ Use a comma to set off a speaker's exact words from the rest of the sentence.
  "Bob Taylor, it's a pleasure to meet you," said Melissa Moore.

- ■ Place periods and commas inside quotation marks.
  "Hello," Bob said. "It's a pleasure to meet you."

- ■ Place an exclamation point or a question mark outside quotation marks when it punctuates the main sentence, and inside when it punctuates the quotation.
  What if someone said to you, "You've won a million dollars!"?
  I would say, "Are you kidding me?"

Exercise

On your own paper, punctuate these sentences correctly.

1. Angie said Do you believe that guy?
2. Was Marta joking when she said Talk about attitude!?
3. Crystal screamed Don't you know who he was?
4. Yeah! Ora shrieked That guy was Phil Axis, the record producer!
5. That guy asked Angie Do you want to be on my record?

Edit

Edit your dialogue. Use the rules and examples in the middle of this page to be sure you've punctuated the dialogue correctly. Also see pages **616.1** and **632.1–632.2**.

Narrative

 3 I need to correct some errors that will confuse my reader.

 2 I need to fix many errors that make my writing hard to read and understand.

1 I need help finding errors and making corrections.

■ Have I used pronouns correctly?

You have used pronouns correctly if they agree with their antecedents. (An *antecedent* is a noun or pronoun that a pronoun replaces or refers to.) A pronoun must agree with its antecedent in number, person, and gender.

A pronoun must agree with its antecedent in number (singular or plural), person (first, second, or third person), and gender (masculine, feminine, neuter, or indefinite). (See pages **708–711**.)

Mr. Lucas **owns 10 horses, and** he **trains** them.

(*Mr. Lucas* is the antecedent for *he*. Both words are singular, third person, and masculine. *Horses* is the antecedent for *them*. Both words are plural, third person, and indefinite.)

 ## Exercise

Write sentences following the directions below.

1. Use a singular first-person pronoun and antecedent.
2. Use a plural third-person pronoun and antecedent.
3. Use a singular third-person masculine pronoun and antecedent.

 Check your pronouns. Review your personal narrative to make sure that you have used pronouns correctly. Use the information above as a guide.

Edit

Conventions
Punctuation
is added and
a pronoun-
antecedent
agreement
problem is
corrected.

After the beep, I said, "Uncle Mark! There's a fire in the

hay field! I called 911 already, but get home quick!"

I hung up the phone and ran outside. I knew we had

my

to do something on our own. If the tall grass around the . . .

Editing ■ Check your writing.

Edit

Check your editing. On a piece of paper, write the numbers 1 to 12. Put a check by the number if you can answer "yes" to that question. If not, continue to edit your narrative for that convention.

Editing Checklist

Conventions

PUNCTUATION

_____ **1.** Do I use end punctuation after all my sentences?

_____ **2.** Do I use commas after longer introductory word groups?

_____ **3.** Do I use commas correctly in compound and complex sentences?

_____ **4.** Do I punctuate my dialogue correctly?

_____ **5.** Do I use apostrophes to show possession *(a girl's book)*?

CAPITALIZATION

_____ **6.** Do I start all my sentences with capital letters?

_____ **7.** Do I capitalize all proper nouns?

SPELLING

_____ **8.** Have I spelled all my words correctly?

_____ **9.** Have I double-checked the words my spell-checker may have missed?

GRAMMAR

_____ **10.** Do I use correct forms of verbs *(had gone,* not *had went)*?

_____ **11.** Do my pronouns agree with their antecedents?

_____ **12.** Do I use the right words *(to, too, two; their, there, they're)*?

■ Add a title.

- Focus on the tone or the overall feeling created by the words in your essay: **Racing Against a Fire**
- Use alliteration, the repetition of a consonant sound: **Face-to-Face with Fire**
- Play with words: **Almost Up in Smoke!**

Publishing ■ Share your essay.

After you have completed revising and editing, you can make a neat final copy of your story to share. Other publishing ideas include recording your narrative, presenting it in a class blog, or simply sharing it with a group of your peers. (See the suggestions below.)

Publish

Make a final copy. When you write your final copy, follow your teacher's instructions or use the guidelines below. (If you use a computer, see pages 76–78 for formatting tips.) Create a clean copy of your personal narrative and carefully proofread it.

■ Focus on presentation.

- Use blue or black ink and write neatly.
- Write your name in the upper left-hand corner of page 1.
- Skip a line and center your title; skip another line and begin your essay.
- Double-space your narrative.
- Indent every paragraph and leave a one-inch margin on all four sides.
- Write your last name and the page number in the upper right-hand corner of every page after the first one.

Record Your Narrative

Produce a recording of your narrative. Use an expressive voice that matches the tone of your work. Give the recording and a printed copy of the narrative to friends and family as a gift.

Create a Class Blog

Encourage all of your classmates to submit their stories to a class blog or Web site. Use graphics to illustrate each narrative.

Perform Your Narrative

Turn your narrative into a script. Assign roles and perform the story for the class or for other audiences. (See pages 323–332 for help.)

Narrative

Rubric for Narrative Writing

Use the following rubric as a guide for assessing your narrative writing. Refer to it whenever you want to improve your writing.

6 Ideas	**5**	**4**
The narrative shares a memorable event. Details bring the essay to life.	The writer shares an interesting experience. Specific details help maintain interest.	The writer tells about an interesting experience. Details need to show, not tell.
Organization		
The structure of the narrative makes it enjoyable and easy to read.	The narrative has a clear beginning, middle, and ending. Transitions are helpful.	For the most part, the narrative is organized. Most of the transitions are helpful.
Voice		
The writer's voice captures the experience for the reader.	The writer's voice sounds natural. Dialogue helps hold the reader's interest.	The writer's voice creates interest in the essay, but dialogue needs to sound more natural.
Word Choice		
The writer's excellent word choice creates a vivid picture of the event.	Specific nouns, verbs, and modifiers create clear images and feelings.	Some stronger nouns, verbs, and/or modifiers would create a clearer picture.
Sentence Fluency		
The sentences are skillfully written to hold the reader's interest.	The sentences show variety and are easy to understand.	The sentences are varied, but some should flow more smoothly.
Conventions		
The narrative has no errors in spelling, grammar, or punctuation.	The narrative has a few minor errors in punctuation, grammar, or spelling.	The narrative has some errors that may distract the reader.

3	**2**	**1**
The writer should focus on one event. Some details do not relate to the essay.	The writer should focus on one experience. More details are needed.	The writer should select an experience and provide details.
The order of events must be corrected. More transitions are needed.	The beginning, middle, and ending all run together. The order is unclear.	The narrative must be organized.
The writer's voice can usually be heard. More dialogue is needed.	The voice is weak. Dialogue is needed.	The writer sounds uninvolved or disinterested in the essay.
More specific nouns, verbs, and modifiers would paint a clearer picture of the event.	Better words are needed. Words are overused or too general to paint a clear picture.	The writer has not considered word choice or has used words incorrectly.
A better variety of sentences is needed. Sentences do not flow smoothly.	Many incomplete or short sentences make the writing choppy.	Few sentences are written well. Help is needed.
The narrative has several errors.	Numerous errors make the narrative hard to read and confusing.	Help is needed to find errors and make corrections.

Evaluating a Personal Narrative

As you read the narrative below, focus on the writer's strengths and weaknesses. (**The essay contains a few errors.**) Then read the student's self-assessment on page **127**.

Musical Chairs

Ever since I began playing trumpet in fifth grade, being first chair in the high school band has been my dream. I had worked up to second chair in freshman band, just behind Luis. Now I was challenging him for first chair.

Luis and I sat in the band room after school, waiting for our director, Ms. Reilly. Luis nervously twirled his trumpet, while I fingered the keys on mine. Had I oiled them enough? I flutter the tabs up and down, making quick little "thumpa-thumpa" sounds in the valve casings.

I had worked for this moment, practicing every night. I had changed my embouchure and breathing to get more volume and a fuller sound. I looked at Luis. He was a good guy, and I felt guilty challenging him.

"I'm sorry about this, Luis," I mumbled.

"Hey, it's okay, Jan." he said. "Ya gotta do what ya gotta do." Then he kind of smirked a little. "Besides, who said you're gonna win"?

I laughed. "Well, I'll give it my best shot."

"Me, too."

Ms Reilly arrived and said, "Okay, let's start. Luis, you can go first." He played the trumpet solo from one of our band pieces. He sounded pretty good. Then I played the same piece. I cracked once. But it wasn't too bad. Before that we had run through some short exercises, playing high notes and low notes. Trills and turns. It was cool—like a "dueling trumpets."

"Very nice! Try this one."

She gave us each another piece of music, and this time I went first. It had some tricky fingering, but I got through it. When Luis played, his staccato notes weren't as clean as mine. I started to relax.

Then Ms. Reilly said, "Let's try a brand new piece." I felt my nerves return. Luis looked worried, too.

"To be fair, I want you to play it together first," Ms. Reilly said. "Ready? Start at the andante. One-two, one-two—"

Narrative

As I got into the piece, I concentrated on the notes. Luis and I both messed up in a few places.

"Now one at a time." Ms. Reilly said. "Jan, you go first."

I was surprised how much easier it seemed the second time. At his turn, Luis made more mistakes than I did. Finally we were finished.

"You both did a great job." Ms. Reilly said. "I'm sorry, Luis, but it looks like Jan gets to be first chair."

Luis gave a half grin and said, "Pretty good, Jan. But you know I'll just have to challenge you next."

"I'll be ready," I said.

Student Self-Assessment

Narrative Rubric Checklist

Title: Musical Chairs
Writer: Jan Maggin

6 Ideas
- Is the essay about an important accomplishment?
- Does it have enough specific details about the event?
- Does it *show* the event rather than *tell* about it?

5 Organization
- Does the beginning grab the reader?
- Does the middle part follow chronological order and increase the narrative tension?
- Does the ending work well?

5 Voice
- Is the dialogue realistic?
- Is the narrative voice natural and consistent?

4 Word Choice
- Do the words have the right connotation?
- Are the nouns and verbs specific?

5 Sentence Fluency
- Is there a good variety of sentences?
- Do the sentences flow smoothly?

4 Conventions
- Does the essay avoid errors in punctuation, spelling, and grammar?
- Is the dialogue punctuated correctly?

OVERALL COMMENTS:

The details of my narrative are complete and clear.

The events are in the right order, except for the part about the exercises before the challenge.

My voice and dialogue sound interesting and natural.

I should have explained technical terms like "embouchure," "trills and turns," and "staccato."

My sentences flow well.

I need to review how to punctuate dialogue.

Review your narrative.
Rate your narrative and write comments about why you gave yourself the scores you did.

Reflecting on Your Writing

You've worked hard to write a personal narrative that your classmates will enjoy. Now take some time to think about your writing. Finish each of the sentence starters below on your own paper. Thinking about your writing will help you see how you are growing as a writer.

My Narrative

1. The strongest part of my personal narrative is . . .

2. The part that still needs work is . . .

3. The main thing I learned about writing a personal narrative is . . .

4. In my next personal narrative, I would like to . . .

5. One question I still have about writing personal narratives is . . .

Narrative Writing
Biographical Narrative

Writing a personal narrative gives you a chance to revisit an experience that affected or changed you. In the same way, writing a biographical narrative offers you an opportunity to re-create a significant event in the life of someone you know. An effective biographical narrative makes the experience come alive for the reader by including dialogue, action, and specific details.

In this chapter, you will read a biographical narrative about the writer's great-grandfather, who became famous in the newspaper industry. Then you will write a biographical narrative of your own.

Writing Guidelines

Subject: An important experience in another person's life
Form: Biographical narrative
Purpose: To share a life-changing event
Audience: Classmates

"To write about people you have to know people, to write about bloodhounds you have to know bloodhounds, to write about the Loch Ness monster you have to find out about it."
—James Thurber

Sample Biographical Narrative

A biographical narrative shares a specific experience from someone else's life. Julie wrote about the day her great-grandfather became a news reporter.

Henry's Big Break

Beginning
The first paragraph sets the scene.

My great-grandfather, Henry A. Benson, is the most famous person in our family. He rose from delivering newspapers in his small hometown of Cross Plains, Texas, to becoming the editor in chief of one of the biggest papers in the state. He tells many stories about his days as a reporter, but his favorite one takes place on a late spring afternoon in 1941. That's the day Great-granddad got his big break.

Middle
The middle part starts right in the middle of the action.

Inside the offices of the *Center State Chronicle*, 15-year-old Henry took a deep breath. The warm air of the print room filled his lungs, and the smell of hot ink lingered in his nose. He stuffed his hands into the pockets of his worn-out jeans so the paper's editor, Mr. Walsh, wouldn't see how nervous he felt.

"Mr. Walsh," Henry said, "I've delivered your paper for three years now. I've never missed one day. If you make me a reporter, I won't let you down."

"Henry," Mr. Walsh replied, "there's a big difference between being a delivery boy and being a reporter. Maybe after you've finished school."

Explanations are added as needed.

Trying not to let his disappointment show, Henry left the newspaper office. What was he going to do? The paper route just didn't earn him enough money to help his mom. He got his battered bicycle and pedaled across town toward home.

Near an old bridge, Henry saw skid marks on the pavement. Tire tracks showed where a car had recently left the road. Henry spotted a sedan lying at the bottom of the ravine.

Details capture specific actions.

Henry flagged down a passing car to fetch an ambulance. Then he scrambled down the ravine. The car's right front tire was shredded, which must have been why the car ran off the road. The driver lay slumped over the

Narrative

steering wheel. He was a middle-aged man wearing a rumpled brown suit. A dark bruise marked the driver's forehead.

"Are you all right?" Henry asked the man.

" . . . Can't move my right arm," the driver mumbled.

Henry opened the car door and took a look. He tried not to let the man see how scared he felt. "It looks broken," Henry said. "I'll do what I can to help until the ambulance gets here."

Henry tried to talk to the injured man to keep him awake, but the man passed out anyway. Henry understood the seriousness of the situation and stayed with the man until an ambulance came. Only when the man was safely on his way to the hospital did it occur to Henry that the accident was newsworthy. Maybe this was the story that could make him a real reporter!

He raced home and typed up an account of the accident. Then he pedaled as fast as he could back to the *Chronicle* offices. Editor Walsh ran the story and began to realize that Henry had the right stuff to become a reporter.

In the years that followed, my great-grandfather learned to be a great reporter. Later, he became one of the most respected newspaper editors in Texas. No matter how famous he became, though, he always loved to tell about the day he got his big break. His story still inspires me whenever I think about what kind of job I would really love.

> **Dialogue adds realism.**

> **Ending**
> The final paragraph explains the importance of the experience.

Respond to the reading. Answer the following questions about the sample biographical narrative.

Ideas (1) What specific event does the writer share? (2) What is the most exciting part of the narrative?

Organization (3) How are the beginning and ending parts different from the middle part?

Voice & Word Choice (4) Which words or phrases help create specific images? Name three or four.

Prewriting ■ Select a topic.

Julie used a cluster to identify possible topics for her biographical narrative. Next to each name, she listed one or two possible story ideas.

Cluster Diagram

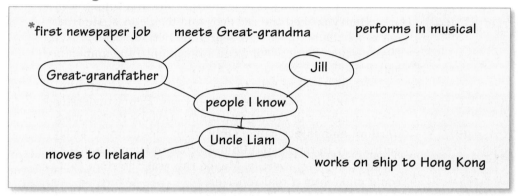

Prewrite

Choose your topic. Create a cluster, naming different people you know and their stories. Put an asterisk (∗) next to the story that you would like to write about.

■ Gather details.

Next you need to gather details for the narrative. Julie wrote freely about her story idea to determine what she remembered about the experience. Here is part of her freewriting.

Freewriting

> My great-grandpa, Henry A. Benson, was a famous news reporter, but he really had to work for everything that he got. He started by delivering papers in a small town. But he wanted to do more, so my great-grandpa asked if he could be a reporter. The editor said that he was too young, but soon Great-grandpa got to prove his ability. . . .

Prewrite

Freewrite to gather details. Write for 10 to 15 minutes about your story idea. Let your ideas flow, writing down everything that comes to mind about the topic.

Prewriting ■ Ask questions.

After reviewing her freewriting, Julie realized that she needed to ask her grandpa a few questions about his dad. Here are some of her questions:

1. Where did Henry live?
2. How old was he when this experience happened?
3. What was the name of the paper and the editor?

Gather more details. Review your freewriting and write down all the questions you have. Talk to someone who knows about the event to find your answers.

■ Organize your details.

A biographical narrative is a type of story, and stories are almost always told chronologically. Julie used a time line to organize the details she had gathered about her great-grandfather's story. Above the line, she listed key events or actions related to the story, and below the line, she listed details.

Time Line

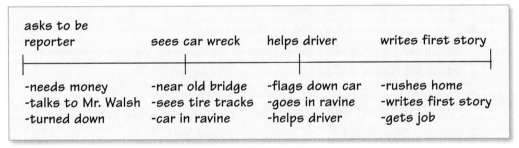

asks to be reporter	sees car wreck	helps driver	writes first story
-needs money	-near old bridge	-flags down car	-rushes home
-talks to Mr. Walsh	-sees tire tracks	-goes in ravine	-writes first story
-turned down	-car in ravine	-helps driver	-gets job

Create a time line. Organize the details of your story. List key events above the line and details below it.

■ Focus on the traits.

Organization The beginning paragraph in the narrative on pages 130–131 introduces the person and his story. The ending paragraph tells what happened because of the experience. In this way, the beginning and ending paragraphs frame the story, which is told in the middle.

Writing ▪ Create your first draft.

Beginning
Middle
Ending

To write your biographical narrative, use your time line of events and details as a guide. Also read through the tips listed on this page. They will help you develop the three main parts of your writing—the beginning, the middle, and the ending.

▪ Write your beginning paragraph.

Set the stage for your story. Introduce the character and his or her story. Give just enough information to grab the reader's interest.

> . . . That's the day Great-granddad got his big break.

▪ Create your middle paragraphs.

Re-create the experience. Let the reader share your experience. Here are four ways to do that.

- ▪ Start right in the middle of the action.
  > Inside the offices of the <u>Center State Chronicle</u>, 15-year-old Henry took a deep breath. The warm air of the print room filled his lungs, and the smell of hot ink lingered in his nose.

- ▪ Provide specific details. Show, don't tell.
  > He stuffed his hands into the pockets of his worn-out jeans so the paper's editor, Mr. Walsh, wouldn't see how nervous he felt.

- ▪ Add dialogue. Reveal the person's character.
  > "Mr. Walsh," Henry said, "I've delivered your paper for three years now. . . ."

- ▪ Include explanations and thoughts as needed.
  > Trying not to let his disappointment show, Henry left the newspaper office. What was he going to do?

▪ Finish with a strong ending paragraph.

Bring your narrative to a close. Tell what happened because of the experience or why it was important.

> In the years that followed, my great-grandfather learned to be a great reporter. . . . His story still inspires me whenever I think about what kind of job I would really love.

Write

Write your first draft. Use your time line (page 133) and the tips above to guide your writing. Your aim is to get all your ideas on paper.

Revising ■ Improve your writing.

Use the following checklist to decide how to improve your writing.

Revising Checklist

Ideas

_____ **1.** Is my subject's story an interesting one?
_____ **2.** Do I include enough specific details?

Organization

_____ **3.** Does my beginning paragraph introduce the person and story?
_____ **4.** Do the middle paragraphs re-create the experience?
_____ **5.** Does the ending tell why the experience was important?

Voice

_____ **6.** Does my interest in the story come through?
_____ **7.** Does the dialogue sound natural?

Word Choice

_____ **8.** Have I used specific nouns?
_____ **9.** Do I capture the experience with vivid verbs and modifiers?

Sentence Fluency

_____ **10.** Do my sentences read smoothly?
_____ **11.** Have I used a variety of long and short sentences?

■ Add a title.

- Be clever: **Accidental Reporter**
- Use an expression: **A Reporter Is Born**
- Use a line from the narrative: **Skid Marks on the Pavement**

Revise

Check your first draft and add a title. Use the checklist above to review your first draft. Then use one of the strategies above or an idea of your own to add a title to your narrative.

Editing ■ Check for conventions.

Once you have revised your narrative, you're ready to edit your writing for conventions. Use the following checklist to guide your editing.

Editing Checklist

Conventions

PUNCTUATION

_____ **1.** Do I use end punctuation correctly?

_____ **2.** Do I use apostrophes to show possession *(Henry's Big Break)*?

_____ **3.** Do I use commas correctly?

CAPITALIZATION

_____ **4.** Do I capitalize all proper nouns?

_____ **5.** Do I capitalize each speaker's first word in quoted dialogue?

SPELLING

_____ **6.** Have I checked my spelling?

GRAMMAR

_____ **7.** Do I use the correct forms of verbs *(didn't earn,* not *didn't earned)*?

_____ **8.** Do my subjects and verbs agree in number *(We were going,* not *We was going)*?

_____ **9.** Do I use the right words *(your, you're)*?

Correct your narrative. Use the checklist above to find and correct any errors. Also ask someone else to check your work. Then create a neat final copy and proofread it.

Edit

Publishing ■ Share your writing.

Sharing your narrative with the subject of your writing (if possible) and with family and classmates is an important part of the writing process.

Share your biographical narrative. If you plan on reading your narrative out loud, be sure to practice first.

Publish

Writing for Assessment
Responding to Narrative Prompts

An important part of life is sharing personal experiences. ("Guess what happened to me.") When you were younger, you may have shared just a few details about each experience. But now that you are older, your personal stories are probably richer and more detailed.

An effective personal story does more than simply tell what happened. It often tells what the writer learned from the experience, and why it is important to him or her. In this chapter, you will learn how to share a personal experience in response to a narrative writing prompt. And besides the story's details, you'll tell why the experience is important to you.

Writing Guidelines

Subject: Narrative prompt
Form: Response to a prompt
Purpose: To demonstrate competence
Audience: Instructor

"Experience is a hard teacher because she gives you the test first, the lesson after."
—Vernon Saunders Law

Prewriting ■ Analyze a narrative prompt.

A prompt is a set of directions that tells you what to write. For example, a narrative prompt tells you to write about a significant personal experience. To effectively respond to a prompt, you must first understand it. The **STRAP questions** below will help you to analyze a narrative prompt.

■ Use the STRAP questions.

<u>S</u>ubject: What specific experience (memorable, life-changing, embarrassing, inspiring) should I write about?

<u>T</u>ype: What type of writing (personal narrative, personal essay, autobiographical article) should I create?

<u>R</u>ole: What role (student, son or daughter, friend, community member) should I assume as the writer?

<u>A</u>udience: Who (principal, parent, city official, classmates) is the intended reader?

<u>P</u>urpose: What is the goal (share, re-create, entertain, illustrate, inspire) of my writing?

Try It!

Analyze these prompts by using STRAP questions for each one.

1. "Help yourself by helping others." Share a personal experience that illustrates this quotation. Your narrative will be in a class booklet for students in your school.
2. Understanding our environment is important. Write an article that relates an experience you had with nature and what you learned from the event. The piece will appear in a science magazine aimed at fourth through sixth graders.
3. Think about a time when you had to work extra hard for something. Write about the experience in a personal narrative intended for a writing contest sponsored by the local newspaper.

Tip

Some prompts do not contain key words for every STRAP question. Use your best judgment to find answers for all the questions.

■ Plan your response.

Once you understand a prompt thoroughly, you can plan your response. The following graphic organizers can help you complete your planning.

Narrative Graphic Organizers

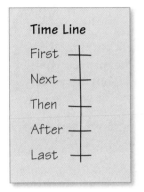

Time Line

First
Next
Then
After
Last

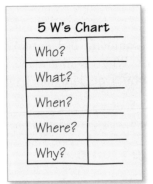

5 W's Chart

Who?	
What?	
When?	
Where?	
Why?	

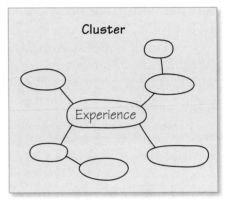

Cluster

Experience

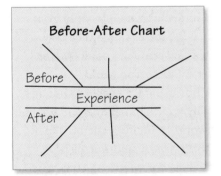

Before-After Chart

Before
Experience
After

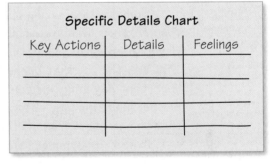

Specific Details Chart

Key Actions	Details	Feelings

Prewrite

Reread the narrative prompts on page 138. Choose one prompt and a graphic organizer from above to organize your response.

Tip

Be sure to use your time wisely. For example, if you have 45 minutes to respond to a prompt, consider using the first 5 to 10 minutes to analyze the prompt and plan your response, and the last 5 minutes to revise and edit it. That leaves 30 to 35 minutes for the actual writing.

Writing ■ Respond to a prompt.

After planning your response, it's time to begin writing. It will be important to keep your audience in mind. Review the following narrative prompt and response.

Sample Narrative Prompt

Think about a time when someone did something that made a significant difference in your life. Write a narrative that captures this important experience and tells what you learned from it. Your story is intended for your classmates.

Sample Response to a Narrative Prompt

The beginning introduces the writer's focus. (underlined)

Each **middle** paragraph presents details about the experience.

Beyond Quitting

Sometimes amazing things happen to people, and from then on, their lives are different. Take, for example, the day Helen Keller learned that there are letters that spell "water." That was the key that opened her mind to the world. An important day in my life was the hot summer evening that my mother made me play softball. <u>Playing in that game taught me that the greatest feeling in the world is facing your own fear.</u>

It was the summer before third grade, and our girls' softball team was facing real pitchers for the first time. The summer before that, the ball had been put on top of a big tee, and we were allowed seven swings to make a hit. Almost every girl hit the ball each time she batted, even if she hit the tee first. When the coaches started pitching, suddenly batting was hard.

By the third week of the season, I had hit the ball a few times. At one embarrassing practice session, I missed every single pitch. From the side, I heard Emily hissing at me. My face got hot, and my throat felt like it had a softball stuck in it. I was starting to hate softball. The next afternoon, when Mom said it was almost time to go play our game, I told her I was sick. She said that I should lie down for a while because I probably ate supper too fast. I knew I had to go through the motions, so I went to my room and lay there. This was hard because I felt fine and just wanted to avoid softball.

Before long, Mom came into my room and said, "Time to go to the game." She didn't even ask if I felt better, or if I really wanted to play. I imagined Emily hissing from the sideline, and suddenly I really did feel sick to my stomach. I started crying so hard that I could barely talk. While I was blubbering, my mother pulled my team T-shirt over my head and guided me to the car. She said that I had to play for the rest of the season, and after that we could talk about whether or not I would play next year. In the meantime, she or Dad would practice with me before every game because practice was what I needed, not quitting.

That night I got two hits, and Emily didn't make a sound. Every week after that, we practiced at home until I got to be one of the best hitters on the team.

The **ending** tells what the writer learned from the experience.

This year, before I started ninth grade, I had the same old sick feeling that I was going to mess up. I was afraid high school was going to be too hard, and someone would make fun of me. I've learned though, that being afraid is part of life, and that I can do whatever is expected of me if I keep working and practicing. I don't think anyone will ever make a movie about my softball experience, but it sure has had a big impact on me.

Practice responding to a narrative prompt. Review the prompt you chose on page **139** and look over the planning you did. Then write a response in the amount of time your teacher gives you.

Write

Revising ■ Improve your response.

Most writing tests allow you to make neat changes to your response, but be sure you know the number and kinds of changes that are allowed.

■ Use the STRAP questions.

The following STRAP questions can serve as a revising guide.

> **Subject:** Does my response focus on a specific personal experience related to the prompt?
>
> **Type:** Have I written the appropriate type of response (narrative, essay, article)?
>
> **Role:** Have I assumed the role indicated in the prompt (student, friend, community member)?
>
> **Audience:** Have I kept my intended audience in mind (principal, parents, city official, classmates)?
>
> **Purpose:** Does my writing accomplish the goal set by the prompt (share, re-create, entertain, illustrate, inspire)?

Improve your work. As you reread your response, ask yourself the STRAP questions. Make changes neatly in the time allotted by your teacher.

Editing ■ Check for conventions.

Finally, it is a good idea to read through your draft again to check for punctuation, capitalization, spelling, and grammar errors.

Conventions

_____ 1. Have I used commas and end punctuation correctly?

_____ 2. Have I capitalized proper nouns and first words of sentences?

_____ 3. Have I checked my spelling?

_____ 4. Do my subjects and verbs agree (*she was*, not *she were*)?

_____ 5. Have I used the right words (*there, they're,* or *their*)?

Check for conventions. Use the checklist above to check your response for punctuation, capitalization, spelling, and grammar errors. Make corrections neatly in the time allotted by your teacher.

Narrative Writing on Tests

The following tips will guide you whenever you are asked to write a response to a narrative prompt.

Before you write . . .

- **Understand the prompt.**
  Use the STRAP questions and remember that a narrative prompt asks you to share or re-create an experience.
- **Plan your response.**
  Spend several minutes planning your response. Use an appropriate graphic organizer to help you. (See page **139**.)

As you write . . .

- **State the focus of your writing in the beginning.**
  Keep your purpose *(to share, to illustrate)* in mind as you write.
- **Be selective.**
  Include specific details that effectively re-create your experience.
- **End in a meaningful way.**
  Tell why the experience has been important to you.

After you write your first draft . . .

- **Check for completeness and correctness.**
  Use the STRAP questions to revise your work. Then check for errors in punctuation, capitalization, spelling, and grammar.

 Plan and write a response. Analyze one of the prompts below using the STRAP questions. Then plan and write your response. Complete your work within the time allotted by your teacher.

Narrative Prompts

- "Experience is the best teacher." In a personal narrative, share a specific time in your life that illustrates this quotation. Make sure to tell what you learned from your experience. Your intended audience is middle school students.
- In an article for your school newspaper, share your most meaningful school-related experience from the past year. Make the experience come alive with vivid details and dialogue.

Narrative

Expository Writing

Expository Writing
Writing a Comparison Essay

Expository writing is the most common form of writing assigned in your classes. If a particular assignment asks you to explain, summarize, illustrate, analyze, classify, or compare, then you are involved in expository writing. In this chapter, you will write a comparison essay about two famous people—perhaps two athletes, two scientists, two musicians, or two leaders.

You will do your best work if you follow these five tips: (1) Select two people who truly interest you. (2) Learn as much as you can about them. (3) Organize your writing around important points of comparison. (4) Engage the reader with some interesting details, including quotations and revealing facts. (5) Share your information clearly and completely.

Writing Guidelines

Subject: **Two famous people**
Form: **Comparison essay**
Purpose: **To show similarities**
Audience: **Classmates**

"I see only one rule: to be clear. If I am not clear, then my entire world crumbles into nothing."
—Margaret Mead

Expository Writing Warm-Up: Key Points of Comparison

When you write a comparison essay, be sure that you focus on key points of comparison between your two topics. Tim Williams was planning a comparison of his two grandfathers. He knew that one important point of comparison was their involvement in World War II. During his planning, he made a T-chart and listed wartime details about each grandfather.

T-Chart

Point of Comparison: Involvement in WWII	
Grandfather Capewell	**Grandfather Williams**
– wanted to join the British army	– wanted to join the U.S. Navy
– denied because of heart murmur	– denied because of poor eyesight
– worked for aviation industry	– accepted in the army
– inspected crashed airplanes	– fought in Europe

Try It!

Think of two people you know well who have things in common—perhaps two aunts, two friends, or two neighbors. Also think of an important or interesting point of comparison between the two people (growing up, involvement in a sport, education, and so on). On a piece of paper, write the point of comparison. Then make a T-chart to list details related to this idea for each person. (See the example above.)

Write your topic sentence.

A specific point of comparison can usually be covered in one paragraph. To plan for his paragraph, Tim wrote this topic sentence, which identified the point of comparison to be covered.

My grandfathers (subjects) **proudly served their countries during World War II** (point of comparison).

Try It!

Using your list of comparison details, write a topic sentence that identifies your subjects and point of comparison. Use the sample sentence above as a guide.

Writing a Comparison Paragraph

A paragraph in a comparison essay should cover one main point of comparison between the two subjects. Tim wrote the following comparison paragraph about his two grandfathers. Remember that a paragraph has three main parts:

- The **topic sentence** introduces the two people and the point of comparison.
- The **body sentences** support the point of comparison.
- The **closing sentence** completes the comparison.

Doing Their Part

Topic Sentence

My grandfathers proudly served their countries during World War II. As soon as the war started, Thomas Capewell, my grandfather in England, wanted to join the British army. As soon as he graduated from high school, John Williams, my grandfather in the United States, wanted to join the navy. Things didn't work out well for either of them. The draft board wouldn't take Thomas because he had a heart murmur as a kid, and the navy

Body

wouldn't take John because his eyesight wasn't good enough. But that didn't stop either of the men. Because Thomas was trained as an engineer, he helped design airplanes for his country. He was also part of a group that inspected enemy warplanes that were shot down. John passed the physical for the United States army and served in the infantry for three years. John was in Germany when the German army surrendered. He said that he and his war buddies really celebrated that night. Both of my

Closing Sentence

grandfathers say that the war taught them more than any other experience in their lives.

Write your own comparison paragraph. Use your planning from page 146 and the paragraph above as a guide for your writing.

Understanding Your Goal

Your goal in this chapter is to write a well-organized expository essay that compares two famous people. The traits listed in the chart below will help you plan and write your essay.

TRAITS OF A COMPARISON ESSAY

- **Ideas**

  Select two famous people to compare. Develop your essay by providing key similarities between these two people.

- **Organization**

  Include a strong beginning and ending. In the middle, set up your points of comparison chronologically—early life, beginning career, middle career, and late career.

- **Voice**

  Engage the reader by using a voice that sounds knowledgeable.

- **Word Choice**

  Select precise words and avoid repetition and unneeded modifiers.

- **Sentence Fluency**

  Write a variety of sentences that smoothly connect your ideas.

- **Conventions**

  Use correct punctuation, capitalization, spelling, and grammar.

Get the big picture. Review the rubric on pages 180–181 before you begin your writing. Use this rubric as a guide to develop your essay and as a tool to assess your completed writing.

"If you would not be forgotten as soon as you are gone, either write things worth reading or do things worth writing."

—Benjamin Franklin

Comparison Essay

In the following expository essay, a professional writer compares two wild-life conservationists who changed the way the world thought about great apes. The notes in the left margin explain the key parts of the essay.

Expository

Beginning
The first paragraph introduces the two people and gives the thesis statement (underlined).

Middle
The topic sentence in each middle paragraph focuses on one main point of comparison.

Women in the Wild

In the first half of the twentieth century, most people thought that great apes were ferocious beasts like King Kong. By the middle of the century, though, a young Englishwoman named Jane Goodall and a young American named Dian Fossey began to change people's minds. By going to live with great apes, Goodall and Fossey taught the world about these gentle giants.

Goodall and Fossey began their careers by following their childhood dreams of working with animals in Africa. In her late twenties, Goodall finally saved up enough money to travel to Cape Town, South Africa, where she met the famous paleontologist Louis Leakey. He hired her as his secretary and by 1960 convinced her to study chimpanzees in the wild. Leakey funded Goodall's expedition to Tanzania, and she took her mother with her. In a speech that Goodall gave in 2002, she said, "I had a wonderful, supportive mother. She encouraged me to follow my ridiculous dream to go to Africa and live with animals ("Jane"). In 1963, Fossey first met Leakey, but she had a harder time impressing him. After paying 14 shillings to look around his dig site, she slipped down a rock slope, landed on his fossil find, sprained her ankle, and because of the pain, threw up on the specimen ("Dian"). Still, by 1966, Leakey had funded an expedition for Fossey to study mountain gorillas in the Congo and Rwanda.

Over the next two decades, Goodall and Fossey became world-renowned primatologists, or ape researchers. Since neither woman was a trained scientist, they shared a unique approach to their research. Instead of numbering the apes like test subjects, the women named them and developed close relationships with them. Goodall discovered that chimpanzees live in extended tribal groups and have individual personalities, emotions, and awareness. Perhaps her most startling discovery, though, was that chimpanzees make tools, stripping leaves off

The writer uses paraphrases, facts, statistics, quotations, and anecdotes to make the comparison clear.

twigs and using the twigs to "fish" termites from their mounds (Shadow). For her part, Fossey learned that gorillas live in small family groups and show compassion even to non-gorillas. Once, when Fossey crouched alone and depressed in the woods, a gorilla named Digit put his arm around her and comforted her (Gorillas). Over the years, both women discovered that great-ape populations are dwindling because of poaching and habitat loss. At Leakey's suggestion, Goodall and Fossey each went to Cambridge to earn PhD's, which helped them fight for the survival of great apes.

Later in their careers, the two women worked hard to save the great apes. Goodall wrote papers and books, traveled and lectured, and created foundations to save chimpanzees and other animals. As a result, the United Nations named her a "Messenger of Peace," and she was the only non-Tanzanian to receive the Medal of Tanzania ("Biography"). Fossey also did these things, but when the gorilla populations she studied were attacked, she declared a public war on poachers. She put a bounty on any poachers and organized patrols to protect gorillas. In 1985, her war ended when she was murdered in her cabin, most likely by a poacher ("Dian").

Ending
The final paragraph reflects on the subjects' importance.

Though Goodall and Fossey were born ten thousand miles apart, each woman followed her dream of going to Africa. They worked with Louis Leakey, wrote and lectured, and set up foundations to save the creatures they loved. Most of all, these two conservationists shared a message that Fossey expressed in her final journal entry: "When you realize the value of all life, you dwell less on what is past and concentrate on the preservation of the future" ("Dian").

Respond to the reading. Answer the following questions.

Ideas (1) Which point of comparison seems the most important? Explain.

Organization (2) How is the comparison of the two women organized—by time, location, or order of importance?

Voice & Word Choice (3) Does the writer sound knowledgeable about the two subjects? Explain.

Prewriting

Your comparison essay will be about two people who share several important similarities. In your prewriting, you will choose two people, gather your details, and organize your thoughts.

Keys to Effective Prewriting

1. Select a topic (two famous people) that interests you and will interest your readers.

2. Research the two people to learn as much as you can about them.

3. Write a thesis statement that focuses your thoughts about the key points of comparison between the two people.

4. Use a point-by-point chronological organization pattern.

5. Organize your details in an outline (or another graphic organizer).

Prewriting ■ Select a topic.

The first step in writing a comparison essay is to choose two people who interest you. To do this, Rafael Hernandez first listed categories of people and chose three categories that interested him. He wrote them across the top of a piece of paper. Next, he listed pairs of athletes, scientists, and leaders/rulers that could be compared. Finally, he selected the two people he wanted to write about.

actors	athletes	leaders/rulers
activists	business people	musicians
artists	explorers	scientists
astronauts	inventors	writers

Famous-People Chart

Athletes	Scientists	Leaders / Rulers
Vijay Singh Tiger Woods	Roy C. Andrews Jack Horner	Queen Elizabeth I Queen Victoria
Sheryl Swoops Diana Taurasi	Marie Curie Gertrude B. Elion	Robert E. Lee Ulysses S. Grant
Jim Thorpe * Jesse Owens		Winston Churchill Franklin Roosevelt

Prewrite

Create a famous-people chart. Choose three categories of people from the list at the top of the page. Write the categories at the tops of three columns. Then under each heading, list pairs of famous people who interest you. Put an asterisk (*) next to the pair you would like to write about.

■ Focus on the traits.

Ideas When you choose two people to compare, focus on two people who you know are similar in a number of ways. Though Ronald Reagan and Henry VIII were both powerful politicians, they may not have had enough in common to prompt a solid comparison essay.

■ Gather details.

Check books, Web sites, and magazines to learn as much as possible about the two people you chose. Rafael used a gathering grid to keep track of the details he found. In parentheses, he listed the source in which he found each piece of information. For additional information, he used note cards. (See the next page.)

Gathering Grid

Questions	Jim Thorpe	Jesse Owens
When and where was he born?	Born in 1888 in a one-room cabin, Prague, Oklahoma (nativeamericans.com)	Born in 1913 in Alabama (jesseowens.com)
What was his family like?	Poor, Native American name "Wa-tho-huck" meant "Bright Path" (All-American)	Poor, moved to Cleveland for better life (Jesse: The Man Who Outran Hitler)
When did his talent first appear?	At the Carlisle Indian School in PA (nativeamericans.com)	At Cleveland East Technical High on track team ("Jesse")
What was his first big success?	Scored 25 touchdowns and 198 points in last season at Carlisle, All-American two years (wmgww.com)	Tied one world record and set three more—all with an injured back! (jesseowens.com)
What was his biggest success?	Pentathlon and decathlon winner at 1912 Olympics, decathlon score stood for 20 years (All-American)	Went to Berlin Olympics in 1936, won four gold medals in front of Hitler (World Book Encyclopedia)
What happened after his biggest success?	Medals stripped for "professionalism," played pro baseball/football, movie extra, Chicago Park Dist. staff (nativeamericans.com)	No endorsement deals, raced against motorcycles and racehorses, became public speaker ("Jesse")

Create a gathering grid. Write questions about the two people you are researching. Then fill in the rest of your grid.

Prewrite

Prewriting ▪ Create note cards.

A gathering grid is an effective way to collect and organize details for an essay. However, sometimes you need more space, especially to record a quotation, to paraphrase important information, or to explain or define something. In these cases, you should use note cards.

Number each new card, and write the question at the top. Then answer the question with a paraphrase, a quotation, or an explanation. If necessary, identify the source of the information at the bottom of the note card.

Sample Note Cards

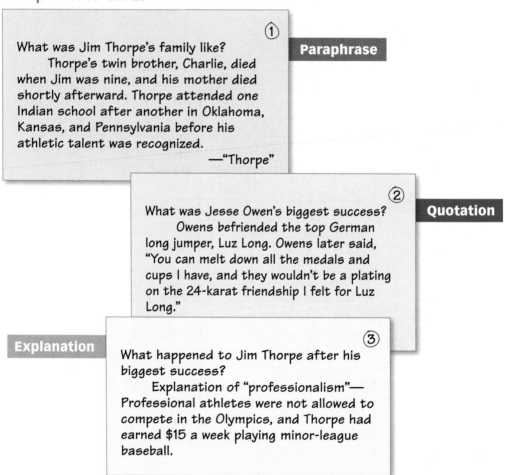

①

What was Jim Thorpe's family like?
    Thorpe's twin brother, Charlie, died when Jim was nine, and his mother died shortly afterward. Thorpe attended one Indian school after another in Oklahoma, Kansas, and Pennsylvania before his athletic talent was recognized.
                                    —"Thorpe"

Paraphrase

②

What was Jesse Owen's biggest success?
    Owens befriended the top German long jumper, Luz Long. Owens later said, "You can melt down all the medals and cups I have, and they wouldn't be a plating on the 24-karat friendship I felt for Luz Long."

Quotation

Explanation

③

What happened to Jim Thorpe after his biggest success?
    Explanation of "professionalism"— Professional athletes were not allowed to compete in the Olympics, and Thorpe had earned $15 a week playing minor-league baseball.

Prewrite

Create note cards. Make note cards like the examples above whenever your answers are too long to fit on your gathering grid.

■ Focus on points of comparison.

After gathering details about your subjects, it's time to decide on the key points of comparison that you will make in your essay. (See pages **146–147** for more information.) After reviewing the assignment goals and his gathering grid, Rafael decided to focus on four points of comparison.

Points of Comparison

– Childhood   – Middle career

– Beginning career   – Late career

Prewrite

Select the points of comparison. Review your gathering grid and decide on three to five important points of comparison that you would like to use. (You can use those shown above if they work with your subjects.)

■ List details.

Next, you should list the details that relate to each subject for each point of comparison. Here is how Rafael listed the details for his first two points of comparison: childhood and beginning career.

Childhood

Jim Thorpe
– born in 1888 in Prague, OK
– very poor
– Native American
 name "Wa-tho-huck" means
 "Bright Path"

Jesse Owens
– born in 1913 in Alabama
– very poor
– African American
– moved to Cleveland
– worked odd jobs, couldn't
 make all track practices

Beginning Career

– led Carlisle Indian football team
 to huge upsets
– named All-American

– track star of East Tech High
– at Ohio State, tied one world
 record and broke three

Prewrite

Arrange your details. List each point of comparison on a piece of paper, leaving seven or eight lines between each one. Then list the appropriate details for your subjects under each point of comparison.

Prewriting ■ Write a thesis statement.

The thesis statement of your essay should name the two people and summarize the main similarity between them. Here is Rafael's thesis statement.

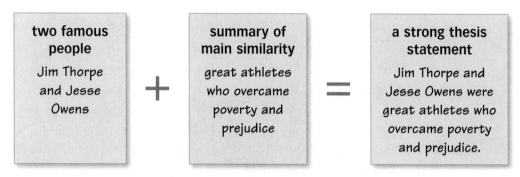

two famous people		summary of main similarity		a strong thesis statement
Jim Thorpe and Jesse Owens	**+**	great athletes who overcame poverty and prejudice	**=**	Jim Thorpe and Jesse Owens were great athletes who overcame poverty and prejudice.

Prewrite

Write your thesis statement. Use the model above to create a thesis statement for your essay. Try different versions until you are satisfied.

■ Outline your essay.

Before you write your first draft, you should outline the main information that you will include in the middle part of the essay to support your thesis statement. Below is the first part of Rafael's sentence outline. (See page **372** for more about outlining.)

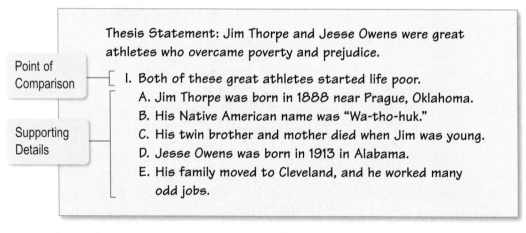

Thesis Statement: Jim Thorpe and Jesse Owens were great athletes who overcame poverty and prejudice.

Point of Comparison

I. Both of these great athletes started life poor.
  A. Jim Thorpe was born in 1888 near Prague, Oklahoma.
  B. His Native American name was "Wa-tho-huk."

Supporting Details

  C. His twin brother and mother died when Jim was young.
  D. Jesse Owens was born in 1913 in Alabama.
  E. His family moved to Cleveland, and he worked many odd jobs.

Prewrite

Prepare a sentence outline. Begin with your thesis statement. Then include each point of comparison (I., II., III.) and supporting details (A., B., C.). You need not include every detail in your outline.

Writing

Now that you have finished prewriting, you're ready to write your first draft. As you write, refer to your outline and your research notes.

Keys to Effective Writing

1. Include a thesis statement in the first paragraph and a topic sentence about a point of comparison in each middle paragraph.

2. Put all your ideas down on paper in your first draft.

3. Use your outline as a guide.

4. Add specific details to explain each point of comparison.

5. Use transition words and phrases to connect your ideas.

6. Write on every other line to leave room for later changes, or double-space if you're working on a computer.

Writing ■ Get the big picture.

Now that you have finished prewriting, you are ready to write a first draft of your essay. The graphic that follows shows how the parts of your essay should fit together. (The example came from the student essay on pages **159–162**.)

BEGINNING

The **beginning** captures the reader's interest, introduces the two famous people, and states the thesis.

Thesis Statement
Jim Thorpe and Jesse Owens were great athletes who overcame poverty and prejudice.

MIDDLE

The **middle** contains a paragraph for each point of comparison and includes supporting details, paraphrases, and quotations.

Topic Sentences
Both of these great athletes started life poor. **(Childhood)**

As young adults, Thorpe and Owens used their natural talents to achieve greatness. **(Beginning career)**

These great American athletes then went on to succeed against the world's best athletes. **(Middle career)**

Following their days of Olympic glory, however, Thorpe and Owens both returned to harsh realities. **(Late career)**

ENDING

The **ending** revisits the thesis and reflects on the importance of the two famous people.

Closing Sentences
Jim Thorpe and Jesse Owens overcame poverty and prejudice to become two of the greatest athletes of all time. Their accomplishments live on in the sports they helped to integrate and in the world they helped to change.

Expository

■ Start your essay.

The beginning of your essay should capture the reader's interest, introduce your two subjects, and state your thesis. Here are some ways to get the reader's attention:

▶ **Beginning**
Middle
Ending

- ■ **Ask a question.**
  Who is the greatest American athlete of all time?
- ■ **Start with a quotation.**
  "Sir," the King of Sweden said to Jim Thorpe, "you are the greatest athlete in the world."
- ■ **Use a surprising statistic.**
  During one Big Ten meet, Jesse Owens tied one world record and set three more—all with an injured back!
- ■ **Connect with the reader.**
  Imagine being a high school athlete who could beat world records.

Beginning Paragraph

Rafael starts his essay by asking a question. He then includes details leading to his thesis statement, which introduces the focus of his writing.

> The writer captures the reader's interest and leads up to his thesis statement (underlined).

> Who is the greatest American athlete of all time? Most people think of people like Muhammad Ali, Jackie Joyner-Kersey, or Babe Ruth. However, there are two other great American athletes that some people may have forgotten about. These two people caught the world's attention many years ago, and they still inspire us today. <u>Jim Thorpe and Jesse Owens were great athletes who overcame poverty and prejudice.</u>

Write

Write your beginning. Use one of the suggestions above to get the reader's interest. Then build to your thesis statement.

■ Focus on the traits.

Organization These transitions may help you make comparisons.

also	by contrast	likewise	similarly
both	each	on the one hand	though
but	however	on the other hand	yet

Writing ▪ Develop the middle part.

Follow your outline to write the middle part of your essay. Be sure to expand on the key ideas with additional information from your note cards.

Beginning

Middle

Ending

Middle Paragraphs

Topic sentences identify each main point of comparison.

A **paraphrase** puts information in the writer's own words.

Facts and **statistics** produce a knowledgeable voice.

Both of these great athletes started life poor. In 1888, Jim Thorpe was born on a farm near Prague, Oklahoma. His parents named him Wa-tho-huck, a Native American name that means "Bright Path" ("Jim"). Still, he didn't have a bright early life. Thorpe's twin brother, Charlie, died when Jim was nine, and his mother died shortly afterward. Thorpe attended one Indian school after another in Oklahoma, Kansas, and Pennsylvania before his athletic talent was recognized. Jesse Owens also had a tough childhood. He was born in 1913 into a poor Alabama family. They moved north to Cleveland, hoping for a better life, but couldn't find one. During high school, Owens worked so many odd jobs that he couldn't make afternoon practices for the track team. However, track coach Charlie Riley recognized Owens' talent and offered to train him in the morning ("Jesse").

As young adults, Thorpe and Owens used their natural talents to achieve greatness. In 1911 and 1912, Thorpe led the Carlisle Indian School varsity football team to victory over powerful teams such as Army, Georgetown, Harvard, and Pittsburgh. Thorpe scored 25 touchdowns and 198 points in his last season, and he was named All-American for two years running ("Jim"). In the same way, Owens became a track star in high school and college. At Cleveland East High School, he tied the world-record time for the 100-yard dash. At Ohio State University, he tied one world record and set three more, all in less than an hour and with an injured back! Owens broke the broad-jump record by placing a handkerchief at the old mark—26 feet 2 1/2 inches—and jumping nearly 6 inches beyond it ("Jesse").

Expository

These great American athletes then went on to succeed against the world's best athletes. Jim Thorpe was chosen to represent the United States in the Stockholm Olympics of 1912. There he easily won the pentathlon and set a decathlon score (8,413 points) that wouldn't be topped for 20 years ("Jim"). The king of Sweden even declared Thorpe "the greatest athlete in the world," to which Jim replied, "Thanks, King" ("Thorpe"). Twenty-four years later, in 1936, Jesse Owens represented this country in the so-called "Hitler Olympics." Adolph Hitler believed the Aryan race was superior, but as he watched, Owens won four gold medals, breaking an Olympic record and a world record. But Owens' greatest accomplishment was winning the hearts of the German people. Even Luz Long, the top German long jumper, befriended Jim in front of Hitler. Owens later said, "You can melt down all the medals and cups I have, and they wouldn't be a plating on the 24-karat friendship I felt for Luz Long" ("Track").

Following their days of Olympic glory, however, Thorpe and Owens both returned to harsh realities. The Olympic committee removed Thorpe's medals because of complaints about his "professionalism." (Professional athletes were not allowed to compete, and Thorpe had earned $15 a week playing minor-league baseball.) Thorpe returned to playing baseball and football, became a Hollywood extra, and finally ended up on the recreation staff of the Chicago Park District ("Jim"). Owens became a "runner-for-hire," racing against ballplayers, motorcycles, or even racehorses ("Biography"). "It was bad enough to have toppled from the Olympic heights to make my living competing with animals," Owens once said, "but the competition wasn't even fair. No man could beat a racehorse, not even for 100 yards" ("Quotes"). Unlike Thorpe, though, Owens kept an optimistic spirit, which launched him into a new career: motivational speaking.

Quotations add insight into Owens' personality.

An **explanation** makes the meaning clear.

Write   **Write your middle paragraphs.** Follow your outline and use transitions to connect your ideas.

Writing ■ End your essay.

Your ending should be strong since it contains the last thoughts for your reader. Here are some ways to create a strong ending.

Beginning

Middle

▶ **Ending**

- ■ **Reflect on the importance of your subjects.**
  Athletes such as Jim Thorpe and Jesse Owens paved the way for other athletes like Mia Hamm and Tiger Woods.

- ■ **Provide an effective quotation.**
  Jesse Owens summed up his winning spirit this way: "Friendships are born on the field of athletic strife and are the real gold of competition. Awards become corroded; friends gather no dust."

- ■ **Include additional information of interest.**
  In 1982, 30 years after his death, the Olympic committee returned Thorpe's medals to his family.

Ending Paragraph

The writer revisits the thesis and reflects on the importance of the subjects.

> Eventually, these two athletes got the recognition they deserved. In 1976, President Ford gave Owens the Medal of Freedom, the highest honor a civilian can receive ("Biography"). In 1982, thirty years after his death, the Olympic committee returned Thorpe's medals to his family ("Jim"). Jim Thorpe and Jesse Owens overcame poverty and prejudice to become two of the greatest athletes of all time. Their accomplishments live on in the sports they helped to integrate and in the world they helped to change.

Write

Write your ending. Write the final paragraph of your essay, using one or more of the strategies above.

"We need important information at the beginning to attract the reader, but what the reader remembers is usually at the end of the paragraph."
—Donald Murray

Revising

When you revise, you improve your writing. You add important new information, delete unnecessary details, change the order of ideas, and rework parts that do not sound right.

Keys to Effective Revising

1. Read your essay aloud to get a feeling for how well it works.

2. Be sure your thesis statement and topic sentences are clear.

3. Check your supporting details. Do they work and are there enough of them?

4. Consider your voice. It should sound knowledgeable and engaging.

5. Check your words and sentences for clarity and variety.

6. Use the editing and proofreading marks inside the back cover of this book.

Revising ■ for Ideas

6 My essay shows the strong similarity between two people, and it is full of supporting details.

5 My essay shows interesting similarities between the two people and one good contrast.

4 My essay shows how the two people are similar, but it could use more details and a better contrast.

When you revise for *ideas*, you assure that the central similarity between the two people is clear. You also decide whether you should include a surprising contrast. The rubric strip above will help you revise.

■ Have I focused on a significant similarity?

You have focused on a significant similarity if you show an *important* way that the two people are alike. Start by checking your thesis statement.

A weak thesis statement: Gloria Estefan is a singer, as was Selena.

A strong thesis statement: Singers Gloria Estefan and Selena helped introduce Latin music to the United States.

Exercise

Read the pairs of thesis statements below. Which one shows a more important similarity between the two people?

1. Queen Elizabeth I and Queen Victoria came to the throne because male heirs could not be found.
   Queen Elizabeth I and Queen Victoria ruled during England's most powerful and profitable periods.
2. Christopher Columbus and Ferdinand Magellan believed they could sail around the world.
   The voyages of Christopher Columbus and Ferdinand Magellan changed the course of European history.
3. Elizabeth Cady Stanton and Susan B. Anthony shared a vision of equality for all women everywhere.
   Elizabeth Cady Stanton and Susan B. Anthony lived in the East but traveled across many states.

Revise

Review your thesis statement. Does it show a significant similarity? If not, rewrite it. Then be sure your main points of comparison fit the thesis.

I need more details that show the similarities between the two people and a contrast.

 I need to address the similarities between the two people.

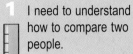 I need to understand how to compare two people.

■ How can a surprising contrast improve my essay?

A surprising contrast will add interest to your essay. The contrast should point out a significant difference between your chosen subjects.

Exercise

Decide which of each pair of contrasts is more surprising.

1. Madeleine Albright and Condoleeza Rice come from different parts of the country.
   Many of Condoleeza Rice's foreign-policy decisions completely overturn those made by Madeleine Albright.

2. Bruce Lee was the most famous martial-arts star, but Jackie Chan is quickly overtaking him.
   Bruce Lee's fighting style was derived from karate and kung fu, while Jackie Chan's style also draws from comedians like Buster Keaton and Charlie Chaplin.

3. Hemingway enjoyed traveling the world, while Faulkner preferred staying in Oxford, Mississippi.
   Hemingway was more popular at first, but Faulkner has become very popular.

Revise

Search for surprising contrasts. Find a few important ways in which your subjects are/were different. Include some contrasts in your essay.

Ideas
A surprising contrast gives insight into both men.

. . . Owens once said, "but the competition wasn't even fair. No man could beat a racehorse, not even for 100 yards" ("Quotes").
Unlike Thorpe, though, Owens kept an optimistic spirit, which launched him into a new career: motivational speaking.

Revising ■ for Organization

 6 The key points of comparison and transitions make the essay engaging.

 5 The beginning, middle, and ending paragraphs provide a clear comparison.

 4 The essay is complete, but the organization in some of the middle paragraphs seems unclear.

To revise for *organization*, be sure that your beginning and ending work well and that each middle paragraph covers a key point of comparison. The rubric strip above can guide your revision.

■ Do my beginning and ending sentences work well?

You know your beginning and ending sentences work well if your writing creates a strong first impression and an even stronger final impression. The best way to find out is to ask a classmate to review these sentences.

Exercise

Ask for a peer response. Have your partner read your beginning and ending and then answer the questions below. (Use the sample responses as a guide.)

Beginning-Ending Review Sheet

1. Do the first few sentences capture your interest? Why or why not? *Mostly. I like sports, so I like knowing about the greatest athletes.*

2. How could I create a stronger beginning? *You could include the names of some famous athletes from the last century.*

3. Do the last few sentences leave you with a final thought? Explain. *They make me think that even if people aren't fair to you during your life, you should just hang on. You'll probably get recognized eventually.*

4. How could I create a stronger ending? *You could use the words "greatest athletes of all time" to refer back to the beginning.*

Revise your beginning and ending. Use your partner's responses to help you improve the beginning and ending of your essay.

Revise

3 The beginning or ending is weak. The middle should have a paragraph for each key point of comparison.

2 The beginning, middle, and ending all run together. Point-by-point organization should be used.

1 The essay should be reorganized.

■ How can I check the organization of the middle part?

Check the organization of the middle to be sure that your comparisons balance. Create a scale diagram for each main point of comparison and weigh the details in it. Here is a sample diagram for a comparison of the early careers of Fred Astaire and Gene Kelly.

Expository

Scale Diagram

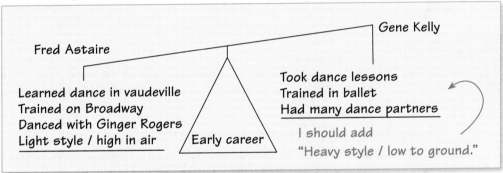

Gene Kelly

Fred Astaire

Learned dance in vaudeville
Trained on Broadway
Danced with Ginger Rogers
Light style / high in air

Early career

Took dance lessons
Trained in ballet
Had many dance partners

I should add
"Heavy style / low to ground."

Revise

Check your point-by-point details. Review your paragraphs. If one seems out of balance, create a scale diagram to compare the weight of details.

Organization
Suggestions from a classmate improve the beginning paragraph.

Who is the greatest American athlete of all time? ∧
other
There are two ∧ great American athletes that some people may have forgotten about. . . .

Most people think of people like Muhammad Ali, Jackie Joyner-Kersey, or Babe Ruth. However,

Revising ■ for Voice

 6 My voice sounds professional and polished from start to finish.

 5 My voice sounds knowledgeable, and it keeps the reader's interest.

4 My voice sounds knowledgeable, but it could be more engaging.

When you revise for *voice*, you add details that make your writing sound knowledgeable and engaging. The rubric strip above can help you revise.

■ Does my writing voice sound knowledgeable?

Your writing voice sounds knowledgeable if you effectively use facts, statistics, and quotations. **Facts** are details that can be proven to be true. **Statistics** are facts that include precise numbers, and **quotations** are someone's exact words.

Exercise

Read the following paragraph and identify at least one fact, one statistic, and one quotation. Tell how these details make the voice sound knowledgeable.

> Though their presidencies came a century apart, Abraham Lincoln and John F. Kennedy both worked to ensure the rights of all citizens. In 1860, Lincoln presided over a nation of 31 million people. Thirteen percent of those, or nearly four million, were slaves ("Census"). Lincoln granted freedom to most of those slaves in the Emancipation Proclamation, but freedom did not translate into equality. "One hundred years of delay have passed since President Lincoln freed the slaves," announced Kennedy on June 11, 1963, "yet their heirs, their grandsons, are not fully free. . . . And this nation, for all its hopes and all its boasts, will not be fully free until all its citizens are free" ("Civil"). Kennedy saw himself as a partner working to complete the job Lincoln had begun.

Revise

Revise for voice. Use facts, statistics, or quotations to make your writing voice sound more knowledgeable.

3 More details and personal connections would improve my voice.

2 My voice sounds uncertain and uninteresting. I should add facts, statistics, quotations, and anecdotes.

1 I need help understanding how to create a strong expository voice.

■ Does my writing voice sound engaging?

Your voice sounds engaging if it creates a personal connection between your topic and your reader. One way to do this is to use an anecdote. An **anecdote** is a little story that reveals something about the person. The following paragraph includes an anecdote about Lincoln:

> Lincoln and Kennedy faced terrible challenges near the end of their presidencies, but they kept their feelings of compassion. For example, during Grant's final advance in the Civil War, Lincoln found three orphaned kittens in the telegraph hut at City Point, Virginia. Lincoln listened to reports of battle while he sat holding the kittens in his lap. "Kitties, thank God you are cats," he said, "and can't understand this terrible strife that is going on" (Sandburg). Lincoln even asked someone on Grant's staff to take care of the kittens. . . .

Revise

Check for anecdotes. Review your research, looking for little stories that reveal something significant about the person you are describing. Consider adding an anecdote to your essay.

Voice

A statistic and an anecdote create a more knowledgeable and engaging voice.

There he easily won the pentathlon and set a decathlon (8,413 points) score ⋀ that wouldn't be topped for 20 years ("Jim"). ⋀ Twenty-four years later, in 1936, Jesse Owens represented this country in the so-called "Hitler Olympics." . . .

The king of Sweden even declared Thorpe "the greatest athlete in the world," to which Jim replied, "Thanks, King."

Revising ■ for Word Choice

 6 Precise word choice makes my essay informative and enjoyable to read.

 5 My words are carefully chosen. I have avoided unnecessary modifiers and repeated words.

 4 Most of my modifiers are necessary, but I should find synonyms for some repeated words.

Revising for *word choice* involves checking to be sure you have not used unnecessary modifiers and have not repeated words too often. The rubric strip above will help you revise.

■ Have I used unnecessary modifiers?

You have used unnecessary modifiers if the adjectives, adverbs, and phrases you include do not make your ideas clearer. Here are traps to avoid:

- **Empty modifiers:** Words like *kind of, sort of, really,* and *totally* don't add to the meaning of your work and should be deleted.

  Carl Sandburg really took the kind of "everyman" approach to poetry.

  Carl Sandburg took the "everyman" approach to poetry.

- **Redundant modifiers:** A strong noun does not need a modifier.

  He wrote about the bloody slaughterhouses of metropolitan Chicago.

  He wrote about the slaughterhouses of Chicago.

- **Strings of modifiers:** One solid modifier is better than two or three.

  His poems use natural, casual, everyday language and dialects.

  His poems use everyday language and dialects.

 ## Exercise

Rewrite each sentence to eliminate unnecessary modifiers.

1. Robert Frost was really very interested in regular, everyday people.
2. Once he even said out loud, "You can be a little ungrammatical if you come from the right part of the country."
3. His most popular and famous poem, "The Road Not Taken," tells of a person taking a walk on a grassy, overgrown trail.
4. What's totally and completely surprising is that this average person actually makes a choice that most people don't make.

Expository

3 I should remove some unnecessary modifiers and repeated words.

2 Too many unnecessary modifiers and repeated words make my essay difficult to follow.

1 I need help to understand how to choose modifiers and avoid word repetition.

■ How do I know if I have repeated a word too often?

The best way to know if you have repeated a word too often is to read your work aloud. Listen for words that are used over and over and replace some of them with synonyms. You can also reword sentences to avoid repetition.

Exercise

Read the following sentences aloud and write down words that are repeated too often. Suggest synonyms or ways to reword the sentences.

1. Carl Sandburg, a poet from Illinois, wrote free-verse poetry about places in Illinois and Illinois's favorite son, Lincoln.
2. Robert Frost lived in New England and wrote about the New England countryside and the people in New England.
3. Frost preferred writing poetry with rhyme and meter because he felt rhyme and meter were important to poetry.
4. Frost avoided free-verse poetry, saying he would rather play tennis with the net down than write free-verse poetry.
5. Whatever type of poetry they preferred, though, both poets won the Pulitzer Prize for Poetry.

Revise   **Check for word repetition.** Read your work aloud and underline words that are used too often. Find synonyms or rewrite sentences to avoid repetition.

Word Choice

A repeated word is deleted and another is replaced with a synonym.

In 1911 and 1912, Thorpe's ~~talent~~ led the Carlisle Indian School

varsity football team to victory over ∧powerful ~~talented~~ teams such as

Army, Georgetown, Harvard, and Pittsburgh. Thorpe scored . . .

Revising ■ for Sentence Fluency

 6 My sentences are skillfully written and easy to follow.

 5 My sentences flow well because I have used a variety of sentence types.

 4 Most of my sentences flow well, but I could use a few more compound or complex sentences.

To revise for *sentence fluency*, be sure you have used a combination of simple, compound, and complex sentences in your writing. The rubric strip above can guide your revision.

■ When should I use compound sentences?

You should use compound sentences to show that two ideas are closely related. You create a compound sentence by joining two simple sentences using a comma and a coordinating conjunction (*and, but, or, nor, for, so,* or *yet*).

Two Simple Sentences
Pocahontas helped the settlers at Jamestown survive.
Sacagawea did the same for the Lewis and Clark expedition.

One Compound Sentence
Pocahontas helped the settlers at Jamestown survive, and Sacagawea did the same for the Lewis and Clark expedition.

 ## Exercise

Use a comma and a coordinating conjunction to join each pair of simple sentences into a compound sentence.

1. Pocahontas's brother captured John Smith.
   Her father decided that Smith had to be put to death.
2. Smith was tied up and helpless.
   Pocahontas embraced him and cradled him in her arms.
3. Tribes were suspicious of the expedition of Lewis and Clark.
   The presence of Sacagawea reduced their suspicions.
4. Sacagawea knew the plants and animals along the route.
   She had lived there many years before.

 Revise

Create compound sentences. Read your work and look for simple sentences with related ideas. Consider joining some with a comma and a coordinating conjunction.

3 More compound and complex sentences would create a better flow.

2 My sentences do not flow. I could create variety with compound and complex sentences.

1 I need help to learn how to create different types of sentences.

■ When should I use complex sentences?

You should use complex sentences to show a relationship between ideas. The ideas may be related by time or place (*when, where*), by cause and effect (*because, in order that*), by comparison (*as if, as though*), or by contrast (*although, whereas*). A subordinating conjunction shows the relationship. (Relative pronouns such as *which* or *that* can also be used to form complex sentences.)

Subordinating Conjunctions

after	because	since	when
although	before	that	where
as if	in order that	though	whereas
as though	provided	unless	while

Two Simple Sentences
Pocahontas traveled to England. She was reunited with John Smith.

Two Complex Sentences
Pocahontas traveled to England where she was reunited with John Smith.
When Pocahontas traveled to England, she was reunited with John Smith.

Revise

Create complex sentences. Review your essay and watch for simple sentences that have a special relationship. Consider joining some of these.

Sentence Fluency
Two simple sentences are joined to form a complex sentence.

Unlike Thorpe, though, Owens kept an optimistic spirit. ~~This~~ which spirit launched him into a new career: motivational speaking.

Revising ■ Improve your writing.

Revise

Check your revising. On a piece of paper, write the numbers 1 to 14. If you can answer "yes" to a question, put a check mark after that number. If not, continue to revise that part of your essay.

Revising Checklist

Ideas

_____ **1.** Have I chosen interesting people to compare?

_____ **2.** Does my thesis statement focus on a significant similarity?

_____ **3.** Do I include details that support my thesis?

Organization

_____ **4.** Does my beginning capture the reader's interest?

_____ **5.** Do I have a middle paragraph for each point of comparison?

_____ **6.** Are the details in each paragraph arranged point by point?

_____ **7.** Does the ending leave the reader with a strong final thought?

Voice

_____ **8.** Does my voice sound knowledgeable?

_____ **9.** Does my voice sound engaging?

Word Choice

_____ **10.** Have I avoided unnecessary modifiers?

_____ **11.** Have I avoided repeating words?

_____ **12.** Have I chosen specific nouns and active verbs?

Sentence Fluency

_____ **13.** Have I used simple, compound, and complex sentences?

_____ **14.** Do my sentences read smoothly?

Revise

Make a clean copy. When you've finished revising, make a clean copy of your essay. This makes editing easier.

Editing

Once you have finished your revisions, you're ready to edit your work for punctuation, capitalization, spelling, and grammar. These rules of English are called *conventions*.

Keys to Effective Editing

1. Edit your work with the help of a dictionary, a thesaurus, and the "Proofreader's Guide." (See pages 604–763.)

2. Check your writing for punctuation, capitalization, spelling, and grammar errors.

3. If you're using a computer, edit on a printed copy. Then enter your changes on the computer.

4. Use the editing and proofreading marks located inside the back cover of this book.

Expository

176

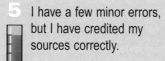

Editing ■ for Conventions

6 My writing is error free, and I have credited my sources correctly.

5 I have a few minor errors, but I have credited my sources correctly.

4 I have errors in conventions and in crediting my sources that must be corrected.

Editing for *conventions* involves checking the punctuation, capitalization, spelling, and grammar of your writing. These two pages will help you correct any comma splices and run-ons you may have. They will also show you how to give credit to sources. The rubric strip above can guide you.

■ Have I fixed any comma splices or run-on sentences?

You can fix comma splices or run-ons by correctly connecting two simple sentences. (A compound sentence needs both a comma and a coordinating conjunction.) You can also correct these errors with a semicolon or by creating two sentences. (See page **557** for more information.)

Comma Splice (coordinating conjunction missing)
Katharine and Audrey Hepburn had the same last name, they weren't sisters.

Corrected Sentence (coordinating conjunction added)
Katharine and Audrey Hepburn had the same last name, but they weren't sisters.

Run-On (comma and coordinating conjunction missing)
Katharine and Audrey Hepburn had the same last name they weren't sisters.

Two Sentences (separated with a period and a capital letter)
Katharine and Audrey Hepburn had the same last name. They weren't sisters.

Exercise

Identify each error as a comma splice or a run-on and correct it.

1. Katharine Hepburn was born in 1907 in Connecticut, Audrey Hepburn was born in 1929 in Belgium.
2. Katharine won her first Oscar for *Morning Glory* she starred in the film the year after Audrey was born.
3. In 1939, Katharine starred in *The Philadelphia Story* on Broadway Howard Hughes bought her the film rights.

Edit

Check for comma splices and run-ons in your essay. Correct any you find.

3 I have errors in conventions and errors in crediting sources that may confuse the reader.

2 I must correct many errors that make my essay confusing and hard to read.

1 I need help finding errors and making corrections.

Expository

■ Have I credited my sources correctly?

You have credited your sources correctly if you have cited them in the text of your paper, using parenthetical citations, and creating a works-cited page. Use the guidelines below and pages **381–384** to cite sources.

- ■ **Cite the author and title** in your text when possible.

    In her autobiography, *Me: Stories of My Life,* Katharine Hepburn shares her struggles and victories.

- ■ **Use the author's last name** or, if the author is unknown, the first significant word from the title in the parenthetical reference.

    Audrey was strongly shaped by her experiences in Nazi-occupied Belgium ("Audrey").

- ■ **Give the page number** if you are citing only part of a work.

    Katharine, likewise, was deeply shaken by the loss of her beloved older brother (Ormand 54).

- ■ **Place the period after** a parenthetical reference.

    Audrey Hepburn's life story appears in a book by her son (Ferrer).

Edit

Credit sources. Review your essay to be sure you have correctly credited your sources. Create a works-cited page (see pages **381–384**).

Conventions
A parenthetical citation credits the source of information.

Thorpe returned to playing baseball and football, became a

Hollywood extra, and finally ended up on the recreation staff

("Jim")

of the Chicago Park District. Owens became a . . .

Editing ▪ Check your writing.

Edit

Check your editing. On a piece of paper, write the numbers 1 to 10. If you can answer "yes" to a question, put a check mark after that number. Continue editing until you can answer "yes" to all the questions.

Editing Checklist

Conventions

PUNCTUATION

_____ **1.** Do I correctly punctuate compound and complex sentences?

_____ **2.** Have I cited sources correctly in my essay?

_____ **3.** Have I correctly formatted a works-cited page?

CAPITALIZATION

_____ **4.** Have I capitalized proper nouns and adjectives?

_____ **5.** Do I begin each sentence with a capital letter?

SPELLING

_____ **6.** Have I spelled all my words correctly?

_____ **7.** Have I double-checked the words my spell-checker may have missed?

GRAMMAR

_____ **8.** Do I use correct forms of verbs (*he saw*, not *he seen*)?

_____ **9.** Do my subjects and verbs agree in number?

____ **10.** Have I used the right words (*there, their, they're*)?

▪ Add a title.

Even when you write informational essays and reports, it's important to engage your reader with an attention-getting title. Here are some ideas:

- Sum up the comparison:
  Natural Talents Bring National Fame
- Be clever:
  Breaking Records and Making History
- Use an idea from your essay:
  Overcoming Poverty and Prejudice

Publishing ▪ Share your essay.

After editing your essay, make a neat final copy, proofread it, and share it. You may post your essay on a Web site, role-play your subjects with a classmate, or turn your writing into a multimedia presentation. (See the suggestions below.)

Make a final copy. Follow your teacher's instructions or use the guidelines below to format your essay. (If you are using a computer, see pages 76–78.) Create a clean final copy of your essay and carefully proofread it.

Publish

▪ Focus on presentation.

- ▪ Use blue or black ink and write neatly.
- ▪ Write your name in the upper left corner of page 1.
- ▪ Skip a line and center your title; skip another line and start your writing.
- ▪ Indent every paragraph and leave a one-inch margin on all four sides.
- ▪ Write your last name and the page number in the upper right corner of every page after page 1.

Post on a Web Site

Upload your paper to a school or personal Web site. Add photos and graphic elements to enhance your comparison.

Role-Play Your Essay

Find a partner and read your comparison essay with that person. Then choose the person each of you will role-play. Finally, improvise a conversation that reveals your similarities (and differences).

Create a Multimedia Presentation

Rework your essay into an effective speech script (see pages 393–403). Create visual aids such as posters or computer slides to complement and strengthen your speech. Give your presentation to the class.

Rubric for Expository Writing

Use this rubric to guide and assess your expository writing. Refer to it to improve your writing using the six traits.

6 Ideas   5   4

6	5	4
Ideas		
The topic, thesis, and details make the essay unforgettable.	The essay is informative with a clear thesis and specific details.	The essay is informative with a clear thesis. More specific details are needed.
Organization		
The organization and transitions make the essay crystal clear and compelling.	The beginning interests the reader. The middle supports the focus. The ending works well. Transitions are used.	The essay is divided into a beginning, a middle, and an ending. Some transitions are used.
Voice		
The writer's voice has the confident, knowledgeable sound of a professional writer.	The writer's voice sounds knowledgeable and confident. It fits the audience.	The writer's voice sounds knowledgeable most of the time and fits the audience.
Word Choice		
The word choice is precise, with just the right nouns, verbs, and modifiers.	Specific nouns and action verbs make the essay clear and informative.	Some nouns and verbs could be more specific.
Sentence Fluency		
The sentences have flair and flavor, and the reader will enjoy them.	The sentences read smoothly.	Most of the sentences read smoothly, but some are short and choppy.
Conventions		
The essay is error free.	The essay has a few minor errors in punctuation, spelling, or grammar.	The essay has some errors in punctuation, spelling, or grammar.

3	**2**	**1**
The thesis of the essay should be clearer, and more specific details are needed.	The topic should be narrowed or expanded. Many more specific details are needed.	The writer should select a new topic.
The beginning or ending is weak. The middle needs a paragraph for each main point. More transitions are needed.	The beginning, middle, and ending all run together. Paragraph breaks and transitions are needed.	The essay should be reorganized.
The writer sometimes sounds unsure, and the voice needs to better fit the audience.	The writer sounds unsure. The voice needs to fit the audience.	The writer needs to learn about voice.
Too many general words are used. Specific nouns and verbs are needed.	General or missing words make this essay difficult to understand.	The writer needs help finding specific words.
Many short, choppy sentences need to be rewritten to make the essay read smoothly.	Many sentences are choppy or incomplete and need to be rewritten.	Most sentences need to be rewritten.
Several errors confuse the reader.	Many errors make the essay difficult to read.	Help is needed to make corrections.

Evaluating a Comparison Essay

Read the comparison essay that follows and focus on its strengths and weaknesses. Then read the student self-assessment on the next page. **(This student essay contains some errors.)**

Men of Letters

Imagine a small pub in Oxford, England, where a group of men get together to read the books they are writing. One man reads a chapter he has just written about Frodo Baggins. Another reads a chapter about the giant lion Aslan. These men are the Inklings, led by J.R.R. Tolkien and C.S. Lewis, who were the first authors of fantasy.

In their early lives, both Tolkien and Lewis were raised by kind, friendly strangers. Tolkien was born in 1892 in South Africa, but after his father's death four years later, his family returned to England. They moved several more times before Tolkien's mother also died. Tolkien was only 12 when he and his brother Hilary became orphans. They were raised by a local priest, and they attended boarding schools as teenagers ("Who"). Lewis also was born to an English family, although they lived in Northern Ireland. After his family returned to England, his mother died. Lewis was only 10 when he and his brother Warnie entered one boarding school after another ("Chronology"). During their boarding-school years, both Lewis and Tolkien fell in love with language and mythology. Lewis enjoyed Greek and Roman mythology while Tolkien focused the Anglo-Saxon myths.

When World War I began, both men joined the British army. Tolkien signed up along with his three closest friends from school. Lewis signed up on his own but met up later with one of his best buddies, Paddy Moore. All of these men fought in the Battle of the Somme, but only Tolkien and Lewis survived. Still, Lewis was seriously injured, and Tolkien came down with "trench fever." They each returned to England where they eventually recovered. These war experiences made a lasting impression on them. Both men later wrote about young people going to war.

Back in England, the two young men found jobs at universities. Lewis went to Oxford and Tolkien went to the University of Leeds. When Tolkien later moved to Oxford, the two professors met each other and became friends. Lewis later wrote, "Friendship is born at that moment when one person says to another, 'What! You too? I thought I was the only one!' " ("Quotes"). Shortly afterward, Tolkien and Lewis created a group called the "Inklings." The group talked about writing, philosophy, and theology. At their meetings, Tolkien read parts of his new novel *The Lord of the Rings*, and C.S. Lewis read parts of his series the Chronicles of Narnia. Both works have become classics of fantasy and have been made into major motion pictures.

Lewis and Tolkien both had a tough childhood. Their parents died when they were young, and they were sent away to boarding schools. Then, both men fought in the War to End All Wars and lost friends and almost died as well. Still, when Lewis and Tolkien finally met each other, they had discovered a real friendship. Lewis described Tolkien and the other Inklings as "those who speak one's own language" (Carpenter). Their friendship helped Lewis and Tolkien create new worlds in their fantasy novels. Millions of other people have gotten to explore these worlds as well.

Student Self-Assessment

Expository Rubric Checklist

Title: Men of Letters
Writer: Bryce Johnson

5 Ideas
- Is the essay informative?
- Does it have a clear thesis?
- Are the details specific?

5 Organization
- Is the beginning interesting?
- Does the middle support the focus?
- Does the ending work well?

4 Voice
- Is the voice knowledgeable?
- Does it sound confident?
- Does the voice fit the audience?

5 Word Choice
- Are the verbs active?

4 Sentence Fluency
- Are the sentences varied?
- Do the sentences read smoothly?

4 Conventions
- Does the essay avoid most errors in punctuation, spelling, or grammar?
- Are sources correctly cited?

OVERALL COMMENTS:

I enjoyed writing my comparison because I like the two authors. Other students were interested because they had seen the movies.

I graded myself down for voice because I forgot to put in any anecdotes.

Many of my sentences start with the subject. I should try to vary them a little more.

I forgot to cite my sources in the third paragraph.

Review your essay. Rate your essay and write comments that explain why you gave yourself the scores you did.

Reflecting on Your Writing

With your comparison essay finished, take a few moments to reflect on this writing experience. On your own paper, finish each sentence starter below. Reflecting helps you to learn more about writing and to apply what you've learned to future assignments.

My Comparison Essay

1. The strongest part of my essay is . . .

2. The part that still needs work is . . .

3. The prewriting activity that worked best for me was . . .

4. The main thing I learned about writing a comparison essay is . . .

5. In my next comparison essay, I would like to . . .

6. One question I still have about writing a comparison essay is . . .

Expository Writing
Explaining a Process

How does a florist arrange a bouquet? What's the best way to find hidden clues in a video game? What are the steps to building a bat house? How do you set up a Web log? When you explain how to do something in an essay, you are doing expository writing.

In this chapter, you'll read a sample expository essay about making jiaozi—Chinese dumplings. Then you will write your own essay based on personal experience and expertise. Your how-to essay should tell the reader what materials are needed and what steps to take to finish the project. Choose a process you know well and care about in order to do your best writing.

Writing Guidelines

Subject: **Something you know how to do or how to make**
Form: **How-to essay**
Purpose: **To explain a process**
Audience: **Classmates**

"Good writing is clear thinking made visible."
—Bill Wheeler

How-To Essay

In the following expository essay, Chen Wei Wu explains how to prepare a traditional Chinese food.

Beginning
The title and opening part identify the topic.

Making Jiaozi

The Chinese dumpling, or jiaozi, is the most popular food in China. There is a common saying in China: "There is nothing more delicious than jiaozi." So you can see that Chinese people have great love for this food. To make your own jiaozi with a basic meat filling, follow these directions:

Making the Dumpling Skins

To make the dumpling skins, you will need three basic ingredients: a small package of white flour, very cold water, and salt. Combine the ingredients in this way:

1. Stir a teaspoon of salt into two cups of very cold water.
2. Then add the water to the flour, a little at a time. Use only as much water as necessary to make workable dough.
3. Knead the dough very well before refrigerating it. (Kneading means to work and press the dough with your hands.)

Middle
The steps are carefully explained.

When you are ready to use the dough, break off a piece about the size of a walnut. Form the piece of dough into a ball and, with a rolling pin, flatten it into a thin, three-inch circle. Continue this process until you have made enough dumpling skins.

Making the Meat Filling

A basic meat filling contains the following ingredients mixed together:

- Ground pork (one pound)
- Finely chopped cabbage (one cup)
- Finely chopped onion (a few tablespoons)
- Grated ginger
- Soy sauce (two tablespoons)
- Minced garlic (one or two cloves)
- Salt and pepper (to taste)

Subheadings and lists (numbered and bulleted) help the reader follow the explanation.

Expository

Special attention is given to design in the essay.

Completing the Dumplings

Form the dumplings in this way:

1. Place one tablespoon of filling in the middle of each skin. Then fold the skin over and seal the dumpling by pressing together both sides. Continue until you have made all of your dumplings.
2. Next, bring a large pot of water to a boil. Add enough dumplings to cover the bottom of the pot. Cover the pot.
3. When it returns to a boil, add a cup of cold water. Cover until the dumplings again come to a boil. Repeat this process one more time, and then the jiaozi are ready. Serve with rice vinegar or soy sauce.

Chinese people put more than 3,000 kinds of stuffing into their dumplings. The ones made in the United States usually are stuffed with a meat filling or with vegetables. By trying this recipe, you will get to enjoy one of the most popular tastes of China.

Ending
Additional information brings the essay to an interesting close.

FLOUR

Respond to the reading. Answer the following questions.

Ideas (1) Will readers be interested in this topic? Explain.

Organization (2) How are the middle paragraphs organized?

Voice & Word Choice (3) What words or phrases show the writer's attention to providing an accurate how-to essay? List three.

Tip

At first, writing an explanation may seem like an easy process. You simply share a set of facts and details with the reader. But once you get started, you'll find that explanations require a lot of work. The details must be clearly stated and logically arranged.

Prewriting ■ Select a topic.

The purpose of your essay is to explain how to do or how to make something. To find a topic for his essay, Chen made a list of things he knew how to do or make. He then put an asterisk next to three topics that he liked the best.

Topics List

Things I know how to do or make:

ride a mountain bike   play shortstop in softball*

make jiaozi*   water-ski

build a bat house   draw Pegasus*

create a blog   make an origami swan

■ Focus your topic.

You should pick a how-to topic that is the "right size" for an essay. A topic that is too narrow won't provide enough information for an essay. One that is too broad may lack focus or run too long. Chen decided that playing shortstop was too broad and drawing Pegasus was too narrow. He selected making jiaozi for his topic because it seemed to be the right size for an essay.

Prewrite

Select a topic and find a focus. Write the heading "Things I know how to do or make." List at least five ideas and put an asterisk (*) next to the two or three topics you like best. Then focus your topic so that it is the right size for your essay.

■ Focus on the traits.

Ideas A good how-to essay is more than just a list of directions. It should include details that will interest and inform the reader. In order to do this, choose a topic that you enjoy and understand well.

■ Gather and organize details.

Ease your reader into the steps of your how-to essay with some background information. Chen used interesting details and a quote about the food to encourage the reader to read on. Other ideas are listed here:

- How you got interested in the topic *(I learned that there are more than 3,000 stuffings for jiaozi.)*
- How you learned to make or do it *(My mother taught me.)*
- Why you enjoy it *(Jiaozi is part of my culture.)*

Once you have your background information, you'll need a list of the materials necessary to complete the process.

Materials List

Dough	Filling	
White flour	Ground pork (one pound)	Grated ginger
Cold water	Finely chopped cabbage (one cup)	Soy sauce (two tablespoons)
Salt		Minced garlic (one or two cloves)
	Finely chopped onion (a few tablespoons)	Salt and pepper (to taste)

Next, you must organize the process logically, as in a time line.

Time Line

Make the dumpling skins —
— Stir salt into cold water
— Add salt water to flour
— Knead dough and refrigerate
— Roll the skins
Make the filling —
— Mix ground pork, chopped cabbage and onion, grated ginger, soy sauce, and minced garlic
Complete the dumplings —
— Place filling on skin and seal
— Boil, adding cold water, repeat

Prewrite

Gather and organize details. Decide how to introduce your topic with background information. List the materials needed. Then write the steps for your how-to topic in proper order, using a time line.

Writing ■ Create your first draft.

The tips below describe how to write each part of the essay. Use these tips as a guide for writing your first draft.

■ Write your beginning paragraph.

The **beginning** grabs the reader's attention, gives some background, and includes the thesis statement. Here are strategies for capturing your reader's interest.

- Give an important detail about the topic.

  Chinese dumplings, or jiaozi, are the most popular food in China.

- Tell what makes the topic fun.

  Chinese dumplings are as much fun to make as they are to eat.

- Open with an intriguing question.

  Do you know what food all Chinese people love?

■ Create your middle paragraphs.

The **middle** paragraphs should tell what materials are needed and share the steps in the process.

- Develop a paragraph (or two) for each step or main point.
- Include details to fully explain each step.
- Use transition words and phrases to connect your ideas.

■ Finish with a strong ending paragraph.

The **ending** must conclude the explanation in a satisfying way. Use one or more of the following strategies.

- Give the reader new information to think about.

  Chinese people put more than 3,000 kinds of stuffing into their dumplings.

- Summarize the process.

  In just a few simple steps, the dumplings are done, steaming hot, and ready to eat.

- Suggest that the reader try the process.

  By trying this recipe, you will get to enjoy one of the most popular tastes of China.

Write

Write your first draft. Use your prewriting work (pages 188–189) and the tips above as a guide for your writing.

Revising ■ Improve your writing.

After you write your first draft, set it aside for a while. When you come back to your writing, use the checklist below as your revising guide.

Revising Checklist

Ideas

_____ 1. Have I focused on an interesting process?
_____ 2. Have I clearly explained the process in easy steps?
_____ 3. Do I provide enough detail for each step?

Organization

_____ 4. Does my essay have a strong beginning, an interesting middle, and a thoughtful ending?
_____ 5. Have I put the how-to steps in a sequential order?
_____ 6. Does each paragraph cover a key step or a main point?
_____ 7. Have I used transitions to connect my ideas?

Voice

_____ 8. Does my voice fit the topic and the audience?
_____ 9. Does my voice show my interest in the topic?

Word Choice

_____ 10. Have I used specific nouns, verbs, and modifiers?
_____ 11. Have I explained any technical or unfamiliar terms?

Sentence Fluency

_____ 12. When I read the essay out loud, do my sentences flow smoothly?
_____ 13. Have I used a variety of sentence types?

Revise

Improve your first draft. Use the checklist as you review your first draft and make changes. (Consider asking a partner to review your writing, too.)

Expository

Editing ▪ Check for conventions.

When you have finished revising, it's time to edit your how-to essay for punctuation, capitalization, spelling, and grammar.

Editing Checklist

Conventions

PUNCTUATION

_____ **1.** Have I used end punctuation correctly?

_____ **2.** Have I used commas correctly in compound and complex sentences?

CAPITALIZATION

_____ **3.** Did I capitalize all proper nouns and proper adjectives?

_____ **4.** Did I capitalize the first word in each sentence?

SPELLING

_____ **5.** Have I caught any errors my spell-checker may have missed?

_____ **6.** Have I double-checked the spelling of any special terms?

GRAMMAR

_____ **7.** Have I used the correct forms of verbs (*I did,* not *I done*)?

_____ **8.** Do my verbs and subjects agree in number?

_____ **9.** Have I used the right word (*to, too, two*)?

Edit your how-to essay. Use the checklist above to edit your work. Ask a partner to check your work, too. Then write a correct final copy and proofread it.

Publishing ▪ Share your writing.

After working so hard on your essay, be sure to share it with friends or family. You can also present your essay as a demonstration speech, a poster, or a Web page.

Publish your essay. Give your writing to classmates or family members to read. Also consider the speech, poster, or Web-page ideas.

Writing for Assessment
Responding to Expository Prompts

Explanations can be tricky. Giving directions or sharing information requires that you thoroughly understand the topic and present your ideas in a clear and concise way. Beyond that, the reader must feel drawn to your explanation because it is interesting. The best explanations begin and end with good information, so the key is to work with solid ideas right from the start.

On a test, you may be asked to write explanations in response to expository prompts. You can create the best responses by following the steps in the writing process. This chapter will show you how to adapt the writing process to response writing, when you have limited time to complete your work.

Writing Guidelines

Subject: **Expository prompt**
Form: **Response essay**
Purpose: **To demonstrate competence**
Audience: **Instructor**

"Never underestimate your reader's intelligence or overestimate his or her information."
—Anonymous

Prewriting ■ Analyze an expository prompt.

Most writing tests ask you to respond to a prompt. A prompt is a set of directions that tells you what to write. It's crucial for you to analyze the prompt carefully so that you write a response that fits the requirements of the test. When you analyze a prompt, answer the following **STRAP questions**:

<u>S</u>ubject: What topic (school schedule, homework policy, healthy living, friendships) should I write about?

<u>T</u>ype: What form (essay, letter, announcement, report, article) of writing should I create?

<u>R</u>ole: What position (student, community member, son or daughter, friend) should I assume as writer?

<u>A</u>udience: Who (classmates, teacher, principal, parents, city council) is the intended reader?

<u>P</u>urpose: What is the goal (inform, explain, evaluate) of my writing?

The following key words are often found in **expository** prompts: *inform, explain, analyze, compare and contrast, outline,* and *define.*

Try It!

Analyze these prompts by using the STRAP questions.

1. The principal has asked for student essays for next year's "Freshman Survival Guide." Write an article that compares and contrasts eighth grade with ninth grade. Focus on providing information to help new freshmen adjust to ninth grade.
2. Your school newspaper is printing a series of articles about heroes and heroines. Write about someone who is a hero or heroine to you. That person may be someone you know or someone you have read about. Explain why you believe this person is heroic.
3. "That's what friends are for." Most people know the word "friend," but everyone has a different idea of what makes a friend. Define the word "friend" and include clear examples.

Tip

Some prompts do not contain key words for every STRAP question. You will have to use your best judgment to answer these questions.

■ Plan your response.

Once you have answered the STRAP questions, you should quickly plan your response. The following graphic organizers can help.

Graphic Organizers

Quick List (Any Essay)

1. First Point
   —Detail 1
   —Detail 2
2. Second Point
   —Detail 1
   —Detail 2
3. Third Point
   —Detail 1
   —Detail 2

**Time Line
(How-To/Process)**

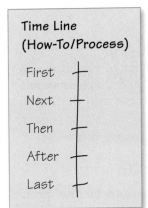

First

Next

Then

After

Last

T-Chart (Two-Part Essay)

Topic:

Part A	Part B
*	*
*	*
*	*
*	*

Venn Diagram (Compare-Contrast)

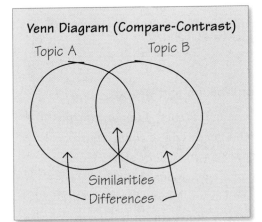

Topic A   Topic B

Similarities
Differences

Cluster (Definition/Classification)

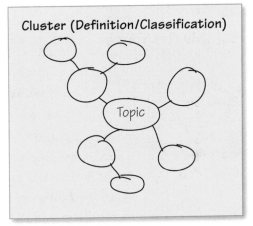

Topic

Prewrite

Reread the expository prompts on page 194. Choose one prompt and use one of the graphic organizers above to quickly organize a response to the prompt.

Tip

Always allow time for prewriting and for revising and editing. For example, with 45 minutes to respond to a prompt, use 5 to 10 minutes to analyze the prompt and plan your response, 30 to 35 minutes for your writing, and the last 5 minutes for revising and editing.

Writing ■ Respond to a prompt.

After answering the STRAP questions and using a graphic organizer to plan your response, it's time to begin writing. Make sure to use a tone and level of language appropriate to your topic and to your audience. Review the sample prompt and response that follow.

Sample Expository Prompt

> What could be done to make your community better? Could something be done to make it safer? Could there be more opportunities for young people? In an essay, explain one idea that you have to improve your community.

Try It!

Answer the STRAP questions for this prompt. Remember that answering these questions will help you understand the prompt and form your response. (See page **194**.)

Sample Response

Beginning
The beginning paragraph states the thesis (underlined).

Make Way for Walking and Biking

You can drive from one end of New London to the other in 15 minutes. On the north end of town, there is a small shopping mall, plus a new grocery store. Our downtown, in the middle of New London, contains a few shops, restaurants, and the Crown Movie Theater. Our medical clinic, another grocery store, and a hardware store anchor the south end of town. What makes New London inconvenient is getting from one shopping area to another—unless you are driving a car. New London would be a better community if it were more accessible for pedestrians and cyclists.

Walking is difficult because there are very few continuous sidewalks. Some sidewalks end halfway down

Expository

a block. In order to continue, you have to walk across front lawns until you come across more sidewalk. If it's wet or muddy, you have to walk in the street. As silly as it sounds, there are parts of town with only one or two small sections of sidewalk on some blocks. If all homeowners were required to have sidewalks, New London would be a safer place to walk.

Middle
Each middle paragraph covers one main point.

Riding a bike is not any safer than walking. The streets in New London are very narrow, and many people park their cars on the street. Riding a bike through this obstacle course can be dangerous. Even experienced cyclists have been known to clip a parked car and crash. It would be impractical to include a bike lane because the streets are so narrow. But many cities have made old railroad paths into bike trails. This could work in New London because we have unused railroad tracks running through town.

Ending
The ending explains the importance of the topic.

We hear a lot about the value of cutting back on driving to save energy. That would certainly be possible if we didn't have to drive everywhere in town. Walking or biking would also give some of us more opportunity to get some exercise. Continuous sidewalks and a bike path would give us different ways to get around New London and clearly make our community a better place to live.

Practice responding to an expository prompt. Review the prompt you chose from page 194, reminding yourself of the STRAP questions and the graphic organizer you have created. Then write a response to the prompt in the amount of time your teacher gives you.

Write

Revising ■ Improve your response.

Most writing tests allow you to make corrections to improve your work, though you should find out ahead of time how many changes are allowed. Always make changes and corrections as neatly as possible. If the test allows revising and editing, use the STRAP questions to guide your changes.

> **Subject:** Does my response focus on the topic in the prompt? Do the main points in my response support the thesis?
> **Type:** Have I followed the correct form (essay, letter, article)?
> **Role:** Have I assumed the position indicated in the prompt?
> **Audience:** Have I used the right level of language for my audience?
> **Purpose:** Does my writing accomplish the goal set forth in the prompt?

Improve your work. Reread your response, asking yourself the STRAP questions above. Make neat changes in the time your teacher allows.

Editing ■ Check your response.

Check your response for punctuation, capitalization, spelling, and grammar. You don't want any careless errors that confuse the reader.

Conventions

_____ 1. Have I used end punctuation for every sentence?
_____ 2. Have I capitalized all proper nouns and first words of sentences?
_____ 3. Have I checked my spelling?
_____ 4. Have I made sure my subjects and verbs agree?
_____ 5. Have I used the right word (there, they're, their)?

Check your conventions. Review your response for punctuation, capitalization, spelling, and grammar. Make neat corrections in the time your teacher allows.

> "Grammar is an ever-evolving set of rules for using words in ways that we can all agree on."
> —Patricia T. O'Conner

Expository Writing on Tests

Use the following tips as a guide whenever you respond to an expository writing prompt.

Before you write . . .

■ **Understand the prompt.**
Review the STRAP questions listed on page **194**.
Remember that an expository prompt asks you to *explain*.

■ **Plan your time wisely.**
Spend several minutes making notes and planning before starting to write. Use the last few minutes to read over what you have written.

As you write . . .

■ **Decide on a focus or thesis for your essay.**
Keep your main idea or purpose in mind as you write.

■ **Be selective.**
Use examples and explanations that directly support your focus.

■ **End in a meaningful way.**
Remind the reader about the importance of the topic.

After you've written a first draft . . .

■ **Check for completeness.**
Use the STRAP questions on page 198 to revise your work.

■ **Check for correctness.**
Check for errors in punctuation, capitalization, spelling, and grammar.

 Plan and write a response. Analyze one of the prompts below using the STRAP questions. Then plan and write a response. Complete your work within the time your teacher gives you.

Expository Prompts

■ Explain why it is good for a person to play a competitive sport, participate in musical performances, or belong to a school organization.

■ Explain how to build something or how to do something. Give your reader enough information to actually do what you are explaining.

Expository

Persuasive Writing

Persuasive Writing
Writing a Position Essay

Don't just sit there; take a stand! That's the position former British Prime Minister Margaret Thatcher took on the topic of debate. She said, "I love argument; I love debate. I don't expect anyone just to sit there and agree with me; that's not their job."

Whether you are a famous politician or a student, you are sure to encounter topics that you feel very strongly about—topics worth debating. Maybe the school board wants to cut the sports budget at your school, or perhaps your city plans to create a landfill near your home. Issues like these are bound to cause differences of opinion in your community and even among your family and friends! What will you do? Will you sit there, or will you take a stand?

Persuasive writing helps you address a difference of opinion. By stating an opinion and defending it, you can convince others to agree with you. In this chapter, you will write a position essay about a local controversy in your community.

Writing Guidelines

Subject: A local controversy in your community
Form: Position essay
Purpose: To defend a position
Audience: Classmates and community members

"Understanding is a two-way street."
—Eleanor Roosevelt

Persuasive Writing Warm-Up: Use support.

When you write a persuasive paragraph or essay, it's important to include plenty of effective supporting details. You can include, among other things, facts, statistics, quotations from experts, and personal experiences. (See pages 569–570 for additional types of details.)

The notebook page below shows supporting details that one student collected to support her opinion about soft-drink machines in schools.

Details for Persuasive Paragraph

Ban "Liquid Candy" in School

personal experience	Some of my friends drink three or four sodas per day in school.
statistics	According to the USDA, teens 25 years ago drank almost twice as much milk as soda pop. Today they drink twice as much soda pop as milk.
facts	The USDA recommends only 40 grams of refined sugar for the entire day.
quotation	"The explosion of candy and soda machines in public schools is a relatively new phenomenon closely paralleling childhood obesity." —WebMD

Try It!

On your own paper, express an opinion about an important topic in your school. Then find at least three different types of details to support your opinion. Use the information above as a guide.

Writing a Persuasive Paragraph

A persuasive paragraph expresses an opinion about a specific topic and contains effective evidence and details to support the opinion. A persuasive paragraph has three main parts:

- The **topic sentence** states the opinion.
- The **body sentences** support the opinion.
- The **closing sentence** revisits the opinion.

Sample Persuasive Paragraph

In the following persuasive paragraph, the student writer expresses her opinion about soda vending machines in her school. She uses all four types of details that she collected on page **202**.

The **topic sentence** states an opinion (underlined).

The **body sentences** support the opinion.

The **closing sentence** reflects on the opinion.

Ban "Liquid Candy" in Our School

The soda machines should be removed from Brooktown Central High School because soft drinks are partly to blame for growing health problems. The average can of soda contains about 40 grams (10 teaspoons) of sugar, and many students at BCHS drink several cans every day. This might not seem like a big problem until you consider that the United States Department of Agriculture (USDA) recommends that an individual consume a maximum of 40 grams of refined sugar for the entire day! The USDA's figures also show that 25 years ago teens drank nearly twice as much milk as soda pop; today they drink twice as much pop as milk. Doctors are seeing the effects of this trend. An article on WebMD reports, "The explosion of candy and soda machines in public schools is a relatively new phenomenon closely paralleling the rise in childhood obesity." Drinking too much soda costs more than money; it can also cost you your health. Schools should not encourage students to buy something that's not good for them.

Persuasive

Write a persuasive paragraph. Review the three parts of a paragraph (top of page) and what they do. Then present your opinion and details from page **202** in a persuasive paragraph about a school-related topic.

Understanding Your Goal

Your goal in this chapter is to write a well-organized persuasive essay that defends a position. The traits listed in the chart below will help you plan and write your essay.

TRAITS OF PERSUASIVE WRITING

- **Ideas**

  Use specific reasons to defend a clear position on a controversial issue in your community.

- **Organization**

  Create a beginning that states your position, a middle that provides support and answers an objection, and an ending that restates your position.

- **Voice**

  Use a persuasive voice that is appropriate for your topic and audience.

- **Word Choice**

  Choose fair and precise words to state and defend your position.

- **Sentence Fluency**

  Write clear, complete sentences with varied beginnings.

- **Conventions**

  Check your writing for errors in punctuation, capitalization, spelling, and grammar.

Get the big picture. Look at the rubric on pages 234–235. You can use that rubric to assess your progress as you write. Your goal is to write a persuasive essay that states and defends your position.

Position Essay

A position essay clearly states where you stand on an issue. By stating and defending your position, you may be able to convince others to agree with you. In this sample essay, the student writer defends his position on keeping open a local home for mentally challenged adults.

Beginning
The beginning introduces the topic and states the position (underlined).

Save Hillhouse

Are you familiar with that big, old house on the hilltop near Beecher and Main Streets? That's Hillhouse, a home for mentally challenged adults. Yesterday, our local newspaper, the *Journal Express*, printed an article about closing Hillhouse. It said that Hillhouse needs more than $100,000 worth of repairs, and there isn't enough money available to get them done. The city wants to close Hillhouse and tear the building down. Is closing it the best way to solve the problem? No. The best solution is to pull together as a community and keep Hillhouse open.

Middle
The first middle paragraph supports the writer's position with statistics and a personal experience.

First, keeping Hillhouse open is very important to the people who live and work there. If Hillhouse shuts down, twenty-six residents will need to find new homes, and seven staff members will lose their jobs. Half of the adults at Hillhouse have lived there for five years or more. For some, it's the only place they have lived since leaving their parents' homes. When I volunteered at Hillhouse, I met a man named John. He is 34 and has been at Hillhouse since he was 18. John has no family, and he thinks of himself as the official caretaker. He is always the first one to welcome a new resident and to make sure that he or she feels like a part of the Hillhouse family. John says that he would make the repairs by himself, if he knew how. Moving from Hillhouse would mean that people like John would have to adjust not only to a new home but to new friends, new caretakers, a new neighborhood, and maybe even a new city!

The second middle paragraph provides interesting facts.

A second reason to keep Hillhouse open is the house itself. Hillhouse was built in 1870, just five years after the Civil War ended. It has had many well-known local owners, and some people in our city want it declared a historical landmark. If the building was made a landmark, then the city could not close it down. As a landmark, it might even be eligible to get some government money to fix it up. Our

Persuasive

local historical society is willing to work with the Heritage Museum to try to get the Hillhouse building on the National Register of Historical Places. Did you know that President William Howard Taft's stepbrother, Charles Phelps Taft, lived in the house at the turn of the twentieth century? Also, several early mayors of our city have lived there.

The third middle paragraph appeals to a sense of community.

Lastly, the best reason for keeping Hillhouse open is to show that our community cares for its people. If we all get together and conduct fund-raisers, organize volunteer efforts, and donate time and money, it will show that our city is a great place to live and that we look out for each other. We can ask businesses to donate materials, and citizens can donate time to help fix things up. You can be sure that the people of Hillhouse would want to help us if we needed them. So let's get busy and help them with what they need.

The last middle paragraph defends the position against an important objection.

Some people think that the residents of Hillhouse should move to Hawthorn Manor, which is more like a nursing home. These people don't understand that the residents don't need daily nursing care. They can do a lot by themselves. Let's help them have some independence and keep their "family" together. Tearing down the house and breaking apart that special family can't be a good thing.

Ending
The ending restates the writer's position.

We need to pull together as a community and keep Hillhouse open. We can all find ways to help with the repairs so that the residents won't need to move, and the staff won't lose their jobs. Maybe Hillhouse can stay open if it is declared a historical landmark. Get involved and help out! Someday soon we could read an article in the *Journal Express* about the amazing way our community solved the Hillhouse problem.

Respond to the reading. Answer the following questions about the sample essay.

Ideas (1) What three reasons support the writer's position?

Organization (2) What method of organization does the writer use (time order, order of importance, order of location)? (3) Which paragraph answers an objection?

Voice & Word Choice (4) Does the writer sound knowledgeable and persuasive? Explain.

Prewriting

Prewriting for a position essay involves selecting a controversial issue in your community, gathering reasons and details to support a position on that issue, and organizing your ideas. Careful prewriting makes persuasive writing easier and more effective.

Keys to Effective Prewriting

1. Choose a controversial local issue in your community. Decide what your position is.

2. Write a clear position statement to guide your writing.

3. Gather the best reasons and details to support your position. Rank the reasons —1, 2, 3—from least important to most important.

4. Select an important objection that you can address.

Prewriting ■ Select a controversy.

A controversy happens when there is a disagreement about an important issue. To find a writing topic, student writer Keefe Collum answered two key questions about local controversies in his community. He put an asterisk next to the controversy that he wanted to write about.

List of Local Controversies

In the past two weeks, what local controversies have been covered most often on the front page of our local newspaper?
- the upcoming school referendum
- rerouting Highway C away from Sanderville Woods *
- building a fire station on the far north side of town
- the need for more security at local sports events

What local controversies have we discussed in class recently?
- the upcoming school referendum
- the city council's decision to make recycling mandatory
- the accuracy of bacteria testing at New Eastland Beach

Prewrite

List controversies. On your own paper, answer the two key questions above. Try to come up with at least three topics for each question. Then choose one controversy that you feel strongly about. Write a sentence that states your position and explain the reason for your choice.

Highway C should be moved away from Sanderville Woods. I picked this issue because I've started to become really interested in wildlife and their habitats. Many birds and animals live in that area, but the highway puts them in great danger. I would like to see our community consider the wildlife for a change when it decides to do something.

■ Focus on the traits.

Ideas Choose an issue that you can defend with several clear, convincing reasons. The more knowledge you have about your topic, the easier it will be for you to defend your position.

■ Gather reasons to support your position.

After you have stated your position, you need to gather reasons to support it. Making a "why" chart helped Keefe gather reasons that supported his position.

"Why" Chart

Why should Highway C be moved away from Sanderville Woods?

Why?			Details
because ②	Deer are getting hit by cars.	• increase in deer population • dead deer on highway • accidents injure people	
because ③	Birds and animals are being driven away by traffic noise.	• sandhill cranes making a comeback in our state • cranes nesting near the woods • noise and exhaust fumes drive cranes away	
because ①	People who live near the woods oppose commercial development and noise in the area.	• built homes near the woods to get away from noise of the city	

Prewrite

Create a "why" chart. Create your own chart. At the top of the chart, write your position in the form of a "why" question. In the boxes below it, write three reasons that answer the question. Then add details about each reason.

■ Focus on the traits.

Organization Persuasive essays are often organized by order of importance. After you have finished your chart, rank your reasons—1, 2, 3—from least important to most important.

Persuasive

Prewriting ■ Gather objections.

Once you have a solid list of reasons that support your position, you should anticipate any arguments that the reader might have. If your position is that something *should* be done, come up with reasons someone might argue that it *should not* be done. By planning how to answer objections, you can make your position even stronger.

■ Identify objections.

Here are several ways to identify objections.

■ Read newspaper articles and listen to local news reports to see how these sources present different sides of an issue.
■ Think about debates you've had about the issue. Try to recall opposing positions and reasons.
■ Ask the opinions of your friends and family. Try to debate positions that differ from yours.

Keefe listed the following objections to his argument.

> County Highway C is a scenic drive.
> County Highway C has become a popular alternate route to Taborville.
> Moving the highway will cost a lot of money. ✳

Gather objections. Use the strategies above to identify and list three objections to your position. Put an asterisk next to the strongest objection.

■ Counter an objection.

Countering an objection is simply arguing against it. Keefe counters the strongest objection in three ways.

> **Moving the highway will cost a lot of money.**
>
> 1. The woods represents years of history and a vital ecosystem.
> 2. No one can put a price tag on natural resources.
> 3. As the city expands, this peaceful place should be saved for future generations.

Counter an important objection. Write down the strongest objection to your argument. Try to counter it in two or three ways.

Writing

Now that you have planned your essay, you are ready to get your ideas on paper.

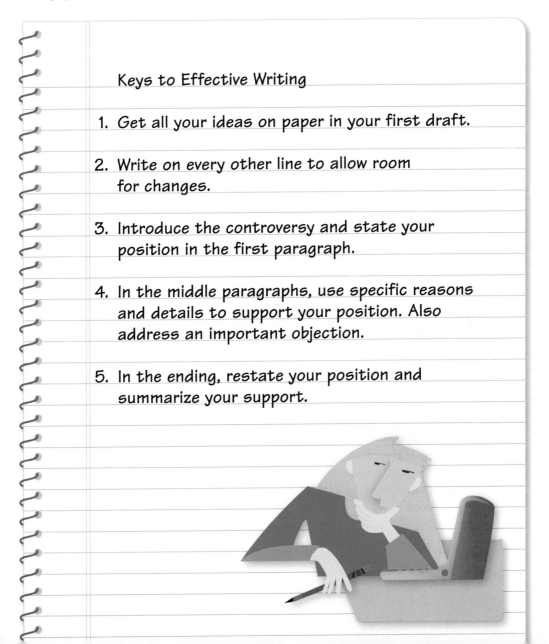

Keys to Effective Writing

1. Get all your ideas on paper in your first draft.

2. Write on every other line to allow room for changes.

3. Introduce the controversy and state your position in the first paragraph.

4. In the middle paragraphs, use specific reasons and details to support your position. Also address an important objection.

5. In the ending, restate your position and summarize your support.

Persuasive

Writing ■ Get the big picture.

As you prepare to write your first draft, study the following graphic to see how the parts of your essay should fit together. (The examples are from the student essay on pages 213–216.)

BEGINNING

The **beginning** introduces the controversial issue and states the writer's position.

Position Statement
Highway C should be rerouted because Sanderville Woods is an irreplaceable community resource.

MIDDLE

The **middle** paragraphs support the writer's position.

Topic Sentences
First of all, relocating Highway C would restore peace and quiet to area neighborhoods.

Another reason for moving the highway away from the woods is to avoid the increasing deer population.

The best reason for relocating Highway C is that its traffic disrupts the habitat of birds and wildlife.

The **last middle** paragraph answers an important objection.

People who oppose rerouting Highway C point out how much it will cost.

ENDING

The **ending** sums up your position and gives the reader something to think about.

Closing Sentence
Relocate Highway C and save Sanderville Woods before it's too late.

■ Start your essay.

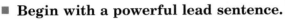

The beginning paragraph of your essay should get the reader's attention, introduce the topic, and state your position.

- **Begin with a powerful lead sentence.**
  Get the reader's attention in the first sentence with a strong opening idea.
  Don't let Sanderville Woods lose its natural beauty and serenity.

- **Provide important background information.**
  Be honest, creative, and even dramatic as you introduce the controversy.
  The quiet woodland paths, ponds, and streams are being invaded by the roar of traffic and the smell of diesel fuel along that stretch of Highway C.

- **Build up to your position statement.**
  Your position statement is the thesis statement for your entire essay. All of the sentences in the beginning paragraph should lead up to your position statement.
  Last week, Calvin County proposed solving the problem by rerouting Highway C away from the woods. . . .

Beginning Paragraph

The controversy is introduced.

> Don't let Sanderville Woods lose its natural beauty and serenity. The quiet woodland paths, ponds, and streams are being invaded by the roar of traffic and the smell of diesel fuel along that stretch of Highway C. Last week, Calvin County proposed solving the problem by rerouting Highway C away from the woods. This idea has become a heated issue. In a poll taken by the Pine Valley Times, 67 percent of those responding agreed with the county's proposal. Even more support is needed. Highway C should be rerouted because Sanderville Woods is an irreplaceable community resource.

The writer's position is stated (underlined).

Write an opening. Write the beginning paragraph of your essay. Does it engage the reader? If not, write another version or two. Choose the one that you like best.

Persuasive

Writing ■ Develop the middle part.

Begin each middle paragraph in your essay with a topic sentence and add details that support it. Refer to your "why" chart (page **209**) for ideas for this part of your essay. Remember to address a significant objection in your last middle paragraph.

■ Use transitions.

Transitions will help you show order of importance in your paragraphs. The following chart includes transitions that could connect your first three middle paragraphs.

Paragraph 1	Paragraph 2	Paragraph 3
First of all, ⟶	Another reason . . . ⟶	The best reason . . .
To begin, ⟶	Also ⟶	Finally,
To start with, ⟶	In addition, ⟶	Most importantly,

Middle Paragraphs

A topic sentence (underlined) introduces each middle paragraph.

First of all, relocating Highway C would restore peace and quiet to area neighborhoods. Before Highway C became a busy road, many people built homes near Sanderville Woods. They wanted a quiet woodland setting where they could relax and enjoy nature. They didn't bargain for a noisy highway.

Another reason for moving the highway away from the woods is to avoid the increasing deer population. What does that mean? The number of deer being hit on the highway has increased 30 percent since last year. Think about it. Hitting a deer can cause a serious accident. Protecting the lives of people as well as animals is an important reason for relocating the highway.

The middle paragraphs build to the most important reason.

The best reason for relocating Highway C is that its traffic disrupts the habitat of birds and wildlife. For example, the marsh at the edge of Sanderville Woods has become a habitat for sandhill cranes. Until recently, sandhill cranes had nearly disappeared in our state. Now they are making a comeback. They nest near Sanderville Woods. The noise and traffic on Highway C may drive them away. Other wild animals, like raccoons and foxes, may be forced to leave the area, too.

People who oppose rerouting Highway C point out how much it will cost. However, no one can put a price tag on natural resources. Sanderville Woods is a gold mine of local history and ecology. In addition, it is a popular place for quiet sports like hiking, snowshoeing, bird-watching, and so on. Many school children enjoy science field trips to Sanderville Woods. It also provides a peaceful habitat for wildlife. This valuable resource should be preserved for future generations.

The last middle paragraph counters an objection.

Write **Write your middle paragraphs.** Construct middle paragraphs that support your position. Make sure to organize your support according to order of importance—from least important to most important reason.

Persuasive

Tip

- **Use transitions** between paragraphs to show order of importance.
- **Include clear reasons** and avoid sounding too emotional.
- **Support your reasons** with facts, statistics, quotations from experts, and personal anecdotes.
- **Respond to a significant objection** by countering it in a thoughtful, reasonable way.

Writing ▪ End your essay.

At this point, you have stated your position, supported it with solid reasons, and responded to an objection. Now you are ready to write your ending paragraph. Follow these guidelines.

- Revisit your position and add a final insight.
- Sum up the main reasons that support your position.
- Sum up your response to the objection.
- Leave the reader with a final thought.

Ending Paragraph

The position is restated.

The paragraph sums up support points and revisits the response to the objection.

The reader is left with a final thought.

> Clearly, Highway C should be moved away from Sanderville Woods. Relocating the highway would restore peace and quiet to area neighborhoods, decrease the number of deer being hit by cars, and, most importantly, help preserve vital wildlife habitat. If current development continues along Highway C, it will become an extended strip mall. From the perspective of long-term value, the cost of rerouting a highway seems smaller than what it would take to re-create a thriving nature preserve complete with marshes and woodlands. Relocate Highway C and save Sanderville Woods before it's too late.

Write your ending and complete a first draft. Write the final paragraph of your essay. Restate your position and summarize your reasons. Leave the reader with something new to think about. Then prepare a copy of your entire essay. Write on every other line if you write by hand, or double-space if you use a computer. This will give you room for revising.

Tip

If you have followed the traditional persuasive essay structure, your first draft should have turned out quite well. That structure follows:

- Introduce the topic and state your opinion.
- Support your opinion.
- Answer an objection.
- Wrap up your argument.

Revising

When you revise, you may add or delete details, rearrange parts of your writing, and work on improving your voice. You should also check your word choice and refine your sentences.

Keys to Effective Revising

1. Read your essay aloud and decide if it sounds convincing.

2. Make sure you have clearly stated your position.

3. Check your paragraphs to make sure that they contain convincing support.

4. Work on your writer's voice so it sounds informed and confident.

5. Check your writing for strong words and varied sentences.

6. Use the editing and proofreading marks found inside the back cover of this book.

Persuasive

Revising ■ for Ideas

6 My position is very well defended and compels the reader to act.	**5** My position is supported with logical reasons, and I respond to an important objection.	**4** Most of my reasons support my position. I respond to an objection.

When you revise for *ideas*, make sure the reasons you use are accurate and logical. Also make sure that you have adequately supported your opinion. The rubric strip above can guide you.

■ How can I avoid errors in logic?

You can avoid errors in logic by eliminating statements that are hard to support. Here are some types of logic errors you should remove from your writing.

■ Statements that jump to a conclusion

> If County Highway C isn't rerouted, Sanderville Woods will be replaced by a strip mall.

This statement is hard to support because you cannot prove that the woods will become a strip mall.

■ Exaggerations

> No one will visit Sanderville Woods if Highway C stays where it is.

To support this statement you must prove that *no one* will visit Sanderville Woods.

Exercise

Identify at least two logic errors in the paragraph below. Explain why they are errors.

1   All kids should have cell phones. A cell phone is handy for calling a
2 family member for a ride or just making plans with a friend. Cell phones can
3 also be safety devices in an emergency. With cell phones, people never have
4 to worry about anything. They can get anything they need.

Revise

Check for logic errors. Read the body of your essay. Look for exaggerations and statements that jump to a conclusion. Revise any errors that you find.

3 I need more supporting reasons and a more convincing response to an objection.

2 I need to rethink my position from start to finish.

1 I need to learn how to defend a position.

■ Have I included adequate support for my opinion?

You have effectively supported your opinion if you include clear, provable details. The following checklist can help you decide how well you have supported your opinion.

_____ **1.** Do you strongly believe in the opinion that you are developing?

_____ **2.** Do you include convincing supporting details? Name the different types of details that you used.

_____ **3.** Do you address an important objection? What other objections are there? How important are they?

Revise

Check your essay. Answer the questions in the checklist above. Continue to work with those parts that you were not able to answer with a "yes."

Persuasive

Ideas
A new detail adds support to the topic sentence.

Don't let Sanderville Woods lose its natural beauty and serenity. The quiet woodland paths, ponds, and streams are being invaded by the roar of traffic⌃along that stretch of *and the smell of diesel fuel* Highway C. Last week, Calvin County proposed solving the problem by rerouting Highway C away from the woods. This

An exaggeration is replaced by a statistic.

idea has become a heated issue. In a poll taken by the Pine Valley Times, ~~almost all~~⌃of those responding agreed with . . . *67 percent*

Revising ■ for Organization

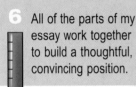 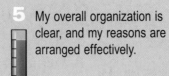 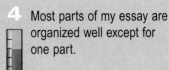

6 All of the parts of my essay work together to build a thoughtful, convincing position.

5 My overall organization is clear, and my reasons are arranged effectively.

4 Most parts of my essay are organized well except for one part.

When you revise for *organization*, you check the structure of your essay. Be sure that your paragraphs are connected in a logical way and your reasons are arranged by order of importance. The rubric strip above can be used as a guide.

■ Is my essay unified?

Your essay is unified if all of the parts work together. If your essay doesn't have unity, the reader won't be able to follow your argument. The following checklist will help you evaluate the unity in your essay.

_____ **1.** Does my first paragraph include my position statement?

_____ **2.** Does the topic sentence of each middle paragraph give a key reason in support of the position statement?

_____ **3.** Do all of the sentences in each paragraph support the topic sentence?

_____ **4.** Does my final paragraph sum up my position?

■ How can I improve unity with transitions?

You can improve unity in your essay by using transitions to tie ideas together between sentences and between paragraphs.

Exercise

Improve the paragraph below by using transitions between sentences or combining some sentences. For a list of transitions, see pages **592–593**.

> A poll shows that 80 percent of students support building a skate park next to North Beach. Some area residents have safety concerns. The park will have a boundary fence. Some residents think skaters might skate outside the fence and get hurt. Residents think the skate park will bring gangs to the beach.

Revise

Check for unity. Revise your essay using the checklist above as a guide. Also check your essay for effective use of transitions.

3 I need to reorganize the middle part of my essay from least important reason to most important.

 2 I need to include a beginning, a middle, and an ending in my essay.

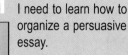 **1** I need to learn how to organize a persuasive essay.

■ Do I present my reasons in the best order?

The reasons in your essay are in the best order if they are presented according to order of importance. Check for order of importance by using the checklist below.

_____ **1.** Does the topic sentence of my first middle paragraph address my least important supporting reason?

_____ **2.** Does the topic sentence of my second middle paragraph address the next important reason?

_____ **3.** Does the topic sentence of my third middle paragraph address the most important reason?

| Position statement |
| Least Important Reason |
| Next Important Reason |
| Most Important Reason |
| Position Summary |

Persuasive

Revise

Check the organization of your essay. Make sure you have built your argument from the least important to the most-important supporting reason. Rearrange any paragraphs that are out of place.

Organization
A transition is changed to improve unity.

A sentence that does not support the topic sentence is removed.

~~Another~~ *The best* reason for relocating Highway C is that its traffic disrupts the habitat of birds and wildlife. For example, the marsh at the edge of Sanderville Woods has become a habitat for sandhill cranes. ~~Each year there is a crane count.~~ Until recently, sandhill cranes had nearly disappeared in our state. Now they are slowly making a comeback. They nest near Sanderville Woods. The noise and traffic on Highway C may drive them away. . . .

Revising ■ for Voice

 6 My knowledgeable voice creates total confidence in my position.

 5 My voice is persuasive and respects my audience. I balance facts and feelings.

 4 My voice respects my audience, but I need to sound more persuasive and knowledgeable.

When you check for *voice*, make sure that you have focused primarily on facts rather than personal feelings in your essay. A knowledgeable-sounding voice will connect with your reader. The rubric strip above will guide your revising.

■ Have I used a knowledgeable-sounding voice?

You have used a knowledgeable-sounding voice if you focus primarily on factual information in your essay. (Persuasive writing succeeds when it contains reliable facts and details that support the main position.) On the other hand, if you focus too heavily on your personal feelings, your voice will sound overly emotional, impulsive, and unconvincing.

Notice the difference between the two passages below. In the first one, the writer sounds too emotional. There is nothing thoughtful or convincing about his voice. In the second passage, the writer effectively balances facts with personal feelings. As a result, he sounds much more convincing.

Overly Emotional Voice

The new rules at the video arcade are the worst. The manager hates kids. He hired a security guard to stand at the door. That makes kids feel like they are being watched all the time. The arcade used to be fun, but now it feels like a prison.

Knowledgeable-Sounding Voice

The video arcade has upgraded its security. The manager became concerned about fights in the arcade, so he hired a security guard. Now, going to the arcade isn't as much fun as it used to be. According to Mike Kuhn, an arcade user, "The security guard creates . . ."

Revise

Check your voice. As you review your essay, make sure that you sound knowledgeable and thoughtful rather than too emotional. Revise accordingly for voice.

3 My voice has a few problems sounding respectful and knowledgeable.

 2 My voice may not respect my audience, and I sound too emotional and unconvincing.

 1 I need to learn how to create a respectful, knowledgeable voice.

■ Do I connect with my audience?

You connect with your audience if, among other things, you address any objections in a respectful way. Your audience may include people who have not made up their minds about the issue, as well as people who feel differently about it. Dealing with an objection in a respectful way will make you sound more convincing. In the following paragraph, the writer addresses an objection in a disrespectful way.

> Extending the landfill to Harrison Road is a really dumb idea. It would mean chopping down lots of trees. People in nice homes on Harrison Road don't want to look at a big, ugly landfill. Everyone knows that a landfill stinks.

 ## Exercise

Rewrite the paragraph above so that it addresses the objection in a respectful way. Trade papers with a classmate. Decide if your partner's voice connects more respectfully with the reader.

Review for voice. Read the paragraph that counters an objection to your position. Does it sound respectful? If not, revise it until it does.

Persuasive

Voice
One sentence is deleted and another is revised to create a more respectful voice.

People who oppose rerouting Highway C point to how

much it will cost. ~~They are being very unreasonable. It is stupid~~
However, no one can
~~to~~ put a price tag on natural resources. Sanderville Woods is

a gold mine of local history and ecology. In addition, . . .

Revising ■ for Word Choice

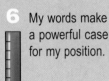
6 My words make a powerful case for my position.

5 Carefully chosen words make my writing persuasive and effective.

4 I have avoided inflammatory (unfair) words, but I need to remove a few qualifiers.

Checking for *word choice* means making sure that you have used the best words to build your argument. It also means making sure that you have not overused qualifying words or used inflammatory words. The rubric strip above can guide you.

■ Did I overuse qualifiers in my essay?

You have overused qualifiers in your essay if too many of your sentences contain words like these: *seems, appears, maybe, somewhat, rather, quite,* or *might.* Such words make a writer sound unsure.

Sentences with Qualifiers

It seems **that the mayor is** somewhat **willing to meet with us.**

Sentences without Qualifiers

The mayor is willing to meet with us.

Exercise

Read the paragraph below. Rewrite it in a straightforward, convincing way.

1   Apparently the mayor will meet with us to discuss our plan. He
2 indicated that he was quite pleased with the proposal we sent him. If he
3 agrees with our position, then maybe we can eventually get a stoplight at
4 the corner by our school. It seems the mayor has already set aside money
5 for a project somewhat like this.

Revise

Check your word choice for balance. Change any sentences that may contain too many qualifying words.

3 I need to change some inflammatory words and remove some qualifiers.

 2 I need to change my unfair language to make a believable position.

 1 I need to learn what words are inflammatory and how to use qualifiers.

■ How can I avoid inflammatory words?

You can avoid inflammatory words by expressing your opinion without blame. Strong language aimed at someone or something only weakens your argument. Here are some examples of inflammatory words.

greedy	foolish	stupid	dumb	so-called
phony	unfit	mean	disgusting	

Note: Being sarcastic can also be inflammatory. Don't call something a great idea when you clearly mean that it is *not* a good idea.

Exercise

Identify inflammatory statements in the paragraph below. Then rewrite the paragraph so that it convinces without blame or sarcasm.

> HGR Inc. is being unreasonable and mean. Their so-called East Side Improvement Plan includes tearing down the recreation center. How ridiculous! That center is where kids go for fun after school. What a brilliant plan—send kids to the streets. HGR should remodel the center and offer more activities.

Revise

Review for inflammatory words. **Read your essay carefully. Rewrite any parts that blame or use sarcasm.**

Word Choice
The argument is strengthened by removing two qualifying words.

Clearly, Highway C should be moved away from Sanderville Woods. ~~Perhaps~~ relocating the highway would restore peace and quiet to area neighborhoods, ~~maybe~~ decrease the number of deer being hit by cars, and, most importantly, help . . .

Revising ▪ for Sentence Fluency

6 My sentences spark the reader's interest in my position.

5 My sentences are skillfully written with varied beginnings.

4 I use different sentence types, and most of the beginnings are varied.

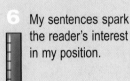
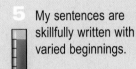
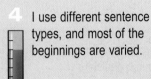

To revise for *sentence fluency*, check to see that you have used different kinds of sentences and that your sentences have varied beginnings. The rubric strip above will help you.

▪ Have I used a variety of sentence types effectively?

You have used different kinds of sentences effectively if they help you develop your argument. Here are the three types of sentences that you can use.

Declarative sentences make statements.
(Most of your sentences should be declarative.)

Interrogative sentences ask questions.
(Asking a question or two in your essay may help you connect with the reader.)

Imperative sentences make commands or requests.
(Use imperative sentences when you want to make a call to action.)

Exercise

Read the following paragraph. How many declarative, interrogative, and imperative sentences does it contain? Where do the interrogative sentences appear? Why? Where do the imperative sentences appear? Why?

1 Signs that old Southport lighthouse is crumbling include chipped
2 mortar and loose bricks. Isn't it time to restore this historic landmark? Even
3 though the lighthouse hasn't been used for years, it has been an important
4 symbol in our community. For many years, it was open to the public. Did
5 you ever climb all those spiraling stairs to the top and look out at the ocean
6 far below? The lighthouse should be fixed so that it can be reopened. Next
7 week, the city council will vote to repair it or tear it down. Call your council
8 person today. Ask for a yes vote.

Revise

Review your sentences. Read your essay. Have you used different kinds of sentences effectively?

3 I use different types of sentences, but I need to vary my sentence beginnings.

 2 Most of my sentences are the same type and begin the same way.

 1 I need to learn about different types of sentences and how to vary the beginnings.

■ Have I varied my sentence beginnings?

You have varied your sentence beginnings if all of your sentences do not begin with the main subject. Compare the following paragraphs.

Similar Beginnings

A bike trail near Lang Road will attract people to other recreation areas in our community. The trail will pass the recreation center, the city playground, and Wentworth Beach. Families can combine a bike ride with other activities along the way. Older kids can use the trail as a safe way to get to places to meet their friends.

Varied Beginnings

A bike trail near Lang Road will attract people to other recreation areas in our community. In addition to the recreation center, the trail will pass the city playground and Wentworth Beach. When families go bike riding, they can enjoy other activities along the way. For older kids, the trail will provide a safe way to get to places to meet their friends.

Revise

Check your sentence beginnings. Read your essay looking at sentence beginnings, especially the subject-followed-by-a-verb pattern. Revise by adding words, phrases, or clauses to the beginnings of some sentences.

Sentence Fluency

An interrogative and an imperative sentence are added.

Another reason for moving the highway away from the
What does that mean?
woods is to avoid the increasing deer population.∧The number of

deer being hit on the highway has increased 30 percent since
Think about it.
last year.∧Hitting a deer can cause a serious accident. . . .

Persuasive

Revising ■ Improve your writing.

Revise

Check your revising. On a piece of paper, write the numbers 1 to 12. If you can answer "yes" to a question, put a check mark after that number. If not, continue to work with that part of your essay.

Revising Checklist

Ideas

_____ **1.** Do I state my position clearly?

_____ **2.** Have I included solid reasons that support my position?

_____ **3.** Do I effectively respond to an important objection?

Organization

_____ **4.** Does the overall structure of my essay work well?

_____ **5.** Are my reasons arranged by order of importance?

_____ **6.** Have I used transitions to create unity in my writing?

Voice

_____ **7.** Is my voice appropriate for my topic?

_____ **8.** Have I shown my audience the proper respect?

Word Choice

_____ **9.** Have I avoided overusing qualifiers?

_____ **10.** Have I removed inflammatory language and sarcasm?

Sentence Fluency

_____ **11.** Have I used different kinds of sentences?

_____ **12.** Do I vary my sentence beginnings?

Revise

Make a clean copy. When you have finished revising, make a clean copy of your essay before you edit. This makes checking for conventions easier.

Editing

After you finish revising your essay, you are ready to edit for *conventions:* punctuation, capitalization, spelling, and grammar.

Keys to Effective Editing

1. Use a dictionary, a thesaurus, and the "Proofreader's Guide" in the back of this book (pages 604–763) to check your writing.

2. Use the editing and proofreading marks inside the back cover of the book to mark your writing.

3. If you are using a computer, edit on a printed computer copy. Then enter your changes on the computer.

4. Check for any words or phrases that may be confusing to the reader.

5. Check your writing for punctuation, capitalization, spelling, and grammar errors.

Editing ■ for Conventions

6 My essay is error free from start to finish.

5 I have one or two errors, but they don't distract the reader.

4 I need to correct a few errors in my paper because they distract the reader.

When you edit for *conventions*, you correct punctuation, grammar, capitalization, and spelling errors. The rubric strip above can guide your editing.

■ Have I correctly punctuated introductory elements?

You have punctuated a long introductory phrase or introductory clause correctly if you have set it off from the rest of the sentence with a comma.

Introductory Prepositional Phrases

With the arrival of winter weather, **the school should be opened earlier.**

Introductory Participial Phrase

Following this proposal, **Ms. Madsen met with the school's security staff.**

Introductory Clause

Whenever the temperature drops below 32, **the doors will open by 7:00 a.m.**

Note: You may omit the comma if an introductory phrase is short.

After school **the main doors remain open until 4:00 p.m.**

Try It!

Rewrite any sentence below that needs a comma. Add the correct punctuation.

1. For the first time in two years we have a chance to change the lunch menu.
2. Before any decision is made students must complete a questionnaire.
3. Providing a new menu the cafeteria staff hopes to meet the dietary needs and tastes of more students.
4. By noon most students have already eaten.

Edit

Check introductory phrases and clauses. Review your essay, looking for long introductory phrases and introductory clauses. Make sure you have punctuated them correctly.

3 I need to correct several errors in my paper because they confuse the reader.

2 I need to correct the many errors because they make my essay difficult to read.

1 I need help finding errors and making corrections.

■ Have I used the correct forms of adjectives?

You have used the correct forms of adjectives if they make the proper comparisons. The *comparative* form compares two people or things; the *superlative* form compares three or more people or things.

- ■ **Comparative adjectives** (*-er, more,* or *less*) compare two things.

    bigger   more profitable   less economical

- ■ **Superlative adjectives** (*-est, most,* or *least*) compare three or more things.

    biggest   most profitable   least economical

Persuasive

Try It!

Correct each underlined adjective below by making it either comparative or superlative.

1. The fall festival will be the challenging project our service club has done.
2. Extra volunteers will make this festival enjoyable than last year's.
3. We believe this will be the great festival in the history of our school!

Edit

Check for forms of adjectives. Add more punch to your essay by including some comparative and superlative adjectives.

Conventions
A comma is added.

The form of an adjective is corrected.

From the perspective of long-term value, the cost of

smaller

rerouting a highway seems ~~small~~ than what it would take to

re-create a thriving nature preserve complete with marshes

and woodlands. Relocate Highway C and save Sanderville . . .

"Fortunately both my wife and my mother-in-law seem to love digging up mistakes in spelling and punctuation. I can hear them in the next room laughing at me."

—Sherwood Anderson

Editing ■ Check for conventions.

Check your editing. On a piece of paper, write the numbers 1 to 9. If you can answer "yes" to a question, put a check mark after that number. If not, continue to edit for that convention.

Edit

Editing Checklist

Conventions

PUNCTUATION

_____ **1.** Do I use end punctuation after all my sentences?

_____ **2.** Do I use commas after long introductory phrases and introductory clauses?

CAPITALIZATION

_____ **3.** Do I start all my sentences with capital letters?

_____ **4.** Do I capitalize all proper nouns and adjectives?

SPELLING

_____ **5.** Have I spelled all words correctly?

_____ **6.** Have I checked the words my spell-checker may have missed?

GRAMMAR

_____ **7.** Do my subjects and verbs agree in number (*She and I are going,* not *She and I is going*)?

_____ **8.** Do my pronouns agree with their antecedents?

_____ **9.** Have I used the correct forms of adjectives?

■ Add a title.

- Sum up the controversy: **Save Sanderville Woods**
- Write a slogan: **Cast a Vote for Peace and Quiet**
- Be creative: **Don't Make Nature Take a Backseat**

Publishing ■ Share your essay.

After writing, revising, and editing your persuasive essay, make a neat final copy to share. You may also present your essay in a debate, publish it in a newspaper, or send it to an official in your community.

Make a final copy. Follow your teacher's instructions or use the guidelines below to format your essay. (If you are using a computer, see pages 76–78.) Create a clean final copy of your essay and carefully proofread it.

■ Focus on presentation.

- Use blue or black ink and write neatly.
- Write your name in the upper left corner of page 1.
- Skip a line and center your title; skip another line and start your writing.
- Indent every paragraph and leave a one-inch margin on all four sides.
- Write your last name and the page number in the upper right corner of every page after page 1.

Contact an Official

Think of a community or state official who has the authority to take action on your issue. Send your essay to that person along with a letter briefly stating your position and asking for help. In the letter, explain that your essay includes important reasons to support your opinion.

Publish a Letter

Reformat your essay as a letter to the editor of your community newspaper. Check submission guidelines. Then submit your letter.

Stage a Debate

Gather a group of family members or friends who hold opposing opinions on your issue. Try to include one neutral person who has not formed an opinion. Stage a debate. Present and defend your position; allow others to present and defend theirs. Then ask the neutral person to form an opinion based on the debate.

Persuasive

Rubric for Persuasive Writing

Refer to the following rubric for guiding and assessing your persuasive writing. Use it to improve your writing using the six traits.

6 Ideas · 5 · 4

6	**5**	**4**
The position is convincingly supported and defended; it compels the reader to act.	The position is supported with logical reasons; an important objection is countered.	Most of the reasons support the writer's position. An objection is addressed.

Organization

All of the parts of the essay work together to build a very thoughtful, convincing position.	The opening states the position, the middle provides clear support, and the ending reinforces the position.	Most parts of the essay are organized adequately except for one part.

Voice

The writer's voice is extremely confident, knowledgeable, and convincing.	The writer's voice is persuasive, knowledgeable, and respectful.	The writer respects the audience but needs to sound more persuasive or knowledgeable.

Word Choice

The writer's choice of words makes a powerful case.	The writer's word choice helps persuade the reader.	The writer avoids inflammatory (unfair) words but needs to remove some qualifiers.

Sentence Fluency

The sentences spark the reader's interest in the essay.	Variety is seen in both the types of sentences and their beginnings.	Variety is seen in most of the sentences.

Conventions

The writing is error free.	Grammar and punctuation errors are few. The reader is not distracted by the errors.	Distracting grammar and punctuation errors are seen in a few sentences.

3	**2**	**1**
More supporting reasons and a more convincing response to an objection are needed.	A clearer position statement is needed. Better support for the position must be provided.	A new position statement and reasons are needed.
Some parts of the essay need to be reorganized.	The beginning, middle, and ending run together.	The organization is unclear and incomplete.
The writer's voice needs to be more persuasive and respectful.	The writer's voice sounds too emotional and unconvincing.	The writer needs to learn about voice in persuasive writing.
The writer needs to change some inflammatory words and remove some qualifiers.	The words do not create a clear message. Some inflammatory words are used.	Word choice for persuasive writing has not been considered.
More variety is needed in the beginnings or kinds of sentences used.	Too many sentences are worded in the same way.	Sentence fluency has not been considered.
There are a number of errors that may confuse the reader.	Frequent errors make the essay difficult to read.	Nearly every sentence contains errors.

Evaluating a Persuasive Essay

Read the position essay below and focus on its strengths and its weaknesses. Then read the student self-assessment on the next page. (**The student essay that follows contains some errors.**)

Open a Teen Center Downtown

Ninth graders get stuck in the middle. We're not kids, but we're still too young to drive. After school, juniors and seniors drive places to meet friends and have fun. We're stuck finding places within walking distance from the high school, or places we can get to on public transportation. Last week, Mayor Steve Ricchio recommended to the common council that it should "seriously consider an after-school program for students at Pine Ridge High." He's right! It's time for a teen center downtown where kids can go after school.

First of all, a downtown teen center would be most convenient. About a third of Pine Ridge students head downtown after school because it's so close to the high school. A teen center downtown would be easy for us to get to. It would also be near the public library, so if we wanted to study with our friends at the teen center, we could get study materials from the library first. Best of all, all city buses stop downtown at the Transit Center, so we would have a way to get home without calling our folks to come and get us.

A downtown teen center would help the relationship between all teens and downtown store owners. Many times, it's cold or rainy outside, so kids hang out in the stores. Store owners don't like this. They either don't let us in at all, or we can only come in two at a time. A teen center would get kids out of the stores and into a place that's better for meeting with friends. That would make both the store owners and us happy.

The most important reason for a downtown teen center is to have a definite place to go after school. Right now, kids hang out on street corners, in coffee shops, and at the park. There isn't much to do in those places, so it's easy to get board. A teen center would provide a safe place where we could listen to music, dance, play games, and have fun with our friends.

The adults in our town believe that teens are troublemakers. In a recent letter to the local newspaper, one adult wrote, "If we provide a place for teens to congregate downtown, there will be nothing but trouble. Downtown will become a dangerous place, and more people will go to the suburbs to shop." This person couldn't be more wrong! A few kids cause trouble, but most kids just want a safe place to study with friends, learn new things, and just have fun.

A downtown teen center is a great idea! It would be easy for us to get to, and it's near places we need to go, like the library. It would get us out of stores and create a place where we can get together and have fun. Best of all, it would help the people of our town see that we are good, law-abiding citizens.

Student Self-Assessment

Persuasive Rubric Checklist

Title: _Open a Teen Center Downtown_
Writer: _Janelle Jones_

__4__ **Ideas**
- Does my essay have a clear position statement?
- Is my position backed with solid reasons?
- Does my essay have any logic errors?

__5__ **Organization**
- Does the beginning introduce the issue and state my opinion?
- Are my reasons arranged by order of importance?
- Does my ending sum up my reasons and opinion and leave the reader with something to think about?

__4__ **Voice**
- Is the tone of my writing appropriate?
- Did I connect with my audience?

__3__ **Word Choice**
- Did I use too many qualifying words?
- Does my essay have any inflammatory words?

__5__ **Sentence Fluency**
- Did I use different kinds of sentences?
- Did I vary my sentence beginnings?

__5__ **Conventions**
- Does my essay avoid most errors in punctuation, spelling, and grammar?

OVERALL COMMENTS:

My position essay shows that I feel strongly about having a teen center downtown. I backed up my opinion with good reasons because my friends and I have talked about it a lot.

I graded down for ideas because I had some logic errors, like including everyone when I just meant some people.

I graded down for voice because I think I sounded too emotional in some places.

My word choice could have been better. I found some blaming words in my essay.

I think I did an excellent job of organizing my essay, and I didn't have many mistakes in conventions, either.

Persuasive

Review your essay. Rate your essay and write comments that explain why you gave yourself the scores you did.

Reflecting on Your Writing

After you finish your position essay, take time to reflect on your writing experience. On your own paper, complete each of the sentences below. This exercise will reinforce what you learned from the writing experience and help you apply that knowledge to future assignments.

My Position Essay

1. The strongest part of my essay is . . .

2. The part that still needs work is . . .

3. The prewriting activity that worked best for me was . . .

4. The main thing I learned about writing a position essay is . . .

5. In my next persuasive essay, I would like to . . .

6. One question I still have about writing a position essay is . . .

Persuasive Writing
Pet-Peeve Essay

If someone is "peevish," it means that they like to complain. A pet peeve is something annoying that someone likes to complain about. Nearly everybody has a pet peeve. You probably have a few of your own. Maybe it bothers you when the neighborhood dog barks every morning, starting around five o'clock. Maybe people talking on cell phones while they drive really burns your toast. Maybe you are annoyed by classmates who tap their pencils on their desks during algebra tests.

Writing about a pet peeve is a form of persuasive writing. In this form, the writer complains about something annoying, without really expecting to change it. A pet-peeve essay gives the writer a chance to vent some frustration, often in an entertaining way.

In this chapter, you'll read a sample pet-peeve essay. Then you'll write your own essay about something that irritates you.

Writing Guidelines

Subject: Something that annoys you
Form: A pet-peeve essay
Purpose: To complain
Audience: Classmates

"A man has to live with himself, and he should see to it that he always has good company."
—Charles Evans Hughes

Pet-Peeve Essay

In the following pet-peeve essay, Devon complains about people who use—or misuse—cell phones in public.

Beginning
The beginning grabs the reader's attention and introduces the pet peeve.

Middle
The writer devotes one paragraph to each way this topic is annoying.

The writer relates an anecdote to illustrate his pet peeve.

A Little Respect, Please!

What is it about cell phone users that makes them think they are the only people in the world? I admit that cell phones are great inventions and help keep people safe and connected when necessary. I keep my cell phone with me at all times to check in with my parents or to talk with my friends. But when used improperly, cell phones can be distracting, annoying, and even downright dangerous!

Just look at people who take or make calls in a theater. There are usually announcements in movies, asking viewers to turn off all cell phones or pagers. True, some people, such as doctors, need to have their phones turned on in case of emergency calls. However, most cell phones can be set to a silent vibrating mode. Then a person can check an incoming call to see if it's important and, if it is, leave the theater to answer it. Yet some people insist on keeping their phones—and ringers—turned on. And I'm always lucky enough to sit next to them. Is the news so vital that the person can't go two hours without getting—or worse, making—a phone call? Why are these people in the theater to begin with if they want to talk?

Then there are the people who think they have to talk extra loud—in public—to be heard on their cell phones. Maybe they have a poor connection and have to shout to be heard, but most cell phones are pretty sensitive and can pick up a whisper. In any case, you'd think a person wouldn't want to discuss personal issues where others can hear them. Sometimes, when waiting in line somewhere, I have had to listen to calls that are downright embarrassing! One time, I couldn't help overhearing a conversation about someone I knew. I heard things I wished I hadn't, and it was really hard to talk to my friend after that! How hard is it for someone to simply say, "Can I call you back later?"

Key facts illustrate the pet peeve.

Probably the worst cell phone misusers are the many people who talk on their phones while driving. I don't mean those who use an earphone, but those who are driving while holding phones up to their ears. Studies have shown that talking on handheld cell phones while driving may cause accidents, because drivers are either distracted or unable to react quickly. Many cities and some states have either introduced or accepted laws against handheld cell phone use by drivers. Some countries, such as Brazil, Japan, and England, have already enacted restrictions. Still, drive on any street or highway, and you will likely see many people yakking away with only one hand on the wheel. When I see those accidents waiting to happen, I want to be far, far away.

Ending
The writer repeats his complaint from a new angle.

So what can I do? I have been tempted to tap an offender on the shoulder and ask him or her to please make the call some other time or place, but I've never done that. I'm too polite. I am also too polite to share my phone conversations in public or disrupt or endanger another person's life with thoughtless or reckless use of a cell phone.

Persuasive

Respond to the reading. Answer the following questions.

Ideas (1) Has the writer chosen a timely topic? Explain.
(2) How does the writer relate the problem to the reader?

Organization (3) How did the writer organize the middle paragraphs?

Voice & Word Choice (4) List three words or phrases that show the writer's annoyance.

Tip

Although a pet peeve like the one you just read may seem minor, an annoyance like cell phone misuse has the power to affect an individual for days on end. Writing about the pet peeve can actually help ease the frustration.

Prewriting ■ Select a topic.

We all suffer annoyances. Your brother uses all the hot water just before you get into the bathroom. Your neighbor lets his dog, well, use your lawn. Your friend chews gum with an open mouth. Even a small problem can really get to you, and it can make a good topic for a pet-peeve essay. To find a topic for his pet-peeve essay, Devon started freewriting about things that annoyed him.

Freewriting

What little things bother me the most? There is always something distracting going on. Yesterday at a movie, someone's cell phone went off. I missed a whole chunk of dialogue because this person answered the call. Maybe I should write about people who aren't considerate about using cell phones in public. They talk so loud. Don't they realize everyone's listening to them? People who use them while driving really bug me. They weave around and are dangerous. How dumb!

Prewrite

Choose your topic. Focus on an average day and freewrite about things that annoy you. Keep writing until you discover something you can complain about in a pet-peeve essay. Pick a topic that is appropriate to share and can be addressed with some humor.

■ Focus on the traits.

Ideas Adding details will make your pet-peeve essay interesting to your audience. Here are two ways to add interesting details.

- **Use an anecdote.** An anecdote is a brief story that illustrates a main point.

  One time, I couldn't help overhearing a conversation about someone I knew. I heard things I wished I hadn't, and . . .

- **Use irony.** Irony is saying one thing and meaning something else.

  And I'm always lucky enough to sit next to them.

Prewrite

Create details. Write one anecdote and one ironic statement about your topic. If you like how they turn out, try to work them into your essay.

■ Organize details.

You can organize a pet-peeve essay by logical order or by order of importance. With **logical order**, all of your reasons are of equal importance. They can be placed in any order, but you must move from one idea to the next in a way that flows well and makes sense.

With **order of importance**, you explain the most important reason either first or last. Placing the most important reason first allows you to reinforce the idea throughout the essay. Placing it last allows you to build up to the best reason. This is the order Devon used in his essay.

Devon's Main Reasons

* Cell phones are disruptive in theaters.   Least important
* Loud private conversations are rude and embarrassing.   ↓
* Using cell phones while driving is dangerous.   Most important

Prewrite ·**Organize your details.** List the main reasons you will use in your essay. Organize them by *logical order* or by *order of importance*.

■ Focus on the traits.

Sentence Fluency Vary your sentences to make your pet-peeve essay read smoothly; remember to vary your sentence beginnings and lengths. Notice how the sentences in the first passage below follow the same basic pattern.

I've had to listen to calls that are downright embarrassing. I couldn't help one time overhearing a conversation about someone I knew. I heard things I wished I hadn't. It was really hard to talk to my friend after that!

Now read the same passage with sentences that are varied. (Some new words have been added.) This writing flows better and is more enjoyable to read.

Sometimes, when waiting in line somewhere, I have had to listen to calls that are downright embarrassing. One time, I couldn't help overhearing a conversation about someone I knew. I heard things I wished I hadn't, and it was really hard to talk to my friend after that!

Writing ■ Create your first draft.

Though a pet-peeve essay is a lighter form of persuasive writing, it still should follow a definite pattern. Use the guidelines below.

■ Write your beginning paragraph.

Start by getting the reader's attention and sharing your thesis or focus statement. Here are several strategies.

- Introduce your pet peeve and tell why it bothers you.
- Ask questions about the topic.
- Use an amusing anecdote about an annoying experience you've had.
- Open with a startling fact or statistic related to your pet peeve.

■ Write your middle paragraphs.

Discuss your pet peeve. Show the reader why the topic annoys you. Use examples, statistics, and anecdotes to illustrate your pet peeve. Organize your middle paragraphs logically or by order of importance.

- Start each paragraph with a well-crafted topic sentence.
- Develop a paragraph for each main point.
- Support each topic sentence with effective details.
- Use transition words and phrases to connect your ideas.

■ Finish with a strong ending paragraph.

Wrap up your essay in a satisfying way. Your ending can be serious and reasonable or entertaining and light. Just make sure that it makes sense within the context of the entire essay. Try one of the following strategies to create a strong ending for your pet-peeve essay.

- Offer a humorous or serious suggestion for solving the problem.
- Summarize your feelings about your pet peeve.
- Suggest ways to handle or adjust to the pet peeve.

Write the first draft. Use your list of reasons and any details you've gathered to write the first draft of your pet-peeve essay. Get all your ideas on paper, including new ones that come to mind as you write.

Write

Revising ■ Improve your essay.

Take a break after finishing your first draft. Let it sit for a while. The following questions can help you decide what to change in your pet-peeve essay.

Revising Checklist

Ideas

_____ **1.** Have I chosen a timely topic and stated my complaint clearly?

_____ **2.** Have I included effective ideas and details to prove my point?

_____ **3.** Do I need to cut any details that are off the topic or unclear?

Organization

_____ **4.** Are my details and paragraphs arranged logically or by order of importance?

_____ **5.** Are my sentences and paragraphs easy to follow?

Voice

_____ **6.** Do the anecdotes I use sound genuine and personal?

_____ **7.** Am I convincing throughout my essay?

Word Choice

_____ **8.** Have I used effective descriptive words?

_____ **9.** Have I avoided name-calling and overly negative words?

Sentence Fluency

_____ **10.** Have I used a variety of sentences?

_____ **11.** Have I used transitions to connect my ideas and my paragraphs?

Revise

Revise your essay. Use the tips above as you review your essay and make changes.

Persuasive

Editing ■ Check for conventions.

After you've revised your pet-peeve essay, it's time to edit it. The following checklist can help you spot any errors in punctuation, mechanics (spelling and capitalization), or grammar.

Editing Checklist

Conventions

PUNCTUATION

_____ **1.** Did I end sentences with the proper punctuation?

_____ **2.** Have I used commas correctly?

_____ **3.** Did I use quotation marks correctly?

MECHANICS

_____ **4.** Did I properly capitalize proper nouns?

_____ **5.** Did I capitalize the beginnings of sentences and direct quotations?

_____ **6.** Did I use a dictionary and/or the computer's spell-checker to check spelling?

GRAMMAR

_____ **7.** Do all my subjects and verbs agree in number?

_____ **8.** Did I use the "Proofreader's Guide" in the back of this book to check grammar?

Edit your essay using the tips above. Mark your changes on the printout. After fixing any errors, create a final copy and proofread it one last time.

Publishing ■ Share your writing.

Your pet-peeve essay may amuse your friends, family, or even the whole world. After you've finished the writing, find a way to share it with others.

Share your pet-peeve essay. Publish your essay in one of the following ways.

- ■ Share copies of your essay with your class.
- ■ Read your essay aloud to friends or family.
- ■ Post your essay on the Web. (Get permission from your teacher and parents first.)

Writing for Assessment
Responding to Persuasive Prompts

Throughout your lifetime, you will have many opportunities to persuade others to agree with you. Perhaps you'll try to convince a friend to see a certain movie, ask a teacher to let you take a makeup exam, or persuade your parents to give you certain privileges. The art of persuasion can be learned. The best arguments are carefully thought out and well structured. They are designed to make your audience think like you do on an issue.

You may be asked to respond to a persuasive prompt on a writing test. Within time limits, you must structure your argument and arrange it in a logical way. This chapter will show you how to use the writing process to create a clear, persuasive response.

Writing Guidelines

Subject: **Persuasive prompt**
Form: **Response essay**
Purpose: **To demonstrate competence**
Audience: **Instructor**

"There is no point asserting what the heart cannot believe."
—Aleksander Solzhenitsyn

Prewriting ■ Analyze a persuasive prompt.

Before you respond to a prompt, you must analyze it to be sure that your response will fit the requirements of the test. One way to analyze a prompt is to answer the following **STRAP questions** about it:

> **Subject:** What topic (lockers, policy, decision, program) should I write about?
>
> **Type:** What form (essay, letter, editorial, article, report) of writing should I create?
>
> **Role:** What position (student, son or daughter, friend, employee) should I assume as the writer?
>
> **Audience:** Who (teacher, principal, parents, classmates, employer) is the intended reader?
>
> **Purpose:** What is the goal (persuade, respond, evaluate, explain, tell, describe) of my writing?

The following key words are often found in **persuasive** prompts: *convince, argue, defend, persuade.*

Try It!

Analyze these prompts by answering the STRAP questions.

1. The school board has decided to eliminate the school art program because of budget constraints. Write a letter arguing for or against the board's decision.

2. Your principal has reduced the number of school assemblies for the year. The school newspaper editor wants you to write about the decision. Write an editorial either defending the decision or urging the principal to reconsider.

3. To promote literacy, the city library is starting a new reading program pairing teens with younger children. Write a newspaper article calling for teens to volunteer for the program.

Tip

Some prompts may not contain key words for every STRAP question. Use your best judgment to answer those questions.

■ Plan your response.

Once you have answered the STRAP questions, you should quickly plan your persuasive response. The following graphic organizers can help you.

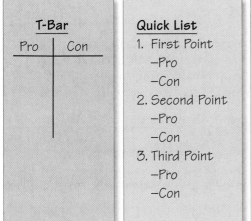

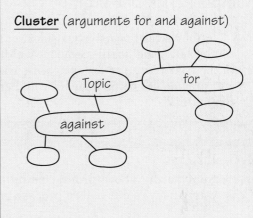

■ Counter an opposing point of view.

Each persuasive graphic organizer includes space for both pro and con arguments. You must consider points from both sides of an issue to see where your strongest argument lies. Facts usually make the strongest arguments; however, your strong feelings about the issue can be important, too.

When planning your persuasive writing, make sure to counter or address at least one opposing point of view. Presenting another opinion tells your reader that you have carefully examined the issue. And effectively countering the point can actually strengthen your overall argument.

Prewrite

Reread the persuasive prompts on page 248. Choose one prompt and use a graphic organizer to plan your response.

Tip

In a timed writing test, plan carefully. Allow yourself time for planning before you write and for revising and editing after you write. For example, if you have 45 minutes to respond to a prompt, use the first 5 to 10 minutes to analyze the prompt and plan your response, the last 5 minutes to revise and edit it, and the 30 to 35 minutes in between for writing.

Persuasive

Writing ▪ Respond to a prompt.

Once you have answered the STRAP questions and planned your response with a graphic organizer, you can begin writing.

Sample Persuasive Prompt

> Your school board is considering funding an after-school student center, but some board members feel it is a waste of funds. Write a letter to the board arguing for or against the center, explaining the benefits it will provide or the problems it could create for students, parents, and the community.

Try It!

Analyze the above prompt using the STRAP questions. Be sure to write your answers out before proceeding.

Sample Response

Beginning
The beginning paragraph states the opinion (underlined).

Dear School Board Members:

    If students are not involved in after-school activities or do not have a job, they may face long afternoons after the final bell rings. Many parents work until 5:00 or later in the evening. Students with time on their hands often look for something to do. Without guidance, they often get into trouble. At the very least, they might just go home and flop in front of the TV. <u>An after-school teen center could create a positive environment for teens.</u>

Middle
Each middle paragraph presents a main supporting point.

    A teen center provides a supervised place for students. In a teen center, adults are always available to make sure nothing inappropriate happens. Students can be with friends in a safe, supervised atmosphere.

    A properly equipped teen center offers a positive place for students, lots of activities, and healthy snacks. Students are encouraged to engage in physical activity. Sports are usually part of a center as well. With a few simple pieces of equipment, students can engage in activities such as table tennis, weight training, or aerobics. If the center has space

Persuasive

outside, a basketball hoop or volleyball court encourages physical activity in good weather. An indoor gym could give students a place to be active even in bad weather.

The teen center could offer homework help. Volunteers could provide assistance. A computer lab supervised by an adult would help students do research, check e-mail, and have some fun. This environment could encourage students to do their homework.

Concession
The writer addresses a possible objection.

Some people might argue that the district can't afford such a facility, but there are ways to make an expensive dream an affordable reality. For one thing, the center could sell snacks and juices to help with expenses. The upper-class students could volunteer to help younger students with class work, earning volunteer service hours for their efforts. Local businesspeople might be willing to mentor students in different areas, working with them at the center. Another resource might be parents. Service organizations could donate materials to help support such a worthy community project. Of course, fund-raisers could be held to support the center.

Ending
The ending offers a final plea and summarizes the argument.

I urge all the school board members to consider the importance of a teen center. The youth of today are the parents and citizens of tomorrow. Through a teen center that offers safe, supervised activities and homework tutoring, you could show us how a community can work together for the betterment of all.

Sincerely,
Alia Santos

Write

Practice responding to a persuasive prompt. Review the prompt you chose on page 249, your answers to the STRAP questions, and your graphic organizer. Then write a response to the prompt in the amount of time your teacher gives you.

Revising ■ Improve your response.

Before you begin a writing test, find out whether you will be allowed to make changes in your writing. If this is allowed, always make your changes and corrections as neatly as possible. The STRAP questions below can help.

> **Subject:** Does my response focus on the topic of the prompt? Do my main points support the opinion stated in the beginning of my response?
>
> **Type:** Have I used the form requested in the prompt (essay, letter, article)?
>
> **Role:** Have I assumed the position called for in the prompt?
>
> **Audience:** Do I use appropriate language for my audience?
>
> **Purpose:** Does my writing accomplish the goal set forth in the prompt?

Improve your work. Reread your response, asking yourself the STRAP questions above. Make whatever changes are necessary to your response.

Editing ■ Check your response.

A final read-through of your essay gives you the chance to check for punctuation, capitalization, spelling, and grammar errors.

Editing Checklist

Conventions

_____ **1.** Have I used end punctuation for every sentence?

_____ **2.** Have I capitalized all proper nouns and the first words of sentences?

_____ **3.** Have I checked my spelling?

_____ **4.** Have I made sure my subjects and verbs agree?

_____ **5.** Have I used the right words (*effect, affect*)?

Check your conventions. Read through your response one final time, checking your punctuation, capitalization, spelling, and grammar. Make all of your corrections neatly in the time allowed.

Persuasive Writing on Tests

Use this guide when preparing to respond to a persuasive writing prompt.

Before you write . . .

- **Understand the prompt.**
  Use the STRAP questions, and remember that a persuasive prompt asks you to use facts and logical reasons to persuade or convince.
- **Plan your time wisely.**
  Spend 5 to 10 minutes planning before starting to write.

As you write . . .

- **Decide on a focus for your essay.**
  Keep your main idea or purpose in mind as you write. Be sure all your points clearly support your argument.
- **Be selective.**
  Use examples that directly support your opinion.
- **End in a meaningful way.**
  Remind the reader about the topic and your point of view.

After you've written a first draft . . .

- **Check for completeness and correctness.**
  Use the STRAP questions to revise your work. Then check for errors in punctuation, capitalization, spelling, and grammar.

Try It!

Plan and write a response. Choose one of the prompts below. Analyze it using the STRAP questions; use a graphic organizer to gather details and plan; then write, revise, and edit your response.

- Your school budget will allow for an additional class to be offered in the coming school year, and your principal has asked students to make suggestions. Write a letter to the principal explaining what class you think should be offered and why.
- As a class project, your English teacher wants to view and analyze a current movie. In preparation for this unit, she would like students to recommend a movie to study. In a memo or an e-mail, convince your teacher to use the movie of your choice.

Persuasive

Response to Literature

Response to Literature
Analyzing a Theme

To analyze means to break down a topic into smaller parts and determine how the parts relate to one another. Sportswriters are often asked to analyze sporting events. For example, a baseball writer may break down a particular game according to three main parts—fielding, pitching, and hitting—and then determine how each part contributed to a team's overall performance.

In this chapter, you will analyze the theme or main point of a short story. You will base your essay on a close examination of two key elements—the **plot** (key events) and **characterization** (the thoughts and actions of the main character).

Writing Guidelines

Subject: **A short story**
Form: **Essay**
Purpose: **To analyze a theme**
Audience: **Classmates**

"What all good story writers certainly have in common is the ability to make the best choices before the story is finished."
—William Boone

■ Writing Warm-Up: Finding Themes

In literature, the **theme** is usually a lesson learned or a statement about life. Sometimes the theme is openly stated in the story but more often it is not. In some long pieces of literature, there may be more than one significant theme. One way to think about literary themes is to consider lessons that are often learned from experience. For example, in *To Kill a Mockingbird*, Scout Finch learns not to prejudge people. Study the cluster of life lessons below. (Some of these lessons are familiar proverbs.)

Cluster

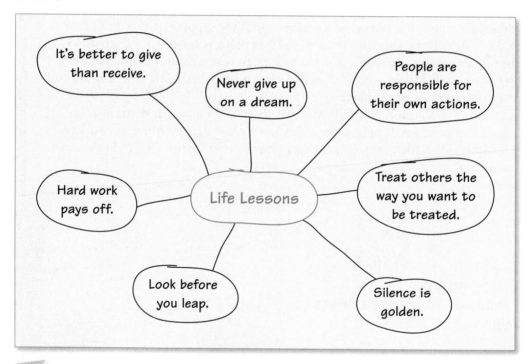

Try It!

Work with a classmate to create a cluster diagram. See how many life lessons you can list. If you get stuck, think of familiar proverbs. Then identify a story you've read that uses one of these life lessons as its theme.

"Reading is actually plunging into one's own identity and, one hopes, emerging stronger than before."

—Amalia Kahana-Carmon

■ Writing an Analysis Paragraph

You can analyze the theme of a short story in one paragraph. Here is one way to develop the analysis:

- In the **topic sentence,** name the title, author, and theme of the story.
- In the **body sentences,** focus on the actions of the main characters.
- In the **closing sentence,** explain how these actions reveal the theme.

Sample Paragraph Analysis

In the following paragraph, a student writer does a brief thematic analysis.

The **topic sentence** introduces the author, the story, and the theme (underlined).

The sentences in the **body** focus on the main characters' actions.

The **closing sentence** analyzes the theme.

Gift Giving

The theme of "The Gift of the Magi" by O. Henry is love means making sacrifices. The main characters' actions and decisions support this theme. A husband and wife named Jim and Della want to give each other a special holiday gift, even though they are poor. Della wants to give Jim a gold chain for his gold watch, and Jim wants to give Della a set of expensive combs for her beautiful, long hair. Jim and Della both sacrifice something they treasure. Della's prized possession is her hair, but she has it cut and sells it to a wig maker so she can afford to buy a gold chain for Jim's watch. Jim's prized possession is his gold watch, but he sells it to buy Della special combs for her hair. When they open their gifts, each of them realizes the sacrifice that the other has made. In the end, their best gift is knowing that they love each other so much that they would sacrifice their prized possessions for one another.

Literature

Write

Write an analysis paragraph. Using the story you identified on the previous page, write a paragraph in which you briefly analyze the story's theme. Be sure to include the three parts explained above.

Understanding Your Goal

Your goal in the rest of the chapter is to write an essay that analyzes a short story in order to reveal its main theme. The chart below lists the key traits of such an essay.

TRAITS OF A RESPONSE TO LITERATURE

- **Ideas**

  Write a thesis statement that explains your interpretation of the theme of the story. Then select specific details to support the statement.

- **Organization**

  Write clear beginning, middle, and ending paragraphs. Use transitions to effectively connect sentences and paragraphs.

- **Voice**

  Sound interested in, and knowledgeable about, the story you are analyzing.

- **Word Choice**

  Quote words and phrases from the story that support the theme. Use literary terms that reveal your understanding of the story.

- **Sentence Fluency**

  Write sentences that read well and flow smoothly.

- **Conventions**

  Correct all punctuation, capitalization, spelling, and grammar errors.

Get the big picture. Review the rubric on pages 290–291 before you begin writing to get an idea of what's ahead. Use the rubrics on pages 274–287 to guide you through the revising and editing steps in the writing process.

Response Essay

Gary Soto's short story, "The No-Guitar Blues," tells about a boy trying to collect enough money to buy a guitar. The response essay below analyzes the story's plot and character development to reveal the main theme.

Beginning
The beginning names the story and author and focuses on the theme (underlined).

Middle
Each middle paragraph explains a different stage in the development of the theme.

Fausto's Guilt

In Gary Soto's short story, "The No-Guitar Blues," the main character, a teenage boy named Fausto, takes advantage of some rich folks. As a result, he is consumed by guilt. The story shows that deep down, people want to do the right thing.

The story begins with Fausto wanting to play guitar in his own band. He wonders how he can get a guitar. Soto uses idioms to illustrate that Fausto's family does not have a lot of money. For example, Fausto worries that if he asks for a guitar, his parents will say, "Money doesn't grow on trees," or "What do you think we are, bankers?" (56). When he does ask for a guitar, his mother replies, "Honey, a guitar costs a lot of money . . . but we'll see" (57).

But Fausto is determined. He hops on a bike and rides north, away from his home near the vacant lot on Olive Street. In the nicer section of Fresno, he goes door-to-door searching for work, hoping to be paid enough to buy a guitar. The author says that Fausto only earns a "grimy, dirt-caked quarter" (58) and one juicy orange. Little does Fausto know that this orange will lead him straight into a lie.

As Fausto sits eating the orange, a sad-eyed dog comes along. Fausto begins feeding it orange slices. Fausto has an idea: "At that moment, a light came on inside Fausto's head" (59). He notices that the dog looks healthy and well fed. He spots a collar and tag, and he realizes that "Roger" probably belongs to rich people. The address is only six blocks away. This is when Fausto decides to tell a lie. He will say that he found Roger near the freeway, and maybe the owners will give him a reward big enough to buy a guitar.

Fausto feels guilty at the thought of lying. The guilt steadily builds. It increases as he stands on the porch knocking on the door. It gets worse as the man and woman of the house are nice and offer him turnovers to eat. The guilt is unbearable when the woman stuffs a $20 bill into Fausto's shirt pocket, a reward for rescuing Roger. Because of his guilt, Fausto tries to give the money back, but the couple insists that he take it. The man says, "You have to. You deserve it, believe me" (60). Fausto takes it. He starts up the street "like a zombie," saying under his breath, "Oh man, I shouldn't have lied" (60).

Middle

The last middle paragraph focuses on decisions that cause the main character to change.

Now, Fausto has a choice to make; he can use the money for a guitar and continue to feel guilty, or he can find a way to get rid of his guilt. He thinks about going to confession, but confession hours are over. Instead, he goes to mass at Saint Theresa's Church. Fausto kneels, prays, and says some Hail Marys, but the guilt stays with him. He cannot stop thinking about lying to the folks who were so nice to him. Finally, when the wicker basket comes his way, Fausto drops the $20 bill inside. Almost immediately, he feels better. The guilt leaves him, and he concentrates on forgetting about the guitar.

Ending

The ending paragraph analyzes the theme.

Fausto has changed. He realizes now that it is wrong to go selfishly after something he wants, not caring about how it might affect others. As he thinks about the kindness of the man and woman and the guilt he felt, Fausto understands that it feels good to do the right thing. In the end, he gets his guitar. His mother gives him an old bass guitarron (an oversized guitar used in Mexican bands) that belonged to his grandfather. It is one of the happiest days of Fausto's life.

Respond to the reading. Answer the following questions about the sample response essay.

Ideas (1) How does the main character change by the end of the story? (2) Which detail in the analysis clearly reveals this theme?

Organization (3) How is the middle part of the response essay organized?

Voice & Word Choice (4) Does the writer sound knowledgeable about the story? Explain.

Prewriting

The writing process begins with prewriting. The first step in writing your essay is to choose a story you have read recently and would like to analyze.

Keys to Effective Prewriting

1. Select an interesting story, one that you have recently read and enjoyed.

2. Identify a main theme in the story.

3. Looking at the beginning, middle, and ending of the story, find the key plot events and the characters' actions that reveal the main theme.

4. Write a clear thesis statement about the theme.

5. Decide how to organize the information in your middle paragraphs.

6. Write a topic sentence for each middle paragraph.

Literature

Prewriting ■ Find topic ideas.

A graphic organizer like the ideas chart below can help you think of possible stories to write about. This chart lists favorite stories, a statement about the basic plot in each story, and a comment about the main character.

Ideas Chart

Story and author	What the story is about	What the main character is like
"The Birds" by Daphne du Maurier	Swarms of birds attack a family living on the coast of England.	Nat is a brave father who tries to protect his family.
"Helen on Eighty-sixth Street" by Wendi Kaufman	A girl tries to understand why her dad went away.	Vita is very smart.
*"Thank You, Ma'm" by Langston Hughes	A teenage boy tries to rob an old lady, and she drags him home with her.	Roger is a tough kid who is not so tough when he gets caught.

Prewrite

Consider possible topics. Make an ideas chart like the one above. List short stories that you have read and liked. For each title, write one sentence that tells what the story is about and one sentence that tells about the main character.

■ Choose a topic.

It will be easier to write your essay if you choose a story that you know and enjoy. Be sure that you have a clear understanding of the story's plot and the actions of the main character. In your analysis, you will be expected to trace the development of the theme through the main character's thoughts, feelings, and actions.

Prewrite

Choose your topic. Review the stories in your chart. Put an asterisk next to the title you choose. Then write a few sentences that explain the reason for your choice. (Perhaps you identify with the main character, enjoy the author's writing style, or so on.)

Prewriting ▪ Find a theme.

Sometimes a theme is clearly stated, but often it is found deep within a story. Here are three ways to uncover a theme.

▪ **Look for clues in the title.**
"Irraweka, Mischief-Maker"

▪ **Look for the author's statements about life.**
"The very best thing in all this world that can befall a man is to be born lucky."
                                                          —Mark Twain, "Luck"

▪ **Identify a life lesson that the main character learns.**
In the short story "To Build a Fire," the main character learns that he must accept his unfortunate fate.

Try It!

Find a theme. Answer the following questions to find the theme of your story. Ask your teacher for help if you still can't identify the theme after answering these questions.

1. Does the title say anything about the main character? If so, what?
2. Does the title say anything about a life lesson? If so, what?
3. Does the author make any statements about life? List them.
4. How does the main character change in the story?
5. What does the main character learn?

Prewrite

Finish this sentence. After answering the "Try It!" questions, complete the sentence below to identify a main theme in your story.

A main theme in my story is _____.

▪ Focus on the traits.

Ideas Authors sometimes use figures of speech to convey ideas to the reader. Figures of speech include *idioms, similes, metaphors,* the *oxymoron* and *hyperbole* (see pages **598–601**). Look for these as you analyze your short story. They often hold clues to theme and character development.

Literature

"My books deal with characters who feel rejected and
have to painfully learn how to deal with other people."

—Alice Childress

Prewriting ▪ Gather details.

One way to gather details for a story analysis is to make a chart of the main character's thoughts, feelings, and actions. The sample chart below is for the essay on pages **269–272**.

Character Chart

Story Title: "Thank You, Ma'm"

Theme: Forgiveness is sweet.

First Stage: The main character's thoughts, feelings, and actions in the **beginning** of the story
— tries stealing a woman's purse
— falls down
— grabbed by the woman and dragged to her apartment

Middle Stage: The main character's thoughts, feelings, and actions in the **middle** part of the story
— fears Mrs. Jones
— wants to run away from her
— admits stealing the purse because he needed money for shoes
— discovers Mrs. Jones understands what it's like to be poor
— wants to be trusted

Final Stage: The main character's thoughts, feelings, and actions in the **last** part of the story
— accepts money from Mrs. Jones for a pair of shoes
— is too proud to say more than thank you

Prewrite

Chart your main character. Make a chart like the one above. List your main character's thoughts, feelings, and actions during the beginning, middle, and ending parts of the story.

■ Use direct quotations.

You can use quotations from the story to show how a character talks, acts, thinks, and feels. The student writer of the essay about "Thank You, Ma'm" gathered the following revealing quotations. Consider what each quotation reveals about the main character.

Sample Quotations

"He did not trust the woman not to trust him. And he did not want to be mistrusted now."
- — not used to being trusted
- — suddenly wants to be trusted

"He looked as if he were fourteen or fifteen, frail and willow-wild."
- — thin, lonely, and scared
- — looks weak, but proves to be strong

"He barely managed to say 'thank you' before she shut the door."
- — got Mrs. Jones's message
- — can't put what he's experienced into words

Try It!

Read the quotations above. Explain what each quotation reveals about the story and the main character.

Gather quotations. Review your character chart (page 264). Make a list of direct quotations that reveal something about the main character.

Prewrite

■ Focus on the traits.

Organization You can't talk about the theme of a short story without also discussing the plot and the main character. (*Theme, plot,* and *characterization* are the three main elements of literature.) As you discuss the plot and characterization, your analysis will naturally be organized chronologically, or by time. However, an analysis can also be organized by order of importance.

"I'd like to explore moral problems, but I don't like to lay down the law about them! Books are for asking questions, not for answering them."

—John Rowe Townsend

Prewriting ■ Write a thesis statement.

Now that you have gathered details, you are ready to write your **thesis statement**—the main point that your paper will illustrate and explain. The thesis statement connects the main character to the theme.

main character		theme		thesis statement
A teenager named Roger	**+**	Forgiveness is sweet.	**=**	Roger learns that forgiveness is sweet.

Form a focus. Write a thesis statement for your response essay using the formula above.

Prewrite

■ Organize the middle paragraphs of your essay.

Each middle paragraph should address a different stage in the development of the theme. The writer of the sample essay on pages **269–272** planned his middle paragraphs by writing a topic sentence for each one.

Topic Sentence 1 (First Stage)

The story begins when Roger grabs a woman's purse.

Topic Sentence 2 (Middle Stage)

Mrs. Jones understands Roger better than he knows.

Topic Sentence 3 (Middle Stage)

Roger, however, still isn't sure about Mrs. Jones.

Topic Sentence 4 (Final Stage)

After supper, Mrs. Jones gives Roger ten dollars to buy some blue suede shoes.

Plan your middle paragraphs. Review your character chart from page 264. Add any important details you may have left out. Write a topic sentence for each middle paragraph of your essay, covering the first, middle, and final stages of your story's theme.

Prewrite

Prewrite → Write ↔ Revise ↔ Edit ↔ Publish →

Writing

Once you have finished your prewriting, you can begin writing your essay. Your thesis statement, character chart, quotations, and topic sentences will guide your writing.

Keys to Effective Writing

1. Write on every other line so that you have room to make changes later.

2. Use your thesis statement and topic sentences to organize your paragraphs.

3. Support your topic sentences with specific details from the story.

4. Refer to your character chart and quotations for details, adding more if needed.

5. Get all of your thoughts on paper.

6. Tie your ideas together with transitions.

Literature

Writing ▪ Get the big picture.

Remember that an essay includes three main parts—the beginning, the middle, and the ending. You are ready to begin writing your response if you have . . .

- discovered the theme,
- written a clear thesis statement that ties the theme to the main character, and
- planned and organized your middle paragraphs.

The chart below shows how the three parts of a response essay fit together. The examples are from the essay on pages **269–272**.

BEGINNING

The **beginning** names the short story and the author, summarizes the story, and states the thesis.

Thesis Statement
By the end of the story, Roger learns that forgiveness is sweet.

MIDDLE

The **middle** paragraphs show different stages in the development of the theme.

Four Topic Sentences
The story begins when Roger grabs a woman's purse.

Mrs. Jones understands Roger better than he knows.

Roger, however, still isn't sure about Mrs. Jones.

After supper, Mrs. Jones gives Roger ten dollars to buy some blue suede shoes.

ENDING

The **ending** paragraph analyzes the theme.

Closing Sentence
Mrs. Jones could have gotten revenge and called the police, but instead, she shows Roger that forgiveness is sweet.

■ Start your essay.

The opening of your analysis should include . . .

- **the title and author of the short story,**
- **background information about the plot and characters, and**
- **your thesis statement.**

▶ Beginning

Middle

Ending

Beginning Paragraph

The sample paragraph below names the title and the author of the short story. It also includes background information about the main character and the plot, and ends with a thesis statement identifying a main theme. (Also see the sample beginning on page **259**.)

> The first part introduces the story and gives the thesis statement (underlined).

"Thank You, Ma'm" by Langston Hughes is a short story about forgiveness. In the story, a boy named Roger tries to steal a woman's purse. The woman surprisingly grabs him and drags him home with her. While at this woman's house, Roger is forced to confront his actions but in a way that seems very positive and helpful. By the end of the story, Roger learns that forgiveness is sweet.

Write

Write your beginning. Write the beginning paragraph of your essay. Include the name of the story and its author, a brief plot summary, and your thesis statement. You may have to write more than one version of this paragraph before it says what you want it to say.

Literature

Tips

If you have trouble getting started, review these tips. One or more of them may trigger your thinking.

- **Talk about your story with a classmate** before you begin to write.
- **Write freely** without worrying about producing the perfect analysis right away. First drafts are often called *rough drafts* for a reason.
- **Include enough details** to support your thesis statement.
- **Show your personal interest** in the story and in your analysis by using precise, careful language.
- **Focus on these key traits of writing**: ideas, organization, and voice.

Writing ■ Develop the middle part.

Each middle paragraph should explore a stage in the development of the story and how it relates to the theme. Your writing should focus on the thoughts, feelings, and actions of the characters during each stage.

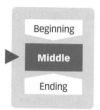

Beginning

Middle

Ending

Middle Paragraphs

These paragraphs show the development of the theme throughout the story.

The first middle paragraph focuses on the first stage of the story.

> The story begins when Roger grabs a woman's purse. Its heaviness makes Roger fall. We know the purse is heavy because of the hyperbole: "It had everything in it but hammer and nails" (211). The woman grabs Roger and shakes him until his teeth rattle. She says, "When I get through with you, sir, you are going to remember Mrs. Luella Bates Washington Jones" (211). Roger struggles to get free, but Mrs. Jones is strong. Hughes writes, "She dragged the boy inside, down a hall, and into a large kitchenette-furnished room at the rear of the house" (212). Finally, she turns Roger loose. In fear, "Roger looked at the door—looked at the woman—looked at the door" (212). However, he doesn't run. Instead, he obeys her order to wash his face. From his "frail and willow-wild" (212) appearance, she guesses he is hungry. But if he is hungry, Roger is too proud to say so. He tells Mrs. Jones that he stole the purse because he wanted money to buy some blue suede shoes.

Each new paragraph begins with a topic sentence (underlined) that introduces a new stage in the story.

> Mrs. Jones understands Roger better than he knows. She says that when she was young she wanted things that she couldn't get. She says that she did bad things, things that she won't tell Roger. This is when the two characters connect. They share an understanding of what it means to be poor.
>
> Roger, however, still isn't sure about Mrs. Jones. He wants to run away, but something also makes him want to stay: "He did not trust the woman not to trust him. And he did not want to be mistrusted now" (213). As Mrs. Jones makes supper, Roger sits on the far side of the room where she can see him. Surprisingly, she isn't watching him. Even more surprising is the fact that she leaves her purse near

The last stage shows how the main character deals with his surprising life lesson.

him. It would be easy for Roger to take it and run, but he doesn't. They eat supper, and it's clear that she cares about him because she doesn't ask about his folks, where he lives, or anything else that will embarrass him.

<u>After supper, Mrs. Jones gives Roger ten dollars to buy some blue suede shoes.</u> She tells him not to make the mistake of stealing someone else's purse. She says, "Shoes come by devilish like that will burn your feet" (214). Then Mrs. Jones leads Roger to the door and reminds him to behave himself. Pride keeps Roger from saying more than "Thank you, ma'm" (214). He wants to say more, but he doesn't. Luella Bates Washington Jones shuts the door, and Roger walks away. They never see each other again.

Write

Write your middle paragraphs. Use your topic sentences, character chart, and direct-quotation list to guide your writing. Try to include one or two figures of speech from the story to enhance the theme for the reader. (For a list of figures of speech, see pages **600–601** in this book.)

■ Create coherence.

When the details of an essay are tied together in a way that produces clear ideas, the essay has **coherence**. Repeating key words is one way to give your writing coherence. In the three examples below, the colored key word creates a transition between two sentences.

From his "frail and willow-wild" (212) appearance, she guesses he is hungry. But if he is hungry, Roger is too proud to say so.

Pride keeps Roger from saying more than "Thank you, ma'm" (214). He wants to say more, but he doesn't.

Surprisingly, she isn't watching him. Even more surprising is the fact that she leaves her purse near him.

Literature

Writing ■ End your essay.

Your essay starts with a thesis statement that connects the theme to a main character in the story. In the middle paragraphs, you show how the theme develops through the plot and the actions of the main character. The ending is your final chance to comment on and explore the theme. Here are some suggestions for this final part of your essay.

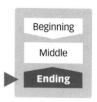

Beginning

Middle

Ending

- Show how a character has changed.
- Use a quotation from the story.
- Predict how the theme might affect the character in the future.
- State the theme as a basic truth or saying about life.

Ending Paragraph

The ending paragraph below shows what Roger learns and states the theme of the short story as a basic truth of life.

The ending explores the main character's actions and restates the theme.

In the beginning of the story, Roger thinks that he can overpower Mrs. Jones and steal her purse. Then, as the story goes on, he learns that she is much stronger than he is, in more ways than one. She is both physically and morally strong. Even though Roger appears "frail and willow-wild," he proves that he, too, is strong and can handle a very humbling experience. There is an old saying that "Revenge is sweet." Mrs. Jones could have gotten revenge and called the police, but instead, she shows Roger that forgiveness is sweet.

Write

Write your ending and form a complete first draft. Using one or more of the suggestions at the top of the page, write the last paragraph of your essay. Then make a clean copy of your essay. Double-space or write on every other line so that you have room for revising.

"Good writing is about making good choices when it comes to picking the tools you plan to write with."
—Stephen King

Revising

Now that your first draft is complete, you are ready to begin the revision process. Focus on ideas, organization, and other key traits to make changes that will improve your writing.

Keys to Effective Revising

1. Read your essay aloud to see whether it holds together from start to finish.

2. Check your thesis statement to be sure it includes the theme of the story.

3. Be sure that each middle paragraph analyzes the thesis statement.

4. Check your voice to see if it sounds knowledgeable.

5. Review your word choice and sentence fluency to be sure that your analysis reads smoothly.

6. Use the editing and proofreading marks inside the back cover of this book.

Literature

Revising ■ for Ideas

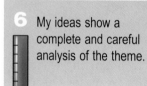 **6** My ideas show a complete and careful analysis of the theme.

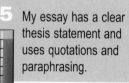 **5** My essay has a clear thesis statement and uses quotations and paraphrasing.

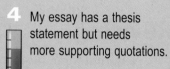 **4** My essay has a thesis statement but needs more supporting quotations.

When you revise for *ideas*, be sure that you have effectively used quotations from the story and that you have clearly paraphrased key ideas. Use the rubric strip above to help you revise.

■ Have I effectively used quotations?

You have effectively used quotations from the text if they clearly and effortlessly support the main points in your analysis. An author's exact words can add a great deal of meaning to your analysis. Here are some effective ways to use quotations from a text.

1. Use story dialogue to help the reader understand a character.
2. Use an author's figure of speech to reinforce an important idea related to the theme.
3. Include a description from the story to show its setting or mood.
4. Cite a specific word or phrase from the text to make an idea clearer.

Try It!

Explain which of the ideas above is illustrated by each sentence below.

1. "She dragged the boy inside, down a hall, and into a large kitchenette-furnished room at the rear of the house" (212).
2. Fausto only earns a "grimy, dirt-caked quarter" (58) . . . .
3. She says, "When I get through with you, sir, you are going to remember Mrs. Luella Bates Washington Jones" (211).
4. Fausto takes it [the money]. He starts up the street "like a zombie," . . . (60).

Tip

Remember that you cannot use an author's exact words as your own. This is called **plagiarism**. Always give the author credit when using a quotation. (See pages **369–370**.)

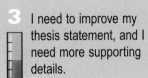

3 I need to improve my thesis statement, and I need more supporting details.

2 I need a thesis statement and supporting details from the text.

1 I need to learn more about how to analyze a theme.

■ Have I paraphrased effectively?

You have paraphrased effectively if you clearly express an author's thoughts and ideas using your own words. (Paraphrasing means using your own words to restate someone else's ideas.)

Author's words: "She was a tiny woman who lit up the room when she entered. Everyone loved Ramona."

Paraphrase: Ramona was small, but her lively personality made everyone notice when she entered the room.

Try It!

Read the paragraph below. Then rewrite it as a paraphrase.

> Luke looked out at the empty field. He imagined himself kicking a field goal and winning the game for his team. A voice behind him said, "Hey, Mahoney." It was Hector Rodrigez, the team running back. "Whoa, dude, what's with the leg cast? Does Coach Karls know you're out for the season?"

Revise

Review your first draft for ideas. Be sure that you have used effective quotations from the story and that you have paraphrased important ideas using your own words.

Ideas
The writer adds a quotation from the story to support the idea of trust.

Roger, however, still isn't sure about Mrs. Jones. He wants to run away, but something makes him want to stay. As Mrs. Jones makes supper, Roger sits on the far side of the room . . .

"He did not trust the woman not to trust him. And he did not want to be mistrusted now" (213).

Literature

Revising ■ for Organization

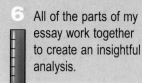 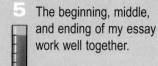 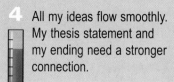

6 All of the parts of my essay work together to create an insightful analysis.	5 The beginning, middle, and ending of my essay work well together.	4 All my ideas flow smoothly. My thesis statement and my ending need a stronger connection.

Organization is the way ideas are arranged in an essay. The beginning, middle, and ending parts should all work well together. The rubric strip above will help you.

■ How can I connect my thesis statement and my final analysis?

You can connect your thesis statement and final analysis by sharing an insight about the story and the theme in your closing sentences.

Try It!

Read the following paragraph analysis. Then explain how the topic sentence (underlined) connects with the closing statement. What does the final statement say about the theme (topic sentence)? What are the flowers compared to?

In the story "The Window Box," Gretchen Bates discovers that beauty lies in the eye of the beholder. Gretchen, a 20-something woman, lives alone in a rundown apartment building. When she looks out her third-story window, she sees only a dark alley below. One cool, autumn day, she sees an old woman in the alley planting something in a window box. She forgets about it until springtime when she sits at her window complaining about the cold draft. Suddenly, she sees a rainbow. Orange, yellow, and purplish-red tulips are spilling out of the window box, bringing life to the dismal alley. Like a sweet-tasting medicine, the colors destroy Gretchen's bitterness. Colorful flowers helped Gretchen to change her attitude. Just like a rainbow brightens a stormy sky, Gretchen learns that there can be beauty, even in a dark alley, if she looks for it.

Review your first draft for connection. Decide if your thesis statement and your final analysis connect.

Revise

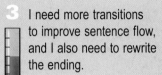

3 I need more transitions to improve sentence flow, and I also need to rewrite the ending.

2 I need clearer topic sentences that relate to the theme.

1 I need to learn how to organize a response to literature.

■ How can I make my ideas flow smoothly?

Your ideas will flow smoothly if you use transitions to connect them. The bold words in the paragraph below are transitions that connect ideas.

> **By nightfall** he was fatigued, footsore, famishing. The thought of his wife and children urged him on. **At last** he found a road which led him in what he knew to be the right direction. It was as wide and straight as a city street. **Yet** it seemed untraveled. No fields bordered it, no dwelling anywhere.
>
> —Ambrose Bierce, "An Occurrence at Owl Creek Bridge"

Try It!

Carefully read the following passage. Then identify the transitional words or phrases that were used to connect ideas.

1   At the beginning of the novel, Alfred Brooks, a high school dropout, has
2   few prospects. He is terrorized by a local gang and worries about losing his
3   best friend to a world of drugs and crime. Then, surprisingly, Brooks decides
4   to try boxing. While getting started, he meets Vito Donatelli, who becomes one
5   of the important influences in his life.

Revise

Review your first draft for idea flow. Make sure that you have used transitions to make your ideas flow smoothly from beginning to end.

Organization
Two transitions are added.

Finally,
∧She turns Roger loose. In fear, "Roger looked at the

door—looked at the woman—looked at the door" (212).
However,
∧He doesn't run. . . .

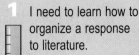
Literature

Revising ■ for Voice

Voice is the way your writing sounds. The rubric strip above and the information below will help you revise your analysis so that it sounds interesting, thoughtful, and natural.

■ Does my voice sound as if I am interested in my analysis?

Your writing voice will sound interesting if you do two things:

1. Show that you truly care about the story.

2. Demonstrate a clear understanding of one of the story's main themes.

NOT INTERESTED

In the passage below, the writer does not sound interested. The ideas are too general.

> The man was unable to move his fingers, but he still got a fire started. If the fire threw off enough heat, he might survive. But then snow from a branch above him fell on the fire and put it out.

INTERESTED

The voice in this passage clearly shows that the writer cares about, and understands, the story he is analyzing.

> The man's fingers were frozen stiff. So he gripped a dry match between his teeth and struck it against his jacket zipper. Surprisingly, the match lit. Then the man carefully set the match on a clump of dry moss, which also caught flame. Ever so gently, he started to build the fire. . . .

Try It!

Write the first five things that come to mind about a short story or novel you have read. Then rewrite your thoughts, making them sound more interesting.

Revise

Check for an interested voice. Read your analysis out loud to see whether you sound interested in the story. Revise any passages that display an uninterested voice.

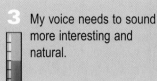

3 My voice needs to sound more interesting and natural.

2 I need to create more voice in my analysis.

1 I need to learn more about voice.

■ Does my voice sound natural and engaging?

Your voice sounds natural and engaging if it reflects your personality and connects with the reader. Keep these tips in mind.

- ■ Your writing should sound the way you do when you talk with a classmate in a "relaxed" classroom setting.
- ■ Imagine yourself reading your essay aloud to the class. Your classmates should enjoy what you have to say. You should use words that they will understand.

■ Keep it natural.

Avoid writing that sounds too formal or too informal.

FORMAL

> The man was extremely shaken by his extraordinary experience, and he was exhilarated to return to his residence.

INFORMAL

> The guy got freaked out by what happened, and then he headed for home.

NATURAL AND ENGAGING

> After his strange experience, the man was happy to go home.

Revise

Check for a natural voice. Reread your essay, marking any sections that sound too formal or too informal. Rewrite them so that they sound natural.

Voice
Overly formal language is rewritten.

After supper, Mrs. Jones gives Roger ten dollars to buy
                                          tells   *not to*
some blue suede shoes. She ~~advises~~ him ~~to never again~~ make
              mistake   *else's*
the ~~transgression~~ of stealing someone's purse.

Literature

Revising ■ for Word Choice

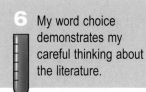
6 My word choice demonstrates my careful thinking about the literature.

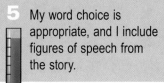
5 My word choice is appropriate, and I include figures of speech from the story.

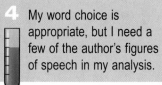
4 My word choice is appropriate, but I need a few of the author's figures of speech in my analysis.

When you revise for **word choice**, make sure to include one or two figures of speech from the story in your analysis. Also make sure that your words effectively reflect the intent of your analysis. Use the rubric above and the information below to help you revise for word choice.

■ Do I use the author's figures of speech to prove a point?

You use figures of speech effectively if they help you prove or support a point in your analysis. Here are some common figures of speech that may appear in a short story.

- A **simile** compares two things using *like* or *as*. (*The dog danced around like loose litter in the wind.*)
- A **metaphor** compares two things without using *like* or *as*. (*At McKinley High School, football is king.*)
- A **hyperbole** is a highly exaggerated statement. (*Her heart melted when she saw the gift.*)
- An **idiom** is an expression that means something different from what the words actually say. (*Mr. Jung has an axe to grind with his landlord.*)

Try It!

Identify the figure of speech used in each literary passage below. Some sentences may have more than one.

1. "[The snapping turtle] struck like springsteel and the branch snapped like a stick of macaroni." ("The Turtle" by George Vukelich)
2. "This intelligence has driven a wedge between me and all the people I once knew." ("Flowers for Algernon" by Daniel Keyes)
3. "Dad hit the ceiling when I brought home my report card." ("Denton's Daughter" by Ellen Lowenberg)
4. "The guns and the dog were an armor against fear." ("The Old Chief Mishlanga" by Doris Lessing)

3 I need to use more appropriate words and include one or two of the author's figures of speech.

2 I need to pay more attention to my word choice.

1 I need to learn more about word choice.

■ Do the words in my analysis have the right feeling?

The words in your analysis have the right feeling, or connotation, if, among other things, they accurately reflect the thoughts and actions of the main character. Read the paragraph below, paying close attention to the underlined words and phrases. These ideas clearly suggest the confused feelings of the main character.

> Robert looks <u>dazed</u> as an official tells him that he has been put under hypnosis as part of his driver's test. Robert <u>slowly nods</u>, as some scary images race through his mind. He was just about to collide with an oncoming vehicle, or <u>so he thought</u>. Now he is in a reclining chair, <u>trying to gather his wits</u>, trying to figure out what he has just experienced. Robert <u>has no idea how to react</u> as he slowly stands up.

Revise

Revise for word choice. Review the way that you use words in your analysis. Do they reflect the thoughts and actions of the main character? Replace words as needed.

Word Choice
New words and phrases are included to create the right feeling.

> The story begins when Roger ~~takes~~ *grabs* a woman's purse.
> Its heaviness makes Roger fall. We know the purse is heavy because of the hyperbole: "It had everything in it but hammer and nails" (211). The woman grabs Roger and shakes him ~~hard.~~ *until his teeth rattle.* She says, "When I get through with you, sir, you are going to remember Mrs. Luella Bates Washington Jones" (211). Roger ~~moves~~ *struggles* to get free, but Mrs. Jones is strong.

Literature

Revising ■ for Sentence Fluency

 6 The sentences in my analysis make my ideas really stand out.

 5 My sentences read smoothly, and I have used the appropriate verb tense.

 4 Most of my sentences read smoothly, but I need to fix some tense shifts.

To revise for **sentence fluency**, check that you have used the correct verb tenses and that your sentences flow smoothly. The rubric strip above will help you.

■ When should I shift tenses in my analysis?

You should not shift tenses in your analysis unless there is good reason to do so. A response to literature (such as an analysis) is usually written in the present tense. Because the plot unfolds in the same way each time you read a story, it makes sense to discuss the story in the present tense.

Present tense: The girl trains **diligently for the city races.**

However, you may need to shift tenses when you include a quotation from the story. Authors often tell their stories using the past tense. *(She smiled. He blushed.)* So when you include a quotation in your analysis, you may shift from the present tense to the past tense. Notice the shift in the example below.

> In "The Cask of Amontillado," Poe **writes**, "He **had** a weak point—this Fortunato—although in other regards he **was** a man to be respected and even feared."

 ## Try It!

Read the example below. Explain how the tenses shift.

1 "The Ransom of Red Chief" begins, "It looked like a good thing: but wait
2 till I tell you. We were down South, in Alabama—Bill Driscoll and myself—when
3 this kidnapping idea struck us." With these words, O. Henry pulls the reader
4 into the action.

 Review your first draft. Read your essay and be sure that you have not shifted tenses without good reason.

Revise

3 I need a variety of sentences and a consistent verb tense to improve the flow of my writing.

2 I need to pay more attention to verb tenses and my sentences.

1 I need to learn more about sentences.

■ Do all of my sentences read smoothly?

Your sentences will read smoothly if you use a variety of sentences. When too many sentences in a paragraph are the same length or follow the same pattern, your writing may sound choppy. Here are three basic types of sentences that you can use.

- **Simple Sentence**
  Eugenia Collier wrote the short story "Marigolds."

- **Compound Sentence**
  Lizabeth's friends view her as a leader, and they follow her example.

- **Complex Sentence**
  After destroying Ms. Lottie's marigolds, Lizabeth learns about compassion.

Try It!

Think of a story you have recently read. Write one simple sentence, one compound sentence, and one complex sentence about the main character.

Revise

Revise for sentence fluency. Be sure that you have used a variety of sentence lengths and patterns in your essay.

Sentence Fluency
Simple sentences are combined for smooth reading.

Then Mrs. Jones leads Roger to the door. ~~She~~ *and* reminds him to behave himself. Pride keeps Roger from saying more than "Thank you, m'am." He wants to say more. ~~He~~ *, but* doesn't.

Literature

Revising ■ Improve your writing.

Revise

Check your revising. On a piece of paper, write the numbers 1 to 12. If you can answer "yes" to a question, put a check mark after that number. If not, continue to work with that part of your essay.

Revising Checklist

Ideas

_____ 1. Have I written a clear thesis statement about the theme?
_____ 2. Have I used quotations from the story to support my analysis?
_____ 3. Have I effectively paraphrased the author's thoughts and ideas?

Organization

_____ 4. Have I written a clear beginning, middle, and ending?
_____ 5. Have I used transitions to connect ideas?
_____ 6. Do my thesis statement and final analysis connect?

Voice

_____ 7. Have I used a natural, engaging voice that fits the story?
_____ 8. Do I sound interested in the story and in my analysis?

Word Choice

_____ 9. Have I included at least one significant figure of speech used by the author?
_____ 10. Do I use words with the right connotation?

Sentence Fluency

_____ 11. Have I used a variety of sentence lengths and patterns?
_____ 12. Have I used the correct verb tenses in my sentences?

Revise

Make a clean copy. When you finish revising your essay, make a clean, double-spaced copy before you begin to edit.

Editing

After you've finished revising your essay, it's time to edit for the following conventions: punctuation, capitalization, spelling, and grammar.

Keys to Effective Editing

1. Use a dictionary, a thesaurus, and the "Proofreader's Guide" in the back of this book (pages 604–763).

2. Check quotations for correct punctuation.

3. Check your writing for correctness of punctuation, capitalization, spelling, and grammar.

4. If you use a computer, edit on a printed copy and enter your changes on the computer.

5. Use the editing and proofreading marks inside the back cover of this book.

Literature

Editing ■ for Conventions

 6 My grammar and punctuation are correct, and the copy is free of spelling errors.

5 I have one or two errors in grammar, spelling, or punctuation, but they won't distract the reader.

 4 I need to correct a few errors in punctuation, spelling, or grammar that may distract the reader.

Conventions are the rules you follow for punctuation, capitalization, spelling, and grammar. To edit for conventions, use the rubric strip above and the information below.

■ How should I cite direct quotations?

You should cite direct quotations using the following method.

1. In most cases, start by giving credit to the author:

O. Henry **writes** . . .

2. Put the direct quotation inside quotation marks.

O. Henry writes, "There was clearly nothing to do but flop down on the shabby little couch and howl. So Della did it."

3. Write the page number from the text you are quoting. Place the number inside parentheses following the quotation. The period for the sentence follows the parentheses.

O. Henry writes, "There was clearly nothing to do but flop down on the shabby little couch and howl. So Della did it" (34).

Try It!

Write one sentence using the information below to show how to cite a direct quotation.

Author: Jack London

Direct quotation: The man flung a look back along the way he had come. The Yukon lay a mile wide and hidden under three feet of ice. On top of this ice were as many feet of snow.

Page number: 48

Edit

Edit for punctuation of quotations. Be sure that you correctly cite any direct quotations that you use.

I need to correct a number of errors.

 I need to fix many errors that make my writing hard to read and understand.

1 I need help making corrections.

■ How should I punctuate compound and complex sentences?

Punctuate compound and complex sentences using these rules.

■ A **compound sentence** is made up of two independent clauses. The clauses must be joined by a semicolon, or by a comma and a coordinating conjunction.

> The story focuses on Celie's family; they face innumerable problems.
>
> Celie's life is extremely difficult, **but** slowly she discovers her true self.

■ A **complex sentence** contains one independent clause (in blue) and one or more dependent clauses (in black). Place a comma after the dependent clause when it comes first in a sentence.

> **As the hardships pile up,** the family discovers an inner strength.

Try It!

Rewrite the two sentences below using correct punctuation.

> Although she invited me to the party I did not want to go.
> It rained hard in the afternoon we played soccer anyway.

Edit for conventions. Check your essay for the correct citations of quotations and the correct punctuation of your compound and complex sentences.

Edit

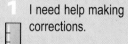
Literature

Conventions
A comma is added to a compound sentence.

A page number is added.

Roger, however, still isn't sure about Mrs. Jones. He wants to run away, but something also makes him want to stay: "He did not trust the woman not to trust him. And he did not want to be mistrusted now." (213).

Editing ■ Check for conventions.

Edit

Check your editing. On a piece of paper, write the numbers 1 to 12. Put a check by the number if you can answer "yes" to that question. If not, continue to edit your essay for that convention.

Editing Checklist

Conventions

PUNCTUATION

_____ **1.** Does each sentence have correct end punctuation?

_____ **2.** Have I used quotation marks and correctly cited direct quotations?

_____ **3.** Do I correctly punctuate compound and complex sentences?

_____ **4.** Have I used parentheses to set off page numbers?

_____ **5.** Do I use apostrophes to show possession *(in Poe's story)*?

CAPITALIZATION

_____ **6.** Do I start all my sentences with capital letters?

_____ **7.** Have I capitalized all proper nouns?

SPELLING

_____ **8.** Have I spelled all my words correctly?

_____ **9.** Have I double-checked the words my spell-checker may have missed?

GRAMMAR

_____ **10.** Have I used correct verb tenses throughout?

_____ **11.** Do my subjects and verbs agree in number (*Marigolds are*, not *Marigolds is*)?

_____ **12.** Have I used the right words *(its, it's)*?

■ Create a title.

- ■ Focus on the theme: **Sweet Forgiveness**
- ■ Refer to the character: **A Not-So-Tough Guy**
- ■ Be creative: **Forget Revenge—Forgive**

Publishing ■ Share your essay.

Now that you've finished writing, revising, and editing your essay, you can think about publishing it! See the suggestions in the boxes below for a variety of ways to present your essay.

Publish

Make a final copy. Follow your teacher's instructions or use the guidelines below to format your paper. (If you are using a computer, see pages 76–78.) Write a final copy of your essay and proofread it for errors.

■ Focus on presentation.

- ■ Use blue or black ink and write neatly.
- ■ Write your name in the upper left corner of page 1.
- ■ Skip a line and center your title; skip another line and start your writing.
- ■ Indent every paragraph and leave a one-inch margin on all four sides.
- ■ Write your last name and the page number in the upper right-hand corner of every page after page 1.

Submit your Essay to a Literary Magazine

Ask your school or public librarian about young adult magazines that accept literary analyses. Submit your essay for publication. (See page 82.)

Give an Oral Presentation

Give a brief summary of the short story and then read your essay to the class. Ask if any of your classmates have read the story. Do they agree with your analysis?

Publish Your Essay Online

If your school has a Web page, submit your essay for publication. You may also explore other online sites that share reviews and analyses by teens.

Literature

Rubric for a Response to Literature

Use this rubric for guiding and assessing your writing. Refer to it whenever you want to improve your writing using the six traits.

6	5	4
Ideas		
The ideas show a complete understanding of the reading.	The essay has a clear focus statement and necessary supporting details.	The essay has a clear focus statement. Unnecessary details need to be cut.
Organization		
All the parts work together to create an insightful essay.	The organization pattern fits the topic and purpose. All parts of the essay are well developed.	The organization pattern fits the topic and purpose. A part of the essay needs better development.
Voice		
The voice expresses interest and complete understanding. It engages the reader.	The voice expresses interest in and understanding of the topic.	The voice expresses interest but needs to show more understanding.
Word Choice		
The word choice reflects careful thinking about the reading.	The word choice, including the use of figures of speech, creates a clear message.	The word choice is clear, but more figures of speech would improve the essay.
Sentence Fluency		
The sentences in the essay make the ideas really stand out.	The sentences are skillfully written and keep the reader's interest.	No sentence problems exist. More sentence variety is needed.
Conventions		
Grammar and punctuation are correct, and the copy is free of all errors.	The essay has one or two errors that do not interfere with the reader's understanding.	The essay has a few careless errors in punctuation and grammar.

3	2	1
The focus statement is too broad. A variety of details are needed.	The focus statement is unclear. More details are needed.	The essay needs a focus statement and details.
The organization fits the essay's purpose. Some parts need more development.	The organization doesn't fit the purpose.	A plan needs to be followed.
The voice needs to be more interesting and express more understanding.	The voice does not show interest in or an understanding of the topic.	The writer needs to understand how to create voice.
The word choice is too general, and more figures of speech are needed.	Little attention was given to word choice.	The writer needs help with word choice.
A few sentence problems need to be corrected.	The essay has many sentence problems.	The writer needs to learn how to construct sentences.
The errors in the essay confuse the reader.	The number of errors make the essay hard to read.	Help is needed to make corrections.

Literature

Evaluating a Response to Literature

Read the following analysis of a short-story theme. Then read the student's self-evaluation on the next page. **(There are errors in the essay below.)**

Dying to Succeed

"The Scarlet Ibis," by James Hurst, is the story of two brothers. One is a disabled boy named Doodle, and the author doesn't say the name of Doodle's older brother. The older boy wants Doodle to be normal because he is embarrassed by the way he looks and acts. Hurst tells us the theme with these words. "Pride is a wonderful, terrible thing, a seed that bears two vines, life and death" (147).

The story begins when Doodle is born. Hurst writes, "He seemed all head, with a tiny body, which was red and shriveled like an old man's." (140) They named him William Armstrong, "which was like tying a big tail on a small kite" (141). Everyone expects William Armstrong to die, but he doesn't. When he surprises everyone and learns to crawl, his older brother names him "Doodle." His brother decides to teach Doodle to be as normal as possible so he won't be an embarrassment to him. The result is mixed.

As Doodle grows, his brother has to haul him around in a cart, which he hates to do. He takes Doodle to Old Woman Swamp. Hidden in the woods near the stream, he persuades, and even forces Doodle to try to walk. He is even mean to Doodle, and he leaves him behind. This makes Doodle cry, "Brother, brother! Don't leave me!" (page 146). Doodle does walk. His brother is proud not only of Doodle but of himself. He says, "Doodle walked only because I was ashamed of having a crippled brother." (147)

One July day, a hurricane comes. This is an important stage in the story. It foreshadows bad times ahead. Around this time, Doodle starts feeling sick a lot. In the days after the hurricane, the family finds a beautiful red bird, called a scarlet ibis, sitting in what they call their "bleeding tree." The hurricane blew it in, and it is out of its environment. It dies and falls to earth, which makes Doodle very sad. He takes the bird to a flower bed and buries it.

That evening, Doodle and his brother go to the swamp. The brother's goal this time is to teach Doodle to row a boat and to swim. He wants Doodle to be as normal as possible when he starts school in the fall. Doodle is tired, but his brother forces him to go on. Soon, a bad storm comes up. The two brothers have to run for home. Doodle can't keep up. His brother runs faster trying to force Doodle to run harder. Doodle puffs, "Brother, brother! Don't leave me! Don't

Jenkins 2

leave me!" (152). Then, everything is quiet. His brother goes back and finds Doodle dead. The author says that the boy cries as he holds his "fallen scarlet ibis" (152).

In the beginning, the brother's pride makes Doodle exceed everyone's expectations of him. In the end, the brother's pride directly contributes to Doodle's death. The brother learns the hard way that pride is both a wonderful and a terrible thing and that it can lead both to life and to death.

Student Self-Assessment

Response Rubric Checklist

Title: "Dying to Succeed"
Writer: David Jenkins

5 Ideas
- Does my analysis focus on an interesting short story?
- Do I have a clear thesis statement?
- Do I include effective supporting details?

5 Organization
- Does the beginning identify the story and the thesis statement?
- Does the middle show how the theme develops?
- Does the ending share a meaningful analysis?

4 Voice
- Does my voice sound natural?
- Do I sound engaging?

4 Word Choice
- Do I use specific nouns and active verbs?
- Have I included one of the author's significant figures of speech?

5 Sentence Fluency
- Do I use tense shifts correctly?
- Do my sentences read smoothly?

5 Conventions
- Do I correctly cite sources?
- Are my punctuation, capitalization, spelling, and grammar correct?

OVERALL COMMENTS:

My first paragraph introduces the story and states the theme, though maybe I should have used a direct quotation to show the boy's personality.

I have a strong beginning, middle, and ending, but I could sound more interested in the story.

I included two important figures of speech from the story, but I didn't discuss them.

I think my paper is free of careless errors, but I'm not sure how to add page numbers to citations.

Literature

Use the rubric. Rate your essay using the rubric on pages 290–291. Write comments about why you gave yourself the scores you did.

Reflecting on Your Writing

Reflect on your finished analysis of a short-story theme by completing each starter sentence below. These comments will help you check your progress as a writer.

My Literature Analysis

1. The strongest part of my essay is . . .

2. The part that most needs change is . . .

3. The main thing I learned about writing an analysis of a theme is . . .

4. In my next response to literature, I would like to . . .

5. Here is one question I still have about writing an analysis of a theme:

6. Right now I would describe my writing ability as . . . (excellent, good, fair, poor)

Writing for Assessment
Responding to Prompts About Literature

You may be asked to respond to a literature prompt on an assessment test. The prompt may be based on a piece of literature that you have previously read or on a story, a poem, or an article provided on the test itself. Your response will show how well you understand the main features of literature. To prepare for this type of writing, pay careful attention to discussions of *plot, character, theme, setting,* and *style* in your English classes.

This chapter will help you respond effectively to literature prompts. You will learn to analyze various types of prompts, to use the writing process in a test situation, and to respond to fiction and nonfiction.

Writing Guidelines

Subject: **Literature prompt**
Form: **Response to a prompt**
Purpose: **To demonstrate competence**
Audience: **Instructor**

"Great literature is simply language charged with meaning to the utmost possible degree."
—George Orwell

"The books that help you the most are those which make you think the most."

—Theodore Parker

Prewriting ■ Analyze a literature prompt.

A prompt about literature asks you to respond to specific characteristics of a story, a poem, a novel, or a nonfiction selection. As you read a prompt, look for key words that tell you exactly what the prompt requires. In the sample prompt below, key words and phrases are underlined. The word *describe* gives the main direction or focus for the response.

Sample Prompt

In the story "The Amigo Brothers," the friendship of two boys is severely tested. Write an essay in which you describe how the crisis between them demonstrates the ideal of true friendship. How do their personal characteristics lead to the crisis and the way it is resolved? How does the author reveal their similarities and differences? Support your thesis with evidence from the story.

Try It!

Copy the following sample prompts on a sheet of paper. Underline key words and phrases for each prompt and make notes about the kinds of supporting information that you would need for your response.

1. Inventor Margaret E. Knight, the subject of Susan Bivin Aller's article "A Lady in a Machine Shop," was remarkably successful. In an essay, explain what characteristics contributed to her achievements. Include specific examples to support your ideas.

2. "Our Son Swears He Has 102 Gallons of Water in His Body," by Naomi Shihab Nye, is a poem about a boy's relationship with his parents. In an essay, discuss the stanza that reveals the most about the relationship. How does this stanza clarify some of the details in the poem?

■ Plan your response.

Once you analyze and understand a prompt, you are ready to plan your response. If a reading selection is provided, read it with the prompt in mind, picking out the information you need for your response. Then form your topic sentence and organize the details.

Sample Prompt and Selection

> **This excerpt from Charles Dickens's "A Christmas Carol" describes Scrooge. In a paragraph, discuss the feeling created by this description. What details create this feeling?**
>
> The <u>cold</u> within him <u>froze</u> his old features, <u>nipped</u> his pointed nose, <u>shriveled</u> his cheek, <u>stiffened</u> his gait; made his <u>eyes red</u>, his thin <u>lips blue</u>; and spoke out shrewdly in his grating voice. A <u>frosty rime</u> was on his head, and on his eyebrows, and his wiry chin. He <u>carried his own low temperature</u> always about with him; he <u>iced his office</u> in the dog-days, and <u>didn't thaw it one degree at Christmas</u>.

The underlined words refer to Scrooge's coldness.

■ Write a topic sentence.

After reading the prompt and selection above, one student wrote the following topic sentence.

> **Dickens's description of Scrooge** (specific topic) **shows a man who is cold to the core** (particular focus related to the prompt).

■ Create a graphic organizer.

The writer used a T-chart to sort details for her response paragraph.

Scrooge	
cold from within him	**cold affected his surroundings**
"froze his old features"	"carried his own low temperature"
"nipped his pointed nose"	"iced his office in the dog-days"
"shriveled his cheek"	"didn't thaw it one degree at Christmas"
"stiffened his gait"	
"eyes red," "lips blue," "frosty rime"	

Literature

Writing ■ Respond to a fiction prompt.

The following prompt and fiction selection show how a student underlined words and phrases and added some notes on a copy of the selection to address the focus of the prompt (red).

Sample Prompt and Selection

Most people are aware that Charles Dickens wrote the famous story "A Christmas Carol." They are less familiar with his other stories, including "The Chimes," celebrating that season of the year. Read the excerpt that follows from "The Chimes," which opens with a description of the winter wind. In an essay, explain how Dickens makes the wind seem more than it really is. **What details create this effect?**

From "The Chimes" by Charles Dickens

There are not, I say, many people who would care to sleep in a church. I don't mean at sermon-time in warm weather (when the thing has actually been done, once or twice), but in the night, and alone. A great multitude of persons will be violently astonished, I know, by this position, in the broad bold day. But it applies to night. It must be argued by night, and I will undertake to maintain it successfully on any gusty winter's night appointed for the purpose, with any one opponent chosen from the rest, who will meet me singly in an old churchyard, before an old church-door; and will previously empower me to lock him in, if needful to his satisfaction, until morning.

The wind is "gusty."

For the night-wind has a dismal trick of wandering round and round a building of that sort, and moaning as it goes; and of trying, with its unseen hand, the windows and the doors; and seeking out some crevices by which to enter. And when it has got in; as one not finding what it seeks, whatever that may

Wind seems human as it plays a "trick," wanders, moans, and uses an "unseen hand."

Soaring and flinging itself down, the wind seems superhuman.

be, it wails and howls to issue forth again: and <u>not content</u> with <u>stalking</u> through the aisles, and gliding round and round the pillars, and tempting the deep organ, <u>soars</u> up to the roof, and strives to rend the rafters: then <u>flings itself despairingly upon the stones below</u>, and passes, <u>muttering</u>, into the vaults. Anon, it comes up stealthily, and <u>creeps along the walls</u>, seeming to read, in whispers, the inscriptions sacred to the dead. At some of these, <u>it breaks out shrilly</u>, as with <u>laughter</u>; and at others, <u>moans and cries</u> as if it were <u>lamenting</u>.

Shrill laughter tied to "lamenting" creates an eerie, scary feeling.

■ Write a thesis statement.

After reading the excerpt and making notes, the student wrote the following thesis statement for his response essay.

> **The narrator presents the wind** (specific topic) **as an intruder that becomes more and more terrifying** (particular focus related to the prompt).

■ Create a graphic organizer.

The writer used a line diagram to organize specific details from the excerpt.

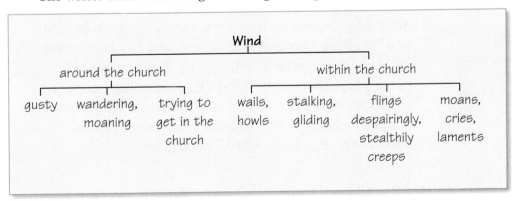

■ Student Response

In this student response to the excerpt from "The Chimes," note how the writer used details from the story to support the thesis statement.

Sleeping in Church?

Beginning
The first paragraph leads up to the thesis statement (underlined).

The excerpt from "The Chimes" by Charles Dickens begins with the idea that isolated, old churches are much different places at night than they are during the daytime. The narrator challenges anyone who doubts this to be locked alone in an old church overnight. The narrator presents the wind as an intruder that becomes more and more terrifying.

Middle
One paragraph focuses on the wind outside the church.

Although the wind is first described as simply "gusty," it soon takes on human qualities, "wandering round . . . moaning as it goes." In addition to the mournful sounds, the wind begins "trying, with its unseen hand, the windows and the doors." The would-be sleeper seems trapped and surrounded by this persistent intruder seeking to get in.

The next paragraph focuses on the wind inside the church.

As if this stalker image were not enough, the wind changes into something superhuman and even more frightening as it enters the building. It starts out "stalking through the aisles" and "gliding round and round the pillars" almost as if in search of some prey. Then something truly alarming happens; the wind "soars up to the roof . . . then flings itself despairingly upon the stones below, and passes, muttering, into the vaults." Clearly the wind is beyond the reach of death itself even as it seems cursed to wander among the graves mournfully "lamenting." The narrator imagines the "moans and cries" are the wind's reactions to the inscriptions on the tombs.

Ending
The closing summarizes the main point.

In an isolated country church at night, the wind is described as a mysterious and frightening intruder. What begins as natural gusts of wind on a winter night takes on a far more terrifying form. The narrator first characterizes the wind as a sinister stalker and then as a haunted spirit moaning among the graves below. Throughout the excerpt, the narrator does his best to describe to anyone brave enough to take the dare what he or she might encounter.

Respond to the reading. Answer the following questions about the student response.

Ideas (1) What part of the topic does the student focus on in the thesis statement? (2) What types of details does the student use to support his thesis?

Organization (3) How does the writer organize the middle part of the response?

Voice & Word Choice (4) Which words or phrases quoted from the story are the most effective? Name two.

Practice Literature Prompt

Whenever you respond to a writing prompt, especially in a timed situation, begin by studying the prompt. Find the key word that indicates what you are to do in the response: *compare, explain, describe,* and so on. Be sure that you understand the prompt and any specific points you need to address in your response before you read the selection. Of course, it is important to quote examples and specific details from the selection to support your thesis. However, it is equally important to share your own insights about the selection.

Practice Prompt and Selection

"An Experiment in Misery" by Stephen Crane is about two friends who are watching a homeless man, and they wonder what it would be like to be in his situation. One of the friends decides to put on some old clothes and pretend to be homeless in order to find out. The following excerpt follows the young man in his new role. Discuss how you think this experience will change his understanding of the homeless. Support your ideas with specific examples from the excerpt.

From "An Experiment in Misery" by Stephen Crane

It was late at night, and a fine rain was swirling softly down causing the pavements to glisten with hue of steel and blue and yellow in the rays of the innumerable lights. A youth was trudging slowly, without enthusiasm, with his hands buried deep in his trousers' pockets, toward the downtown places where beds can be hired for coppers. He was clothed in an aged and tattered suit, and his derby was a marvel of dust-covered crown and torn rim. He was going forth to eat as the wanderer may eat, and sleep as the homeless sleep. By the time he had reached City Hall Park he was so completely plastered with yells of "bum" and "hobo," and with various unholy epithets that small boys had applied to him at intervals, that he was in a state of the most profound dejection. The sifting rain saturated the old velvet collar of his overcoat, and as the wet cloth pressed against his neck, he felt that there no longer could be pleasure in life. He looked about him searching for an outcast of highest degree that they two might share miseries, but the lights threw a quivering glare over rows and circles of deserted benches that glistened damply, showing patches of wet sod behind them. It seemed that their usual freights had fled on this night to better things. There were only squads of well-dressed Brooklyn people who swarmed toward the bridge.

The young man loitered about for a time and then went shuffling off down Park Row. In the sudden descent in style of the dress of the crowd he felt relief, and as if he were at last in his own country. He began to see tatters that matched his tatters. In Chatham Square there were aimless men strewn in front of saloons and lodging-houses, standing sadly, patiently, reminding one vaguely of the attitudes of chickens in a storm. He aligned himself with these men, and turned slowly to occupy himself with the flowing life of the great street.

Through the mists of the cold and storming night, the cable cars went in silent procession, great affairs shining with red and brass, moving with formidable power, calm and irresistible, dangerful and gloomy, breaking silence only by the loud fierce cry of the gong. Two rivers of people swarmed along the sidewalks, spattered with black mud which made each shoe leave a scar-like impression. Overhead, elevated trains with a shrill grinding of the wheels stopped at the station, which upon its leg-like pillars seemed to resemble some monstrous kind of crab squatting over the street. The quick fat puffings of the engines could be heard. Down an alley there were somber curtains of purple and black, on which street lamps dully glittered like embroidered flowers.

Respond to a literature prompt. Read the practice prompt again to make sure that you understand its focus. Then carefully reread the fiction selection by Stephen Crane. Next, form a thesis statement, quickly arrange your main supporting details in a graphic organizer, and write your essay. After you finish, check your work for conventions.

Literature

■ Respond to a nonfiction prompt.

The following prompt and nonfiction selection show how a student underlined words and phrases related to the prompt's focus. The writer also jotted notes in the margin of the selection in order to put together a brief outline before writing his response essay.

Prompt and Selection

The following excerpt from Booker T. Washington's autobiography is about part of his childhood. What caused Washington to remember what his life had been like when he was young? As Washington recalls these experiences, what does he realize about his childhood? Using examples from your own childhood or from the experiences of people you know, explain whether or not you think that your generation will look back with some of the same feelings that Washington had.

From *Up from Slavery: An Autobiography*
by Booker T. Washington

Cause for
Washington
to recall his
youth

What he
realizes
about his
childhood

Washington's
feelings
about his
childhood

I was asked not long ago to tell something about the sports and pastimes that I engaged in during my youth. Until that question was asked it had never occurred to me that there was no period of my life that was devoted to play. From the time that I can remember anything, almost every day of my life has been occupied in some kind of labour; though I think I would now be a more useful man if I had had time for sports. During the period that I spent in slavery I was not large enough to be of much service, still I was occupied most of the time in cleaning the yards, carrying water to the men in the fields, or going to the mill, to which I used to take the corn, once a week, to be ground. The mill was about three miles from the plantation. This work I always dreaded. The heavy bag of corn would be thrown across the back of the horse, and the corn divided about evenly on each side; but in some way, almost without exception, on these trips, the corn would so shift as to become unbalanced and would fall off the horse, and often I would fall with it. As I was not strong enough to reload the corn upon the horse, I would have to wait, sometimes for many hours, till a chance passer-by came along who would help me out of my trouble. The hours while waiting for someone were usually spent in crying. The time consumed in this way made me late in reaching the mill, and by the time I got my corn ground and reached home it would be far into the night. The road was a lonely one, and often led through dense forests. I was always frightened. The woods were said to be full of soldiers who had deserted from the army, and <u>I had been told that the first thing a deserter did to a Negro boy when he found him alone was to cut off his ears.</u> Besides, <u>when I was late in getting home I knew I would always get a severe scolding or a flogging.</u>

Washington's fears and experiences

■ Write a thesis statement.

After reading the excerpt, the student writer developed the following thesis statement for his response essay.

> **Young people today, like Washington in his childhood** (specific topic)**, are not being given enough chances to play** (particular focus related to the prompt).

■ Create a graphic organizer.

The student used a simple outline to plan his response.

> I. Parents today forget kids need to play.
> II. Some kids are locked into too much organized activity.
> III. I got to play as a kid.
> IV. Today's kids may grow up like Booker T., regretting their lack of true play time.

■ Student Response

The following essay is a student response to the prompt and excerpt from Booker T. Washington's autobiography.

Instant Replay

Beginning
The first paragraph identifies the author of the selection, uses a quotation, and builds up to the thesis statement (underlined).

The feeling that I get when I read Booker T. Washington's description of his early life is that he didn't really have a childhood. He says, "There was no period of my life that was devoted to play." Washington had never really thought about this until someone asked him "to tell something about the sports and pastimes" of his youth. He described having to spend his time doing dangerous and difficult chores, sometimes followed by "a severe scolding or a flogging." Of course, today's children are free from the terrible abuses of slavery. However, it is possible that young people today, like Washington in his childhood, are not being given enough chances to play.

Middle
The first middle paragraph gives examples of why kids today may relate to Washington's lack of free time.

Booker T. Washington "always dreaded" some of the things he had to do, but it wasn't the hardship that seemed to haunt him. Later in life, when he thought back on his childhood, he regretted not having had a chance to play sports—to do something just for the fun of it. It's possible that some kids today may look back on their early years in the same way. Many of my friends spent almost all their grade-school years being hauled around by their parents to music lessons, scout meetings, church retreats, and organized baseball or soccer games.

This frantic pace continued all summer, when some of them also had to attend summer school.

I was lucky, because my dad never made me take part in anything as a kid unless it was something I really wanted to do. Having the time to just play in my neighborhood was a great thing. We had a tree house, played catch, rode our bikes, and just fooled around. Now I'm in high school, and I'm ready to improve my skills in soccer and golf, my favorite sports.

Ending
The ending compares the lives of kids today with Washington's early experience and revisits the thesis.

It may not seem that the lives of kids today and the life of Booker T. Washington would have much in common. There's no doubt that childhood for me was far better than his experiences during slavery. However, Washington's autobiography reminds me that having the freedom to play like a kid is a really important thing. I'm afraid that some kids who are growing up today will wonder later, as Washington did, whether they might have been better grown-ups if they had been allowed to act more like children.

Literature

Respond to the reading. Answer the following questions about the student response.

Ideas (1) What is the thesis of the student response? (2) What details does the student use to support the thesis? Name two or three.

Organization (3) How is this response organized—chronologically, spatially (by location), or logically?

Voice & Word Choice (4) Which words and phrases indicate the student's attitude toward the topic? Name two.

Practice Writing Prompt

Whether you are reading and responding to fiction or nonfiction, remember that the author of the selection carefully chose the words to create a character, establish a setting, share information, arouse an emotion, and so on. You also need to carefully choose your words when you respond to a literature prompt.

Practice Prompt and Selection

The excerpt that follows is from a speech that Patrick Henry delivered on March 23, 1775. The final words of the speech became an inspiration to those who wanted to go to war against the British. In an essay, explain why Patrick Henry's speech was so effective. What reasons did Henry give his fellow colonists for rebelling? Why did he think that fighting was a better alternative than peace? What words, phrases, or sentence structures of Henry's seem especially convincing? Support your ideas with examples from the speech.

From Patrick Henry's
"Give Me Liberty or Give Me Death" speech

There is no longer any room for hope. If we wish to be free—if we mean to preserve inviolate those inestimable privileges for which we have been so long contending—if we mean not basely to abandon the noble struggle in which we have been so long engaged, and which we have pledged ourselves never to abandon until the glorious object of our contest shall be obtained—we must fight! I repeat it, sir, we must fight! An appeal to arms and to the God of hosts is all that is left us! They tell us, sir, that we are weak; unable to cope with so formidable an adversary. But when shall we be stronger? Will it be the next week, or the next year? Will it be when we are totally disarmed, and when a British guard shall be stationed in every house? Shall we gather strength by irresolution and inaction? Shall we acquire the means of effectual resistance by lying supinely on our backs and hugging the delusive phantom of hope, until our enemies shall have bound us hand and foot? Sir, we are not weak if we make a proper use of those means which the God of nature hath placed in our power. The millions of people, armed in the holy cause of liberty, and in such a country as that which we possess, are invincible by any force which our enemy can send against us. Besides, sir, we shall not fight our battles alone. There is a just God who presides over the destinies of nations, and who will raise up friends to fight our battles for us. The battle, sir, is not to the strong alone; it is to the vigilant, the active, the brave. Besides, sir, we have no election. If we were base enough to desire it, it is now too late to retire from the contest. There is no retreat but in submission and slavery! Our chains are forged! Their clanking may be heard on the plains of Boston! The war is inevitable—and let it come! I repeat it, sir, let it come.

It is in vain, sir, to extenuate the matter. Gentlemen may cry, Peace, Peace—but there is no peace. The war is actually begun! The next gale that sweeps from the north will bring to our ears the clash of resounding arms! Our brethren are already in the field! Why stand we here idle? What is it that gentlemen wish? What would they have? Is life so dear, or peace so sweet, as to be purchased at the price of chains and slavery? Forbid it, Almighty God! I know not what course others may take; but as for me, give me liberty or give me death!

Literature

Respond to a writing prompt. Read the practice prompt on the previous page again to be sure that you understand its focus. Then reread the selection. Next, form a thesis statement, briefly list your main ideas in a graphic organizer, and write your response essay. Use the revising and editing tips on the next page to check your response before turning it in.

Revising ■ Improve your response.

Always review your response at the end of a writing test. Make any changes and corrections as neatly as possible. Use the following questions to help you revise your response.

- **Ideas:** Does my thesis statement address the focus of the prompt? Do the details support the thesis?

- **Organization:** Have I included a beginning, a middle, and an ending? Does each paragraph have a focus? Did I conclude with an insight about the literature selection?

- **Voice:** Do I sound clear in my thinking?

- **Word Choice:** Do the words that I use reflect my clear understanding of the literature selection? Have I avoided any unnecessary repetition?

- **Sentence Fluency:** Are all of my sentences complete? Do my sentences flow smoothly from one to the next?

Revise

Improve you work. Reread your practice response, asking yourself the questions above. Make any changes neatly.

Editing ■ Check your response.

In your final read-through, check your punctuation, capitalization, spelling, and grammar.

Conventions

_____ **1.** Have I used end punctuation for every sentence?

_____ **2.** Have I capitalized all proper nouns and first words of sentences?

_____ **3.** Have I checked the spelling in my work?

_____ **4.** Have I made sure my subjects and verbs agree?

_____ **5.** Have I put quotation marks around the exact words that I quoted from the selection?

Edit

Check your response. Read over your work, looking for errors in punctuation, capitalization, spelling, and grammar. Make corrections neatly.

Responding to Literature on Tests

Use the following tips as a guide whenever you respond to a prompt about literature. These tips will help you respond to both fiction and nonfiction selections.

Before you write . . .

- **Be clear about the time limit.**
  Plan enough time for prewriting, writing, and revising.
- **Understand the prompt.**
  Be sure that you know what the prompt requires. Pay special attention to the key word that tells you what you need to do.
- **Read the selection with the focus of the prompt in mind.**
  Take notes that will help you form your thesis. If you're working on a copy of the selection, underline important details.
- **Form your thesis statement.**
  The thesis statement should identify the specific topic plus the focus of the prompt.
- **Make a graphic organizer.**
  Jot down main points and possible quotations for your essay.

As you write . . .

- **Maintain the focus of your essay.**
  Keep your thesis in mind as you write.
- **Be selective.**
  Use examples from your graphic organizer and the selection to support your thesis.
- **End in a meaningful way.**
  Start by revisiting the thesis. Then try to share a final insight about the topic with the reader.

After you write a first draft . . .

- **Check for completeness and correctness.**
  Use the questions on page **310** to revise your essay. Then check for errors in punctuation, capitalization, spelling, and grammar.

Try It!

Plan and write a response. Read a prompt your teacher supplies. Analyze it, read the selection, form a thesis statement, list ideas in a graphic organizer, and write your essay. Then revise and edit your response. Try to complete your work within the time your teacher gives you.

Literature

Creative Writing

Writing Stories

Writing about your own experiences is fairly easy, and so is writing about people that you know well. You simply tap into your memory and write. However, writing made-up stories is another matter. While the starting point for a story may be a real experience, the end result should be something new and imaginative.

To write effective stories, you must understand how stories develop. Usually, there is a main character doing some activity, and a problem, or conflict, occurs. The story then unfolds around the main character's attempts to solve the problem. You will begin to understand basic story structure if you read a variety of short stories and novels. The information in this chapter will get you started on your own story writing.

Writing Guidelines

Subject: Getting to know someone
Form: Short story
Purpose: To engage and entertain
Audience: Classmates

"I try to give the readers a slice out of life."
—Stephen Crane

The Shape of Stories

Think of a special experience in your life: a concert, family trip, school play, championship game, or some other event. The best experiences gradually build in excitement to a high point—a big payoff—that really makes the event memorable. The best fictional stories do the same thing; they follow a classic plot line that builds to a climax.

Begin with the plot.

The plot refers to the events or actions that move a story along from start to finish. A plot has five parts: *exposition, rising action, climax, falling action,* and *resolution.* The plot line below shows how these parts work together.

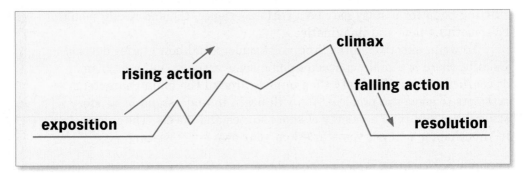

Exposition

The *exposition* is the beginning part of a story in which the main character, conflict, and setting are introduced. The conflict is the problem that the main character faces. The setting is where and when the action takes place.

Juan Lopez is about to leave school and head to the park. In one hand, he carries a copy of Conrad Richter's *The Light in the Forest,* and in the other hand, a suspension slip. He's been skipping classes, and now the principal has made his skipping official. "What do you want to do with your life?" the principal yells after him, the same thing Juan's father yelled that morning.

Rising Action

In a short story, the *rising action* usually includes at least two or three important actions involving the main character and his or her problem. This builds suspense into the story.

First Action: Juan finishes *The Light in the Forest*, the story of a young man in Colonial America who is torn between two cultures. Juan, who recently moved to the United States from Puerto Rico, understands that feeling.

Second Action: Juan remembers hearing about a vision quest, in which a young Native American leaves his family and travels into the wilderness to discover his guardian spirit. (*Guardian* means "one who protects.")

Third Action: Juan looks for a guardian spirit. He sees a squirrel looking for food, and wishes he weren't stuck here, cold and hungry, on the park bench. He sees geese flying south and wishes he could fly to Puerto Rico.

Climax

The *climax* is the moment of truth or the most exciting action, when the character confronts her or his problem head-on. All the action leads up to the climax. In the best stories, the main character is changed by the climax.

A crow lands in front of Juan. The big, strong bird stares at him with calm confidence. The crow nods at Juan and then flies off, leaving a black feather. Juan has just found his guardian.

Falling Action

The *falling action* involves the main character as he or she learns how to deal with life after the moment of truth.

Juan walks home through the cold, dark streets and knows that he, like the crow, will overcome this harsh northern place. He'll show his principal, his father, and himself that he can succeed.

Resolution

The *resolution* brings the story to a natural, thought-provoking, or surprising conclusion. (In some stories, it's hard to tell the difference between the falling action and resolution because they are so closely related.)

Juan arrives home, and his father meets him at the door. "Where have you been?" Juan holds up the suspension slip and says, "I've been in a bad place, but I'm not there anymore. And it's more important where I'm going."

Creative Writing

Sample Story

Read and enjoy the sample story by Gabe Roberts. The side notes indicate how the story develops from the exposition to the resolution.

Exposition
The writer identifies the characters, setting, and conflict.

Jack and Jill

"This creative writing?"

Jill looked up from the poem she had been laboring over. Looming in the classroom doorway was a tall, unkempt boy swathed in a dingy green military coat. A set of earphones embraced his neck, which showed hints of shaving stubble and grime.

"Yes, it is," replied Mrs. Hawkins, reading the crumpled slip he thrust at her. "John Powers."

"Jack," the boy mumbled, his eyes lowered beneath a shock of black hair.

"Jack," repeated Mrs. Hawkins with a smile. "Why don't you take that empty seat next to Jill there?"

The boy flopped into the seat, sending an unpleasant mix of stale smoke and body odor wafting across the aisle. Jill wrinkled her nose in distaste, then forced a weak smile. She was about to speak when the boy flipped up his coat collar and sank down, his long legs stretching to hook under the desk in front of him. *Fine,* thought Jill, shrugging slightly. *You don't want to be friendly, it's okay with me.* She turned her attention to wrestling with the poem once more.

Rising Action
Dialogue and details add to the suspense of the story.

A few days later, Jill got to class early and noticed Jack hunched over behind Mrs. Hawkins's desk, reading one of the teacher's poetry books. He looked different—his face seemed softer somehow, and his lips moved as he read. He chuckled softly, and she heard him murmur the word "quoth" once out loud, then again. "Quoth." Like he was tasting a new flavor. He looked up quickly and saw her.

"Whatcha starin' at?"

"N-nothing!" His face had fallen back to the old menacing hardness, and Jill backed out of the room, deciding to wait until the others got there.

After class, she approached Mrs. Hawkins to talk about Jack.

"He doesn't belong in creative writing," Jill complained. "He never writes anything, never talks in class, and in workshops he's absolutely useless. He never even smiles!"

"But he never disrupts class, either," the teacher smiled. "And he is listening. Does anyone ever talk to him? Jill, you're a writer. The most important thing a writer can learn is how to see beneath the surface. Jack didn't just appear on this earth sullen and alone. Don't you wonder what's behind that mask?"

Jill thought of Jack, shuffling down the hallway, his headphones firmly in place as though to drown out the world around him. She wondered if there could be more to him than she realized.

She watched Jack on the bus after school, his ever-present headphones plugged into his MP3 player. His hands made tiny flickers against the books on his lap, tapping a rhythm that Jill couldn't hear. His eyes, half closed, seemed focused on something only he could see.

Suddenly, she heard a shriek from a few seats back, where some younger students were sitting. A couple of bullies had grabbed a smaller child's stuffed animal and were tossing it around in a game of keep-away.

The toy was flying through the air, when a long arm in a green sleeve shot out and snagged it. Holding the toy, Jack swung himself up, his head nearly touching the top of the bus as he headed toward the back.

"Siddown!" yelled the bus driver, and Jack slid into the seat behind Jill, turning to face the kids in the back.

"Knock it off, you jerks," Jack growled, and at his dark look the bullies cowered into the back of their seats. "This yours?" he softy asked the crying child, who nodded. "Nice," Jack said, stroking the soft golden lion. "He got a name?"

"Simba," the child said softly, wiping his eyes.

"Good name. I had a tiger called Kiko." He handed the stuffed animal back to the child. "You hold onto Simba real tight, okay?" Jack whispered.

"Kay."

Jack smiled then, and with a jolt, Jill saw that he had a big gap where a tooth was missing. Jack turned and saw her looking at him, and his smile quickly closed.

"I'm Jill," she said. "From creative writing class?"

"I know," he said, starting to pull his earphones up into place. Jill's hand flashed out to stop him.

"Hey, do you like poetry? Maybe you could help me figure out what to do with this poem I'm trying to write for class." Jill reached for her backpack and shifted back to sit next to Jack. When she looked up again, she smiled at him.

After the smallest hesitation, he smiled back.

Prewriting ▪ Plan your writing.

Professor John Tolkien was grading exams when he scribbled a now-famous line: "In a hole in the ground there lived a Hobbit." Tolkien didn't know what a Hobbit was or why it lived in the ground. Even so, a single character in a setting inspired him to write *The Hobbit* and a series of other fantastic stories.

Remember that most short stories start with a main character doing some activity, and a conflict occurs. As you start planning your story, identify at least the main character and her or his problem.

▪ Create characters.

Your story should be about getting to know someone. So think of two characters: a main character plus someone he or she learns about. Remember, though, not to embarrass anyone by making any of your characters too much like actual people.

The best stories have characters that you enjoy reading about and grow to care about. Don't, however, include so many characters that the reader becomes confused.

▪ Develop a conflict.

Your main character can be in conflict with another person, with him- or herself, with nature, with society, or with fate. The main character in the sample story on pages **316–317** is primarily in conflict with herself: Jill is having a hard time dealing with a new student in her creative writing class.

▪ Establish a setting.

The *Hobbit* was set in "a hole in the ground" long ago. Your setting can be any place that allows your main character to deal with the conflict. Limit yourself, though, to one main location and a brief span of time.

▪ Consider the action.

The conflict requires the main character to act, so list two or three actions that could move your story along. Also consider the climax, or moment of truth.

Plan your story. Think of at least two characters for your story, a conflict, and a setting. You could also list one or two actions that result from the conflict.

Prewrite

Writing ■ Create your first draft.

Build your story with a few interesting characters, realistic dialogue, and believable action. Also consider the following points about story writing.

■ Start your story.

To get the reader's attention, try starting your story in one of the following ways: (The sample story begins with dialogue.)

- **Start with an exciting action.**

  The dog lunged at Ming, and she climbed higher in the tree.

- **Begin with dialogue.**

  "I need to see some I.D.," said the security guard.

- **Make a surprising statement.**

  David wasn't worried about the trees along the ski trail;

  it was the bear that concerned him.

As you develop the beginning of your story, you should name the setting, introduce the main character, and identify the conflict.

■ Develop the action.

Place your characters in the first challenging action. Then build suspense with each new action or struggle, leading up to the climax.

- Create dialogue that sounds real and natural. Let the words reflect what the characters think and feel.
- Include sensory details. What do the characters see, hear, smell, taste, or feel?
- *Show* instead of *tell* what is happening. For example, instead of writing "Joe was happy," write "Joe's face split into a grin." Instead of writing "The boat was in trouble," write "A wave crashed over the side and swamped the boat."

■ Bring the story to a close.

After the climax, work quickly through the rest of the story. Show how the climax has changed your main character, and tell how she or he will act or live from now on. The ending of your story will fall into place if the other parts of your story work well together.

Write your first draft. Use your planning from page 318 plus the information above as a general guide for your writing.

Creative Writing

320

Revising ■ Improve your story.

Ask yourself the following questions when you review and revise your first draft. (Also see page 322.)

Story Checklist

_____ Do my characters talk and act like real people?
_____ Does the conflict really test my main character?
_____ Do all the actions build toward the climax?
_____ Does the main character learn about another person?

Revising in Action
An unneeded idea is deleted, and a new idea is added.

"N-nothing!" His face had fallen back to the old menacing hardness ~~when he saw her,~~ and Jill backed out of the room.
  deciding to wait until the others got there

Editing ■ Check for style and accuracy.

When you edit your revised story, check for capitalization, punctuation, grammar, and spelling errors.

Editing in Action
A spelling error is fixed.

Punctuation is corrected.

A set of earphones embraced his neck, which showed hints of shaveing stubble and grime.

"Yes, it is," replied Mrs. Hawkins, reading the crumpled slip he thrust at her. "John Powers."

Revise and edit your story. Use the information above to help you revise and edit the first draft of your story.

Revise

Story Patterns

Many short stories follow a basic pattern. Here are brief descriptions of some popular short-story patterns.

The Quest

The main character goes on a journey into the unknown, overcomes a number of obstacles, and returns either victorious or wiser. Heroic myths follow this pattern, but so do many modern stories.

A young woman fights for the right to join an all-male sports team.

The Discovery

The main character follows a trail of clues to discover an amazing secret. Mystery and suspense novels use this pattern.

A curious young man discovers that the bully at school is . . .

The Rite of Passage

A difficult experience changes the main character in a significant and lasting way. These stories are also called *Coming of Age* stories.

A young soldier learns about responsibility while on the battlefield.

The Choice

The focus in this type of story is a decision the main character must make. Tension builds as the decision approaches.

A young adult must decide to follow the crowd or follow her own conscience.

The Union

Two people fall in love, but they are held apart by a number of obstacles. Their struggle to come together only causes their love to grow stronger. Sometimes they succeed, and sometimes they fail.

A young deaf man falls in love with a gifted violinist and then struggles to understand the music he can't hear.

The Reversal

In this pattern, the main character follows one course of action until something causes him or her to think or act in a different way.

A young woman quits school, but then discovers her true love is painting and enrolls in an art school.

Creative Writing

Elements of Fiction

The following terms describe elements of literature. This information will help you discuss and write about novels, poetry, essays, and other literary works.

Antagonist The person or force that works against the hero of the story (See *protagonist*.)

Character A person or an animal in a story

Conflict A problem or clash between two forces in a story
- **Person vs. person** A problem between characters
- **Person vs. himself or herself** A problem within a character's own mind
- **Person vs. society** A problem between a character and society, the law, or some tradition
- **Person vs. nature** A problem with an element of nature, such as a blizzard or a hurricane
- **Person vs. destiny** A problem or struggle that appears to be beyond a character's control

Mood The feeling a piece of literature creates in a reader

Narrator The person or character who tells the story, gives background information, and fills in details between dialogue

Plot, Plot Line See pages 314–315.

Point of View The angle from which a story is told
- In **first-person point of view,** one character is telling the story.
- In **third-person point of view,** someone outside the story is telling it.
- In **omniscient point of view,** the narrator tells the thoughts and feelings of all the characters.
- In **limited omniscient point of view,** the narrator tells the thoughts of one character at a time.
- In **camera view** (objective), the narrator records the action from his or her own point of view without any other characters' thoughts.

Protagonist The main character or hero in a story (See *antagonist*.)

Setting The place and time period in which a story takes place

Theme The author's message about life or human nature

Tone The writer's attitude toward his or her subject (*angry, humorous,* and so on)

Writing Plays

Playwriting has been a powerful means of communication for thousands of years, dating back to ancient Greece. Plays have changed in style through the years, but they still follow the same basic structure. A play tells a story with a beginning, a middle, and an ending. The main character is challenged and somehow changed by the events as they unfold.

Playwriting is a special form of creative writing. While plays are meant to be performed, they are often read as well. The story is "told" by the characters—their **dialogue** and their **actions**. Additional information in the form of **stage directions** helps the reader visualize what is happening.

In this chapter, you will read a play about the high school dating scene. Then you will develop a play of your own about a changing relationship.

Writing Guidelines

Subject: Changing relationships
Form: Play
Purpose: To entertain
Audience: Classmates

"Everything that I have written is closely related to something that I have lived through."

— Henrik Ibsen

Sample Play

In the following play by Brandi Lee, the main character discovers that she may be dating the wrong boy. The side notes identify key points in the development of the play.

Friends and More

Characters: **Gina**, a high school student
Jared, Gina's boyfriend
Beth, Gina's friend
Pete, Gina's best friend

(Gina and Jared are on a platform in a pool of light. Beth and Pete sit in chairs, one on each side of the stage.)

GINA: You're breaking our date?

JARED: Look, Gina, you want to go to that concert. I don't. My dad said he'll take me fishing, and I'd rather do that.

BETH: *(A light comes up on her.)* Jerk!

JARED: You could come with us. It would be fun!

PETE: *(A light comes up on him.)* Not for the fish!

GINA: No, that's all right. You should spend some time with your dad. *(The lights go down on Beth and Pete.)*

JARED: Great. I'll call you tomorrow, okay?

GINA: Sure.

(Beth rises and approaches Gina. Gina is practicing her ballet, doing deep and graceful dips.)

BETH: He dumped you? Oh, Gina, you poor thing!

JARED: *(His light comes up.)* Jeez, it's just a date! *(Light goes down.)*

GINA: *(Laughing and continuing her practicing.)* He broke a date, Beth, not my heart! Besides, he didn't dump me. We're still together.

BETH: Then why are you going to this concert alone? *(Gina stops dancing.)*

GINA: You want to come?

BETH: You have got to be kidding! Ask Pete! He loves that stuff.

Beginning
The characters and the problem are introduced.

(Pete rises and approaches Gina.)

Middle
The interplay between the characters builds suspense.

PETE: A concert? Sure. Did Jared wimp out on you again?

GINA: What do you mean?

PETE: I mean, you always come to me whenever he doesn't want to do something.

GINA: I do?

JARED: *(Light comes up)* She does?

BETH: Um-hmmm. *(Beth and Pete lean forward and listen.)*

GINA: I'm sor—I didn't mean to make you feel—

PETE: It's okay, Gina. I don't mind. I like doing stuff with you.

GINA: Well, that's why we're friends.

JARED: *(To Beth)* See, they're just friends.

PETE: *(Sighs)* Right. Friends.

BETH: Oh, yes. *(All characters' lights go down.)*

Middle
Stage directions set the scene.

(Gina and Jared move chairs together on the platform and sit facing the audience as though taking notes in school. Pete sits on a chair off to the side. Lights come up on platform.)

JARED: *(Whispering as though in class)* So how was your concert?

GINA: Shhh. Fine.

JARED: Sorry you had to go alone.

GINA: *(Whispering)* I didn't go alone. I went with Pete.

JARED: Oh, good. I'm glad you had fun.

GINA: You're not jealous that I went with Pete?

JARED: No. Should I be?

PETE: *(A light comes up on him.)* Gee, thanks. *(His light goes down. Beth's light comes up.)*

BETH: Well, maybe just a little. *(Her light goes down.)*

GINA: No.

JARED: You know, this works out great. You like to do things I don't, and Pete likes the same stuff you do.

GINA: Yes, he does.

Middle
The characters work out the problem.

JARED: I think it's great that you have so much fun with him.

GINA: *(Realization)* Yeah, we do have fun.

PETE: *(Light comes up on Pete and Beth and they look at each other.)* And there it is.

BETH: Surprise! *(Her light goes down.)*

JARED: *(Realization)* You have a lot more fun with him than with me, don't you? *(Pete turns and observes.)*

BETH: *(Her light comes up.)* Aha! *(Her light goes down.)*

GINA: *(Looks at Jared)* Yes, I do. *(They both nod.)* I'm sorry, Jared.

Ending
The main character sets a new course of action.

JARED: *(Shrugs)* Yeah. Still friends, right?

GINA: *(Smiles)* Sure. Maybe we can go fishing sometime.

(Jared laughs as Pete rises and approaches Gina. Jared moves to Pete's chair.)

GINA: Hey, Pete! Would you like to go to a movie?

PETE: What, doesn't Jared like movies now?

BETH: *(Her light comes up.)* Ouch!

GINA: It doesn't matter. I want to go with you. What do you say?

PETE: I say, that's what friends are for.

GINA: Friends. Yeah, well, we can work on that.

(They exit between the chairs. Jared and Beth watch them go out, then look at each other and smile. The lights go out.)

Respond to the Reading Answer the following questions about the play.

Ideas (1) What is the conflict or problem in the play?

Organization (2) How do the stage directions help organize the play?

Voice & Word Choice (3) How does the writer make the dialogue sound realistic? Give three examples.

Prewriting ■ Select a conflict.

A play explores a conflict in the life of the main character. In the play you will write in this chapter, your main character should deal with a changing relationship.

When Brandi planned her play, she made a list of conflicts or problems that she could write about. Then she placed an asterisk beside the one that interested her the most.

List of Conflicts

Becoming a friend with an elderly neighbor
Dealing with a new coach
* Breaking up with a boy- or girlfriend
Working for a demanding employer
Making a new friend

Make a list of possible conflicts. Your list may include one or two of the ideas in Brandi's list. Then put an asterisk next to the conflict that interests you the most.

■ Choose a main character.

After choosing a conflict, Brandi thought about a main character for her play. She felt this person should be a teenager. Not surprisingly, she decided on a teenage girl as her main character.

What would this main character be like? Brandi wrote freely about her to find out. Read part of Brandi's freewriting below:

Sample Freewriting

I'll call the main character Gina. She's 16 and cute, with long hair. She's really into the arts—especially classical music and ballet. She plays the oboe in the school orchestra. She's not into team sports right now, but would like to be. Gina is very easygoing and has a boyfriend named Jared. . . .

Select a main character. After you decide upon the main character, form your first thoughts about this person by writing freely about him or her.

■ Identify other characters.

Brandi considered additional characters to include in her play. She listed three of them and described each one in a sentence.

Character List

> Jared—He is Gina's current boyfriend.
> Beth—She is Gina's friend who understands relationships.
> Pete—He is another friend with interests similar to Gina's.

Prewrite

List additional characters for your play. Depending on the conflict, you may need only one or two more characters. Describe each one in a sentence or two.

■ Plan the starting point.

Writing a play is a process of discovery. The story line will take shape *during* the process of writing. All you really need is a starting point. Brandi clustered possible starting points that would lead into the conflict of breaking up. Then she starred the one she wanted to use.

Cluster Diagram

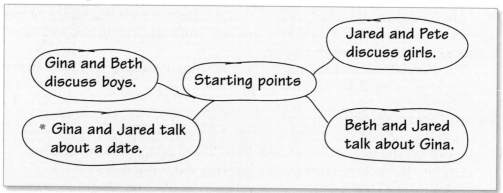

Jared and Pete discuss girls.

Gina and Beth discuss boys.

Starting points

* Gina and Jared talk about a date.

Beth and Jared talk about Gina.

Prewrite

Cluster possible starting points. Think of actions that will naturally lead into the conflict of your play. Star the starting point that you will use.

Try It!

Consider listing other actions or discussions that might take place in your play. But don't try to do too much planning at this point.

■ Think about stage directions.

Part of developing a play is deciding where and how the action will take place on stage. For the most part, you give this information in **stage directions**. These directions appear at the beginning and also within the play, whenever it is important to say what a character is doing on stage.

Brandi decided to have all four characters on stage at all times. A light shines on them when they talk or do something. Here are the simple stage directions at the beginning of Brandi's play.

Stage Directions

(Gina and Jared are on the platform in a pool of light. Beth and Pete sit in chairs, one on each side of the stage.)

Prewrite

Plan your initial stage directions. Describe where and how the opening action of your play takes place. Try to keep things simple.

■ Learn stage terminology.

Below is a diagram of the basic acting areas on a typical stage and the shorthand used to refer to each area. All stage directions are given from the point of view of an actor facing the audience. So moving to the actor's left and toward the audience would be called *down left* or *DL*.

Stage Diagram

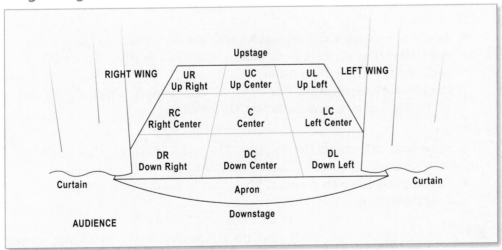

Creative Writing

Writing ■ Create your first draft.

In your play, remember to let your characters tell the story through what they say and do in response to the play's conflict. As you develop your play, have the characters reveal their personalities. The main character in the sample play is developed in the following ways.

From what she says, the reader learns that Gina is understanding:

> GINA: No, that's all right. You should spend some time with
> your dad.

From what she does, the reader learns (in the stage directions) that she is easygoing:

> GINA: *(Laughing and continuing her practicing.)* He broke a date,
> Beth, not my heart!

From what others say, the reader realizes Gina takes Pete for granted:

> PETE: I mean, you always come to me whenever he [Jared] doesn't
> want to do something.

■ Develop the three parts.

Keep in mind the interplay of action and dialogue in a play. Use the following guide to help you write your play.

Beginning

- ■ **Introduce the characters and the conflict.** Refer to your starting point on page **328** for help.
- ■ **Share background information** that your audience needs to understand the conflict.

Middle

- ■ **Add complications.** Introduce small problems that the character must overcome on the way to solving the main conflict. This will heighten the dramatic tension.
- ■ **Create a clear climax.** The climax is the point at which the main character makes a decision about the problem.

Ending

- ■ **Show the effects of the climax.** The main character should show or discuss any personal changes caused by her or his decision.
- ■ **Bring your play to a close.** Wrap up the action with a clear, definite ending.

Write your first draft. Use the information above as a guide as you develop your play.

Revising ■ Improve your writing.

Read your play out loud or have someone else read it to you. Change any lines that sound forced or unnatural. Ask these questions as you revise.

Revising Checklist

Ideas

_____ **1.** Is the conflict believable?

_____ **2.** Have I built suspense into the play?

_____ **3.** Does each character's personality come through in the play?

Organization

_____ **4.** Does my play build to a climax?

_____ **5.** Have I included enough stage directions?

Voice

_____ **6.** Does the dialogue sound natural?

Sentence Fluency

_____ **7.** Are all of the ideas easy to follow?

Editing ■ Check for conventions.

Use the following checklist as a guide when you check your play for proper formatting and for conventions.

Editing Checklist

Conventions

_____ **1.** Does the play follow basic script form?

_____ **2.** Have I checked for punctuation and capitalization?

_____ **3.** Have I checked for spelling errors?

Revise and edit your writing. Use the checklist above as a guide when you revise and edit the first draft of your play.

Revise

Creative Writing

Sample Advertising Script

You can create a commercial by writing an ad script. The following script satirizes (attacks with humor and sarcasm) get-rich-quick schemes.

The beginning establishes the setting and provides the first images.

PYRAMIDZ R US
Desert Exterior—Day

The Giza plateau sizzles beneath the sun, with two completed pyramids and the Great Pyramid half-built. While overseers bark, work gangs in loincloths haul gigantic stones across rolling logs. One beleaguered worker wears a sticker that says "Hello, I'm Jason." He staggers up in front of the camera and wipes his forehead.

JASON
Pyramid building is such a grind. Blazing sunlight, ten-ton stones—there's got to be a better way. . . .

ANNOUNCER (Voice–Over)
Now there is!

The middle uses a voice–over to convey a message.

FADE TO: INTERIOR BASEMENT—NIGHT
Jason sits on an old recliner. He flips through a telephone directory and dials a phone on an old TV tray.

JASON
Hello? I'm calling from Jason Industries. How would you like to make a million dollars this year? . . . Yes? Have I got a pyramid scheme for you!

The ad pokes fun at telemarketing.

ANNOUNCER (Voice–Over)
That's right—Pyramidz R Us can help you set up your own pyramid scheme. Like a pharaoh, you'll rise to the top by keeping everybody else on the bottom.

A pyramid of cash erupts from the floor under Jason's chair, carrying him up out of the house until he is high in the sky. He laughs joyously.

The ending includes a slogan and a strong final image.

JASON
Don't just make a pile of cash. Make a pyramid of it!

Try It!

Write an ad script. Think of a product or service to promote—or satirize. Create a commercial using images and words to convey your point.

Writing Poetry

What is a poem? Robert Frost says, "Poetry is when an emotion has found its thought and the thought has found words."

That captures the process you use to create a poem. First, you recall a powerful feeling. Then, when the feeling is stirred up within you, your thoughts pour out in words. Finally, you polish your poem so that it best conveys your feeling to the reader.

In this chapter, you will learn to write a free-verse poem that shows a special feeling. You will also learn about two special forms of poetry: a blues poem and a senryu poem.

Writing Guidelines

Subject: Sharing a special feeling
Form: Free-verse poem
Purpose: To entertain
Audience: Friends, family, and classmates

"You will not find poetry anywhere unless you bring some of it with you."
—Joseph Joubert

Sample Free-Verse Poem

Free-verse poems have a structure of their own and rarely rhyme. However, poets craft the sound and structure of each free-verse poem to make sure it conveys the right feeling. Deangelo Piccioni's free-verse poem expresses his feelings about a statue at a closed drive-in restaurant in his neighborhood.

The Smiling Chef

The restaurant is closed
    permanently

Still he stands
    bright-eyed with
    a mustached grin lifting
    rosy cheeks
    above a perfect red
    bow tie

And that thumb raised to say,
    "The food here is great!"

But the parking lot is empty
    permanently

All that remains
    is the vague scent of burgers
    and this cheery statue

Maybe his raised thumb is saying,
    "Can you give me a lift
    outta here?"

—Deangelo Piccioni

Respond to the reading. On your own paper, reflect on the ideas, organization, and voice of the free-verse poem above.

Ideas (1) What feeling does this poem give you? Explain why.

Organization (2) The poem is divided into six stanzas. How does their arrangement share the focus of the poem?

Voice & Word Choice (3) What words or phrases give this poem an upbeat tone? List at least three.

Prewriting ■ Choose a topic.

Think about a time or an event that gave you a special feeling. If you keep a diary or journal, look there for "mood memories," or page through a photo album for ideas. Then again, you could just look at the world around you. Deangelo listed the following topic ideas. He then put an asterisk next to the topic he wanted to share in a poem.

List

Topic Ideas	Feelings
playing basketball—excitement	
biking down a steep hill—thrilling	
listening to Green Day—awestruck	
* statue at the old drive-in—cheerfulness	
talking to my older sister on the phone—closeness	

Prewrite

Gather possible topics. Make a list of topics, ideas, and feelings for your poem. Then put an asterisk next to the one that you want to write about in a poem.

■ Gather details.

Like a painting, a poem creates a picture. As you think about your topic idea, consider different sights, sounds, smells, and so on. Deangelo created the following chart about a statue at a closed restaurant.

Sensory Chart

See	Hear	Smell	Taste	Feel
big raised thumb	silent parking lot	old asphalt faint smoke scent		coarse statue material
mustached grin				flecks of paint
smiling eyes		old burger grease		cheerfulness and optimism
flushed cheeks				sad/funny
red bow tie				

Prewrite

Gather details. Make a chart like the one above to gather sensory details about your topic idea.

Creative Writing

Prewriting ■ Use poetic techniques.

Poets often use figures of speech and special sound techniques in their writing. (See pages **340–341**.) For example, Deangelo uses *personification, repetition*, and *rhythm* in his poem.

■ Use personification.

Personification gives personality to an animal, object, or idea.

> **And that thumb raised to say,**
> **"The food here is great!"**

■ Add repetition.

Repetition emphasizes a word or phrase and can unify a poem.

> **The restaurant is closed**
> **permanently**

> **But the parking lot is empty**
> **permanently**

Consonance is the repetition of consonant sounds anywhere in words. (Also see *alliteration* on page **340**.) The repetition of the *r* sound in the following words adds a pleasing rhythm to the poem.

> **. . . lifting rosy cheeks above a perfect red bow tie.**

Explore poetic techniques. In your sensory chart, underline any ideas that suggest one of the techniques above.

Prewrite

Writing ■ Develop your first draft.

The first draft of a poem should spill onto the page. These guidelines will help you write freely.

- ■ **Think** about the idea and feeling you have chosen. Scan your sensory chart for details.
- ■ **Let** the mood or feeling generated by the topic guide your writing.
- ■ **Write** whatever comes to mind.

Write your first draft. Use the guidelines above as you write your poem. Also experiment with personification, repetition, and consonance.

Write

Revising ▪ Focus on the traits.

During the revising process, you improve your poem until it conveys the feeling you intend. In particular, look at the following traits.

- ▪ **Ideas** Do I use effective sensory details? Have I shared personal feelings or insights?
- ▪ **Organization** Do I use line breaks and indents to control the flow of my poem?
- ▪ **Voice** Do I sound interested in the poem's message?
- ▪ **Word Choice** Are my words precise? Have I used poetic techniques?
- ▪ **Sentence Fluency** Do the lines of the poem have an appealing rhythm?

Revise

Revise your poem. Using the questions above as a guide, revise your poem until it is the best that it can be.

Editing ▪ Check for errors.

Because poems are more concise than other types of writing, every word and punctuation mark is important. Careful editing is necessary.

- ▪ **Conventions** Is my poem free of errors that could distract the reader?

Edit

Edit your poem. Poems sometimes break the rules, but never by accident. Edit your poem for careless errors and make a neat final copy.

Presenting ▪ Share your poem.

Poetry is meant to be shared. Here are some ways to do that.

- ▪ **Post it.** Put it on a bulletin board, a Web site, or your refrigerator.
- ▪ **Submit it.** Send your poem to a contest or magazine.
- ▪ **Perform it.** Read your poem aloud to friends and family.
- ▪ **Send it.** Create an e-mail attachment with photos, animation, or other special effects.

Publish

Present your poem. Allow other people to read or hear what you have created. Ask your teacher for other publishing ideas.

Sample Blues Poem

A **blues poem** follows the tradition of blues music. You express yourself about something that gets you down—and end up feeling good! Some blues poems use rhyme and repeated lines like a song; others are more like free verse. Leida Sulzman wrote a rhyming poem about being bored.

The Saturday Morning Blues

Well, it's Saturday morning,
And I've got nothing to do.
I said it's Saturday morning,
But I've got nothing to do.
I'm just sitting here on the couch,
With the boring old Saturday morning blues.

All I have is a rhyming dictionary
To keep myself amused.
Just a rhyming dictionary
For me to peruse.
Guess I could try writing a poem,
But I can't seem to get enthused.

Maybe I should go outside and exercise,
So I don't just sit here and stew.
I guess I could go outside and skate awhile
Up and down the avenue.
I could skate across a parking lot,
Along the hypotenuse.

I'll need my helmet, knee and elbow pads,
So that I don't get a bruise.
You have to use that safety gear,
If you don't want to be transfused.
Now I'm going to go get my skate stuff,
And bid this boring room adieu.

—Leida Sulzman

Tip

- **Choose a topic.** Think about something that gives you the blues.
- **Gather details.** Make a chart of details about the topic.
- **Write your poem.** Convey your feelings to the reader in a fun way.

Write

Write your first draft. Use the tips above to guide your writing. Experiment with repetition, rhyme, and rhythm, but don't worry about getting things perfect.

Sample Senryu Poems

A **senryu** (pronounced *sĕń-rē-ü*) is similar to a haiku. Both types of poems have three unrhymed lines, with five syllables in the first line, seven in the second line, and five in the last line. However, instead of focusing on an image from nature, as the haiku does, the senryu deals with human nature, and always with a touch of humor or irony.

**Laughing so hard we
forget what we are saying—
which brings more laughter**

**A heart in sand could
last forever, if not for
the nearby ocean**

**Like a helpful book
with an attractive cover—
the smiling teacher**

Write

Write your own senryu. Think of something that amuses you about human nature and compose a senryu about it.

Special Poetry Techniques

Poets use a variety of special techniques, and these two pages define the most important ones.

Figures of Speech

- A **simile** *(sĭm'ə-lē)* compares two unlike things with the word *like* or *as*.

  The water in the cooler burbled
  like a happy baby.

- A **metaphor** *(mĕt'ə-fôr)* compares two unlike things without using *like* or *as*.

  His fingers were acrobats tumbling
  down the row of keys.

- **Personification** *(pər-sŏn'ə-fĭ-kā'shən)* is a technique that gives human traits to something that is nonhuman.

  Distant mountains call, "Come closer."

- **Hyperbole** *(hī-pûr'bə-lē)* is an exaggerated statement, often humorous.

  She sliced a piece of cake so thin
  it fluttered to the plate.

Sounds of Poetry

- **Alliteration** *(ə-lĭt'ə-ra'shən)* is the repetition of consonant sounds at the beginning of words.

  A jester's job
  is to joust with jibes.

- **Assonance** *(as'ə-nəns)* is the repetition of vowel sounds anywhere in words.

  Still he stands
  bright-eyed

- **Consonance** *(kon'sə-nəns)* is the repetition of consonant sounds anywhere in words.

  A jester's job
  is to joust with jibes.

- **Line breaks** help control the rhythm of a poem. The reader naturally pauses at the end of a line. There's also added emphasis on the last word in a line.

    a mustached grin lifting
      rosy cheeks
      above a perfect red
      bow tie

- **Onomatopoeia** *(on´ə-mat´ə-pē´ə)* is the use of words that sound like what they name.

    The campfire hissed and popped for attention.

- **Repetition** *(rĕp´i-tĭsh´ən)* uses the same word or phrase more than once, for emphasis or for rhythm.

    Inching across the walk,
    inching across the driveway,
    inching across the lawn,
    and oh-so-slowly up the fence.

- **Rhyme** means using words whose endings sound alike.

    End rhyme happens at the end of lines.
      What wonder
      in thunder!

    Internal rhyme happens within lines.
      Asking for crackers, and other snacks

- **Rhythm** *(rĭth´əm)* is the pattern of accented and unaccented syllables in a poem. The rhythm of free-verse poetry tends to flow naturally, like speaking. Traditional poetry follows a more regular pattern, as in the following example.

    What wonder
    in thunder!

Creative Writing

Try It!

Write your own example for one or more of the techniques explained on these two pages. Then expand one of your examples into a complete poem.

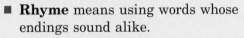

Research Writing

Report Writing
Research Skills

How would you describe intelligence? Most people are impressed when someone has in-depth knowledge about a certain topic. However, intelligence means more than knowing facts. It also means knowing where to find information when you need it. To be an effective researcher, you need to know how to find reliable information. With the increased reliance on sources of information on the Internet, it is essential to know which sources you can trust, and which ones you can't trust.

In this chapter, you will learn how to use the Internet and the library, and you will also learn how to weigh the merits of the sources you find. These skills will prove valuable in the classroom and in the world of work.

- **Primary vs. Secondary Sources**
- **Evaluating Sources of Information**
- **Using the Internet**
- **Using the Library**
- **Using Reference Books**

"Knowledge is of two kinds. We know the subject ourselves, or we know where we can find information upon it."
—Samuel Johnson

Primary vs. Secondary Sources

Primary sources are original sources. These sources (*diaries, people, events, surveys*) inform you directly, not through another person's explanation or interpretation. Ideally, when you research a topic, you should find as much primary information as possible. (See below.)

Primary sources include . . .

- **Diaries, Journals, and Letters** You can often find these in museums, in libraries, or at historic sites.
- **Presentations** A speaker at a museum or a historic site can give you firsthand information, but be aware of the presenter's own interpretation of events.
- **Interviews** Talk to an expert on your research topic. You can do this by phone, e-mail, or letter.
- **Surveys and Questionnaires** These tools help you gather a great deal of data from many people.
- **Observation and Participation** Your own observations of a person, a place, or an event provide excellent firsthand information. Participating in an event can give you insights that cannot be discovered through the reports of others.

Secondary sources are third-person accounts found in research done by other people. Much of the news (*television, radio, Internet, books, magazines*) can be considered a secondary source of information. Keep in mind that, by their very nature, secondary sources represent filtered information that may contain biases or misunderstandings.

Primary Sources	Secondary Sources
1. Reading the journal of a mountain climber	1. Exploring a Web site about mountain climbing
2. Listening to a presentation by a mountain climber	2. Reading a magazine article about mountain climbing
3. Interviewing a mountain climber	3. Watching a TV documentary about a mountain climber

Try It!

List primary sources you might use to learn about the governor of your state. Also list secondary sources you might use to write about deep-sea exploration.

Evaluating Sources of Information

You may find a lot of information about your research topic. But before you use any of it, decide whether or not the information is dependable. Use the following questions to help you decide about the reliability of your sources.

Is the source a primary source or a secondary source?

You can usually trust the information you've collected yourself, but be careful with secondary sources. Although many of them are reliable, they can contain outdated or incorrect information.

Is the source an expert?

An expert knows more about a subject than other people. Using an expert's thoughts and opinions can make your paper more believable. If you aren't sure about a source's authority, ask a teacher or librarian what he or she thinks.

Is the information accurate?

Sources that people respect are usually very accurate. Big-city newspapers (*New York Times* or *Chicago Tribune*) and well-known Web sites (CNN or ESPN) are reliable sources of information. Little-known sources that do not support their facts or that contain errors may not be reliable.

Tip

Be especially cautious about the accuracy of information on the Internet. While there is an incredible amount of information available on the Net, there is also a lot of misinformation.

Is the information fair and complete?

A reliable source should provide information fairly, covering all sides of a subject. If a source presents only one side of a subject, its information may not be accurate. To make themselves sound better, politicians and advertisers often present just their side of a subject. Avoid sources that are one-sided, and look for those that are balanced.

Is the information current?

Usually, you want to have the most up-to-date information about a subject. Sometimes information changes, and sources can become outdated quickly. Check the copyright page in a book, the issue date of a magazine, and the posting date of online information.

Research

Using the Internet

Because you can access many resources by surfing the Web, the Internet is a valuable research aid. You can find government publications, encyclopedia entries, business reports, and firsthand observations on the Internet. The increasing speed of modern computers makes the Internet even more inviting. When researching on the Internet, keep in mind the following points.

■ Remember these points.

■ **Use the Web wisely.** Sites that include *.edu, .org,* and *.gov* in the Web address are often reliable. These sites are from educational, nonprofit, or government agencies. If you have questions about the reliability of a site, talk to your teacher. (See also page **345**.)

■ **Try several search engines.** Because there is an enormous amount of information on the Web, no one search engine can handle it all. So employ at least two search engines when you surf the Web. Enter keywords to start your research or enter specific questions to zero in on your topic.

When you type a term into a search engine's input box, the search engine scans its database for matching sites. Then the engine returns recommendations for you to explore.

■ **Take advantage of links.** When you read a page, watch for links to other sites. These may offer different perspectives or points of view on your topic.

■ **Experiment with keywords.** Sometimes you must ask a number of different questions or use different keywords to find the information you need. Remember to check the date of the Web site. Abandoned Web sites may contain outdated information.

■ **Ignore Web sites that advertise research papers for sale.** Using these sites is dishonest. Teachers and librarians can recognize and verify when a paper is someone else's work.

■ **Learn your school's Internet policy.** Using the computer at school is a privilege. To maintain that privilege, follow your school's Internet policy and any guidelines your parents may have set.

Try It!

Go to *www.thewritesource.com* and click on "Research Links." Practice using some of the search engines shown on that page to research a topic of your choice. What differences between search engines did you notice?

Using the Library

The Internet may be a good place to initiate your research, but a library is often a more valuable place to continue your research. A library offers materials that are more in-depth and reliable than what you find on the Internet. Most libraries contain the following resources.

Books

- **Reference** books include encyclopedias, almanacs, dictionaries, atlases, and directories, plus resources such as consumer information guides and car-repair manuals. Reference books provide a quick review or overview of research topics.
- **Nonfiction** texts are a good source of facts that can serve as a foundation for your research. Check the copyright dates to be sure you are reading reasonably up-to-date information. (Some libraries organize nonfiction using the Library of Congress system, but most libraries use the Dewey decimal system as shown on page **349**.)
- **Fiction** can sometimes aid or enhance your research. For example, a historical novel can reveal people's feelings about a particular time in history. (Fiction books are grouped together in alphabetical order by the authors' last names.)

Periodicals

Periodicals (*newspapers* and *magazines*) are grouped together in a library. Use the *Readers' Guide to Periodical Literature* to find articles in periodicals. (See page **354**.) You will have to ask the librarian for older issues.

The Media Section

The media section of your library includes DVD's, CD-ROM's, CD's, cassettes, and videotapes. These resources can immerse you in an event. Keep in mind, however, that directors and screenwriters may present events in a way that accommodates their personal views.

Computers

Computers are available in most libraries, and many are connected to the Internet, although there may be restrictions on their use.

 Try It!

Visit your school or public library. Familiarize yourself with the floor plan so that you will know exactly where to look for resources.

Research

■ Use the computer catalog.

Some libraries still use a card catalog located in a cabinet with drawers. Most libraries, however, have put their entire catalog on computer. Each system varies a bit, so ask for help if you're not sure how the system in your library works. A **computer catalog** lists the books held in your library and affiliated systems. It lets you know if a book is available or if you must wait for it.

■ Use a variety of search methods.

When you are using a computer catalog, you can find information about a book with any of the following methods:

1. If you know it, enter the **title** of the book.
2. If you know the **author** of the book, enter the first and last names.
3. A general search of your **subject** will also help you find books on your topic. Enter either the subject or a related keyword.

Sample Computer Catalog Screen

The key to the right identifies the types of information provided for a particular resource, in this case, a book. Once you locate the book you need, make note of the call number. You will use this to find the book on the shelf.

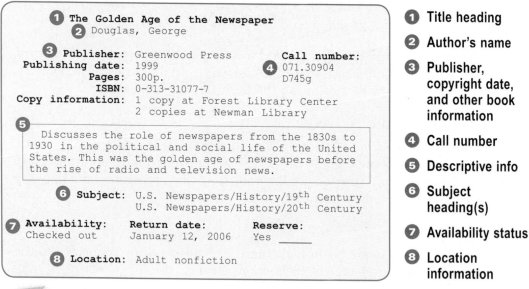

Try It!

Use a computer catalog to find a book about a topic that interests you. Read all of the information on the catalog screen and then locate the book.

■ Understand call numbers.

All nonfiction books in the library have **call numbers**. The books are arranged on the shelves according to these numbers. Call numbers are usually based on the **Dewey decimal classification** system, which divides nonfiction books into 10 subject categories.

000–099	**General Works**	500–599	**Sciences**
100–199	**Philosophy**	600–699	**Technology**
200–299	**Religion**	700–799	**Arts and Recreation**
300–399	**Social Sciences**	800–899	**Literature**
400–499	**Languages**	900–999	**History and Geography**

A call number often has a decimal in it, followed by the first letter of an author's name. Note how the following call numbers are ordered on the shelves.

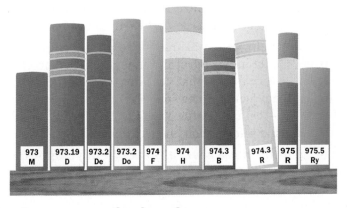

| 973 M | 973.19 D | 973.2 De | 973.2 Do | 974 F | 974 H | 974.3 B | 974.3 R | 975 R | 975.5 Ry |

■ Identify the parts of a book.

Each part of a book provides valuable information. The *title page* includes the title of the book, the author's name, and the publisher's name and city. The *copyright page* follows with the year the book was published. The *preface, foreword,* or *introduction* comes before the table of contents and tells why the book was written. The *table of contents* lists the names and page numbers of sections and chapters in the book. At the end of the book, you may find at least one *appendix*, containing various maps, tables, and lists. Finally, the *index* is an alphabetical list of important topics and their page numbers in the book.

Try It!

For a book from your library, write down its title and call number, its publisher's name and city, the year it was published, and the heading and page numbers for one section in the table of contents.

Using Reference Books

A reference book is a special kind of nonfiction book that contains specific facts or background information. The reference section includes encyclopedias, dictionaries, almanacs, and so on. Usually, reference books cannot be checked out, so you must use them in the library.

■ Refer to encyclopedias.

An encyclopedia is a set of books (or a CD-ROM) that contains basic information on topics from A to Z. Topics are arranged alphabetically. Here are some tips for using encyclopedias.

Tips for Using Encyclopedias

- **At the end of an article, there is often a list of related articles.**
  You can read these other articles to learn more about your topic.

- **The index can help you find out more about your topic.**
  The index is usually in a separate volume or at the end of the last volume. It lists every article that contains information about a topic. For example, if you look up "newspapers" in the index, you would find a list of articles—"United States Media," "Freedom of the Press," and so on—that include information on that topic. (See below.)

- **Libraries usually have several sets of encyclopedias.**
  Review each set and decide which one best serves your needs. (Always check with your teacher first to see if you can use an encyclopedia as a source for your research.)

Sample Encyclopedia Index

Encyclopedia volume

United States News Media U: 383 with pictures

Associated Press **A: 340**

Free Press **F: 213**

Page numbers   Yellow Journalism **Y: 135–137**

See also the list of related articles in the United States News Media *article.*

Related topics

United States Magazines **U: 393**

United States Penny Press **U: 394**

Day, Benjamin **D: 85**

Political Factors **U: 395**

■ Consult other reference books.

Most libraries contain several types of reference books in addition to encyclopedias.

Almanacs

Almanacs are books filled with facts and statistics about many different subjects. *The World Almanac and Book of Facts* contains celebrity profiles; statistics about politics, business, and sports; plus consumer information.

Atlases

Atlases contain detailed maps of the world, continents, countries, and so on. They also contain statistics and related information. Specialized atlases cover topics like outer space and the oceans.

Dictionaries

Dictionaries contain definitions of words and their origins. Biographical dictionaries focus on famous people. Specialized dictionaries deal with science, history, medicine, and other subjects.

Directories

Directories list information about groups of people, businesses, and organizations. The most widely used directories are telephone books.

Periodical Indexes

Periodical indexes list articles in magazines and newspapers. These indexes are arranged alphabetically by subject.

- The *Readers' Guide to Periodical Literature* lists articles from many publications. (See page **354**.)
- The *New York Times Index* lists articles from the *New York Times* newspaper.

Other Reference Books

Some reference books do not fit into any one category but are recognized by their names:

- *Facts on File* includes thousands of short but informative facts about events, discoveries, people, and places.
- *Facts About the Presidents* presents information about all of the American presidents.
- *Bartlett's Familiar Quotations* lists thousands of quotations from famous people.

Research

■ Check a dictionary.

A dictionary gives many types of information:

- **Guide words:** These are the first and last words on the page. Guide words show whether the word you are looking for will be found alphabetically on that page.
- **Entry words:** Each word defined in a dictionary is called an entry word. Entry words are listed alphabetically.
- **Etymology:** Many dictionaries give etymologies (word histories) for certain words. An etymology tells what language an English word came from, how the word entered our language, and when it was first used.
- **Syllable divisions:** A dictionary tells you where you may divide a word.
- **Pronunciation and accent marks:** A dictionary tells you how to pronounce a word and also provides a key to pronunciation symbols, usually at the bottom of each page.
- **Illustrations:** For some entries, an illustration, photograph, or drawing is provided.
- **Parts of speech:** A dictionary tells you what part(s) of speech a word is, using these abbreviations:

n.	**noun**	*tr. v.*	**transitive verb**	*adj.*	**adjective**
pron.	**pronoun**	*interj.*	**interjection**	*adv.*	**adverb**
intr. v.	**intransitive verb**	*conj.*	**conjunction**	*prep.*	**preposition**

- **Spelling and capitalization:** The dictionary shows the acceptable spelling, as well as capitalization, for words. (For some words, more than one spelling is given.)
- **Definitions:** Some dictionaries are large enough to list all of the meanings for a word. Most standard-size dictionaries, however, will list only three or four of the most commonly accepted meanings. Take time to read all of the meanings to be sure that you are using the word correctly.

Try It!

Ask your teacher for three words you can look up in the dictionary.

1. Identify the part(s) of speech for each word.
2. Provide the first one or two meanings for each word.
3. Identify the etymology (if given) for each word.

Sample Dictionary Page

Guide words —

Entry word —

cir·cle (sûr′kəl) *n.* **1.** A plane curve everywhere equidistant from a given fixed point, the center. **2.** A planar region bounded by a circle. **3.** Something, such as a ring, shaped like such a plane curve. **4.** A circular course, circuit, or orbit. **5.** A traffic circle. **6.** A curved section or tier of seats in a theater. **7.** A series or process that finishes at its starting point or repeats itself; a cycle. **8.** A group of people sharing an interest, activity, or achievement. **9.** A territorial or administrative division, esp. of a province, in some European countries. **10.** A sphere of influence or interest; domain. **11.** *Logic* A vicious circle. ❖ *v.* **-cled, -cling, -cles** —*tr.* **1.** To make or form a circle around; enclose. **2.** To move in a circle around. —*intr.* To move in a circle. —*idiom:* **circle the wagons** To take a defensive position. [ME *cercle* < OFr. < Lat. *circulus,*

Etymology —

dim. of *circus,* circle < Gk. *kirkos, krikos.*] —**cir′cler** (-klər) *n.*

circle graph *n.* See **pie chart.**

Syllable divisions —

cir·clet (sûr′klĭt) *n.* A small circle, esp. a circular ornament. [ME *cerclet* < OFr., dim. of *cercle,* circle. See CIRCLE.]

Pronunciation and accent marks —

cir·cuit (sûr′kĭt) *n.* **1a.** A closed, usu. circular line that goes around an object or area. **b.** The region enclosed by such a line. **2a.** A path or route that returns to its starting point. **b.** The act of following such a path or route. **c.** A journey made on such a path or route. **3.** *Electronics* **a.** A closed path followed by an electric current. **b.** A configuration of electrically or electromagnetically connected components or devices. **4a.** A regular or accustomed course from place to place; a round: *the lecture circuit.* **b.** The area or district thus covered, esp. a territory under the jurisdiction of a judge in which periodic court sessions are held. **5a.** An association of theaters among which plays, acts, or films move for presentation. **b.** A group of nightclubs, show halls, or resorts at which entertainers appear in turn. **c.** An association of teams or clubs. **d.** A series of competitions held in different places. ❖ *intr. & tr.v.* **-cuit·ed, -cuit·ing, -cuits** To make a circuit or circuit of. [ME, circumference < OFr. < Lat. *circuitus,* a going around < p. part. of *circumīre,* to go around : *circum-,* circum- + *īre,* to go; see **ei-** in App.]

Illustration —

circuit simple electrical circuit system

Parts of speech —

circuit board *n. Computer Science* An insulated board on which interconnected circuits and components such as microchips are mounted or etched.

circuit breaker *n.* An automatic switch that stops the flow of electric current in an overloaded electric circuit.

Spelling —

circuit court *n.* A state court that holds sessions at several different places within a judicial district.

cir·cu·i·tous (sər-kyōō′ĭ-təs) *adj.* Being or taking a roundabout, lengthy course. [< Med.Lat. *circuitōsus* < Lat. *circuitus,* a going around. See CIRCUIT.] —**cir·cu′i·tous·ly** *adv.* —**cir·cu′i·ty, cir·cu′i·tous·ness** *n.*

circuit rider *n.* A cleric who travels from church to church.

cir·cuit·ry (sûr′kĭ-trē) *n., pl.* **-ries 1.** The design of or a detailed plan for an electric circuit. **2.** Electric circuits considered as a group.

cir·cu·lar (sûr′kyə-lər) *adj.* **1.** Of or relating to a circle. **2a.** Shaped like or nearly like a circle; round. **b.** Moving in or forming a circle. **3.** Circuitous; roundabout. **4.** Using a premise to prove a conclusion that in turn is used to prove the premise: *a circular argument.* **5.** Addressed or distributed to a large number of persons. ❖ *n.* A circular printed advertisement, directive, or notice. [ME *circuler* < AN < Lat. *circulāris* < *circulus,* circle. See CIRCLE.] —**cir′cu·lar′i·ty** (-lăr′ĭ-tē) *n.* —**cir′cu·lar·ly** *adv.*

circular function *n.* See **trigonometric function.**

Definitions —

cir·cu·lar·ize (sûr′kyə-lə-rīz′) *tr.v.* **-ized, -iz·ing, -iz·es 1.** To publicize with circulars. **2.** To canvass or poll using a questionnaire. —**cir′cu·lar·i·za′tion** (-lər-ĭ-zā′shən) *n.*

ă	pat	oi	boy
ā	pay	ou	out
âr	care	ŏŏ	took
ä	father	ōō	boot
ĕ	pet	ŭ	cut
ē	be	ûr	urge
ĭ	pit	th	thin
ī	pie	*th*	this
îr	pier	hw	which
ŏ	pot	zh	vision
ō	toe	ə	about,
ô	paw		item

Stress marks:
′ (primary);
′ (secondary), as in
lexicon (lĕk′sĭ-kŏn′)

■ Find magazine articles.

Periodical guides are located in the reference or periodical section of the library. These guides alphabetically list topics and articles found in magazines, newspapers, and journals. Some guides are printed volumes, some are CD-ROM's, and some are on library Web sites. Ask your librarian for help.

Readers' Guide to Periodical Literature

The *Readers' Guide to Periodical Literature* is a well-known periodical reference source and is found in most libraries. The following tips will help you look up your topic in this resource:

- Articles are always listed alphabetically by author and topic.
- Some topics are subdivided, with each article listed under the appropriate subtopic.
- Cross-references refer to related topic entries where you may find more articles pertinent to your topic.

Sample *Readers' Guide* Format

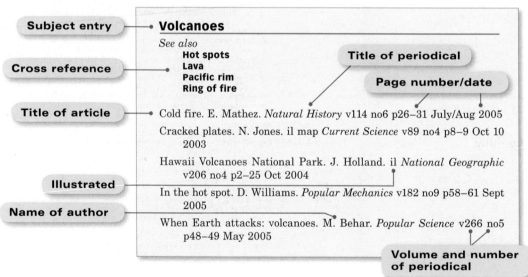

Tip

When you find a listing for your topic, write down the name and issue date of the magazine and the title and page numbers of the article. Your librarian may get the periodical for you, or you may need to find it yourself.

Research Writing
Research Report

Morning news, noon news, nightly news, special news reports, newspapers, news channels, news stations, newsmagazines, the Internet—the news media bombards us on all sides with late-breaking stories. Obviously, this hasn't always been the case. Ancient kings waited weeks or months for runners bearing news from the frontier, and the common people seldom knew about events outside their own communities. How then has our modern news media come into existence?

This chapter will help you to write a research paper about an important aspect in the development of the news media in the United States. In the process, you may gain a better understanding of how and why the media operates as it does.

Writing Guidelines

Subject: **An important development in the history of the news media in the United States**
Form: **Research report**
Purpose: **To research and present historical information**
Audience: **Classmates**

"There's no use getting into a writing schedule until you've done the [research] and you have the material."

—Tom Wolfe

Title Page and Outline

Gabriella Neuhoff chose to write her research report about the start of the penny press in the United States in the 1830s. You can read her report starting on the next page. Below are the title page and outline of her paper. Some teachers require a title page and an outline. If your teacher does, follow any special instructions he or she may give you.

A Penny for Your Paper

Gabriella Neuhoff
Mr. Delnoce
English
9 May 2006

Title Page
Center the title one-third of the way down the page. Center and double-space the writer information two-thirds of the way down the page.

Outline
Center the title one inch from the top of the page. Double-space throughout.

i

A Penny for Your Paper

Introduction: The creation of the penny press paved the way for the modern daily newspaper.

I. Colonial newspapers in America were different from those today.
   A. They needed government authorization.
   B. John Peter Zenger was tried for libel for criticizing the governor.
   C. Freedom of the press became the focus of Zenger's trial.

II. Early newspapers were different from ours in other ways, too.
   A. Commercial papers had advertisements, ship schedules, product prices, money conversion tables.
   B. Political papers contained stuffy political statements.
   C. News in both types was out of date.
   D. These papers were mainly for the wealthy.

III. In the early 1800s, more people began to read newspapers.
   A. They liked interesting items like the police court reports.
   B. The nation was changing and growing.
   C. The masses were ready for a new type of paper.

Sample Research Report

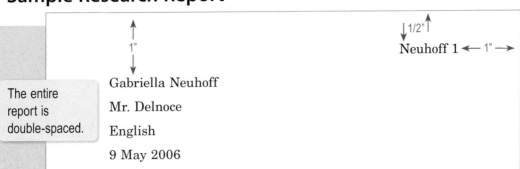

↓1/2"↑
Neuhoff 1 ←— 1" —→

↑1"↓

Gabriella Neuhoff

Mr. Delnoce

English

9 May 2006

A Penny for Your Paper

The entire report is double-spaced.

Have you ever seen newsboys in a movie shouting "Extra! Extra! Read all about it!"? Have you ever wondered why newspapers include an entertainment section and an opinion page? Would you like to know who the first Washington news correspondent was? You can find answers to these questions by studying the

Beginning
The writer introduces her topic and states her thesis (underlined).

←— 1" —→ start of the "penny press" in the 1830s. The creation of the penny press paved the way for the modern daily newspaper.

Before the Penny Press

Colonial newspapers in America were different from those today. For one thing, they could not be published without the approval of the government. In 1690, the publisher of the first newspaper in the colonies found this out the hard way. The government arrested him and destroyed all copies of his paper because he didn't get proper approval. In another case, John Peter Zenger published articles in the New York Weekly Journal that criticized the governor. Authorities arrested Zenger and tried him for libel (Public). Freedom of the press became the focus of his

Middle
The first middle paragraphs tell about the topic's history.

↑1"↓

Research

Neuhoff 2

famous trial in 1735. He was eventually set free.

The early newspapers were different from ours in many other ways, too. Colonial papers were usually "4-page weeklies containing local ads, . . . local hearsay, and large, unedited chunks of . . . news from the London press" (Public). Even after the American Revolution, newspapers lacked interesting and timely news. Commercial papers "were filled with advertisements, ship schedules, . . . product prices, money conversion tables, and stale news," and political papers "contained staid [stuffy] political discourses in addition to yesterday's or last week's or last month's news" (Thompson 2). These newspapers were expensive and read mostly by wealthy citizens.

Because of increased literacy in the early 1800s, more people began to read newspapers. Common people paid special attention to the more interesting sections, especially the coverage of the police court (Thompson 2). This was also a time of great change for the nation. The country elected Andrew Jackson, the first unaristocratic president. More immigrants were entering the country, and cities were growing rapidly (Younes 14). The stage was set for the penny press, a new type of newspaper that would appeal to the masses.

Ellipses show that words have been left out of a quotation.

Brackets show that a word has been added to explain something.

A source and page number are identified in parentheses.

Neuhoff 3

The Rise of the Sun

In 1833, Benjamin Day, the owner of a printing
company in New York, started the Sun, the first successful
penny paper. Walking to work each day, he passed
Chatham Street, where street vendors sold items for
a penny (Thompson 8). Day thought he could make a
penny newspaper to sell on the street. On September 3,
1833, he sold the first edition of the Sun. It was only a
single sheet of paper, folded in the middle. On the front
page, Day printed advertisements copied from other
papers. The other three pages contained a mix of ads
and news from other papers, two humorous tall tales,
and the police report copied from the Courier & Enquirer
(10–11). His paper was an instant success. Soon Day had
enough new ads to make the paper profitable even with
its penny price.

Day quickly realized that he needed help. While he
managed the business, someone would have to attend
the courts each day and write the police report. A man
named George Wisner became Day's court reporter and
partner (Thompson 13). Day and Wisner didn't always
agree, and the paper reflected their different opinions
(15–17). This debate of ideas set the Sun apart from the
older, more conservative political newspapers.

Day also needed help selling the paper. He decided
to use a system known as the "London plan." Under this

The next part
of the report
focuses on the
penny press.

Each paragraph
begins with a
topic sentence,
followed by
supporting
details.

Neuhoff 4

plan, he offered newspapers at a reduced rate to people who then sold their copies and pocketed the profit. The first person to join him was a 10-year-old boy. Before long, "newsboys" were selling the papers all over New York (Thompson 12–13), and the <u>Sun</u> became the most popular paper in the city.

The Trumpeting of the <u>Herald</u>

In 1835, James Gordon Bennett started another successful penny paper in New York called the <u>Herald</u>. Bennett had lived in many places, from Canada to South Carolina, and had gained valuable experience as a writer and an editor. Historians say that he was America's first Washington news correspondent, for the <u>New York Enquirer</u>. These experiences helped prepare Bennett to start his own paper (Douglas 27–29). Bennett started out alone, in a dark cellar room, using a plank and two boxes as a desk. However, before long, the <u>Herald</u> would outsell the <u>Sun</u>. In fact, at its best, the <u>Herald</u> sold more copies worldwide than even the most respected European papers (Younes 16).

Bennett knew how to get the attention of readers. They liked the <u>Herald</u> because Bennett wrote opinion pieces that were "saucy, impertinent [disrespectful], and funny" (Thompson 34). Bennett also filled his paper with sensational news stories that made the <u>Sun</u> seem tame by comparison, and he placed these

Headings help the reader understand the report's organization.

Information from a key source is paraphrased.

The writer's last name and page number appear on every page.

stories on the front page to gain more attention. Many historians give Bennett the credit for the first "crisis news reporting," based on his eyewitness news about New York City's Great Fire of 1835 and his writing about the Jewett murder trial (Douglas 30). The Herald also quickly became the best source of Wall Street news (Thompson 59). Along with these stories, Bennett included entertainment news. All of these things helped make the Herald a great success.

The Conscience of the Tribune

In 1841, Horace Greeley started another penny newspaper in New York. It was called the Tribune. Like the Sun and the Herald, the Tribune relied on advertising for its main income, and it included sensational stories to attract readers. However, Greeley believed that a newspaper should do more than just make money. He thought it should keep people informed about important events and educate them about important ideas.

The Tribune gave readers crime stories and stories about local events, but it "downplayed sensational stories by placing them on inside pages" (Thompson 97). This paper also included poetry and literature by respected authors. Under Greeley's direction, the Tribune showed "a social conscience in its news columns and reform-minded editorials" (98).

Quotations from experts add authority to the report.

The <u>Tribune</u> soon rivaled the <u>Herald</u> as the most popular paper of the time, and through the <u>Tribune</u>, Greeley became a well-known national figure. He influenced the opinion of Americans everywhere on topics like "labor, education, [and] temperance" (Thompson 112). Greeley showed that a newspaper could help shape a nation.

After the Penny Press

Modern newspapers continue to focus on disaster and crime news, along with editorials and stories about business and entertainment. Also, topics in the public interest continue to appear in the news, just as they did in the <u>Tribune</u>. The obligation to the public that today's newspaper reporters and editors feel, originated with the penny press. Further, modern newspapers still "rely heavily on advertising as a main source of income and that is also a main reason they are still being offered at relatively low prices today" (Vance). All these things show that "the age of modern-day journalism began with the penny press" (Thompson 3). The free press that grew from those early papers has helped to shape our nation, just as the Founding Fathers had hoped.

Ending
The conclusion discusses the topic in relation to the present.

The final sentence leaves the reader with something to think about.

Neuhoff 7

Works Cited

Douglas, George H. The Golden Age of the Newspaper.
      Westport, CT: Greenwood, 1999.

A separate page alphabetically lists sources cited in the paper.

Public Affairs Television. "Milestones in the History
      of Media and Politics." Now with Bill Moyers.
      Kristin Miller. 2005. Public Affairs Television.
      27 April 2005 <http://www.pbs.org/now/politics/
      mediahistory.html>.

Second and third lines are indented five spaces.

Thompson, Susan. The Penny Press. Northport, AL:
      Vision, 2004.

Vance, Jennifer. "The Penny Press." A Brief History of
      Newspapers in America. 29 April 2005 <http://
      iml.jou.ufl.edu/projects/Spring04/Vance/
      pennypress.html.>

Younes, Robert. "In for a Penny." American Publisher
      1 Oct. 2005: 14+.

Respond to the reading. After you have finished reading the sample research report, answer the following questions.

Ideas (1) What is the focus or main idea of this paper?
(2) List at least three facts that support this main idea.

Organization (3) How do the headings help organize the report?

Voice & Word Choice (4) Does the writer sound knowledgeable about her topic? Explain.

Research

Prewriting

To get to the top of a mountain, you must take one step at a time. The same is true of a research project. First, you need to choose an interesting topic. Next, you must carefully research the topic, establish a thesis, and plan your writing. Then you'll be ready to write.

Keys to Effective Prewriting

1. For your topic, choose an interesting event in the history of the news media in the United States.

2. List questions you want to have answered about the topic.

3. Be sure that there is enough information available about your topic.

4. Use a gathering grid to organize your research questions and answers. Use note cards to keep track of longer answers. (See pages 367–368.)

5. Be careful to cite the sources of any information you paraphrase or quote.

6. Write down the publication details of all your sources as you do your research.
   (See page 370.)

■ Select a topic.

When you are assigned a research report, your teacher will suggest a general subject area. Your job is to identify an interesting specific topic within that subject area. To consider possible topics about the news media, Gabriella decided to make a time line of developments that she had learned about in her history textbook. She then circled the topic she wanted to research.

Time Line

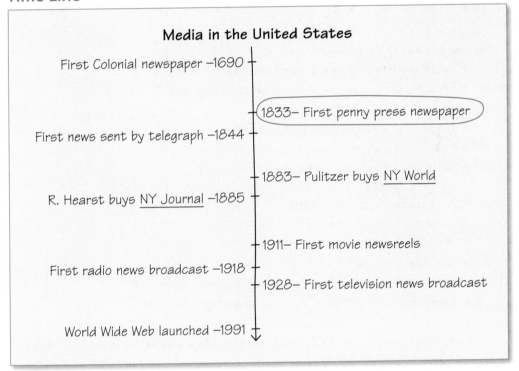

Media in the United States

First Colonial newspaper −1690

1833− First penny press newspaper

First news sent by telegraph −1844

1883− Pulitzer buys NY World

R. Hearst buys NY Journal −1885

1911− First movie newsreels

First radio news broadcast −1918

1928− First television news broadcast

World Wide Web launched −1991

Prewrite

Review possible topics. For a research report on news media in the United States, you may choose one of the topics in the sample time line above. Or you can consider other possible topics, including those listed below.

- How the "New Journalism" has shaped reporting
- The significance of the Hearst/Pulitzer conflict
- The *Progressive* magazine and the H-bomb
- The effect of advertising dollars on news coverage

Prewrite

Select a topic. Choose one specific topic for your research report. Then, on your own paper, explain the reason for your choice in a brief freewriting.

Research

■ Size up your topic.

An effective research report about a historical event related to the media in the United States should cover three basic areas: (1) the circumstances before the event, (2) how the event came about, and (3) how the event affected the development of the media.

Gabriella checked an encyclopedia and did a quick Internet search for basic facts about her topic. She took notes on her findings.

Research Notes

Before the Penny Press
- Colonial American newspapers printed for the wealthy
- Papers devoted to business or political parties

How It Came About
- The Sun started in New York in 1833
- Paper priced at a penny
- News that appealed to the common people
- Herald followed
- Bennett an outspoken editor
- Horace Greeley Tribune
- Tried to be unbiased

After the Penny Press
- Papers reporting current news
- Newspapers as people's main source of information

With these basic facts in hand, Gabriella knew that she could find enough information to write a research report about the penny press. She decided to focus on the first three penny newspapers: the *Sun*, the *Herald*, and the *Tribune*. She was confident that she could find more facts and details about these papers.

Prewrite

Size up your topic. Do some initial research about your topic using an encyclopedia and the Internet. List the key details you find. Will you be able to find enough information to write a research report? If not, consider another topic. (In most cases, your teacher will not want you to use an encyclopedia as an actual resource for your research report.)

Prewriting ▪ Use a gathering grid.

A gathering grid can help you organize your research. Gabriella used a grid to guide her research about the first penny papers. Down the left-hand side, she listed questions she needed to answer about her topic. Across the top, she listed sources she found to answer those questions. For answers too long to fit in the grid, Gabriella used note cards. (See page **368**.)

Gathering Grid

PENNY PRESS	Public Affairs Television (Web site)	The Penny Press (book)	The Golden Age of the Newspaper (book)	"In for a Penny" (magazine article)
1. What was the media like before the penny press?	Newspapers were "mouthpieces for political parties."	See note card #1.	Most colonial papers were published weekly. page 2	
2. How did the penny press come about?	Day's <u>Sun</u> and Bennett's <u>Herald</u> appealed to the masses with sensational stories and a low price.	Growing literacy, prosperity, and public education provided a new audience. page 2	See note card #2.	
3. What effect has the penny press had on modern media?			"In many ways, the age of modern day journalism began with the penny press." page 3	See note card #3.

Prewrite

Create a gathering grid. Make a list of questions about your topic in the left-hand column. Across the top, list sources you will use. Fill in the grid with answers you find. Use note cards for longer, more detailed answers.

Research

Prewriting ■ Create note cards.

While a gathering grid allows you to see all your research at a glance, sometimes an answer needs more space. Use note cards when that is the case. Number each new card and write the question at the top. Then answer the question with a paraphrase (see page **369**), a quotation, or a list. At the bottom of each card, identify the source of the information (including a page number if appropriate).

Note cards

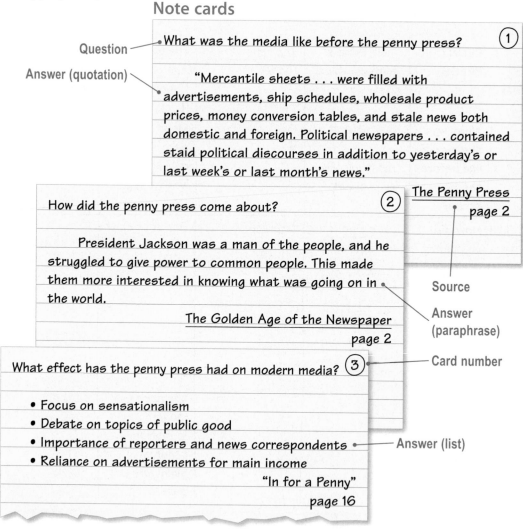

Question — •What was the media like before the penny press?   ①

Answer (quotation) —
"Mercantile sheets . . . were filled with advertisements, ship schedules, wholesale product prices, money conversion tables, and stale news both domestic and foreign. Political newspapers . . . contained staid political discourses in addition to yesterday's or last week's or last month's news."

The Penny Press
page 2

How did the penny press come about?   ②

President Jackson was a man of the people, and he struggled to give power to common people. This made them more interested in knowing what was going on in the world.

The Golden Age of the Newspaper
page 2

Source

Answer (paraphrase)

Card number

What effect has the penny press had on modern media?   ③

• Focus on sensationalism
• Debate on topics of public good
• Importance of reporters and news correspondents
• Reliance on advertisements for main income

Answer (list)

"In for a Penny"
page 16

Prewrite

Create note cards. Make note cards like the examples above whenever your answers are too long to fit on your gathering grid.

■ Avoid plagiarism.

When you develop an essay or a report, you must give credit for information that is not your own or not common knowledge. Using other people's words and ideas without giving them credit is called **plagiarism**, and it is a form of intellectual stealing. Here are two ways to avoid plagiarism.

- **Paraphrase:** It's usually best to put ideas you find into your own words, so that your paper sounds like you. This is called *paraphrasing*. Still, you must give credit to the source of the idea.

- **Quote:** Sometimes it's best to use the exact words of a source to add authority to your report. Be sure you enclose those words in quotation marks and give credit to the source.

Paraphrase

> What effect has the penny press had on modern media? (4)
>   Newspapers today are cheap to buy because they get most of their money from advertising, just like the penny papers.
>
>   Vance Web site

Quote

> What effect has the penny press had on modern media? (4)
>   "Newspapers rely heavily on advertising as a main source of income and that is also why they are still being offered at relatively low prices today."
>
>   Vance Web site

Try It!

Read this excerpt from "In for a Penny." Then label two note cards with the question "What was the media like before the penny press?" On one card, *quote* a sentence from the excerpt. On the other, *paraphrase* the selection.

> In the earliest days of American newspapers, publishers could be arrested and tried for criticizing the government. In fact, the more accurate the criticism, the more damaging it was considered, and the greater the publisher's guilt. That changed when John Zenger was arrested in 1734 for publishing articles that criticized the governor of the New York colony. Andrew Hamilton argued to the jury that a law intended to protect the king in England should not be used to forbid complaint against a corrupt governor. The jury returned a verdict of "not guilty," setting a precedent for freedom of the American press.

Research

Prewriting ■ Keep track of your sources.

As you conduct your research, keep track of the sources you use so that you can correctly cite them in your final report. You'll need the following information:

- **Book:** Author's name. Title. Publisher and city. Copyright date.
- **Magazine:** Author's name. Article title. Magazine title. Date published. Page numbers.
- **Newspaper:** Author's name. Article title. Newspaper title. City. Date published. Section. Page numbers.
- **Internet:** Author's name (if listed). Page title. Site title. Date posted or copyright date (if listed). Site sponsor. Date visited. Page address.
- **Videocassette or DVD:** Title. Distributor. Release date.

Source Notes

<u>Source Notes</u>

Book
Susan Thompson. <u>The Penny Press</u>. Vision Press. Northport, Alabama. 2004.

Magazine
Robert Younes. "In for a Penny." <u>American Publisher</u>. October 1, 2005. Pages 14–17 and 21.

Newspaper
Jerry Large. "Steady Trickle Alters the Flow of the Mainstream." <u>The Seattle Times</u>. February 17, 2003. Section C. Page 3.

Internet
No author. "Newspapers in the Boston Public Library (Background)." <u>Boston Public Library</u>. Last updated August 2001. Visited May 9, 2005. http://www.bpl.org/research/microtext/newsbpl.htm

Interview
Ralph Faraday. E-mail. January 31, 2006.

Video
<u>The American Experience: Emma Goldman</u>. PBS, 2004.

Prewrite

List sources. Keep a list of each of your sources with the information shown above. Whenever you find a new source, add it to the list.

■ Write your thesis statement.

Once your research is completed, you should write a thesis statement. The thesis statement identifies the main idea of your paper, serving as the focus of your report. The following formula will help you write your thesis statement.

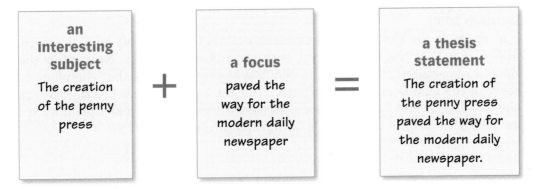

an interesting subject	a focus	a thesis statement
The creation of the penny press	**+** paved the way for the modern daily newspaper	**=** The creation of the penny press paved the way for the modern daily newspaper.

Sample Thesis Statements

The invention of the electric telegraph (an interesting subject) had a profound effect on people in this country (a focus).

The science of weather forecasting (an interesting subject) has saved millions of lives by predicting dangerous storms (a focus).

The global spread of radio and television (an interesting subject) helped to bring down the Berlin Wall and end the Cold War (a focus).

Prewrite

Form your thesis statement. Review your research notes and choose the main point you want to make about your topic. Using the formula above, write a thesis statement for your report. You may have to write more than one version of the thesis statement before it says exactly what you want it to say.

Research

Prewriting ■ Outline your ideas.

One way to organize and plan your report is to make an outline. An outline maps the ideas you plan to include in your paper. You can use either a topic outline or a sentence outline. A topic outline lists ideas as words or phrases; a sentence outline lists them as full sentences. (For an example of a topic outline, see page **590**.)

Below is the first part of a sentence outline for the report on pages **356–363**. Notice that the writer begins with the thesis statement. Next, after the Roman numerals (I., II., III., . . .), she lists the major points that she plans to cover in the middle part of her report. After the capital letters (A., B., C., . . .), she includes the details that support the major points. (Each major point serves as the topic sentence for a middle paragraph in the report.)

Sentence Outline

Remember, in an outline, if you have a I, you must have at least a II. If you have an A, you must have at least a B.

Thesis
Statement

Major Point
(I., II.)

Supporting
Details
(A., B., C.)

THESIS STATEMENT: The creation of the penny press paved the way for the modern daily newspaper.

I. Colonial newspapers in America were different from those today.
   A. They needed government authorization.
   B. John Peter Zenger was tried for libel for criticizing the governor.
   C. Freedom of the press became the focus of Zenger's trial.

II. The early newspapers were different from ours in many other ways, too.
   A. . . .
   B. . . .

Prewrite

Create your outline. Write a sentence outline for your report, using the details from your research. Be sure that each topic sentence (I., II., III., . . .) supports the thesis statement and that each detail (A., B., C., . . .) supports its topic sentence. Use your outline as a guide for writing the first draft of your report.

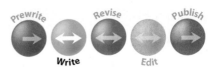

Writing

With your research and planning completed, you are ready to write the first draft of your research report. Don't worry about getting everything perfect in this first draft. For now, just get your ideas on paper in a way that makes sense to you. The following key points will help.

Keys to Effective Writing

1. Use your first paragraph to get your reader's attention, introduce your topic, and present your thesis statement.

2. In the next paragraph or two, explain how things were before your important event took place.

3. In the next several paragraphs, tell how the event came about.

4. In the final part of your report, discuss how the event influenced or affected the news media in this country.

5. Remember to cite, within your report, the sources of any ideas you paraphrase or quote; also list those sources alphabetically on a works-cited page.

CITING SOURCES IN YOUR REPORT

Credit the sources of ideas and facts you use in your report.

When You Have All the Information

- The most common type of credit (citation) lists the author's last name and page number.

  In 1829, young Benjamin Day moved to New York to seek his fortune (Thompson 5).

- If you name the author in your report, just include the page number in parentheses.

  What made the Herald a success, George Douglas says, was the personality of its owner and editor (27).

When Some Information Is Missing

- If a source does not list an author, use the title and page number. (If the title is long, use only the first word or two.)

  "The press played an important role in the American Colonies' fight against British authorities and eventually for independence from Britain" ("Background" 302).

- If neither the author nor a page number are available, use the title alone.

  When John Peter Zenger published articles criticizing the governor in the New York Weekly Journal in 1735, he was jailed and tried for libel (Public).

- Some sources (especially Internet sites) do not use page numbers. In those cases, include just the author (or, if the author is not listed, the title).

  "The changes made to the newspaper during the penny press era set a precedent for the way newspapers operate today" (Vance).

Try It!

Rewrite the following sentence, citing Randall P. Bezanson's article "Profits and Press Freedom" from *Human Rights*, page 20.

As a free and self-governing people, Americans depend upon the news media for information, and they expect that media to be independent in its own judgment.

Writing ■ Start your research report.

The opening paragraph of your research report should grab the reader's attention, introduce your topic, and present your thesis statement. Consider using one of the following effective ways to begin your opening paragraph.

- **Ask an interesting question.**

    > Have you ever seen newsboys in a movie shouting "Extra! Extra! Read all about it!"?

- **Start with a quotation.**

    > "Before the coming of the penny press, newspapers weren't really news," says writer Robert Younes in an article called "In for a Penny."

- **Start with an interesting fact.**

    > When George Day started publishing the *Sun* in 1833, he was mainly looking for a way to save his new printing business.

Beginning Paragraph

This beginning paragraph starts with an interesting question and ends with the thesis statement (underlined).

> Have you ever seen newsboys in a movie shouting "Extra! Extra! Read all about it!"? Have you ever wondered why newspapers include an entertainment section and an opinion page? Would you like to know who the first Washington news correspondent was? You can find answers to these questions by studying the start of the "penny press" in the 1830s. <u>The creation of the penny press paved the way for the modern daily newspaper.</u>

Write

Write your opening paragraph. Make sure to grab the reader's interest in the beginning, then introduce your topic, and end with a clear thesis statement. You may have to write more than one version of this paragraph before it says exactly what you want it to say.

Writing ■ Develop the middle part.

The middle part of your report should support or explain your thesis statement. Start by explaining what things were like before the event. Then discuss the development of the event in detail.

Each middle paragraph should cover one major point. This major point is presented in the topic sentence and followed by supporting details. Use your sentence outline as a guide for your writing.

Middle Paragraphs

The first middle paragraphs tell what the media was like before the event.

Colonial newspapers in America were different from those today. For one thing, they could not be published without the approval of the government. In 1690, the publisher of the first newspaper in the colonies found this out the hard way. The government arrested him and destroyed all copies of his paper because he didn't get proper approval. In another case, John Peter Zenger published articles in the New York Weekly Journal that criticized the governor. Authorities arrested Zenger and tried him for libel (Public). Freedom of the press became the focus of his famous trial in 1735. He was eventually set free.

All the details in each paragraph support the topic sentence (underlined).

The early newspapers were different from ours in many other ways, too. Colonial papers were usually "4-page weeklies containing local ads, . . . local hearsay, and large, unedited chunks of . . . news from the London press" (Public). Even after the American Revolution, newspapers lacked interesting and timely news. Commercial papers "were filled with advertisements, ship schedules, . . . product prices, money conversion tables, and stale news," and political papers "contained staid [stuffy] political discourses in addition to

Sources are cited in parentheses.

yesterday's or last week's or last month's news" (Thompson 2). These newspapers were expensive and read mostly by wealthy citizens.

Because of increased literacy in the early 1800s, more people began to read newspapers. Common people paid special attention to the more interesting sections, especially the coverage of the police court (Thompson 2). This was also a time of great change for the nation. The country elected Andrew Jackson, the first unaristocratic president. More immigrants were entering the country, and cities were growing rapidly (Younes 14). The stage was set for the penny press, a new type of newspaper that would appeal to the masses.

In 1833, Benjamin Day, the owner of a printing company in New York, started the Sun, the first successful penny paper. Walking to work each day, he passed Chatham Street, where street vendors sold items for a penny (Thompson 8). Day thought he could make a penny newspaper to sell on the street. On September 3, 1833, he sold the first edition of the Sun. It was only a single sheet of paper, folded in the middle. On the front page, Day printed advertisements copied from other papers. The other three pages contained a mix of ads and news from other papers, two humorous tall tales, and the police report copied from the Courier & Enquirer (10–11). His paper was an instant success. Soon Day had enough new ads to make the paper profitable even with its penny price.

Day quickly realized that he needed help. While he managed the business, someone would have to attend the courts each day and write the police report. A man named George Wisner became Day's court reporter and partner (Thompson 13). Day and Wisner didn't always agree, and the paper reflected their different opinions (15–17). This debate of ideas set the Sun apart from the older, more conservative political newspapers.

Information from the source is paraphrased.

The next middle paragraphs explain how the event came about.

Sentences are arranged so that the reader can easily follow the ideas.

Research

A new term, the "London plan," is explained.

Day also needed help selling the paper. He decided to use a system known as the "London plan." Under this plan, he offered newspapers at a reduced rate to people who then sold their copies and pocketed the profit. The first person to join him was a 10-year-old boy. Before long, "newsboys" were selling the papers all over New York (Thompson 12–13), and the Sun became the most popular paper in the city.

In 1835, James Gordon Bennett started another successful penny paper in New York called the Herald. Bennett had lived in many places, from Canada to South Carolina, and had gained valuable experience as a writer and an editor. Historians say that he was America's first Washington news correspondent, for the New York Enquirer. These experiences helped prepare Bennett to start his own paper (Douglas 27–29). Bennett started out alone, in a dark cellar room, using a plank and two boxes as a desk. However, before long, the Herald would outsell the Sun. In fact, at its best, the Herald sold more copies worldwide than even the most respected European papers (Younes 16).

The author's interest in the subject is evident in the voice and word choice.

Bennett knew how to get the attention of readers. They liked the Herald because Bennett wrote opinion pieces that were "saucy, impertinent [disrespectful], and funny" (Thompson 34). Bennett also filled his paper with sensational news stories that made the Sun seem tame by comparison, and he placed these stories on the front page to gain more attention. Many historians give Bennett the credit for the first "crisis news reporting," based on his eyewitness news about New York City's Great Fire of 1835 and his writing about the Jewett murder trial (Douglas 30). The Herald also quickly became the best source of Wall Street news (Thompson 59). Along with these stories, Bennett included entertainment news. All of these things helped make the Herald a great success.

In 1841, Horace Greeley started another penny newspaper in New York. It was called the Tribune. Like the Sun and the Herald, the Tribune relied on advertising for its main income, and it included sensational stories to attract readers. However, Greeley believed that a newspaper should do more than just make money. He thought it should keep people informed about important events and educate them about important ideas.

The Tribune gave readers crime stories and stories about local events, but it "downplayed sensational stories by placing them on inside pages" (Thompson 97). This paper also included poetry and literature by respected authors. Under Greeley's direction, the Tribune showed "a social conscience in its news columns and reform-minded editorials" (98).

The Tribune soon rivaled the Herald as the most popular paper of the time, and through the Tribune, Greeley became a well-known national figure. He influenced the opinion of Americans everywhere on topics like "labor, education, [and] temperance" (Thompson 112). Greeley showed that a newspaper could help shape a nation.

> The transition "however" introduces an important point.

> Quotations are worked smoothly into the writing.

Write your middle paragraphs. Keep these tips in mind as you write.

- Write a topic sentence for each paragraph and support it with details.
- Refer to your outline for direction. (See page 372.)
- Give credit to all your sources. (See page 374.)

Research

Writing ■ End your research report.

Your ending paragraph should summarize your research report and bring it to a thoughtful close. To accomplish that, use the following guidelines.

- Tell how the event influenced or affected modern media.
- Restate the thesis.
- Leave the reader with something to add to his or her understanding of the topic.

Ending Paragraph

The report's conclusion discusses the topic's effect on modern media.	Modern newspapers continue to focus on disaster and crime news, along with editorials and stories about business and entertainment. Also, topics in the public interest continue to appear in the news, just as they did in the Tribune. The obligation to the public that today's newspaper reporters and editors feel, originated with the penny press. Further, modern
The writer restates the thesis (underlined).	newspapers still "rely heavily on advertising as a main source of income and that is also a main reason they are still being offered at relatively low prices today" (Vance). All these things show that "the age of modern-day journalism began with the
The reader is left with a final idea to think about.	penny press" (Thompson 3). The free press that grew from those early papers has helped to shape our nation, just as the Founding Fathers had hoped.

Write your ending paragraph and review your first draft. Draft your ending paragraph using the guidelines above. Then read your draft to make sure it is complete. Check your research notes and outline to make sure you haven't forgotten any important details. In the margins and between the lines, make notes about anything you should change.

Tip

Think of your research report as one-half of a conversation with a reader you invent. Talk to your silent partner in a sincere and honest voice. Research reports should be informative *and* engaging.

■ Create your works-cited page.

The purpose of a works-cited page at the end of a research report is to allow the reader to locate the sources you used. Pages **381–384** show the standard format for common types of sources. Some sources will not match these formats exactly, so simply give as much detail as possible.

Books

The standard works-cited entry for a book uses the following format.

Author or editor (if available, last name first). **Title** (underlined). **City where the book was published: Publisher, copyright date.**

> Douglas, George H. The Golden Age of the Newspaper. Westport, CT: Greenwood, 1999.

If a book has two or three authors, list them in the order they appear on the title page. Reverse only the name of the first author. (Example: Brentano, Margaret, and Nicholson Baker.) For a book with four or more authors, list only the first author, followed by "et al."

A Single Work from an Anthology

To list an essay or a short story from an anthology, include the title of that work in quotation marks, followed by the title of the anthology and the editor.

> Ashabranner, Brent. "Helping Hands." Read All About It: Great Read-Aloud Stories, Poems, and Newspaper Pieces for Preteens and Teens. Ed. Jim Trelease. New York: Penguin, 1993.

An Article in a Familiar Reference Work

It is not necessary to list full publication details for dictionaries, encyclopedias, or other familiar reference works. If the article is initialed, check the index of authors for the author's full name.

Author (if available). **Article title** (in quotation marks). **Title of the encyclopedia** (underlined). **Edition** (if available). **Date published.**

> "Day, Benjamin Henry." Columbia Encyclopedia. 2000.

Periodicals

Periodicals are publications issued on a regular, scheduled basis. This includes magazines, scholarly journals, and newspapers.

A Magazine

If a magazine is published weekly or biweekly, include the full date (day, month, year). If it is published monthly, bimonthly, or less often, include only the month and year. For an article not running on continuous pages, list the first page followed by a "+" sign.

> **Author** (if available, last name first). **Article title** (in quotation marks). **Title of the magazine** (underlined) **Date** (day, month, year): **Page numbers of the article.**

> Younes, Robert. "In for a Penny." American Publisher 1 Oct. 2005: 14+.

A Scholarly Journal

Scholarly journals are identified by volume number rather than by full date of publication.

> **Author** (if available, last name first). **Article title** (in quotation marks). **Title of the journal** (underlined) **Volume number. Issue number** (if each issue begins with page 1) **Year published** (in parentheses): **Page numbers of the article.**

> Postman, Neil. "The Information Age: A Blessing or a Curse?" Harvard International Journal of Press/Politics 9.2 (2004): 3-10.

A Newspaper

> **Author** (if available, last name first). **Article title** (in quotation marks). **Title of the newspaper** (underlined) **Date** (day, month, year), **edition** (if listed): **Section letter and page numbers of the article.**

> Large, Jerry. "Steady Trickle Alters the Flow of the Mainstream." The Seattle Times 17 Feb. 2003: C3.

Online Sources

Online sources include Web pages, documents in Internet databases, and e-mail messages.

A Web Page

> **Author** (if available). **Page title** (if available, in quotation marks). **Site title** (underlined). **Name of sponsor** (if available). **Date published** (if available). **Date found. Electronic address** (in angle brackets).

> "Newspapers in the Boston Public Library (Background)." Boston Public Library. August 2001. 9 May 2005 <http://www.bpl.org/research/microtext/newsbpl.htm>.

If you must include a line break in a URL (Web address), do so only after a slash, and do not add a hyphen.

An Article in an Online Service

Libraries often subscribe to online services where articles are kept. To cite such an article, first give any details about the original print version. (See "Periodicals" on page **382**.) Then list the database if known (underlined), the service, and the library. Next, give your date of access followed by the URL for the home page of the service (if known). If no URL is given for the article itself, give a keyword or path statement instead, if appropriate.

> Weston, Beth Turn. "Papers for a Penny." Cobblestone Mar. 2005: 47. MasterFILE Premier. EBSCOHost. Burlington Public Library. 22 Mar. 2005 <http://search.epnet.com>. Keyword: newspaper history.

Use semicolons to separate the links in a path statement. (Example: Path: Publishing; Journalism; History.)

E-Mail to the Author (Yourself)

> **Writer** (last name first). **Type of message** ("E-mail to the author"). **Date received.**

> Faraday, Ralph. E-mail to the author. 31 Jan. 2006.

Other Sources

Your research may include other sources, such as television programs, video documentaries, and personal interviews.

A Television or Radio Program

> **Episode title, if given** (in quotation marks). **Program title** (underlined). **Series title** (if any). **Name of the network. Call letters and city of the local station** (if any). **Broadcast date.**

> "NOVA scienceNOW." Nova. PBS. WMVS, Milwaukee. 19 Oct. 2005.

Video, DVD, Slide Program

> **Title** (underlined). **Type of medium** (filmstrip, slide program). **Distributor, date released.**

> The American Experience: Emma Goldman. DVD. PBS, 2004.

An Interview by the Author (Yourself)

> **Person interviewed** (last name first). **Description** (Personal interview, Telephone interview, etc.). **Date of interview.**

> Faraday, Ralph. Personal interview. 19 Feb. 2006.

Write

Format your sources. Check your report and your list of sources (page 370) to see which sources you actually used. Then follow these directions.

1. Write out the information for each of your sources using the guidelines above and on the previous three pages. Use a sheet of paper or note cards.
2. Arrange your sources in alphabetical order.
3. Create your works-cited page. (See the example on page 363.)

Revising

Your focus during drafting is to get your thoughts on paper in a logical order. During the revising step, you make changes to ensure that your thoughts are clear and interesting, that your organization is easy to follow, that your voice sounds knowledgeable, and so on.

Keys to Effective Revising

1. Read your entire draft to get an overall sense of your research report.

2. Review your thesis statement to be sure that it clearly states your main point about the topic.

3. Make sure your beginning engages the reader. Then check that your ending leaves the reader with something to think about.

4. Be sure that the middle part clearly and completely supports the thesis statement.

5. Make sure that you sound knowledgeable and interested in the topic.

6. Check for effective word choice and sentence fluency.

Improve your writing.

A first draft is never a finished paper. There is always room for improvement. In the following sample paragraphs, Gabriella makes several important revisions. Each improves the *ideas, organization, voice, word choice,* or *sentence fluency* in the writing.

More precise words improve word choice.

A subheading is added.

A transition is added for better fluency.

Wording is changed to create the active voice.

Have you ever seen newsboys in a movie shouting "Extra! Extra! Read all about it!"? Have you ever wondered why newspapers include an entertainment section and an opinion page? Would you like to know who the first Washington news ~~reporter~~ *correspondent* was? You can find answers to these questions by studying the start of the "penny press" in the 1830s. The creation of the penny press ~~made~~ *paved the* way for the modern daily newspaper.

Before the Penny Press

∧Colonial newspapers in America were different from those today. ∧*For one thing,* They could not be published without the approval of the government. In 1690, the publisher of the first newspaper in the colonies found this out the hard way. *The government arrested him and destroyed all copies of his paper* ∧~~He was arrested and all copies of his paper were destroyed~~ because he didn't get proper approval. In another case, John Peter Zenger published articles in the New York Weekly Journal that criticized the governor. Authorities arrested Zenger and tried him for libel (Public). Freedom of the press became the focus of his famous trial in 1735. He was eventually set free.

The early newspapers were different from ours in many other ways, too. Colonial papers were usually "4-page weeklies containing local ads, . . . local hearsay, and large, unedited chunks of . . . news from the London press" (Public). Even after the American Revolution, newspapers lacked interesting and timely news. These newspapers were expensive and read mostly by wealthy citizens. Commercial papers "were filled with advertisements, ship schedules, . . . product prices, money conversion tables, and stale news," and political papers "contained staid [stuffy] political discourses in addition to yesterday's or last week's or last month's news" (Thompson 2).

> A sentence is moved to improve organization.

Because of increased literacy in the early 1800s, more people began to read newspapers. Common people paid special attention to the more interesting sections, especially the coverage of the police court (Thompson 2). This was also a time of great change for the nation. The country elected Andrew Jackson, the first unaristocratic president. More immigrants were entering the country, and cities were growing rapidly (Younes 14). The stage was set for the penny press, a new type of newspaper that would appeal to the masses.

> An idea is added for clarity.

Revise

Revise your research report and add subheadings. Check your first draft for problems with ideas, organization, voice, word choice, and sentence fluency. Make any needed changes. Also look for logical breaks in your report and add appropriate subheadings.

Revising ■ Use a traits checklist.

On a piece of paper, write the numbers 1 to 13. If you can answer "yes" to a question, put a check mark after that number. Continue to revise until you can answer all of the questions with a "yes."

Revising Checklist

Ideas

_____ **1.** Have I chosen an interesting event to write about?

_____ **2.** Does my thesis statement clearly state the main idea of my paper?

_____ **3.** Do I include enough details to support my thesis?

_____ **4.** Do I give credit for ideas that I have paraphrased or quoted from other sources?

Organization

_____ **5.** Does my beginning paragraph capture the reader's interest and introduce my topic?

_____ **6.** Do my first middle paragraphs explain what things were like before this event?

_____ **7.** Do my next middle paragraphs detail how the event developed?

_____ **8.** Does my ending relate the event to present-day media?

Voice

_____ **9.** Does my voice sound knowledgeable and engaging?

Word Choice

_____ **10.** Have I used specific nouns and active verbs?

_____ **11.** Do I avoid unnecessary modifiers?

Sentence Fluency

_____ **12.** Do my sentences read smoothly?

_____ **13.** Have I used a variety of sentence beginnings and lengths?

Prewrite   Revise   Publish
Write   Edit

Editing

When you have finished revising your research paper, all that remains is checking for conventions: spelling, punctuation, capitalization, and grammar.

Keys to Effective Editing

1. Read your research report out loud and listen for words or phrases that may be incorrect.

2. Use a dictionary, a thesaurus, your computer's spell-checker, and the "Proofreader's Guide" in the back of this book.

3. Look for errors in punctuation, capitalization, spelling, and grammar.

4. Check your report for proper formatting. (See pages 356–363.)

5. If you use a computer, edit on a printed copy. Then enter your changes on the computer.

6. Use the editing and proofreading marks inside the back cover of this book. Check all citations for accuracy.

■ Check for conventions.

After revising the first draft of her report, Gabriella checked the new version carefully for punctuation, spelling, and usage errors. She also asked a classmate to look it over. The passage below shows some of Gabriella's editing changes.

A spelling error is corrected.

An error in verb tense is corrected.

A capitalization error is marked.

A missing citation is added.

The Rise of the <u>Sun</u>

In 1833, Benjamin Day, the owner of a printing company in New York, started the <u>Sun</u>, the first ~~succesful~~ *successful* penny paper. Walking to work each day, he passe~~s~~ *d* Chatham Street, where street vendors sold items for a penny (Thompson 8). Day thought he could make a penny newspaper to sell on the street. On September 3, 1833, he sold the first edition of the <u>Sun</u>. It was only a single sheet of paper, folded in the middle. On the front page, <u>d</u>ay printed advertisements copied from other papers. The other three pages contained a mix of ads and news from other papers, two humorous tall tales, and the police report copied from the <u>Courier & Enquirer</u>. *(10–11)* His paper was an instant success. Soon Day had enough new ads to make the paper profitable even with its penny price.

Edit

Check your work for conventions. Use your computer spell-checker and grammar checker to correct your work. Then print a copy of your report and read it carefully for errors the computer cannot catch. Use the editing and proofreading marks on the inside back cover of this book.

Editing ■ Use a checklist.

On a piece of paper, write the numbers 1 to 12. If you can answer "yes" to a question, put a check mark after that number. Continue editing until you can answer all of the questions with a "yes."

<u>Editing Checklist</u>

Conventions

PUNCTUATION

_____ **1.** Do I correctly punctuate all my sentences?

_____ **2.** Have I correctly punctuated citations in my research paper?

_____ **3.** Do I use quotation marks around all quoted words from my sources?

_____ **4.** Do I use underlining for all italicized words? *

_____ **5.** Have I correctly formatted the works-cited page?

CAPITALIZATION

_____ **6.** Have I capitalized proper nouns and adjectives?

_____ **7.** Do I begin each sentence with a capital letter?

SPELLING

_____ **8.** Have I spelled all my words correctly?

_____ **9.** Have I double-checked the words my spell-checker may have missed?

GRAMMAR

_____ **10.** Do I use the correct forms of verbs (*he saw*, not *he seen*)?

_____ **11.** Do my subjects and verbs agree in number?

_____ **12.** Have I used the right words (*there, their,* or *they're*)?

＊ The documentation guidelines in this chapter follow the MLA format. (MLA stands for Modern Language Association.) MLA suggests that writers of research papers use underlining instead of italics for titles and specialized words. However, always follow your teacher's instructions.

Research

Editing ■ Add a title.

Make sure that you have considered a title before you share your research report. Writer Randall VanderMey says that a title, like a good fish bait, should entice the reader. Each of the following approaches will help you write an effective title:

- Provide a creative hook:
  From Penny Press to Free Press

- Identify the topic of your report with special attention given to the sound and the rhythm of the words:
  A Penny for Your Paper

- Directly state the key point of your report:
  The Birth of the Modern Newspaper

- Focus on a theme that runs though your paper:
  Common News for Common People

Publishing ■ Share your report.

When you have finished your editing and proofreading, make a neat final copy to share. Consider making extra copies for family and friends.

Make your final copy. Use the following guidelines to format your report. (Also see pages 76–78 for instructions about designing on a computer.) Create a clean final copy and share it with your classmates and family.

Publish

■ Focus on presentation.

- Use blue or black ink and double-space the entire paper.

- Write your name, your teacher's name, the class, and the date in the upper left corner of page 1.

- Skip a line and center your title; skip another line and start your writing.

- Indent every paragraph and leave a one-inch margin on all four sides.

- For a research paper, you should write your last name and the page number in the upper right corner of every page of your report.

- If your teacher requires a title page and outline, follow your teacher's instructions. (See page 356.)

Making Oral Presentations

Speaking in front of a group can be exciting, but it can also be scary. If the thought of any formal speaking situation makes you nervous, you are not alone. Speaking in front of a group is a common fear, but one that you can overcome.

Just think of speaking as a type of performance. You may already perform quite well on a basketball court, in a band, in a play, or at a dance. With planning and practice, you will also be able to give effective oral presentations.

In this chapter, you will learn how to prepare and present an oral presentation based on a research report you have written. You will also learn how to turn your presentation into a multimedia report.

- Planning Your Presentation
- Creating Note Cards
- Considering Visual Aids
- Practicing Your Speech
- Delivering Your Presentation
- Evaluating a Presentation
- Preparing a Multimedia Report

"Lend thy serious hearing to what I shall unfold."
—Shakespeare

Planning Your Presentation

To transform a research report into an oral presentation, you need to consider your purpose, your audience, and the content of your report.

■ Determine your purpose.

Your purpose is your reason for giving a presentation.

- **Informative** speeches educate by providing valuable information.
- **Persuasive** speeches argue for or against something.
- **Demonstration** speeches show how to do or make something.

■ Consider your audience.

As you think about your audience, keep the following points in mind.

- **Be clear** so that listeners understand your main points immediately.
- **Anticipate questions** the audience might have and answer them. This helps keep the audience connected.
- **Engage the listeners** through thought-provoking questions, revealing anecdotes, interesting details, and effective visuals.

■ Review your report.

During an oral report, your audience obviously cannot go back and listen again to anything you have said, so you must be sure to share your ideas clearly from beginning to end. Review your report to see how the different parts will work in an oral presentation. Use the following questions as a review guide.

- Will my opening grab the listeners' attention?
- What are the main supporting points that listeners need to know?
- How many supporting details should I include for each main point?
- What visual aids can I use to create interest in my topic? (See page **398**.)
- Will the ending part have the proper impact on the listener?

Try It!

Adapt your research report. Rework any parts of your report that need to be adjusted to work well in an oral presentation. Pay special attention to the beginning and ending parts, which should be written out word for word. (See the next page for example adaptations.)

■ Rework your report.

To create a more effective oral presentation, you may need to rewrite certain parts of your report. The new beginning below grabs the listeners' attention by using short, punchy phrases and asking questions. The new ending makes a more immediate connection with the beginning.

Written Report (page 357)

> Have you ever seen newsboys in a movie shouting "Extra! Extra! Read all about it!"? Have you ever wondered why newspapers include an entertainment section and an opinion page? Would you like to know who the first Washington news correspondent was? You can find answers to these questions by studying the start of the "penny press"...

Oral Introduction

> "Extra! Extra! Read all about it! Latest news! Shocking stories! Political scandals! Just a penny a paper!" These are the things newsboys shouted to sell penny newspapers in the early 1800s. Creators of the penny press in the United States paved the way for modern daily newspapers.

Written Report (page 362)

> Modern newspapers continue to focus on disaster and crime news, along with editorials and stories about business and entertainment. Also, topics in the public interest continue to appear in the news, just as they did in the Tribune. The obligation . . .

Oral Conclusion

> So when you hear the cry "Extra! Extra!" in a movie, remember those enterprising men who advanced the idea of a people's press. Although the penny press was sensational, it developed and influenced a national readership and established the foundation for the media of today.

Presentations

Creating Note Cards

If you are giving a prepared speech rather than an oral reading of your report, you should use note cards to help you remember your ideas. The guidelines below will help you make effective cards.

■ Follow these note-card guidelines.

Write out your entire introduction and conclusion on separate note cards. In the body of your speech, write one point per card, along with specific details. Clearly number your cards.

- Place each main point on a separate note card, using key words and phrases to help you remember your details.
- Number each card.
- Note the main idea at the top of each card.
- Write supporting ideas on the lines below the main idea.
- Highlight any ideas you especially want to emphasize.
- Mark cards that call for visual aids.

■ Consider the three main parts.

As you prepare your note cards, keep the following points in mind about the three parts of your oral presentation: the introduction, the body, and the conclusion.

- **The introduction** should grab the listeners' attention, identify the topic and the focus of your presentation, and provide any essential background information about the topic. (See pages **394–395**.)
- **The body** should contain the main points from your report that you want to cover. Present these points in such a way that they have the most impact on the listener. Also jot down the visual aids that you plan to use. (See the bold notes on the sample cards on page **397**.)
- **The conclusion** should restate your focus and leave the listener with a final thought about your topic. (See pages **394–395**.)

Try It!

Create your note cards. Review the note cards on the following page. Then create cards for your introduction, main points, and conclusion. Make notes on the cards where you want to use visual aids.

■ Sample Note Cards

Below are the note cards Gabriella used for her oral presentation. Note how she arranged and marked her details on each card.

Introduction   1
    "Extra! Extra! Read all about it!
Latest news! Shocking stories! Political
scandals! Just a penny a paper!" These
are the things newsboys shouted to se
penny newspapers in the early 1800s.
Creators of the penny press in the
United States paved the way for moder

Before the Penny Press   2
   – Publisher of first American paper
     (1690) arrested
   – New York Weekly Journal, John
     Zenger trial, 1735
   – papers not about current news

Benjamin Day—Sun   3
   – Day's background
   – paper launched September 3, 1833
   – hired George Wisner to help
   – began "London plan" of newsboys
     selling
show sample ad

James Bennett—Herald   4
   – Bennett's background
   – sensationalism, called "crisis news
     reporting"
   – financial news
sample front page

Horace Greeley—Tribune 1841   5
   – Greeley's background
   – Tribune downplayed sensational stories
   – interested in ideas and what's
     happening—affected opinions
     across the nation
   – more intellectual appeal
show photo and front page

Legacy of the Penny Press   6
   – popped up all over U.S.
   – showed preoccupation with crisis,
     disaster, and crime news
   – reporters began to feel obligation
     to the public
show chart of features

Conclusion   7
    So when you hear the cry "Extra!
Extra!" in a movie, remember those
enterprising men who advanced the idea of
a people's press. Although the penny press
was sensational, it developed and influenced
a national readership and established the
foundation for the media of today.

Considering Visual Aids

Consider using visual aids during your speech. They can make your presentation clearer and more meaningful. Here are some examples.

Posters	include words, pictures, or both.
Photographs	help people see what you are talking about.
Charts	explain points, compare facts, or show statistics.
Maps	identify or locate specific places being discussed.
Objects	show the audience important items related to your topic.
Computer slides	project your photographs, charts, and maps onto a screen and turn your speech into a multimedia presentation. (See pages 402–403.)

■ Indicate when to present visuals.

Write notes in the margins of your note cards to indicate where a visual aid would be helpful. Gabriella considered the following visuals for her presentation about the penny press.

- A sample ad from Benjamin Day's newspaper
- Front page of James Bennett's newspaper
- Photo of Horace Greeley and the front page of his newspaper
- Chart listing the main features of penny press newspapers

Try It!

List possible visual aids. Identify two or three visual aids you could use in your presentation. Explain how and when you would use each one.

Tip

When creating visual aids, keep these points in mind.

- **Make them big.** Your visuals should be large enough for everyone in the audience to see.

- **Keep them simple.** Use labels and short phrases rather than full sentences.

- **Make them eye-catching.** Use color, bold lines, and simple shapes to attract the audience.

Practicing Your Speech

Practice is the key to giving an effective oral presentation. Knowing what to say and how to say it will help eliminate those "butterflies" speakers often feel. Here are some hints for an effective practice session.

- **Arrange your note cards in the proper order.** This will eliminate any confusion as you practice.
- **Practice in front of a mirror.** That way you can check your posture and eye contact and determine if your visuals are easy to see.
- **Practice in front of others.** Friends and family can help you identify parts that need work.
- **Record a practice presentation.** A tape recording will let you know if you sound interested and if your voice and message are clear. (A videotape of your presentation would be even better.)
- **Time yourself.** If your teacher has set a time limit, practice staying within it.
- **Speak clearly.** Do not rush your words, especially later when you are in front of your audience.
- **Work on eye contact.** Look down only to glance at a card.
- **Speak up.** Your voice will sound louder to you than it will to the audience. Rule of thumb: if you sound *too* loud to yourself, you are probably sounding just right to your audience.
- **Look interested and confident.** This will help you engage the listeners.

Practice Checklist

To review each practice session, ask yourself the following questions.

_____ **1.** Did I appear at ease?
_____ **2.** Could my voice be heard and my words understood?
_____ **3.** Did I sound like I enjoyed and understood my topic?
_____ **4.** Were my visual aids interesting and used effectively?
_____ **5.** Did I feel like I was rushing through my speech?
_____ **6.** Did I miss anything I wanted to say?

Try It!

Practice your presentation. Practice your speech before your family or friends. Also consider videotaping your speech.

Presentations

Delivering Your Presentation

When you deliver a speech, concentrate on your voice and body language. Voice quality and body language communicate as much as your words do.

■ Control your voice.

Volume, tone, and *pace* are three aspects of your formal speaking voice. If you can control these three aspects of voice, your listeners will clearly follow your ideas.

- **Volume** is the loudness of your voice. Imagine you are speaking to someone in the back of the room and adjust your volume accordingly.
- **Tone** expresses your feelings. Be enthusiastic about your topic and let your voice show that.
- **Pace** is the speed at which you speak. For the most part, speak at a relaxed pace.

Tip

You can make an important point by slowing down, by pausing, by increasing your volume, or by emphasizing individual words.

■ Consider your body language.

Your body language (*posture, gestures,* and *facial expressions*) plays an important role during a speech. Follow the suggestions given below to communicate effectively.

- **Assume a straight but relaxed posture.** This tells the audience that you are confident and prepared. If you are using a podium, let your hands rest lightly on the surface.
- **Pause before you begin.** Take a deep breath and relax.
- **Look at your audience.** Try to look toward every section of the room at least once during your speech.
- **Think about what you are saying** and let your facial expressions reflect your true feelings.
- **Point to your visual aids** or use natural gestures to make a point.

Try It!

Deliver your presentation. As you deliver your speech, make sure to control your voice and exhibit the proper body language.

Evaluating a Presentation

Evaluate a presentation using the following evaluation sheet. Circle the description that best fits each assessed area. Then offer two comments: one positive comment and one helpful suggestion.

Peer Evaluation Sheet

Speaker _____ Evaluator _____

1. ### Vocal Presentation

   Volume:
   Clear and loud   Loud enough   A little soft   Mumbled

   Pace:
   Relaxed   A little rushed or slow   Rushed or slow   Hard to follow

   Comments:

   a. _____

   b. _____

2. ### Physical Presentation

   Posture:
   Relaxed, straight   A bit stiff   Fidgeted a lot   Slumped

   Eye contact:
   Excellent contact   Made some contact   Quick glances   None

   Comments:

   a. _____

   b. _____

3. ### Information

   Thought provoking   Interesting   A few good points   No ideas

   Comments:

   a. _____

   b. _____

4. ### Visual Aids

   Well used   Easy to follow   Not clear   None used

   Comments:

   a. _____

   b. _____

Preparing a Multimedia Report

You can enhance an oral report using electronic aids such as slides and sound. In order to use these effectively, you must plan exactly where each slide or sound bite will fit into your speech.

Here is a planning script for a multimedia report on the penny press. What will be *seen* appears in the "Video" column, and what will be *heard* appears in the "Audio" column.

Planning Script

Video	Audio
1. Title Screen: "The Penny Press"	1. SPEAKER: Introduction SOUND: Music begins.
2. Slide 2: "Before the Penny Press" and picture of newsboys on city streets, early 1800s	2. SPEAKER: Read background of penny press. SOUND: Newspaper presses, boys' voices calling "Extra! Extra!"
3. Slide 3: Photo of Benjamin Day next to a picture of the NY Sun front page	3. SPEAKER: Give background of Benjamin Day and the Sun. SOUND: Ragtime music VOICE: Quotation about Day
4. Slide 4: Photo of Bennett and Herald	4. SPEAKER: Give background of James Bennett and the Herald. SOUND: Ragtime music VOICE: Quotation about Bennett
5. Slide 5: Photo of Greeley and Tribune	5. SPEAKER: Give background on Horace Greeley and the Tribune. SOUND: Ragtime music VOICE: Quotation about Greeley
6. Slide 6: Map of U.S. with New York pinpointed with large flag	6. SPEAKER: Explain impact of papers. SOUND: Music becomes Western.
7. Slide 7: Same map, with flags wherever other papers appeared	7. SPEAKER: Tell of spread of papers. SOUND: Music continues.
8. Slide 8: Pictures of printing presses then and now, side by side	8. SPEAKER: Conclusion SOUND: Printing presses running

Multimedia Report Traits Checklist

Use the following checklist to help you improve your multimedia report. When you can answer all of the questions with a "yes," your report is ready.

Revising Checklist

Ideas

_____ **1.** Have I included the main ideas from my written report in my multimedia report?

_____ **2.** Have I effectively supported my main ideas?

_____ **3.** Does each slide or sound bite suit the audience and the purpose of the report?

Organization

_____ **4.** Do I state the topic in my introduction?

_____ **5.** Do I include the important main points in the body?

_____ **6.** Do I restate my focus in the conclusion?

Voice

_____ **7.** Do I sound interested and enthusiastic?

_____ **8.** Is my voice clear, relaxed, and expressive?

Word and Multimedia Choices

_____ **9.** Are the words and pictures on each slide easy to read and see?

_____ **10.** Have I chosen the best audio and video clips?

Presentation Fluency

_____ **11.** Does my report flow smoothly from point to point?

Conventions

_____ **12.** Is each slide free of grammar, spelling, capitalization, and punctuation errors?

Writing Across the Curriculum

Writing in Science

Simply put, science is a system of knowledge obtained by applying the scientific method—a method of testing hypotheses and drawing conclusions about the natural world. Throughout time, applying the scientific method has been one of the most powerful ways for human beings to learn about their world. In science classes—biology, life science, astronomy, or geology—you can learn how to explore the world for yourself and make many fascinating discoveries.

This chapter covers the types of science writing that will help you deepen your understanding of the world around you. It will also allow you to share that understanding with others.

- Taking Classroom Notes
- Taking Reading Notes
- Keeping a Learning Log
- Writing Guidelines: Lab Report
- Writing Guidelines: Cause-Effect Essay
- Writing Guidelines: Science-Article Summary
- Other Forms of Writing in Science

"Nothing in life is to be feared. It is only to be understood."

—Marie Curie

Taking Classroom Notes

Note taking helps you focus on the information in a lecture, understand new material, and remember what's important. Here are tips on taking notes.

Before You Take Notes . . .

- **Set up your notes.** Use a three-ring binder so that you can add handouts to your notes, or use a notebook with a folder in the back.
- **Date each entry** and write down the topic.
- **Organize each page.** Consider using a two-column format, with lecture information on the left and questions on the right.

As You Take Notes . . .

- **Listen for key words.** Pay attention to information that comes after words like *for instance, as a result,* or *most importantly.*
- **Write down information the teacher puts on the board** or on an overhead. This is often the most important material.
- **Use your own words** as much as possible.
- **Write down any questions you may have** in the second column.
- **Draw pictures.** Use quick sketches to capture complex ideas.

After You Take Notes . . .

- **Reread your notes** after class. Add information to clarify your notes as necessary.
- **Research answers** to any questions that you wrote.
- **Review notes before the next class** to be ready for discussions.
- **Study your notes** to prepare for tests and exams.

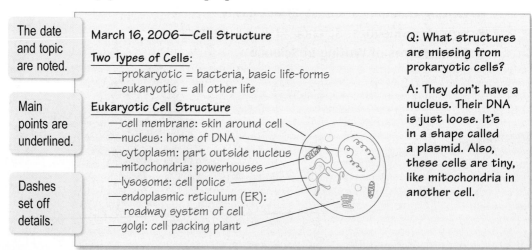

The date and topic are noted.

Main points are underlined.

Dashes set off details.

March 16, 2006—Cell Structure

Two Types of Cells:
— prokaryotic = bacteria, basic life-forms
— eukaryotic = all other life

Eukaryotic Cell Structure
— cell membrane: skin around cell
— nucleus: home of DNA
— cytoplasm: part outside nucleus
— mitochondria: powerhouses
— lysosome: cell police
— endoplasmic reticulum (ER): roadway system of cell
— golgi: cell packing plant

Q: What structures are missing from prokaryotic cells?

A: They don't have a nucleus. Their DNA is just loose. It's in a shape called a plasmid. Also, these cells are tiny, like mitochondria in another cell.

Taking Reading Notes

Taking notes while you read can increase your understanding and recall of a text. Here are some tips on taking reading notes.

Before You Take Notes . . .

- **Write the date, chapter, book, and topic** at the top of each entry.
- **Organize each page.** Try using a two-column format with wide margins. Put notes on the left and thoughts or questions on the right.
- **Quickly skim the assignment.** Read the title, introduction, headings, and chapter summaries. Look at graphics and charts.

As You Take Notes . . .

- **Write down headings or subtopics.** Note the most important details under each.
- **Put ideas in your own words** to be sure you understand the material.
- **Summarize graphics.** Write down or sketch the main ideas.
- **List vocabulary words.** Look up definitions later.

After You Take Notes . . .

- **Review your notes.** Write down any thoughts or questions you may have. Find answers and add them to your notes.

March 16, 2006   Chapt. 10   BioWorld   Cell structure and function

Reflections and questions are listed in the second column.

* Plant/animal cells both have membranes. Only plants have cell walls (rigid).
1. Cell walls are made of cellulose.
2. They protect a cell from damage.
3. They give a plant its shape.

* Plant/animal cells have cytoplasm. Only plant cells have chloroplasts.
1. Oval, green-colored structures
2. Absorb sunlight, convert water and CO_2 into food (photosynthesis)

Flexible plant parts (leaves) have thinner cell walls.

Q: What is cytoplasm?

A: The liquid environment, mostly water, where cell activity happens.

Try It!

Take notes on the next chapter you read for a class assignment.

Keeping a Learning Log

A **learning log** is a specialized journal in which you reflect on ideas and facts you are learning in class. In a learning log, you write about new concepts by connecting them to previous knowledge or experience. Here are some tips for keeping a learning log.

Before You Make an Entry . . .

- **Set up your learning log** in a three-ring binder or notebook.
- **Write the date and topic of each entry.**
- **Leave wide margins** so that you have room for reflections and questions.

As You Make an Entry . . .

- **Summarize key concepts** and compare them to familiar ideas.
- **Apply new ideas** to what you know and have experienced.
- **Write down questions** that you have about the topic.
- **Predict how the new ideas** may prove helpful in the future.
- **Make a connection** by explaining what the new ideas mean to you.

After You Make an Entry . . .

- **Review your entries** to see how well you understand the class material.
- **Research any questions** you have and write down answers.
- **Continue your reflections** by writing new observations in the margins.

Tip

One way to approach your learning log is to stop and write. Stop in the middle of your reading or just after a lecture and freewrite immediate thoughts about what you've just learned. This can reveal how well you understand the material. Knowing which concepts are most difficult for you can help you better prepare for exams.

Try It!

Follow the guidelines above to set up your own learning log. Then, after a lecture or while reading an assignment, stop and write, reflecting on what you are learning. Explain what the ideas mean to you personally.

■ Learning-Log Entries

Here are sample learning-log entries from a student in an earth science class. The student reflects on the ideas raised in class, analyzing them and applying them to her own life.

Sample Learning Log

The date and topic are given, and ideas from the class are reviewed.

The student reflects on the topic and writes a question.

Another entry shows the student's growing understanding.

Answers to questions are also recorded.

October 19—Global Warming

Today we talked about global warming, which was confusing. Mr. Gull said that most scientists agree it is happening, and they have many ways to show it, like glaciers and ice caps melting and trees growing on the tundra where they never grew before.

Partly, I wonder why it matters if things get warmer. People say there was an ice age for tens of thousands of years, and then things got warmer. Maybe the earth just changes. That's the way it goes.

If global warming is real, how come it's been so cold around here lately?

October 23—Greenhouse Gases

Mr. Gull showed us an experiment with two clear-plastic zip-type bags. He filled one with air and zipped it. The other one he breathed into over and over before zipping it. Then he shined a hot light through each bag. The one with the regular air let the heat come right through—I could feel it on my hand. But the heat didn't come through the bag full of old breath (carbon dioxide). The CO_2 caught and held the heat. It's a greenhouse gas. The earth's CO_2 holds the sun's heat.

Why can't plants keep up? They take CO_2 and turn it into oxygen. Won't more CO_2 just mean bigger plants and more oxygen? Mr. Gull said that deforestation and destruction of plants in the oceans means the plants can't keep up with all the CO_2 people produce.

So, where does all the carbon dioxide come from? It's from breathing and from burning things. Ever since people discovered fire, they've been burning things—wood, coal, gasoline, natural gas. Unless people begin to get energy from cleaner sources, the planet will just keep heating up.

Writing Guidelines ■ Lab Report

A **lab report** follows the scientific method. The report states a hypothesis, provides a method for testing it, records observations, and offers conclusions. Here are guidelines for creating a lab report.

Prewriting

- **Select a topic.** Follow your science teacher's assignment or (if given a choice) select a topic that interests you.
- **Plan the experiment.** Follow the planning your teacher provides. If you have selected the experiment, study it, gather materials, and make sure you understand each step.
- **Follow the proper format.** Use the lab-report format provided by your teacher or follow the lab-report model on page **411**, which is divided into seven separate parts.

Writing

- **Lay the groundwork.** State the purpose of your experiment— what it is designed to prove—and list materials needed. Also note the variables you will use in your test. Then write your hypothesis, explaining what you expect your experiment to prove.
- **Describe the procedure.** Use specific language to make each step clear.
- **Record your observations.** Describe exactly what happens during the experiment in chronological order.
- **Write a conclusion.** Tell whether your hypothesis was correct or not. Explain why.

Revising

- **Improve your writing.** Review your first draft for *ideas, organization,* and *voice.* Ask these questions: *Have I clearly stated my purpose, hypothesis, and conclusion? Have I described the experiment in chronological order and included enough details?*
- **Improve your style.** Check your *word choice* and *sentence fluency* by asking these questions: *Have I correctly used and explained scientific terms? Do my sentences read smoothly?*

Editing

- **Check for conventions.** Proofread your report for errors in punctuation, capitalization, spelling, and grammar. Fix any errors.
- **Prepare a final copy.** Make a neat final copy of your lab report.

Science

■ Lab Report

The lab report below describes an in-class experiment dealing with acid-base reactions. The acid used is vinegar and the base is baking soda.

Sample Lab Report

The beginning states the purpose, the materials, the variables, and the hypothesis.

Acid-Base Reactions

PURPOSE: Show how an acid-base reaction is affected by foreign materials.

MATERIALS: Two 2-liter beakers, 3 cups water, 2 cups vinegar, 2 tsp. baking soda, 6 raisins

VARIABLES: Time and ingredients

HYPOTHESIS: The raisins will not change the acid-base reaction at all; the vinegar-baking soda reaction will still produce CO_2 bubbles.

The middle outlines the procedure and records observations.

PROCEDURE: I labeled the beakers A (test) and B (control). I poured 1.5 cups of water into each beaker and added 1 tsp. of baking soda to each beaker. I stirred each mixture until the powder dissolved in the water. Then I dropped the 6 raisins into beaker A. Afterward, I slowly poured 1 cup of vinegar into each beaker.

OBSERVATIONS: After a minute or so, the solution in each beaker began to bubble. Both solutions bubbled like carbonated soda, with bubbles clinging to the side of the beaker. The raisins in beaker A rose to the top of the liquid and then sank again. They continued to move up and down for the entire period.

The ending tells whether the hypothesis was correct or not and why.

CONCLUSION: My hypothesis was correct. The raisins did not affect the reaction. That's because the skin of the raisins isn't acidic or basic. (I wonder what would happen if the raisins were cut open.) However, the reaction did affect the raisins. The CO_2 bubbles formed by the acid-base reaction stuck to the raisins, causing them to rise to the top of the solution. The gas bubbles were released at the surface, causing the raisins to sink again. I was surprised that the acid-base reaction continued as long as it did.

Try It!

Perform a science experiment assigned by your teacher or devise one that interests you. Describe it completely in a lab report.

Writing Guidelines ■ Cause-Effect Essay

Nature is full of causes and effects, and a science essay that explains them is called a cause-effect essay. It is common in a cause-effect essay to focus on one cause (the topic) and show its many effects. Follow these guidelines when you create a cause-effect essay.

Prewriting

- **Select a topic.** If your teacher does not assign a topic, review your class notes, learning log, or textbook for ideas. Choose a topic that shows a clear cause-effect relationship.
- **Gather details.** Research your topic so that you understand it thoroughly. Write down the cause and its effects. (Consider using a graphic organizer like the one on page **588**.)
- **Outline your essay.** Write a thesis statement that names your topic (the cause) and the part you will focus on (the effects). Then write down the important details that explain the cause and the effects.

Writing

- **Connect your ideas.** Use your planning as a guide when you write your essay. Create a beginning that introduces the topic and leads to your thesis statement. Write a middle that explains the effects. Each middle paragraph should refer to a separate effect. Write an ending that reflects on the cause and its effects. (Refer to the model on the next page for ideas.)

Revising

- **Improve your writing.** Review your first draft for *ideas, organization,* and *voice.* Ask these questions: *Does my essay clearly illustrate a cause and its effects? Does my essay include enough details? Does my voice sound knowledgeable and appropriate?*
- **Improve your style.** Check your *word choice* and *sentence fluency,* asking these questions: *Have I correctly used and defined any scientific terms? Do my ideas flow smoothly from one to another?*

Editing

- **Check for conventions.** Proofread your essay for errors in punctuation, capitalization, spelling, and grammar.
- **Prepare a final copy.** Make a neat final copy of your cause-effect essay and check it for errors.

■ Cause-Effect Essay

In this essay a student explains the effects of climbing above 25,000 feet.

Sample Essay

The **beginning** introduces the topic (cause) and leads to the thesis statement.

Each **middle** paragraph explains an effect of the lack of oxygen on mountain climbers.

The **ending** summarizes and emphasizes that the rewards of mountain climbing come with great risks.

Into the Death Zone

Mountain climbers must overcome many dangers, and those who climb the world's highest peaks must deal with the greatest danger of all, the death zone. Hundreds of people have climbed above 25,000 feet and returned. They all know that a prolonged stay above that elevation will cause death because the air only holds a third as much oxygen as it does at sea level.

One effect of oxygen deprivation is pulmonary edema. Pulmonary edema is caused by the inability of the lungs to exchange gases and get rid of toxins. All climbers suffer from this condition to a degree, but some risk death if they do not immediately descend to much lower levels. A few mountain climbers cough so hard that they break ribs as their lungs battle for oxygen.

The high altitude and lack of oxygen also affect the brain. The prolonged lack of oxygen causes the brain to swell, and in serious cases death follows quickly. Even breathing bottled oxygen cannot completely compensate for the oxygen-starved brain. Climbers are so impaired at times that they make foolish, often fatal mistakes. Climbers report hallucinations and headaches. One person who successfully climbed Everest found he could not even appreciate what he had done once he reached the peak.

The lack of oxygen also punishes the rest of the body. Hypothermia and frostbite are common because the body's metabolic functions need oxygen to operate efficiently. Climbers stumble, fatigue easily, endure frozen fingers and toes, and suffer nausea. A climber unable to walk is probably doomed because no one else will have the strength to help him or her.

Mountain climbing delivers spectacular rewards, and that is one reason why people risk so much. However, even the best-equipped climbers cannot endure the death zone for long. The lack of oxygen simply challenges climbers beyond their limits. Though climbers may reach their goals, they must quickly leave the place where no human was ever meant to live.

Writing Guidelines ■ Science-Article Summary

Scientists do a great deal of reading to keep up with new discoveries in their fields. The ability to read and summarize an article helps scientists and students alike. Use the guidelines below when you summarize a science article.

Prewriting

- **Find an article.** Browse periodicals like *National Geographic* or *Popular Science*, looking for articles that relate to your class work. Also check Internet sites like *www.nasa.gov* or *www.scitech.gov* and page through your science textbook.
- **Read the article.** Read the selection quickly to get its overall message. Then reread it more carefully for details.
- **Focus on the summary.** Write down the main idea of the article.
- **Gather details.** For your summary, select only the most important details that support the main point of the article. Your summary should be no more than one-third the length of the original.

Writing

- **Connect your ideas.** Write your topic sentence, stating the main point of the reading. Then follow with the key supporting details and an effective closing sentence.
- **Paraphrase information.** Use your own words for the summary. Avoid plagiarism by not copying phrases and sentences from the article itself.

Revising

- **Improve your writing.** Review your first draft for *ideas, organization,* and *voice.* Ask these questions: *Have I identified the main idea of the article? Have I included only the most important details? Have I used a topic sentence, body sentences, and a closing sentence? Have I put the ideas in my own words?*
- **Improve your style.** Check on your *word choice* and *sentence fluency,* asking these questions: *Have I used specific nouns and active verbs? Does my summary read smoothly?*

Editing

- **Check for conventions.** Proofread your summary for errors in punctuation, capitalization, spelling, and grammar.
- **Prepare a final copy.** Make a neat final copy of your summary.

■ Science-Article Summary

The following article, "The Debate on Cloning," is summarized in the student paragraph "Clones Aren't Just Copies."

The Debate on Cloning

Cloning—the process of creating genetically identical organisms—has been a common science-fiction theme for more than 50 years. Today, cloning is making headlines around the world. The first cloned mammal was Dolly the sheep in 1997. Since then, scientists have cloned cats, deer, goats, horses, pigs, and endangered species like the banteng, gaur, and mouflon. Some commercial ventures even provide genetic clones of beloved pet dogs and cats.

In the science of reproductive cloning, the DNA of one animal is transplanted into the nucleus of an egg. The egg is then carried to term by a female of the same species or a similar one.

Advocates of reproductive cloning support the new science as a way to improve medical research. They claim that cloning can provide many medical advances: infertile couples can have children; genetically compatible organs or skin can be created for accident victims; and gene therapies may help doctors cure diseases like Alzheimer's or Parkinson's. However, the immediate use for reproductive cloning is to repopulate endangered animal species.

Opponents of cloning argue that the science faces great ethical problems. They consider it immoral to create life to use it selectively or destroy it in a lab. Indeed, the science-fiction stories that first explored the idea of human cloning depicted the horror of these kinds of abuses. Other opponents of human cloning point to legal issues. In the United States, for example, the constitutional guarantees of rights to individuals would cover any clone at birth. Opponents of cloning argue that the medical advances that cloning offer would come at an unthinkable ethical price.

The science of cloning continues to move forward. Like any science, it has potential to heal or harm. While scientists push the frontiers, opponents continue to protest. The debate is not likely to be resolved soon and may still be raging when the first human clone is old enough to speak for him- or herself.

Sample Summary

Clones Aren't Just Copies

Topic Sentence

Despite deep concerns, cloning has moved from science fiction to science fact. Dolly the sheep was the first cloned mammal in 1997, and more animals have been cloned since then. Supporters say this technology can help infertile couples,

Body Sentences

provide organs for transplants, and cure diseases through gene therapies. Cloning also can help save endangered species. Opponents argue that cloning raises serious ethical concerns, especially in human cloning. They say that human clones should

Closing Sentence

have rights and should not be test subjects. **Cloning isn't science fiction anymore, but science has not been able to dismiss long-standing ethical questions.**

Try It!

Write a summary of an assigned article or of one that interests you. Follow the writing guidelines on the previous page.

Other Forms of Writing in Science

Process Essay

Biology—Write a process essay that describes a chronic illness or condition. Sample topics include arteriosclerosis, emphysema, cancer, or osteoporosis. Tell how the condition begins, how it progresses, and what it leads to.

Classification Essay

Climate Science—Write a classification essay about weather phenomena: types of cyclonic storms, types of fronts, types of clouds, or types of lightning.

Problem-Solution Essay

Life Science—Write a problem-solution essay about a current problem of conservation, such as disappearing wetlands, dying amphibians, or nonnative species. Suggest possible solutions to the problem.

Definition Essay

Geology—Write an essay that defines a major geological feature and explains how it came into being. Consider features like the Ring of Fire, the Great Barrier Reef, the forests of Petrified Forest National Park, the Great Lakes, or the Rocky Mountains.

Opposing-Views Essay

Earth-Space Science—Write an opposing-views essay about a controversial proposal in earth-space science: whether the moon should be mined, whether planets like Mars should be "terraformed" to make them earthlike, and so forth.

Position Essay

Any Science—Read about controversial new theories in biology, earth-space science, or any other area of science that interests you. Choose one theory and write a position essay that explains and defends it against opposing viewpoints.

Writing in Social Studies

In social studies, you are often asked to gather and interpret information from a variety of sources (texts, charts, graphs, maps, photos, and so on) and then respond to the information in writing. Learning to read and interpret data are important skills that will help you succeed when writing about key issues related to social studies.

This chapter models several types of writing you may be asked to do in your social studies classes. It addresses the descriptive report as well as responding to an editorial cartoon and responding to a series of documents.

- **Taking Notes**
- **Keeping a Learning Log**
- **Writing Guidelines: Descriptive Report**
- **Writing Guidelines: Editorial-Cartoon Response**
- **Writing Guidelines: Document-Based Essay**

"I was brought up to believe that the only thing worth doing was to add to the sum of accurate information in the world."

—Margaret Mead

Taking Notes

Taking complete and accurate notes helps you understand new material. Effective notes are also one of your main resources when reviewing for tests and when completing writing assignments. Here are tips for taking notes.

Before You Take Notes . . .

- **Write the topic and date** at the top of each page.
- **Do your assigned reading** before you come to class. That will make it easier to follow what is being discussed. (See page **407**.)

As You Take Notes . . .

- **Listen to lectures carefully** and write down the main ideas.
- **Write down** what the teacher writes on the board or on an overhead.
- **Use your own words** for the most part.
- **Note new or unfamiliar terms** and add definitions later.
- **Condense information.** Write your notes in phrases and lists rather than in complete sentences.

After You Take Notes . . .

- **Review your notes** as soon as possible. Add information to clarify your notes.
- **Find answers** to any questions you still have.

The date and topic are noted.

Main points are underlined.

Dashes set off details.

September 5, 2006

Themes for the Geographer

Describing a place:
- location (where it is)
- features (what it's like)
- region (how places are similar/different)
- movement (how people move from place to place)
- human-environment interaction (how people and animals relate to the physical world)

Geography is the study of the earth's surface features and how humans and animals interact with them.

Try It!

Follow the tips and sample above the next time you take notes in class.

Keeping a Learning Log

A **learning log** is a specialized notebook in which you reflect on ideas and facts you are learning in class. Here are some tips on keeping a learning log.

Before You Make an Entry . . .

- **Write the date and topic** each time you make an entry.

As You Make an Entry . . .

- **Summarize key concepts** that you learned.
- **Connect to the material** by explaining what the ideas mean to you.
- **Write down questions** that you have.

After You Make an Entry . . .

- **Review your entries** to see how well you understand the class material. Also research the questions you have.

The date and topic are given.	**September 5, 2006** *Geography and Geographers*
New information is reviewed.	Today we learned what geography is and how geographers do their work. I think it's fun to look at maps. Whenever my family goes on road trips, I am the map reader.
A personal connection is made.	I like visiting the forest, but I'm always happy to get home to the ocean shore where I can see for miles.
An assignment is discussed.	We learned about the five themes of geography. Each place is described by where it is, what it's like, how it's like other places, how people get around there, and how they interact with their surroundings. I need to write a descriptive report using these five themes.

What's the point of studying geography?

It helps you see connections between land and people.

Try It!

Freewrite for 5 minutes after your next class. Try to make a personal connection with what you learned.

Writing Guidelines ■ Descriptive Report

Often in social studies, you will need to describe an event, a place, or a time in history. Use the following guidelines when you create a descriptive report.

Prewriting

- **Select a topic.** If your teacher does not assign a topic, you should choose a specific event, time, or place that relates to your course work and that you would like to know more about.
- **Gather details.** Learn all you can about your topic. Read books and Web-site articles. Study maps, graphs, and charts. All of this information will help you write a clear and interesting description.
- **Outline your report.** Organize your notes so that related details are together. If you are describing an event, consider organizing your details in chronological order. If you are describing a place, consider organizing your details by order of location or by some other logical order.

Writing

- **Connect your ideas.** Start by introducing your topic. Let the reader know the focus of your description. (Perhaps you will describe a place using the five themes of geography.) In the middle part, describe the topic using a clear and effective method of organization. Write an ending that sums up the topic.

Revising

- **Improve your writing.** Review your first draft for *ideas*, *organization*, and *voice*. Ask yourself if you have included details that help the reader clearly understand what you are describing.
- **Improve your style.** Check for *word choice* and *sentence fluency*. Ask these questions: *Have I correctly used and explained new terms? Do my sentences read smoothly?*

Editing

- **Check for conventions.** Proofread your report for errors in punctuation, capitalization, spelling, and grammar.
- **Prepare a final copy.** Make a neat final copy of your descriptive report. Proofread this copy before sharing it.

■ Descriptive Report

In this report, a student describes the city of Chicago, using the five themes of geography.

Sample Report

Heart of the Midwest

Writers have called Chicago the "Windy City" to describe the wind off Lake Michigan. Carl Sandburg called it the "City of the Big Shoulders" when he wrote about Chicago's hardworking labor force. However, it's unlikely that anyone has ever described Chicago using the five themes of geography: location, features, region, movement, and human-environment interaction.

Location: Located in both the Northern and Western Hemispheres, Chicago is at about 42 degrees latitude and 87 degrees longitude in northeastern Illinois. Lake Michigan forms its eastern boundary.

Features: Chicago sits on a flat tract of land. The city's most unique geographical feature is its beautiful lake shore that borders the Loop, the city's downtown business district. The city's climate is one of extremes. Chicago experiences freezing winter temperatures and occasional heavy snowstorms. Then in summer, the temperature and humidity can almost reach tropical levels.

Region: Chicago is the most populous city in the Midwest region. Politically speaking, Chicago tends to be liberal, just like other large urban areas. A strong work ethic among the city's people means that many major industries and businesses have located in the region.

Movement: Many visitors arrive by air at O'Hare International Airport, one of the world's busiest airports, or at Midway Airport. Chicago provides public transportation for residents and tourists alike, including commuter trains and "el trains" (short for elevated trains). Cars, trucks, buses, and taxis crowd the city streets and expressways. Chicago is also a major Great Lakes port.

Human-Environment Interaction: As Chicago has grown, land has become more scarce. That is why developers have constructed skyscrapers in the Loop. The Sears Tower in Chicago is now the nation's tallest building. Businesses, such as those located on Navy Pier, have also expanded out into the lake on huge piers. Housing in the city and suburbs extends to the north, south, and west.

It's hard to describe a city as complex as Chicago. However, using the five themes of geography is a good starting point.

Writing Guidelines ■ Editorial-Cartoon Response

Often in social studies, you will be asked to respond to an editorial cartoon, which uses words and images to comment on timely issues. Typically, editorial cartoons make their point through caricatures, symbols, labels, and brief captions. (A *caricature* is an exaggerated representation of a person, group, place, or thing.) Use the following guidelines to help you respond to an editorial cartoon.

Prewriting

■ **Study the cartoon.** Carefully review the elements (*caricatures, symbols, text*) in the cartoon. If you're not sure about a particular element, ask someone for help.

■ **Gather details.** List the different elements of the cartoon on a piece of paper. Write a brief description next to the element. (The two examples below relate to the cartoon on the next page.)

Caricature of NASA: NASA is represented by a young boy.

Slingshot: The slingshot may symbolize that the space program is "winging it."

■ **Plan your response.** Identify the main point of the cartoon. Next, write a topic sentence for your response that focuses on the main point. Then determine which details from the cartoon you will include to support the topic sentence.

Writing

■ **Connect your ideas.** Start with your topic sentence. In the body sentences of your response, include the key details. End with a closing sentence that reminds the reader of the main point of the cartoon.

Revising

■ **Improve your writing.** Ask yourself if you have clearly and completely explained the editorial cartoon. Revise accordingly.

■ **Improve your style.** Check for *word choice* and *sentence fluency*.

Editing

■ **Check for conventions.** Proofread your response for errors in punctuation, capitalization, spelling, and grammar.

■ **Prepare a final copy.** Make a neat final copy of your response.

■ Editorial Cartoon

Sample Response

Student writer Mai Yang wrote the following paragraph after taking some time to interpret the editorial cartoon shown above.

Slingshot Space Program

This editorial cartoon suggests two main problems with the United States space program. First, NASA is represented by a young boy pulling back a slingshot. This image suggests that NASA may be "winging" it with the space program, rather than spelling out a specific plan for the future. Just shooting rocket after rocket into space may not be serving the American public. Second, the space program is funded by the American taxpayers. And, as the cartoon suggests, taxpayers are being stretched to the limit to pay for NASA, not to mention all other government programs. The helpless taxpayer appears to have no control over what is happening. All in all, this cartoon raises some critical questions about NASA.

Try It!

Locate a political cartoon in an area newspaper or on the Internet. Respond to the cartoon using the information on page **422** and the sample above as a guide.

Writing Guidelines ▪ Document-Based Essay

In social studies class, you may be asked to respond to a question or prompt based on a series of documents. The documents may include excerpts from books, magazines, letters, diaries, or other text sources. They may also include graphic documents, such as photos, maps, political cartoons, tables, or graphs.

In most cases, you will have several documents on the same subject to read and analyze. Along the way, you may be asked to answer a question about each document. Your main job, however, will be to write an extended essay using all the documents.

Prewriting

- **Read all the information thoroughly.** That includes your responses to questions for each document.
- **Look for clue words.** Make sure you understand your main task. Words such as *compare, explain, define,* and so on, indicate the type of thinking and writing you are to do. (See page **526**.)
- **Analyze each document.** Consider how the documents relate to each other and the main question or prompt you must answer.
- **Organize your facts.** Create an outline that pulls together information from all the documents and from your own previous knowledge.

Writing

- **Write your introductory paragraph.** Introduce the topic, give background information, and restate the question as a thesis statement.
- **Write the body of your essay.** Reword each main point in your outline as a topic sentence for a paragraph that explains part of your thesis. Include plenty of supporting detail in each paragraph.
- **Write a concluding paragraph** that briefly restates your position.

Revising

- **Improve your writing.** Review your essay for *ideas, organization,* and *voice.* Then check for *word choice* and *sentence fluency.*

Editing

- **Check for conventions.** Proofread your essay for errors in punctuation, capitalization, spelling, and grammar.
- **Prepare a final copy.** Make a neat final copy of your essay.

Social Studies

■ Sample Documents

Introduction: In many tropical areas around the world, rain forests are being cut down or burned in a process known as deforestation. At the current rate of deforestation, the rain forests will be gone within 100 years.

Document One

Deforestation and Biodiversity

Worldwide, some 80 million species of plants and animals comprise the biodiversity of earth. Tropical rain forests—covering only 7 percent of the total land area of earth—are home to more than half of all these species. Earth is believed to have tens of millions of species, yet scientists have only given names to about 1.5 million of them.

Many of the rain forests' plants and animals can only be found in very localized areas because they require a unique habitat. This makes them especially vulnerable to deforestation. Every day, species are disappearing as the tropical rain forests are cleared. The exact rate of extinction is unknown. However, estimates indicate that up to 137 species disappear worldwide each day.

The loss of countless species could have a serious impact on the planet. The very plant, animal, and insect species that are being lost today could well hold the key to preventing cancer or curing AIDS.

Source: earthobservatory.nasa.gov

> Only the most important information is included in the summary.

Task: Summarize the main concern of deforestation as presented in this document. Why is it important?

_____ The majority of earth's 80 million species of plants and animals live in rain forests. Approximately 137 species are probably becoming extinct each day due to loss of habitat caused by deforestation. It is not known how this will affect the world, but it could mean losing a chance to cure life-threatening diseases.

Document Two

Causes of Deforestation

Deforestation is the process of cutting down trees and clearing forests. Today, most of the tree clearing is done in tropical rain forests for agricultural purposes. On a large scale, corporate farms deforest huge tracts of land to provide grazing space for large herds of cattle. Commercial loggers contribute to the problem by harvesting trees for timber and wood pulp. On a much smaller scale, subsistent farmers cut down trees to open up a few acres for crops.

The causes of deforestation are complex. The global economy drives the need for money in economically deprived tropical countries. Governments of poor countries sell logging concessions to pay off debts to other countries, to fund government agencies, and to support new industries. Deforestation by individual farmers is driven by the basic need for food.

Other reasons for deforestation include constructing towns for growing populations or building dams to create large reservoirs of water. However, these two reasons account for only a small part of the total deforestation of rain forests.

Source: earthobservatory.nasa.gov

A word or two is all that is needed to list the answers for this task.

Task: Make a chart listing the groups who cause deforestation and the reasons they do it.

Farmers	Businesses	Governments
– food	– make money	– pay off debts
– earn a living	– raise beef cattle	– fund government agencies
	– logging (timber, pulp)	– support new industries

Document Three

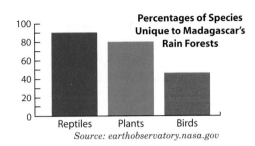

Percentages of Species Unique to Madagascar's Rain Forests

Source: *earthobservatory.nasa.gov*

Graph information is changed to text form.

Task: Explain the information in the bar graph. State at least two of the percentages in a different mathematical form (ratio, fraction, and so on).

Two percentages are stated in other ways.

_____The bar graph shows species unique to Madagascar's rain forests. That means they are found no where else in the world. Nine out of ten of this island's reptiles, four-fifths of its plants, and 46 percent of its birds exist only in Madagascar._____

Document Four

Rain Forests of the World

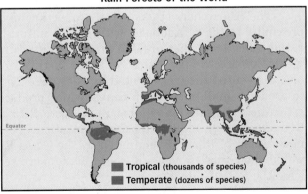

Equator

■ **Tropical** (thousands of species)
■ **Temperate** (dozens of species)

Previous knowledge is used to answer this question.

Task: Based on this map, tell why there are probably fewer species of plants and animals in temperate rain forests than there are in tropical rain forests.

_____Temperate rain forests are farther from the equator. They are cooler and have a wider range of temperatures that many tropical rain-forest species can not tolerate._____

Document Five

We can't save all the forests. Let's say, hypothetically, that we can save 10 percent. We have to decide: What do we set aside? What do we let be destroyed?

> —*Chris Raxworthy, Curator, Herpetology Department,*
> *American Museum of Natural History, New York*

Task: What position does this quotation represent?

<u>This quotation says that deforestation cannot</u>
<u>just stop. A plan is needed to determine which rain</u>
<u>forests to save.</u>

The main point is restated.

Document Six

Buzz from Rain Forest Good for Coffee Farms

Those coffee beans you're grinding might be better tasting and more bountiful thanks to rain-forest bees. And that discovery by a Kansas University researcher could give Central American farmers a powerful incentive to stop destroying the bees' habitat. . . .

The researchers studied crop production as it related to proximity to the rain forests, which are a natural bee habitat. They found coffee trees that grew in areas heavily pollinated by bees had yields 20 percent higher than in areas farther from the bees. They also discovered the trees visited by bees were 27 percent less likely to produce small, misshapen beans, which produce inferior coffee. . . .

Michener said many farmers in Costa Rica clear-cut forest land to make way for additional coffee plantations. He said he hoped the new research, when disseminated by the Costa Rican government, would show those farmers it would make more sense financially to keep the forests intact.

> —*The Lawrence Journal-World,* Lawrence, Kansas

Task: What's one way to save rain forests?

<u>One way to save rain forests is to prove their value to local</u>
<u>people who live near them.</u>

■ Document-Based Essay

In this essay, a student writes an essay that pulls together the information presented in six original documents.

Task: Extended Essay

Using all six documents provided and your own knowledge about this topic, write an essay in which you explain why deforestation occurs, what it leads to, and what can be done about it.

Sample Essay

Is There Hope for the World's Rain Forests?

DOCUMENTS 1, 2, AND 4
The thesis is stated in the opening paragraph.

Deforestation of tropical rain forests occurs because economically challenged tropical nations find it difficult to compete in a world market. However, even though deforestation appears to make life better for people in the short term, it is impossible to replace the tropical rain forests. The world's temperate rain forests just don't offer the same variety of species. The nations of the world should try to reduce the loss of valuable plant and animal life since such loss is affecting the world in a devastating way in the long term.

DOCUMENT 2
An overview of reasons for deforestation is presented.

In all cases, rain forests are destroyed for economic reasons. Farmers cut down trees on a few acres to grow crops or graze animals. A majority of people in these countries rely on the land to eat and to earn a living. In many areas, large logging businesses destroy huge areas of rain forest for lumber. On cleared land, corporate farms graze cattle for the world beef market. Governments also destroy rain forests by promoting industry to help pay debts. They also use some rain-forest land to construct new towns and dams for growing populations.

DOCUMENT 1
The importance of habitat is emphasized and previous knowledge is shared.

Losing rain forests means losing plants, reptiles, birds, and other wildlife. The majority of the world's species call rain forests home, so any loss of rain forest is a loss of vital habitat. Some species may live in more than one of the world's rain forests, but that isn't always true. Rain forests

DOCUMENT 3
Specific facts from a graph emphasize the uniqueness of the rain-forest ecosystem.

are very unique ecosystems. For example, in the rain forests of Madagascar, 90 percent of the reptiles live nowhere else on earth. The same is true for 80 percent of Madagascar's plants and 46 percent of its birds. Many rain forest species are still unknown to humans, so the exact effect of their loss to the world is uncertain. However, any plant or animal that becomes extinct might have been the source of a cure for disease.

DOCUMENTS 1, 2, AND 4
The causes and effects of deforestation are revisited.

While the future of tropical rain forests is uncertain, two facts remain. As many as 137 species may be lost each day because rain-forest habitat is being destroyed. The world's few temperate rain forests don't support plants and animals being lost in the tropical rain forests. Populations of rain-forest countries keep growing, and so economic pressure keeps increasing for individuals, businesses, and governments who rely on rain forests for income.

DOCUMENTS 5 AND 6
The conclusion points to one way to slow or stop deforestation.

Scientists seem to agree that it may be impossible to stop deforestation. Instead, they call for a plan to slow the process. Questions remain about which rain forests will contribute most to the world and humankind. More research could find ways to prove the value of saving rain forests. For instance, in Costa Rica, researchers found that pollination by rain-forest bees increased nearby coffee crops 20 percent. More could be done to find out what people living in rain forests already know about the medical values of plants and animals so that people around the world would understand the value of saving irreplaceable rain forests.

Essay Checklist

_____ **1.** Do all the ideas in my essay support and relate to my thesis statement?

_____ **2.** Do I cover all the issues named in the task or prompt?

_____ **3.** Do I summarize my main points in the conclusion?

_____ **4.** Do I refer to information from all the documents?

_____ **5.** Do I include some of my own knowledge about this topic?

_____ **6.** Have I checked my punctuation, grammar, and spelling?

Writing in Math

Your understanding of mathematics rests upon a foundation laid down during your early years—from counting to adding to subtracting and on and on. Through the years, you have continued to build concept upon concept, much as construction workers frame in a building floor by floor.

When you attempt to explain a math concept in writing, you may discover you have gained a greater understanding of the idea. You may also find that striving to put math into words can actually improve your writing.

- Taking Notes
- Keeping a Learning Log
- Writing Guidelines: Article Summary
- Writing Guidelines: Problem Analysis
- Writing Guidelines: Creation of a Chart or Graph
- Writing Guidelines: Response to a Math Prompt
- Other Forms of Writing in Math

"The safest words are always those which bring us most directly to fact."
—Charles H. Parkhurst

Taking Notes

Using your own words to write down mathematical steps and formulas can help you understand and remember them. Here are some note-taking tips.

Before You Take Notes . . .

- **Use a three-ring binder** to store your notes so that you can add handouts, worksheets, and so on.
- **Write the topic and date** at the beginning of each entry.

As You Take Notes . . .

- **Write down** what the teacher puts on the board or overhead. This information often contains main concepts, math terms, definitions, formulas, and important examples.
- **Put concepts in your own words.** Also write down questions you have about the material.
- **Draw pictures.** Use diagrams to help you visualize a process.

After You Take Notes . . .

- **Find answers** to your questions.
- **Study your notes** before the next class and again before exams.

Sample Notes

May 3, 2007
Two-Step Equations
- variable—represents the unknown
- inverse operation—doing the opposite (subtract, not add)
- solving for the variable—getting the variable alone on one side of the equation

Solving Two-Step Equations
1. Subtract (or add) the number without the variable to both sides.
2. Divide (or multiply) by the number attached to the variable on both sides of the equation.
3. Substitute the answer into the equation to check it.

Problem: Tulip bulbs cost $0.75 each plus $3.00 for shipping. With $14.00, how many bulbs can you order?

Form an equation: Let x represent the number of tulip bulbs. Then
$0.75x + 3.00 = 14.00$

(1) Subtract 3.00 from both sides.
$0.75x + 3.00 - 3.00 = 14.00 - 3.00$
$0.75x = 11.00$

(2) Divide by 0.75 on both sides.
$$\frac{0.75x}{0.75} = \frac{11.00}{0.75} \qquad x = 14.67$$
You can buy 14 bulbs.

(3) Check your solution.
$0.75 (14) + 3.00 = 13.50.$
You have $0.50 remaining.

Keeping a Learning Log

In a learning log, you record new ideas and puzzle over questions related to what you are studying. Here are some tips for keeping a learning log.

Before You Write . . .

- **Set up the log.** Use a notebook or a section of your binder.
- **Date each entry** so you can find it easily.
- **Leave wide margins** for writing questions and answers.

As You Write . . .

- **Reflect on what you learn** by writing about what you understand and what you're still questioning.
- **Summarize key concepts** and think about how they connect to your own experience and to other ideas you have learned in math.

After You Write . . .

- **Review your log** before a test or when you study a new theorem.
- **Answer any questions** you may still have.

Sample Learning Log

May 3, 2007   Exponents

Exponents: n is the exponent in X^n (X to the nth power). An exponent tells how often the base is used as a factor.

$A^4 = A \times A \times A \times A$ (A to the 4th power)

1. When multiplying same-base variables with exponents, ADD exponents.
$A^x \times A^y = A^{x+y}$ $A^3 \times A^2 = A^5$

2. When raising a variable with an exponent to another power, MULTIPLY exponents.
$(A^x)^y = A^{xy}$ $(A^3)^2 = A^6$

3. When raising more than one variable to a power, raise BOTH by that exponent.
$(AB)^x = A^x B^x$ $(AB)^3 = A^3 B^3$

Base? Number raised to n^{th} power
Factor? Multiplying number
$3^4 = 3 \times 3 \times 3 \times 3 = 81$ (3=base)

1. product of powers
$2^3 \times 2^2 = 2^5 = 32$

2. power of a power
$(2^3)^2 = 2^6 = 64$

3. power of a product
$(2 \times 3)^3 = 2^3 \times 3^3 = 8 \times 27 = 216$

Try It!

Write a learning log entry about a topic you studied in math class.

Writing Guidelines ▪ Article Summary

You often encounter statistics or data analysis in the articles, books, or news stories you read. Use the following guidelines when you are asked to summarize a math-related article.

Prewriting

- **Find an article.** Choose a newspaper or magazine article that uses statistics and figures to support a story, a position, or an issue.
- **Read the article.** Read the selection first to get its overall message. Then reread it carefully, paying attention to details.
- **Find the focus.** Write down the main idea of the article.
- **Gather details.** Select only the most important details that support the main idea of the article. Arrange the details in the most logical order.

Writing

- **Write your first draft.** Write your topic sentence, stating the main point of the reading. Supply supporting details. Close with a sentence that summarizes your thoughts.

Revising

- **Improve your writing.** Review your first draft for *ideas, organization,* and *voice.* Ask these questions: *Have I identified the main idea of the article? Have I included only the most important details? Have I explained any math concepts in clear language?*
- **Improve your style.** Check on your *word choice* and *sentence fluency.* Ask these questions: *Have I used specific nouns and active verbs? Does my summary read smoothly?*

Editing

- **Check for conventions.** Proofread your summary for errors in punctuation, capitalization, spelling, and grammar.
- **Prepare a final copy.** Make a neat final copy of your summary.

Try It!

Write a summary. Find an article containing math data. Follow the tips above as you write your summary paragraph.

■ Math Article and Summary

A student read the following article in the newspaper and wrote a brief summary, including a graph to illustrate the statistics in the article.

Teen Reading Habits Examined

Parents today are frequently reminded to monitor what their children are watching on television, downloading on the computer, or listening to on their MP3 players. Curiously, you seldom hear of parents being warned to monitor what books their children are checking out from the public library. Many libraries maintain a policy of no restrictions as to what young people may check out, and the Putnam City Library is no different. According to City Librarian Anna LaGrange, "If they have a card, they can check out anything."

While this might seem disconcerting to most parents, there is good news. According to Ms. LaGrange, the majority of books being read by young people in Putnam seem to be age appropriate. "While we don't censor reading materials, I keep records of what is checked out," she says. "Our teens make excellent choices of reading materials." She offers the following statistics from the past year to support her claim.

The books most often checked out in the past 12 months have been classified by the Young Adult Library Services Association (YALSA) as "Books that don't make you blush." These include teen romances, modern novels, and classics and contain no objectionable themes or language. Nearly 27% of books checked out by Putnam teens fall into this category. Mysteries are checked out by 21% of the city's teens and include adult mysteries as well as those for young adults. Science fiction runs a close third at 18%, and historical fiction is also popular, with a 16% readership. Health-related books capture 9% of our teens' interest. These can be either fiction, including medical thrillers, or nonfiction. The remaining 7% are books that contain inappropriate adult themes or language.

"While there is some wiggle room in the categories, on the whole, our children appear to be reading age-appropriate material," says Ms. LaGrange. She still encourages parents to talk with their children about their reading, and offers this advice to parents: "You judge what is appropriate. Read what your child is reading, and read good books on your own. Set an example, and then you can set your guidelines."

Sample Summary

Teen Reading: Right on Track

The article "Teen Reading Habits Examined" shows the types of books teenagers are checking out of the Putnam City Library. Statistics quoted by librarian Anna LaGrange indicate that student interests tend to be appropriate to their ages. Books most often checked out by local teens appear to be unobjectionable novels, classics, and mysteries. Science fiction and historical fiction also appear to be widely read, followed by health-related works. Only a few students check out books that might be unacceptable. The librarian suggests that parents should know what their children are reading.

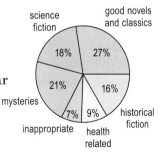

Types of Literature Checked Out by Teens at Putnam City Library

Writing Guidelines ■ Problem Analysis

In math class, you learn how to analyze problems by stating specific *assumptions, evaluations,* and *explanations* about them.

- **Assumptions** are statements that are believed to be true. These could be formulas or statements about variables. They provide the structure for solving the problem.

    Evaluate and solve 6x - (x+y), for x=4 **and** y=5 (assumptions)

- **Evaluations** are the calculations and manipulations needed to get to the answer. For this problem, show your work by replacing unknown variables (x or y) with their values.

    6(4) - (4+5) = 6(4) - 9 = 24 - 9 = 15 (evaluations)

- **Explanations** make any complex process clearer to the reader by explaining problem-solving steps.

    I solved this by replacing x and y with their assumed values;
    if x=4 and y=5, then the answer to 6x - (x+y) is 15 (explanation).

Prewriting

- **Select a topic.** If your teacher does not assign a specific math problem, review your learning log or textbook for ideas.
- **Study the problem.** Be sure you understand your assignment. Then write down assumptions you find in its instructions.
- **Plan the steps.** Write down each step in the correct order.

Writing

- **Write your first draft.** First, introduce the problem and explain it step-by-step, identifying any variables. Next, evaluate the problem by sharing all work. Finally, state your explanation.

Revising

- **Improve your writing.** Review your *ideas, organization,* and *voice. Do you identify the assumptions and explain the process clearly?*
- **Improve your style.** Check *word choice* and *sentence fluency. Have you correctly used and defined any math terms?*

Editing

- **Check for conventions.** Check punctuation, grammar, and spelling.
- **Prepare a final copy.** Make a neat final copy of your work.

■ Analysis of a Problem

To analyze math problems, you need to show your work. Read the prompt and determine the assumptions (A). In the middle, show the calculations and manipulations (B–D). End with an explanation of the process (E).

Sample Analysis

For the past 50 years, kids have enjoyed coiled-spring toys. In those five decades of production, 3,030,000 miles of wire weighing 50,000 tons have been coiled, with each spring toy starting as 80 feet of wire.

(A) What assumptions can be made from the above information?

One toy uses 80 feet of wire. In 50 years, 3,030,000 miles and 50,000 tons of wire were used for the toys.

(B) Explain how to find out the number of toys made and then solve.

There are 5,280 feet in one mile. Divide 5,280 by 80 to find out how many toys are in one mile of wire (66). Multiply 66 times 3,030,000 to find out how many toys were produced in 50 years (199,980,000).

(C) Explain how to find out how much 1 mile of wire weighs and then solve.

A ton weighs 2,000 pounds. First multiply 2,000 times 50,000 to find out how many pounds all the wire weighs (100,000,000 pounds). Divide that by 3,030,000 miles to find the pounds per mile (33 pounds).

(D) The 3,030,000 miles of wire could go around the equator 126 times. What is the length of the equator? What is the diameter of Earth?

Divide 3,030,000 by 126 to find the equator (24,048 miles). Find Earth's diameter by dividing 24,048 by 3.14 (7,659 miles).

(E) List known values and definitions you need to solve the questions.

I needed to know the number of feet in a mile, the number of pounds in a ton, that the length of the equator equals Earth's circumference, that circumference equals diameter times pi, and that pi is about 3.14.

Try It!

Eight public swimming pools hold a total volume of 17,500 cubic meters of water. Each pool is 1.75 meters deep and is half as wide as it is long. What assumptions can you make from this information? Explain how to find the dimensions of the pools. What do you need to know to find the dimensions? Use the example above as a model.

Math

Writing Guidelines ■ Creation of a Chart or Graph

Sometimes figures, numbers, or statistics are best communicated in charts and graphs, which can express the relationship between facts at a glance.

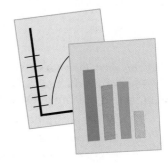

- **Charts** often list the most important details from an article, such as the prices of certain grocery items. Tables are sometimes called charts.
- **Graphs** can plot the points of different variables to show how numbers change over time or in relation to other factors.

Prewriting

- **Select a topic.** If your teacher does not assign a specific topic, review your class notes, learning log, or textbook for ideas. Choose a topic from which you can develop a chart or graph.
- **Gather details.** Research your topic and write down the primary details. Use a chart if you are listing numbers. Develop a chart or a graph to show the relationship between variables.

Writing

- **Design your chart or graph.** Include the most important ideas and details on your chart or graph. Experiment to find the best way to display your information so that a reader understands it.

Revising

- **Improve your chart or graph.** Ask these questions: *Have I correctly used and defined any mathematical terms? Is the information clear, easy to follow, and labeled properly? Have I double-checked any calculations made to create this chart or graph?*

Editing

- **Check for conventions.** Check your work for errors in punctuation, capitalization, spelling, and grammar.
- **Prepare a final copy.** Make a neat final copy of your chart or graph and proofread it again.

■ Graphic Response

Yuri's teacher gave his class the following assignment about banking statistics.

Sample Assignment and Response

Many people borrow money to buy a car. The length of time they take to pay back the loan may range from two to six years. The chart below shows the monthly payments on a loan of $15,000 at 6 percent interest.

1. What can you tell, from the chart at the right, about the relationship between the length of the loan and the monthly payment?
2. Identify the independent and the dependent variables.
3. Graph the data.
4. Is the relationship between the variables clearer on the graph or in the chart? Explain your answer.

Length of Loan	Monthly Payment
Two years	$664.81
Three years	$456.33
Four years	$352.28
Five years	$289.99
Six years	$248.59

Yuri B.
Math 9, Period 7

The student answers each question.

1. If you borrow money for a longer time, your monthly payment is lower.
2. The independent variable is the number of years; the dependent variable is the monthly payment. The monthly payment depends on the length of the loan.
3. See the graph.

He makes a graph to show his answer.

4. The graph is clearer. You can spot the relationship of time against the payment.

Monthly Payments (in dollars)

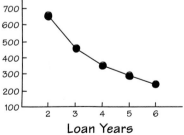
Loan Years

Try It!

Figure out the total payment for each loan. Graph the data. The total payment is your dependent variable and time is the independent variable.

Writing Guidelines ■ Response to a Math Prompt

Math prompts are like word problems. To solve mathematical test prompts, you need good reading and thinking skills. By approaching the prompt one step at a time, you can solve the problem and explain your solution. Use the following guidelines when responding to a math test prompt.

Prewriting

- **Read the prompt.** Read the prompt carefully to understand it completely. Some problems have more than one part. Always pay attention to the directions in the prompt, performing the requested actions only.
- **Gather details and data.** Find the details given in the prompt as assumptions. Write down the data you will use to solve the prompt.

Writing

- **Build your solution.** Decide how to use the assumptions and data to solve the problem. Set up the mathematical formula or equation and show all your work.

Revising

- **Improve your response.** Reread the prompt after you do your calculations. If the problem has more than one part, be sure to answer every part. Always double-check your math to be sure your solution is correct.

Editing

- **Check for conventions.** Check your solution for errors in punctuation, capitalization, spelling, and grammar.
- **Prepare a final copy.** Make a neat final copy of your solution.

Try It!

Find a prompt and write a response. Choose a practice prompt from your math textbook or one recommended by your teacher. Follow the tips above to write your solution to the test prompt.

■ Response to a Math Prompt

Toni's algebra class was assigned the following math prompt. Toni's response below answers each question and shows all the work of her solution.

Solving Systems of Equations

A. Solve one of the problems below using the appropriate method or methods—graphing, substitution, or elimination.

B. Justify your reason for choosing the method and explain how to solve the problem.

C. Solve the system of equations and show all your work.

1. $-5x + 2y = 14$ **2.** $y = -2x + 7$ **3.** $y = 4$
   $-3x + y = -2$ $y = 4x - 5$ $3x - y = 5$

Toni Ortiz
Math 9, Period 4

A. I chose to solve problem #1 using both elimination and substitution.

B. The system of two equations is set up to use this method. I first have to multiply the bottom equation by -2 (because the top equation has a positive 2y I need to balance out). Then I can add the two equations together to "eliminate" the y variable (reduce it to 0). That shows the solution to the x variable. I then use substitution to solve for the y variable.

C. Steps of Solution

$-5x + 2y = 14$	$-5x + 2y = 14$	$-3(18) + y = -2$
$-2(-3x + y = -2)$	$+\ 6x - 2y = 4$	$-54 + y = -2$
	$\overline{\quad x \quad\quad = 18}$	$+\ \ 54 \qquad\quad 54$
		$\overline{\qquad\qquad y = 52}$

Solution of (x, y) is (18, 52)

> This student breaks the answer into steps.

> She shows all her work and gives the final answer.

Other Forms of Writing in Math

Descriptive Writing

Geometry—Write a descriptive paragraph or essay using your knowledge of geometric shapes to describe your home.

Definition

Any Math—Write a detailed expository paragraph that defines a major mathematical concept, such as *coefficients, complementary angles, inductive reasoning, Pythagorean rule,* or *tessellation.*

Narrative

Personal Finance—Write a paragraph or an essay about converting currency while you are on a trip (real or imagined) to another country. Ask your teacher for help in finding the most up-to-date currency conversion rates.

Any Math—Write an anecdote or a longer narrative to tell about a time you used math skills in your daily life.

Classification

Geometry—Write a classification paragraph or essay about different types of polyhedrons: the five regular polyhedra, the different types of pyramids, and so on. Organize your writing to compare and contrast if you wish.

Position

Any Math—Read about controversial new theories in math or economics that interest you. Choose one theory and write a position essay that supports the theory and defends it against opposing viewpoints.

Process

Any Math—Write a process paragraph or essay about the history and development of calculators from the abacus to today's computers.

Writing in the Applied Sciences

In some classes, you learn by reading a textbook, listening to lectures, and taking notes. In other classes, you learn by doing. Family and consumer science (FACS) and technical education (Tech Ed) are considered applied science classes because they give you hands-on experience.

Many teachers of applied sciences use writing assignments to complement the hands-on part of the class. After completing a project, students reflect on their experience, analyzing what went right as well as what went wrong.

In this section, you will learn about taking notes and keeping a learning log in a FACS or Tech Ed class. Then you will review forms of writing often assigned in these classes.

- Taking Notes
- Keeping a Learning Log
- Writing Guidelines: Process Essay
- Writing Guidelines: Essay of Identification
- Writing Guidelines: Persuasive Poster
- Other Forms of Practical Writing

"I hear and I forget; I see and I remember; I write and I understand."

—Chinese Proverb

Taking Notes

Effective note taking is especially valuable in the applied sciences.

Before You Take Notes . . .

- **Keep your notes in a three-ring binder** so you can add work sheets and additional notes.
- **Write the date** at the beginning of each entry.
- **Divide your paper into two columns.** Write steps of a process on the left and comments, reasons, or other data on the right. Or put reading notes on the left and classroom notes on the right.

As You Take Notes . . .

- **Jot down important instructions** as they are given.
- **Don't write down every word.** Use phrases and lists.
- **Draw diagrams and graphic organizers** to help you remember.

After You Take Notes . . .

- **Review your notes** and highlight main ideas.
- **Study your notes** during a project or before a test.
- **Form study groups** for sharing notes and asking questions.

Oct. 12, 2005   Hybrid engines

A parallel hybrid engine has a fuel tank to run the gas engine and batteries to run the electric motor.

The gas and electric engines both connect to the transmission. Either one can turn the axle on its own, or they can turn it together.

A series hybrid engine is different. It uses a gas-driven generator to run the electric motor or recharge the batteries.

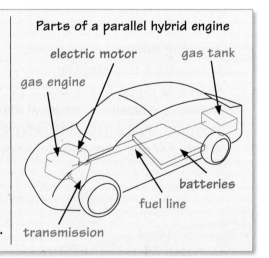

Parts of a parallel hybrid engine

electric motor   gas tank

gas engine

batteries

fuel line

transmission

Try It!

Prepare a binder for notes and take notes in your next class.

Keeping a Learning Log

A learning log is a journal with entries about the things you are learning in a specific class. In this type of journal, you can reflect on new ideas, puzzle over questions, and add drawings or comments on a project.

Before You Write . . .

- **Use a spiral notebook** or a section of your three-ring binder.
- **Date each entry.**
- **Leave wide margins** for writing questions and, later, for answers.

As You Write . . .

- **Reflect on what you are learning.** Include what you experienced, what you wonder about, what worked and didn't work.
- **Predict what will come next.** Think about how the material connects to other classes or to what you already know.

After You Write . . .

- **Review your log** before a test and when you need an idea for a project.
- **Answer any questions** you may have written in the margins.

November 9, 2005—FACS

Sleeves are so complicated! I tried to save time by using only one row of basting stitches along the top edge of the sleeve, but I ended up with tucks when I tried to attach the sleeve to the bodice. I had to start over!

A sculptor must see a statue inside a block of marble, but a tailor must see a shirt inside out and right side out at the same time.

Of course, there are tricks, like pressing seams open before attaching pieces. That makes the seams lie flat so they are easier to match. I'll get the hang of this soon!

What's the point of two rows of basting stitches? They keep the shoulders from looking puffy.

Try It!

Set up a learning log in a notebook or in a section of your three-ring binder. Be sure to date each entry.

Writing Guidelines ▪ Process Essay

A process essay tells how to do something or how something works. You could write about how to make tortilla pinwheels, or you could describe how gas burns in an internal-combustion engine. Your goal in a process essay is to explain each step clearly and completely.

Prewriting

- **Select a topic.** If your teacher does not assign a specific topic, review your notes, manual, or textbook for ideas. Think of things you have made, skills you have mastered, or processes you have observed. Consider topics with steps or with a chain of causes and effects.
- **Gather details.** Freewrite about the topic, writing everything you know about it. Research the various steps in your notes, manual, or textbook. Then list needed materials or ingredients, equipment, and the steps in the process.
- **Plan and organize.** Outline your essay. First, list the materials and equipment. Then, in chronological order, list the steps of the process.

Writing

- **Connect your ideas.** Write a beginning paragraph, introducing the topic. Then discuss materials, ingredients, or equipment in the order used. Afterward, write about each step. The steps should logically follow each other, allowing the reader to understand the process. Use transition words and phrases to connect your ideas.

Revising

- **Improve your writing.** Review your first draft for *ideas, organization*, and *voice*. Ask these questions: *Is the process clear? Have I described all necessary materials or equipment? Do I have the steps in time order? Is my essay interesting to read?* Work with a partner to get suggestions for revision. Use the expository rubric (pages 180–181) as a final check of your revising.
- **Improve your style.** Check your *word choice* and *sentence fluency*. Ask these questions: *Have I used correct terminology? Does each step lead naturally to the next step?* Revise to improve your essay.

Editing

- **Check for conventions.** Check punctuation, spelling, and grammar.
- **Prepare a final copy.** Make a neat final copy of your essay.

■ A Recipe

Luz chose to explain the process of making tortilla pinwheels step-by-step.

The **beginning** introduces the topic.

The **middle** paragraphs list materials needed and explain the process.

The **ending** concludes with serving suggestions.

Tasty Tortilla Pinwheels

Tortillas aren't just for tacos anymore. Try this tasty appetizer, which is easy to make and delicious.
- 2 8-oz. packages cream cheese
- 1 package dry ranch dressing mix
- 2 green onions
- 4 12-inch flour tortillas
- 1 small jar diced pimentos
- 3 jalapeño peppers, no seeds
- 3 green chili peppers
- 8 oz. black olives

Before you begin, be sure you have kitchen gloves handy to protect your hands from the juice of the jalapeño peppers. Also be careful not to rub your eyes when handling the peppers.

To begin, soften the cream cheese in a microwave. Set the microwave on medium power for 30 seconds at a time until the cheese is spreadable. Blend with the dry ranch dressing mix.

Next, finely chop the green onions and add to the cream-cheese mixture. Spread the mixture onto the four tortillas, covering all the way to the edges.

Drain the pimentos on paper towels. Meanwhile, wearing kitchen gloves, chop the jalapeños and discard the seeds. Dice the chiles and the olives. Sprinkle all ingredients evenly on the four tortillas.

Starting on one side of the first tortilla, roll tightly. Do the same for each of the others. Wrap each in wax paper and chill at least two hours. When firm, unwrap from the wax paper, slice each tortilla into 1-inch-thick slices, and arrange on a plate.

Serve pinwheel tortillas as a colorful appetizer at your next family gathering or just as a tasty snack anytime.

Write a process essay. Select a process you know very well. Follow the guidelines on page 446 as you write your essay. Be sure to list any materials necessary and provide the steps in chronological order.

Writing Guidelines ■ Essay of Identification

An essay of identification names tools or the parts of a machine. It then explains what each of these items does and how they work together.

Prewriting

- **Select a topic.** If your teacher doesn't assign a specific topic, think of tools you use in class or machines that help you perform a task. Select a topic that has several elements to be identified.
- **Gather details.** Freewrite about your topic, describing it and telling what it is used for. Then think about how the different parts relate to each other.
- **Plan and organize.** Decide on the best order for arranging your information. If you are describing saws, for example, you could start with the most common (handsaw) and work up to the most unusual (radial-arm saw). If you are describing parts of a machine, you could organize them spatially (front to back, top to bottom, or left to right).

Writing

- **Connect your ideas.** Introduce the items or parts you will write about. Then devote a paragraph to each item, identifying it, describing it, and telling its uses. (Two closely related items can be covered in one paragraph.) Write an ending that explains how the items relate to each other, or sum up the essay in another way.

Revising

- **Improve your writing.** Review your writing for *ideas, organization,* and *voice.* Ask these questions: *Have I identified, described, and explained each item? Have I presented the items in the best order? Do I sound interested and knowledgeable?* Add, cut, or move details to improve your essay. Use the expository rubric on pages **180–181** as a final check of your revising.
- **Improve your style.** Check your *word choice* and *sentence fluency* to make sure that everything is stated clearly and effectively. Ask these questions: *Have I chosen specific words and explained technical terms? Do my sentences flow smoothly?*

Editing

- **Check for conventions.** Check punctuation, spelling, and grammar.
- **Prepare a final copy.** Make a neat final copy of your essay.

■ Essay of Identification

Ravi wrote the following essay of identification for his Drafting I class.

T-square

45° triangle

30°–60° triangle

Protractor

The beginning introduces the tools used.

> When I first started drafting, I couldn't believe people could make such complicated drawings using such simple tools. Now, with a T-square, a couple of triangles, and a protractor, I can make complex drawings of my own.

Each middle paragraph identifies a tool, describes it, and explains its uses.

> The T-square is a straight plastic or metal measuring stick with a guide piece attached to one end at a right angle (90°). By placing the guide along the side of the drafting table, the T-square establishes the horizontal axis. The T-square is used to line up the paper and draw any horizontal line on it.

> The T-square works with two triangles to make vertical lines and various angles. The 45° triangle has one angle at 90° and two others at 45°. The 30°–60° triangle has one angle at 90°, one at 30°, and another at 60°. Each triangle is set on the T-square and used to draw lines. By using both triangles together, the following angles can be created: 75°, 105°, 120°, 135°, and 150°.

> Another tool used with the T-square is the protractor. It is a semicircle with a straight side. The curved side is marked by degrees to help create any angles between 0° and 180°. The drafter aligns the protractor with one side of the angle. A mark is made through the hole in the center of the straight side for the vertex of the angle. Another dot is marked at the angle desired, and the two dots are connected to create the second side of the angle.

The ending reflects on the importance of all the tools.

> With these simple tools, drafters have drawn entire cathedrals. At first, I couldn't do more than draw a few lines, but now I can draw just about anything I can imagine.

Write an essay of identification. Identify tools or parts of a machine. Define each item, show how it works, and tell how it relates to the others.

Writing Guidelines ■ Persuasive Poster

A well-designed poster uses words and images to make a point quickly, clearly, and persuasively. In applied sciences, posters can convince the reader to attend important events, follow procedures, and avoid dangerous situations.

Prewriting

■ **Select a topic.** If your teacher doesn't assign a specific topic, think of things you'd personally like to promote—events, rules and safety procedures, or policies to keep the workplace running smoothly. Select a topic that you feel strongly about.

■ **Gather details.** Brainstorm a list of the points you wish to make. Think of as many as you can, and then select the most important ones. Write a slogan or catchphrase that sums up your points. Also think of a call to action: something you want the reader to do.

Writing

■ **Design your poster.** Sketch out your poster on a standard sheet of paper. Experiment with different elements—main headings, bullet points, and graphics. Also try various typestyles and colors. Your poster should be both eye catching and easy to read.

■ **Compare designs.** Review your designs, checking for *ideas*, *organization*, and *voice*. Ask these questions: *Which design effectively delivers my overall message, has the clearest organization, and is most convincing and eye catching?* Choose the best one and add, cut, or rearrange elements to improve your poster.

Revising

■ **Improve your poster's message.** Review your poster for *word choice* and *sentence fluency*. Ask these questions: *Do I use the best words to get my point across? Do I use command words to ask my reader to act? Do my ideas flow smoothly?* Make your revisions.

Editing

■ **Check for conventions.** Look for errors in punctuation, spelling, capitalization, and grammar. Use the persuasive rubric on pages 234–235 as a final check of your revising and editing.

■ **Prepare a final copy.** Transfer your corrected poster to a large piece of poster board. Proofread this final copy before posting it.

■ Safety Posters

The following posters for a shop class focus on safety and courtesy. You can try a variety of colors, type fonts, and images to present your message.

Command words get attention.

A graphic emphasizes the message.

Color highlights important words.

STAY SAFE IN SHOP!

Wear goggles **and hearing-protection equipment.**

Use tool guards!

Check tools **before using them.**

Walk, **don't run.**

Keep **your brain in gear!**

A question catches the reader's attention.

Short, parallel sentences get to the point.

Color highlights important words.

WHY SHOULD YOU KEEP THIS SHOP CLEAN?

Spills **can cause accidents.**

Dirty tools **can be dangerous.**

Messes **can waste time.**

Oily rags **can cause fires.**

Try It!

Create a persuasive poster promoting an event, highlighting classroom rules, or encouraging safety or courtesy.

Other Forms of Practical Writing

Lab Report

Foods Class—Write a lab report based on an observation of yeast at various temperatures. Report your hypothesis about what will happen. Then note your observations and summarize the results.

Observation/Accident Report

Metal Shop—Observe students working on their projects and write a report on their use of equipment (tools and safety).

Letter and E-mail Message

Living-on-Your-Own Class—Write a letter of complaint about a product you recently bought that does not work properly. Include a detailed description of the problem and the action needed to remedy the situation. Keep your language neutral, cool, and professional.

Press Release

Any Class—Write a press release promoting a current class project. Focus on the positive aspects of the project as well as its importance to the general public.

Résumé

Career Explorations Class—Write your résumé for a career that interests you. Include your education and relevant talents and abilities. Add personal qualifications and name two references.

Work Order and Estimate

Auto Shop—Examine an engine that needs a tune-up. Write a description of the work that should be done along with a cost estimate for parts and labor charges. Explain the need for each item.

Writing in the Arts

Studying works of art or music can stimulate your mind and trigger many questions. Why did a painter use a particular medium? How did a composer develop his or her style? How has sculpting changed over time? How do different types of music affect people's feelings? Why do different countries have different styles of music?

As you study these creative fields, let writing deepen your understanding and enjoyment of the arts. This chapter will help you write learning-log entries, essays, and reports about the arts.

- ■ **Taking Classroom Notes**
- ■ **Keeping a Learning Log**
- ■ **Writing Guidelines: Response to a Prompt**
- ■ **Writing Guidelines: Research Report**
- ■ **Other Forms of Writing in the Arts**

"Art is a lie which makes us realize the truth."

—Picasso

454

Taking Classroom Notes

Even though most of your work in art and music classes is applied (you paint, you sing, you play an instrument), there are times to take notes.

Take notes when . . .

- **your teacher writes information on the board or an overhead.**
  This information is obviously important. Copying it into your notes helps make the information part of your own thinking. Be sure to write down new vocabulary words, as well as names, dates, and key phrases.
- **you have a demonstration in class.**
  Your class may view slides of art pieces or listen to recordings of various musical styles. Taking notes will help you keep track of the individual works.
- **you have a guest speaker/performer.**
  Professional artists may demonstrate or discuss their work. Your notes can help you participate during a question-and-answer session after the presentation.

Tip

- Date each entry and give it a heading so you can quickly find the topic.
- Copy new vocabulary words and leave space so that you can fill in definitions or examples later.
- Write down hints or memory joggers to help you remember a name, term, or concept.
- Draw sketches to help you recall individual works.
- Mark the spot in your notes where you got lost so that you can come back and ask about it later.
- Divide your page into two columns (one side wider than the other). Write classroom notes in the wider column and questions in the other.
- Find a "study buddy" who will compare notes, go over questions, or review for tests with you.

Try It!

Set up a notebook for your art or music class with a wide right column and a narrower left column (see page **455**). Take notes during class.

Keeping a Learning Log

In any project-based class, such as art or music, a learning log can help you keep track of, and reflect on, your progress. Julia wrote the following entries in her learning log as she worked on a watercolor project. Notice that she divided her log, using the left side for the steps in the project and the right side for comments about her progress.

Sample Entries

Steps in watercolor painting	December 12
1. Tape the paper on the newspaper on the table.	Mr. Anderson told us to use scratch paper to practice on, but I won't need it.
2. Wet the paper and let it dry.	Last time I didn't do this, and the paper curled when I painted on it.
3. Make a light sketch.	Pressing too hard on the pencil made dents in the paper. Paint may pool in the dents.
4. Some ways to paint Wet on wet Wet on dry Dry on wet Dry on dry	Wet on wet made a nice background wash, but my sky and grass smeared together. Next time I'll use scratch paper for a new technique.
5. Fill large areas first.	Dry on wet worked better. The colors didn't bleed so much. I left space for my tree.
6. Use the smaller brush for details.	The paper was still too wet, and the details bled into the wash. Paint pooled in the pencil lines, but it looked kind of cool, so I used a dry brush to pull some of the paint out. It made nice shadows, blending out of the darker colors. I liked layering colors and got some nice effects. A light yellow wash over the dry, finished painting gave it a hazy look.

Try It!

Set up a learning log for your art or music class. Keep one side for class notes or instructions and the other side for your own comments.

Writing Guidelines ■ Response to an Art Prompt

Sometimes you will be asked to write a short essay in response to a prompt about art or music. This type of writing can be a regular class assignment or part of a test. In either case, responding to a prompt allows you to apply what you have learned about a specific work. Here are guidelines to follow as you write.

Prewriting

- **Understand the prompt.** Read through the prompt and focus on what it is asking you to do. Is the purpose of your response to explain, compare, describe, persuade?
- **Gather your details.** Go through your notes and any research materials you are allowed to use. Highlight or jot down the details that will help you respond to the prompt. Be sure to record the sources you use for quotations or facts.
- **Organize your details.** Decide on the best way to organize your information. Check the prompt for clues. For example, if the prompt is "compare and contrast the Roman Empire with the British Empire," you know you will be organizing details to show how the two topics are similar and different.

Writing

- **Write freely.** Use your notes as a guide, but don't worry too much about getting everything right. Just get all your ideas down on paper. Most short-response essays are one paragraph long. However, if a prompt calls for more than one main point, you should use a new paragraph for each main point.

Revising

- **Improve your writing.** Read your draft and cut any details that don't fit the prompt. Also add any information that will clarify your ideas or help answer the prompt. Be as complete as possible.
- **Improve your style.** Check your word choice and sentence fluency to make sure that your response reads smoothly.

Editing

- **Check for conventions.** Look for errors in spelling, punctuation, and grammar.
- **Prepare your final copy.** If necessary, and if time permits, copy your response onto a clean sheet of paper and proofread it a final time.

■ Response to an Art Prompt

In the following response, Roy Jones evaluates a painting.

Prompt

Evaluate Georges Seurat's *Sunday Afternoon on the Island of La Grande Jatte.* Answer the questions in one or more paragraphs.
1. What are the important technical aspects of the painting? How did critics of the time react? **2.** What types of people are in the painting? Are any social comments being expressed?

Sample Response

The writer uses a separate paragraph to cover each main point of the answer.

The writer uses in-text citations to indicate sources of specific ideas.

The writer uses specific details and examples to show his understanding of the topic.

Response #1
The primary technical aspect of the painting is that it is composed entirely of dots of color. Seurat didn't mix colors on the palette. Instead, he let the colors be mixed naturally by the eye of the observer. Seurat's dots create a soft, hazy look.
Another interesting technical aspect of the painting is the composition. Most of the people are in profile. Only one woman and her child are full face. The people create vertical lines in the painting. Curves in the umbrellas, boat sails, and the riverbank soften those vertical lines.
When Seurat's work first came out, the technique of pointillism was new. The critics mostly hated it, even sneering at its first exhibition at the Independants (WebMuseum, Paris).

Response #2
Subjects in the painting appear to be middle-class people enjoying a holiday by the river. Some occupations are revealed by the way people are dressed. Two men in uniforms can be seen in the distance. There are two exceptions to the middle class. The couple on the far right appear to be wealthy. They stand extra straight, and the lady has a pet monkey on a leash. Interestingly, the only person dressed like a worker dominates the lower left-hand corner, and he is also the only person in the painting with a detailed face. Perhaps that was Seurat's way of snubbing the middle class.

Try It!

Respond to a short-essay prompt your teacher will supply about a topic you are studying. Write a one- or two-paragraph answer.

Writing Guidelines ■ Research Report

At some time, you may be asked to do a research report on an aspect of art or music. You may write a biographical piece about an artist or a musician, or an expository piece about a certain artistic style or time period. The following guidelines will help you write your report.

Prewriting

- **Gather what you know.** List what you already know about the subject and any questions you may have.
- **Begin your research.** Do an overview of your subject. Read articles and excerpts from books to find a specific area of the subject that interests you. Then choose a specific topic suitable for the length of your paper. The shorter your paper, the more focused your topic should be. Once you have narrowed your topic, write a thesis statement.
- **Plan and organize.** Decide on the type of organization you will use. For example, chronological order is effective when you are writing a biography. If you are explaining an art style, you may decide to put your main points in order of importance.

Writing

- **Connect your ideas.** Introduce your topic in the first paragraph and include the thesis statement for your report. As you begin writing, pretend you are explaining your topic out loud to a classmate.

Revising

- **Improve your writing.** Check your writing for *voice. Do you sound interested and knowledgeable? Do you include all the information you need to examine the topic?*
- **Improve your style.** Check your *word choice* and *sentence fluency* to make sure that everything is stated clearly and effectively. *Are your ideas easy to follow? Do your words effectively express your ideas? Do you connect your sentences and paragraphs with transitions? Does each sentence flow naturally into the next?*

Editing

- **Check for conventions.** Look for and correct any errors in punctuation, spelling, and grammar.
- **Prepare a final copy.** After you have made your changes, write a neat final copy and give it another proofreading.

■ Research Report

You can learn about music by studying famous composers and their works. Tam wondered how modern classical music began and whether one composer played a key role in developing that style. After doing some research, he wrote the following essay on Aaron Copland.

Sample Report

Aaron Copland: Our Nation's Musical Voice

Aaron Copland's life spanned nearly all of the twentieth century. Copland was an innovative composer who eventually became the musical voice of the United States.

Born in New York on November 14, 1900, Copland learned to play piano from his older sister. By the age of 15, he had already decided to be a composer and took a mail-order course on harmony. Later on he studied harmony and counterpoint with Rubin Goldmark. Goldmark had a classical background, but Copland was more modern.

Even though Copland would develop a uniquely American sound, he actually left the United States in 1921 to study in Paris. Jazz was a strong influence there, just as it was in the United States. The jazz of Paris was different, though, and Copland returned home after three years with some new sounds and rhythms. Soon he completed his first large work, the ballet *Grohg*.

Copland's special style emerged in the second half of the 1920s. His jazz rhythms were important in his early work, including his *Piano Concerto* (1926). He produced new works that blended elegance with a concise, compact style (Washington State University).

In the 1930s, Copland developed a more popular sound. Trying to escape the economic troubles of the Depression, people were attracted to the upbeat sounds of the radio and theater. Copland understood this and created a series of ballets that boosted American pride. His ballet music for *Billy the Kid, Rodeo,* and *Appalachian Spring* (which earned him a Pulitzer Prize) celebrated the American spirit.

The introduction presents the thesis statement for the report.

The body of the report is organized in chronological order, beginning with the composer's early life and then moving decade by decade.

Copland visited Mexico often during this period and began using that country's folk sounds and rhythms in his music. He also visited Cuba and South America, seeking to create "American music for all Americans" (Aaron Copland Collection, Library of Congress). His music became the music of the masses: people felt his music, and they responded to it.

Movies were also very popular in the 1930s, and this was not lost on Copland. He saw a new way to introduce classical music to America. During the 1940s, he composed scores for many movies. These have been called "popular" works by some critics, but the music definitely added an important dimension to fine films such as *Of Mice and Men, Our Town, The Red Pony,* and *The Heiress,* for which Copland won an Academy Award for best score.

During the 1950s and 1960s, Copland began to do less composing. Instead, he traveled all over the world, conducting his work and the work of others. By the 1970s, Copland had pretty much stopped composing. He stopped conducting in 1983. He wrote more than 60 articles and essays and five books about music. Throughout his later career, he helped young American composers, encouraged school music programs, and lectured around the world, promoting music until he died at age 90 on December 2, 1990, in Tarrytown, New York.

Copland had a passion for bringing music to the masses. His style influenced some of the best composers of modern music. Copland's music became a tribute to the pioneer spirit that formed our great nation. He remains to this day the ultimate American composer.

Try It!

Write a research report related to an area of art or music that interests you. Use the guidelines on page 458 and the model above as a guide.

Review a piece of writing. Read over something that you have recently written. Try to find two or three sets of sentences that you could combine. Write the combined sentences to see how they sound.

Other Forms of Writing in the Arts

Here are some more ways to explore the arts through writing.

Expository Writing

- Explain how basic sculpting tools are used.
- Examine the parts of a musical instrument and describe how each contributes to the final sound.
- Explain how to throw a pot.
- Review a book about a composer, musician, or band.
- Summarize a review of a concert or an art exhibit.

Descriptive Writing

- Describe the composition of a painting.
- Describe your feelings when listening to different types of music.
- Describe the use of color and texture in a painting.

Persuasive Writing

- Write a proposal for building a school sculpture garden.
- Write a letter to the school board requesting new jazz choir uniforms.
- Write an editorial addressing cuts in the school music program.

Narrative Writing

- Write about a time that music had a major impact in your life.
- Tell about the first time you worked on a group art project.
- Tell about a concert you attended.
- Write a journal entry as though you were Beethoven.

Creative Writing

- Create an imaginary encounter between Bach and John Lennon.
- Write a myth to fit an instrumental piece of music.
- Write about the music you would find on a distant, inhabited planet.
- Write a parody of a popular song, relating it to your school.
- Write a poem about a piece of art.

Tools of Learning

Listening and Speaking

Effective listening and speaking are often called *people skills* or *group skills*. They help you succeed in the classroom, in extracurricular activities, and in the workplace. You've been using these skills for, well, for as long as you can remember. But you probably have not been using them as effectively as you could be.

Good listening requires practice. No one can listen with complete attention for very long unless they really concentrate and practice effective listening skills. Similarly, effective speaking takes effort. No one can speak convincingly without thinking first and being prepared. This chapter will help you improve your listening and speaking skills.

- Listening in Class
- Speaking in Class
- A Closer Look at Listening and Speaking

"Some people talk simply because they think sound is more manageable than silence."
—Margaret Halsey

Listening in Class

When you really listen, you're doing more than simply hearing what is being said. Listening involves effort. The following tips will help you become a better listener.

- **Know why you're listening.** What is the speaker trying to tell you? Will there be a test? Are you being given an assignment?
- **Listen for the facts.** The 5 W's and H—*Who? What? When? Where? Why?* and *How?*—will help you identify the most important information.
- **Take notes.** When you hear important information, write it down in your notebook. Also write down questions and comments in the margins. Review and complete your notes as soon after class as possible.
- **Put the speaker's ideas into your own words.** Paraphrase the speaker's key points as you take notes. Add your own comments.

Try It!

Take notes in your own words. In your notes, practice putting ideas in your own words and adding your own comments.

Magna Carta (1215)

means "great charter"
- King John's barons forced him to sign it
- signed at Runnymede near Windsor
basis for all modern laws
- set the stage for due process and parliamentary rule
- forerunner of Declaration of Independence and U.S. Constitution
revised throughout history—of more than 60 original clauses only 2 remain intact
- #39 (no judgment until proven guilty)
- #40 (equal justice in courts for all citizens)
Importance: Established equality among all— even rulers

Mostly the nobles wanted to set limits on the monarchy's control.

Gradually the Magna Carta extended to all English citizens.

Speaking in Class

Speaking in class is a skill everyone needs to master. A good classroom discussion depends on cooperation. These basic strategies will help you and your classmates become better speakers.

Before You Speak . . .

- **Listen** carefully and take notes.
- **Think** about what others are saying.
- **Wait** until it's your turn to speak.
- **Plan** how you can add something positive to the discussion.

As You Speak . . .

- **Use a loud, clear voice.**
- **Stick to the topic.**
- **Avoid repeating** what's already been said.
- **Support your ideas** with examples, facts, or anecdotes.
- **Maintain eye contact** with others in the group or class.

Tip

- Focus your comments on ideas, not on personalities.
- Ask meaningful questions.
- Summarize what's been agreed upon in the discussion.
- Mention another person's comments and expand on them constructively.

Try It!

Play "Who, Where, and When." Exercise your speaking skills by completing the following game.

1. Form groups of five students. Have each group choose a speaker.
2. The speaker looks at the lists below and chooses one person, one place, and one time period. Then the speaker begins to speak like that person, in that place, at that time.
3. The one who guesses the person, place, and time becomes the speaker.

People	Places	Times
nanny	playground	Roman Empire
salesperson	restaurant	Colonial days
scientist	the opera	Civil War
cowhand	an art museum	1930s
computer technician	flea market	present day

A Closer Look at Listening and Speaking

Improving your listening and speaking skills will help you increase your confidence and effectiveness. Follow these basic guidelines to carry on productive conversations and discussions.

Good Listeners . . .	Good Speakers . . .
■ think about what the speaker is saying. ■ stay focused so that they are prepared to respond thoughtfully. ■ pay attention to the speaker's tone of voice, gestures, and facial expressions. ■ interrupt only when necessary to ask questions.	■ speak loudly and clearly. ■ maintain eye contact with their listeners. ■ emphasize their main ideas by changing the tone and volume of their voice. ■ respect their audience by explaining and clarifying information that may be confusing. ■ use gestures and body language effectively to enhance their message.

Try It!

Focus on speaking and listening skills by doing the activity below.

1. Pick two classmates and number yourselves 1, 2, and 3.
2. Person 1 will take person 2 aside and read the paragraph below.
3. Person 2 will then take person 3 aside and try to repeat the paragraph from memory.
4. Person 3 will then try to repeat the paragraph from memory to the first two classmates.
5. Compare the original paragraph to what person 3 reports.

Gregor Mendel is credited with our modern-day theory of genetics. Interestingly, he was not a scientist, but an Augustinian monk who taught high school science in the nineteenth century. Thinking that the environment was the key to why plants developed as they did, he discovered heredity was far more important. He became more and more involved in his experiments and spent seven years crossing plants and recording the results. What he learned became the foundation of modern genetics.

Taking Notes

Taking notes is an active approach to learning, one that gets you personally involved in the learning process. In your high school classes, notes help you learn as you read textbooks, listen to lectures in class, and complete homework assignments. You begin to understand even the most complex ideas as you put information into your own words. Note taking also helps you focus on and organize the information you need to study for tests.

This chapter presents strategies for taking notes while reading a text, listening to a lecture, or attending a meeting. As you master this useful skill, note taking will become one of your most important learning tools.

- Taking Classroom Notes
- Taking Reading Notes
- Taking Minutes for a Meeting

"Make your writing useful."
—William Zinsser

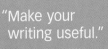

Taking Classroom Notes

Your teacher may give a lecture to explain an important subject, introduce a new topic, or help the class review for a test. The following tips will help you take clear, organized lecture notes.

Guidelines for Class Notes

1. **Write the topic and date at the top of each page.** Number your pages so that you can sort them out if they get mixed up.

2. **Listen carefully.** This is the key to taking good notes. If you get busy writing, you may miss important clues. For example, if a teacher says, "There are six steps in flying a hot-air balloon," listen for the six steps. Also listen for key words such as *first, second, next,* or *most importantly.*

3. **Use your own words.** You can't write down everything your teacher says. Instead, try to put the main points into your own words. You can fill in the details later.

4. **Begin taking notes right away** or you may miss something important. It's hard to catch up while taking notes.

5. **Write quickly, but be neat.** Your notes won't be helpful if you can't read them.

6. **Condense information.**
   - Use lists, phrases, and abbreviations (*p = page, ex = for example*).
   - Skip the small, unnecessary words, such as articles (*a, an, the*).
   - Shorten some words (*intro* for *introduction, chap* for *chapter*).
   - Use numbers and symbols (*1st, 2nd, +, ↑, ↓,=*).
   - Develop a personal shorthand (*w = with, w/o = without*).

7. **Draw sketches and diagrams** to explain something more quickly than in words.

8. **Copy important information** your teacher writes on the board.

9. **Ask your teacher** to explain something you don't understand, to repeat something, or to please slow down.

Try It!

Review some of your recent class notes in light of the guidelines above. How could you improve your note-taking skills? Explain.

■ Set up your notes.

Keep your notes in a notebook, preferably one for each subject. You can also take notes on loose-leaf paper kept in a three-ring binder, which lets you add or remove pages as needed. Write only on one side of the paper. This makes it easier to read and find portions of your notes.

page 14

How a Submarine Dives   Nov. 17

Theory
- Buoyancy keeps the sub floating above or at some point below the surface.
- Ballast causes the sub to dive beneath the surface.

Four parts of a submarine
1. double hull
2. ballast tanks
3. compressed-air tanks
4. crew quarters

Steps in submerging a submarine
1. Close all air valves and hatches.
2. Fill ballast tanks with water.
3. Angle bow planes to help the sub dive.
4. Level off for underwater travel.

Controlling the submarine
- Increase or decrease engine speed to drive the sub forward.
- Reverse engines to move sub backward.
- Adjust bow planes and rudders to control left/right and up/down motion.
- Bring the sub to surface by forcing compressed air into ballast tanks to push water out.

Leave wide margins.

Skip a line between main ideas.

Make sketches.

Use bullets or numbers in lists.

■ Review your notes.

As you read over your notes, circle any words that may not be spelled correctly. Also underline any words or phrases that you don't understand. Look up these words in a dictionary or textbook glossary. Then write each word and its meaning in the margin of your notes.

1. **Write any questions you have in the margin.** Then look for the answers on your own. If you can't find an answer, ask a teacher or classmate. Write the answer near the question.

2. **Use a highlighter** to mark the most important notes. You can use a different colored pen to circle or underline key ideas instead.

3. **Rewrite your notes.** Making a neat, organized copy of your notes gives you another chance to learn the material.

4. **Review your notes.** Look over your notes before the next class, especially if you are having a test or class discussion.

---

page 14

How a Submarine Dives   Nov. 17

Theory
  • Buoyancy keeps the sub floating above or at some point below the surface.

Buoyancy =
water
making
things float

  • Ballast causes the sub to dive beneath the surface.

conning tower

Four parts of a submarine

Ballast =
something
that adds
stability

1. double hull
2. ballast tanks
3. compressed-air tanks
4. crew quarters

1
2
3
4

valves

Steps in submerging a submarine
  1. Close all air valves and hatches.
  2. Fill ballast tanks with water.
  3. Angle bow planes to help the sub dive.
  4. Level off for underwater travel.

Can it dive
if a valve
is stuck
open?

Controlling the submarine
  • Increase or decrease engine speed to drive the sub forward.

Taking Reading Notes

Taking notes while you read an assignment is easier than taking notes during a lecture. You can stop to write at any time, which means you can write more neatly and carefully. Here are some tips for taking reading notes.

Guidelines for Reading Notes

1. **Preview the assignment.** Look through your assignment to see what your reading is about. Look at the title, introduction, headings, and chapter summary. Also look at any pictures, maps, or graphics. (See pages **602–603**.)

2. **Quickly read the entire assignment** once before taking notes. This gives you an overview of the material and allows you to pick out the main ideas.

3. **Take notes while reading a second time.** Start taking notes as you read your assignment again. Read the material slowly and stop at new ideas or words.

   - **Write down the important information.**
   - **Put notes in your own words.** Don't just copy passages from the book. You learn more when you rewrite ideas in your words. (See pages **483–490** for more information on summaries and paraphrases.)
   - **Use headings or subtitles.** Headings and subtitles help to organize your notes. Write down the important information under each heading or subtitle.
   - **Include notes about pictures, charts, and illustrations.** You can also make quick sketches of these visual elements.
   - **Use graphic organizers.** (See pages **588–589**.)
   - **List and define any new words.** Look up each word in the glossary or in a dictionary. Write down the appropriate meaning in your notes. Also write down the number of the page where the word is located. This way you can easily find it again.

4. **Learn more.** See "Critical Reading" on pages **473–482** for more information on taking reading notes.

Try It!

For your next reading assignment, take notes using the tips above.

Taking Minutes for a Meeting

Recording the minutes of a meeting is another form of note taking. Minutes must be well organized and include everything from who is present to what is discussed and decided. Always report minutes in an objective (impersonal) voice. To record minutes during a meeting, you must listen carefully and write down information accurately. Below are some tips to follow.

Guidelines for Taking Minutes

- Begin with the organization's name, the date, location, and topic of the meeting.
- Record what time the meeting begins.
- List those present (or absent). Indicate who led the meeting and who recorded the minutes.
- Note "old business" (from a previous meeting) that is discussed or resolved.
- Note "new business" (plans or decisions to be handled in the current meeting).
- Record any votes taken and their result.
- Record when the meeting is adjourned.

McPherson High School Student Government Minutes
Date: October 12, 2006
Location: Room 115 (Mr. Troskas, Faculty Liaison)
Topic: Weekly Meeting

Attending
Madonna Armando, Maretta Cabaso, Ray Cadavico, James Conlan, Burt DiPerri (recording), Andreas Gallin, Rex Girtz, Tara Lehrer, Jonelle Levin, Sabrina Mocaryn, Wyatt Moody, Joey Righetti, Tamara Seung (chair), Lavinia Sidle, Carla Zacaggi

Old Business
Homecoming Committee: Supplies were purchased for gym decorations. Tara still needs volunteers to help with setup after school on October 26.

Fund-Raiser Committee: With last Friday's dance receipts, there is $460 in the fund. Another $40 is needed to pay for the homecoming band in two weeks.

New Business
Blood Drive: The local Blood Center, Principal Jackson, and Mr. Troskas all agreed to having the 14th Annual Blood Drive on February 8 & 9, 2007. Bring suggestions for a theme/title for the drive to next week's meeting.

School Spirit Committee: Fan attendance has been down at all nonvarsity sports events. Ideas for how to raise awareness included posters in halls and morning sports announcements. Joey will talk to Principal Jackson about adding announcements.
- Vote: 10 to 5 to paint posters for the halls next Monday evening (October 16) instead of tonight.

Meeting Time: 2:45 pm – 4:00 pm

Take minutes to tell what was discussed and decided upon by a group. When you take minutes, record only the main points, not all the details, of a discussion. Be sure to accurately record any votes or official action taken.

Critical Reading

Does this ever happen to you? You read a paragraph, a page, or a chapter in a textbook—put the book down—and say, "I can't remember a thing!" Unfortunately, many students have that experience. However, the good news is that you *can* remember important information that you read. The way to do that is by reading critically.

Critical reading involves a number of important steps, including *surveying* a reading assignment, *questioning* what the text is about, *taking notes* as you read, and so on. If you have a tested reading plan in mind, and carry out that plan, you will be in control of your reading. This chapter gives you an effective critical-reading method to follow.

- **Critical Reading: SQ3R**
- **Before You Read**
- **As You Read**
- **After You Read**
- **Reading Fiction**
- **Reading Poetry**

"Meaning doesn't reside ready-made in the text or in the reader; it happens during the transaction between reader and text."
— Louise Rosenblatt

Critical Reading: SQ3R

An effective reading technique for all types of nonfiction is the SQ3R method. SQ3R stands for the five steps in this reading process: *survey, question, read, recite,* and *review.* The steps in this technique are explained below.

Before you read . . .

- **Survey** Preview the reading assignment for its general content. Read titles, subtitles, headings, and subheadings to see what is being covered. Take note of illustrations and terms in bold or italic type. Also read just the first and last paragraphs.

- **Question** Ask yourself what you already know about the topic of the reading. Write down questions you still want answered. To get started, you could turn the text's titles, subtitles, headings, and subheadings into questions. Asking questions keeps you actively involved while reading.

As you read . . .

- **Read** Read slowly and carefully. Look for the main idea in each paragraph, section, or chapter. Try to answer questions you have already identified. At different points, also ask these questions: *What does this mean? How does it connect with previous material? What will come next?* Take notes as you go along. Take the time to read difficult parts slowly. (Reread them if necessary.)

- **Recite** Test your comprehension of the material by summarizing the main points out loud. Reciting is one of the most valuable parts of SQ3R. After you read a page, section, or chapter, try to answer the 5 W's and H *(Who? What? Where? When? Why?* and *How?)* about that part. Reread any parts as needed.

After you read . . .

- **Review** Assess your knowledge by reviewing your notes. See how well you understand the entire reading assignment. Ask these questions: *Have all my questions been answered? Can I summarize each main section? Can I summarize or outline the whole assignment?* Consider outlining the material (or using another type of graphic organizer) to help you remember what you have read.

 Critical reading means looking beyond surface details and thinking carefully about the information that is presented.

Before You Read

Try to get the big picture with each assignment.

Survey the reading.

To begin, **survey** or preview the text. This will give you a general understanding of the main points. Use the following guidelines:

- **Scan** chapter titles, subtitles, headings, and boldfaced type.
- **Identify the purpose of the material:** to inform, to persuade, to entertain.
- **Read** the first and last paragraphs.
- **List** the topic and the main points you identify.

Below, Marcus *surveys* the opening part of an article. He writes his notes on a copy of the article.

Sample Survey Notes

On Our Borders: Immigrants and Terrorists

Terrorism in the United States

    Terrorism is a relatively new threat to the United States. Before the first attack on the World Trade Center in 1993, foreign terrorists had not successfully attacked a target on U.S. soil. Other countries—including Russia, Spain, and the United Kingdom—have dealt with terrorists for decades. Since 9/11, defending the security of our borders against terrorism has emerged as one of the key issues in this country.

Immigration Policies and a Protected Nation

    All citizens want to feel protected against terrorism. However, tighter security may jeopardize civil liberties in this country. So a critical debate has developed between those individuals who want tighter immigration policies and people who are concerned that those policies will harm the American way of life. . . .

Purpose:
to inform

Topic:
connection between immigration and terrorism

Key Points:
terrorism in the U.S.

policies protecting immigrants/ the nation

Try It!

Survey a reading assignment. Choose a reading assignment from any of your classes. Identify its purpose, main topic, and the key points.

Question the material.

After you have surveyed the entire text, ask **questions** about the reading. Use the following guidelines:

- **Ask what you already know** about the topic.
- **List questions** that you still want answered. Also ask the 5 W and H questions.
- **Turn headings and main points into questions.** For example, if the chapter title is "Scientific Discoveries of the Ancient World," your questions might be "What were those scientific discoveries? Who made them?"

Below, Marcus turned the main headings into questions and formed other questions that occurred to him. Next to his questions, he noted things he already knew about the topic.

Sample Question Notes

"On Our Borders: Immigrants and Terrorists"   Already Know:

1. How do terrorists get into this country?   Terrorists came to the
2. Does "borders" refer to national borders or   U.S. legally and attacked
   other borders?   the World Trade Center
3. What are U.S. immigration policies?   more than once.
4. How do U.S. policies compare to policies   I think that "borders"
   in other countries?   might refer to more than
5. What rights do immigrants have?   just national borders.
6. How would our country change if   I want to be safe from
   immigration policies changed?   terrorists, but I also want
   immigrants to be able to
   come to the U.S.

Try It!

Ask questions. Write down questions you have about the reading assignment you surveyed. Also note what you already know about the topic.

As You Read

Once you have surveyed the assignment and formed questions about it, you are ready to read carefully. Try to turn your reading into a conversation with the text. Respect what the writer has to say even as you question certain parts. And stay open to the unexpected.

Read (and take notes).

Always have a goal in mind when you read. Use the following guidelines to read the material and answer the questions you listed.

- **Read slowly** so that you don't miss anything.
- **Reread parts** that seem challenging.
- **Write down boldfaced key concepts.**
- **Define key concepts** using context or a dictionary.
- **Record any additional questions** you may have.
- **Keep the following questions in mind** as you read:
  - What does this mean?
  - How does it connect with what I already know about the topic?
  - What will probably come next?

Try It!

Read your chosen assignment critically. Take careful notes as you go along, using the guidelines above.

Recite out loud.

After you complete the entire reading, it's time to reinforce what you have learned. Reciting or repeating the information out loud is an effective way to evaluate how well you understand information. Use the following guidelines:

- **Recite the key points** without looking at your notes.
- **Answer the 5 W's and H** (*Who? What? Where? When? Why?* and *How?*) about the material.
- **Discuss (and answer) your other questions** about the topic.
- **Identify any new questions** that occur to you.

Try It!

Recite what you have learned from your reading assignment. Use the guidelines above to help you complete this step.

After You Read

Having completed the first four steps in the SQ3R method, it's time to review the reading. Reviewing will help you see how well you understand the material.

Review the material.

A final **review** of your reading assignment will make the information part of your own thinking. Use the following guidelines:

- **Go over your notes** one section at a time.
- **Keep searching for answers** if you have any unanswered questions.
- **Ask for help** if you cannot figure something out on your own.
- **Add illustrations or graphic organizers** to your notes to make complex ideas clearer.
- **Summarize the reading** at the end of your notes.

In the example below, Marcus summarized the entire article in a paragraph and added his own thoughts in the margin.

Sample Summary

"On Our Borders"—Summary

This point/counterpoint article argues both sides of immigration policies in the United States and discusses how to change these policies to deal with terrorism. Disagreements arise over limiting the freedoms of both U.S. citizens and immigrants. Tougher restrictions could lead to problems with global trade. Both sides agree something must be done to combat terrorism, but excluding immigrants goes against the ideals of this nation, which has always welcomed new citizens from around the globe.

The U.S. needs to track student and tourist visas more effectively. Don't those systems need fixing, too?

Why do politicians make this an immigration issue? (I would like to do more research on this.)

Try It!

Review your reading assignment. Go over your notes and summarize the assignment. Be sure to include all the main ideas.

Reading Fiction

Fiction uses made-up characters and events to reveal what is real or true about life. This makes fiction a great way to learn. Here are some tips for reading fiction.

Before you read . . .

- **Learn something about the author** and his or her other works.
- **React thoughtfully** to the title and opening pages.

As you read . . .

- **Identify** the following story elements: *setting, tone, main characters, central conflict,* and *theme.*
- **Predict** what will happen next.
- **Write** your reactions to the short story or novel in a reading journal as you go along.
- **Think** about the characters and what they do.
  - What motivates the characters?
  - Have you encountered people similar to these characters?
  - Have you faced situations similar to the ones faced by the main characters?
  - Would you have reacted in the same way?
- **Consider** how the author's life may have influenced the story.
- **Notice** the author's style and word choice. (See pages **298–299**.)
  - How effectively has the author used literary devices?
  - Why do you think the author used a particular word or phrase?
- **Discuss** the story with others who are reading it.

After you read . . .

- **Consider** how the main character changes during the course of the story. Often, this is the key to understanding a work of fiction.
- **Determine** the story's main message or theme; then decide how effectively this message is communicated.

Try It!

Use the information above as a guide to help you better understand and enjoy the next short story or novel you read.

React to fiction.

The excerpt below is from the short story "Ghosts in the House" by Rob King. The margin notes reveal one student's reactions, which she wrote on a photocopy of the story. She makes observations, asks questions, and defines a term.

From "Ghosts in the House"

More than anything, I'll miss this.

This simile helps me to "see" the setting.

Terrell sat on an old crate by the attic window and watched the sun set. It turned his neighborhood gold. From this window, even the worn-out rooftops shone like the streets of heaven.

"This is my house." The words sounded hollow. Somebody had bought the place to make it a parking lot. "This is *my* house."

Actually, it wasn't. The house had been abandoned for 10 years, and most of the neighborhood kids called it the "haunted house." Four years ago, Terrell explored it and liked it so well, he made it his own. He and his friends called themselves "the Ghosts," and they fixed up their Haunt and hung there every afternoon.

The dialogue sounds real.

" 'Sup?" said Junior, coming up the stairs.

Terrell knocked knuckles with him. "Last day for the Ghosts."

Junior flopped down on the old beanbag. "Nah, we'll always be the Ghosts."

"What're Ghosts without a Haunt?"

Bill climbed in through the fire escape. " 'Sup?"

"I'm surprised you came," Terrell said.

Bill slouched against the wall. "It couldn't last forever, T. Two more years, and we'll graduate anyway."

Why do the boys think the house is theirs?

Terrell said, "This is *our* house. We grew up here. Who can grow up in a parking lot?"

There was nothing more to say. Outside, the rooftops gave up their gold and became cracked black asphalt. Bill left, and then Junior. That left only Terrell and his window and the house that wasn't his.

Violators means "people who break or disregard the law."

On the next day, the house was padlocked, and a sign was taped on the door: "PRIVATE PROPERTY. KEEP OUT. VIOLATORS WILL BE PROSECUTED."

The Ghosts weren't violators. They took care of this place, and it took care of them.

*"The job of the poet is to render the world—
to see it and report it without loss. . . . "*
—Mark Van Doren

Reading Poetry

You shouldn't expect to understand a poem completely in one reading, especially if it is lengthy or complex. In fact, each time you read a poem over again, you will probably discover something new about it. Reacting to poetry in a reading journal will also help you to appreciate it more. (See the next page.) Here are some strategies for reading poetry.

First Reading

- **Read the poem** at your normal reading speed to gain an overall first impression.
- **Jot down brief notes** about your immediate reaction to the poem.

Second Reading

- **Read the poem again**—out loud, if possible. Pay attention to the sound of the poem.
- **Note examples of sound devices** in the poem—alliteration, assonance, rhyme (see pages **340–341**). Finding a poem's phrasing and rhythm can help you discover its meaning.
- **Observe** the punctuation, spacing, and special treatment of words and lines.
- **Think** about what the poem is saying.

Third Reading

- **Identify** the type of poem you're reading. Does this poem follow the usual pattern of that particular type? If not, why not?
- **Determine** the literal sense or meaning of the poem. What is the poem about? What does it seem to say about its topic?
- **Look for** figurative language in the poem. How does this language—metaphors, similes, personification, symbols—support or add to the meaning of the poem? (See pages **340–341**.)

 Try It!

Use the strategies above as a guide the next time you read a poem.

Critical Reading

React to poetry.

The untitled poem below is by Stephen Crane. The notes on a copy of the poem show one student's reactions. He makes observations, asks questions, identifies figurative language, and so forth. Whenever you read a challenging poem, try to react to it in several different ways.

The poet starts with a metaphor for truth.

What does "whence" mean?

XXVII

"Truth," said a traveler,
"Is a rock, a mighty fortress;
Often have I been to it,
Even to its highest tower,
From whence the world looks black."

The second stanza parallels the first.

"Truth," said a traveler,
"Is a breath, a wind,
A shadow, a phantom;
Long have I pursued it,
But never have I touched
The hem of its garment."

The poem uses repetition to make a point.

The third stanza comments on the second.

And I believed the second traveler;
For truth was to me
A breath, a wind,
A shadow, a phantom,
And never had I touched
The hem of its garment.

This poem does not rhyme or have a regular rhythm.

The poem uses irony as each traveler describes truth in opposite terms. The same contrast is seen in the words often and never.

Tip

Do a 5 to 10 minute freewriting when you finish reading a poem. Write down anything you can about the poem. Relate it to other poems you have read.

Summarizing and Paraphrasing

Have you ever explained something to another person and found that, in making the explanation, you suddenly understood the topic better yourself? The same thing happens when you summarize or paraphrase a reading assignment. When you read a text and then put the main ideas into your own words, real understanding begins to take place.

When you summarize an article, you highlight its main points and arguments without writing down every single detail. Paraphrasing is similar to summarizing, except that paraphrasing requires you to interpret the main points and then put them in your own words. This chapter presents examples of both kinds of writing and shows you how to write concise summaries and accurate paraphrases.

- Sample Article and Summary
- Guidelines for Summarizing
- Summarize an Article
- Strategies for Paraphrasing
- Sample Paragraphs and Paraphrases
- Paraphrase a Paragraph

"It's good to rub and polish our brain against that of others."

—Montaigne

Sample Article

The following article is about a Native American tribe called the Mandan.

The Nearly Forgotten People

The Mandan tribe lived in what is now North Dakota, where they achieved a level of technology that was unique on the North American Great Plains. The Mandan lived in houses and tended gardens at the same time that neighboring nomadic tribes followed the buffalo. In the 1700s, the Mandan had twelve thriving villages along the Missouri River. Because smallpox ravaged the tribe in the early 1800s, the Mandan have been mostly forgotten in American popular culture. However, their living descendents and historians have passed on important information about them.

At one time, Mandan communities centered on a sacred cedar pole and a central plaza. The Mandan dwelled in sod-enclosed houses that were erected upon frames of wooden timbers. These structures were sturdy enough that people could sit on top of them. In fact, they used the buildings as makeshift grandstands to watch the elaborate ceremonies they held around their community's sacred pole.

Mandan tribal society had distinct male and female roles. Mandan women maintained elaborate and productive gardens, growing maize (corn), beans, pumpkins, sunflowers, and squash. They made baskets and were the only potters among all the Plains Indians. They used small, tub-shaped watercraft called "bull boats," made by stretching animal hide over a framework of sticks. The men served as hunters and warriors and were responsible for the tribe's spiritual life.

Although the Mandan were more agrarian than most of their neighboring cultures, they still relied upon the buffalo as a staple of survival just as other Plains tribes did. A Mandan buffalo hunt was generally preceded by an elaborate dance performed (sometimes for days) by hunters who had already slain buffalo. The hunters danced until a herd of buffalo was spotted. Then the hunt would commence.

By 1804, smallpox had reduced the Mandan to two large villages. In 1837, the Mandan were stricken for the last time, when smallpox swept through both of the remaining villages and reduced the tribal population from some sixteen hundred to only a few dozen. Yet, because of those survivors and others who have studied their culture, the Mandan are remembered to this day.

Summarizing

Sample Summary

The following paragraph is a student summary of the preceding article. Pay special attention to the three main parts: the topic sentence, the body, and the closing sentence. (See the side notes.)

The **topic sentence** expresses the main idea.

Each sentence in the body summarizes one or even two paragraphs from the article.

The **closing sentence** adds the article's concluding thoughts.

The Mandan Tribe

The Mandan were a tribe of Native Americans living along the Missouri River in an area of the Great Plains that would become North Dakota. Unlike the nomadic tribes of the Great Plains, the Mandan were farmers who lived in permanent villages and sturdy houses. The women did most of the work and were skilled at gardening, making pots and baskets, and even building tub-like boats. The Mandan, like other Plains Indians, hunted buffalo. The men were the hunters, and they would do a dance that could last for days before they'd go hunting. **In the early 1800s, the tribe was nearly wiped out by smallpox, but the memory of the Mandan still lives on.**

Respond to the reading. Answer the following questions.

Ideas (1) What main points from the article does the summary focus on? Name two. (2) What details are *not* included? Name two.

Organization (3) How is the summary paragraph organized?

Voice & Word Choice (4) How does the writer show that she or he has a clear understanding of the article? Identify two phrases or ideas from the summary in your explanation.

Tip

An effective summary includes only the necessary facts. Names, dates, times, places, and similar information are usually necessary, but examples and descriptive details are not. A summary should answer two questions: *What is the most important idea in the reading? What information supports this idea?*

Guidelines for Summarizing

Follow the guidelines below whenever you are asked to write a summary.

Prewriting

- Select an article on a topic that interests you or relates to a subject you are currently studying. Make a photocopy of the article if possible.
- Read the article once, quickly. Then read it again, underlining passages (if working from a photocopy) or taking notes on the key details.
- Think about the article. Identify and write down the main idea. For example, here is the main idea of the sample article: **The Mandan were a tribe of Native Americans living along the Missouri River in an area of the Great Plains that would become North Dakota.**

Writing

Write a summary paragraph.

- Write a topic sentence that states the main idea of the article.
- Write body sentences that communicate the most important ideas of the article in your own words.
- Conclude by reminding your reader of the main point of the article. (A summary should *not* contain your personal opinions.)

Revising **and** Editing

Read and revise your summary and make necessary changes. Also edit for conventions. Ask yourself the following questions:

Ideas	Do I correctly identify the article's main idea in my topic sentence? Do my body sentences contain only the most important details from the article?
Organization	Does my paragraph arrange ideas in the same order that the article does?
Voice	Does my voice sound informed and interested?
Word Choice	Have I used my own words for the most part? Are there terms that need to be defined?
Sentence Fluency	Have I varied sentence structures and lengths?
Conventions	Have I eliminated all errors in punctuation, spelling, and grammar?

Summarize an article.

The following article is about the evolution and history of the horse.

Full Circle

The spread of horses around the world is well documented. Archaeologists report that horses first appeared on the plains of North America more than 55 million years ago. Then, about 8 to 10 thousand years ago, horses disappeared from the Western Hemisphere. It was not until the first Spanish expeditions to the New World that the horse returned to its original home.

By about 2.5 million years ago, ancestors of all modern breeds of horses had multiplied across the plains of the Americas and into the rest of the world, probably crossing to Asia on the Siberian land bridge that regularly rose above sea level during that time.

The horse disappeared from the Americas about 8000 B.C., but by then *Equus,* the scientific name for these animals, was already well established in Asia and Europe (as the horse and donkey) and in Africa (as the zebra). Several hypotheses seek to explain the horse's disappearance from the Western Hemisphere. Horses and other large animals all became extinct when humans migrated to the Americas. It is possible that these early humans killed off the horse through hunting. Alternately, a devastating disease might have destroyed them. In any event, there were no horses around as early human cultures developed in the Americas.

It was A.D. 1519 before the horse was finally returned to the continent of its origin. The Spanish conquistador Hernando Cortez took horses with him to Mexico. These animals quickly increased their numbers. In 1532, horses were taken to Peru. Within three years, wild horses were roaming the lush grass *pampas* of Argentina.

The horse moved north from Mexico, as well. By 1594, native tribes in northern Mexico were using horses, and in 1598 a band of Native Americans drove a herd all the way to what is now New Mexico. Less than 100 years later, Ute and Shoshone tribes brought the horse onto the Great Plains, and soon other tribes had horses, too.

Today, wild horses again range over the Western Hemisphere. No doubt, they will remain with humankind for many centuries to come.

Try It!

Summarize the article above. Write a summary paragraph about this article, using the guidelines provided on page 486.

Strategies for Paraphrasing

A paraphrase is a type of summary that is very effective for clarifying or explaining the meaning of an important passage that you would like to use in your research. A summary is shorter than the original text and attempts to state its meaning. A paraphrase, on the other hand, is sometimes longer than the original material and tries to *interpret* its meaning. Use the following strategies as a guide when you paraphrase.

Follow a plan: In order to complete an effective paraphrase, you must follow a series of important steps. There are no shortcuts.

- **Review the entire passage.** This will help you identify the main point and purpose of the material.
- **Carefully read the passage.** If necessary, reread parts that seem especially important or challenging.
- **Write your paraphrase.** Be sure your interpretation is clear and complete. For the most part, use your own words. (See below.)
- **Check your paraphrase.** Make sure that you have captured the tone and meaning of the passage.

Use your own words: Avoid the original writer's words as much as possible. Exceptions include key words (*tribe, repertory theater*) or proper nouns (*Iroquois, Lake Erie, New York*).

- **Consult a dictionary.** Refer to a dictionary to help you think of new ways to express certain terms or ideas.
- **Refer to a thesaurus.** Find synonyms to use in place of words in the original text. For example, if the writer is describing an empire, a thesaurus will suggest synonyms such as *domain, realm,* and *kingdom.* Pick the synonym that fits the context of the passage.

Capture the original voice: In a paraphrase, you should try to communicate the original writer's opinions and feelings. Read the examples that follow.

Original News Report

> Councilman Davis Miller declared that he is tired of kids with skateboards taking over the city parks and parking lots.

- **Paraphrase lacking voice:** Councilman Miller commented about the teenage skateboarders gathering in the city parks and parking lots.
- **Paraphrase with the proper voice:** Councilman Miller complained about the teenage skateboarders overwhelming the city parks and parking lots.

Sample Paragraphs and Paraphrases

The following expository paragraph from a longer article describes tribes of early American people.

> The League of the Iroquois was a confederacy of Native American tribes living in what is now the state of New York. From east to west, these tribes were the Mohawk, Oneida, Onondaga, Cayuga, and Seneca. Archaeological evidence suggests that the Iroquois lived along the lower Great Lakes for several centuries before the first European settlers arrived in North America. For all this time, the League stood united against hostile tribes to the north, west, and south.

A student wrote the following paraphrase to demonstrate her understanding of the above paragraph.

> Five tribes of Native Americans living in the area of New York State formed a confederacy, which is like a nation, called the League of the Iroquois. The tribes were the Seneca, Cayuga, Onondaga, Oneida, and Mohawk. They lived along Lake Erie and Lake Ontario for hundreds of years before Europeans arrived on the continent. They acted as allies of one another against neighboring tribes.

The following paragraph is a brief published review of a play performed at an area theater.

> The new comedy, *Who, Me?*, at the local repertory theatre is a major disappointment, considering the talent of the cast and the excellent musical accompaniment. The actors do the best they can with material that is at best trite and at worst boring. The playwright's political ranting obscures the plot, and there is no significant plot development.

A student wrote this paraphrase of the review, taking care to reflect the writer's opinion in his paraphrase.

> You might be wasting your time if you go to the repertory theater's comedy <u>Who, Me?</u> The main problem seems to be a poor script, and good actors and musicians aren't enough to save it. The author of the play goes on and on about his political beliefs, and nothing happens with the plot.

Paraphrase a paragraph.

Here are three sample paragraphs. As you read them, you will see that each one has a specific main idea and a distinct author's voice.

There exists a common misconception that the spread of European settlers across North America was inevitably bad news for the wild animals on the continent. Certainly the populations of large predators, such as wolves, cougars, and grizzly bears, suffered almost to the point of extinction. Other animals, however, thrived even as the population of humans increased. White-tailed deer, for example, maintain far higher populations amid the cornfields of farm country than they ever did in a pre-Columbian forest. Likewise, raccoons, coyotes, and squirrels are all thought to be more populous now than ever before.

Near Mexico City rise two structures called the Pyramid of the Sun and the Pyramid of the Moon. Built long before the coming of the conquistadores, they even predate the Aztecs by many hundreds of years. The two pyramids are part of the complex known as Teotihuacán. The people who built it have been lost from the annals of history. Teotihuacán was certainly a center of religion and ritual, but it had been abandoned for centuries before the great clash of cultures that occurred in Mexico about 1520.

Coach Renault has a rosy prediction for the Clinton Cougars' chances in the upcoming Division I football season. Star quarterback Derek "Duke" Wilson returns, having led the conference in passing and touchdowns last year. Also returning is running back Jeff Roberts, who blistered opposing defenses and school record books with his performance last year. Both lines are also intact, and a promising array of underclassmen forms a solid nucleus of receivers, linebackers, and defensive backs.

Try It!

Paraphrase a paragraph. Paraphrase one of the paragraphs above. Communicate all important details and the author's point of view, in your own words. Use the strategies on page 488 to guide you.

Understanding Writing Assignments

Writing is really thinking on paper. The type of thinking that you do depends on the writing assignment. In an English class, you may be asked to analyze a poem or evaluate a newspaper article. In a history class, you may be asked to explain a piece of legislation or to apply an event to your own experience. The key to doing well on these writing assignments is to understand the requirements of each.

This chapter explains the six basic levels of thinking as they relate to various writing assignments. The levels are *recalling, understanding, applying, analyzing, synthesizing,* and *evaluating.* It is important to know that as you work on an assignment, you will often use more than one type of thinking.

- **Types of Assignments**
- **Levels of Thinking**
- **Planning Your Writing Time**

"I learn by going where I have to go."
—Theodore Roethke

Types of Assignments

Throughout your school career, you will most often be assigned the following three basic types of writing.

Types	Examples
Specific You are given a specific topic.	Explain how an internal combustion engine works.
Open-ended You are given the chance to select your own topic.	Write a biographical essay about a person of significance who lived during the 1920s.
Combination You are given a subject area from which to choose a topic. This type of assignment is part specific and part open-ended.	Describe a key cultural event that occurred in the United States during the 1960s.

Try It!

Label each assignment below as open-ended, specific, or a combination.

1. Describe the features of a planet, a moon, or an asteroid in our solar system.

2. Explain the causes and effects of a tsunami.

3. Write a historical fiction story set in any time period.

■ Understand your task.

Different types of writing assignments require you to use different levels of thinking. These levels can range from simply recalling information to understanding, applying, analyzing, synthesizing, or evaluating it. (See the next page.) That is why it is so important that you clearly understand each assignment before you get started. Once you know exactly what you have to do, you can confidently plan, and carry out, your writing.

Levels of Thinking

The chart on this page describes the levels of thinking inherent in different types of assignments; the next six pages give a closer look at each one.

Whenever you are asked to . . .   **Be ready to . . .**

RECALL ⟶ **Remember what you have learned.**

underline	circle
list	match
name	label
cluster	define

- collect information
- list details
- identify or define key terms
- remember main points

UNDERSTAND ⟶ **Explain what you have learned.**

explain	review
summarize	restate
describe	cite

- give examples
- restate important details
- tell how something works

APPLY ⟶ **Use what you have learned.**

change	illustrate
do	model
demonstrate	show
locate	organize

- select the most important details
- organize information
- explain a process
- show how something works

ANALYZE ⟶ **Break down information.**

break down	rank
examine	compare
contrast	classify
tell why	

- carefully examine a subject
- identify important parts
- make connections and comparisons

SYNTHESIZE ⟶ **Shape information into a new form.**

combine	connect
speculate	design
compose	create
predict	develop
invent	imagine

- invent a better way of doing something
- blend the old with the new
- predict or hypothesize (make an educated guess)

EVALUATE ⟶ **Judge the worth of information.**

recommend	judge
criticize	argue
persuade	rate
convince	assess
weigh	

- point out a subject's strengths and weaknesses
- evaluate its clarity, accuracy, value, and so on
- convince others of its value/worth

Recall information.

The most basic type of thinking you use in school is **recalling**. This type of thinking is needed when you are asked to remember and repeat what you have learned in class.

You recall when you . . .

- supply details such as dates or other facts.
- identify or define key terms.
- remember main points.

Recalling

Your teachers will give very few writing assignments that only require recalling information. However, you may encounter test questions that ask you simply to recall. Multiple-choice, fill-in-the-blank, and short-answer questions are examples of test questions asking students to recall information.

Directions: Underline the correct answer in each set of parentheses.

1. The civil rights leader who, in the spring of 1941, threatened to organize a march in Washington to protest racial segregation was *(Frederick Douglass, A. Philip Randolph)*.

2. On June 6, 1944, American, British, and Canadian armies invaded the mainland of Europe at *(Berlin, the Ardennes Forest, Normandy)*.

Directions: Define each term by completing the sentence.

1. The "dollar-a-year" men were _____

   _____

2. Lobbyists are _____

   _____

3. Rosie the Riveter was _____

   _____

Try It!

Review your notes from a recent classroom lecture, underlining key ideas. Set the notes aside and write down all of the details you can recall. Check your notes again to see how much you were able to remember.

Understand information.

Understanding is a level of thinking that is more advanced than simply recalling facts and information. You show that you understand something when you can write about it in your own words.

You understand when you . . .

- explain how something works.
- provide reasons for something.
- summarize or rewrite information in your own words.

Understanding

Often, you will be asked to show understanding by writing an essay or a paragraph. The following assignment asks the student to explain an executive order, which requires that the student understand it. (Graphic organizers, charts, or maps can also be used to show understanding.)

Directions: Explain some of the reasons for President Roosevelt's signing of Executive Order #8802, which prohibited racial discrimination in hiring, in March of 1941.

By 1941, the president could see that the United States would be drawn into World War II, which was already being waged in Europe and China. He felt that it was very important for American industries to be working at top speed. Still, many companies in the South were refusing to hire African American workers. An important civil rights leader named A. Philip Randolph was trying to organize a march in Washington, D.C., to protest this discrimination. Roosevelt was afraid this march would disrupt the country. He made a deal with Randolph and signed the executive order banning discrimination in exchange for the march being called off.

Try It!

Write a paragraph that summarizes a detailed newspaper article. Be sure to use your own words.

Apply information.

When you are **applying** information, you must be able to use what you have learned to demonstrate, show, or model something. For example, using a manual to help you set up your computer requires you to apply the information from the manual to the job.

You apply when you . . .

- think about how you can use information.
- organize information so that it meets your specific needs.

Applying

Sometimes you will be asked to apply one type of information to another situation or idea. This assignment asks the writer to apply a specific concept to a foreign-policy decision made by Germany during World War II.

Assignment: Define the concept of *Lebensraum* and show how it applied to Nazi foreign policy during World War II.

The term *Lebensraum*, which means "living space" in German, was the idea that people should spread out from their homeland to occupy lands around them. The term became Hitler's main motive for World War II, and he saw Eastern Europe as a desirable "living space" for the German people. The first phase of Hitler's plan was to invade and take over countries such as Czechoslovakia and Poland. In these countries, he set up concentration camps meant to depopulate the countryside and make room for his people. At the same time, Hitler initiated so-called "eugenics" programs to produce more Germans to fill the emptied space. War and genocide were the natural results of applying the concept of *Lebensraum*. Whenever a country claims that it needs "living space," its neighbors should prepare for war.

Try It!

Write a paragraph explaining what would happen if there were suddenly no gasoline in the world.

Assignments

Analyze information.

You **analyze** information when you are able to break it down into parts that you can further explain.

You analyze when you . . .

- show how things are similar or different.
- identify which things are most important.
- arrange things in groups or categories.
- describe a process.
- discuss causes and/or effects.

Analyzing

Assignments that ask you to analyze information may require you to compare and contrast, discuss causes and effects, and so on. In this assignment, the writer discusses the causes of dramatic changes in the capital of the United States.

Assignment: In 1939, Washington, D.C., was a small city on the banks of the Potomac River. By 1945, it was one of the most important places in the world. Why did it change so much and so quickly?

During the 1930s, many citizens of the United States were "isolationists." They wanted this country to keep to itself. When World War II broke out in 1939, the U.S. had a small army. However, when the U.S. became involved in the war, isolationists could do nothing to stop it. The army expanded into one of the world's largest, and industries built more ships, tanks, and airplanes than anyone thought possible. This expansion was managed from Washington, D.C. Every bit of office space was used, and many temporary buildings were erected for government offices. More African Americans and women were hired than ever before, and the city more than doubled in population. Due to its distance from the fighting, Washington became the center for the Allied command.

Try It!

Think of a recent news event. Write a detailed paragraph describing the actions (causes) that led up to the event.

Synthesize information.

When you employ reasoning to combine parts into a whole, you are **synthesizing**.

You synthesize when you . . .

- add new ideas to existing information.
- use information to create a story, a poem, or other creative work.
- predict what will happen based on information that you have learned.

Synthesizing

The same thing that makes synthesizing a challenge also makes it fun: you get to use your imagination. This assignment asks the writer to use information to create imaginary diary entries about life in Washington, D.C., during World War II.

Assignment: Imagine that you are a "government girl" or a "dollar-a-year man" arriving in Washington, D.C., early in 1942. Write several diary entries about your life in this new city.

March 8, 1942—I arrived by bus after a long trip north from Montgomery, Alabama. There were lots of other young women on the bus, and the terminal in Washington was absolutely full of soldiers. In a very old building, I found a tiny apartment that I am sharing with five other girls.

March 12, 1942—Getting a job was easy because everyone needs workers who know how to type. I am working for the city draft board, helping young men (boys, really) fill out registration forms. We have a temporary office set up in a high school. Some of the boys act really tough, but I can tell that most of them are scared.

May 1, 1942—The cherry blossoms are blooming, and it is really beautiful. I got a letter from my brother Charlie, who is in the army in North Africa. I can't help but think of him every time I process new draftees.

Try It!

Imagine living in the United States during World War II. Write several diary entries about what you might see and experience.

Assignments

Evaluate Information.

When you are asked to express your opinion about an important issue, or to discuss the good and the bad points of a subject, you are **evaluating**. Evaluating is an advanced form of thinking that requires more thorough understanding and analysis of information.

You evaluate when you . . .

- give your opinion and support it.
- identify both the good and the bad points of a subject.

Evaluating

An effective evaluation is based on information. It often begins by identifying an overall opinion, or evaluation, and then adds supporting facts and details. This assignment asks the writer to evaluate the effects of a historical period.

Assignment: Can you think of two positive effects of the United States' involvement in World War II? If so, describe and discuss them.

The United States' involvement in World War II helped improve racial equality in the country. African Americans fought in the armed forces and performed very well. The Tuskegee Airmen, African American fighter pilots trained in Alabama, were one notable example. Besides that, minorities were hired for war jobs in areas that were closed to them previously.

Another positive effect was the end of the United States' isolationism. This country helped form the United Nations after the war and invited the organization to have its offices in New York. This showed that the U.S. was ready to play a positive role in world affairs.

Try It!

Write a paragraph discussing some of the positive or negative aspects of a topic you are studying in one of your classes.

Planning Your Writing Time

Be sure that you completely understand a writing assignment before you begin. Use the following guidelines.

1. **Read the directions** carefully.
2. **Focus on key words**—"describe," "evaluate," and so on—in order to understand the requirements of the assignment.
3. **Ask questions** if necessary.
4. **Plan your time** so that you can complete your work without rushing. (See the schedule below.)
5. **Review and revise** your writing.

The following schedule was created by a student who was asked to write a research report for a history class. The report was due in two weeks.

Sample Schedule

Week One

Day 1 PREWRITING
- Review the assignment.
- Search for a topic.

Day 2 PREWRITING
- Choose a topic.
- Start doing research.

Day 3 PREWRITING
- Gather and organize details.
- Find a focus for the report.

Day 4 WRITING
- Begin the first draft.

Day 5 WRITING
- Complete the first draft.

Week Two

Day 1 REVISING
- Revise the draft for ideas, organization, and voice.

Day 2 REVISING
- Ask a peer to review the draft.

Day 3 REVISING
- Check word choice and sentence fluency.

Day 4 EDITING
- Check the report for convention errors.
- Proofread the final copy.

Day 5 PUBLISHING
- Share the final copy.

■ Schedule a timed writing.

If you must complete your writing in one sitting, such as during a single class period, it is especially important to plan your work. For example, you might use 5 to 10 minutes at the beginning of the period to plan your writing, 30 to 40 minutes to write your draft, and 5 to 10 minutes at the end to make any necessary changes.

Improving Your Vocabulary

The words you know and use are important for three reasons: (1) They shape your thinking; (2) They influence how you communicate with your world; and (3) They affect how the world responds to you. You can improve your vocabulary by studying new subjects, having new experiences, increasing the amount of reading that you do, and listening carefully to other people. (Learning about any new subject requires learning the vocabulary that goes with it.)

This chapter contains a detailed glossary of prefixes, suffixes, and roots that will help you to learn many new words. By understanding these different word parts, you'll be able to figure out the meaning of even challenging words like *megalopolis* and *psychosomatic*. Consider this glossary as a special resource, much like a dictionary, that you can refer to again and again.

- **Understanding Word Parts**
- **Prefixes**
- **Suffixes**
- **Roots**

"We all come from the factory wired for language."
—Patricia T. O'Conner

Understanding Word Parts

Some English words such as *ground, age,* and *clock* are called base words. They cannot be broken down into word parts. However, many English words are made of prefixes, suffixes, and roots. Knowing the meanings of these parts can help you figure out the meanings of the words they form.

Unicyclist combines . . .

- the prefix *uni* (meaning *one*)
- the root *cycle* (meaning *wheel*)
- the suffix *ist* (meaning *a person who*)
  A *unicyclist* is a person who rides a one-wheeled vehicle.

Monochromatic combines . . .

- the prefix *mono* (meaning *one*)
- the root *chrom* (meaning *color*)
- the suffix *ate* (meaning *make*)
- the suffix *ic* (meaning *nature of*)
  A *monochromatic* painting is made of one color.

Try It!

Look through the following pages of prefixes, suffixes, and roots. Then write down the parts, their meanings, and a final definition for each of the following words.

1. geocentric
2. empathetic
3. synchronize
4. volcanology
5. bibliophile

■ Learn new words.

You already know and use many common prefixes, suffixes, and roots every day. To improve your speaking and writing vocabulary, study the meanings of prefixes, suffixes, and roots that are not familiar to you. The following pages contain nearly 500 word parts. Here is how to use these pages:

1. Scan the pages until you come to a word part that is new to you.
2. Learn its meaning and at least one of the sample words listed.
3. Apply your knowledge as you encounter new words in your course work.

Prefixes

Prefixes are those word parts that come *before* the root words (*pre* = before). Depending upon its meaning, a prefix changes the intent, or sense, of the base word. As a skilled reader, you will want to know the meanings of the most common prefixes in order to figure out the meanings of unfamiliar words.

a, an [not, without] amoral (without a sense of moral responsibility), atypical, atom (not cuttable), apathy (without feeling), anesthesia (without sensation)

ab, abs, a [from, away] abnormal, abduct, absent, avert (turn away)

acro [high] acropolis (high city), acrobat, acronym, acrophobia (fear of height)

ambi, amb [both, around] ambidextrous (skilled with both hands), ambiguous

amphi [both] amphibious (living on both land and water), amphitheater

ante [before] antedate, anteroom, antebellum, antecedent (happening before)

anti, ant [against] anticommunist, antidote, anticlimax, antacid

be [on, away] bedeck, belabor, bequest, bestow, beloved

bene, bon [well] benefit, benefactor, benevolent, benediction, bonanza, bonus

bi, bis, bin [both, double, twice] bicycle, biweekly, bilateral, biscuit, binoculars

by [side, close, near] bypass, bystander, by-product, bylaw, byline

cata [down, against] catalog, catapult, catastrophe, cataclysm

cerebro [brain] cerebral, cerebellum

circum, circ [around] circumference, circumnavigate, circumspect, circular

co, con, col, com [together, with] copilot, conspire, collect, compose

coni [dust] coniosis (disease that comes from inhaling dust)

contra, counter [against] controversy, contradict, counterpart

de [from, down] demote, depress, degrade, deject, deprive

deca [ten] decade, decathlon, decapod

di [two, twice] divide, dilemma, dilute, dioxide, dipole, ditto

dia [through, between] diameter, diagonal, diagram, dialogue (speech between people)

dis, dif [apart, away, reverse] dismiss, distort, distinguish, diffuse

dys [badly, ill] dyspepsia (digesting badly), dystrophy, dysentery

em, en [in, into] embrace, enslave

epi [upon] epidermis (upon the skin, outer layer of skin), epitaph, epithet

eu [well] eulogize (speak well of, praise), euphony, euphemism, euphoria

ex, e, ec, ef [out] expel (drive out), ex-mayor, exorcism, eject, eccentric (out of the center position), efflux, effluent

extra, extro [beyond, outside] extraordinary (beyond the ordinary), extrovert, extracurricular

for [away, off] forswear (to renounce an oath)

fore [before in time] forecast, foretell (to tell beforehand), foreshadow

hemi, demi, semi [half] hemisphere, demitasse, semicircle (half of a circle)

hex [six] hexameter, hexagon

homo [man] Homo sapiens, homicide (killing man)

hyper [over, above] hypersensitive (overly sensitive), hyperactive

hypo [under] hypodermic (under the skin), hypothesis

il, ir, in, im [not] illegal, irregular, incorrect, immoral

in, il, im [into] inject, inside, illuminate, illustrate, impose, implant, imprison

infra [beneath] infrared, infrasonic

inter [between] intercollegiate, interfere, intervene, interrupt (break between)

intra [within] intramural, intravenous (within the veins)

intro [into, inward] introduce, introvert (turn inward)

macro [large, excessive] macrodent (having large teeth), macrocosm

mal [badly, poorly] maladjusted, malady, malnutrition, malfunction

meta [beyond, after, with] metaphor, metamorphosis, metaphysical

mis [incorrect, bad] misuse, misprint

miso [hate] misanthrope, misogynist

mono [one] monoplane, monotone, monocle, monochrome

multi [many] multiply, multiform

neo [new] neopaganism, neoclassic, neophyte, neonatal

non [not] nontaxable (not taxed), nontoxic, nonexistent, nonsense

ob, of, op, oc [toward, against] obstruct, offend, oppose, occur

oct [eight] octagon, octameter, octave, octopus

paleo [ancient] paleoanthropology (pertaining to ancient humans), paleontology (study of ancient life-forms)

para [beside, almost] parasite (one who eats beside or at the table of another), paraphrase, paramedic, parallel, paradox

penta [five] pentagon (figure or building having five angles or sides), pentameter, pentathlon

per [throughout, completely] pervert (completely turn wrong, corrupt), perfect, perceive, permanent, persuade

peri [around] perimeter (measurement around an area), periphery, periscope, pericardium, period

poly [many] polygon (figure having many angles or sides), polygamy, polyglot, polychrome

post [after] postpone, postwar, postscript, posterity

pre [before] prewar, preview, precede, prevent, premonition

pro [forward, in favor of] project (throw forward), progress, promote, prohibition

pseudo [false] pseudonym (false or assumed name), pseudopodia

quad [four] quadruple (four times as much), quadriplegic, quadratic, quadrant

quint [five] quintuplet, quintuple, quintet, quintile

re [back, again] reclaim, revive, revoke, rejuvenate, retard, reject, return

retro [backward] retrospective (looking backward), retroactive, retrorocket

se [aside] seduce (lead aside), secede, secrete, segregate

self [by oneself] self-determination, selfish, self-employed, self-service,

sesqui [one and a half] sesquicentennial (one and one-half centuries)

sex, sest [six] sexagenarian (sixty years old), sexennial, sextant, sextuplet, sestet

sub [under] submerge (put under), submarine, substitute, subsoil

suf, sug, sup, sus [from under] sufficient, suffer, suggest, support, suspend

super, supr [above, over, more] supervise, superman, supernatural, supreme

syn, sym, sys, syl [with, together] system, synthesis, synchronize (time together), synonym, sympathy, symphony, syllable

trans, tra [across, beyond] transoceanic, transmit (send across), transfusion

tri [three] tricycle, triangle, tripod, tristate

ultra [beyond, exceedingly] ultramodern, ultraviolet, ultraconservative

un [not, release] unfair, unnatural, unknown

under [beneath] underground, underlying

uni [one] unicycle, uniform, unify, universe, unique (one of a kind)

vice [in place of] vice president, viceroy, vice admiral

Numerical Prefixes

Prefix	Symbol	Multiples and Submultiples	Equivalent	Prefix	Symbol	Multiples and Submultiples	Equivalent
tera	T	10^{12}	trillionfold	centi	c	10^{-2}	hundredth part
giga	G	10^{9}	billionfold	milli	m	10^{-3}	thousandth part
mega	M	10^{6}	millionfold	micro	u	10^{-6}	millionth part
kilo	k	10^{3}	thousandfold	nano	n	10^{-9}	billionth part
hecto	h	10^{2}	hundredfold	pico	p	10^{-12}	trillionth part
deka	da	10	tenfold	femto	f	10^{-15}	quadrillionth part
deci	d	10^{-1}	tenth part	atto	a	10^{-18}	quintillionth part

Suffixes

Suffixes come at the end of a word. Very often a suffix will tell you what kind of word it is part of (noun, adverb, adjective, and so on). For example, words ending in *-ly* are usually adverbs.

able, ible [able, can do] capable, agreeable, edible, visible (can be seen)

ade [result of action] blockade (the result of a blocking action), lemonade

age [act of, state of, collection of] salvage (act of saving), storage, forage

al [relating to] sensual, gradual, manual, natural (relating to nature)

algia [pain] neuralgia (nerve pain)

an, ian [native of, relating to] Canadian, African, Floridian

ance, ancy [action, process, state] assistance, allowance, defiance, truancy

ant [performing, agent] assistant, servant

ary, ery, ory [relating to, quality, place where] dictionary, bravery, dormitory

ate [cause, make] liquidate, segregate (cause a group to be set aside)

cian [having a certain skill or art] musician, beautician, magician, physician

cule, ling [very small] molecule, ridicule, duckling (very small duck), sapling

cy [action, function] hesitancy, prophecy, normalcy (function in a normal way)

dom [quality, realm, office] freedom, kingdom, wisdom (quality of being wise)

ee [one who receives the action] employee, nominee (one who is nominated), refugee

en [made of, make] silken, frozen, oaken (made of oak), wooden, lighten

ence, ency [action, state of, quality] urgency, difference, conference

er, or [one who, that which] baker, miller, teacher, racer, amplifier, doctor

escent [in the process of] adolescent (in the process of becoming an adult), obsolescent, convalescent

ese [a native of, the language of] Japanese, Vietnamese, Portuguese

esis, osis [action, process, condition] genesis, hypnosis, neurosis, osmosis

ess [female] actress, goddess, lioness

et, ette [a small one, group] midget, octet, baronet, majorette

fic [making, causing] scientific, specific

ful [full of] frightful, careful, helpful

fy [make] fortify (make strong), simplify, amplify

hood [order, condition, quality] manhood, womanhood, brotherhood

ic [nature of, like] metallic (of the nature of metal), heroic, poetic, acidic

ice [condition, state, quality] justice, malice

id, ide [a thing connected to or belonging to] fluid, fluoride

ile [relating to, suited for, capable of] missile, juvenile, senile (related to being old)

ine [nature of] feminine, genuine, medicine

ion, sion, tion [act of, state of, result of] contagion, aversion, infection (state of being infected)

ish [origin, nature, resembling] foolish, Irish, clownish (resembling a clown)

ism [system, manner, condition, characteristic] heroism, alcoholism, Communism

ist [one who, that which] artist, dentist

ite [nature of, quality of, mineral product] Israelite, dynamite, graphite, sulfite

ity, ty [state of, quality] captivity, clarity

ive [causing, making] abusive (causing abuse), exhaustive

ize [make] emphasize, publicize, idolize

less [without] baseless, careless (without care), artless, fearless, helpless

ly [like, manner of] carelessly, forcefully, quickly, lovingly

ment [act of, state of, result] contentment, amendment (state of amending)

ness [state of] carelessness, kindness

oid [resembling] asteroid, spheroid, tabloid, anthropoid

ology [study, science, theory] anthropology, biology, geology, neurology

ous [full of, having] gracious, nervous, spacious, vivacious (full of life)

ship [office, state, quality, skill] friendship, authorship, dictatorship

some [like, apt, tending to] lonesome, threesome, gruesome

tude [state of, condition of] gratitude, multitude (condition of being many), aptitude

ure [state of, act, process, rank] culture, literature, rupture (state of being broken)

ward [in the direction of] eastward, forward, backward

y [inclined to, tend to] cheery, crafty, faulty

Vocabulary

Roots

A *root* is a base upon which other words are built. Knowing the root of a difficult word can take you a long way toward figuring out its meaning—even without a dictionary. For that reason, learning the following roots will be very valuable to you as you read.

acer, acid, acri [bitter, sour, sharp] acrid, acerbic, acidity (sourness), acrimony

acu [sharp] acute, acupuncture

ag, agi, ig, act [do, move, go] agent (doer), agenda (things to do), agitate, navigate (move by sea), ambiguous (going both ways), action

ali, allo, alter [other] alias (a person's other name), alibi, alien (from another place), alloy, alter (change to another form)

alt [high, deep] altimeter (a device for measuring heights), altitude

am, amor [love, liking] amiable, amorous, enamored

anni, annu, enni [year] anniversary, annually (yearly), centennial (occurring once in 100 years)

anthrop [man] anthropology (study of mankind), philanthropy (love of mankind), misanthrope (hater of mankind)

anti [old] antique, antiquated, antiquity

arch [chief, first, rule] archangel (chief angel), architect (chief worker), archaic (first, very early), monarchy (rule by one person), matriarchy (rule by the mother)

aster, astr [star] aster (star flower), asterisk, asteroid, astronomy (star law), astronaut (star traveler, space traveler)

aud, aus [hear, listen] audible (can be heard), auditorium, audio, audition, auditory, audience, ausculate

aug, auc [increase] augur, augment (add to; increase), auction

auto, aut [self] autograph (self-writing), automobile (self-moving vehicle), author, automatic (self-acting), autobiography

belli [war] rebellion, belligerent (warlike or hostile)

bibl [book] Bible, bibliography (list of books), bibliomania (craze for books), bibliophile (book lover)

bio [life] biology (study of life), biography, biopsy (cut living tissue for examination)

brev [short] abbreviate, brevity, brief

cad, cas [to fall] cadaver, cadence, caducous (falling off), cascade

calor [heat] calorie (a unit of heat), calorify (to make hot), caloric

cap, cip, cept [take] capable, capacity, capture, reciprocate, accept, except, concept

capit, capt [head] decapitate (to remove the head from), capital, captain, caption

carn [flesh] carnivorous (flesh eating), incarnate, reincarnation

caus, caut [burn, heat] caustic, cauterize (to make hot, to burn)

cause, cuse, cus [cause, motive] because, excuse (to attempt to remove the blame or cause), accusation

ced, ceed, cede, cess [move, yield, go, surrender] procedure, secede (move aside from), proceed (move forward), cede (yield), concede, intercede, precede, recede, success

centri [center] concentric, centrifugal, centripetal, eccentric (out of center)

chrom [color] chrome, chromosome (color body in genetics), chromosphere, monochrome (one color), polychrome

chron [time] chronological (in order of time), chronometer (time measured), chronicle (record of events in time), synchronize (make time with, set time together)

cide, cise [cut down, kill] suicide (killing of self), homicide (human killer), pesticide (pest killer), germicide (germ killer), precise (cut exactly right), incision, scissors

cit [to call, start] incite, citation, cite

civ [citizen] civic (relating to a citizen), civil, civilian, civilization

clam, claim [cry out] exclamation, clamor, proclamation, reclamation, acclaim

clud, clus, claus [shut] include (to take in), conclude, claustrophobia (abnormal fear of being shut up, confined), recluse (one who shuts himself away from others)

cognosc, gnosi [know] recognize (to know again), incognito (not known), prognosis (forward knowing), diagnosis

cord, cor, cardi [heart] cordial (hearty, heartfelt), concord, discord, courage, encourage (put heart into), discourage (take heart out of), core, coronary, cardiac

corp [body] corporation (a legal body), corpse, corpulent

cosm [universe, world] cosmic, cosmos (the universe), cosmopolitan (world citizen), cosmonaut, microcosm, macrocosm

crat, cracy [rule, strength] democratic, autocracy

crea [create] creature (anything created), recreation, creation, creator

cred [believe] creed (statement of beliefs), credo (a creed), credence (belief), credit (belief, trust), credulous (believing too readily, easily deceived), incredible

cresc, cret, crease, cru [rise, grow] accrue (to grow), crescendo (growing in loudness or intensity), concrete (grown together, solidified), increase, decrease

crit [separate, choose] critical, criterion (that which is used in choosing), hypocrite

cur, curs [run] concurrent, current (running or flowing), concur (run together, agree), incur (run into), recur, occur, precursor (forerunner), cursive

cura [care] curator, curative, manicure (caring for the hands)

cycl, cyclo [wheel, circular] Cyclops (a mythical giant with one eye in the middle of his forehead), unicycle, bicycle, cyclone (a wind blowing circularly, a tornado)

deca [ten] decade, decalogue, decathlon

dem [people] democracy (people-rule), demography (vital statistics of the people: deaths, births, and so on), epidemic (on or among the people)

dent, dont [tooth] dental (relating to teeth), denture, dentifrice, orthodontist

derm [skin] hypodermic (injected under the skin), dermatology (skin study), epidermis (outer layer of skin), taxidermy (arranging skin; mounting animals)

dict [say, speak] diction (how one speaks, what one says), dictionary, dictate, dictator, dictaphone, dictatorial, edict, predict, verdict, contradict, benediction

doc [teach] indoctrinate, document, doctrine

domin [master] dominate, predominant, dominion, domain

don [give] donate, condone

dorm [sleep] dormant, dormitory

dox [opinion, praise] doxy (belief, creed, or opinion), orthodox (having the correct, commonly accepted opinion), heterodox (differing opinion), paradox (contradictory)

drome [run, step] syndrome (run-together symptoms), hippodrome (a place where horses run)

duc, duct [lead] produce, induce (lead into, persuade), seduce (lead aside), reduce, aqueduct (water leader or channel), viaduct, conduct

dura [hard, lasting] durable, duration, endurance

dynam [power] dynamo (power producer), dynamic, dynamite, hydrodynamics

endo [within] endoral (within the mouth), endocardial (within the heart), endoskeletal

equi [equal] equinox, equilibrium

erg [work] energy, erg (unit of work), allergy, ergophobia (morbid fear of work), ergometer, ergonomic

fac, fact, fic, fect [do, make] factory (place where workers make goods of various kinds), fact (a thing done), manufacture, amplification, confection

fall, fals [deceive] fallacy, falsify

fer [bear, carry] ferry (carry by water), coniferous (bearing cones, as a pine tree), fertile (bearing richly), defer, infer, refer

fid, fide, feder [faith, trust] confidante, Fido, fidelity, confident, infidelity, infidel, federal, confederacy

fila, fili [thread] filament (a single thread or threadlike object), filibuster, filigree

fin [end, ended, finished] final, finite, finish, confine, fine, refine, define, finale

fix [attach] fix, fixation (the state of being attached), fixture, affix, prefix, suffix

flex, flect [bend] flex (bend), reflex (bending back), flexible, flexor (muscle for bending), inflexibility, reflect, deflect

flu, fluc, fluv [flowing] influence (to flow in), fluid, flue, flush, fluently, fluctuate (to wave in an unsteady motion)

form [form, shape] form, uniform, conform, deform, reform, perform, formative, formation, formal, formula

fort, forc [strong] fort, fortress (a strong place), fortify (make strong), forte (one's strong point), fortitude, enforce

fract, frag [break] fracture (a break), infraction, fragile (easy to break), fraction (result of breaking a whole into equal parts), refract (to break or bend)

gam [marriage] bigamy (two marriages), monogamy, polygamy (many spouses or marriages)

gastr(o) [stomach] gastric, gastronomic, gastritis (inflammation of the stomach)

gen [birth, race, produce] genesis (birth, beginning), genetics (study of heredity), eugenics (well born), genealogy (lineage by race, stock), generate, genetic

geo [earth] geometry (earth measurement), geography (earth writing), geocentric (earth centered), geology

germ [vital part] germination (to grow), germ (seed; living substance, as the germ of an idea), germane

gest [carry, bear] congest (bear together, clog), congestive (causing clogging), gestation

gloss, glot [tongue] glossary, polyglot (many tongues), epiglottis

glu, glo [lump, bond, glue] glue, agglutinate (make to hold in a bond), conglomerate (bond together)

grad, gress [step, go] grade (step, degree), gradual (step-by-step), graduate (make all the steps, finish a course), graduated (in steps or degrees), progress

graph, gram [write, written] graph, graphic (written, vivid), autograph (self-writing, signature), graphite (carbon used for writing), photography (light writing), phonograph (sound writing), diagram, bibliography, telegram

grat [pleasing] gratuity (mark of favor, a tip), congratulate (express pleasure over success), grateful, ingrate (not thankful)

grav [heavy, weighty] grave, aggravate, gravity, gravitate

greg [herd, group, crowd] congregation (a group functioning together), gregarian (belonging to a herd), segregate (tending to group aside or apart)

helio [sun] heliograph (an instrument for using the sun's rays to send signals), heliotrope (a plant that turns to the sun)

hema, hemo [blood] hemorrhage (an outpouring or flowing of blood), hemoglobin, hemophilia

here, hes [stick] adhere, cohere, cohesion

hetero [different] heterogeneous (different in birth), heterosexual (with interest in the opposite sex)

homo [same] homogeneous (of same birth or kind), homonym (word with same pronunciation as another), homogenize

hum, human [earth, ground, man] humus, exhume (to take out of the ground), humane (compassion for other humans)

hydr, hydra, hydro [water] dehydrate, hydrant, hydraulic, hydraulics, hydrogen, hydrophobia (fear of water)

hypn [sleep] hypnosis, Hypnos (god of sleep), hypnotherapy (treatment of disease by hypnosis)

ignis [fire] ignite, igneous, ignition

ject [throw] deject, inject, project (throw forward), eject, object

join, junct [join] adjoining, enjoin (to lay an order upon, to command), juncture, conjunction, injunction

juven [young] juvenile, rejuvenate (to make young again)

lau, lav, lot, lut [wash] launder, lavatory, lotion, ablution (a washing away), dilute (to make a liquid thinner and weaker)

leg [law] legal (lawful; according to law), legislate (to enact a law), legislature, legitimize (make legal)

levi [light] alleviate (lighten a load), levitate, levity (light conversation; humor)

liber, liver [free] liberty (freedom), liberal, liberalize (to make more free), deliverance

liter [letters] literary (concerned with books and writing), literature, literal, alliteration, obliterate

loc, loco [place] locality, locale, location, allocate (to assign, to place), relocate (to put back into place), locomotion (act of moving from place to place)

log, logo, ogue, ology [word, study, speech] catalog, prologue, dialogue, logogram (a symbol representing a word), zoology (animal study), psychology (mind study)

loqu, locut [talk, speak] eloquent (speaking well and forcefully), soliloquy, locution, loquacious (talkative), colloquial (talking together; conversational or informal)

luc, lum, lus, lun [light] translucent (letting light come through), lumen (a unit of light), luminary (a heavenly body; someone who shines in his or her profession), luster (sparkle, shine), Luna (the moon goddess)

magn [great] magnify (make great, enlarge), magnificent, magnanimous (great of mind or spirit), magnate, magnitude, magnum

man [hand] manual, manage, manufacture, manacle, manicure, manifest, maneuver, emancipate

mand [command] mandatory (commanded), remand (order back), mandate

mania [madness] mania (insanity, craze), monomania (mania on one idea), kleptomania, pyromania (insane tendency to set fires), maniac

mar, mari, mer [sea, pool] marine (a soldier serving on shipboard), marsh (wetland, swamp), maritime (relating to the sea and navigation), mermaid (fabled sea creature, half fish, half woman)

matri [mother] maternal (relating to the mother), matrimony, matriarchate (rulership of women), matron

medi [half, middle, between, halfway] mediate (come between, intervene), medieval (pertaining to the Middle Ages), Mediterranean (lying between lands), mediocre, medium

mega [great, million] megaphone (great sound), megalopolis (great city; an extensive urban area including a number of cities), megacycle (a million cycles), megaton

mem [remember] memo (a reminder), commemoration (the act of remembering by a memorial or ceremony), memento, memoir, memorable

meter [measure] meter (a metric measure), voltameter (instrument to measure volts), barometer, thermometer

micro [small] microscope, microfilm, microcard, microwave, micrometer (device for measuring small distances), omicron, micron (a millionth of a meter), microbe (small living thing)

migra [wander] migrate (to wander), emigrate (one who leaves a country), immigrate (to come into the land)

mit, miss [send] emit (send out, give off), remit (send back, as money due), submit, admit, commit, permit, transmit (send across), omit, intermittent (sending between, at intervals), mission, missile

mob, mot, mov [move] mobile (capable of moving), motionless (without motion), motor, emotional (moved strongly by feelings), motivate, promotion, demote, movement

mon [warn, remind] monument (a reminder or memorial of a person or an event), admonish (warn), monitor, premonition (forewarning)

mor, mort [mortal, death] mortal (causing death or destined for death), immortal (not subject to death), mortality (rate of death), mortician (one who prepares the dead for burial), mortuary (place for the dead, a morgue)

morph [form] amorphous (with no form, shapeless), metamorphosis (a change of form, as a caterpillar into a butterfly), morphology

multi [many, much] multifold (folded many times), multilinguist (one who speaks many languages), multiped (an organism with many feet), multiply

nat, nasc [to be born, to spring forth] innate (inborn), natal, native, nativity, renascence (a rebirth, a revival)

neur [nerve] neuritis (inflammation of a nerve), neurology (study of nervous systems), neurologist (one who practices neurology), neural, neurosis, neurotic

nom [law, order] autonomy (self-law, self-government), astronomy, gastronomy (art or science of good eating), economy

nomen, nomin [name] nomenclature, nominate (name someone for an office)

nov [new] novel (new, strange, not formerly known), renovate (to make like new again), novice, nova, innovate

nox, noc [night] nocturnal, equinox (equal nights), noctilucent (shining by night)

numer [number] numeral (a figure expressing a number), numeration (act of counting), enumerate (count out, one by one), innumerable

omni [all, every] omnipotent (all-powerful), omniscient (all-knowing), omnipresent (present everywhere), omnivorous

onym [name] anonymous (without name), synonym, pseudonym (false name), antonym (name of opposite meaning)

oper [work] operate (to labor, function), cooperate (work together)

ortho [straight, correct] orthodox (of the correct or accepted opinion), orthodontist (tooth straightener), orthopedic (originally pertaining to straightening a child), unorthodox

pac [peace] pacifist (one for peace only; opposed to war), pacify (make peace, quiet), Pacific Ocean (peaceful ocean)

pan [all] panacea (cure-all), pandemonium (place of all the demons, wild disorder), pantheon (place of all the gods in mythology)

pater, patr [father] paternity (fatherhood, responsibility), patriarch (head of the tribe, family), patriot, patron (a wealthy person who supports as would a father)

path, pathy [feeling, suffering] pathos (feeling of pity, sorrow), sympathy, antipathy (feeling against), apathy (without feeling), empathy (feeling or identifying with another), telepathy (far feeling; thought transference)

ped, pod [foot] pedal (lever for a foot), impede (get the feet in a trap, hinder), pedestal (foot or base of a statue), pedestrian (foot traveler), centipede, tripod (three-footed support), podiatry (care of the feet), antipodes (opposite feet)

pedo [child] orthopedic, pedagogue (child leader; teacher), pediatrics (medical care of children)

pel, puls [drive, urge] compel, dispel, expel, repel, propel, pulse, impulse, pulsate, compulsory, expulsion, repulsive

pend, pens, pond [hang, weigh] pendant pendulum, suspend, appendage, pensive (weighing thought), ponderous

phil [love] philosophy (love of wisdom), philanthropy, philharmonic, bibliophile, Philadelphia (city of brotherly love)

phobia [fear] claustrophobia (fear of closed spaces), acrophobia (fear of high places), hydrophobia (fear of water)

phon [sound] phonograph, phonetic (pertaining to sound), symphony (sounds with or together)

photo [light] photograph (light-writing), photoelectric, photogenic (artistically suitable for being photographed), photosynthesis (action of light on chlorophyll to make carbohydrates)

plac [please] placid (calm, peaceful), placebo, placate, complacent

plu, plur, plus [more] plural (more than one), pluralist (a person who holds more than one office), plus (indicating that something more is to be added)

pneuma, pneumon [breath] pneumatic (pertaining to air, wind, or other gases), pneumonia (disease of the lungs)

pod (see *ped*)

poli [city] metropolis (mother city), police, politics, Indianapolis, Acropolis (high city, upper part of Athens), megalopolis

pon, pos, pound [place, put] postpone (put afterward), component, opponent (one put against), proponent, expose, impose, deposit, posture (how one places oneself), position

pop [people] population, populous (full of people), popular

port [carry] porter (one who carries), portable, transport (carry across), report, export, import, support, transportation

portion [part, share] portion (a part; a share, as a portion of pie), proportion (the relation of one share to others)

prehend [seize] comprehend (seize with the mind), apprehend (seize a criminal), comprehensive (seizing much, extensive)

prim, prime [first] primacy (state of being first in rank), prima donna (the first lady of opera), primitive (from the earliest or first time), primary, primal, primeval

proto [first] prototype (the first model made), protocol, protagonist, protozoan

psych [mind, soul] psyche (soul, mind), psychiatry (healing of the mind), psychology, psychosis (serious mental disorder), psychotherapy (mind treatment), psychic

punct [point, dot] punctual (being exactly on time), punctuation, puncture, acupuncture

reg, recti [straighten] regiment, regular, regulate, rectify (make straight), correct, direction

ri, ridi, risi [laughter] deride (mock, jeer at), ridicule (laughter at the expense of another, mockery), ridiculous, derision

rog, roga [ask] prerogative (privilege; asking before), interrogation (questioning; the act of questioning), derogatory

rupt [break] rupture (break), interrupt (break into), abrupt (broken off), disrupt (break apart), erupt (break out), incorruptible (unable to be broken down)

sacr, sanc, secr [sacred] sacred, sanction, sacrosanct, consecrate, desecrate

salv, salu [safe, healthy] salvation (act of being saved), salvage, salutation

sat, satis [enough] satient (giving pleasure, satisfying), saturate, satisfy (to give pleasure to; to give as much as is needed)

sci [know] science (knowledge), conscious (knowing, aware), omniscient (knowing everything)

scope [see, watch] telescope, microscope, kaleidoscope (instrument for seeing beautiful forms), periscope, stethoscope

scrib, script [write] scribe (a writer), scribble, manuscript (written by hand), inscribe, describe, subscribe, prescribe

sed, sess, sid [sit] sediment (that which sits or settles out of a liquid), session (a sitting), obsession (an idea that sits stubbornly in the mind), possess, preside (sit before), president, reside, subside

sen [old] senior, senator, senile (old; showing the weakness of old age)

sent, sens [feel] sentiment (feeling), consent, resent, dissent, sentimental (having strong feeling or emotion), sense, sensation, sensitive, sensory, dissension

sequ, secu, sue [follow] sequence (following of one thing after another), consequence, sequel, subsequent, prosecute, consecutive (following in order), second (following "first"), ensue, pursue

serv [save, serve] servant, service, preserve, subservient, servitude, conserve, deserve, reservation, conservation

sign, signi [sign, mark, seal] signal (a gesture or sign to call attention), signature (the mark of a person written in his or her own handwriting), design, insignia (distinguishing marks)

simil, simul [like, resembling] similar (resembling in many respects), assimilate (to make similar to), simile, simulate (pretend; put on an act to make a certain impression)

sist, sta, stit [stand] persist (stand firmly; unyielding; continue), assist (to stand by with help), circumstance, stamina (power to withstand, to endure), status (standing), state, static, stable, stationary, substitute (to stand in for another)

solus [alone] soliloquy, solitaire, solitude, solo

solv, solu [loosen] solvent (a loosener, a dissolver), solve, absolve (loosen from, free from), resolve, soluble, solution, resolution, resolute, dissolute (loosened morally)

somnus [sleep] insomnia (not being able to sleep), somnambulist (a sleepwalker)

soph [wise] sophomore (wise fool), philosophy (love of wisdom), sophisticated

spec, spect, spic [look] specimen (an example to look at, study), specific, aspect, spectator (one who looks), spectacle, speculate, inspect, respect, prospect, retrospective (looking backward), introspective, expect, conspicuous

sphere [ball, sphere] stratosphere (the upper portion of the atmosphere), hemisphere (half of the earth), spheroid

spir [breath] spirit (breath), conspire (breathe together; plot), inspire (breathe into), aspire (breathe toward), expire (breathe out; die), perspire, respiration

string, strict [draw tight] stringent (drawn tight; rigid), strict, restrict, constrict (draw tightly together), boa constrictor (snake that constricts its prey)

stru, struct [build] construe (build in the mind, interpret), structure, construct, instruct, obstruct, destruction, destroy

sume, sump [take, use, waste] consume (to use up), assume (to take; to use), sump pump (a pump that takes up water), presumption (to take or use before knowing all the facts)

tact, tang, tag, tig, ting [touch] contact, tactile, intangible (not able to be touched), intact (untouched, uninjured), tangible, contingency, contagious (able to transmit disease by touching), contiguous

tele [far] telephone (far sound), telegraph (far writing), television (far seeing), telephoto (far photography), telecast

tempo [time] tempo (rate of speed), temporary, extemporaneously, contemporary (those who live at the same time), pro tem (for the time being)

ten, tin, tain [hold] tenacious (holding fast), tenant, tenure, untenable, detention, content, pertinent, continent, obstinate, abstain, pertain, detain

tend, tent, tens [stretch, strain] tendency (a stretching; leaning), extend, intend, contend, pretend, superintend, tender, extent, tension (a stretching, strain), pretense

terra [earth] terrain, terrarium, territory, terrestrial

test [to bear witness] testament (a will; bearing witness to someone's wishes), detest, attest (bear witness to), testimony

the, theo [God, a god] monotheism (belief in one god), polytheism (belief in many gods), atheism, theology

therm [heat] thermometer, therm (heat unit), thermal, thermostat, thermos, hypothermia (subnormal temperature)

thesis, thet [place, put] antithesis (place against), hypothesis (place under), synthesis (put together), epithet

tom [cut] atom (not cuttable; smallest particle of matter), appendectomy (cutting out an appendix), tonsillectomy, dichotomy (cutting in two; a division), anatomy (cutting, dissecting to study structure)

Vocabulary

tort, tors [twist] torture (twisting to inflict pain), retort (twist back, reply sharply), extort (twist out), distort (twist out of shape), contort, torsion (act of twisting, as a torsion bar)

tox [poison] toxic (poisonous), intoxicate, antitoxin

tract, tra [draw, pull] tractor, attract, subtract, tractable (can be handled), abstract (to draw away), subtrahend (the number to be drawn away from another)

trib [pay, bestow] tribute (to pay honor to), contribute (to give money to a cause), attribute, retribution, tributary

turbo [disturb] turbulent, disturb, turbid, turmoil

typ [print] type, prototype (first print; model), typical, typography, typewriter, typology (study of types, symbols), typify

ultima [last] ultimate, ultimatum (the final or last offer that can be made)

uni [one] unicorn (a legendary creature with one horn), unify (make into one), university, unanimous, universal

vac [empty] vacate (to make empty), vacuum (a space entirely devoid of matter), evacuate (to remove troops or people), vacation, vacant

vale, vali, valu [strength, worth] valiant, equivalent (of equal worth), validity (truth; legal strength), evaluate (find out the value), value, valor (value; worth)

ven, vent [come] convene (come together, assemble), intervene (come between), venue, convenient, avenue, circumvent (come or go around), invent, prevent

ver, veri [true] very, aver (say to be true, affirm), verdict, verity (truth), verify (show to be true), verisimilitude

vert, vers [turn] avert (turn away), divert (turn aside, amuse), invert (turn over), introvert (turn inward), convertible, reverse (turn back), controversy (a turning against; a dispute), versatile (turning easily from one skill to another)

vic, vicis [change, substitute] vicarious, vicar, vicissitude

vict, vinc [conquer] victor (conqueror, winner), evict (conquer out, expel), convict (prove guilty), convince (conquer mentally, persuade), invincible (not conquerable)

vid, vis [see] video, television, evident, provide, providence, visible, revise, supervise (oversee), vista, visit, vision

viv, vita, vivi [alive, life] revive (make live again), survive (live beyond, outlive), vivid, vivacious (full of life), vitality

voc [call] vocation (a calling), avocation (occupation not one's calling), convocation (a calling together), invocation, vocal

vol [will] malevolent, benevolent (one of goodwill), volunteer, volition

volcan, vulcan [fire] volcano (a mountain erupting fiery lava), volcanize (to undergo volcanic heat), Vulcan (Roman god of fire)

volvo [turn about, roll] revolve, voluminous (winding), voluble (easily turned about or around), convolution (a twisting)

vor [eat greedily] voracious, carnivorous (flesh eating), herbivorous (plant eating), omnivorous (eating everything), devour

zo [animal] zoo (short for zoological garden), zoology (study of animal life), zodiac (circle of animal constellations), zoomorphism (being in the form of an animal), protozoa (one-celled animals)

The Human Body

capit	head	gastro	stomach	osteo	bone
cardi	heart	gloss	tongue	ped	foot
corp	body	hema	blood	pneuma	breathe
dent	tooth	man	hand	psych	mind
derm	skin	neur	nerve	spir	breath

Writing Business Letters

Well-written business letters are designed to get results. People in the workplace write business letters to apply for jobs, request information, promote products, make complaints, or answer questions. In addition, carefully written letters serve as accurate records, especially for businesses, organizations, and governing bodies. While telephone conversations and e-mails are frequently used to exchange information, letters are still regarded as the most reliable form of communication. In other words, if something is important, put it in writing.

As a student, you can also write business letters to get things done. You can request help, apply for jobs or admission to schools, or persuade others to support worthy causes. Developing good letter-writing skills will help you now and for years to come.

- **Writing a Business Letter**
- **Parts of a Business Letter**
- **Creating an E-Mail Message**
- **Sending a Letter**

"Make the most of yourself, for that is all there is of you."
—Ralph Waldo Emerson

Writing a Business Letter

If you need information, resources, or a recommendation from an individual or group, a request letter is an effective way to accomplish this task. In the following letter, Justin Dobbs requests a job recommendation from a former employer. (See the writing tips on the next page.)

The letter follows the correct format. (See pages **516–517**.)

717 Main Street
Sandusky, OH 44870
May 12, 2006

Mr. Sam Spencer
Sandusky Register
314 West Market Street
Sandusky, OH 44870

Dear Mr. Spencer:

The **beginning** introduces the request.

I delivered papers for you for two years when I was in seventh and eighth grade. Now I am at the end of my freshman year at Sandusky High School, and I am applying for a summer job at a Dollar General grocery store. Mr. Perkins, the store manager, asked me if I could get a reference from a previous employer. I immediately thought of you because you were my first employer.

The **middle** provides details of the request.

If you could give me a recommendation, please call Mr. Perkins at the store's office number, 555-1234, before May 18. If you have any questions, you can reach me at 555-1086.

The **ending** expresses thanks.

Thank you for considering my request. If you could do this for me, I would be very grateful.

Sincerely,

Justin Dobbs

Justin Dobbs

Business Letters

"The best advice on writing I've ever received is: 'Write with authority.'"

—Cynthia Ozick

Writing Tips for Letters of Request

Use the following tips as a guide whenever you write a letter of request.

Before you write . . .

- **Determine your purpose.**
  Know exactly what you are requesting.
- **Gather information.**
  Collect information that supports your request, including specific dates, names, places, and so on. Also think about the best way to organize the information.
- **Consider your reader.**
  Decide what your reader must know to respond to your request.

As you write . . .

- **Keep it short.**
  Stay focused on the main idea and make your point quickly.
- **State your request.**
  Be specific about what you are asking the reader to do.
- **Be courteous.**
  Be polite.
- **Focus on the outcome.**
  What do you want the reader to do, and when, and how?

After you've written a first draft . . .

- **Check for completeness.**
  Be sure that your main point is clear and that you have included all important information.
- **Check for appropriate voice.**
  Did you use a respectful, sincere tone?
- **Check for correctness.**
  Double-check the address and spelling of all names. Correct errors in punctuation, capitalization, spelling, and grammar.

Try It!

Write a request letter to the appropriate person or organization, politely asking for help. (Send the letter or simply treat it as a school assignment.)

Parts of a Business Letter

1. The **heading** includes the writer's complete address and the date. Write the heading at least one inch from the top of the page, at the left-hand margin.

2. The **inside address** includes the reader's name and address (including the company name).
   - If the person has a title, be sure to include it. (If the title is short, write it on the same line as the name. If the title is long, write it on the next line.)
   - If you are writing to an organization or a business—but not to a specific person—begin the inside address with the name of the organization or business.

3. The **salutation** is the greeting. Always put a colon after the salutation.
   - If you know the reader's name, use it in your greeting.
     Dear Mr. Perkins:
   - If you don't know the name of the person who will read your letter, use a salutation like one of these:
     Dear Store Manager:
     Dear Sir or Madam:

4. The **body** is the main part of the letter. Do not indent the paragraphs in your letter; instead, double-space between them. The body is organized into these parts: (1) the beginning states why you are writing, (2) the middle provides the needed details, and (3) the ending focuses on what should happen next.

5. The **complimentary closing** comes after the body. Use *Sincerely* or *Yours truly* to close a business letter. Capitalize only the first word of the closing and put a comma after the closing.

6. The **signature** ends the letter. If you are using a computer, leave four spaces under the closing; then type your name. Write your signature in the space between the closing and the typed name.

Tip

Check the help file in the word-processing program on your computer to see if it has templates (built-in patterns) that will help you set up your business letters. However, make sure that the templates closely follow the format of the letter on the next page before you use any of them.

Business-Letter Format

1

717 Main Street
Sandusky, OH 44870
May 8, 2006

Four to Seven Spaces

2

Mr. Anthony Perkins, Manager
Dollar General
1622 Cleveland Road
Sandusky, OH 44870

3

Dear Mr. Perkins:

Double Space

I noticed the sign in your store window about an opening for a stocker/bagger. I asked my friend James Leonard, who works for you, about it. He said the best way to apply for a job would be to send you a letter of application.

Double Space

4

I am a freshman at Sandusky High School, and I would be able to start work on June 4, the day after school gets out for summer vacation. I have had one extended job before this as a paper carrier for the *Sandusky Register*. I had that job for two years during seventh and eighth grade. My boss, Mr. Spencer, said that I was the only carrier who never had a customer complaint. If I work for you this summer at Dollar General, I would also be interested in working part-time during the school year, if there is an opening.

Double Space

If you would like more information, please call me at 555-1086. You can also reach me at my father's e-mail address <rdobbs@insight.com>. Thanks for considering me. I look forward to hearing from you.

Double Space

5

Yours truly,

6

Justin Dobbs   Four Spaces

Justin Dobbs

Creating an E-Mail Message

E-mail has become an important, quick communication tool for teachers, students, and parents. However, in spite of e-mail's delivery speed, it still takes time to write a good message. In the following e-mail, a student asks a teacher for advice on a research project.

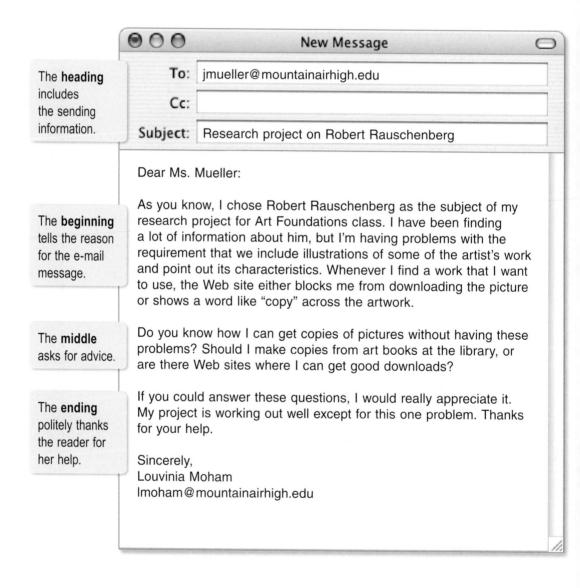

The **heading** includes the sending information.

To: jmueller@mountainairhigh.edu

Cc:

Subject: Research project on Robert Rauschenberg

Dear Ms. Mueller:

The **beginning** tells the reason for the e-mail message.

As you know, I chose Robert Rauschenberg as the subject of my research project for Art Foundations class. I have been finding a lot of information about him, but I'm having problems with the requirement that we include illustrations of some of the artist's work and point out its characteristics. Whenever I find a work that I want to use, the Web site either blocks me from downloading the picture or shows a word like "copy" across the artwork.

The **middle** asks for advice.

Do you know how I can get copies of pictures without having these problems? Should I make copies from art books at the library, or are there Web sites where I can get good downloads?

The **ending** politely thanks the reader for her help.

If you could answer these questions, I would really appreciate it. My project is working out well except for this one problem. Thanks for your help.

Sincerely,
Louvinia Moham
lmoham@mountainairhigh.edu

Tips for Writing E-Mail Messages

Show respect for the recipient of your e-mail messages. Check your spelling, punctuation, and grammar, just as you would in a more formal business letter.

Before you write . . .

- **Jot down the main points you want to make.**
  List other necessary details.
- **Complete the e-mail heading.**
  Fill in the address line by typing in each character of the address or by using your address book's automatic fill-in feature. Then write a subject line that briefly indicates the reason for the e-mail message.

As you write . . .

- **Greet the reader and give your reason for writing.**
  Start with a polite greeting. Then give the reason for your e-mail.
- **Use a conversational but proper tone.**
  Be sure your sentences are clear and complete. Even if you use an informal voice, your grammar should be correct.
- **Briefly state your main points.**
  Include only the most important information.
- **End politely.**
  Close with "Sincerely," or another appropriate closing. Type your name below it and add your e-mail address (if you wish).

After you write a first draft . . .

- **Read over your e-mail.**
  Be sure your message is clear and complete.
- **Check attachments.** Don't forget to include any attachments you refer to in your message.
- **Check for correctness.**
  Check for errors in punctuation, capitalization, spelling, and grammar.
- **Finally, press "send."**

Try It!

Think of a school-related situation that may require an e-mail. Write a message about the matter to a teacher or a fellow student. (You may send the e-mail or simply treat it as a class assignment.)

Sending a Letter

Letters sent through the mail will get to their destinations faster if they are properly addressed and stamped. Always include a ZIP code.

■ Address the envelope.

Place the writer's name and address in the upper left corner of the envelope and the destination name and address in the center. Then put correct postage in the upper right corner of the envelope.

JUSTIN DOBBS
717 MAIN ST
SANDUSKY OH 44870

MR SAM SPENCER
SANDUSKY REGISTER
314 W MARKET ST
SANDUSKY OH 44870

There are two acceptable forms for addressing an envelope: the older, traditional form and the new form preferred by the postal service.

Traditional Form	Postal Service Form
Ms. Theresa Chang	MS THERESA CHANG
Goodwill Industries	GOODWILL INDUSTRIES
9200 Wisconsin Avenue	9200 WISCONSIN AVE
Bethesda, MD 20814-3896	BETHESDA MD 20814-3896

■ Follow U.S. Postal Service guidelines.

1. Capitalize everything and leave out ALL punctuation.

2. Use the list of common address abbreviations located on page **660**. Use numerals rather than words for numbered streets and avenues (9TH AVE NE, 3RD ST SW).

3. If you know the ZIP + 4 code, use it.

Taking Tests

Teachers give tests to check how well you are learning. You may feel nervous while taking tests and have trouble remembering the important information, but this shouldn't happen if you are prepared. This is true of any test—objective, essay, or standardized. Plan properly, and you will perform at your best.

The preparation should start with your class work. Make sure that you understand the subjects you are studying. This means you must pay attention in every class, take good notes, and complete each assignment. You must also understand the test-taking process. This means you should know how to study for, and take, different types of tests.

This chapter will help you plan your test-taking strategies and make test taking less stressful for you. It includes tips for studying and for taking three types of tests.

- **Preparing for a Test**
- **Test-Taking Tips**
- **Taking Objective Tests**
- **Taking Essay Tests**
- **Taking Standardized Tests**
- **Tips for Standardized Tests**

"Man's mind, stretched to a new idea, never goes back to its original dimensions."
—Oliver Wendell Holmes

Preparing for a Test

In order to prepare for a test, you must know what to expect. Usually, you can expect a test to cover whatever you've learned in class. Every day in class, take good notes and review them often. Keep your graded assignments so you can look them over later. Follow the cycle below to do your best on every test.

Test-Prep Cycle

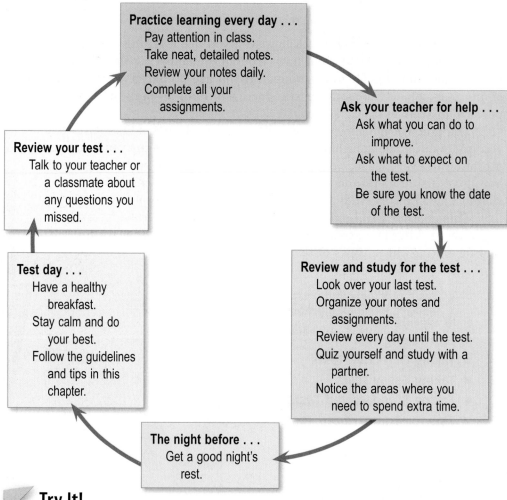

Practice learning every day . . .
Pay attention in class.
Take neat, detailed notes.
Review your notes daily.
Complete all your
    assignments.

Ask your teacher for help . . .
Ask what you can do to
    improve.
Ask what to expect on
    the test.
Be sure you know the date
    of the test.

Review your test . . .
Talk to your teacher or
a classmate about
any questions you
missed.

Review and study for the test . . .
Look over your last test.
Organize your notes and
    assignments.
Review every day until the test.
Quiz yourself and study with a
    partner.
Notice the areas where you
    need to spend extra time.

Test day . . .
Have a healthy
    breakfast.
Stay calm and do
    your best.
Follow the guidelines
    and tips in this
    chapter.

The night before . . .
Get a good night's
    rest.

Try It!

Think of the ways you prepared for your last test. Did you leave out any of the above steps? See if you can improve your test scores by following this test-prep cycle.

Test-Taking Tips

- **Listen carefully** as your teacher gives directions, makes any corrections, or provides other information. And don't try to get a head start while your teacher is talking. You may miss important comments such as these:

> "You have 30 minutes to finish the test."

> "Make this change in number three."

> "Write your answer to the final question on the back of the test sheet."

- **Put your name on the test right away.**
- **Take a quick look at the entire test.** This will help you decide how much time to spend on each section or question.
- **Begin the test.** Read the instructions before answering each set of questions. Do exactly what they tell you to do.
- **Read each question carefully.** Be sure you understand the question completely before answering it.
- **Answer all of the questions you are sure of first.** Then go back to the other questions and do your best to answer each one. Keep track of the time as you work on the more difficult questions.
- **Check over your answers when you finish the test.** If you skipped any really hard questions, try to answer them now.

Try It!

Review these tips right before your next test and then put them into practice. Upon completion of the test, determine how closely you followed this advice.

Taking Objective Tests

Tests often have four different types of objective questions: true/false, matching, multiple-choice, and fill-in-the-blanks.

True/False

In a true/false test, you decide if a statement is correct or incorrect. Most true/false questions focus on the details, so read each statement carefully.

- **Look for absolutes and qualifiers.** Statements with absolutes such as *always, never, all,* and *none* are often false. Statements that use qualifiers such as *often, rarely,* and *seldom* are more likely to be true.

  <u>False</u> 1. The Speaker of the House always presides over Senate sessions. *(When the Speaker is away, the president pro tem presides.)*

  <u>True</u> 2. Political parties sometimes make it difficult for Congress to pass a bill.

- **Test each part.** Even if only one word or phrase in a statement is false, then the entire statement is false.

  <u>False</u> 3. The legislative and the executive branch have the power to override the veto of a bill. *(Only the legislative branch has that power.)*

- **Watch for negatives.** Words such as *don't, can't, doesn't,* and *wasn't* can be confusing, so make sure you know what the statement means.

  <u>False</u> 4. The power to zone property doesn't belong to local governments.

Matching

In matching tests, you are asked to match items from one column to those in another column.

- **Read both columns before answering any questions.** This helps you find the best match for each item.
- **Match the items you know first.** If each answer is used only once, cross out the letter or number after you've used it.
- **Find grammar clues.** For example, plural subjects need plural verbs.

  <u>C</u> 1. metabolism   A. Compounds that link with peptides to act as chemical messengers

  <u>A</u> 2. amino acids   B. Fundamental components of all living cells that are made of substances like enzymes and hormones

  <u>B</u> 3. proteins   C. The sum of all chemical reactions in an organism

Multiple-Choice

In multiple-choice questions, you choose the right answer from several possibilities.

- **Read each question carefully.** Usually, you will be asked to choose the best answer. Sometimes your choices may include "all of the above" or "none of the above."

  1. All of the following are branches of government except

      A. Legislative   C. Executive

      (B.) Presidential   D. Judicial

- **Anticipate the answer.** Before reading the choices, try to answer the question or complete the sentence. That will help you recognize the right answer.
- **Read each choice.** It's tempting to choose the first answer that seems close, but there may be another choice that is better.
- **Consider the "all of the above" answer carefully.** If there is even one statement that you are sure is false, do not choose "all of the above." If there is one statement that you are sure is true, do not choose "none of the above."
- **Eliminate the wrong or unlikely choices first.**

  2. Washington was elected as the first president of the United States in

      A. 1620 *(too early)*   C. 1789

      B. 1776 *(too early)*   D. 1813 *(too late)*

Fill-in-the-Blanks

Fill-in-the-blank questions require you to complete a missing part of a statement.

- **Check the number of blanks.** Often, there is one for each word.

  1. Monosaccharides and disaccharides are __simple__ __carbohydrates__ .

- **Check for grammar clues.** If there is an *a* before the blank, the answer should begin with a consonant. If there is an *an* before the blank, the answer should begin with a vowel.

  2. An educated guess or explanation based on current logic and data is called a ___hypothesis___ .

Try It!

Which types of objective questions are the most difficult for you? Which tips can you use to help you on your next test?

Taking Essay Tests

Many students feel that the essay questions are the hardest part of a test because, unlike other questions, possible answers are not given. Essay-test prompts require you to show how facts and supporting details are connected. The next few pages offer tips for taking an essay test.

■ Understand and restate the prompt.

- **Read the question carefully.**
- **Underline the key words** that explain what you are being asked to do. Here are some key words and their explanations.

Compare . . . . . tell how things are alike.
Contrast . . . . . tell how things are different.
Cause . . . . describe how one thing has affected another.
Define . . . . give a clear, specific meaning for a word or an idea.
Describe . . . . . use sensory details to explain how something looks, sounds, and so on.
Evaluate . . . . . . make a value judgment supported by facts or examples.
Explain . . . . use details and facts to tell what something means or how it works, or give reasons that tell why.
Identify . . . . . . answer the question using one or more of the 5 W's.
Illustrate . . . . . use examples to show how something works or why it's important.
Prove . . . . use facts and details to tell why something is true.
Review . . . . create an overall picture of the topic.
Summarize . . . tell the main idea and key points about the topic.

- **Rephrase the prompt into a thesis statement.** It often works well to drop the key word from your thesis statement.

    Prompt: Explain how a flat tax would affect people with low income levels.

    Thesis Statement: A flat tax would affect low-income people in a negative way because most of them would have to pay a higher percentage of their income in taxes.

Try It!

Turn each essay-test prompt below into a thesis statement.

1. Compare the effectiveness of a space shuttle and a space station.
2. Identify some of the major sources of water pollution.

■ Plan a one-paragraph response.

Tests may include one or more prompts that call for a paragraph response rather than a full-length essay. The following guidelines will help you write an effective one-paragraph response to a prompt.

- ■ **Read the prompt carefully.** Underline the key words or phrases.
- ■ **Identify what the prompt is asking you to do** (explain, compare, prove, define).
- ■ **Plan your response.**
  1. **Turn the prompt into a topic sentence.**
  2. **Include at least three supporting details.** Keep your topic sentence in mind when you select these details.

Prompt

Briefly explain the reason for the formation of the United Nations.

Planning Notes

Topic Sentence: The United Nations was formed after World War II to help countries work together.

Supporting details:
1. Prevent future wars
2. Help countries in conflict find peace
3. Defend human rights
4. Support nations in trouble
5. Promote social and economic progress

Response

Formation of the United Nations

The United Nations was formed after World War II to help countries work together. The founders of the United Nations wanted to protect future generations from the devastating effects of war. They believed the United Nations could help countries in conflict find peaceful solutions. They also wanted to defend human rights throughout the world, but especially in developing regions. Other priorities were to provide assistance for nations in crisis and promote social and economic progress in every country.

■ Plan an essay response.

Some essay prompts require you to respond with a full-length essay. The following tips will help you write a clear, well-organized response essay.

- ■ **Read the prompt** and restate it as a thesis statement.
- ■ **Plan your response** by collecting and outlining details that support your thesis.
- ■ **Write your essay answer.** Include your thesis statement in your opening paragraph. Each main point of your outline becomes the topic sentence for a body paragraph. In the final paragraph, write a meaningful conclusion that shows you truly understand the topic.

Prompt

Evaluate the effectiveness of the United Nations. Give at least three reasons to support your response.

Planning Notes

Thesis Statement: Since its creation, the United Nations has helped those in need by improving health care, defending human rights, and assisting struggling countries.

Outline:
I. Improving health care
    A. Provides immunizations and safe water
    B. Fights against the spread of diseases
    C. Results in increased life expectancy
II. Defending human rights
    A. Offers assistance to women, children, and refugees
    B. Created Universal Declaration of Human Rights
III. Assisting struggling countries
    A. Provides about one-third of the world's food aid
    B. Has given more than $1 billion in aid for disasters

Try It!

Plan and respond to the following prompt: "Evaluate the effectiveness of _____ in your school." (Fill in the blank with a topic.)

Essay Response

The following essay response follows the outline on page **528**. The thesis statement appears at the end of the beginning paragraph. In the final paragraph, the writer restates the reasons she uses to defend her position on the prompt.

Sample Essay Response

Effectiveness of the United Nations

Clearly, the United Nations is more than a peacekeeping organization. In fact, billions of dollars raised by the United Nations have had a positive impact on people around the world. Since its creation, the United Nations has helped those in need by improving health care, defending human rights, and assisting struggling countries.

There are millions of people around the world whose health has improved because of the United Nations. With the help of other organizations, the United Nations provides immunizations and safe drinking water. This group has also led the fight against the spread of diseases such as malaria and AIDS. As a result, the life expectancy of people throughout the world has increased.

The United Nations has also worked very hard to defend human rights. The United Nations has created the Universal Declaration of Human Rights to describe the freedoms and rights of all people. This declaration has triggered programs to assist women and children. It has also prompted the United Nations to protect refugees when their freedoms are threatened and they are forced to leave their homes.

Countries facing all kinds of crises are a priority for the United Nations as well. More than one-third of the world's food aid comes from a United Nations' agency. Each year, more than $1 billion is raised to help countries affected by natural disasters or war. In addition, another $1 billion is provided to help struggling countries develop.

Although the United Nations is known for supplying peacekeeping troops, and often faces criticism for its efforts to keep peace, it has other benefits for people around the world. Health care, human rights, and disaster aid are three of its most important roles in touching the lives of people.

Taking Standardized Tests

At certain times throughout your school life, you will be required to take standardized tests. The guidelines below will help you take these tests.

Before the test . . .

- **Know what to expect.** Ask your teacher what subjects will be covered on the standardized test, what format will be used, and what day the test will be given.
- **Get a good night's rest.** Also be sure to eat breakfast before any test.
- **Be prepared.** Bring extra pens, pencils, and erasers. Make sure to have enough blank paper for notes, outlines, or numerical calculations.

During the test . . .

- **Listen to the instructions and carefully follow directions.** Standardized tests follow strict guidelines. You will be given exact instructions on how to fill in information and supply answers.
- **Pace yourself.** In general, don't spend more than one minute on an objective question; move on and come back to it later.
- **Keep your eyes on your own work.** Don't worry if others finish before you.
- **Match question numbers to answer numbers.** If you skip a question in the question booklet, be sure to skip the corresponding number on your answer sheet. Every few questions, double-check the question number against your answer sheet.
- **Answer every question.** As long as there is no penalty for incorrect answers, you should always answer every question. First eliminate all the choices that are obviously incorrect, and then use logic to make your best educated guess.
- **Review your answers.** If you have time left, make sure that you've answered all the questions and haven't made any accidental mistakes. In general, don't change an answer unless you are sure that it's wrong. If you need to change an answer, erase the original answer completely.

After the test . . .

- **Make sure you have filled in all information correctly.**
- **Erase any unnecessary marks before turning in your test.**

Tips for Standardized Tests

Standardized tests in language arts assess your skills in areas such as vocabulary, word analysis, conventions, and reading comprehension. Below are tips for responding to these kinds of questions.

Vocabulary and Word Analysis

Some questions on standardized tests assess your vocabulary knowledge. You are tested on your ability to identify a word's literal and figurative meanings, usage, concept, power, or origin.

1. Which underlined word has the most negative connotation?

   A. The man's testimony was unfounded.

   B. The man's testimony was malicious.

   C. The man's testimony was damaging.

   D. The man's testimony was hurtful.

Conventions

These questions assess your command of the conventions of grammar, sentence structure, spelling, and punctuation.

2. Read the following sentence.

   I realize that our school cannot afford brand-new uniforms every year, but absolutely we can surely replace uniforms that are faded and torn.

   Which is the BEST way to improve the underlined part of the sentence?

   A. but surely we can replace uniforms that are faded and torn.

   B. yet absolutely we can replace faded and torn uniforms.

   C. but we can replace uniforms that are faded and torn absolutely.

   D. yet uniforms that are faded and torn we can surely replace.

Reading Comprehension and Literary Responses

In this section of a test, you are given a text passage to read. Then you answer questions about it. These questions test your comprehension and ability to draw conclusions. Use the following guidelines to help you answer these kinds of questions efficiently.

- **Skim the questions before you read the passage.**
- **Read the passage quickly but carefully.**
- **Read all the choices before deciding which answer is best.**

Tests

Basic Elements of Writing

Using Words Effectively

In the world of fashion, style comes and goes. One year, hip-hugger jeans with bell-bottoms are in style, and the next year, high-waisted, straight-legged jeans are all the rage. In her book, *Sisterhood of the Traveling Pants,* Ann Brashares claims that "you must never double-cuff the pants. It's tacky." But in the world of fashion, "never" is a very short time.

It's different in the world of writing; good style is always in fashion. If you place just the right word in just the right spot, your writing will be in style tomorrow and next month and next year. This chapter discusses the parts of speech, showing you how to improve your use of words.

- ■ **Nouns**
- ■ **Pronouns**
- ■ **Verbs**
- ■ **Adjectives**
- ■ **Adverbs**
- ■ **Prepositions**
- ■ **Conjunctions**
- ■ **Checking Your Word Choice**

"Remember that the basic rule of vocabulary is *use the first word that comes to your mind, if it is appropriate and colorful.*"
—Stephen King

Nouns ▪ Use specific nouns.

Since a noun names something, the more specific your nouns are, the more colorful and more precise your writing will be. Specific nouns pin down exactly **whom** and **what** you are writing about. Proper nouns (names of actual people, places, and things) are the most specific nouns you can use. Always capitalize proper nouns.

Vague and Dull
The **guy** walked out of the **building** and handed me the **papers**.

Specific and Interesting
The **policeman** walked out of the **courthouse** and handed me the **subpoena**.

The **exterminator** walked out of the **basement** and handed me the **bill**.

Extremely Specific and Interesting
Albert Einstein walked out of the **Kaiser Wilhelm Institute for Physics** and handed me the **"General Theory of Relativity."**

Try It!

Rewrite each numbered sentence, replacing the general nouns with specific ones. Create three versions of each sentence. Include some proper nouns.

Example: The **person** was a **man**.
> The superhero was Sarcasm Man.
> The Viking was Eric the Red.
> The pirate was Three-Toed Jack.

1. The **food** was good.
2. The **man** climbed out of the **car** and waved the **book**.
3. The **storm** battered the **house** and the **truck**.

FYI

Besides being **common** or **proper**, nouns can be **concrete** or **abstract**. A concrete noun names a thing that is tangible (*can* be seen, heard, smelled, tasted, or touched).

telephone	**spaghetti**	**letters**	**Mia Hamm**

An abstract noun names a thing that *cannot* be seen, heard, smelled, tasted, or touched.

loyalty	**freedom**	**soccer**	**Coriolis effect**

Word Style

■ Create appositives.

An **appositive** is an explanatory word, phrase, or clause that renames or adds more information about the noun or pronoun that comes before it.

Appositive Word

My oldest sister, Carla, **loves sports.** ("Carla" renames "sister.")

Appositive Phrase

Carla, my oldest sister, **loves sports.**

("My oldest sister" adds information about "Carla.")

Appositive Clause

My oldest sister, who is named Carla, **loves sports.**

("Who is named Carla" adds information about "sister.")

Try It!

Rewrite each of the following sentences, using your imagination to create an appositive after each **boldfaced** noun. Your appositives should use other nouns to rename or add information to the preceding noun or pronoun.

1. Carla's favorite **sports** have no varsity teams at our school.
2. She created an after-school student **club** dedicated to her favorite sports.
3. The club will become citywide if Carla can convince nearby **schools** to start their own clubs.
4. **Carla** can be extremely convincing.
5. Carla and her **friends** have really changed sports in our **city**.

FYI

Some appositives are **restrictive**—which means that they *restrict* the meaning of the word they rename.

   • Carla's friend **Judy** is a great tennis player.

The appositive "Judy" restricts the meaning of "friend" by identifying *which* friend. After all, Carla has other friends. A restrictive appositive is not set off with commas.

A **nonrestrictive** appositive doesn't restrict the meaning of the word it renames.

   • Carla's best friend, **Frances**, is an athlete as well.

"Frances" does not restrict the meaning of "friend" because Carla can have only one best friend. The nonrestrictive appositive is set off by commas.

Pronouns ■ Establish voice with pronouns.

The form of a personal pronoun indicates its number *(singular* or *plural)*, its person *(first, second,* or *third)*, its case *(nominative, possessive,* or *objective)*, and its gender *(masculine, feminine,* or *neuter)*. You can use these versatile words to establish the voice of your writing.

- ■ **Write in the first person** to focus on personal thoughts, feelings, and experiences. Use this voice in freewriting, journals, personal narratives, and so on.

   I really blew it at play practice last night. I was late making my entrance, *and* I forgot my line.

- ■ **Write in the second person** to speak directly to your reader, as in letters and e-mail messages. Some fiction writers experiment with this voice, but it should be avoided in formal writing assignments.

   Before you log off, you will want to save your work to a backup file.

- ■ **Write in the third person** to focus on the subject, not yourself. Use this voice in most formal writing and in stories that are not about you.

   Conflicts may be unavoidable, but they can provide an opportunity to improve friendships among students.

Try It!

Identify the *person* in which these sentences are written *(first, second,* or *third)*. Then rewrite each sentence, changing the person of the pronouns. What effect does each change have on the voice of the writing?

1. When the team of horses hauled our wagon to the crest of the hill, we saw that the wildfire had destroyed our farm.

2. You looked in dread at your barn, gutted and blackened, and your house, still smoldering, and saw that everything you owned was in ruins.

3. She stepped down from their wagon and put her feet on the sooty stalks of corn she and her husband had planted.

4. I said, "We should be glad. We all survived, and our land has been fertilized by this fire."

5. You plowed the ash under and rebuilt your home and barn, and the next year, your crops were more bountiful than ever.

■ Create suspense with indefinite pronouns.

Usually, writers use pronouns and antecedents that are specific and precise. Notice how each **pronoun** in the following story has a clear **antecedent**. (An *antecedent* is the noun that the pronoun refers to or replaces.)

> David **had nearly drifted off when** he **heard Joe outside. David sat up.** Joe **wasn't supposed to be awake. Still,** he **was walking outside the tent.**
>
> **"Are** you **out there, Joe?" The footsteps stopped.** David **listened. "I can hear you,** Joe**. What do** you **want?"**
>
> He **finally answered, "The flashlight."**

You can create suspense by using indefinite pronouns such as *something, somebody, nobody, nothing,* and *anything.* This version of the story *withholds* information from the reader, creating suspense.

> **David had nearly drifted off when he heard** something **outside. He sat up.** Nobody **was supposed to be awake. Still,** someone **or** something **was walking outside the tent.**
>
> **"Is** somebody **out there?" The footsteps stopped. David listened. "I can hear you. What do you want?"**
>
> Someone **finally answered,** "Everything."

Try It!

Write your own suspenseful scene, using indefinite pronouns to withhold information from the reader. You might set your scene in a subway at night, a classroom before a major test, or an abandoned mine. Below is a list of indefinite pronouns to choose from.

Singular				Plural	Singular/Plural
another	each	more	one	both	all
anybody	everybody	nobody	some	few	any
anyone	everyone	no one	somebody	many	most
anything	everything	nothing	someone	several	none

Note: For academic essays, use specific pronouns and antecedents because they make your writing clear and answer the reader's questions. But for personal narratives and fictional stories, use indefinite pronouns when you want to keep your reader guessing.

Word Style

Verbs ▪ Use verbs to *show* instead of *tell*.

Verbs can be described as *static* or *dynamic*. Static verbs use the passive voice. Dynamic verbs use the active voice and add interest to your writing.

- ▪ **Static verbs** are *be* verbs that *tell* what happens.

  Jim **was** excited about the letter from Kurt Vonnegut.

- ▪ **Dynamic verbs** are *action* verbs that *show* what happens.

  Jim **whooped** and **waved** the letter from Kurt Vonnegut.

Try It!

Read the following sentences, each with a static verb. Then choose a dynamic verb or two and build a new sentence that shows instead of tells.

Example: Jim usually was glum when there was mail.

> Jim usually moped when the mail slid through the slot.

1. On Tuesday, Jim was excited.
2. His brother was jealous about the letter.
3. Jim was tough to put up with.

▪ Use specific verbs.

Verbs can also be *general* or *specific*. Some writers prop up general verbs by adding modifiers, but a specific verb is always a better choice.

Instead of writing . . .	Write . . .
angrily looked	scowled
looked with amazement or shock	gaped
intently looked	stared

Try It!

Replace these general verbs and modifiers with specific verbs. Use a thesaurus if you get stuck.

1. quietly said
2. stepped on heavily
3. moved with speed
4. loudly spoke
5. eagerly took
6. hit hard

 Use dynamic, specific verbs. Complete the following story starter, using as many dynamic and specific verbs as you can.

Just as our helicopter shot over the snowy peak, the blizzard began. . . .

■ Understand onomatopoeia.

Some verbs simply tell the reader what is happening. Other verbs seem to let the reader actually *hear* the action. The English language has more verbs than any other language on the globe, and many of those verbs make the sounds they describe. (The term *onomatopoeia* is used to identify these types of words.) Here are some examples.

Plain Verbs	laugh	break	eat	yell
Onomatopoetic Verbs	chuckle giggle snicker guffaw cackle bray	crack smash shatter crunch rip split	gulp gobble chomp swallow nibble gnaw	holler bellow blare shriek roar blast

Poets regularly use onomatopoeia in their poems; careful prose writers do, too. Onomatopoetic verbs work well even in articles and reports.

Plain Verbs

The railroad crossing alarm sounded, Dad applied the brakes, the car rolled to a stop, and a freight train went past our bumper.

Onomatopoetic Verbs

The railroad crossing alarm clanged, Dad stomped on the brakes, the car screeched to a stop, and a freight train screamed past our bumper.

Try It!

Use a thesaurus, if necessary, to find two onomatopoetic synonyms for each of the following plain verbs:

shake   cut   speak   cry   fly

Use onomatopoeia. Think of a noisy setting that you know well—perhaps the cafeteria, a busy intersection, or the garage where a friend's band is practicing. Write a one-paragraph description of the noisy setting and use at least two or three onomatopoetic verbs in your writing.

Word Style

Adjectives ■ Use objective and subjective adjectives.

In terms of style, adjectives can be objective or subjective, depending on what they describe.

- **Objective adjectives** focus on the noun itself, describing qualities that anyone can objectively see.

  The tall, thin **farmer ambled toward the** short, stout **dog.**

- **Subjective adjectives** focus on the writer's feelings about the noun.

  The gangly **farmer ambled toward the** pudgy **dog.**

Each type of adjective has its place. When you want to create a factual, knowledgeable voice (as in expository essays and research reports), consider using objective adjectives. When you want to create an emotional, personal voice (as in personal narratives and some persuasive essays), consider using subjective adjectives.

Try It!

In each word pair below, decide which adjective is objective and which is subjective.

1. empty—pointless
2. lush—fertile
3. old—haggard
4. warm—inviting
5. unique—peculiar

6. huge—staggering
7. baffling—complex
8. small—cozy
9. vibrant—colorful
10. amorphous—blobby

FYI

You can create a subtle effect by using objective and subjective adjectives together.

> Niagara Falls is a **huge, staggering** cascade.
> The Mesopotamian landscape once was a **lush, fertile** Eden.
> I sought out a **warm, inviting** corner of the library.

This technique should be used sparingly to provide special emphasis.

Use objective and subjective adjectives. Create a T-graph, writing objective adjectives on one side and subjective adjectives on the other. Try to list four of each. Then spend 5 minutes freewriting a paragraph that uses as many of the adjectives as you can.

■ Emphasize adjectives.

When you want to focus on the specific qualities of a person, a place, a thing, or an idea, you can create emphasis by varying the placement of adjectives in the sentence. Here are some techniques to try.

■ **Place the adjectives at the beginning of the sentence.**

> Cold, hungry, and weary, the prospector staggered into town with his last nugget of gold.

■ **Place adjectives at the end of the sentence.**

> He looked dejected. He felt defeated. For this one man, prospecting had been many things, but most of all it had been hard.

■ **Place adjectives after the noun.**

> In the town bank, the teller, shifty eyed and suspicious, stared at the prospector as he hiked up to the window.

■ **Repeat an adjective to emphasize it.**

> The prospector released a gusty sigh and handed over the gold nugget. "It's been a bad day at the end of a bad month at the end of a bad year. Give me some good news."

■ **Contrast adjectives within a sentence.**

> The teller lifted the nugget to his long face and took a short look. "The bad news is that this here's fool's gold." He grinned. "The good news is that there's a diamond stuck in it."

■ **Create a series of adjectives.**

> The prospector felt confused, amazed, elated.

Try It!

Write an ending to the story of the prospector and the teller. Experiment with different strategies for emphasizing adjectives.

FYI

As with nouns and verbs, adjectives can be general or specific; specific adjectives are usually better. Write about a *brisk* wind rather than a *cold* wind, or a *grating* sound instead of an *annoying* sound.

Adverbs ■ Answer questions.

An adverb (or a phrase or clause that functions as an adverb) answers questions such as *how? when? where? why? to what degree? how often?* The great advantage of the adverb is that it can be placed almost anywhere. Different adverb positions create different effects.

■ **Begin with an adverb.** Start a sentence with an adverb to emphasize the quality of the action.

> Abruptly, **the party ended.**
> (adverb emphasizing *how*)

> When Mrs. Jones walked in, **the party ended.**
> (adverb clause emphasizing *when*)

■ **Interrupt the flow of the sentence.** To give special emphasis to an adverb (word, phrase, or clause), place it in the middle of the sentence.

> **Mrs. Jones** deliberately **and** ferociously **met her son's gaze.**

> **Mrs. Jones,** with eyes like heat-seeking missiles, **met her son's gaze.**

■ **End with an adverb.** Place the adverb (word, phrase, or clause) at the end of the sentence, set off by a comma or a dash, to create a strong sense of finality.

> **Young Mr. Jones replied, "I'm sorry, Mom—**very.**"**

> **Young Mr. Jones replied, "I'm sorry, Mom,** more than you know.**"**

FYI

Even though adverbs can be placed almost anywhere in a sentence, there are still a few places they should not appear. For example, adverbs should not appear between a verb and a direct or an indirect object.

> Don't **write:** Mrs. Jones scowled as her son opened **slowly** the door.
> Do **write:** Mrs. Jones scowled as her son **slowly** opened the door.

Also, an adverb that answers the question *when* should not appear between the subject and the verb.

> Don't **write:** The other party guests **at that moment** shouted, "Surprise!"
> Do **write:** **At that moment,** the other party guests shouted, "Surprise!"

Experiment with adverb placement. Write an ending to the story about the surprise party for Mrs. Jones. Include adverbs, and experiment with placing them in different positions throughout the sentence.

■ Avoid unnecessary adverbs.

Adverb abuse is a sad fact of bad writing. Eliminate adverbs from your work when they contribute nothing to the meaning.

- ■ **Eliminate redundant adverbs.** Adverbs are often not needed if you use strong verbs.

  Recently, the energy secretary growled angrily at the press.

  Recently, the energy secretary growled at the press.

- ■ **Drop telling adverbs.** Don't try to persuade by overusing adverbs such as *absolutely, apparently, certainly, clearly, definitely,* and *undoubtedly.* These words are usually unnecessary to the real meaning. They only emphasize the writer's bias.

  Obviously, politicians can't continue to let fuel prices rise.

  Politicians can't continue to let fuel prices rise.

- ■ **Avoid unnecessary amplifiers.** Speakers of British English commonly use *rather, really,* and *quite,* even though these words don't add any meaning to an idea. These words are not commonly used in American English, which is much more direct.

  Consumers are really quite bothered by these rather high prices.

  Consumers are bothered by these high prices.

Try It!

Read the following paragraph and identify unneeded adverbs.

1 When ancient plants and animals died completely, their bodies were
2 totally compacted to create coal, oil, and natural gas. These creatures certainly
3 transferred the carbon in their bodies to the fossil fuels we now obviously use.
4 When we burn up those fuels, we quite undoubtedly let out all that carbon into
5 the atmosphere again. This practice very definitely must stop before the world
6 turns back into a really hot planet.

FYI

Hopefully is a problem adverb: Hopefully, hybrid cars will help reduce pollution.

What the writer means is "I hope hybrid cars will help reduce pollution," but the sentence actually means "Hybrid cars will help reduce pollution with hope." So avoid beginning sentences with *hopefully.*

Word Style

Prepositions ▪ Accelerate your verbs.

When a verb in a sentence shows movement, prepositions will direct the action. Consider the following simple sentence and notice how the prepositions extend and direct the motion of the verb *paddled*. This technique creates a strong sense of continuing action and is useful in writing about exciting events.

> The kayaker paddled over a six-foot plunge, through a boiling cauldron, between towering rocks, down a channel of white water, and over a waterfall.

▪ Create an appropriate mood.

In contrast to using multiple prepositional phrases to direct action, you can use a single prepositional phrase with multiple objects to create a dreamy, thoughtful feeling.

> Marlene lingered beside the sun-dappled meadow, the corral where the foals trotted with their mothers, the barn her great-grandfather had built with his own hands, and the farmhouse that now bore the sign "For Sale."

Try It!

Complete each of the following sentence starters twice. First, complete the starter with a series of prepositional phrases to create strong, continuing action. Then try using a single preposition with multiple objects to create a thoughtful mood. (Some prepositions are listed below. See page **732** for more.)

1. A quarter horse galloped . . .

2. An old man sauntered . . .

3. The race car roared . . .

4. Some music blared . . .

above	behind	for	off	to
across	below	from	on	toward
after	beneath	in	onto	under
along	beside	inside	on top of	until
among	between	into	out	up
around	by	like	over	upon
at	down	near	past	within
away from	during	of	through	without

Experiment with prepositions. Freewrite for 5 minutes about a recent experience you have had. If the experience was fast paced and full of action, try using a series of prepositional phrases to extend the action of the verb. If the experience was quiet and reflective, try using a single preposition with many objects.

■ **Create emphasis.**

Sometimes, prepositions work without calling attention to themselves. At other times, the preposition takes center stage, as in Abraham Lincoln's address at Gettysburg:

" . . . **that government** of **the people,** by **the people, and** for **the people shall not perish from the earth.**"

You can use prepositional phrases to expand a sentence and create emphasis in a number of ways.

- ■ **Begin a sentence with a series of prepositional phrases.** Use the phrases to build anticipation in the mind of the reader.

    On **a dreamy evening,** after **a day of blazing sun,** under **the green arms of a chestnut tree, we met.**

- ■ **Use several prepositions with a single object.** In the style of Mr. Lincoln, create a string of prepositional phrases that have the same object but a different preposition.

    I'd rather have people laugh with **me than** at **me, let alone** without **me.**

- ■ **Use a single preposition with several objects.** Create a strong rhythm by varying the objects but not the preposition.

    The army fought through **the barricades,** through **the city streets, and** through **the enemy lines.**

Try It!

Add prepositional phrases to the sentences below. Try a different strategy for each sentence.

1. The elk raised his antlered head.
2. Cyclists rode.
3. The reforms were denied.

FYI

Prepositions have a unique function: they turn nouns into modifiers. Take the noun *pajamas*. Add a preposition—*in pajamas*—and the combination becomes a modifier. Now you can add more modifiers—*in red-striped pajamas*, or *in the red-striped pajamas that Winston Churchill wore during the London air raids*. A single preposition can unlock a world of meaning.

 Word Style

Conjunctions ▪ Create rhythm with "and."

Instead of using commas to connect words, groups of words, and sentences, you can use the word *and*.

lions, tigers, and bears

lions and tigers and bears (oh my!)

This technique is called *polysyndeton*, which means "many conjunctions." Note how this gives every item special emphasis, doing as much to separate the items as to join them. This technique creates rhythm and emphasis.

The civil rights movement and the Watergate scandal and the equal rights movement changed the United States profoundly during the '60s and '70s.

You may have used this same technique when you were trying to describe a hectic day.

After school, I ran laps and took a shower and worked in the deli and finished my homework and crawled into bed.

Try It!

List the things you plan to do on Saturday. After you have four or five items, write a sentence with the list as a standard series, including commas and a single "and." Next, rewrite the sentence using polysyndeton. Then do the same for the main things that you would like to do next summer.

Tip

Limit your use of this technique to times when you want to create a special effect. In the following excerpt from "After the Storm," Hemingway uses polysyndeton to create a sense of chaos. In the hands of a less skillful writer, this may have become simply a rambling sentence.

> "It was dark and there was water standing in the street and no lights and windows broke and boats all up in the town and trees blown down and everything all blown and I got a skiff and went out and found my boat where I had her inside Mango Bay and she was all right only she was full of water."

■ Use subordinating conjunctions.

A subordinating conjunction shows the relationship between two clauses. Such conjunctions can show time, cause and effect, and logical connections.

Showing Time
After the mayor finished her speech, the press asked her questions.

> after, as, as long as, before, since, till, until, when, while

Showing Cause and Effect
She said the city budget was tight **because** spring floods required expensive cleanup.

> because, if/then, in order that, provided that, since, so that

Showing Logical Connections
"**Although** money is tight," the mayor said, "we have enough to keep the city running."

> although, as if, as though, that, though, unless, whereas, while

When two short sentences express ideas that are related by time, cause and effect, or a logical relationship, consider combining them with a subordinating conjunction.

Try It!

Combine the following pairs of sentences by selecting a subordinating conjunction showing the relationship between the ideas.

1. The spring rains raised the river to record heights.
   Public facilities along the river were flooded.
2. The cleanup effort after the flood helped the whole city.
   The whole city should be willing to pay for the cost.
3. Next year's budget will also be tight.
   The city will continue to look for sources of funds.
4. New funds will be found.
   Improvements will be made to the storm sewers.

Tip

If the clause with the subordinating conjunction comes first, place a comma after the clause. If the clause with the conjunction comes last, you usually do not need a comma. Use a comma, however, if the clause begins with a conjunction that expresses a contrast, such as *although, even though,* or *while.*

Word Style

Checking Your Word Choice

Writers often have difficulty evaluating and improving word choice. They see the essay, the paragraphs, the sentences, but somehow they gloss right over the individual words. Improving your word choice is just a matter of *looking*. The following scavenger hunt can help you evaluate the word choice in all your writing.

Word-Choice Scavenger Hunt

1. Find the three most specific nouns in your work. Teddy Roosevelt, piranha, expedition

2. Find the three most general nouns in your work and suggest specific nouns to replace them. boat (dugout), river (Amazon), disease (malaria)

3. Find three verbs with strong onomatopoeia. pelted, trundled, slogged

4. Find three verbs that could be stronger and suggest replacements. wanted (longed for), tried (struggled), got (snatched)

5. Find your most effective objective adjective. detailed (plan)

6. Find your most effective subjective adjective. fanatical (vision)

7. Find three adverbs that could be cut or replaced. suddenly, very, extremely

8. Find one sentence in which you have emphasized adjectives or prepositions. Wounded, bleeding, and antagonized, Roosevelt pulled the speech from his breast pocket, showed the bullet hole in it, and declared, "It takes more than that to kill a bull moose!"

9. Find three subordinating conjunctions you used. when, although, despite

---

Try It!

Review your first draft of a current writing assignment. Evaluate your word choice by completing the scavenger hunt above.

Understanding Sentence Style

Writer Patricia T. O'Conner says that a well-written sentence really is "a triumph of engineering." On its own, an effective sentence states a complete thought, using just enough words and no more. As part of a longer piece of writing, it carries an important idea and connects the reader with the ideas that come before and after it.

To become sentence-smart, make reading and writing important in your life. Read anything and everything that you can get your hands on, and write regularly on your own. Your personal reading and writing will help you develop an ear for good sentences. In addition, follow the guidelines in this chapter for writing sentences.

- Sentence Balance
- Sentence Length
- Sentence Variety
- Sentence Combining
- Sentence Problems
- Sentence Modeling

"Don't be afraid to throw more than one verb in a sentence. I think *She twisted and fell* is more exciting than *She twisted. She fell to the ground.*"

—Martyn Godfrey

Sentence Balance ■ Use parallel construction.

You can create balance in sentences by using **parallel construction**. This means repeating similar grammatical elements (words or phrases) to give your writing rhythm. Here are some ways to make your sentences parallel.

Sentence Elements	Example	Technique Used
Words— All words in a series should be the same *parts of speech*.	**Not parallel:** Opera can amuse, sadden, or make you think. **Parallel:** Opera can **amuse**, **sadden**, or **inspire**.	All the words in the series are **verbs**.
	Parallel: Opera can be **amusing**, **depressing**, or **inspiring**.	All the words in the series are **adjectives**.
Phrases— All phrases in a series should be the same *type*.	**Not parallel:** The audience members reacted to the show by jumping to their feet, cheering for an encore, and with calls of "Bravo!" **Parallel:** The audience members reacted to the show by **jumping to their feet**, **cheering for an encore**, and **calling "Bravo!"**	All the phrases are **participial phrases** (they start with -*ing* words).
	Parallel: The audience began **to cheer**, **to jump to their feet**, and **to call "Bravo!"**	All the phrases are **infinitive phrases** (they start with *to*).

Try It!

Rewrite each of the following sentences, using parallel construction.

1. I enjoy swimming, to play computer games, and when we go to the movies.
2. When I choose music, I listen to jazz, rock, and chilling out to Latin rhythms.
3. Our library contains study tables, computer stations, and it has a reading corner.
4. Korean summers are hot, it rains a lot, and humid.

Sentence Length ▪ Write short sentences.

The length of your sentences contributes to the effect you wish to establish in a piece of writing. Short sentences often make a strong point.

Creating Suspense

Short sentences add excitement to your writing by suggesting suspense. Compare the two paragraphs below.

> **The room had always presented an uncomfortable feeling, but now, as the door slowly opened with a long, creaky sound, the inside seemed even less welcoming.**

> With an eerie creak, the door slowly opened. The room had never before seemed so frightening.

Stepping Up the Pace

Short sentences help create a sense of speed and urgency by pulling the reader through a fast-moving situation. Again, compare the examples below.

> **As the door opened with a weird creak, a spider ominously disappeared into the shadows. The dark room loomed, and I found that my feet were rooted to the ground, even as my mind was filled with thoughts of what awaited me.**

> The door creaked. A spider disappeared into the shadows. Inside, the room was dark. My feet wouldn't move, but my imagination raced.

Emphasizing Key Points

Short sentences set among longer ones create emphasis.

> **I called out into the darkness for the assurance that someone human would join me.** There was no answer. **Moving through the darkness, I tentatively eased my barefoot way across the cool wooden floor, hoping to find a light switch, a lamp, a candle.** I found none. **I tried to take a deep breath, to focus on adjusting my eyes to the blackness. The silence was thick as cotton, stuffing my ears and muffling even the sound of my heartbeat.** Then I heard a crash.

Try It!

Write an ending to the story beginning above. Use some short sentences to create suspense, speed, or emphasis.

Sentence Style

■ Write long sentences.

Long sentences can effectively package important information. Here are three ways to build longer, more intricate sentences.

Type of Long Sentence	Uses	Example
Loose sentences express the main clause or idea near the beginning and follow with modifiers.	Add layers to the main idea, creating a more informative sentence.	**We ran drill after drill,** all the time with Coach Mayland encouraging us to pick up the pace.
Periodic sentences postpone the most important or most surprising idea until the end.	Add a sense of suspense as the reader works through to the main idea.	Following Coach's threats to make us run the "stops," **we almost immediately improved our footwork.**
Cumulative sentences place the main idea in the middle, with modifying phrases and clauses coming before and after.	Create a detailed, complex sentence.	Once we finished the passing drills, **Coach finally blew his whistle,** signaling a much-needed water break.

Try It!

Copy each of the following sentences on your own paper. Then underline the main clause or idea and identify the type of each sentence—either loose, periodic, or cumulative.

1. The tornado swept through the town, leaving a trail of destruction that shocked everyone.

2. Because the tornado was completely unexpected, it caused extensive damage, including uprooted trees, broken windows, and twisted road signs.

3. Within a matter of minutes during a warm summer evening, a small town changed forever.

Sentence Variety ■ Vary sentence beginnings.

In paragraphs and essays, varied sentence beginnings can make your writing interesting. Here are some different beginnings that will add variety to your sentences.

Beginning with a Subject

Chaya **spilled some of the chemicals used in the safety drill.**

The other students **followed safety procedures.**

Beginning with a Modifying Word or Phrase

Quickly, **they pulled on safety gloves and switched on the ventilation hoods.**

Standing quietly at the door, **the teacher made notes on a clipboard.**

As the seconds ticked by, **the class worked to clean up the chemicals.**

Because they had gone through the practice many times, **the students knew exactly what to do.**

Try It!

All of the sentences below begin with the subject. Create sentence variety by rewriting some of the sentences to begin with modifying words, phrases, or clauses.

1. Chelsey and her sister Kara both need rides from their after-school activities.
2. Chelsey volunteers at the city's homeless shelter two days a week.
3. Kara has soccer practice every day at the high school.
4. Their mother's office is not far from the shelter.
5. She picks Chelsey up after work.
6. Chelsey sometimes has to wait if her mother works late.
7. The girls' father picks up Kara at practice.
8. He often finishes work early, so he reads in the car until practice is over.
9. The girls would like to get their own car someday so their parents don't always have to pick them up.

Sentence Style

■ Expand sentences.

You can use the 5 W's and H—*Who? What? Where? When? Why? How?*—to expand short sentences. For example, look at this basic sentence:

> **Spices were important trade items.**

Now see how using the 5 W's and H adds details and makes the sentence longer and more interesting.

Who?	Spices were important trade items **to European customers**.
What?	Spices **such as cinnamon and pepper** were important trade items to European customers.
Where?	Spices **from the East**, such as cinnamon and pepper, were important trade items to European customers.
When?	Spices from the East, such as cinnamon and pepper, were important trade items to European customers **in the thirteenth century**.
Why?	Spices from the East, such as cinnamon and pepper, were important trade items to European customers, **providing them a way to make plain food taste better**.
How?	Spices such as cinnamon and pepper, **brought with great difficulty in caravans from the East**, were important trade items to European customers in the thirteenth century.

Tip

Usually, you will not use all of the 5 W's and H in one sentence. Be careful not to overload a sentence with details.

Try It!

Using the 5 W's and H to add details, rewrite one of the sentences below. Use as many details as you can without making the sentence cumbersome.

1. The employees loaded the trucks.

2. The mall bustled.

3. People hurried along.

Sentence Combining ▪ Combine short, choppy sentences.

Sentence combining is the act of making one smoother, more detailed sentence from two or more short sentences.

Using a Series of Words

Ideas from short sentences can be combined into one sentence using a series of words.

- ▪ **Three Short Sentences:**
  Medications **may cause insomnia.**
  Caffeine **may keep you from sleeping.**
  Poor eating habits **may also bring on sleep problems.**

- ▪ **Combined Sentence:**
  Medications, caffeine, and poor eating habits may cause insomnia.

Using a Series of Phrases

These are all acceptable sentences, but see what happens when they are combined. The ideas flow more smoothly.

- ▪ **Three Short Sentences:**
  Carlos loves to play video games.
  He loves to watch movies.
  He loves to surf the Net.

- ▪ **Combined Sentence:**
  Carlos loves to play video games, watch movies, and surf the Net.

Try It!

Combine each group of short sentences into one smoother sentence.

1. Headaches can cause insomnia. Worry can cause a loss of sleep. Illness can cause insomnia.

2. Insomnia can be brought on by stress. Insomnia can be caused by excitement. Insomnia can be the result of outside noise.

3. Insomnia produces irritability. Sleeplessness causes nervousness. It also triggers memory problems.

4. Taking a warm bath can help you overcome insomnia. Drinking warm milk can help you sleep. Listening to soft music can help you sleep.

Using Other Types of Phrases

Ideas from shorter sentences can also be combined into one sentence by using phrases.

- **Short Sentences:**

    Most students need to be rested in order to do well.
    They need to do well in their classes.

- **Combined Using a Prepositional Phrase:**

    Most students need to be rested in order to do well in their classes.

- **Short Sentences:**

    Newborns are babies in their first few days of life.
    They need 17 hours of sleep per day.

- **Combined Using an Appositive Phrase:**

    Newborns, babies in their first few days of life, need 17 hours of sleep per day.

Try It!

Combine each set of short sentences into one sentence using a phrase.

1. Some adults are not getting enough sleep.
   These adults are in their working years.

2. Older adults need less sleep than young adults do.
   Older adults are people over 60.

3. Young adults really should sleep nine to ten hours per day.
   They should sleep this long during their formative years.

4. Dreams often last several hours.
   Dreams are an important part of sleep.

5. Thomas Edison took many short naps throughout the day.
   He was a very famous inventor.

6. Sleep is a time for the body to heal itself.
   Sleep is essential for good health.

Review a piece of writing. Read over something that you have recently written. Try to find two or three sets of sentences that you could combine. Write them as combined sentences to see how they sound.

Sentence Problems ▪ Avoid sentence errors.

Avoid the following sentence problems when you write—or correct them as you revise.

Correcting Run-On Sentences

Run-on sentences occur when two sentences are joined without punctuation or without a connecting word (*and, but, or*).

- **Run-On Sentence:** Wing-walking was a popular stunt during the 1920s Ormer Locklear is credited with popularizing the activity among young daredevils.

- **Corrected as Two Sentences:** Wing-walking was a popular stunt during the 1920s. Ormer Locklear is credited with popularizing the activity among young daredevils.

- **Corrected as a Compound Sentence:** Wing-walking was a popular stunt during the 1920s, and Ormer Locklear is credited with popularizing the activity among young daredevils.

Eliminating Comma Splices

Comma splices occur when a comma is placed between two independent clauses without a conjunction.

- **Comma Splice:** Locklear liked to think he was providing a real service, he claimed he was showing people that anything was possible if they tried.

- **Corrected as Two Sentences:** Locklear liked to think he was providing a real service. He claimed he was showing people that anything was possible if they tried.

- **Corrected as a Compound Sentence:** Locklear liked to think he was providing a real service, and he claimed he was showing people that anything was possible if they tried.

Try It!

Read the following paragraph. On your own paper, rewrite any run-on or comma splice, fixing the error.

(1) Wing-walking was not limited to men many women also tried the stunt high above the ground. (2) Gladys Ingle became famous for transferring from one plane's wing to another, she also practiced archery on the moving plane's wing. (3) Mabel Cody shared the adventurous spirit of her uncle "Buffalo Bill" Cody the daredevil became the first woman to successfully transfer from a boat to an airplane. (4) The first African American woman pilot was Bessie Coleman. She was best known as a parachute jumper.

Sentence Style

Fixing Fragments

A fragment is not a sentence because it does not communicate a complete thought. In a sentence fragment, a subject, a predicate, or both are missing.

Fragment: Became a national park in 1919. (A subject is needed.)

The Grand Canyon became a national park in 1919.

Fragment: Sure-footed burros down paths in the canyon. (A predicate is needed.)

Sure-footed burros walk down paths in the canyon.

Fragment: Through the canyon. (A subject and a predicate are needed.)

People raft through the canyon.

Try It!

Rewrite each of the following fragments as a complete sentence. (Some of the examples are complete sentences.)

1. More than 270 miles long, 15 miles wide, and 5,000 feet deep.
2. The Colorado River carved out the Grand Canyon.
3. At the bottom of the canyon.
4. The river has been cutting the rock for six million years.
5. Filled with high ridges and deep valleys.
6. The rock formation known as "The Alligator" amazes people.
7. John Wesley Powell, the first geologist to explore the area.
8. Traveled through the canyon in a small boat.
9. The dangerous journey was completed in 1869.

Rewriting Rambling Sentences

Rambling sentences are those that seem to go on and on. Their parts are connected by coordinating conjunctions. While not grammatically incorrect, these sentences are hard to read. As a rule, if your sentence has more than two coordinating conjunctions, try to divide it into shorter sentences.

Rambling: The man in line in front of us had two little children, and he was having trouble keeping them quiet so Raul started doing some of his magic tricks and the children didn't make a sound until their dad got their tickets.

Better: The man in line in front of us had two little children. He was having trouble keeping them quiet, so Raul started doing some of his magic tricks. The children didn't make a sound until their dad got their tickets.

Moving Misplaced Modifiers

Misplaced modifiers are modifiers that have been placed incorrectly in a sentence. A modifier should be as close as possible to the word it modifies.

Misplaced: After finishing the last song, the press met with the singer.

(Did the press sing?)

Corrected: After finishing the last song, the singer met with the press.

Correcting Dangling Modifiers

A dangling modifier appears to modify a word that isn't in the sentence. It "dangles" because it's not attached to anything.

Dangling: Fighting for breath, the finish line seemed very far away.

(Who or what is fighting for breath?)

Corrected: Fighting for breath, Kali thought the finish line seemed very far away.

Try It!

Rewrite each of the sentences below so that it does not contain a misplaced modifier.

1. The boat puttered down the river loaded with excited tourists.
2. Hanging from the trees, we could see hundreds of monkeys.
3. Skewered by a spear, our guide removed the wriggling fish.

Changing Double Subjects

Do not use a pronoun immediately after the subject.

Double Subject: Felix's letter jacket it needs to be cleaned.

Corrected: Felix's letter jacket needs to be cleaned.

Correcting Double Negatives

Do not use two negative words together, like *never* and *no*, or *not* and *no*. Also, do not use *hardly, barely,* or *scarcely* with a negative word.

Double Negative: She never saw no one run so fast.

Corrected: She never saw anyone run so fast.

Try It!

Rewrite each of the sentences below so that it does not contain a double subject or a double negative.

1. Blue whales they are the largest mammals on earth.
2. The female blue whale she can be up to 110 feet long.
3. A baby blue whale doesn't eat no solid foods.

Sentence Style

Sentence Modeling ■ Write stylish sentences.

Many painters learn to paint by copying famous works of art. Writers, too, can learn to write better by modeling sentence patterns used by professional writers.

Model: **I bought a jug of milk and fell off my bike, breaking the glass jug, cutting my leg.**

—Thylias Moss, "Wings"

New Sentence: **I found an album of family photographs and paged through it, enjoying each photo, losing track of time.**

Try It!

Select two of the sentences below and write your own sentences, modeling the sentence structure as closely as possible.

1. The steam from the kettle had condensed on the cold window and was running down the glass in tear-like trickles.

   —Jessamyn West, "Sixteen"

2. His hands were white and small, his frame was fragile, his voice was quiet, and his manners were refined.

   —James Joyce, "A Little Cloud"

3. Jim dipped his hand into the trough and stirred the moon to broken, swirling streams of light.

   —John Steinbeck, "The Murder"

4. As in so many past experiences, our hopes had been blasted, and the shadow of deep disappointment settled upon us.

   —Martin Luther King, Jr., "Letter from Birmingham Jail"

5. In the darkness, Mr. Shiftlet's smile stretched like a weary snake waking up by a fire.

   —Flannery O'Connor, "The Life You Save May Be Your Own"

6. In cotton-picking time the late afternoons revealed the harshness of Black Southern life, which in the early morning had been softened by nature's blessing of grogginess, forgetfulness, and the soft lamplight.

   —Maya Angelou, *I Know Why the Caged Bird Sings*

Writing Effective Paragraphs

Writer Donald Hall calls a paragraph a "maxi-sentence" or a "mini-essay." What he means is this: A paragraph is a special unit of writing that does more than the typical sentence and less than the typical essay. If you can write strong paragraphs, you can develop effective essays, articles, and research papers.

A paragraph is made up of a group of sentences focused on one topic. A paragraph can tell a story, describe, share information, or express an opinion. Whatever form a paragraph takes, it must contain enough details to give the reader a complete picture of the topic. The first sentence usually identifies the topic, the middle sentences support it, and the last sentence wraps things up.

- The Parts of a Paragraph
- Types of Paragraphs
- Writing Guidelines
- Types of Details
- Patterns of Organization
- Modeling Paragraphs
- Connecting Paragraphs in Essays
- Paragraph Traits Checklist

"Writing is the solid construction of thoughts."
—Donald Murray

The Parts of a Paragraph

A typical paragraph consists of three main parts: a **topic sentence**, the **body sentences**, and a **closing sentence**. A paragraph can develop an explanation, an opinion, a description, or a narrative. Whatever form a paragraph takes, it must contain enough information to give readers a complete picture of the topic. The following expository paragraph provides information about a remarkable breed of dog. Notice that each detail in the body supports the topic sentence.

Gentle Giants

Topic Sentence

Of all dogs, perhaps the greatest helper breed has been the Newfoundland. Because of their Canadian origin and English breeding, "Newfs" are ideally suited for life by the water. They boast great lung capacity, an oily outer fur, and webbed feet! This gentle animal is a natural retriever; at 150 pounds, it can easily bring a drowning human to safety. However, the dog's usefulness through the centuries has not been limited to lifesaving. These large canines

Body

can lug as much as 2,000 pounds, and in their native province, they were once used to haul fishing nets as well as carts of fish, milk, or mail. At one time, Newfs were part of a sailing ship's crew, sometimes used to swim a line to land in choppy waters. If a ship were sinking, the animals would be sent with lifelines to rescue drowning crew members. Newfs are as gentle as they are strong and can be loving, protective companions

Closing Sentence

to children. Indeed, this huge, devoted dog is one of the greatest partners to bless humankind.

Respond to the Reading. What main idea about the topic does this paragraph communicate? What specific details support this idea?

A Closer Look at the Parts

Whether a paragraph stands alone or is part of an extended piece of writing, it contains three elements.

The Topic Sentence

A **topic sentence** tells the reader what your paragraph is about. The topic sentence should do two things: (1) name the specific topic of the paragraph and (2) identify a particular feeling or feature about the topic. Here is a simple formula for writing a topic sentence.

    a specific topic
\+   a particular feeling or feature about the topic

= **an effective topic sentence**

    Newfoundland dogs
\+   perhaps the greatest helper breed

= **Of all dogs, perhaps the greatest helper breed has been the Newfoundland.**

Tip

The topic sentence is *usually* the first sentence in a paragraph. However, it can also be located elsewhere. For example, you can present details that build up to an important summary topic sentence at the end of a paragraph.

The Body

The sentences in the **body** of the paragraph should all support the idea expressed in the topic sentence. Each sentence should add new details about the topic.

- Use specific details to make your paragraph interesting.

  These large canines can lug as much as 2,000 pounds, and in their native province, they were once used to haul fishing nets, as well as carts of fish, milk, or mail.

- Organize your sentences in the best possible order: time order, order of importance, classification, and so on. (See pages **571–574**.)

The Closing Sentence

The **closing sentence** comes after all the body details have been presented. This sentence can remind the reader of the topic, summarize the paragraph, or link the paragraph to the next one.

  Indeed, this huge, devoted dog is one of the greatest partners to bless humankind.

Paragraphs

Types of Paragraphs

There are four basic types of paragraphs: *narrative*, *descriptive*, *expository*, and *persuasive*. Notice how the details support the topic sentence in each of the following paragraphs.

Narrative Paragraph

A **narrative paragraph** tells a story. It may draw from the writer's personal experience or from other sources of information. The details should answer the 5 W's *(who? what? when? where?* and *why?)*. A narrative paragraph is almost always organized chronologically, or according to time.

My Watch Dog

Topic Sentence

My morning routine is unusual because it has been established by my dog, Rolph. By nature, I'm not an early riser, but unfortunately for me, Rolph is always ready to go by 5:30 in the morning. He snorts and grunts for a while, but if I don't get out of bed, he'll start to bark. I can assure you that this works better than any alarm clock. Before I know it, I'm stumbling downstairs in my pajamas to let

Body

Rolph outside. By the time I get my face washed and teeth brushed, he's barking again, wanting to come in. Just after 6:00, he has to be fed; otherwise, he follows me around panting and drooling until I put his food out. Then he needs his exercise, so I take him for a walk through the park. Thanks to Rolph,

Closing Sentence

I'm wide awake by 7:00 when I catch the bus for school. By then, Rolph is heading up to my room for his morning nap.

Respond to the reading. What transitional words or phrases does the writer use to indicate the passage of time? Find three. What tone does the writer use—serious, entertaining, or surprising? Explain.

Write a narrative paragraph. Write a narrative paragraph in which you share an experience dealing with a pet or some other animal. Make sure to answer the 5 W's. (Follow the guidelines on page 568.)

Descriptive Paragraph

A **descriptive paragraph** provides a detailed picture of a person, a place, an object, or an event. This type of paragraph should contain a variety of sensory details—specific sights, sounds, smells, tastes, and textures.

Topic Sentence

Body

Closing Sentence

A Champion Mix

My dog, Rolph, has the look of a strange mix of breeds. His nose is pointed like a German shepherd, but his ears are long and floppy, suggesting some spaniel in his DNA. His eyes are as blue as arctic skies, hinting of a gene pool that includes a little husky or malamute somewhere in the history. His fur, gray streaked with black, has a large white patch on his chest, suggesting some schnauzer blood. When I pet his rough coat, I feel brushlike bristles along his back, yet the fluff around his head is curly and soft—almost poodlelike. His tail is soft, too, but bushy, perhaps conjuring up some collie heritage. (My mom says Rolph can dust a coffee table in nothing flat if he's in a good mood and we position him just right.) Rolph's "woof" is deep enough to belong to a Saint Bernard, but when he gets excited he yips like a little Chihuahua! When he is running free in the park, someone may even mistake him for a nimble purebred retriever. Although Rolph appears as though he was assembled from a crazy collection of leftover pieces, he is a champion to me.

Respond to the reading. What senses are covered in this paragraph? Which two or three details seem especially descriptive?

Write a descriptive paragraph. Write a paragraph that describes something that is important to you. Use sensory details in your description. (Follow the guidelines on page 568.)

Expository Paragraph

An **expository paragraph** shares information about a specific topic. Expository writing presents facts, gives directions, defines terms, explains a process, and so forth. It should clearly inform the reader.

Topic Sentence

Body

Closing Sentence

The Nose Knows

To a dog, the sense of smell is everything. The structure of a dog's nose accounts for its extraordinary sense of smell. Generally, the longer the dog's nose, the keener its sense of smell is. The wetness of the outer area of a dog's nose helps the animal detect and collect odors. Inside the nose, dogs have 25 times more smell receptors than humans. Sniffing activates these receptors, which send the odor "messages" to the olfactory lobe in the dog's brain. This lobe is four times larger than the corresponding area in the human brain and allows dogs to sort out and pinpoint many specific layers of smells. Dogs can pick up odors in concentrations 100 million times lower than humans can detect! A dog uses its sense of smell to evaluate its world, an ability that has proven to be of enormous help to humans. Some dogs can find people trapped in avalanches or collapsed buildings, while others are trained to hunt for those who have not survived. Patrol dogs prove invaluable for sniffing out drugs, smuggled goods, and bombs. Scientists are even exploring the medical "miracle" that dogs seem to be able to smell certain kinds of cancers before they are detected through lab tests. While we may not always agree with a dog about what does or does not smell delightful, we can surely appreciate the marvel that is a dog's nose.

Respond to the reading. What is the specific topic of this paragraph? What supporting facts or examples does the writer include? Name three or four of them.

Write an expository paragraph. Write a paragraph that shares information about a specific topic. Make sure to include plenty of details that support the topic. (Follow the guidelines on page 568.)

Paragraphs

Persuasive Paragraph

A **persuasive paragraph** expresses an opinion and tries to convince the reader that the opinion is valid. To be persuasive, a writer must include effective supporting reasons and facts.

Topic Sentence

Body

Closing Sentence

Not So Fast . . . Or So Far

Sled dogs in the Iditarod race in Alaska should not be exposed to unnecessary health risks. The Iditarod race covers an incredible distance, approximately 1,150 miles, and takes a dog team from 9 to 14 days to complete. That amount of running in the course of that number of days puts an incredible strain on the dogs. In most of the Iditarod races, at least one dog has died. Causes of death include "strangulation in the towlines, internal bleeding from sled gouges, liver injuries, heart failure, and pneumonia" (Facts 2). Sled dogs are bred to obey commands under any circumstances, so they will continue to run even if they are injured or sick. Even if a dog wanted to stop, it couldn't because it is tied into the sled harness. A dog that happens to hesitate or fall could be trampled to death. Some health experts, including veterinarians, say that the number of deaths is not very surprising. With 800 dogs in the race, one or two deaths should be expected. That many deaths would just naturally occur over a two-week period. While that may be true, it must be remembered that the dogs have no choice but to run. As a result, race promoters must do everything possible to reduce health risks to these animals.

Respond to the reading. What is the writer's opinion in the paragraph? What reasons does the writer include to support the opinion? Name two.

Write a persuasive paragraph. Write a paragraph expressing your opinion about an event or an activity. Include at least two or three strong reasons that support your opinion. (Follow the guidelines on page 568.)

Writing Guidelines ■ Develop a paragraph.

Before you begin your writing, make sure you understand the requirements of the assignment. Then follow the steps listed below.

Prewriting ■ Select a topic and details.

- Select a specific topic that meets the requirements of the assignment.
- Collect facts, examples, and other details about your topic.
- Write a topic sentence stating what your paragraph will be about. (See page **563**.)
- Decide on the best way to organize the supporting details. (See pages **571–574**.)

Writing ■ Create the first draft.

- Start your paragraph with the topic sentence.
- Follow with sentences that support your topic. Use your planning as a general guide.
- Connect your ideas and sentences with transitions.
- Close with a sentence that restates your topic, gives a final thought, or, in the case of an essay, leads into the next paragraph.

Revising ■ Improve your writing.

- Add information if you need to say more about your topic.
- Move sentences that aren't in the best order.
- Delete sentences that don't support the topic.
- Rewrite any sentences that are unclear.

Editing ■ Check for conventions.

- Check the revised draft for punctuation, capitalization, grammar, and spelling errors.
- Write a neat final copy and proofread it one last time.

Tip

When you write a paragraph, remember that the reader wants to . . .

- learn something. *(Offer new and interesting information.)*
- hear the writer's voice. *(Let your personality come through in the writing.)*

Types of Details

There are many types of details you can include in paragraphs (and in longer forms of writing). The purpose of your writing determines which details you should use. The key types are explained below and on the following page.

Facts are *details* that can be proven.

> Carnivores are animals that derive most of their sustenance from eating meat.

> In 2004, the Boston Red Sox won the World Series by sweeping the St. Louis Cardinals.

Statistics present *numerical information* (numbers) about a specific topic.

> A recent survey found that 16 percent of Whitewater High School students have family pets.

> Whole-grain bread contains up to six times more dietary fiber than regular white bread.

Examples are *statements that illustrate a main point.*

> Every region presents climate-related challenges *(main point)*. Southeastern coastal regions are subject to hurricanes. The Great Plains are vulnerable to tornadoes, while the northern regions experience howling blizzards and periods of dangerous subzero temperatures.

Anecdotes are *brief stories* that help to make a point about a topic. They can be much more effective than a matter-of-fact list of details.

> Abraham Lincoln had a dry wit and a sharp sense of humor. Two men once asked him to settle an argument they were having about the proper proportion of the length of a man's legs to his torso. After acknowledging the seriousness of the matter, Lincoln concluded:
>
> "After much thought and consideration, not to mention mental worry and anxiety, it is my opinion, all side issues being swept aside, that a man's lower limbs, in order to preserve harmony of proportion, should be at least long enough to reach from his body to the ground."

Paragraphs

Quotations are *people's statements* repeated word for word. Quotations can provide powerful supporting evidence.

> Some people are concerned that bilingual education is a threat to English as our national language. This is obviously not the case, since the ultimate goal is to help all students become speakers of English. James Crawford, author of *Hold Your Tongue*, states, "Bilingualism is as American as apple pie—and has been ever since this nation's beginnings."

Definitions give the *meaning* of unfamiliar terms. Definitions of technical terms are especially important for the reader. Defining such terms makes your writing clear.

> That painting has a lot of texture because it is a fresco, a painting applied directly onto wet plaster.

> Manatees, large aquatic mammals sometimes called sea cows, can be found in the warm coastal waters of Florida.

Reasons answer *why* and can explain or justify ideas.

> High school athletes should avoid using creatine, a common training supplement. In the short term, creatine may cause diarrhea, nausea, dehydration, and cramping. While these side effects are rare, high school football players have been hospitalized for dehydration from using creatine. In the long term, taking creatine may lead to serious kidney problems and muscle tears. Some experts also believe that if athletes overload on creatine, their bodies may stop producing it naturally.

Comparisons address the *similarities or differences* between two things. It is especially helpful to compare something new or unknown to something your reader understands.

> Switzerland celebrates its founding on August 1st, much like the United States celebrates its independence on July 4th. Switzerland, however, is more than 700 years old, while the United States is little more than 200 years old.

Try It!

Find examples in this book's writing samples of any four types of details listed on the previous two pages. Write the examples and the pages where you found them on your own paper.

Patterns of Organization

On the following four pages, sample paragraphs show basic patterns of organization. Reviewing these samples can help you organize your own writing.

Chronological Order

Chronological (time) **order** is effective for explaining a process or sharing a story. Information is organized by what happens first, second, third, and so on. The paragraph below explains how to focus a microscope.

Time Line

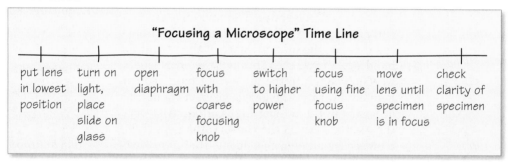

"Focusing a Microscope" Time Line

| put lens in lowest position | turn on light, place slide on glass | open diaphragm | focus with coarse focusing knob | switch to higher power | focus using fine focus knob | move lens until specimen is in focus | check clarity of specimen |

A Clear Specimen

Topic Sentence

Knowing how to focus a microscope properly can save you time and frustration when viewing slides. Start with the lens on its lowest power—that's the shortest objective lens. Then turn on the viewing light and place your slide on the glass stage with the specimen centered. Open the diaphragm all the way to get the most light. Next, look through the eyepiece and begin focusing by slowly turning the coarse focus knob (the large outer knob) until the specimen is in focus. Reposition the slide as needed.

Body

At this point, switch to a higher power, but be careful not to touch the coarse focus knob again. Adjusting the coarse focus knob could scratch or crack the slide. Only use the smaller fine focus knob if you need to adjust the focus. Then slowly move the lens up until your specimen is in focus. Once you are satisfied with your focus, check to see if your specimen looks faint. If it does look faint,

Closing Sentence

try closing the diaphragm a little. This will make your specimen brighter. Your specimen will now be easy to identify and observe.

Paragraphs

Order of Location

Order of location (spatial organization) is effective for organizing a description. It provides unity by arranging details in a logical way—left to right, top to bottom, and so on. A student who described Casa Loma, a castle located in Toronto, Canada, used the graphic organizer shown at the right to help him arrange his details.

Topic Sentence

Body

Closing Sentence

The Canadian Castle

Visiting Casa Loma in Toronto is like visiting another time and place—a time of royalty and elegance. The mammoth entranceway, with its high stone arches, sets the tone for the magnificence of the rest of the building. As you step through the enormous wooden doors into the huge front hall, you can't help but stare at the gargoyles peering down at you from the 60-foot-high ceiling. Also on the ground floor is the conservatory, which is crowned by an enormous dome that is made of stained glass. Moving up the massive staircase, you come to the second floor, which includes the ornate main bedroom suites as well as a balcony overlooking the main hall. Some of the bedrooms even have secret passageways leading to other places in the castle. Next, take the elevator or stairway up to the third floor, where you will find the Queen's Own Rifles Museum and the servants' quarters. If you are adventurous, another staircase will lead you to the open Norman tower. From this breathtaking command post, you can gaze south, across the city of Toronto, which appears to be bowing humbly to this magnificent structure. Casa Loma is based on the vision—and the money— of Sir Henry Mill Pellatt, a wealthy Canadian who always wanted his own castle.

First Floor
arched
   entrance
huge front hall
60-foot ceiling
gargoyles
conservatory

Second Floor
balcony
main bedrooms
   —secret
   passages

Third Floor
Queen's
   Own Rifles
   Museum
servants'
   quarters

Tower
open Norman
   tower
city of Toronto
   below

Respond to the reading. What other ways could the writer have approached and organized a description of Casa Loma? Name two.

Classification

Classification is used when you need to break a topic down into categories and subcategories to help the reader better understand it. The following paragraph classifies the divisions of food according to kosher dietary laws. The writer used the following line diagram to help plan her writing.

Line Diagram

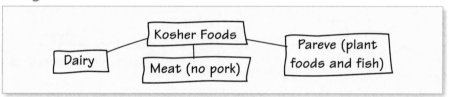

Keeping Kosher

Topic Sentence

Body

Closing Sentence

My friend Rachel's family keeps kosher, meaning they follow the Jewish dietary laws that divide food into three groups: dairy, meat, and pareve. Dairy foods include milk, cheese, and butter, as well as many prepared foods and mixes that contain milk products such as whey. Anything that contains dairy products must never be eaten with meat. The meat group includes beef, chicken, and lamb, but never ham or other pork products. Some dry mixes or powders may have meat flavorings or fat in them, and these, too, should never be served with dairy foods. Foods that are neither dairy nor meat are called pareve and include vegetables, fruits, and grains. Pareve foods may be eaten with either dairy or meat foods. Fish is also considered pareve, but it is not mixed with meat in a recipe and is usually served on a separate plate in a meat meal. (Shellfish such as lobster or shrimp are never kosher.) People who keep kosher often have two sets of dishes, utensils, and pots—one for dairy and one for meat—and some even go so far as to have separate dishwashers! I think it would be hard to remember all the rules, but my friend Rachel says keeping kosher is easy once you get used to it.

 Respond to the reading. Answer this question: What facts or details did you learn about the topic? Name three.

Comparison and Contrast

Organizing by **comparison** shows the similarities or differences between two subjects. To compare dairy farming of the past with that of today, one student used a Venn diagram. After organizing her details, she found that the two styles were more different than alike. Those differences are explained in her paragraph.

Venn Diagram

Then	Both	Now
family farms	sanitary conditions	owned by corporations
cows roamed free	affected by varying weather, prices	cows penned in "drylots"
all natural—no Rbgh		hormones used—Rbgh
milked twice a day	milk picked up by trucks	milked 3 times a day
milk cans		"bulk" tanks

Farming Then and Now

Topic Sentence

The family farm of the '50s had little in common with the modern dairy farm. Of course, dairy farms have always held sanitary conditions as a top priority, and farmers have always been at the mercy of both the weather and milk prices. The family farm gave way to farms owned by corporations and run by accountants. On the family farm, cows grazed rich pastures between milkings, while on modern farms, every inch of land is utilized for crops. That means many herds spend their lives in large barns or drylots (pens with no grass) with no room to roam. All feed and supplements were natural in the past, but today, hormones might be administered to promote milking three times a day rather than twice. Old-time farmers used individual milking machines: rubber cups suctioned the milk into a steel container. The machines were then emptied into a larger milk can, which was placed in a cooler until the milk truck came to pick it up. Today, the suction cups lead to sterile pipelines that run the milk directly into a large tank, which is then pumped into huge tanker trucks. Farming today is less of a personal relationship between farmer and animal and more of an efficient business.

Body

Closing Sentence

Modeling Paragraphs

When you come across paragraphs that you really like, practice writing examples of your own that follow the author's pattern of writing. This process is called **modeling**. Follow these guidelines:

Guidelines for Modeling

- **Find a paragraph** you would like to model.
- **Think of a topic** for your practice writing.
- **Follow the pattern** of the paragraph as you write about your own topic. (You do not have to follow the pattern exactly.)
- **Build your paragraph** one sentence or idea at a time.
- **Review your work** and change any parts that seem confusing.
- **Save your writing** and share it with your classmates.

End with the topic sentence.

Sometimes a writer presents the topic sentence at the end of the paragraph. The details build suspense gradually until the final sentence, which serves as an effective summary (topic) sentence.

> My toes curl in pain. Stepping forward only makes it worse because my ankles start to stiffen. Then the cramping begins in my calf as the pain moves up my body. My teeth also start to chatter uncontrollably. I wrap my arms around myself, hoping to gather a little warmth. Finally, I decide to take action because procrastinating only prolongs the agony. So I hold my breath and leap forward. My body momentarily goes into shock as I hit the cold water. I gasp and then relax. I have made my first dive into the lake.

Respond to the reading. What is the topic of the paragraph? In which sentence is this topic identified? Which details build suspense into the paragraph? Name two or three of them.

Try It!

Write your own narrative paragraph modeled after the sample above. Refer to the guidelines near the top of the page to help you complete your writing.

> "Good writing has an aliveness that keeps the reader reading from one paragraph to the next."
> —William Zinsser

Answer a question.

A topic sentence is usually a statement, but it doesn't have to be. A writer can ask a question in a topic sentence. The remaining sentences in the paragraph answer the question. In the expository paragraph that follows, the writer asks and answers a question about a common fastening device, the zipper.

Have you ever wondered what makes a zipper work? A zipper works because the slide either joins or separates the two sides of the track. The key to understanding this is knowing that the two sides have perfectly matched teeth. Each tooth has a hook on the top and a hollow on the bottom. In order to join the sides, the moving slide wedges each hook into the hollow of the tooth directly across from it. When all of the hooks and hollows are joined, the zipper is closed. To open the zipper, the slide pops each hook out of its hollow. A zipper won't work if there is a piece of thread tangled in the works, a tooth is broken, or the hooks and hollows are not properly lined up. Of course, understanding this process will not make you feel any less upset when a zipper gets stuck.

 Respond to the reading. What is the topic of this paragraph? In which sentence is the main idea about the topic identified? Does the writer supply enough supporting details? Explain.

Try It!

Write your own expository paragraph modeled after the sample above. Refer to the guidelines for modeling near the top of page **575** to help you complete your writing.

Connecting Paragraphs in Essays

To write strong essays, you must organize the ideas within each paragraph and then organize the paragraphs within the essay. The guidelines that follow will help you connect the paragraphs in your essay.

- **Be sure that your paragraphs are complete.** Each one should contain an effective topic sentence and supporting details.

- **Identify the topic and thesis (focus) of your essay** in the beginning paragraph. Start with some interesting details to get the reader's attention. Then share the focus of your writing.

- **Develop your ideas** in the middle paragraphs. Each middle paragraph should include information that explains and supports your focus. Often, the paragraph that contains the most important information comes right after the beginning paragraph or right before the final paragraph.

- **Review one or more of the main points in your essay** in the closing paragraph. The last sentence usually gives the reader a final interesting thought about the topic.

- **Use transition words or phrases** to connect the paragraphs. Transitions help the reader follow an essay from one paragraph to the next. In the sample below, the transitions are shown in red.

. . . Since that time, blue jeans have become much more than a symbol of the American West and are worn around the world.

In addition to jeans, other symbols of American culture include athletic shoes and sports jerseys. These two symbols have become especially important with the international popularity of basketball. . . .

For several reasons, many fashion trends have begun in the United States. Because of our wealth, free time, and technology, it's easy to understand why . . .

Try It!

Turn to pages **592–593** to see examples of transition words and phrases. On your own paper, list the transitions that you have used in your writing. *Special Challenge:* Find one or two writing samples that use some of the transitions from pages **592–593**.

Paragraphs

Sample Essay

Read this sample essay about leadership. Notice how the three parts—the beginning, the middle, and the ending—work together.

Becoming a Leader

Who is a leader? The simple answer is "someone who leads." But there isn't anything simple about leadership. As basketball coach Howard Brown states, "Leading a team, and getting the players to work toward a common goal, takes skill and a lot of effort." So how does someone take on this important role? To become a leader, a person must develop three main traits.

First of all, leaders must be confident. They must believe in their own abilities and know that these abilities will help the group reach its goals. This confidence comes mainly through training and experience. True leaders are willing to make decisions and stand behind them even when faced with detractors. Leaders know what needs to be done, and they act accordingly. They also make decisions based on good personal judgment, along with the wise input of others.

Second, leaders must display good work habits. Effective leaders lead by example, working longer and harder than the rest of the group. In many cases, a group's effort—or lack of it—will be a direct reflection of the leader's example. Leaders also keep up with the latest developments related to the group's work. In other words, true leaders change with the times and grow as individuals.

Third, and most important, leaders must earn the respect of the group. This respect is earned in a number of ways. Leaders must be organized, laying out an effective plan or schedule for the group to follow. They help the individuals in the group improve and grow. In addition, effective leaders treat everyone fairly and honestly. They offer praise when it is earned and criticism when it is necessary.

Becoming a good leader truly does take a lot of effort. A person earns that position by being confident, hardworking, and respected by others. There is an English proverb that says, "A smooth sea never made a skilled mariner." A leader, like a skilled mariner, has sailed and conquered rough seas and, from that experience, has learned how to lead.

Respond to the reading. What transitions are used to connect the middle paragraphs in this essay? Does the writer present his most important supporting reason in the first middle paragraph or in the last middle paragraph? Why does he organize his reasons in this way?

Paragraph Traits Checklist

Use the checklist below as a basic guide when you review your paragraphs. If you answer "no" to any of the questions, continue to work with that part of your paragraph.

Revising Checklist

Ideas

_____ **1.** Have I selected a specific topic?

_____ **2.** Have I supported the topic with specific details?

Organization

_____ **3.** Is my topic sentence clear?

_____ **4.** Have I organized the details in an effective order?

Voice

_____ **5.** Do I sound interested in, and knowledgeable about, my topic?

_____ **6.** Does my voice fit the assignment and my audience?

Word Choice

_____ **7.** Do I use specific nouns, verbs, and modifiers?

_____ **8.** Do I define any unfamiliar terms?

Sentence Fluency

_____ **9.** Have I written clear and complete sentences?

_____ **10.** Do I vary my sentence beginnings and lengths?

Conventions

_____ **11.** Have I checked for punctuation, capitalization, and grammar errors?

_____ **12.** Have I checked for spelling errors?

Paragraphs

A Writer's Resource

A Writer's Resource

Writer Sholem Asch says, "Writing comes more easily if you have something to say." That is so true. If you know a lot about a topic, and have strong feelings about it, you're ready to write. But what about those times when you can't think of a writing topic, or you're not sure how to develop a writing idea? Then you should turn to this section for help.

This chapter contains tips and guidelines to help you complete any writing assignment. You'll find strategies for selecting topics, organizing details, writing thesis statements, and so on. Once you become familiar with this chapter, you'll always have something interesting to say in your writing.

- Finding a Topic
- Knowing the Different Forms
- Collecting and Organizing Details
- Creating an Outline
- Using Transitions
- Writing Thesis Statements
- Writing Great Beginnings and Endings
- Integrating Quotations
- Learning Key Writing Terms
- Using Writing Techniques
- Adding Graphics to Your Writing

"You can't wait for inspiration. You have to go after it with a club."
—Jack London

Finding a Topic

In writing, everything starts with an idea. Sometimes your teacher will supply a general writing subject. Suppose your teacher assigns a paper on the Great Depression. It's a huge subject—you still need to find a specific writing topic. These two pages show different ways that students approached this task.

Use a cluster diagram.

Cho used a cluster diagram to find her topic. She wrote the general subject in the center and then broke it down into three categories. Each category became another cluster. Cho could see which topic had the most information and looked most interesting to her. She decided to write about the New Deal.

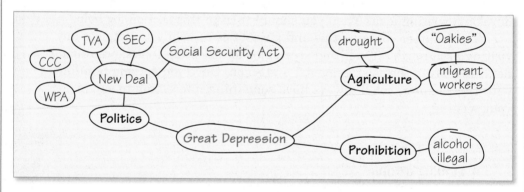

Try freewriting.

Jennifer tried freewriting. She wrote for 10 to 15 minutes about what she already knew about the subject as well as questions she had about it. Jennifer's freewriting led her to research and write about entertainment during the Great Depression.

> The movie we saw about the Depression was depressing! What did people do for fun during that time? I know they went to movies. How could they afford them? My grandma has some dishes her mother got when she went to the movies. That's weird. What was that all about? What kind of movies did people watch back then? Did they go to movies to take their minds off the Depression? What other types of entertainment did people find?

Review a "Basics of Life" list.

There are certain things people need to live a full life. Below is a list of these categories, called the "Basics of Life." By selecting one category and applying it to your subject, you can zero in on a topic. Randall selected the category "freedom/rights" and decided to explore civil rights during the Great Depression.

food	friends	land/property	heat/fuel
work/occupation	purpose/goals	community	natural resources
clothing	love	science	personality/identity
faith/religion	senses	plants/vegetation	recreation/hobbies
communication	machines	freedom/rights	trade/money
exercise	intelligence	energy	literature/books
education	history/records	rules/laws	health/medicine
family	agriculture	tools/utensils	art/music

Use visual images.

Sometimes topic ideas are all around you. Juana used the Internet to help her find her topic. She was fascinated by the Depression-era images of dust storms and grasshopper damage, so she decided to research and write about the causes and effects of the Dust Bowl.

Use writing prompts.

Every day is full of experiences that make you think. You do things that you feel good about. You hear things that make you angry. You wonder how different things work. You are reminded of a past experience. These everyday thoughts can make excellent starting points for writing. As you write about one of these prompts, a number of specific topics will come to mind.

Best and Worst

My most memorable day in school
My best hour
My encounter with a bully

It could only happen to me!

A narrow escape from trouble
I was so shocked when . . .
My life began in this way.
My strangest phone conversation
If only I had done that differently
Whatever happened to my . . .

Quotations

"Someone who makes no mistakes does not usually make anything."

"When people are free to do as they please, they usually imitate each other."

"More is not always better."

"It is easier to forgive an enemy than a friend."

"Never give advice unless asked."

"Honesty is the best policy."

"Know thyself."

"Like mother, like daughter."

"Like father, like son."

I was thinking.

Everyone should know . . .
Where do I draw the line?
Is it better to laugh or cry?
Why do people like to go fast?
I don't understand why . . .

First and Last

My first game or performance
My last day of_____
My last visit with _____

School, Then and Now

The pressure of tryouts
Grades—are they the most important part of school?
Finally, a good assembly
What my school really needs is . . .
A teacher I respect
I'm in favor of more . . .

People and Places

Who knows me best? What does he or she know?
Getting along with my brother, sister, or friend
A person I admire
My grandparents' house
The emergency room
A guided tour of my neighborhood

Use sample topics.

People, places, experiences, and information you encounter all offer springboards for writing. Here are some topic ideas for descriptive, narrative, expository, and persuasive writing.

Descriptive

People: favorite relative, coach, friend, teacher, doctor or veterinarian, brother or sister, homeless person, local store worker

Places: band room, park, mall, art museum, wood shop, corner garage, observatory, science lab, laundromat, library, mountaintop, city street

Things: wedding cake, salt and pepper shakers, cell phone, locker, snowy road, bracelet, griffin, old car, photograph, potted plant, fish tank

Animals: buffalo, coyote, alley cat, goldfish, gorilla, mosquito, pigeon, opossum, whale, ostrich, wolverine, penguin, dove, porpoise

Narrative

Stories: trying out for a team, choosing a pet from a shelter, volunteering at a nursing home or day care, riding in an ambulance, acting in community theater, working on a farm, going fishing or hunting

Expository

Comparison-Contrast: football and rugby, baseball and cricket, the United States and Australia, squid and octopus, guitar and violin, U.S. Congress and British Parliament, tulip and Venus flytrap

Cause/Effect: shrinking polar ice caps, identity theft, deforestation, AIDS, drought, lab experiment, cosmetic surgery, rabies, rainbows

Classification: kinds of clouds, types of popular music, branches of the military, groups of vertebrates, kinds of cameras, types of waves

Persuasive

School: carrying backpacks to class, giving special privileges to students who earn them, offering weighted grades, opening a student lounge, adding a cafeteria vegetable bar

Home: getting a larger allowance, rotating chores, extending computer time, having parental blocks on TV channels, taking music/dance/karate lessons

Community: adding corner stoplights, building or repairing sidewalks, creating bicycle paths, extending weekend curfews, allowing skateboards on sidewalks, creating a teen center

Resource

Knowing the Different Forms

Finding the right form for your writing is just as important as finding the right topic. When you are selecting a form, be sure to ask yourself who you're writing for (your *audience*) and why you're writing (your *purpose*).

Anecdote	A brief story that helps to make a point
Autobiography	A writer's story of his or her own life
Biography	A writer's story of someone else's life
Book review	An essay offering an opinion about a book, not to be confused with *literary analysis*
Cause and effect	A paper examining an event, the forces leading up to that event, and the effects following the event
Character sketch	A brief description of a specific character showing some aspect of that character's personality
Descriptive writing	Writing that uses sensory details that allow the reader to clearly visualize a person, a place, a thing, or an idea
Editorial	A letter or an article offering an opinion, an idea, or a solution
Essay	A thoughtful piece of writing in which ideas are explained, analyzed, or evaluated
Expository writing	Writing that explains something by presenting its steps, causes, or kinds
Eyewitness account	A report giving specific details of an event or a person
Fable	A short story that teaches a lesson or moral, often using talking animals as the main characters
Fantasy	A story set in an imaginary world in which the characters usually have supernatural powers or abilities
Historical fiction	An invented story based on an actual historical event
Interview	Writing based on facts and details obtained through speaking with another person
Journal writing	Writing regularly to record personal observations, thoughts, and ideas

Literary analysis	A careful examination or interpretation of some aspect of a piece of literature
Myth	A traditional story intended to explain a mystery of nature, religion, or culture
Novel	A book-length story with several characters and a well-developed plot, usually with one or more subplots
Personal narrative	Writing that shares an event or experience from the writer's personal life
Persuasive writing	Writing intended to persuade the reader to follow the writer's way of thinking about something
Play	A form that uses dialogue to tell a story, usually meant to be performed in front of an audience
Poem	A creative expression that may use rhyme, rhythm, and imagery
Problem-solution	Writing that presents a problem followed by a proposed solution
Process paper	Writing that explains how a process works, or how to do or make something
Profile	An essay that reveals an individual or re-creates a time period
Proposal	Writing that includes specific information about an idea or a project that is being considered for approval
Research report	An essay that shares information about a topic that has been thoroughly researched
Response to literature	Writing that is a reaction to something the writer has read
Science fiction	Writing based on real or imaginary science and often set in the future
Short story	A short fictional piece with only a few characters and one conflict or problem
Summary	Writing that presents the most important ideas from a longer piece of writing
Tall tale	A humorous, exaggerated story about a character or animal who does impossible things
Tragedy	Literature in which the hero fails or is destroyed because of a serious character flaw

Resource

Collecting and Organizing Details

Use graphic organizers.

Graphic organizers can help you gather and organize your details for writing. Clustering is one method (see page **582**). These two pages show other useful organizers.

Cause-Effect Organizer

Use to collect and organize details for cause-effect essays.

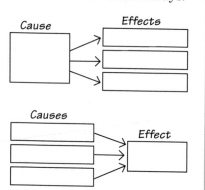

Problem-Solution Web

Use to map out problem-solution essays.

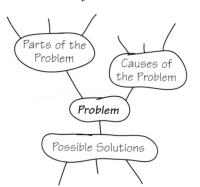

Time Line

Use for personal narratives to list actions or events in the order they occurred.

Subject: _____

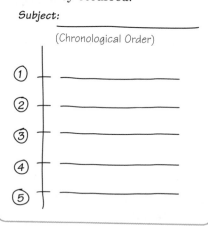

Evaluation Collection Grid

Use to collect supporting details for essays of evaluation.

Subject: _____

Points to Evaluate	Supporting Details
1.	
2.	
3.	
4.	

Resource

Venn Diagram

Use to collect details to compare and contrast two topics.

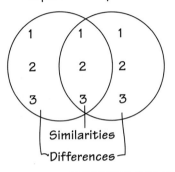

Topic A   Topic B

Similarities

Differences

Line Diagram

Use to collect and organize details for academic essays.

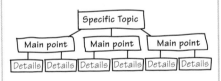

Specific Topic

Main point | Main point | Main point

Details | Details | Details | Details | Details | Details

Process (Cycle) Diagram

Use to collect details for science-related writing, such as how a process or cycle works.

Topic: _____

(Chronological Order)

Step 1 → Step 2 → Step 3

Step 1 → Step 2 → Step 3 (cycle)

5 W's Chart

Use to collect the *Who? What? When? Where?* and *Why?* details for personal narratives and news stories.

Subject: _____

Who?	What?	When?	Where?	Why?

Definition Diagram

Use to gather information for extended definition essays.

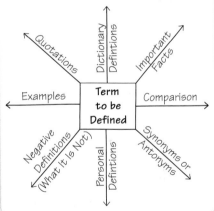

Quotations | Dictionary Definitions | Important Facts

Examples | **Term to be Defined** | Comparison

Negative Definitions (What It Is Not) | Personal Definitions | Synonyms or Antonyms

Sensory Chart

Use to collect details for descriptive essays and observation reports.

Subject: _____

Sights	Sounds	Smells	Tastes	Textures

Creating an Outline

An **outline** organizes a set of facts or ideas by listing main points and subpoints. An effective outline shows how topics or ideas fit together. A well-designed outline serves as a frame for an effective essay.

There are two types of outlines: *topic outlines* and *sentence outlines*. (See the samples below and on the next page.)

A Topic Outline

In a **topic outline**, main points and details appear as phrases rather than as complete sentences. Topic outlines are useful for short essays, including essay-test answers. The information after the Roman numerals (I., II., III., and so on) identifies the main points in the essay. The information after the capital letters (A., B., C., and so on) identifies the details that support the main points.

Sample Topic Outline

I. History of driver safety problems in Formula-One cars
  A. Bad accidents at the start
  B. Hazards due to the course
  C. Hazards due to the cars
II. Modifications to cars
  A. Single-shell construction and cockpit survival cells
  B. Fire extinguishers
  C. Escape systems
III. Modifications to driver equipment
  A. Helmet improvements
  B. Head-and-neck support systems
  C. Fireproof clothes
IV. Modifications to racetracks
  A. Track improvements
  B. Medical services upgraded

Note: Information for the opening and closing paragraphs is not included in this outline for an essay about safety in Formula-One cars.

Tip

In an outline, if you have a "I.," you must have at least a "II." If you have an "A.," you must have at least a "B.," and so on.

A Sentence Outline

A **sentence outline** is a detailed plan for writing. In this type of outline, the ideas are explained in complete sentences. This type of outline is useful for longer writing assignments like research reports and formal essays.

Sample Sentence Outline

I. Driver safety wasn't always a primary concern in Formula-One racing.
   A. Races have a history of bad accidents.
   B. The courses include hills and hairpin turns.
   C. The cars are the fastest in the world and jockey for position.
II. Many safety modifications have been made to cars.
   A. The body shell and cockpit survival cell are stronger now.
   B. Each car has several fire extinguishers.
   C. Escape systems allow drivers to escape after an accident.
III. Modifications have improved driver equipment.
   A. Helmets are stronger and lighter.
   B. The new head-and-neck support systems prevent spinal injuries.
   C. All clothing is fireproof.
IV. Modifications have made racetracks safer.
   A. Improvements in track layout help prevent crashes.
   B. Rescue and medical services are only seconds away.

A Quick List

Use a **quick list** when there is no time for an outline. A quick list organizes ideas in the most basic way, but it will still help you organize or structure your writing.

Sample Quick List

Formula-One Safety
- history of accidents
- safety modifications in cars
- modifications in driver equipment
- modifications in racetracks

Resource

Using Transitions

Transitions can be used to connect one sentence to another sentence within a paragraph, or to connect one paragraph to another within a longer essay or report. The lists below show a number of transitions and how they are used.

Each colored list below is a group of transitions that could work well together in a piece of writing.

Words used to show location

above	around	between	inside	outside
across	behind	by	into	over
against	below	down	near	throughout
along	beneath	in back of	next to	to the right
among	beside	in front of	on top of	under

Above	In front of	On top of
Below	Beside	Next to
To the left	In back of	Beneath
To the right		

Words used to show time

about	during	yesterday	until	finally
after	first	meanwhile	next	then
at	second	today	soon	as soon as
before	to begin	tomorrow	later	in the end

First	To begin	Now	First	Before
Second	To continue	Soon	Then	During
Third	To conclude	Eventually	Next	After
Finally			In the end	

Words used to compare things

likewise	as	in the same way	one way
like	also	similarly	both

In the same way	One way
Also	Another way
Similarly	Both

Words used to contrast (show differences)

| but | still | although | on the other hand |
| however | yet | otherwise | even though |

On the other hand   Although
Even though   Yet
Still   Nevertheless

Words used to emphasize a point

| again | truly | especially | for this reason |
| to repeat | in fact | to emphasize | |

For this reason   Truly   In fact
Especially   To emphasize   To repeat

Words used to conclude or summarize

| finally | as a result | to sum it up | in conclusion |
| lastly | therefore | all in all | because |

Because   As a result   To sum it up   Therefore
In conclusion   All in all   Because   Finally

Words used to add information

again	another	for instance	for example
also	and	moreover	additionally
as well	besides	along with	other
next	finally	in addition	

For example   For instance   Next   Another
Additionally   Besides   Moreover   Along with
Finally   Next   Also   As well

Words used to clarify

| in other words | for instance | that is | for example |

For instance   For example
In other words   Equally important

Writing Thesis Statements

An effective thesis statement tells the reader specifically what you plan to write about. In a longer essay or research report, your thesis statement generally comes at the end of the opening paragraph. It serves as a guide to keep you on track as you develop your writing.

The Process at Work

A thesis statement usually takes a stand or expresses a specific feeling about, or feature of, your topic. Write as many versions as it takes to hit upon the statement that sets the right tone for your writing. The following formula can be used to form your thesis statements.

> **A specific topic** (*Egypt's magnificent Sphinx*)
> + **a particular stand, feeling, or feature**
>   (*is being destroyed by pollution.*)
> _____
> = **an effective thesis statement.**

Sample Thesis Statements

Writing Assignment: Research report about a historical event
Specific Topic: The Monroe Doctrine
Thesis Statement: The Monroe Doctrine **(topic)** benefited England as much as it did the United States **(particular stand)**.

Writing Assignment: Persuasive essay about a school problem
Specific Topic: Litter on the school grounds
Thesis Statement: The excessive litter on the school grounds **(topic)** reflects negatively on our school **(particular feeling)**.

Writing Assignment: Analysis of a character in a story
Specific Topic: "A Christmas Memory" by Truman Capote
Thesis Statement: "A Christmas Memory" by Truman Capote **(topic)** examines the bond between a young boy and his special guardian **(particular feature)**.

Thesis Checklist

Be sure that your thesis statement . . .

_____ identifies a limited, specific topic,
_____ focuses on a particular feature or feeling about the topic,
_____ is stated in one or more clear sentences,
_____ can be supported with convincing facts and details, and
_____ meets the requirements of the assignment.

Writing Great Beginnings

The opening paragraph of an essay should grab the reader's attention, introduce your topic, and present your thesis. To start your opening paragraph, try one of these approaches.

- **Start with an interesting fact.**
  King Kong by director Peter Jackson is a remake of the famous 1933 motion picture.

- **Ask an interesting question.**
  Did you know that the original King Kong was only eighteen inches tall?

- **Start with a quotation.**
  In the original *King Kong*, fictional showman Carl Denham said, "Why, the whole world will pay to see this"—and he was right.

Try a beginning strategy.

If you have trouble coming up with a good opening paragraph, follow the step-by-step example below.

First sentence—**Grab the reader's attention.**
Start with a sentence that catches your reader's attention (see above).

> Did you know that the original King Kong was only eighteen inches tall?

Second sentence—**Give some background information.**
Provide some background information about the topic.

> During most of the movie, Kong was actually a posable or movable model covered with rabbit fur.

Third sentence—**Introduce the specific topic of the essay.**
Introduce the topic in a way that builds up to the thesis statement.

> Stop-motion animation was just one of the techniques used to bring Kong to life.

Fourth sentence—**Give the thesis statement.**
Write the thesis statement of the paper (see page **594**).

> Many special effects pioneered in the original *King Kong* appear in movies today.

Resource

Developing Great Endings

The closing paragraph of a paper should summarize your thesis and leave the reader with something to think about. When writing your closing paragraph, use two or more of the following ideas.

- Review your main points.
- Emphasize the special importance of one main point.
- Answer any questions the reader may still have.
- Draw a conclusion and put the information in perspective.
- Provide a final significant thought for the reader.

Try an ending strategy.

If you have trouble coming up with an effective closing paragraph, follow the step-by-step example below.

First sentence—**Reflect on the topic.**
Start by reflecting on the material presented previously about the topic.

Movie special effects have come a long way since 1933.

Second sentence—**Add another point.**
Include a final point of interest that you didn't mention before.

Computer-generated imagery (CGI) used today would astound early filmmakers.

Third sentence—**Emphasize the most important point.**
Stress the importance of one or more key points that support the thesis.

Despite the new technology, however, many basic techniques remain the same, including the use of miniatures, animation, and matte paintings.

Fourth sentence—**Wrap up the topic or draw a conclusion.**
Add one final thought about the topic or draw a conclusion from the points you've presented in the writing.

No matter how special effects are achieved, they continue to delight movie audiences everywhere.

Integrating Quotations

Always choose quotations that are clear and appropriate for your writing. Quotations should *support* your ideas, not replace them.

Try strategies for using quotations.

Use the strategies below to get the most from quoted material in your writing.

- **Use quotations to support your own thoughts and ideas.**
  Effective quotations can back up your main points or support your arguments.

  > Doing what you know to be right will build your self-esteem. As Mark Twain noted, "A man cannot be comfortable without his own approval." That is why it is so important to let your conscience guide your actions.

- **Use quotations to lend authority to your writing.**
  Quoting an expert shows that you have researched your topic and understand its significance.

  > Albert Einstein observed the growth of nuclear power with concern, stating, "I know not with what weapons World War III will be fought, but World War IV will be fought with sticks and stones." His disturbing comment reminds us that a nuclear war would result in unthinkable destruction.

- **Use quotations that are succinct and powerful.**
  Any quotation that you use must add value to your writing.

  > Clearly, the education we provide our students today will determine the success of our future. As Benjamin Franklin put it, "An investment in knowledge always pays the best interest." A well-funded education system greatly benefits and enriches society.

Common Quotation Problems to Avoid

Keep these problems in mind when you consider using quotations.

- **Don't plagiarize.**
  Cite sources for all quotations (and paraphrases).

- **Don't use long quotations.**
  Keep quotations brief and to the point.

- **Don't overuse quotations.**
  Use a quotation only if you can't share the idea as powerfully or effectively in another way.

Learning Key Writing Terms

Here's a glossary of terms that describe aspects of the writing process.

Balance Arranging words or phrases in a way to give them equal importance

Body The main part of a piece of writing, containing details that support or develop the thesis statement

Brainstorming Collecting ideas by thinking freely about all the possibilities; used most often with groups

Central idea The main point of a piece of writing, often stated in a thesis statement or a topic sentence

Closing sentence The summary or final part in a piece of writing

Coherence The logical arranging of ideas so they are clear and easy to follow

Dialogue Written conversation between two or more people

Emphasis Giving great importance to a specific idea in a piece of writing

Exposition Writing that explains and informs

Figurative language Language that goes beyond the normal meaning of the words used, often called "figures of speech"

Focus (thesis) The specific part of a topic that is written about in an essay

Generalization A general statement that gives an overall view, rather than focusing on specific details

Grammar The rules that govern the standard structure and features of a language

Idiom A phrase or an expression that means something different from what the words actually say

That answer was really out in left field. (This means the answer was not even close to being correct.)

Next year you'll sing a different tune. (This means you'll think differently.)

Jargon The special language of a certain group or occupation
The weaver pointed out the fabric's unique warp and woof.
Computer jargon: byte   icon   server   virus

Limiting the subject	Narrowing a general subject to a more specific one
Literal	The actual dictionary meaning of a word; a language that means exactly what it appears to mean
Loaded words	Words slanted for or against the subject **The new tax bill** helps the rich **and** hurts the poor.
Logic	Correctly using facts, examples, and reasons to support a point
Modifiers	Words, phrases, or clauses that limit or describe another word or group of words
Objective	Writing that gives factual information without adding feelings or opinions (See *subjective*.)
Poetic license	A writer's freedom to bend the rules of writing to achieve a certain effect
Point of view	The position or angle from which a story is told (See page **322**.)
Prose	Writing in standard sentence form
Purpose	The specific goal of the writing
Style	The author's unique choice of words and sentences
Subjective	Writing that includes the writer's feelings, attitudes, and opinions (See *objective*.)
Supporting details	Facts or ideas used to sustain the main point
Syntax	The order and relationship of words in a sentence
Theme	The main point or unifying idea of a piece of writing
Thesis statement	A statement of the purpose, or main idea, of an essay
Tone	The writer's attitude toward the subject
Topic	The specific subject of a piece of writing
Topic sentence	The sentence that carries the main idea of a paragraph
Transitions	Words or phrases that connect or tie ideas together
Unity	A sense of oneness in writing in which each sentence helps to develop the main idea
Usage	The way in which people use language (*Standard* language follows the rules; *nonstandard* language does not.)
Voice	A writer's unique personal tone or feeling that comes across in a piece of writing

Resource

Using Writing Techniques

Experiment with some of these techniques in your own essays and stories.

Allusion A reference to a familiar person, place, thing, or event
Mario threw me my mitt. "Hey, Babe Ruth, you forgot this!"

Analogy A comparison of similar ideas or objects to help clarify one of them
There is no frigate like a book, to take us lands away.
—Emily Dickinson

Anecdote A brief story used to illustrate or make a point
It is said that the last words John Adams uttered were "Thomas Jefferson survives." Ironically, Jefferson had died just a few hours earlier. Both deaths occurred on July 4, 1826—the 50th anniversary of the Declaration of Independence shepherded by the two great men. (This ironic anecdote intensifies the importance of both men in our nation's history.)

Colloquialism A common word or phrase suitable for everyday conversation but not for formal speech or writing
"Cool" and "rad" are colloquialisms suggesting approval.

Exaggeration An overstatement or a stretching of the truth to emphasize a point (See *hyperbole* and *overstatement*.)
We opened up the boat's engine and sped along at a million miles an hour.

Flashback A technique in which a writer interrupts a story to go back and relive an earlier time or event
I stopped at the gate, panting. Suddenly I was seven years old again, and my brother was there, calling me "chicken" from the edge of the stone well. Then I opened my eyes and heard only the crickets chirping. The years, the well, and my brother were gone. I turned back to the road, determined to get home before nightfall.

Foreshadowing Hints about what will happen next in a story
As Mai explained why she had to break their date, she noticed Luke looking past her. Turning, she saw Meg smiling—at Luke.

Hyperbole (hi-púr-bə-lē) Exaggeration used to emphasize a point
The music was loud enough to make your ears bleed.

Irony An expression in which the author says one thing but means just the opposite
As we all know, there's nothing students love more than homework.

Juxtaposition	Putting two words or ideas close together to create a contrasting of ideas or an ironic meaning **Ah, the sweet smell of fuel emissions!**
Local color	The use of details that are common in a certain place
Metaphor	A figure of speech that compares two things without using the words *like* or *as* **The sheep were** dense, dancing clouds **scuttling across the road.**
Overstatement	An exaggeration or a stretching of the truth (See *exaggeration* and *hyperbole*.) **If I eat one more piece of turkey,** I will burst!
Oxymoron	Connecting two words with opposite meanings **small fortune, cruel kindness, original copy**
Paradox	A true statement that says two opposite things **As I crossed the finish line dead last, I felt a surge of triumph.**
Parallelism	Repeating similar grammatical structures (words, phrases, or sentences) to give writing rhythm We cannot undo, we will not forget, **and** we should not ignore **the pain of the past.**
Personification	A figure of speech in which a nonhuman thing is given human characteristics **The computer spit out my disk.**
Pun	A phrase that uses words that sound the same in a way that gives them a funny effect **I call my dog Trousers because he** pants **so much.**
Simile	A figure of speech that compares two things using *like* or *as* **Her silent anger was** like a rock wall, **hard and impenetrable.**
Slang	Informal words or phrases used by a particular group of people **cool it hang out shoot the curl**
Symbol	A concrete object used to represent an idea
Understatement	The opposite of exaggeration; using very calm language to call attention to an object or an idea **". . . except for an interruption caused by my wife falling out of the car, the journey went very well."** **—E. B. White**

Resource

Adding Graphics to Your Writing

Graphics can enhance your writing by explaining your ideas in a visual manner. You can create graphics by hand or design them on a computer program and paste them into your document. Be sure to refer to the graphic in the text of your paper, either in the body of a paragraph or in a parenthetical reference.

Line Graphs

Line graphs show change or trends across a period of time. A line graph is drawn as an L-shaped grid, with the horizontal axis showing time and the vertical axis denoting quantity. Dots are plotted and connected to show changes. The stages are clearly labeled as well as the quantity figures.

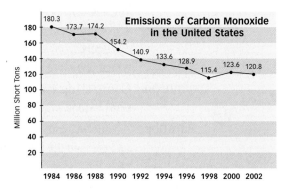

Bar Graphs

Bar graphs use columns representing the subjects of the graph. Unlike the line graph, it does not show how things change over time but is used to show comparisons. The bars may run horizontally or vertically. Label each axis clearly so the reader can easily see and understand the information.

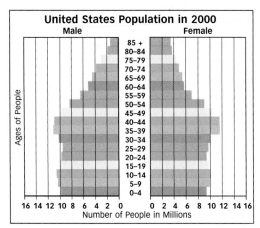

Pie Graphs

Pie graphs show all the proportions and percentages of a whole, along with how those percentages relate to each other. Use a different color for each section. You can either add a key explaining each color or label the graph itself if the graph is large enough.

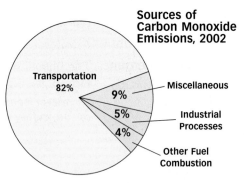

Tables

Tables can organize information in a convenient manner. Most tables have rows (going across) and columns (going down). Rows contain one set of details, while columns contain another. At the right is a sample flight table, showing how far it is from one place to another. Check one place's column against the other's row.

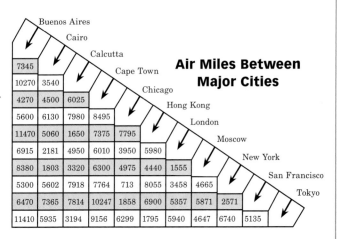

Air Miles Between Major Cities

Buenos Aires	Cairo	Calcutta	Cape Town	Chicago	Hong Kong	London	Moscow	New York	San Francisco	Tokyo
7345										
10270	3540									
4270	4500	6025								
5600	6130	7980	8495							
11470	5060	1650	7375	7795						
6915	2181	4950	6010	3950	5980					
8380	1803	3320	6300	4975	4440	1555				
5300	5602	7918	7764	713	8055	3458	4665			
6470	7365	7814	10247	1858	6900	5357	5871	2571		
11410	5935	3194	9156	6299	1795	5940	4647	6740	5135	

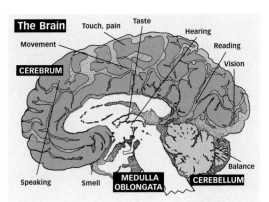

The Brain — Touch, pain — Taste — Hearing — Movement — Reading — Vision — CEREBRUM — Speaking — Smell — MEDULLA OBLONGATA — CEREBELLUM — Balance

Diagrams

Diagrams are drawings that show how something is constructed, how it works, or how its parts relate to each other. A diagram may leave out parts to show you only what you need to learn.

Maps

Maps can be used to illustrate many different things, from political boundaries to population issues to weather conditions. Use color or patterns to show differences.

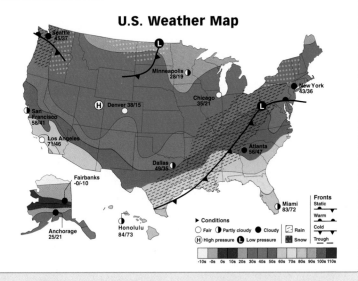

U.S. Weather Map

Seattle 45/37 — Minneapolis 28/19 — New York 43/36 — Chicago 35/21 — San Francisco 58/41 — Denver 38/15 — Los Angeles 71/46 — Atlanta 56/47 — Dallas 49/35 — Fairbanks -0/-10 — Anchorage 25/21 — Honolulu 84/73 — Miami 83/72

Conditions: Fair, Partly cloudy, Cloudy, Rain, High pressure, Low pressure, Snow

Fronts: Static, Warm, Cold, Trough

-10s -0s 0s 10s 20s 30s 40s 50s 60s 70s 80s 90s 100s 110s

Resource

Proofreader's Guide

Marking Punctuation

Period

605.1 At the End of a Sentence

Use a **period** at the end of a sentence that makes a statement, requests something, or gives a mild command.

(Statement) **The man who does not read good books has no advantage over the man who can't read them.**

—Mark Twain

(Request) **Please bring your folders and notebooks to class.**

(Mild command) **Listen carefully so that you understand these instructions.**

NOTE: It is not necessary to place a period after a statement that has parentheses around it and is part of another sentence.

My dog Bobot (I don't quite remember how he acquired this name) **is a Chesapeake Bay retriever—a hunting dog—who is afraid of loud noises.**

605.2 After an Initial or an Abbreviation

Place a period after an initial or an abbreviation (in American English).

Ms.   Sen.   D.D.S.   M.F.A.   M.D.   Jr.   U.S.   p.m.   a.m.
Edna St. Vincent Millay   Booker T. Washington   D. H. Lawrence

NOTE: When an abbreviation is the last word in a sentence, use only one period at the end of the sentence.

Jaleesa eyed each door until she found the name Fletcher B. Gale, M.D.

605.3 As a Decimal Point

A period is used as a decimal point.

New York City has a budget of $46.9 **billion to serve its** 8.1 **million people.**

Exclamation Point

605.4 To Express Strong Feeling

Use the **exclamation point** (sparingly) to express strong feeling. You may place it after a word, a phrase, or a sentence.

"That's not the point," said Wangero. "These are all pieces of dresses Grandma used to wear. She did all this stitching by hand. Imagine!**"**

—Alice Walker, "Everyday Use"

Question Mark

606.1 Direct Question

Place a **question mark** at the end of a direct question.

> Now what? I wondered. Do I go out and buy a jar of honey and stand around waving it? How in the world am I supposed to catch a bear?
>
> —Ken Taylor, "The Case of the Grizzly on the Greens"
>
> Where did my body end and the crystal and white world begin?
>
> —Ralph Ellison, *Invisible Man*

When a question ends with a quotation that is also a question, use only one question mark, and place it within the quotation marks.

> On road trips, do you remember driving your parents crazy by asking, "Are we there yet?"

NOTE: Do *not* use a question mark after an indirect question.

> Out on the street, I picked out a friendly looking old man and asked him where the depot was.
>
> —Wilson Rawls, *Where the Red Fern Grows*

606.2 To Show Uncertainty

Use a question mark within parentheses to show uncertainty.

> This summer marks the 20th season (?) of the American Players Theatre.

606.3 Short Question Within a Sentence

Use a question mark for a short question within parentheses.

> We crept so quietly (had they heard us?) past the kitchen door and back to our room.

Use a question mark for a short question within dashes.

> Maybe somewhere in the pasts of these humbled people, there were cases of bad mothering or absent fathering or emotional neglect—what family surviving the '50s was exempt?—but I couldn't believe these human errors brought the physical changes in Frank.
>
> —Mary Kay Blakely, *Wake Me When It's Over*

Periods and Question Marks

 Write the correct end punctuation for each of the following sentences. Also write the instances where a period is needed as a decimal point or after an initial or abbreviation (as shown in red).

Example: Bill Gates, worth an astounding $46 5 billion, became interested in writing software at age 13

$46.5   13.

1. That was back in 1968—wasn't that before personal computers were even around

2. Gates went to Harvard, but he did not graduate

3. William H Gates III wanted to work at his own company instead

4. Few people question if that was a good decision

5. Gates had a hunch that personal computers would become common in homes and offices

6. The company he founded developed software for these personal computers

7. That company did $36 8 billion in business in 2004

8. Mr Gates and his wife, Melinda, are noted philanthropists

9. Only someone like John D Rockefeller knows how it feels to be as generous as the Gateses with a personal fortune

10. Can you imagine giving away $28 8 billion

11. That is the amount of money the Gateses have given to the Gates Foundation since 2000

 ## Model

Model the following sentences to practice using question marks.

Mara couldn't help but dream (did she really have a chance?) about her eligibility for the competition.

Could it be possible that she was asking, "How can I be a member of this team? What must I do?"

Comma

608.1 Between Two Independent Clauses

Use a **comma** between two independent clauses that are joined by a coordinating conjunction *(and, but, or, nor, for, yet, so)*.

I wanted to knock on the glass to attract attention, but I couldn't move.
—Ralph Ellison, *Invisible Man*

NOTE: Do not confuse a sentence containing a compound verb for a compound sentence.

I had to burn her trash and then sweep up her porches and halls.
—Anne Moody, *Coming of Age in Mississippi*

608.2 To Separate Adjectives

Use commas to separate two or more adjectives that *equally* modify the same noun. (Note: Do not use a comma between the last adjective and the noun.)

Bao's eyes met the hard, bright lights hanging directly above her.
—Julie Ament, student writer

A Closer Look

To determine whether adjectives modify equally—and should, therefore, be separated by commas—use these two tests:

1. Shift the order of the adjectives; if the sentence is clear, the adjectives modify equally. (In the example below, *hot* and *smelly* can be shifted and the sentence is still clear; *usual* and *morning* cannot.)

2. Insert *and* between the adjectives; if the sentence reads well, use a comma when the *and* is omitted. (The word *and* can be inserted between *hot* and *smelly*, but *and* does not make sense between *usual* and *morning*.)

Matty was tired of working in the hot, smelly kitchen and decided to take her usual morning walk.

608.3 To Separate Contrasted Elements

Use commas to separate contrasted elements within a sentence. Often the word or phrase that is set off is preceded by *not*.

Since the stereotypes were about Asians, and not African Americans, no such reaction occurred.
—Emmeline Chen, "Eliminating the Lighter Shades of Stereotyping"

Commas 1

- Between Independent Clauses
- To Separate Adjectives

 Indicate where commas are needed in the following sentences by writing the commas along with the words that surround them (as shown in red).

Example: Walt and Wade are twins but they are not identical.
. . . twins, but . . .

1. Walt is a tall dark-haired man.

2. Wade is the slightly shorter twin and he has long curly hair.

3. Wade enjoys long productive computer sessions or quick video games.

4. Walt enjoys those pursuits, too yet he is also a talented musician.

5. His blue bass guitar is his constant companion so he's always ready to jam.

6. Wade playfully calls his brother's wailing soulful rhythms "the bass-ment."

7. Despite their differences, the friendly intelligent brothers get along well.

8. They go to see the same movies or they hit the beach together.

9. They both plan to go to college but they'll attend different schools.

Model

Model the following sentences to practice using commas between independent clauses and to separate adjectives.

I have caught rattlesnakes with a forked stick and my bare hands, but I'm not ashamed to say I jumped back from that cage.
—Daniel P. Mannix, "A Running Brook of Horror"

It was a small, black-covered book . . . with that ageless look that some books have.
—Robert Sheckley, "Feeding Time"

Punctuation

Comma *(continued)*

610.1 To Set Off Appositives

A specific kind of explanatory word or phrase called an **appositive** identifies or renames a preceding noun or pronoun.

Benson, our uninhibited and enthusiastic Yorkshire terrier, **joined our family on my sister's fifteenth birthday.**

—Chad Hockerman, student writer

NOTE: Do not use commas with *restrictive appositives.* A restrictive appositive is essential to the basic meaning of the sentence.

Sixteen-year-old student Ray Perez **was awarded an athletic scholarship.**

610.2 Between Items in a Series

Use commas to separate individual words, phrases, or clauses in a series. (A series contains at least three items.)

Dad likes meat, vegetables, and a salad **for dinner.** (words)

I took her for walks, read her stories, and made up games for her to play. (phrases)

—Anne Moody, *Coming of Age in Mississippi*

NOTE: Do not use commas when all the words in a series are connected with *or, nor,* or *and.*

Her fingernails are pointed and **manicured** and **painted a shiny red.**

—Carson McCullers, "Sucker"

610.3 After Introductory Phrases and Clauses

Use a comma after an introductory participial phrase.

Determined to finish the sweater by Friday, my grandmother knit night and day.

Use a comma after a long introductory prepositional phrase or after two or more short ones.

In the oddest places and at the strangest times, my grandmother can be found knitting madly away.

NOTE: You may omit the comma if the introductory phrase is short.

Before breakfast my grandmother knits.

Use a comma after an introductory adverb (subordinate) clause.

After the practice was over, Tina walked home.

NOTE: A comma is not used if an adverb clause *follows* the main clause and is needed to complete the meaning of the sentence.

Tina practiced hard because she feared losing.

However, a comma is used if the adverb clause following the main clause begins with *although, even though, while,* or another conjunction expressing a contrast.

Tina walked home, even though it was raining very hard.

Commas 2

- ■ To Set Off Appositives
- ■ Between Items in a Series

 Indicate where commas are needed in the following sentences by writing the commas along with the words that surround them (as shown in red). If no commas are needed, write "none needed."

Example: One of my cousins Pablo got the hiccups the other day and couldn't get rid of them.

One of my cousins, Pablo, . . .

1. The person who holds the world record for hiccups Charles Osborne had them for 68 years—from 1922 to 1990.

2. Hiccups are the result of an involuntary contraction of the diaphragm a large, convex muscle located underneath the lungs.

3. The diaphragm becomes irritated from eating or drinking too much swallowing too much air or feeling nervous.

4. The muscle contracts, causing a sudden gulp of air.

5. The glottis the opening of the air passage closes quickly, and this is what makes the "hic" sound.

6. Although scientists know *how* hiccups come about, they don't know why; hiccups serve no known function.

7. Hiccups can last a few minutes several hours or (as mentioned) many years.

Model

Model the following sentences to practice using commas between items in a series and to set off appositives.

> More and more Americans are appalled by the ravages of industrial progress, by the defacement of nature, by man-made ugliness.
>
> —John William Gardner, *No Easy Victories*

> Months before he had lost his heart to young Elise, the blue-eyed, yellow-haired daughter of the lecturer.
>
> —Arthur Conan Doyle, "The Great Keinplatz Experiment"

Comma *(continued)*

612.1 To Enclose Parenthetical Elements

Use commas to separate parenthetical elements, such as an explanatory word or phrase, within a sentence.

> **They stood together,** away from the pile of stones in the corner, **and their jokes were quiet, and they smiled rather than laughed.**
>
> —Shirley Jackson, "The Lottery"
>
> **Allison meandered into class,** late as usual, **and sat down.**

612.2 To Set Off Nonrestrictive Phrases and Clauses

Use commas to set off **nonrestrictive** (unnecessary) clauses and participial phrases. A nonrestrictive clause or participial phrase adds information that is not necessary to the basic meaning of the sentence. For example, if the clause or phrase (in red) were left out in the two examples below, the meaning of the sentences would remain clear. Therefore, commas are used to set them off.

> **The Altena Fitness Center and Visker Gymnasium,** which were built last year, **are busy every day.** (nonrestrictive clause)
>
> **Students and faculty,** improving their health through exercise, **use both facilities throughout the week.** (nonrestrictive phrase)

Do not use commas to set off a **restrictive** (necessary) clause or participial phrase, which helps to define a noun or pronoun. It adds information that the reader needs to know in order to understand the sentence. For example, if the clause and phrase (in red) were dropped from the examples below, the meaning wouldn't be the same. Therefore, commas are *not* used.

> **The handball court** that has a sign-up sheet by the door **must be reserved.**
> The clause identifies which handball court must be reserved.
> (restrictive clause)
>
> **Individuals** wanting to use this court **must sign up a day in advance.**
> (restrictive phrase)

A Closer Look: *That* and *Which*

Use *that* to introduce restrictive (necessary) clauses; use *which* to introduce nonrestrictive (unnecessary) clauses. When the two words are used in this way, the reader can quickly distinguish necessary and unnecessary information.

> The treadmill that monitors heart rate is the one you must use.
> (The reader needs the information to find the right treadmill.)
>
> This treadmill, which we got last year, is required for your program.
> (The main clause tells the reader which treadmill to use; the other clause gives additional, unnecessary information.)

Commas 3

- To Enclose Parenthetical Elements
- To Set Off Nonrestrictive Phrases and Clauses

 Indicate where commas are needed in the following sentences by writing the commas along with the words that surround them (as shown in red).

Example: My mom who is really into her exercise program is always trying to get me off the couch.

... mom, who is really into her exercise program, is ...

1. She claims that aerobic exercise which gets oxygen to the brain would help me get better grades.

2. Mom feeling she is right about this usually manages to get me moving.

3. Yesterday I walked fast around our block the kind lined with nice shade trees exactly eight times.

4. That was a long hike which was just what I needed.

5. Back home I popped in a DVD one I'd seen already and made some microwave popcorn.

6. Mom having heard about a test I had the next day came in to talk.

7. Soon we were both eating popcorn while she quizzed me on my history notes which is probably why I got a B on the test today.

Model

Model the following sentences to practice using commas to enclose parenthetical elements and to set off nonrestrictive phrases.

It was growing dark before, drunk with sun and air, we all stumbled sleepily back to the houses.

—Frances Fowler, "The Day We Flew the Kites"

Farther down, in the land of the Crows and Blackfeet, the plain is yellow.

—M. Scott Momaday, "A Kiowa Grandmother"

Comma *(continued)*

614.1 To Set Off Dates

Use commas to set off items in a date.

On September 30, 1997, my little sister entered our lives.

He began working out on December 1, 2005, but quit by May 1, 2006.

However, when only the month and year are given, no commas are needed.

He began working out in December 2005 but quit by May 2006.

When a full date appears in the middle of a sentence, a comma follows the year.

On June 7, 1924, my great-grandfather met his future wife.

614.2 To Set Off Items in Addresses

Use commas to set off items in an address. (No comma is placed between the state and ZIP code.)

Mail the box to Friends of Wildlife, Box 402, Spokane, Washington 20077.

When a city and state (or country) appear in the middle of a sentence, a comma follows the last item in the address.

Several charitable organizations in Juneau, Alaska, pool their funds.

614.3 In Numbers

Use commas to separate numerals in large numbers in order to distinguish hundreds, thousands, millions, and so forth.

1,101   25,000   7,642,020

614.4 To Enclose Titles or Initials

Use commas to enclose a title or initials and names that follow a surname (a last name).

Letitia O'Reilly, M.D., is our family physician.

Hickok, J. B., and Cody, William F., are two popular Western heroes.

Commas 4

- To Set Off Dates
- To Set Off Items in Addresses
- In Numbers

 Indicate where commas are needed in the following sentences by writing the commas along with the words that surround them (as shown in red).

Example: Here are some facts about Washington D.C. the capital of the United States.

. . . Washington, D.C., the . . .

1. On July 16 1790 Congress made it possible for George Washington to select our capital's present location.

2. It rests on the banks of the Potomac River, 35 miles southwest of Baltimore Maryland.

3. While the site was being prepared, Philadelphia Pennsylvania served as the temporary capital from 1790 to 1800.

4. Finally, Congress convened for the first time in the new capital on November 21 1800.

5. The transfer of the government from Philadelphia to Washington D.C. wasn't finished until June 1801.

6. Presently, the population of the capital city is 572059 (302693 female and 269366 male).

7. You can write to the City Museum of Washington D.C. 801 K Street Mount Vernon Square Washington D.C. 20001 for more information.

 ## Model

Model the following sentences to practice using commas in dates, addresses, and numbers.

My best friend, who was born on August 31, 1993, lives at 2745 Market Place Drive, Phoenix, Arizona 85062.

If I lived in Chicago, Illinois, and wanted to visit Seattle, Washington, I would have to travel 2,052 miles.

Comma *(continued)*

616.1 To Set Off Dialogue

Use commas to set off the speaker's exact words from the rest of the sentence. (It may be helpful to remember that the comma is always to the left of the quotation mark.)

"It's like we have our own government," **adds Tanya, a 17-year-old squatter.**

—Kyung Sun Yu and Nell Bernstein, "Street Teens Forge a Home"

616.2 To Set Off Interjections

Use a comma to separate an interjection or a weak exclamation from the rest of the sentence.

Hey, **how am I to know that a minute's passed?**

—Nathan Slaughter and Jim Schweitzer, *When Time Dies*

616.3 To Set Off Interruptions

Use commas to set off a word, a phrase, or a clause that interrupts the movement of a sentence. Such expressions usually can be identified through the following tests: (1) They may be omitted without changing the meaning of a sentence. (2) They may be placed nearly anywhere in the sentence without changing its meaning.

For me, well, it's just a good job gone!

—Langston Hughes

The safest way to cross this street, as a general rule, is with the light.

616.4 In Direct Address

Use commas to separate a noun of direct address from the rest of the sentence. A *noun of direct address* is the noun that names the person(s) spoken to.

"You wouldn't understand yet, son, but your daddy's gonna make a transaction. . . . "

—Lorraine Hansberry, *A Raisin in the Sun*

616.5 For Clarity or Emphasis

You may use a comma for clarity or for emphasis. There will be times when none of the traditional rules call for a comma, but one will be needed to prevent confusion or to emphasize an important idea.

It may be that those who do most, dream most. (emphasis)

—Stephen Leacock

What the crew does, does affect our voyage. (clarity)

Commas 5

- ■ To Set Off Dialogue
- ■ To Set Off Interruptions

 Indicate where commas are needed in the following sentences by writing the commas along with the words that surround them (as shown in red).

Example: Wolves as you may be aware completely disappeared from Yellowstone National Park by the 1970s.

Wolves, as you may be aware, completely . . .

1. These animals are very efficient predators, and this not surprisingly has given the wolf a bad name.

2. "As a child, I remember singing a song about the big bad wolf" says my grandpa.

3. Cruel eradication programs were in reality the cause of the wolf's decline.

4. During the past century as a matter of fact "humans . . . killed an estimated two million wolves" says CNN reporter Jack Hamann.

5. A 1995 wolf reintroduction program however has been successful in Yellowstone, even though it is controversial.

6. Ranchers for example worry about wolves wandering off parkland to prey on livestock.

7. I hope that, with education and cooperation, no one will again say "The only good wolf is a dead wolf."

Model

Model the following sentences to practice using commas to set off dialogue and interruptions.

"My son will go to school," he said, and the neighbors were hushed.

—John Steinbeck, *The Pearl*

The room, to tell the truth, was a barren, cold place with dirty walls.

Semicolon

618.1 To Join Two Independent Clauses

Use a **semicolon** to join two or more closely related independent clauses that are not connected with a coordinating conjunction. (Independent clauses can stand alone as separate sentences.)

I did not call myself a poet; I told people I wrote poems.

> —Terry McMillan, "Breaking Ice"

Silence coated the room like a layer of tar; not even the breathing of the 11 Gehad made any sound.

> —Gann Bierner, "The Leap"

NOTE: When independent clauses are especially long or contain commas, a semicolon may punctuate the sentence, even though a coordinating conjunction connects the clauses.

We waited all day in that wide line, tired travelers pressing in from all sides; and when we needed drinks or sandwiches, I would squeeze my way to the cafeteria and back.

618.2 With Conjunctive Adverbs

A semicolon is used *before* a conjunctive adverb (with a comma after it) when the word connects two independent clauses in a compound sentence. (Common conjunctive adverbs are *also, besides, finally, however, indeed, instead, meanwhile, moreover, nevertheless, next, still, then, therefore,* and *thus.*)

"I am faced with my imminent demise; therefore, life becomes a very precious thing."

> — Amy Taylor, "AIDS Can Happen Here!"

618.3 To Separate Groups That Contain Commas

A semicolon is used to separate groups of words that already contain commas.

Every Saturday night my little brother gathers up his things—goggles, shower cap, and snorkel; bubble bath, soap, and shampoo; tapes, stereo, and rubber duck—and heads for the tub.

Semicolons

■ **To Join Two Independent Clauses**

 Indicate where a semicolon is needed in the following sentences by writing the semicolon along with the words that surround it (as shown in red).

Example: Aliens from outer space are still a popular subject movies like *Independence Day, Signs*, and *Men in Black* attest to that.

. . . subject; movies . . .

1. Recently, the imagined aliens are unfriendly indeed, they are the "let's-take-over-the-earth" variety.

2. Long ago, people were crazy about the movie *Close Encounters of the Third Kind* however, this movie's aliens were a more friendly type.

3. You wanted to meet these guys you wanted to take a ride in their brightly lit, saucer-shaped spacecraft!

4. Their spaceship was gargantuan it dwarfed the Devils Tower National Monument in Wyoming!

5. Area 51, a military facility north of Las Vegas, is shrouded in secrecy at the center of this 60-square-mile plot of land, a site once used to test the U-2 spy plane, is an air base the government will not discuss.

6. Many unidentified flying object (UFO) stories are connected with this place Area 51 has become the symbol for the government's alleged UFO cover-up.

7. Whatever you choose to believe about aliens, they remain an interesting topic plenty of stories are yet to be told.

 ## Model

Model the following sentences to practice using semicolons to join two independent clauses.

No one dared touch the bowls of steaming food; instead, they sat quietly, waiting to be invited.

—Lois Krenzke, "The Long Table"

The small fox trembled a moment; it had heard something, a warning.

Colon

620.1 After a Salutation

Use a **colon** after the salutation of a business letter.

Dear Judge Parker: **Dear Governor Whitman:**

620.2 Between Numerals Indicating Time

Use a colon between the hours, minutes, and seconds of a number indicating time.

8:30 p.m.   **9:45 a.m.**   **10:24:55**

620.3 For Emphasis

Use a colon to emphasize a word, a phrase, a clause, or a sentence that explains or adds impact to the main clause (also see **650.3**).

> **His guest lecturers are local chefs who learn a lesson themselves: Homeless people are worth employing.**
> —Beth Brophy, "Feeding Those Who Are Hungry"

620.4 To Introduce a Quotation

Use a colon to formally introduce a quotation, a sentence, or a question.

> **Directly a voice in the corner rang out wild and clear: "I've got him! I've got him!"**
> —Mark Twain, *Roughing It*

620.5 To Introduce a List

A colon is used to introduce a list.

> **I got all the proper equipment: scissors, a bucket of water to keep things clean, some cotton for the stuffing, and needle and thread to sew it up.**
> —Joan Baez, *Daybreak*

A Closer Look

Do not use a colon between a verb and its object or complement, or between a preposition and its object.

> **Incorrect:** Min has: a snowmobile, an ATV, and a canoe.
> **Correct:** Min has plenty of toys: a snowmobile, an ATV, and a canoe.
> **Incorrect:** I watch a TV show about: cooking wild game.
> **Correct:** I watch a TV show about a new subject: cooking wild game.

620.6 Between a Title and a Subtitle

Use a colon to distinguish between a title and a subtitle, volume and page, and chapter and verse in literature.

Encyclopedia Americana IV: 211   Psalm 23:1–6

Colons

- For Emphasis
- To Introduce a List

 Indicate where a colon is needed in the following sentences by writing the colon along with the words that surround it (as shown in red).

Example: Hawaii is a beautiful tropical paradise in my grandmother's mind a place she has only dreamed of visiting.

... mind: a place ...

1. Grandmother remembers the exact day that Hawaii became the 50th state in the Union August 21, 1959.

2. The Aloha State is composed of many islands, seven of which are inhabited Niihau, Kauai, Oahu, Molokai, Lanai, Maui, and Hawaii.

3. Niihau has been privately owned since 1864 and has an interesting nickname the Forbidden Island.

4. The owners are determined to preserve the traditional ways of life on Niihau, including their native language Hawaiian.

5. The 200 residents of the island still hunt and fish with traditional tools ropes, knives, spears, and nets.

6. Because this is an arid, flowerless island, residents make leis of another material tiny seashells.

7. Tourists can visit this paradise for half-day tours, reaching the island in a classy helicopter the Agusta 109A.

8. While there, they can spend a few hours at one of the pristine beaches, doing what Hawaiian vacations are famous for swimming, snorkeling, and just plain relaxing.

 ## Model

Model the following sentences to practice using colons for emphasis and to introduce a list.

Tilly received a surprise birthday gift: a round-trip ticket to Hawaii! She's busy packing the essentials: sunscreen, bathing suits, sandals, straw hats, a camera, film—and more sunscreen.

Test Prep

Read the following paragraphs. From the choices given on the next page, write the letter of the correct way to punctuate each underlined part. If it is already correct, choose "D."

What does the future <u>hold.</u> If you were asked this question in the mid-
1
twentieth <u>century here's</u> what you may have <u>envisioned,</u> flying automobiles,
2 **3**
space travel to distant planets, and lifelike robots acting as servants. Movies
and books of that era are fascinating to look at now.

The 1930 movie *Just Imagine* depicted the future of 1980. People had
numbers rather than <u>names and</u> the government arranged all marriages.
4
Several movies from the 1970s and 1980s depicted a future world run by
computers. The *Mad Max* series of <u>movies on the other hand</u> showed a <u>bleak</u>
5 **6**
<u>orderless</u> future. Fortunately, none of these ideas has come to pass . . . yet.

Unfortunately, some predictions have come true. Two of Aldous
Huxley's <u>books *Brave New World*</u> and <u>*Ape and Essence,* which</u> were
7 **8**
published in the 1930s and 1940s, described many of the social problems
we see <u>today; terrorism,</u> overpopulation, the loss of natural <u>resources and</u>
9 **10**
widespread drug use. In movies, destruction caused by huge bombs was
depicted before the nuclear age was a reality.

On the brighter side, movies and books that dreamed of "picture
phones" have of course, become a dream come true. (These dreams didn't
go far <u>enough, indeed,</u> no one saw the Internet coming!) And while human
11
travel to distant planets hasn't <u>evolved scientists</u> have been able to explore
12
beyond our galaxy with the help of a kind of robot.

No one knows what tomorrow has in store for <u>us, but</u> based on
13

technologies in development <u>today we</u> can make educated guesses. Many
                            14
predict a cashless <u>future, all</u> financial transactions will take place
                    15
electronically. Some see cures for <u>AIDS cancer,</u> and the common cold. And
                                    16
a few envision molecular transport, as in *Star Trek*. Whatever we predict,

people of the future will either laugh—or be in awe of our insight.

1. A hold!
  B hold?
  C hold,
  D correct as is

2. A century, here's
  B century. Here's
  C century; here's
  D correct as is

3. A envisioned.
  B envisioned;
  C envisioned:
  D correct as is

4. A names and,
  B names: and
  C names, and
  D correct as is

5. A movies, on the other hand,
  B movies, on the other hand
  C movies on the other hand,
  D correct as is

6. A bleak orderless,
  B bleak, orderless
  C bleak; orderless
  D correct as is

7. A books *Brave New World,*
  B books *Brave, New World*
  C books, *Brave New World*
  D correct as is

8. A *Ape and Essence* which
  B *Ape and Essence* which,
  C *Ape, and Essence* which
  D correct as is

9. A today: terrorism
  B today: terrorism,
  C today terrorism
  D correct as is

10. A resources, and
  B resources and,
  C resources, and,
  D correct as is

11. A enough indeed;
  B enough, indeed;
  C enough; indeed,
  D correct as is

12. A evolved scientists,
  B evolved; scientists
  C evolved, scientists
  D correct as is

13. A us but
  B us but,
  C us. but
  D correct as is

14. A today, we
  B today; we
  C today we,
  D correct as is

15. A future all
  B future; all
  C future all,
  D correct as is

16. A AIDS cancer
  B AIDS, cancer
  C AIDS, cancer,
  D correct as is

Hyphen

624.1 In Compound Words

Use the **hyphen** to make some compound words.

great-great-grandfather   maid-in-waiting   three-year-old

624.2 To Create New Words

Use a hyphen to form new words beginning with the prefixes *self-, ex-, all-,* and *half-*. Also use a hyphen to join any prefix to a proper noun, a proper adjective, or the official name of an office. Use a hyphen before the suffix *-elect*.

self-**contained**   ex-**governor**   all-**inclusive**   half-**painted**
pre-**Cambrian**   mid-**December**   **president**-elect

Use a hyphen to join the prefix *great-* only to the names of relatives.

great-**aunt,** great-**grandfather** (correct)   **great-hall** (incorrect)

624.3 To Form an Adjective

Use a hyphen to join two or more words that serve as a single adjective (a single-thought adjective) before a noun.

In real life I am a large, big-boned **woman with rough,** man-working **hands.**
                                        —Alice Walker, "Everyday Use"

Use common sense to determine whether a compound adjective might be misread if it is not hyphenated. Generally, hyphenate a compound adjective that is composed of . . .

- a phrase   heat-and-serve **meal**   off-and-on **relationship**
- a noun + adjective   oven-safe **handles**   book-smart **student**
- a noun + participle (*ing* or *ed* form of a verb)   bone-chilling **story**

A Closer Look

When words forming the adjective come after the noun, do not hyphenate them.

In real life I am large and big boned.

When the first of these words is an adverb ending in *-ly,* do not use a hyphen.

delicately prepared **pastry**

Also, do not use a hyphen when a number or a letter is the final element in a single-thought adjective.

class B **movie**

624.4 To Join Letters and Words

Use a hyphen to join a capital letter or lowercase letter to a noun or participle. (Check your dictionary if you're not sure of the hyphenation.)

T-**shirt**   Y-**turn**   G-**rated**   x-**axis**

Punctuation

Hyphens 1

- To Create New Words
- To Form an Adjective

 For each sentence below, write the words that should be hyphenated (as shown in red). Some sentences contain two hyphenated words.

Example: Every spring, Nebraska's Platte River welcomes thousands upon thousands of long necked sandhill cranes to its banks.
long-necked

1. Many birders come to see the cranes and enjoy the three day Rivers and Wildlife Celebration held each March.

2. Long ago there were many wetlands along the Platte that offered nutrient rich worms, snails, and frogs to the migrating birds.

3. Because of water diversion projects, the Platte River is not the lush roosting place it once was.

4. In the 1970s, the National Audubon Society purchased a 1,248 acre sanctuary along an 80 mile stretch of the Platte to help the cranes and other wildlife.

5. Although dried up wetlands imposed food source changes on the cranes, they have proved to be adaptable creatures.

6. Cranes search cow pies for half digested corn or newly hatched grubs; they also feast on machine harvested corn left behind in the fields.

7. The sandhill cranes and other birds still look to the Platte as a fattening up stopover on their way to northern nesting grounds.

 ## Model

Model the following sentences to practice using hyphens to create new words and to form adjectives.

By mid-June the self-assured little boy had earned fifty dollars doing errands for the neighbors.

That is what the two Helens and I were talking about the day we had lunch in a room up in a high-rise motel near the Kansas City airport. We had lunch there at the end of a two-day conference on families.
—Jane Howard, "All Happy Clans Are Alike"

Hyphen *(continued)*

626.1 **Between Numbers and Fractions**

Use a hyphen to join the words in compound numbers from *twenty-one* to *ninety-nine* when it is necessary to write them out (see **658.3**).

Use a hyphen between the numerator and denominator of a fraction, but not when one or both of those elements are already hyphenated.

    four-tenths   **five-sixteenths**   **(7/32) seven thirty-seconds**

626.2 **In a Special Series**

Use hyphens when two or more words have a common element that is omitted in all but the last term.

    The ship has lovely two-, four-, or six-person cabins.

626.3 **To Join Numbers**

Use a hyphen to join numbers indicating the life span of a person or the score in a contest or a vote.

    We can thank Louis Pasteur (1822–1895) for pasteurized milk.

    In the 2000 Rose Bowl, Wisconsin defeated Stanford 17–9.

626.4 **To Prevent Confusion**

Use a hyphen with prefixes or suffixes to avoid confusion or awkward spelling.

    re-create (not *recreate*) the image   **re-cover (not *recover*) the sofa**

626.5 **To Divide a Word**

Use a hyphen to divide a word, only between its syllables, at the end of a line of print. Always place the hyphen after the syllable at the end of the line—never before a syllable at the beginning of the following line.

Guidelines for Dividing with Hyphens

1. Always divide a compound word between its basic units: **sister-in-law**, not **sis-ter-in-law.**

2. Avoid dividing a word of five or fewer letters: **paper, study, July.**

3. Avoid dividing the last word in a paragraph.

4. Never divide a one-syllable word: **rained, skills, through.**

5. Never divide a one-letter syllable from the rest of the word: **omit-ted**, not **o-mitted.**

6. When a vowel is a syllable by itself, divide the word after the vowel: **epi-sode**, not **ep-isode.**

7. Never divide abbreviations or contractions: **shouldn't**, not **should-n't.**

8. Never divide the last word in more than two lines in a row.

Hyphens 2

- Between Numbers and Fractions
- To Join Numbers

 For each sentence below, write the numerals or words that should be hyphenated (as shown in red). You may use more than one hyphen in some sentences.

Example: Wolfgang Amadeus Mozart (1756 1791) wrote his first compositions at age four.
(1756–1791)

1. Mozart's father took Wolfgang on an extended tour of Italy (1769 1773).

2. A mule is genetically one half horse and one half donkey.

3. Being sure-footed, a mule can serve as a good pack animal for 20 30 years of its life.

4. A four fifths majority vote in the Senate would settle the matter once and for all.

5. "Ninety nine out of a hundred people use this brand," bragged the salesperson.

6. A late fourth-quarter score of 112 110 kept the fans on their feet.

7. Forty eight of our classmates rode the school bus to the state championship game, and thirty two rode in private cars.

8. Fran Tarkenton completed 3,686 passes during his 1961 1978 professional football career.

9. Although he might have expected it, my uncle's college career (1968 1972) was not interrupted by a tour of duty in Vietnam.

Model

Model the following sentences to practice using hyphens between numbers and to join numbers.

> Twenty-one other children went to school with him in first grade; in twelfth grade, ninety-five.
> Yemen's coastal plain is 20-50 miles wide (32-80 kilometers).

Apostrophe

628.1 In Contractions

Use an **apostrophe** to show that one or more letters have been left out of a word group to form a contraction.

> hadn't – *o* **is left out**   they'd – *woul* **is left out**   it's – *i* **is left out**

NOTE: Use an apostrophe to show that one or more numerals or letters have been left out of numbers or words in order to show special pronunciation.

> class of '99 – *19* **is left out**   g'day – *ood* **is left out**

628.2 To Form Singular Possessives

Add an apostrophe and *s* to form the possessive of most singular nouns.

> Spock's **ears**   Captain Kirk's **singing**   **the** ship's **escape plan**

NOTE: When a singular noun ends with an *s* or a *z* sound, you may form the possessive by adding just an apostrophe. When the singular noun is a one-syllable word, however, you usually add both an apostrophe and an *s* to form the possessive.

> San Carlos' **government** (or) San Carlos's **government** (two-syllable word)
>
> Ross's **essay** (one-syllable word)   **The** class's **field trip** (one-syllable word)

628.3 To Form Plural Possessives

The possessive form of plural nouns ending in *s* is usually made by adding just an apostrophe.

> students' **homework**   bosses' **orders**

For plural nouns not ending in *s,* an apostrophe and *s* must be added.

> children's **book**   men's **department**

A Closer Look

It will help you punctuate correctly if you remember that the word immediately before the apostrophe is the owner.

> girl's **guitar** (*girl* **is the owner**)   boss's **order** (*boss* **is the owner**)
> girls' **guitar** (*girls* **are the owners**)   bosses' **order** (*bosses* **are the owners**)

628.4 To Show Shared Possession

When possession is shared by more than one noun, use the possessive form for the last noun in the series.

> Hoshi, Linda, and Nakiva's **water skis** (All three own the same skis.)
>
> Hoshi's, Linda's, and Nakiva's **water skis** (Each owns her own skis.)

Apostrophes 1

- ■ **In Contractions**
- ■ **To Form Singular Possessives**

 Write the word or words from the following sentences that need apostrophes.

Example: Central Americas seven countries include Nicaragua, Guatemala, El Salvador, Panama, Honduras, Costa Rica, and Belize.
Central America's

1. Its basically an isthmus connecting North and South America.

2. Guatemalas Sierra Madre mountain range has more than 30 volcanoes.

3. Most of the regions volcanoes arent active, but some are.

4. Panamas canal provides ships a means to go quickly from the Atlantic to the Pacific Ocean.

5. Along with Belize and Costa Rica, Honduras popularity as a tourist destination is growing.

6. The countrys ancient ruins, beaches, rain forests, and mountains attract foreigners.

7. Native Hondurans dont mind the influx of tourist dollars.

8. Belize wasnt independent until 1993; before that, it was known as British Honduras.

9. Belizes coral reefs offer superior scuba diving.

Model

Model the following sentence to practice using an apostrophe in contractions and to show special pronunciation. Note that this use is often employed in dialogue.

"Why not 'fess up, Jimmy? Confession's good for the soul, they say."

—Stephen King, "The Little Sisters of Eluria"

Apostrophe *(continued)*

630.1 To Show Possession with Indefinite Pronouns

Form the possessive of an indefinite pronoun by placing an apostrophe and an *s* on the last word (see **704.1** and **706.3**).

everyone's   **anyone's**   **somebody's**

630.2 To Show Possession in Compound Nouns

Form the possessive of a compound noun by placing the possessive ending after the last word.

the secretary of the interior's (singular) **agenda**
her lady-in-waiting's (singular) **day off**

If forming a possessive of a plural compound noun creates an awkward construction, you may replace the possessive with an *of* phrase. (All four forms below are correct.)

their fathers-in-law's (plural) **birthdays**
or **the birthdays of their fathers-in-law** (plural)
the ambassadors-at-large's (plural) **plans**
or **the plans of the ambassadors-at-large** (plural)

630.3 To Express Time or Amount

Use an apostrophe and an *s* with an adjective that is part of an expression indicating time or amount.

a penny's worth   **today's business**   **this morning's meeting**
yesterday's news   **a day's wage**   **a month's pay**

630.4 To Form Certain Plurals

Use an apostrophe and *s* to form the plural of a letter, a number, a sign, or a word discussed as a word.

B – B's   **C** – C's   **8** – 8's   **+** – +'s   *and* – *and*'s

Ms. D'Aquisto says our conversations contain too many *like's* **and** *no way's***.**

NOTE: If two apostrophes are called for in the same word, omit the second one.

Follow closely the *do's* **and** *don'ts* **(not** *don't's***) on the checklist.**

Punctuation

Apostrophes 2

- ■ **To Show Possession with Indefinite Pronouns**
- ■ **To Show Possession with Compound Nouns**

 Write the possessive form of the underlined words in the following sentences.

Example: The <u>middle class</u> aspirations are sometimes hindered by its members' collective debt.
middle class's

1. "I presume that this is <u>nobody</u> paper airplane," the teacher remarked.

2. The look on the <u>passerby</u> face was one of despair.

3. It is best that <u>one</u> thoughts converge prior to action.

4. Crystal borrowed her <u>brother-in-law</u> power drill.

5. Do not look at <u>one another</u> papers.

6. Not everyone accepts the <u>president-elect</u> agenda for the country.

7. <u>Everybody</u> opinion is valued in my ethics class.

8. The <u>post office</u> heavy glass doors are difficult to open.

9. My <u>half sister</u> mother lives in Ontario.

10. Is this <u>someone</u> towel?

11. The <u>nine-year-old</u> ability to play the piano was astounding.

Model

Model the following sentence to practice using an apostrophe to show possession with indefinite pronouns.

There is no greater joy nor greater reward than to make a fundamental difference in someone's life.

—Sister Mary Rose McGeady

Quotation Marks

632.1 To Set Off Direct Quotations

Place **quotation marks** before and after the words in direct quotations.

"Just come to a game," he pleads. "You'll change your mind."
—Sandra Lampe, "Batter UP!"

In a quoted passage, put brackets around any word or punctuation mark that is not part of the original quotation. (See **644.3**.)

If you quote only part of the original passage, be sure to construct a sentence that is both accurate and grammatically correct.

Much of the restructuring of the Postal Service has involved "turning over large parts of its work to the private sector."

632.2 Placement of Punctuation

Always place periods and commas inside quotation marks.

"Dr. Slaughter wants you to have liquids, Will," Mama said anxiously. "He said not to give you any solid food tonight."
—Olive Ann Burns, *Cold Sassy Tree*

Place an exclamation point or a question mark *inside* quotation marks when it punctuates the quotation and *outside* when it punctuates the main sentence.

"Am I dreaming?"   **Had she heard him say, "Here's the key to your new car"?**

Always place semicolons or colons outside quotation marks.

I wrote about James Joyce's "The Dead"; I found it thought provoking.

632.3 For Long Quotations

If you quote more than one paragraph, place quotation marks before each paragraph and at the end of the last paragraph (Example A). If a quotation has more than four lines on a page, you may set it off from the text by indenting 10 spaces from the left margin (block form). Do not use quotation marks either before or after the quoted material, unless they appear in the original (Example B).

Example A

Example B

Quotation Marks 1

- **To Set Off Direct Quotations**
- **Placement of Punctuation**

 Write the following dialogue, placing quotation marks correctly.

Example: Hey, what's up? asked Raheema.
"Hey, what's up?" asked Raheema.

I'm trying to plan my class schedule for next year, Steve answered.

Are you going to take a foreign language? she asked.

I don't know, said Steve. There are a lot of other courses I want to take, like drama.

Yeah, me, too. Well, I'm going to take Chinese, Raheema said, rising from her seat.

Did Steve hear her right? Did he really hear her say, I'm going to take Chinese?

What did you say? he asked.

I said, Raheema answered, I'm going to get some take-out Chinese. Do you want any?

 ## Model

Write a sentence that quotes part of this passage. Use quotation marks correctly.

When I first signed with the Chicago Bulls in 1984, the NBA's Uniform Player's Contract included a clause that prohibited players from certain activities during the off-season, including playing the game.

—Michael Jordan, *For the Love of the Game*

Quotation Marks *(continued)*

634.1 **Quotation Marks Within Quotations**

Use single quotation marks to punctuate a quotation within a quotation. Use double quotation marks in order to distinguish a quotation within a quotation within a quotation.

> **"For tomorrow," said Mr. Botts, "read 'Unlighted Lamps.'"**
>
> **Sue asked, "Did you hear Mr. Botts say, 'Read "Unlighted Lamps"'?"**

634.2 **For Special Words**

You may use quotation marks (1) to distinguish a word that is being discussed, (2) to indicate that a word is unfamiliar slang, or (3) to point out that a word is being used in a special way.

> **(1) A commentary on the times is that the word** "honesty" **is now preceded by** "old-fashioned."
>
> —Larry Wolters
>
> **(2) I . . . asked the bartender where I could hear** "chanky-chank," **as Cajuns called their music.**
>
> —William Least Heat-Moon, *Blue Highways*
>
> **(3) Tom pushed the wheelchair across the street, showed the lady his** "honest" **smile . . . and stole her purse.**

NOTE: You may use italics (underlining) in place of quotation marks in each of these three situations. (See **636.3.**)

634.3 **To Punctuate Titles**

Use **quotation marks** to punctuate titles of songs, poems, short stories, one-act plays, lectures, episodes of radio or television programs, chapters of books, unpublished works, electronic files, and articles found in magazines, newspapers, encyclopedias, or online sources. (For punctuation of other titles, see **636.2.**)

> "Santa Lucia" (song)
>
> "The Chameleon" (short story)
>
> "Twentieth-Century Memories" (lecture)
>
> "Affordable Adventures" (magazine article)
>
> "Dire Prophecy of the Howling Dog" (chapter in a book)
>
> "Dancing with Debra" (television episode)
>
> "Miss Julie" (one-act play)

NOTE: You do not need to use quotation marks in the titles of your own writing.

Quotation Marks 2

- Quotation Marks Within Quotations
- For Special Words
- To Punctuate Titles

 Write the word or words that should be enclosed in quotation marks in the following sentences.

Example: Marina and Dale moved to the dance floor when the deejay played Can't Get You Outta My Head as the last song.
"Can't Get You Outta My Head"

1. Dale shuffled his feet a bit and swung his arms slightly; he called this dancing.

2. "You should find the article Time Management for Students on the school Web site," the advisor said.

3. Ms. Poland got quite a variety of answers when she asked us to define the word morality.

4. Kenny explained, "When I asked him about my application, he said, Come on in, and we'll talk it over."

5. "I just finished reading a clever little story by Isaac Asimov, A Loint of Paw, and it really got me thinking," said Grant.

 ## Model

Model the following sentence to practice using quotation marks within quotations.

"This song has invaded my brain, and I don't even know the name of it," Lee said. "Maybe 'Bear It' or 'Dare It' or something like that—it's driving me nuts."

—Claire Ziffer, "Just Instinct"

Italics (Underlining)

636.1 Handwritten and Printed Material

Italics is a printer's term for a style of type that is slightly slanted. In this sentence, the word *happiness* is printed in italics. In material that is handwritten or typed on a machine that cannot print in italics, underline each word or letter that should be in italics.

> **My Ántonia is the story of a strong and determined pioneer woman.**
> (printed)
> **Willa Cather's My Ántonia describes pioneer life in America.**
> (typed or handwritten)

636.2 In Titles

Use italics to indicate the titles of magazines, newspapers, pamphlets, books, full-length plays, films, videos, radio and television programs, book-length poems, ballets, operas, paintings, lengthy musical compositions, sculptures, cassettes, CD's, legal cases, and the names of ships and aircraft. (For punctuation of other titles, see **634.3**.)

> *Newsweek* (magazine)   *Cold Sassy Tree* (book)
> *Shakespeare in Love* (film)   *Law & Order* (television program)
> *Caring for Your Kitten* (pamphlet)   *Hedda Gabler* (full-length play)
> *Chicago Tribune* (newspaper)   *The Thinker* (sculpture)

NOTE: Punctuate one title within another title as follows:

> **"Clarkson's 'Breakaway' Hits the Waves"**
> (title of a song in title of an article)

636.3 For Special Uses

Use italics for a number, letter, or word that is being discussed or used in a special way. (Sometimes quotation marks are used for this reason. See **634.2**.)

> **I hope that this letter *I* on my report card stands for *incredible* and not *incomplete*.**

636.4 For Foreign Words

Use italics for foreign words that have not been adopted into the English language; also use italics for scientific names.

> **The voyageurs—tough men with natural *bonhomie*—discovered the shy *Castor canadensis*, or North American beaver.**

Italics (Underlining)

- **In Titles**
- **For Special Uses**
- **For Foreign Words**

 Write and underline the word or words that should be italicized in the following sentences.

Example: There is a certain je ne sais quoi about the new restaurant; it's become quite popular.

je ne sais quoi

1. A large number 9 is the only image on the restaurant's sign.

2. A positive review appeared in the magazine Out and About.

3. Grandpa's directions read, "When you hit the fork in the road (where it splits like the letter Y), follow it left."

4. Chester's singing on Linkin Park's Collision Course CD is awesome.

5. Helenium autumnale, also known as the common sneezeweed, is a member of the aster family.

6. When did the word bad start to mean its opposite?

7. Reality shows such as American Idol cost television networks less than other types of shows.

8. In the United States, the highest-grossing film of 2004 was Shrek 2.

9. The 1954 legal case Brown v. Board of Education, by a unanimous Supreme Court decision, mandated integration in all public schools.

 ## Model

Model the following sentence to practice using italics (underlining) for special uses.

    I do not evolve; I *am*.

                           —Pablo Picasso, *The Art*

Parentheses

638.1 To Set Off Explanatory Material

You may use **parentheses** to set off explanatory or added material that interrupts the normal sentence structure.

Benson (our dog) sits in on our piano lessons (on the piano bench), much to the teacher's surprise and amusement.

—Chad Hockerman, student writer

NOTE: Place question marks and exclamation points within the parentheses when they mark the added material.

Ivan at once concluded (the rascal!) that I had a passion for dances, and . . . wanted to drag me off to a dancing class.

—Fyodor Dostoyevsky, "A Novel in Nine Letters"

638.2 With Full Sentences

When using a full sentence within another sentence, do not capitalize it or use a period inside the parentheses.

And, since your friend won't have the assignment (he was just thinking about calling you), you'll have to make a couple more calls to actually get it.

—Ken Taylor, "The Art and Practice of Avoiding Homework"

When the parenthetical sentence comes after the period of the main sentence, capitalize and punctuate it the same way you would any other complete sentence.

They kiss and hug when they say "hello," and I love this. (In Korea, people are much more formal; they just shake hands and bow to each other.)

—Sue Chong, "He Said I Was Too American"

NOTE: For unavoidable parentheses within parentheses (. . . [. . .] . . .), use brackets. Avoid overuse of parentheses by using commas instead.

Diagonal

638.3 To Show a Choice

Use a **diagonal** (also called a *slash* or forward slash) between two words, as in *and/or*, to indicate that either is acceptable.

Press the load/eject button.
Don't worry; this is indoor/outdoor carpet.

638.4 When Quoting Poetry

When quoting more than one line of poetry, use a diagonal to show where each line of poetry ends. (Insert a space on each side of the diagonal.)

I have learned not to worry about love; / but to honor its coming / with all my heart.

—Alice Walker, "New Face"

Parentheses and Diagonals

 Write the word or words that should be enclosed in parentheses or divided by a slash. (Use the correct punctuation.)

Example: Aunt Joanie my mom's sister is my favorite relative.
(my mom's sister)

1. When Octavio and Jude went snowboarding I was working and so couldn't go, they met Olympic medal winner Danny Kass.

2. Dad glared as he said, "This is not an either or decision, Son. Just do what I told you to do."

3. Travon lucky dog! already has a job lined up for the summer.

4. Lots of kids go to Skate U the local roller rink on Friday nights.

5. To adjust the dryer's alarm volume, turn the high low knob accordingly.

6. Now that Colleen has her room to herself her sister is away at college, she can play her music as loud as she likes it.

7. Rhea was walking her dog on the 16th? or 17th? when she witnessed a car crash into a stoplight.

Model

Model the following sentence to practice using parentheses with full sentences.

> **Donleavy looked at the audience once (on reflection, I'm sure that he wanted only to reassure himself that we were really there), adjusted his glasses, and began to read from a sheaf of papers.**
>
> —Maya Angelou, "Graduation"

Model

Write the lyrics to a favorite song to practice using diagonals when quoting poetry.

> **The revolving door / Insanity every floor / Skyscraping, paper chasing / What are we working for?**
>
> —Lauryn Hill, "Mystery of Inequity"

Dash

640.1 To Indicate a Sudden Break

Use a **dash** to indicate a sudden break or change in the sentence.

Near the semester's end—and this is not always due to poor planning—**some students may find themselves in a real crunch.**

NOTE: Dashes are often used in place of commas. Use dashes when you want to give special emphasis; use commas when there is no need for emphasis.

640.2 To Set Off an Introductory Series

Use a dash to set off an introductory series from the clause that explains the series.

A good book, a cup of tea, a comfortable chair—**these things always saved my mother's sanity.**

640.3 To Set Off Parenthetical Material

You may use a dash to set off parenthetical material—material that explains or clarifies a word or a phrase.

A single incident—a tornado that came without warning—**changed the face of the small town forever.**

640.4 To Indicate Interrupted Speech

Use a dash to show interrupted or faltering speech in dialogue.

Sojourner: Mama, why are you—

Mama: Isabelle, do as I say!

—Sandy Asher, *A Woman Called Truth*

640.5 For Emphasis

Use a dash to emphasize a word, a series, a phrase, or a clause.

After years of trial and error, Belther made history with his invention—the unicycle.

After several hours of hearing the high-pitched yipping, Petra finally realized what it was—coyote pups.

Dashes

- ■ **To Set Off An Introductory Series**
- ■ **To Set Off Parenthetical Material**
- ■ **For Emphasis**

 A word, a phrase, or a clause follows each sentence below. Write the sentences to include those words, set off by one or two dashes.

Example: The book she left on the bed was probably some kind of hint. (*Cleaning in a Snap!*)

The book she left on the bed—<u>Cleaning in a Snap!</u>— was probably some kind of hint.

1. The nine-day tournament over, a voice came over the loudspeaker announcing the winner. (my brother)

2. Many Native Americans are involved in the conservation movement today. (whose ancestors treated the land with respect)

3. No household will run smoothly without them. (scissors, tape, and string)

4. The museum would like to feature Mr. Saraee's car in an exhibit. (a 1954 Ferrari convertible)

5. It is strongly suggested that everyone make a $5 donation at the dance. (although not required)

Model

Model the following sentences to practice using dashes for emphasis and to set off an introductory series.

There is but one success—to be able to spend your life in your own way.

—Christopher Morley, *Where the Blue Begins*

A tie, a little plastic comb, and a belt—those are three gifts that my grandparents thought I needed.

Ellipsis

642.1 To Show Omitted Words

Use an **ellipsis** (three periods with one space before and after each period) to show that one or more words have been omitted in a quotation.

(Original)

We the people of the United States, in order to form a more perfect Union, establish justice, insure domestic tranquility, provide for the common defense, promote the general welfare, and secure the blessings of liberty to ourselves and our posterity, do ordain and establish this Constitution for the United States of America.

—Preamble, *U.S. Constitution*

(Quotation)

"We the people . . . in order to form a more perfect Union . . . establish this Constitution for the United States of America."

642.2 At the End of a Sentence

If words from a quotation are omitted at the end of a sentence, place the ellipsis after the period that marks the conclusion of the sentence.

"Five score years ago, a great American, in whose symbolic shadow we stand, signed the Emancipation Proclamation. . . . But one hundred years later, we must face the tragic fact that the Negro is still not free."

—Martin Luther King, Jr., "I Have a Dream"

NOTE: If the quoted material is a complete sentence (even if it was not complete in the original), use a period, then an ellipsis.

(Original)

I am tired; my heart is sick and sad. From where the sun now stands I will fight no more forever.

—Chief Joseph of the Nez Percé

(Quotation)

"I am tired. . . . From where the sun now stands I will fight no more forever."

or

"I am tired. . . . I will fight no more. . . . "

642.3 To Show a Pause

Use an ellipsis to indicate a pause.

I brought my trembling hand to my focusing eyes. It was oozing, it was red, it was . . . it was . . . a tomato!

—Laura Baginski, student writer

Punctuation

Ellipses

- **To Show Omitted Words**
- **To Show a Pause**

 For each of the following paragraphs, select the least important information to replace with ellipses. Write the shortened paragraphs on your paper.

Example: Taneka Sills, a local girl who is a member of the high school forensics team, has been awarded a scholarship to the Young People's Peace Camp in Tillamook, Oregon.

Taneka Sills . . . has been awarded a scholarship to the Young People's Peace Camp in Tillamook, Oregon.

1. Simple braids are easy to make. First, divide the hair into three equal sections. You may fasten each with a small band at the bottom, if desired. Next, pull the section on the right into the middle of the two others; then do the same with the section on the left. Continue to alternate until the braid is the desired length (or you run out of hair!). Use a covered rubber band to tie the ends together, and finish with a hair decoration or barrette.

2. Polar bears live in a place where not many other animals live, on the coasts of the Arctic Ocean. They are powerful swimmers and can easily go 25 miles back and forth from the coast to drifting icebergs. Male polar bears can reach 10 feet tall and 1,700 pounds. The bears' heavy, white fur even covers the soles of their feet—a feature not seen in any other bear—to help them walk on the ice. The polar bear's only enemy is the human, and because of overhunting, the species is threatened.

Model

Model the following sentence to practice using an ellipsis to indicate a pause.

"Tell me something: those little plants there . . ." she said, nonchalantly, pointing to some rushes growing tall in the midst of the lagoon, "where do they put down their roots?"

—Italo Calvino, "The Aquatic Uncle"

Brackets

644.1 To Set Off Clarifying Information

Use **brackets** before and after words that are added to clarify what another person has said or written.

"They'd [the sweat bees] get into your mouth, ears, eyes, nose. You'd feel them all over you."

—Marilyn Johnson and Sasha Nyary, "Roosevelts in the Amazon"

NOTE: The brackets indicate that the words *the sweat bees* are not part of the quotation but were added for clarification.

644.2 Around an Editorial Correction

Place brackets around an editorial correction inserted within quoted material.

"Brooklyn alone has 8 percent of lead poisoning [victims] nationwide," said Marjorie Moore.

—Donna Actie, student writer

NOTE: The brackets indicate that the word *victims* replaced the author's original word.

Place brackets around the letters *sic* (Latin for "as such"); the letters indicate that an error appearing in the material being quoted was made by the original speaker or writer.

"When I'm queen," mused Lucy, "I'll show these blockheads whose [*sic*] got beauty and brains."

644.3 To Set Off Added Words

Place brackets around comments that have been added to a quotation.

"Congratulations to the astronomy club's softball team, which put in, shall we say, a 'stellar' performance." [groans]

Punctuation Marks

´	Accent, acute	,	Comma	( )	Parentheses
`	Accent, grave	†	Dagger	.	Period
'	Apostrophe	—	Dash	?	Question mark
*	Asterisk	/	Diagonal/Slash	" "	Quotation marks
{ }	Brace	¨ (ü)	Dieresis	§	Section
[ ]	Brackets	. . .	Ellipsis	;	Semicolon
^	Caret	!	Exclamation point	~	Tilde
(ç)	Cedilla	-	Hyphen	___	Underscore
^	Circumflex	...	Leaders		
:	Colon	¶	Paragraph		

Brackets

- To Set Off Clarifying Information
- Around an Editorial Correction

 Follow the directions for each activity below.

Example: In the following quotation, the speaker is talking about influenza. Use words in brackets to clarify the quotation.

"People hear about so many other diseases," said Dr. Pintar, "but we need to remember that this disease continues to exert a high toll on human life."

"People hear about so many other diseases," said Dr. Pintar, "but we need to remember that this disease [influenza] continues to exert a high toll on human life."

1. In the following quotation, the speaker is talking about the earth. Use words in brackets to clarify the quotation.

"By measuring the level of decay of radioactive material in rocks, we can figure out how old it is," Jung noted.

2. In the following quotation, replace the speaker's use of the word *hypertrichosis* with *excessive hair*. Place brackets around your editorial correction.

"My father's hypertrichosis bothered him," she related.

3. Quote the following statement and show that the error was made by the original writer, Gary Sumter. (Use the word *sic* enclosed in brackets.)

The storm wreaked it's havoc for hundreds of miles along the coast.

Model

Model the following sentence to practice using brackets to set off clarifying information.

There is no frigate [sailing vessel] like a book, to take us lands away.

—Emily Dickinson

Test Prep

Read the following paragraphs. From the choices given below each paragraph, write the letter of the correct way to punctuate each underlined part. If it is already correct, choose "D."

The movie "You've Got Mail" is actually a remake of the 1940 film *"The Shop Around the Corner."* While the previous film focused on a romance conducted through the post office, the newer one (made in 1998) had the romance happening through e mail.

1. A "Youv'e Got Mail"
   B *You've Got Mail*
   C "You've Got Mail"
   D correct as is

2. A *The Shop Around the Corner.*
   B "The Shop Around the Corner."
   C "The Shop Around the Corner".
   D correct as is

3. A (made) in 1998
   B (made in 1998
   C made in 1998)
   D correct as is

4. A e'mail
   B "e" mail
   C e-mail
   D correct as is

Sasha asked, "Do you know whose hat this is"? She held up a red and white striped knit stocking cap.

Patrick said, "Its either Jacks' or Zack's hat, I'm pretty sure."

5. A this is?
   B this is?"
   C this is"
   D correct as is

6. A a-red-and-white
   B a red-and-white
   C a red and-white
   D correct as is

7. A "It's
   B It's
   C "Its'
   D correct as is

8. A Jacks' or Zacks' hat
   B Jack's or Zack's hat
   C Jacks or Zack's hat
   D correct as is

"The Black Eyed Peas released a new <u>album, Kent said. Have</u>
                                              9
you heard any songs from it?"

"<u>Iv'e heard "Union"</u> a few times," said Fiona.
        10
"Is this album as good as the one before it, <u>*Elephunk*?" he asked.</u>
                                                     11

"I think <u>its the Pea's</u> best one," she said.
          12

9. A album," Kent said. Have
   B album, Kent said. "Have
   C album," Kent said. "Have
   D correct as is

10. A "I've heard "Union"
    B "Iv'e heard 'Union
    C "I've heard 'Union'
    D correct as is

11. A *Elephunk*"?
    B '*Elephunk*'?"
    C '*Elephunk*?'"
    D correct as is

12. A it's the Peas'
    B its' the Peas
    C it's the Pea's
    D correct as is

In general, <u>dont make a U turn</u> at an intersection with a
                  13
traffic light. Also, when <u>someones' view</u> of your car may be obstructed,
                                14
such as on a hill or a curve, do not do so. Always observe <u>the right of way</u>
                                                              15
<u>rules</u>. <u>It's everyones' responsibility</u> to prevent striking another vehicle
              16
or pedestrian.

13. A don't make a U turn
    B do'nt make a U-turn
    C don't make a U-turn
    D correct as is

14. A someone's view
    B someones view
    C someones" view
    D correct as is

15. A the-right-of-way rules
    B the right of-way rules
    C the right-of-way rules
    D correct as is

16. A Its everyone's responsibility
    B It's everyones responsibility
    C It's everyone's responsibility
    D correct as is

Checking Mechanics

Capitalization

648.1 Proper Nouns and Adjectives

Capitalize proper nouns and proper adjectives (those derived from proper nouns). The chart below provides a quick overview of capitalization rules. The pages following explain some specific rules of capitalization.

Capitalization at a Glance

Names of people	Alice Walker, Matilda, Jim, Mr. Roker
Days of the week, months	Sunday, Tuesday, June, August
Holidays, holy days	Thanksgiving, Easter, Hanukkah
Periods, events in history	Middle Ages, the Battle of Bunker Hill
Official documents	Declaration of Independence
Special events	Elgin Community Spring Gala
Languages, nationalities, religions	French, Canadian, Islam
Political parties	Republican Party, Socialist Party
Trade names	Oscar Mayer hot dogs, Pontiac Sunbird
Official titles used with names	Mayor John Spitzer, Senator Feinstein
Formal epithets	Alexander the Great
Geographical names	
Planets, heavenly bodies	Earth, Jupiter, the Milky Way
Continents	Australia, South America
Countries	Ireland, Grenada, Sri Lanka
States, provinces	Ohio, Utah, Nova Scotia
Cities, towns, villages	El Paso, Burlington, Wonewoc
Streets, roads, highways	Park Avenue, Route 66, Interstate 90
Landforms	the Rocky Mountains, the Sahara Desert
Bodies of water	Yellowstone Lake, Pumpkin Creek
Buildings, monuments	Elkhorn High School, Gateway Arch
Public areas	Times Square, Sequoia National Park

Capitalization 1

■ **Proper Nouns and Adjectives**

 For each sentence below, write the words that should be capitalized (as shown).

Example: On the friday before the labor day weekend, mr. rayda invited us to his house in michigan.

Friday, Labor Day, Mr. Rayda, Michigan

1. Richard the lionhearted was the king of england for 10 years.

2. Of the five great lakes, only lake michigan is entirely within the united states.

3. Admission to the coronation ball required dressing in a renaissance-era costume.

4. When salvadore began going to hershey high school, he spoke fluent italian and a little english.

5. Although erica likes her car, she'd really like a mazda miata.

6. The december 2004 tsunami affected many countries surrounding the bay of bengal.

7. The only interstate highway that runs from canada to mexico is interstate 5 (from san diego to blaine, washington).

8. Is neptune or pluto the farthest planet from the sun?

9. A small part of russian land is lodged between lithuania and poland.

Model

Model the following sentences to practice capitalizing proper nouns and adjectives.

> Though a June or July birthday celebration was offered many times, Shavonda insisted that she celebrate her birthday on the day she was born: December 25.

> After driving all day and night, we arrived at the grounds of the Washington Monument just in time for the march, and joined the section of Southern delegates.

> —Anne Moody, "Coming of Age in Mississippi"

Capitalization *(continued)*

650.1 First Words

Capitalize the first word of every sentence, including the first word of a full-sentence direct quotation.

> **The crowd was quiet. A girl whispered, "I hope it's not Nancy," and the sound of her whisper reached the edges of the crowd.**
>
> —Shirley Jackson, "The Lottery"

650.2 Sentences in Parentheses

Capitalize the first word in a sentence enclosed in parentheses, but do not capitalize the first word if the parenthetical appears within another sentence.

> **Shamelessly she winked at me and grinned again. (That grin! She could have taken it off her face and put it on the table.)**
>
> —Jean Stafford, "Bad Characters"
>
> **Damien's aunt (she's a wild woman) plays bingo every Saturday night.**

650.3 Sentences Following Colons

Capitalize the first word in a complete sentence that follows a colon when (1) you want to emphasize the sentence or (2) the sentence is a quotation.

> **When we quarreled and made horrible faces at one another, Mother knew what to say: "Your faces will stay that way, and no one will marry you."**

650.4 Sections of the Country

Capitalize words that indicate particular sections of the country; do not capitalize words that simply indicate direction.

> **Mr. Johnson is from the Southwest.** (section of the country)
>
> **After moving north to Montana, he had to buy winter clothes.** (direction)

650.5 Certain Religious Words

Capitalize nouns that refer to the Supreme Being, the word *Bible,* the books of the Bible, and the names for other holy books.

> **God   Jehovah   the Lord   the Savior   Allah   Bible   Genesis**

650.6 Titles

Capitalize the first word of a title, the last word, and every word in between except articles (*a, an, the*), short prepositions, and coordinating conjunctions. Follow this rule for titles of books, newspapers, magazines, poems, plays, songs, articles, films, works of art, photographs, and stories.

> ***Washington Post***   **"The Diary of a Madman"**   ***Nights of Rain and Stars***

Capitalization 2

- Sentences in Parentheses
- Sections of the Country
- Titles

 For the paragraphs below, write the line number along with the words that should be capitalized (as shown in red below).

Example: 1. Midwest

1   When my uncle was growing up in the midwest during the 1960s,

2   he loved to listen to his little transistor radio. He could hear all kinds

3   of rock music, but his favorite bands were the "hot rod" groups. (the

4   genre was born in California but soon spread east.) Uncle Will and

5   his friends tuned in to that music as it became popular in their area.

6   They'd sing along to Jan and Dean's "Drag city" and "Dead man's

7   curve." They'd turn up the radio when the Beach Boys' "Little deuce

8   coupe" came on, and they'd dream about having their own hot rods

9   when they heard "Boss drag at Hot Rod beach."

10   By 1970, Uncle Will's family moved to the south, and the hot

11   rod craze had dried up. His next musical obsession was (naturally)

12   southern rock. He has some great stories about that time in his

13   life (this was in his late teens) and shares them with me often. It's

14   interesting to hear about someone's life through his love of music.

Model

Model the following sentence to practice capitalizing sections of the country and titles.

> We watched the University of Texas Longhorn Band (known as the Show Band of the Southwest) play "The Eyes of Texas."

Model

Model this sentence to practice *not* capitalizing a sentence in parentheses when it appears within another sentence.

> They play cops and robbers (only they call it "Jail") and throw things at one another—snowballs in winter, rose hips in fall.
>
> —E. B. White, "Education"

Capitalization *(continued)*

652.1 Words Used as Names

Capitalize words like *father, mother, uncle,* and *senator* when they are used as titles with a personal name or when they are substituted for proper nouns (especially in direct address).

> **We've missed you, Aunt Lucinda!** (*Aunt* is part of the name.)
>
> **I hope Mayor Bates arrives soon.** (*Mayor* is part of the name.)

A Closer Look

To test whether a word is being substituted for a proper noun, simply read the sentence with a proper noun in place of the word. If the proper noun fits in the sentence, the word being tested should be capitalized; otherwise, the word should not be capitalized.

> **Did Mom (Sue) say we could go?** (*Sue* works in this sentence.)
>
> **Did your mom (Sue) say you could go?** (*Sue* does not work here.)

NOTE: Usually the word is not capitalized if it follows a possessive —*my, his, your*—as it does in the second sentence above.

652.2 Letters

Capitalize the letters used to indicate form or shape.

> **U-turn   I-beam   S-curve   T-shirt   V-shaped**

652.3 Organizations

Capitalize the name of an organization, an association, or a team.

> **Lake Ontario Sailors   American Indian Movement   Democratic Party**

652.4 Abbreviations

Capitalize abbreviations of titles and organizations. (Some other abbreviations are also capitalized. See pages 660–662.)

> **AAA   CEO   NAACP   M.D.   Ph.D.**

652.5 Titles of Courses

Capitalize words like *sociology* and *history* when they are used as titles of specific courses; do not capitalize these words when they name a field of study.

> **Who teaches History 202?** (title of a specific course)
>
> **It's the same professor who teaches my sociology course.** (a field of study)

NOTE: The words *freshman, sophomore, junior,* and *senior* are not capitalized unless they are part of an official title.

> **Rosa is a senior this year and is in charge of the Senior Class Banquet.**

Capitalization 3

- Organizations
- Abbreviations
- Titles of Courses

 For each of the following sentences, correctly capitalize or lowercase any word or word groups that are incorrect.

Example: The national audubon society is an Organization especially
interested in birds.

National Audubon Society, organization

1. Ms. Kincaid, who teaches biology II, is a member.

2. Other Conservation and Animal-Welfare organizations are the
national wildlife federation (NWF) and the american society for the
prevention of cruelty to animals (aspca).

3. The goal of the world wildlife fund (wwf) is "to build a future where
people live in harmony with nature."

4. The Natural resources defense council (Nrdc) is an environmental
group that takes action to protect wildlife and wild places.

5. We've learned about many of these groups in cultural geography,
taught by Mr. Lee.

6. In addition, Luisa Rane, the president of the school's
environmentalist club, made a presentation during earth science I.

7. I think I would like to get involved with greenpeace international.

Model

Model the following sentences to practice capitalizing abbreviations
and the names of organizations.

**Members of the International Ecology Society (IES) try to attain a
better understanding of all life forms.**

Mechanics

Plurals

654.1 Most Nouns

Form the **plurals** of most nouns by adding *s* to the singular.

cheerleader – cheerleaders   wheel – wheels   crate – crates

654.2 Nouns Ending in *sh, ch, x, s,* and *z*

Form the plurals of nouns ending in *sh, ch, x, s,* and *z* by adding *es* to the singular.

lunch – lunches   dish – dishes   mess – messes   fox – foxes

EXCEPTION: When the final *ch* sounds like *k*, add an *s* (*monarchs*).

654.3 Nouns Ending in *y*

The plurals of common nouns that end in *y*—preceded by a consonant—are formed by changing the *y* to *i* and adding *es*.

fly – flies   jalopy – jalopies

Form the plurals of nouns that end in *y*—preceded by a vowel—by adding only an *s*.

donkey – donkeys   monkey – monkeys

NOTE: Form the plurals of all proper nouns ending in *y (Kathys)* by adding *s*.

654.4 Nouns Ending in *o*

The plurals of nouns ending in *o*—preceded by a vowel—are formed by adding an *s*.

radio – radios   rodeo – rodeos   studio – studios   duo – duos

The plurals of most nouns ending in *o*—preceded by a consonant—are formed by adding *es*.

echo – echoes   hero – heroes   tomato – tomatoes

EXCEPTION: Musical terms always form plurals by adding *s*.

alto – altos   banjo – banjos   solo – solos   piano – pianos

654.5 Nouns Ending in *ful*

Form the plurals of nouns that end in *ful* by adding an *s* at the end of the word.

two tankfuls   three pailfuls   four mouthfuls

NOTE: Do not confuse these examples with *three pails full* (when you are referring to three separate pails full of something) or *two tanks full*.

654.6 Compound Nouns

Form the plurals of most compound nouns by adding *s* or *es* to the important word in the compound.

brothers-in-law   maids of honor   secretaries of state

Plurals 1

- Regular Nouns
- Nouns Ending in *sh, ch, x, s,* and *z*
- Nouns Ending in *y, o,* and *ful*

 Write the correct plurals of the underlined word or words in each sentence.

Example: Alahandra picked two <u>bunch</u> of <u>flower</u> for the kitchen table.
　　　　　bunches, flowers

1. The hidden <u>box</u> that Jake came upon intrigued him.

2. Some <u>job</u> offer several paid <u>holiday</u> per year.

3. The <u>piccolo</u> played the song over and over while the <u>dancer</u> gathered.

4. My aunts came from the <u>arbor</u> with <u>apronful</u> of <u>grape</u> for the special recipe.

5. We had a garden stew with lots of <u>potato</u>, onions, and <u>carrot</u> for supper, and cobbler made with <u>mango</u> for dessert.

6. The warm spell hatched many <u>insect</u> and brought new <u>buzz</u> to the evening air.

7. Soon the <u>boy</u> arrived at the campsite with <u>armful</u> of firewood.

8. The neighborhood looked interesting with its different-colored <u>chimney</u>.

9. Besides taking many biology <u>class</u>, Cecily toured the nation's major <u>zoo</u> and wrote a thesis to complete her major.

10. She plans to take several long <u>journey</u> to study exotic wildlife.

11. We wanted to get a picture, but the camera <u>battery</u> were dead.

Exercise

Write the plurals of the following words. Then use as many of the plurals as you can in one sentence.

　　handful, library, halo, wish, address, toy, sky

Plurals *(continued)*

656.1 **Nouns Ending in *f* or *fe***

Form the plurals of nouns that end in *f* or *fe* in one of two ways: if the final *f* sound is still heard in the plural form of the word, simply add *s;* but if the final *f* sound becomes a *v* sound, change the *f* to *ve* and add *s.*

Plural ends with *f* sound: roof – roofs; chief – chiefs

Plural ends with *v* sound: wife – wives; loaf – loaves

NOTE: Several words are correct with either ending.

Plural ends with either sound: hoof – hooves/hoofs

656.2 **Irregular Spelling**

A number of words form a plural by taking on an irregular spelling.

crisis – crises	**child – children**	**radius – radii**
criterion – criteria	**goose – geese**	**die – dice**

NOTE: Some of these words are acceptable with the commonly used *s* or *es* ending.

index – indices/indexes   cactus – cacti/cactuses

Some nouns remain unchanged when used as plurals.

deer   sheep   salmon   aircraft   series

656.3 **Words Discussed as Words**

The plurals of symbols, letters, numbers, and words being discussed as words are formed by adding an apostrophe and an *s.*

Dad yelled a lot of *wow's* and *yippee's* when he saw my A's and B's.

NOTE: You may omit the apostrophe if it does not cause any confusion.

the three R's or Rs   YMCA's or YMCAs

656.4 **Collective Nouns**

A collective noun may be singular or plural depending upon how it's used. A collective noun is singular when it refers to a group considered as one unit; it is plural when it refers to the individuals in the group.

The class was on its best behavior. (group as a unit)

The class are preparing for their final exams. (individuals in the group)

If it seems awkward to use a plural verb with a collective noun, add a clearly plural noun such as *members* to the sentence, or change the collective noun into a possessive followed by a plural noun that describes the individuals in the group.

The class members are preparing for their final exams.

The class's students are preparing for their final exams.

Plurals 2

- Nouns Ending in *f* or *fe*
- Irregular Spellings
- Words Discussed as Words

 For each sentence below, write the plural form of the word or words in parentheses.

Example: Not too long ago, when you saw (goose) in the sky, it meant winter was near.

geese

1. Now, however, it seems that a number of environmental (crisis) have changed weather patterns.

2. My grandparents say that they learned the 3 (R) in school—reading, 'riting, and 'rithmetic.

3. In the 1950s, it was usually the case that (man) went to work, (woman) stayed home, and (child) played outside—a lot.

4. Different religions naturally have different (belief).

5. The (leaf) on our maple tree are turning orange already.

6. The fisherman grinned as he showed us the nice-sized (salmon) and (trout) he had caught.

7. I've heard the (ABC) one too many times from my four-year-old sister.

8. Dad says we use too many *(no way)* and *(whatever)* in our conversations.

9. Board games usually involve throwing (die).

10. Our scrapping outdoor cat seems to have far more than the usual "nine (life)."

11. Long run-on sentences often have many *(and)* and *(so)* in them.

 ## Model

Write sentences using plurals of these words:

cactus, mouse, ox, shrimp, and **moonfish**

Numbers

658.1 Numerals or Words

Numbers from one to nine are usually written as words; numbers 10 and over are usually written as numerals. However, numbers being compared or contrasted should be kept in the same style.

8 to 11 years old   eight to eleven years old

You may use a combination of numerals and words for very large numbers.

1.5 million   3 billion to 3.2 billion   6 trillion

If numbers are used infrequently in a piece of writing, you may spell out those that can be written in no more than two words.

ten   twenty-five   two hundred   fifty thousand

658.2 Numerals Only

Use numerals for the following forms: decimals, percentages, chapters, pages, addresses, phone numbers, identification numbers, and statistics.

26.2   8 percent   Highway 36   chapter 7
pages 287-89   July 6, 1945   44 B.C.E.   a vote of 23 to 4

Always use numerals with abbreviations and symbols.

8%   10 mm   3 cc   8 oz   90° C   24 mph   6' 3"

658.3 Words Only

Use words to express numbers that begin a sentence.

Fourteen students "forgot" their assignments.

NOTE: Change the sentence structure if this rule creates a clumsy construction.

Clumsy: *Six hundred thirty-nine* teachers were laid off this year.

Better: This year, 639 teachers were laid off.

Use words for numbers that come before a compound modifier if that modifier includes a numeral.

They made twelve 10-foot sub sandwiches for the picnic.

658.4 Time and Money

If time is expressed with an abbreviation, use numerals; if it is expressed in words, spell out the number.

4:00 A.M. (or) four o'clock

If an amount of money is spelled out, so is the currency; use a numeral if a symbol is used.

twenty dollars (or) $20

Numbers

- Numerals or Words
- Numerals Only
- Words Only

For each sentence below, write the underlined numbers the correct way. If a number is already correctly presented, write "correct."

Example: The teacher assigned pages <u>two hundred thirty</u> to <u>two hundred forty-five</u>.

230 to 245

1. A <u>nineteen forty-eight</u> flood in Woodland, Washington, caused $ <u>two hundred million</u> worth of damage.

2. The firebrick can withstand a temperature of at least <u>two thousand 760</u> degrees Fahrenheit.

3. The giant Ferris wheel at the 1893 World's Columbian Exposition in Chicago was <u>two hundred fifty</u> feet high; the next year, England built a Ferris wheel that was <u>three hundred twenty-eight</u> feet high.

4. The Chicago wheel had <u>thirty-six</u> cars, and each could hold <u>60</u> passengers; the London wheel had <u>40</u> cars, and each could hold <u>thirty</u> passengers.

5. When you think that these wheels were as high as <u>25-</u> or <u>32-</u>story buildings, it's amazing that they found people brave enough to ride them!

6. The museum offers art classes for children <u>six</u> to <u>13</u> years old.

7. <u>10</u> kids want cheese-and-sausage pizza; that's <u>fifty</u> percent of us.

8. The shop class ordered <u>14 12-foot</u> boards.

9. The Milky Way is <u>one hundred fifty thousand</u> light-years in diameter.

Exercise

Complete this sentence with your own numbers.

The team has won _____ out of nine games, with their best game ending at ____–____.

Mechanics

Abbreviations

660.1 Formal and Informal Abbreviations

An **abbreviation** is the shortened form of a word or phrase. Some abbreviations are always acceptable in both formal and informal writing:

Mr.   Mrs.   Jr.   Ms.   Dr.   a.m. (A.M.)   p.m. (P.M.)

NOTE: In most of your writing, you do not abbreviate the names of states, countries, months, days, or units of measure. However, you may use the abbreviation U.S. after it has been spelled out once. Do not abbreviate the words *Street, Company,* and similar words, especially when they are part of a proper name. Also, do not use signs or symbols (%, &, #, @) in place of words. The dollar sign, however, is appropriate with numerals ($325).

660.2 Correspondence Abbreviations

United States

Standard		Postal
Alabama	Ala.	AL
Alaska	Alaska	AK
Arizona	Ariz.	AZ
Arkansas	Ark.	AR
California	Calif.	CA
Colorado	Colo.	CO
Connecticut	Conn.	CT
Delaware	Del.	DE
District of Columbia	D.C.	DC
Florida	Fla.	FL
Georgia	Ga.	GA
Guam	Guam	GU
Hawaii	Hawaii	HI
Idaho	Idaho	ID
Illinois	Ill.	IL
Indiana	Ind.	IN
Iowa	Iowa	IA
Kansas	Kan.	KS
Kentucky	Ky.	KY
Louisiana	La.	LA
Maine	Maine	ME
Maryland	Md.	MD
Massachusetts	Mass.	MA
Michigan	Mich.	MI
Minnesota	Minn.	MN
Mississippi	Miss.	MS
Missouri	Mo.	MO
Montana	Mont.	MT
Nebraska	Neb.	NE
Nevada	Nev.	NV
New Hampshire	N.H.	NH
New Jersey	N.J.	NJ
New Mexico	N.M.	NM
New York	N.Y.	NY
North Carolina	N.C.	NC
North Dakota	N.D.	ND
Ohio	Ohio	OH
Oklahoma	Okla.	OK
Oregon	Ore.	OR
Pennsylvania	Pa.	PA
Puerto Rico	P.R.	PR
Rhode Island	R.I.	RI
South Carolina	S.C.	SC
South Dakota	S.D.	SD
Tennessee	Tenn.	TN
Texas	Texas	TX
Utah	Utah	UT
Vermont	Vt.	VT
Virginia	Va.	VA
Virgin Islands	V.I.	VI
Washington	Wash.	WA
West Virginia	W.Va.	WV
Wisconsin	Wis.	WI
Wyoming	Wyo.	WY

Canadian

	Standard	Postal
Alberta	Alta.	AB
British Columbia	B.C.	BC
Labrador	Lab.	NL
Manitoba	Man.	MB
New Brunswick	N.B.	NB
Newfoundland	N.F.	NL
Northwest Territories	N.W.T.	NT
Nova Scotia	N.S.	NS
Nunavut		NU
Ontario	Ont.	ON
Prince Edward Island	P.E.I.	PE
Quebec	Que.	QC
Saskatchewan	Sask.	SK
Yukon Territory	Y.T.	YT

Addresses

Standard		Postal
Apartment	Apt.	APT
Avenue	Ave.	AVE
Boulevard	Blvd.	BLVD
Circle	Cir.	CIR
Court	Ct.	CT
Drive	Dr.	DR
East	E.	E
Expressway	Expy.	EXPY
Freeway	Fwy.	FWY
Heights	Hts.	HTS
Highway	Hwy.	HWY
Hospital	Hosp.	HOSP
Junction	Junc.	JCT
Lake	L.	LK
Lakes	Ls.	LKS
Lane	Ln.	LN
Meadows	Mdws.	MDWS
North	N.	N
Palms	Palms	PLMS
Park	Pk.	PK
Parkway	Pky.	PKY
Place	Pl.	PL
Plaza	Plaza	PLZ
Post Office Box	P.O. Box	PO BOX
Ridge	Rdg.	RDG
River	R.	RV
Road	Rd.	RD
Room	Rm.	RM
Rural	R.	R
Rural Route	R.R.	RR
Shore	Sh.	SH
South	S.	S
Square	Sq.	SQ
Station	Sta.	STA
Street	St.	ST
Suite	Ste.	STE
Terrace	Ter.	TER
Turnpike	Tpke.	TPKE
Union	Un.	UN
View	View	VW
Village	Vil.	VLG
West	W.	W

661.1 Other Common Abbreviations

abr. abridged; abridgment
AC, ac alternating current
ack. acknowledge; acknowledgment
acv actual cash value
A.D. in the year of the Lord (Latin *anno Domini*)
AM amplitude modulation
A.M., a.m. before noon (Latin *ante meridiem*)
ASAP as soon as possible
avg., av. average
BBB Better Business Bureau
B.C. before Christ
B.C.E. before the Common Era
bibliog. bibliographer; bibliography
biog. biographer; biographical; biography
C 1. Celsius **2.** centigrade **3.** coulomb
c. 1. circa (about) **2.** cup
cc 1. cubic centimeter **2.** carbon copy
CDT, C.D.T. central daylight time
C.E. of the Common Era
chap. chapter
cm centimeter
c.o., c/o care of
COD, C.O.D 1. cash on delivery **2.** collect on delivery
co-op. cooperative
CST, C.S.T. central standard time
cu., c cubic
D.A. district attorney
d.b.a. doing business as
DC, dc direct current
dec. deceased
dept. department
DST, D.S.T. daylight saving time
dup. duplicate
DVD digital video disc
ea. each
ed. edition; editor
EDT, E.D.T. eastern daylight time
e.g. for example (Latin *exempli gratia*)
EST, E.S.T. eastern standard time
etc. and so forth (Latin *et cetera*)
ex. example
F Fahrenheit
FM frequency modulation
F.O.B., f.o.b. free on board
ft foot
g 1. gram **2.** gravity
gal. gallon
gloss. glossary
GNP gross national product
hdqrs, HQ headquarters
HIV human immunodeficiency virus

Hon. Honorable (title)
hp horsepower
HTML hypertext markup language
Hz hertz
ibid. in the same place (Latin *ibidem*)
id. the same (Latin *idem*)
i.e. that is (Latin *id est*)
illus. illustration
inc. incorporated
IQ, I.Q. intelligence quotient
IRS Internal Revenue Service
ISBN International Standard Book Number
Jr., jr. junior
K 1. kelvin (temperature unit) **2.** Kelvin (temperature scale)
kc kilocycle
kg kilogram
km kilometer
kn knot
kW kilowatt
l liter
lat. latitude
lb, lb. pound (Latin *libra*)
l.c. lowercase
lit. literary; literature
log logarithm
long. longitude
Ltd., ltd. limited
m meter
M.A. master of arts (Latin *Magister Artium*)
Mc, mc megacycle
M.C., m.c. master of ceremonies
M.D. doctor of medicine (Latin *medicinae doctor*)
mdse. merchandise
mfg. manufacturing
mg milligram
mi. 1. mile **2.** mill (monetary unit)
misc. miscellaneous
ml milliliter
mm millimeter
mpg, m.p.g. miles per gallon
mph, m.p.h. miles per hour
MS 1. manuscript **2.** Mississippi **3.** multiple sclerosis
Ms., Ms title of courtesy for a woman
MST, M.S.T. mountain standard time
neg. negative
N.S.F., n.s.f. not sufficient funds
oz, oz. ounce
PA 1. public-address system **2.** Pennsylvania
pct. percent
pd. paid

PDT, P.D.T. Pacific daylight time
PFC, Pfc. private first class
pg., p. page
P.M., p.m. after noon (Latin *post meridiem*)
P.O. 1. personnel officer **2.** purchase order **3.** postal order; post office **4.** (also p.o.) petty officer
pop. population
POW, P.O.W. prisoner of war
pp. pages
ppd. 1. postpaid **2.** prepaid
PR, P.R. 1. public relations **2.** Puerto Rico
P.S. post script
psi, p.s.i. pounds per square inch
PST, P.S.T. Pacific standard time
PTA, P.T.A. Parent-Teachers Association
qt. quart
RF radio frequency
RN registered nurse
R.P.M., rpm revolutions per minute
R.S.V.P., r.s.v.p. please reply (French *répondez s'il vous plaît*)
SASE self-addressed stamped envelope
SCSI small computer system interface
SOS 1. international distress signal **2.** any call for help
Sr. 1. senior (after surname) **2.** sister (religious)
ST standard time
St. 1. saint **2.** strait **3.** street
std. standard
syn. synonymous; synonym
TBA to be announced
tbs, tbsp tablespoon
TM trademark
tsp teaspoon
UHF, uhf ultra high frequency
UPC universal product code
UV ultraviolet
V 1. *Physics:* velocity **2.** *Electricity:* volt **3.** volume
V.A., VA Veterans Administration
VHF, vhf very high frequency
VIP *Informal:* very important person
vol. 1. volume **2.** volunteer
vs. versus
W 1. *Electricity:* watt **2.** *Physics:* (also w) work **3.** west
whse., whs. warehouse
wkly. weekly
w/o without
wt. weight
yd yard (measurement)

Mechanics

Acronyms and Initialisms

662.1 Acronyms

An **acronym** is a word formed from the first (or first few) letters of words in a phrase. Even though acronyms are abbreviations, they require no periods.

    radar radio detecting and ranging
    CARE Cooperative for American Relief Everywhere
    NASA National Aeronautics and Space Administration
    VISTA Volunteers in Service to America
    LAN local area network

662.2 Initialisms

An **initialism** is similar to an acronym except that the initials used to form this abbreviation are pronounced individually.

    CIA Central Intelligence Agency
    FBI Federal Bureau of Investigation
    FHA Federal Housing Administration

662.3 Common Acronyms and Initialisms

ADD	attention deficit disorder	**MADD**	Mothers Against Drunk Driving
AIDS	acquired immunodeficiency syndrome	**MRI**	Magnetic Resonance Imaging
AKA	also known as	**NASA**	National Aeronautics and Space Administration
ATM	automatic teller machine	**NATO**	North Atlantic Treaty Organization
BMI	body mass index	**OPEC**	Organization of Petroleum-Exporting Countries
CD	compact disc	**OSHA**	Occupational Safety and Health Administration
DMV	Department of Motor Vehicles	**PAC**	political action committee
ETA	expected time of arrival	**PDF**	portable document format
FAA	Federal Aviation Administration	**PETA**	People for the Ethical Treatment of Animals
FCC	Federal Communications Commission	**PIN**	personal identification number
FDA	Food and Drug Administration	**PSA**	public service announcement
FDIC	Federal Deposit Insurance Corporation	**ROTC**	Reserve Officers' Training Corps
FEMA	Federal Emergency Management Agency	**SADD**	Students Against Destructive Decisions
FTC	Federal Trade Commission	**SUV**	sport utility vehicle
FYI	for your information	**SWAT**	Special Weapons and Tactics
GPS	global positioning system	**TDD**	telecommunications device for the deaf
HDTV	high-definition television	**VA**	Veterans Administration
IRS	Internal Revenue Service		
IT	information technology		
JPEG	Joint Photographic Experts Group		
LCD	liquid crystal display		
LLC	limited liability company		

Abbreviations

In the following paragraph, some abbreviations are used incorrectly. If an underlined abbreviation is used incorrectly, write out what it stands for; if it is used correctly, write "correct."

Example: 1. *correct*

A survey of **(1)** Mrs. Reynolds' **(2)** apt. building at 1610 North Bunting **(3)** Rd., Sarton, **(4)** Ore., revealed that her property line is marked incorrectly. The neighboring **(5)** whse., owned by Roy Mitchel, **(6)** Jr., encroaches on the Reynolds property by 1 1/2 **(7)** ft. in the **(8)** NW corner of the lot. In a meeting on **(9)** Feb. 24 with **(10)** Mr. Mitchel and his wife, **(11)** Dr. Annemarie Tolbert, **(12)** Mrs. Reynolds agreed to a legal redefinition of the property line in exchange for a one-time cash payment of $32,500 to be made by 11:59 **(13)** p.m. **(14)** CST on **(15)** Mar. 15, 2006.

Model

Model the following acronyms and initialisms to come up with your own abbreviations. (Write at least one acronym and one initialism.)

> scuba – self-contained underwater breathing apparatus
> NOW – National Organization for Women
> IQ – intelligence quotient
> CPA – certified public accountant

Spelling Rules

664.1 Write *i* before *e*

Write *i* before *e* except after *c,* or when sounded like *a* as in *neighbor* and *weigh.*

> **relief   receive   perceive   reign   freight   beige**

EXCEPTIONS: There are a number of exceptions to this rule, including these: *neither, leisure, seize, weird, species, science.*

664.2 Words with Consonant Endings

When a one-syllable word *(bat)* ends in a consonant *(t)* preceded by one vowel *(a),* double the final consonant before adding a suffix that begins with a vowel *(batting).*

> **sum—summary   god—goddess**

NOTE: When a multisyllable word *(control)* ends in a consonant *(l)* preceded by one vowel *(o),* the accent is on the last syllable *(con trol´),* and the suffix begins with a vowel *(ing)*—the same rule holds true: double the final consonant *(controlling).*

> **prefer—preferred   begin—beginning**
> **forget—forgettable   admit—admittance**

664.3 Words with a Silent *e*

If a word ends with a silent *e,* drop the *e* before adding a suffix that begins with a vowel. Do not drop the *e* when the suffix begins with a consonant.

> **state—stating—statement   like—liking—likeness**
> **use—using—useful   nine—ninety—nineteen**

EXCEPTIONS: *judgment, truly, argument, ninth*

664.4 Words Ending in *y*

When *y* is the last letter in a word and the *y* is preceded by a consonant, change the *y* to *i* before adding any suffix except those beginning with *i.*

> **fry—fries—frying   hurry—hurried—hurrying   lady—ladies**
> **ply—pliable   happy—happiness   beauty—beautiful**

When *y* is the last letter in a word and the *y* is preceded by a vowel, do not change the *y* to *i* before adding a suffix.

> **play—plays—playful   stay—stays—staying   employ—employed**

IMPORTANT REMINDER: Never trust your spelling even to the best spell-checker. Use a dictionary for words your spell-checker does not cover.

Spelling 1

 Find the 10 words that are misspelled in the following paragraph and write them correctly. (Each misspelled word is in the "Commonly Misspelled Words" list on pages 666–667.)

Example: 1. *abruptly*

The music world changed abrubtly in August 1981: MTV broadcast its first music video. Twenty-five years later, record companies offen spend millions on a three-minute video—even more if the video is part of a movie campagne. Imagine what it must cost to design and build one of those elaberate sets! (Some videos, of course, have sevral sets.) Then figure in a veriety of other costs, such as computer-generated animation, costumes and jewelery, and props. Sometimes an orchestra must be "rented." It adds up fast. The most ixpensive video, at an apsurd $7 million, was for Michael Jackson's song "Scream," feachering his sister, Janet. Are we entertained yet?

Model

Model the following sentences to practice using the spelling rules that deal with adding a suffix.

Sometimes [the songs] are more than my real life and, conversely, my life is more than just my songs.

—Melissa Etheridge

To stop the flow of music would be like the stopping of time itself: incredible and inconceivable.

—Aaron Copland

Commonly Misspelled Words

A

abbreviate
abrupt
absence
absolute (ly)
absurd
abundance
academic
accelerate
accept (ance)
accessible
accessory
accidentally
accommodate
accompany
accomplish
accumulate
accurate
accustom (ed)
ache
achieve (ment)
acknowledge
acquaintance
acquired
across
address
adequate
adjustment
admissible
admittance
adolescent
advantageous
advertisement
advisable
aggravate
aggression
alcohol
alleviate
almost
alternative
although
aluminum
amateur
analysis
analyze
anarchy
ancient
anecdote
anesthetic

annihilate
announce
annual
anonymous
answer
anxious
apologize
apparatus
apparent (ly)
appearance
appetite
applies
appreciate
appropriate
approximately
architect
arctic
argument
arithmetic
arrangement
artificial
ascend
assistance
association
athlete
attendance
attire
attitude
audience
authority
available

B

balance
balloon
bargain
basically
beautiful
beginning
believe
benefit (ed)
biscuit
bought
boycott
brevity
brilliant
Britain
bureau
business

C

cafeteria
caffeine
calculator
calendar
campaign
canceled
candidate
catastrophe
category
caught
cavalry
celebration
cemetery
certificate
changeable
chief
chocolate
circuit
circumstance
civilization
colonel
colossal
column
commercial
commitment
committed
committee
comparative
comparison
competitively
conceivable
condemn
condescend
conference
conferred
confidential
congratulate
conscience
conscientious
conscious
consequence
consumer
contaminate
convenience
cooperate
correspondence
cough
coupon

courageous
courteous
creditor
criticism
criticize
curiosity
curious
cylinder

D

dealt
deceitful
deceive
decision
defense
deferred
definite (ly)
definition
delicious
descend
describe
description
despair
desperate
destruction
development
diameter
diaphragm
diarrhea
dictionary
dining
disagreeable
disappear
disappoint
disastrous
discipline
discrimination
discuss
dismissal
dissatisfied
dissect
distinctly
dormitory
doubt
drought
duplicate
dyeing
dying

E

earliest
efficiency
eighth
elaborate
eligible
eliminate
ellipse
embarrass
emphasize
employee
enclosure
encourage
endeavor
English
enormous
enough
enrichment
enthusiastic
entirely
entrance
environment
equipment
equipped
equivalent
especially
essential
eventually
exaggerate
examination
exceed
excellent
excessive
excite
executive
exercise
exhaust (ed)
exhibition
exhilaration
existence
expensive
experience
explanation
exquisite
extinguish
extraordinary
extremely

FG

facilities
familiar
fascinate
fashion
fatigue (d)
feature
February
fiery
financially
flourish
forcible
foreign
forfeit
fortunate
forty
fourth
freight
friend
fulfill
gauge
generally
generous
genuine
glimpse
gnarled
gnaw
government
gradual
grammar
gratitude
grievous
grocery
guard
guidance

H

happiness
harass
harmonize
height
hemorrhage
hereditary
hindrance
hoping
hopping
hospitable
humorous

hygiene
hymn
hypocrisy

ignorance
illiterate
illustrate
imaginary
immediately
immense
incidentally
inconvenience
incredible
indefinitely
independence
indispensable
industrial
industrious
inevitable
infinite
inflation
innocence
inoculation
inquiry
installation
instrumental
intelligence
interesting
interfere
interrupt
investigate
irregular
irresistible
issuing
itinerary
jealous (y)
jewelry
journal
judgment

KL

knowledge
laboratory
laugh
lawyer
league
legacy
legalize
legitimate
leisure

liaison
license
lightning
likable
liquid
literature
loneliness

MN

maintenance
maneuver
manufacture
marriage
mathematics
medieval
memento
menagerie
merchandise
merely
mileage
miniature
miscellaneous
mischievous
misspell
moat
mobile
mortgage
multiplied
muscle
musician
mustache
mutual
mysterious
naive
nauseous
necessary
neither
neurotic
nevertheless
ninety
nighttime
noticeable
nuclear
nuisance

OP

obstacle
obvious
occasion
occupant
occupation

occurred
occurrence
official
often
omitted
opinion
opponent
opportunity
opposite
optimism
ordinarily
organization
original
outrageous
pamphlet
parallel
paralyze
partial
particularly
pastime
patience
peculiar
pedestal
performance
permanent
permissible
perseverance
personal (ly)
personality
perspiration
persuade
petition
phenomenon
physical
physician
picnicking
planned
playwright
plead
pneumonia
politician
ponder
positively
possession
practically
precede
precious
preference
prejudice
preparation
presence
prevalent
primitive

privilege
probably
proceed
professional
professor
prominent
pronounce
pronunciation
protein
psychology
puny
purchase
pursuing

QR

qualified
quality
quantity
questionnaire
quiet
quite
quizzes
recede
receipt
receive
recipe
recognize
recommend
reference
referred
regard
regimen
religious
repel
repetition
residue
responsibility
restaurant
rheumatism
rhythm
ridiculous
robot
roommate

S

sacrifice
salary
sandwich
satisfactory
scarcely
scenic

schedule
scholar
science
secretary
seize
separate
sergeant
several
severely
sheriff
shrubbery
siege
signature
signify
silhouette
similar
simultaneous
sincerely
skiing
skunk
society
solar
sophomore
souvenir
spaghetti
specific
specimen
statue
stomach
stopped
strength
strictly
submission
substitute
subtle
succeed
success
sufficient
supersede
suppose
surprise
suspicious
symbolism
sympathy
synthetic

TU

tariff
technique
temperature
temporary
tendency

thermostat
thorough (ly)
though
throughout
tongue
tornado
tortoise
tragedy
transferred
tremendous
tried
trite
truly
unanimous
undoubtedly
unfortunately
unique
unnecessary
until
urgent
usable
usher
usually

V

vacuum
vague
valuable
variety
vengeance
versatile
vicinity
villain
visibility
visual

W

waif
Wednesday
weird
wholly
width
women
wrath
wreckage

Y

yesterday
yield
yolk

Steps to Becoming a Better Speller

1. **Be patient.**
   Becoming a good speller takes time.

2. **Check the correct pronunciation of each word you are attempting to spell.**
   Knowing the correct pronunciation of a word can help you remember its spelling.

3. **Note the meaning and history of each word as you are checking the dictionary for pronunciation.**
   Knowing the meaning and history of a word provides you with a better notion of how the word is properly used, and this can help you remember its spelling.

4. **Before you close the dictionary, practice spelling the word.**
   Look away from the page and try to "see" the word in your mind. Then write it on a piece of paper. Check your spelling in the dictionary; repeat the process until you are able to spell the word correctly.

5. **Learn some spelling rules.**
   For four of the most useful rules, see page **664**.

6. **Make a list of the words that you often misspell.**
   Select the first 10 and practice spelling them.

   STEP A: Read each word carefully; then write it on a piece of paper. Check to see that you've spelled it correctly. Repeat this step for the words that you misspelled.

   STEP B: When you have finished your first 10 words, ask someone to read them to you as you write them again. Then check for misspellings. If you find none, congratulations! (Repeat both steps with your next 10 words, and so on.)

7. **Write often.**

"There is little point in learning to spell if you have little intention of writing."
—Frank Smith

Spelling 2

For each sentence below, fill in the blank with the correct word from the list of "Commonly Misspelled Words" (pages 666–667).

Example: A person who has p_____c__ can wait calmly.
patience

1. You may not operate a car without a driver's l_____.

2. _____x_____ is an important part of physical fitness.

3. Zaida has not played in any professional tournaments yet; she still plays at the a_____ level.

4. Some sodas have as much _____f f_____ in them as coffee does.

5. Seth is always _____g his hair different colors.

6. Juries should assume a person's i___n_____ until guilt is proven.

7. Keep the dogs in s_____ kennels; they cannot be together.

8. Angel used a small v_____ to suck up the crumbs in the crevices of his car.

9. A cross is a r_____g_____ icon.

10. Angus kept asking Dom for the test answers, but Dom's _____s c_____ wouldn't let him do it.

11. These garlic potatoes are so d_____s, I'll have another serving!

Model

Model the following sentences to practice using the spelling rules for words ending in *y*.

She was overjoyed that the guests liked her curried lamb.

We were praying that the cub's pitiful whines would end soon.

Test Prep

Read the following paragraphs. From the choices given on the next page, write the letter of the correct way to express each underlined part. If it is already correct, choose "D."

Although the United States was an ally of the Soviet Union during

world war II, tensions afterward led to a period of time known as the
__1__

Cold War. In particular, Western democracies disputed the Soviet Union's

takeover of east european states. A vivid symbol of the Cold War was the
__2__

Berlin Wall, separating west berlin from the territory of East Germany.
__3__

The conflict never heated up into a full-scale war, but both the East

and the West perceived each other as hostile, leading to the arms race. In
__4__

nineteen forty-nine, the Soviets tested their first a-bomb. Of course,
__5__   __6__

the u.s. had already used the bomb on Japan; nevertheless, president
__7__   __8__

Truman's response was to further build up conventional and nuclear

weapons. That the country took the Soviet "threat" very seriously was

evident in its placement of Nike missiles around major U.S. cities. the
__9__

hidden rockets, designed as antiaircraft weapons, were stored underground

and could be raised into fireing position when needed. The first Nike
__10__

missiles in 1954 carried conventional explosives and had a range of

25 miles; 4 years later the range was not only increased to seventy-five
__11__   __12__

miles, but the missiles could carry nuclear warheads as well. The

development of intercontinental ballistic missiles (IcbM's) in the late '50s
__13__

made the Nike missile system obsolete. These self-propelled, unmanned

missiles had a range of many thousand of miles and could be controlled
__14__

remotely. They are still in use today.

Most analysts would agree that the Cold War fizzled as the Soviet Union broke up in the early '90s. The countries involved now cooperate on issues rather than focus on <u>destroing</u> each other. The current advances in
15
international space exploration, for example, show that hostility between nations can be overcome—and that former <u>allies can be allies</u> again.
16

1. **A** World war II
   B World War II
   C world War II
   D correct as is

2. **A** East European states
   B East European States
   C east European states
   D correct as is

3. **A** West Berlin
   B west Berlin
   C West berlin
   D correct as is

4. **A** east and the west
   B east and the West
   C East and the west
   D correct as is

5. **A** 1949
   B nineteen fourty-nine
   C 19 forty-nine
   D correct as is

6. **A** 1st a-bomb
   B first A-bomb
   C first A-Bomb
   D correct as is

7. **A** The U.S.
   B the U.S.
   C the US
   D correct as is

8. **A** president truman's
   B President truman's
   C President Truman's
   D correct as is

9. **A** U.S. citys. The
   B U.S. cities. The
   C U.S. citys. the
   D correct as is

10. **A** raised into firing
   B raised into fiering
   C raiseed into firing
   D correct as is

11. **A** 25 miles; four years
   B twenty-five miles; 4 years
   C 25 mile; four years
   D correct as is

12. **A** seventy-five mile
   B 75 mile
   C 75 miles
   D correct as is

13. **A** IcBM's
   B icbms
   C ICBM's
   D correct as is

14. **A** many thousands of mile
   B many thousands of miles
   C many thousand of mile
   D correct as is

15. **A** distroing
   B distroying
   C destroying
   D correct as is

16. **A** allys can be allys
   B Allies can be Allies
   C allys can be allies
   D correct as is

Understanding Idioms

Idioms are phrases that are used in a special way. You can't understand an idiom just by knowing the meaning of each word in the phrase. You must learn it as a whole. For example, the idiom *bury the hatchet* means "to settle an argument," even though the individual words in the phrase mean something much different. This section will help you learn some of the common idioms in American English.

apple of his eye	Eagle Lake is the apple of his eye. (something he likes very much)
as plain as day	The mistake in the ad was as plain as day. (very clear)
as the crow flies	New London is 200 miles from here as the crow flies. (in a straight line)
at a snail's pace	My last hour at work passes at a snail's pace. (very, very slowly)
axe to grind	The manager has an axe to grind with that umpire. (disagreement to settle)
bad apple	There are no bad apples in this class. (a bad influence)
beat around the bush	Don't beat around the bush; answer the question. (avoid getting to the point)
benefit of the doubt	Everyone has been given the benefit of the doubt at least once. (another chance)
beyond the shadow of a doubt	Beyond the shadow of a doubt, this is my best science project. (for certain)
blew my top	When I saw the broken statue, I blew my top. (showed great anger)
bone to pick	Alison had a bone to pick with the student who copied her paper. (problem to settle)
brain drain	Brain drain is a serious problem in some states. (the best students moving elsewhere)
break the ice	The nervous ninth graders were afraid to break the ice. (start a conversation)
burn the midnight oil	Devon had to burn the midnight oil to finish his report. (work late into the night)

Idioms

bury the hatchet	**My sisters were told to** bury the hatchet **immediately.** (settle an argument)
by the skin of her teeth	**Anna avoided an accident** by the skin of her teeth. (just barely)
champing at the bit	**The skiers were** champing at the bit **to get on the slopes.** (eager, excited)
chicken feed	**The prize was** chicken feed **to some people.** (not worth much money)
chip off the old block	**Frank's just like his father. He's a** chip off the old block. (just like someone else)
clean as a whistle	**My boss told me to make sure the place was as** clean as a whistle **before I left.** (very clean)
cold shoulder	**I wanted to fit in with that group, but they gave me the** cold shoulder. (ignored me)
crack of dawn	**Ali delivers his papers at the** crack of dawn. (first light of day, early morning)
cry wolf	**If you** cry wolf **too often, no one will believe you.** (say you are in trouble when you aren't)
dead of night	**Hearing a loud noise in the** dead of night **frightened Bill.** (middle of the night)
dirt cheap	**A lot of clothes at that store are** dirt cheap. (inexpensive, costing very little money)
doesn't hold a candle to	**That award** doesn't hold a candle to **a gold medal.** (is not as good as)
drop in the bucket	**The contributions were a** drop in the bucket. (a small amount compared to what's needed)
everything from A to Z	**That catalog lists** everything from A to Z. (a lot of different things)
face the music	**Todd had to** face the music **when he broke the window.** (deal with the punishment)
fish out of water	**He felt like a** fish out of water **in the new math class.** (someone in an unfamiliar place)
fit for a king	**The food at the athletic banquet was** fit for a king. (very special)

flew off the handle	Bill flew off the handle **when he saw a reckless driver near the school.** (became very angry)
floating on air	Celine was floating on air **at the prom.** (feeling very happy)
food for thought	The boys' foolish and dangerous prank gave us food for thought. (something to think about)
get down to business	After sharing several jokes, Mr. Sell said we should get down to business. (start working)
get the upper hand	The wrestler moved quickly on his opponent in order to get the upper hand. (gain the advantage)
give their all	Student volunteers give their all **to help others.** (work as hard as they can)
go fly a kite	Charlene stared at her nosy brother and said, "Go fly a kite." (go away)
has a green thumb	Talk to Mrs. Smith about your sick plant. She has a green thumb. (is good at growing plants)
has a heart of gold	Joe has a heart of gold. (is very kind and generous)
hit a home run	Rhonda hit a home run **with her speech.** (succeeded, or did well)
hit the ceiling	When my parents saw my grades, they hit the ceiling. (were very angry)
hit the hay	Exhausted from the hike, Jamal hit the hay **without eating supper.** (went to bed)
in a nutshell	Can you, in a nutshell, **tell us your goals for this year?** (in summary)
in one ear and out the other	Sharl, concerned about her pet, let the lecture go in one ear and out the other. (without really listening)
in the black	My aunt's gift shop is finally in the black. (making money)
in the nick of time	Janelle caught the falling vase in the nick of time. (just in time)
in the red	Many businesses start out in the red. (in debt)
in the same boat	The new tax bill meant everyone would be in the same boat. (in a similar situation)

iron out	Joe will meet with the work crew to iron out their complaints. (solve, work out)
it goes without saying	It goes without saying that saving money is a good idea. (it is clear)
it stands to reason	It stands to reason that your stamina will increase if you run every day. (it makes sense)
keep a stiff upper lip	Keep a stiff upper lip when you visit the doctor. (be brave)
keep it under your hat	Keep it under your hat about the pop quiz. (don't tell anyone)
knock on wood	My uncle knocked on wood after he said he had never had the flu. (did something for good luck)
knuckle down	After wasting half the day, we were told to knuckle down. (work hard)
learn the ropes	It takes every new employee a few months to learn the ropes. (get to know how things are done)
leave no stone unturned	The police plan to leave no stone unturned at the crime scene. (check everything)
lend someone a hand	You will feel good if you lend someone a hand. (help someone)
let's face it	Let's face it. You don't like rap. (let's admit it)
let the cat out of the bag	Tom let the cat out of the bag during lunch. (told a secret)
look high and low	We looked high and low for Jan's dog. (looked everywhere)
lose face	In some cultures, it is very bad to lose face. (be embarrassed)
needle in a haystack	Trying to find a person in New York is like trying to find a needle in a haystack. (something impossible to find)
nose to the grindstone	With all of these assignments, I have to keep my nose to the grindstone. (working hard)
on cloud nine	After talking to my girlfriend, I was on cloud nine. (feeling very happy)
on pins and needles	Nancy was on pins and needles during the championship game. (feeling nervous)

Idioms

out the window	**Once the rain started, our plans were** out the window. (ruined)
over and above	Over and above **the required work, Will cleaned up the lab.** (in addition to)
pain in the neck	**Franklin knew the report would be a** pain in the neck. (very annoying)
pull your leg	**Cary was only** pulling your leg. (telling you a little lie as a joke)
put his foot in his mouth	**Lane** put his foot in his mouth **when he answered the question.** (said something embarrassing)
put the cart before the horse	**Tonya** put the cart before the horse **when she sealed the envelope before inserting the letter.** (did something in the wrong order)
put your best foot forward	**When applying for a job, you should** put your best foot forward. (do the best that you can do)
red-letter day	**Sheila had a** red-letter day **because she did so well on her math test.** (very good day)
rock the boat	**I was told not to** rock the boat. (cause trouble)
rude awakening	**Jake will have a** rude awakening **when he sees the bill for his computer.** (sudden, unpleasant surprise)
save face	**His gift was clearly an attempt to** save face. (fix an embarrassing situation)
see eye to eye	**We** see eye to eye **about the need for a new school.** (are in agreement)
shake a leg	**I told Mako to** shake a leg **so that we wouldn't be late.** (hurry)
shift into high gear	**Greg had to** shift into high gear **to finish the test in time.** (speed up, hurry)
sight for sore eyes	**My grandmother's smiling face was a** sight for sore eyes. (good to see)
sight unseen	**Liz bought the coat** sight unseen. (without seeing it first)
sink or swim	**Whether you** sink or swim **in school depends on your study habits.** (fail or succeed)

spilled the beans	Suddenly, Jose realized that he had spilled the beans. (revealed a secret)
spring chicken	Although Mr. Gordon isn't a spring chicken, he sure knows how to talk to kids. (young person)
stick to your guns	Know what you believe, and stick to your guns. (don't change your mind)
sweet tooth	Chocolate is often the candy of choice for those with a sweet tooth. (a love for sweets, like candy and cake)
take a dim view	My sister will take a dim view of that movie. (disapprove)
take it with a grain of salt	When you read that advertisement, take it with a grain of salt. (don't believe everything)
take the bull by the horns	It's time to take the bull by the horns so the project gets done on time. (take control)
through thick and thin	Those two girls have remained friends through thick and thin. (in good times and in bad times)
time flies	Time flies as you grow older. (time passes quickly)
time to kill	Grace had time to kill, so she read a book. (extra time)
to go overboard	The class was told not to go overboard. A $50.00 donation was fine. (to do too much)
toe the line	The new teacher made everyone toe the line. (follow the rules)
tongue-tied	He can talk easily with friends, but in class he is usually tongue-tied. (not knowing what to say)
turn over a new leaf	He decided to turn over a new leaf in school. (make a new start)
two peas in a pod	Ever since kindergarten, Lil and Eve have been like two peas in a pod. (very much alike)
under the weather	Guy was feeling under the weather this morning. (sick)
wallflower	Joan knew the other girls thought she was a wallflower. (a shy person)
word of mouth	Joseph learns a lot about his favorite team by word of mouth. (talking with other people)

Idioms

Using the Right Word

a lot ■ *A lot* (always two words) is a vague descriptive phrase that should be used sparingly.

> "You can observe a lot just by watching."
>
> — Yogi Berra

accept, except ■ The verb *accept* means "to receive" or "to believe"; the preposition *except* means "other than."

> The principal accepted the boy's story about the broken window, but she asked why no one except him saw the ball accidentally slip from his hand.

adapt, adopt ■ *Adapt* means "to adjust or change to fit"; *adopt* means "to choose and treat as your own" (a child, an idea).

> After a lengthy period of study, Malcolm X adopted the Islamic faith and adapted to its lifestyle.

affect, effect ■ The verb *affect* means "to influence"; the verb *effect* means "to produce, accomplish, complete."

> Ming's hard work effected an A on the test, which positively affected her semester grade.

The noun *effect* means the "result."

> Good grades have a calming effect on parents.

aisle, isle ■ An *aisle* is a passage between seats; an *isle* is a small island.

> Many airline passengers on their way to the Isle of Capri prefer an aisle seat.

all right ■ *All right* is always two words (not *alright*).

allusion, illusion ■ *Allusion* is an indirect reference to someone or something; *illusion* is a false picture or idea.

> My little sister, under the illusion that she's movie-star material, makes frequent allusions to her future fans.

already, all ready ■ *Already* is an adverb meaning "before this time" or "by this time." *All ready* is an adjective meaning "fully prepared."

NOTE: Use *all ready* if you can substitute *ready* alone in the sentence.

> Although I've already had some dessert, I am all ready for some ice cream from the street vendor.

Using the Right Word 1

a lot; accept, except; **adapt, adopt;** affect, effect; **aisle, isle;** all right

 Read the following paragraphs. If an underlined word is used incorrectly, write the correct word. If it's correct as is, write "OK."

Example: 1. *OK*

Located in the middle of the Irish Sea between Liverpool and Belfast, the (1) <u>Isle</u> of Man is an independent country of approximately 77,000 people. (2) <u>Alot</u> of British people live there, but about half the population is native, known as Manx.

The island's status as an offshore financial center has had a positive (3) <u>affect</u> on the Manx economy. Current unemployment is only 1 percent, so a growing population of foreigners (4) <u>except</u> jobs on the Isle of Man to take advantage of the economic possibilities. Soon, they (5) <u>adopt</u> the island as their home—and (6) <u>adopt</u> to the damp climate. The island's weather is (7) <u>effected</u> by the Gulf Stream that runs through the Irish Sea, and there is not a wide fluctuation in temperatures: 68°F in summer and 48°F in winter. The precipitation is rain and fog (8) <u>accept</u> for snow that sometimes falls in late February or early March.

In the town of Douglas, young people visit shops and cafes, leisure centers, and bowling alleys. They descend the (9) <u>isles</u> at cinemas to see the latest movies. The area also boasts sports and facilities such as the new skateboard, in-line skating, and BMX area. That sounds (10) <u>all right</u>!

Model

Model the following sentences to practice using the words *already* and *all ready* correctly.

> Advice is what we ask for when we already know the answer but wish we didn't.
>
> —Erica Jong

> I've prepared everything we need; I believe we're all ready to leave now.

altogether, all together ▪ *Altogether* means "entirely." The phrase *all together* means "in a group" or "all at once."

> **"There is altogether too much gridlock," complained the Democrats. All together, the Republicans yelled, "No way!"**

among, between ▪ *Among* is used when speaking of more than two persons or things. *Between* is used when speaking of only two.

> **The three of us talked among ourselves to decide between going out or eating in.**

amount, number ▪ *Amount* is used for bulk measurement. *Number* is used to count separate units. (See also *fewer, less*.)

> **A substantial amount of honey spilled all over a number of my CD's.**

annual, biannual, semiannual, biennial, perennial ▪ An *annual* event happens once every year. A *biannual* or *semiannual* event happens twice a year. A *biennial* event happens every two years. A *perennial* event is one that is persistent or constant.

> **Dad's annual family reunion gets bigger every year.**
> **We're going shopping at the department store's semiannual white sale.**
> **Due to dwindling attendance, the county fair is now a biennial celebration.**
> **A perennial plant persists for several years.**

anyway ▪ Do not add an *s* to *anyway*.

ascent, assent ▪ *Ascent* is the act of rising or climbing; *assent* is "to agree to something after some consideration" (or such an agreement).

> **We completed our ascent of the butte with the assent of the landowner.**

bad, badly ▪ *Bad* is an adjective. *Badly* is an adverb.

> **This apple is bad, but one bad apple doesn't always ruin the whole bushel.**
> **In today's game, Ross passed badly.**

base, bass ▪ *Base* is the foundation or the lower part of something. *Bass* (pronounced like *base*) is a deep sound. *Bass* (pronounced like *class*) is a fish.

beside, besides ▪ *Beside* means "by the side of." *Besides* means "in addition to."

> **Mother always grew roses beside the trash bin. Besides looking nice, they also gave off a sweet smell that masked odors.**

Using the Right Word 2

altogether, all together; among, between; **amount, number**; annual, biannual, biennial, perennial; **ascent, assent**; bad, badly

 Write the correct choice from those given in parentheses.

Example: Shawn is such a cheerful guy—he seems to have *(an annual, a perennial)* smile on his face.

     a perennial

1. The *(amount, number)* of gray wolves in Minnesota increased tenfold from 1967 to the present.

2. *(Altogether, All together)*, they numbered about 3,020 in 2004.

3. The consensus *(among, between)* experts is that the population will continue to grow.

4. The volunteer firefighters hold their *(biannual, biennial)* pancake breakfast every March and September.

5. Mom and Dad go to each one since their *(bad, badly)* accident a few years ago.

6. Everyone was surprised at Cruz's rapid *(ascent, assent)* to a leadership position in the student government.

7. He didn't do *(bad, badly)* in his first year's elections.

8. He is *(altogether, all together)* a great candidate for almost any office.

9. The *(amount, number)* of support he can count on is staggering.

10. People often *(ascent, assent)* to vote for him after meeting him just once.

11. Maybe he can fit in a political internship *(among, between)* high school and college.

 ## Model

Model the following sentence to practice using the word *anyway*.

Courage is being scared to death—but saddling up anyway.
        —John Wayne

board, bored ■ *Board* is a piece of wood. *Board* is also an administrative group or council.

The school board approved the purchase of fifty 1- by 6-inch pine boards.

Bored is the past tense of the verb "bore," which may mean "to make a hole by drilling" or "to become weary out of dullness."

Watching television bored Joe, so he took his drill and bored a hole in the wall where he could hang his new clock.

brake, break ■ *Brake* is a device used to stop a vehicle. *Break* means "to separate or to destroy."

I hope the brakes on my car never break.

bring, take ■ *Bring* suggests the action is directed toward the speaker; *take* suggests the action is directed away from the speaker.

Bring home some garbage bags so I can take the trash outside.

can, may ■ *Can* suggests ability while *may* suggests permission.

"Can I go to the mall?" means "Am I physically able to go to the mall?"
"May I go to the mall?" asks permission to go.

capital, capitol ■ The noun *capital* refers to a city or to money. The adjective *capital* means "major or important." *Capitol* refers to a building.

The state capital is home to the capitol building for a capital reason. The state government contributed capital for its construction.

cent, sent, scent ■ *Cent* is a coin; *sent* is the past tense of the verb "send"; *scent* is an odor or a smell.

For thirty-seven cents, I sent my girlfriend a mushy love poem in a perfumed envelope. She adored the scent but hated the poem.

cereal, serial ■ *Cereal* is a grain, often made into breakfast food. *Serial* relates to something in a series.

Mohammed enjoys reading serial novels while he eats a bowl of cereal.

chord, cord ■ *Chord* may mean "an emotion" or "a combination of musical tones sounded at the same time." A *cord* is a string or a rope.

The guitar player strummed the opening chord to the group's hit song, which struck a responsive chord with the audience.

chose, choose ■ *Chose* (chōz) is the past tense of the verb *choose* (chooz).

Last quarter I chose to read Chitra Divakaruni's *The Unknown Errors of Our Lives*—a fascinating book about Indian immigrants.

Using the Right Word 3

board, bored; brake, break; **can, may;** capital, capitol; **cent, sent, scent**

 Select the correct word from the list above to complete each sentence. (One word is used twice.)

Example: I'll give you $12 for that CD, and not one _____ more.
  cent

1. My mechanic says my car needs _____ work.

2. A typical business start-up needs a _____ infusion of several thousand dollars.

3. Although most teens love summer, some are _____ by the lack of intellectual stimulation.

4. Most teachers require that you ask whether you _____ leave to use the washroom.

5. As Moira walked down the hall, the _____ of her perfume lingered after her.

6. Rap the egg sharply with a knife to _____ its shell.

7. We climbed up the grand staircase in the _____ to get to our senator's office.

8. My makeshift shelf consisted of a _____ laid across two milk crates.

9. _____ you help me move this sofa?

10. I _____ a job application to the zoo.

11. I hope I _____ get the job.

Model

Model the following sentences to practice using the words *can* and *may* correctly.

No one can make you feel inferior without your consent.
                                    —Eleanor Roosevelt, *This Is My Story*

Conscience is the inner voice that warns us somebody may be looking.
                                    —H. L. Mencken, *A Mencken Chrestomathy*

Right Word

coarse, course ■ *Coarse* means "rough or crude"; *course* means "a path or direction taken." *Course* also means "a class or a series of studies."

> Fletcher, known for using coarse language, was barred from the golf course until he took an etiquette course.

complement, compliment ■ *Complement* refers to that which completes or fulfills. *Compliment* is an expression of admiration or praise.

> Kimberly smiled, thinking she had received a compliment when Carlos said that her new Chihuahua complemented her personality.

continual, continuous ■ *Continual* refers to something that happens again and again with some breaks or pauses; *continuous* refers to something that keeps happening, uninterrupted.

> Sunlight hits Iowa on a continual basis; sunlight hits Earth continuously.

counsel, council ■ When used as a noun, *counsel* means "advice"; when used as a verb, it means "to advise." *Council* refers to a group that advises.

> The student council counseled all freshmen to join a school club. That's good counsel.

desert, dessert ■ The noun *desert* (dĕz´ərt) refers to barren wilderness. *Dessert* (dĭ zûrt´) is food served at the end of a meal.

> The scorpion tiptoed through the moonlit desert, searching for dessert.

The verb *desert* (dĭ zûrt´) means "to abandon"; the noun *desert* (dĭ zûrt´) means "deserved reward or punishment."

> The burglar's hiding place deserted him when the spotlight swung his way; his subsequent arrest was his just desert.

die, dye ■ *Die* (dying) means "to stop living." *Dye* (dyeing) is used to change the color of something.

different from, different than ■ Use *different from* in a comparison of two things. *Different than* should be used only when followed by a clause.

> Yassine is quite different from his brother.
> Life is different than it used to be.

farther, further ■ *Farther* refers to a physical distance; *further* refers to additional time, quantity, or degree.

> Alaska extends farther north than Iceland does. Further information can be obtained in an atlas.

fewer, less ■ *Fewer* refers to the number of separate units; *less* refers to bulk quantity.

> Because we have fewer orders for cakes, we'll buy less sugar and flour.

Using the Right Word 4

coarse, course; counsel, council; **die, dye**; farther, further; **fewer, less**

 Write the correct choice from those given in parentheses.

Example: Rae's *(coarse, course)* hair frizzed whenever it was humid.

coarse

1. Last week, she sought the *(counsel, council)* of a trusted stylist.

2. The stylist encouraged Rae to *(die, dye)* her hair.

3. Quincy runs every other day; he enjoys trying to find a different *(coarse, course)* each week.

4. He is building his strength slowly, so he attempts to run a little *(farther, further)* each time he goes out.

5. He finds that he experiences *(fewer, less)* incidents of being totally out of breath now that he runs so often.

6. The Norwood city *(counsel, council)* meets once a month at city hall.

7. Tomorrow the members will *(farther, further)* discuss the drought's effect on local farmers.

8. Their crops will *(die, dye)* if we don't get rain soon.

9. The area has had *(fewer, less)* rain than it did during the drought of '86.

Model

Model the following sentences to practice using the words *farther* and *further* correctly.

Gratitude is merely the secret hope of further favors.

—Francois de La Rochefoucauld

The farther behind I leave the past, the closer I am to forgiving my own character.

—Isabelle Eberhardt

flair, flare ■ *Flair* refers to style or natural talent; *flare* means "to light up quickly" or "burst out" (or an object that does so).

Ronni was thrilled with Jorge's flair for decorating—until one of his strategically placed candles flared, marring the wall.

good, well ■ *Good* is an adjective; *well* is nearly always an adverb. (When *well* is used to describe a state of health, it is an adjective: He was happy to be *well* again.)

The CD player works well.

Our team looks good this season.

heal, heel ■ *Heal* means "to mend or restore to health." A *heel* is the back part of a foot.

Achilles died because a poison arrow pierced his heel and caused a wound that would not heal.

healthful, healthy ■ *Healthful* means "causing or improving health"; *healthy* means "possessing health."

Healthful foods build healthy bodies.

hear, here ■ You *hear* with your ears. *Here* means "the area close by."

heard, herd ■ *Heard* is the past tense of the verb "hear"; *herd* is a large group of animals.

hole, whole ■ A *hole* is a cavity or hollow place. *Whole* means "complete."

idle, idol ■ *Idle* means "not working." An *idol* is someone or something that is worshipped.

The once-popular actress, who had been idle lately, wistfully recalled her days as an idol.

immigrate, emigrate ■ *Immigrate* means "to come into a new country or environment." *Emigrate* means "to go out of one country to live in another."

Martin Ulferts immigrated to this country in 1882. He was only three years old when he emigrated from Germany.

imply, infer ■ *Imply* means "to suggest or express indirectly"; *infer* means "to draw a conclusion from facts." (A writer or speaker implies; a reader or listener infers.)

Dad implied by his comment that I should drive more carefully, and I inferred that he was concerned for both me and his new car.

Using the Right Word 5

good, well; heal, heel; **healthful, healthy;** hear, here; **hole, whole**

 Write the correct choice from those given in each set of numbered parentheses.

Example: 1. healthful

There are questions about whether or not certain dietary supplements are, in fact, **(1)** *(healthful, healthy)*. People **(2)** *(hear, here)* all kinds of claims from the manufacturers. But do the supplements **(3)** *(heal, heel)* people of any medical conditions? Can they make weak, inactive people strong and **(4)** *(healthful, healthy)* again? Or is the supplement industry just a big **(5)** *(hole, whole)* where gullible people throw their money?

Since supplements are not regulated by the federal government, it is hard to find **(6)** *(good, well)*, solid evidence one way or the other. It's possible that supplements will work **(7)** *(good, well)* in some people and not in others. While only man-made pharmaceuticals might work **(8)** *(hear, here)*, herbal supplements might do fine there. But because supplements may actually be harmful to some individuals, the **(9)** *(hole, whole)* issue is an important one.

Some people rely solely on supplements, but many use a combination of therapies. For instance, I use a homeopathic ointment on my sore **(10)** *(heal, heel)*, but I also take ibuprofen for the pain. I take the most **(11)** *(healthful, healthy)* approach when it comes to taking care of myself.

Model

Model the following sentences to practice using the words *good* and *well* correctly.

> **In spite of everything I still believe that people are really good at heart.**
> —Anne Frank

> **People forget how fast you did a job—but they remember how well you did it.**
> —Howard Newton

Right Word

insure, ensure ■ *Insure* means "to secure from financial harm or loss." *Ensure* means "to make certain of something."

To ensure that you can legally drive that new car, you'll have to insure it.

it's, its ■ *It's* is the contraction of "it is." *Its* is the possessive form of "it."

It's hard to believe, but the movie *Shrek* still holds its appeal for many kids.

later, latter ■ *Later* means "after a period of time." *Latter* refers to the second of two things mentioned.

Later that year we had our second baby and adopted a stray kitten. The latter was far more welcomed by our toddler.

lay, lie ■ *Lay* means "to place." *Lay* is a transitive verb. (See **716.1**.)

Lay your books on the big table.

Lie means "to recline," and *lay* is the past tense of *lie*. *Lie* is an intransitive verb. (See **716.1**.)

In this heat, the children must lie down for a nap. Yesterday they lay down without one complaint. Sometimes they have lain in the hammocks to rest.

lead, led ■ *Lead* (lēd) is the present tense of the verb meaning "to guide." The past tense of the verb is *led* (lĕd). The noun *lead* (lĕd) is a metal.

We were led along the path that leads to an abandoned lead mine.

learn, teach ■ *Learn* means "to acquire information." *Teach* means "to give information."

I learn better when people teach with real-world examples.

leave, let ■ *Leave* means "to allow something to remain behind." *Let* means "to permit."

Would you let me leave my bike at your house?

lend, borrow ■ *Lend* means "to give for temporary use." *Borrow* means "to receive for temporary use."

I told Mom I needed to borrow $18 for a CD, but she said she could only lend money for school supplies.

like, as ■ When *like* is used as a preposition meaning "similar to," it can be followed only by a noun, pronoun, or noun phrase; when *as* is used as a subordinating conjunction, it introduces a subordinate clause.

You could become a gymnast like her, as you work and practice hard.

medal, meddle ■ *Medal* is an award. *Meddle* means "to interfere."

Some parents meddle in the awards process to be sure that their kids get medals.

Using the Right Word 6

it's, its; later, latter; **learn, teach;** lend, borrow; **medal, meddle**

For each paragraph below, choose the correct words from the list above to fill in the blanks.

Example: 1. *it's*

Clayton Dyer is a professional bass fisherman who was born without one arm and both of his legs. You can imagine that **(1)**_____ not easy to operate his boat and manipulate the rods, but Clayton has won more than one **(2)**_____ during his career. He has won 25 tournaments. When disabled children ask Clayton to **(3)**_____ them how to fish, he gladly does so. He says, "If I could **(4)**_____ how to fish, anyone can!"

My sister Mykaela loves to **(5)**_____ in my business. Once, I was trying to avoid facing my dad over a scratch on his car. I "repaired" the finish using some nail polish that matched **(6)**____color. She piped up, "You might think that's the right thing to do now, but you'll regret it **(7)**_____!" Recently she overheard me asking a friend to **(8)**_____ me some money. Mykaela said, "You shouldn't **(9)**_____ money from friends!" I don't know whether I should argue with her or ignore her. (Usually, I choose the **(10)**_____.)

Model

Model the following sentences to practice using the words *learn* and *teach* correctly.

A critic is a legless man who teaches running.

—Channing Pollock

We could never learn to be brave and patient if there were only joy in the world.

—Helen Keller

metal, mettle ■ *Metal* is a chemical element like iron or gold. *Mettle* is "strength of spirit."

> **Grandad's mettle during battle left him with some metal in his shoulder.**

miner, minor ■ A *miner* digs for valuable ore. A *minor* is a person who is not legally an adult. A *minor* problem is one of no great importance.

moral, morale ■ A *moral* is a lesson drawn from a story; as an adjective, it relates to the principles of right and wrong. *Morale* refers to someone's attitude.

> **Ms. Ladue considers it her moral obligation to go to church every day.**
> **The students' morale sank after their defeat in the forensics competition.**

passed, past ■ *Passed* is a verb. *Past* can be used as a noun, an adjective, or a preposition.

> **That old pickup truck passed my sports car! (verb)**
> **Many senior citizens hold dearly to the past. (noun)**
> **Tilly's past life as a circus worker must have been . . . interesting. (adjective)**
> **Who can walk past a bakery without looking in the window? (preposition)**

peace, piece ■ *Peace* means "tranquility or freedom from war." *Piece* is a part or fragment.

> **Grandma sits in the peace and quiet of the parlor, enjoying a piece of pie.**

peak, peek, pique ■ A *peak* is a high point. *Peek* means "brief look" (or "look briefly"). *Pique*, as a verb, means "to excite by challenging"; as a noun, it is a feeling of resentment.

> **The peak of Dr. Fedder's professional life was his ability to pique children's interest in his work. "Peek at this slide," he said to the eager students.**

pedal, peddle, petal ■ A *pedal* is a foot lever; as a verb, it means "to ride a bike." *Peddle* means "to go from place to place selling something." A *petal* is part of a flower.

> **Don Miller paints beautiful petals on his homemade birdhouses. Then he pedals through the flea market every weekend to peddle them.**

personal, personnel ■ *Personal* means "private." *Personnel* are people working at a particular job.

plain, plane ■ *Plain* means "an area of land that is flat or level"; it also means "clearly seen or clearly understood."

> **It's plain to see why settlers of the Great Plains had trouble moving west.**

Plane means "flat, level"; it is also a tool used to smooth the surface of wood.

> **I used a plane to make the board plane and smooth.**

Using the Right Word 7

miner, minor; past, passed; **peace, piece**; pedal, peddle, petal;
personal, personnel

 Write the correct choice from those given in parentheses.

Example: Would you care for a *(peace, piece)* of lasagna?

    piece

1. Soraya supervises all the maintenance *(personal, personnel)* at the hospital.

2. I haven't been feeling well for the *(past, passed)* few days, but I'm sure it's just a *(miner, minor)* bug.

3. We don't see many people who *(pedal, peddle, petal)* products door-to-door these days.

4. A *(miner, minor)* who does not take precautions is likely to get lung disease.

5. It's an uncomfortable situation when someone's *(personal, personnel)* hygiene leaves a little to be desired.

6. As Rohan *(past, passed)* his old girlfriend's house, he unconsciously hit the brake *(pedal, peddle, petal)*.

7. The *(peace, piece)* demonstrations of the 1960s affected public opinion about the Vietnam War.

8. This poor flower has just one *(pedal, peddle, petal)* left clinging to its stem.

 ## Model

Model the following sentences to practice using the words *passed* and *past* correctly.

> Soon silence will have passed into legend.
>
>   —Jean Arp, "Sacred Silence"

> The future, according to some scientists, will be exactly like the past, only far more expensive.
>
>   —John Sladek

Right Word

poor, pour, pore ■ *Poor* means "needy or pitiable." *Pour* means "to cause to flow in a stream." A *pore* is an opening in the skin.

Tough exams on late spring days make my poor pores pour sweat.

principal, principle ■ As an adjective, *principal* means "primary." As a noun, it can mean "a school administrator" or "a sum of money." *Principle* means "idea or doctrine."

His principal concern is fitness. (adjective) The principal retired. (noun)
During the first year of a loan, you pay more interest than principal. (noun)
The principle of *caveat emptor* is "Let the buyer beware."

quiet, quit, quite ■ *Quiet* is the opposite of "noisy." *Quit* means "to stop." *Quite* means "completely or entirely."

quote, quotation ■ *Quote* is a verb; *quotation* is a noun.

The quotation I used was from Woody Allen. You may quote me on that.

real, really, very ■ Do not use *real* in place of the adverbs *very* or *really*.

Mother's cake is usually very (not *real*) tasty, but this one is really stale!

right, write, wright, rite ■ *Right* means "correct or proper"; it also refers to that which a person has a legal claim to, as in copyright. *Write* means "to inscribe or record." A *wright* is a person who makes or builds something. *Rite* refers to a ritual or ceremonial act.

Write this down: It is the right of the shipwright to perform the rite of christening—breaking a bottle of champagne on the stern of the ship.

ring, wring ■ *Ring* means "encircle" or "to sound by striking." *Wring* means "to squeeze or twist."

At the beach, Grandma would ring her head with a large scarf. Once, it blew into the sea, so she had me wring it out.

scene, seen ■ *Scene* refers to the setting or location where something happens; it also may mean "sight or spectacle." *Seen* is a form of the verb "see."

Serena had seen her boyfriend making a scene; she cringed.

seam, seem ■ *Seam* (noun) is a line formed by connecting two pieces. *Seem* (verb) means "to appear to exist."

The ragged seams in his old coat seem to match the creases in his face.

set, sit ■ *Set* means "to place." *Sit* means "to put the body in a seated position." *Set* is transitive; *sit* is intransitive. (See **716.1**.)

How can you just sit there and watch as I set all these chairs in place?

Using the Right Word 8

poor, pour, pore; quiet, quit, quite; **scene, seen**; seam, seem

 Select the correct word from the list above to complete each sentence.

Example: Yellow police tape often surrounds the _____ of a crime.
scene

1. Many teenagers know what happens when too much sebum clogs a _____.

2. Simon _____ his job last month.

3. He was _____ fortunate to find another one so soon.

4. Three more years until graduation might _____ like a long time—but to your parents, it's not.

5. Grandma says she is _____ in terms of cash but rich in many other ways.

6. Have you ever _____ a tornado?

7. Sometimes the bus is actually a _____ place to think.

8. The mistake most first-timers make when applying wallpaper is not matching a _____.

9. The pitcher doesn't have a spout, so it's difficult to _____ from it.

Model

Model the following sentences to practice using the words *quiet* and *quite* correctly.

Full bottles are quiet; it's the empty ones that make all the noise.
—Chinese proverb

Nothing is quite as bad as being without privacy and lonely at the same time.
—Alexander Theroux

Right Word

sight, cite, site ■ *Sight* means "the act of seeing"; a *sight* is what is seen. *Cite* means "to quote" or "to summon," as before a court. *Site* means "location."

> In her report, the general contractor cited several problems at the downtown job site. For one, the loading area was a chaotic sight.

sole, soul ■ *Sole* means "single, only one"; *sole* also refers to the bottom surface of the foot. *Soul* refers to the spiritual part of a person.

> As the sole inhabitant of the island, he put his heart and soul into his farming.

stationary, stationery ■ *Stationary* means "not movable"; *stationery* refers to the paper and envelopes used to write letters.

steal, steel ■ *Steal* means "to take something without permission"; *steel* is a type of metal.

than, then ■ *Than* is used in a comparison; *then* tells when.

> Abigail shouted that her big brother was bigger than my big brother. Then she ran away.

their, there, they're ■ *Their* is a possessive personal pronoun. *There* is an adverb used to point out location. *They're* is the contraction for "they are."

> They're a well-dressed couple. Do you see them there, with their matching jackets?

threw, through ■ *Threw* is the past tense of "throw." *Through* means "from beginning to end."

> Through seven innings, Egor threw just seven strikes.

to, too, two ■ *To* is a preposition that can mean "in the direction of." *To* is also used to form an infinitive. (See **726.2**) *Too* means "also" or "very." *Two* is a number.

vain, vane, vein ■ *Vain* means "valueless or fruitless"; it may also mean "holding a high regard for oneself." *Vane* is a flat piece of material set up to show which way the wind blows. *Vein* refers to a blood vessel or a mineral deposit.

> The vain prospector, boasting about the vein of silver he'd uncovered, paused to look up at the turning weather vane.

vary, very ■ *Vary* means "to change." *Very* means "to a high degree."

> Though the weather may vary from day to day, generally, it is very pleasant.

Using the Right Word 9

steal, steel; than, then; **their, there, they're;** threw, through;
to, too, two

 Read the following paragraphs. If a numbered word is used incorrectly, write the correct word. If it's correct as is, write "OK."

Example: 1. Then

Sometimes it's not practical to build a bridge by sinking supports into the ground. **(1)** Than a suspension bridge is the answer. Early suspension bridges were made of rope and wood. Today, **(2)** their roadways supported by cables made of thousands of individual **(3)** steal wires bound tightly together. Huge main cables rest on top of high towers and extend from one end of the bridge **(4)** to the other. Anchorage systems at both ends are embedded in rock or concrete blocks. The cables are spread over a large area for **(5)** too reasons: to distribute **(6)** they're load, and to prevent them from breaking free.

Suspension bridges can span distances far longer **(7)** then any other kind of bridge. Currently, the longest bridge (at about 6,500 feet) is over the Akashi Strait in Japan. Since it is an earthquake-prone area **(8)** their, the bridge must withstand great forces of nature. As with most other suspension bridges, it must remain standing as 150-mph winds blast **(9)** threw its cables, **(10)** too. For these reasons, suspension bridges are built to be somewhat flexible. Fortunately, this type of bridge is usually quite pleasing to the eye, as well.

Model

Model the following sentences to practice using the words *then* and *than* correctly.

> All you need in this life is ignorance and confidence; then success is sure.
>
> —Mark Twain

> You can no more win a war than you can win an earthquake.
>
> —Jeannette Rankin

Right Word

vial, vile ■ A *vial* is a small container for liquid. *Vile* is an adjective meaning "foul, despicable."

It's a vile job, but someone has to clean these lab vials.

waist, waste ■ *Waist* is the part of the body just above the hips. The verb *waste* means "to spend or use carelessly" or "to wear away or decay"; the noun *waste* refers to material that is unused or useless.

Her waist is small because she wastes no opportunity to exercise.

wait, weight ■ *Wait* means "to stay somewhere expecting something." *Weight* refers to a degree or unit of heaviness.

ware, wear, where ■ *Ware* refers to a product that is sold; *wear* means "to have on or to carry on one's body"; *where* asks "in what place?" or "in what situation?"

The designer boasted, "Where can anybody wear my ware? Anywhere."

way, weigh ■ *Way* means "path or route." *Weigh* means "to measure weight" or "to have a certain heaviness."

My dogs weigh too much. The best way to reduce is a daily run in the park.

weather, whether ■ *Weather* refers to the condition of the atmosphere. *Whether* refers to a possibility.

Due to the weather, the coach wondered whether he should cancel the meet.

which, that ■ Use *which* to refer to objects or animals in a nonrestrictive clause (set off with commas). Use *that* to refer to objects or animals in a restrictive clause. (For more information about these types of clauses, see **612.2**.)

The birds, which stay in the area all winter, know where the feeders are located. The food that attracts the most birds is sunflower seed.

who, whom ■ Use *who* to refer to people. *Who* is used as the subject of a verb in an independent clause or in a relative clause. *Whom* is used as the object of a preposition or as a direct object.

To whom do we owe our thanks for these pizzas? And who ordered anchovies?

who's, whose ■ *Who's* is the contraction for "who is." *Whose* is a pronoun that can show possession or ownership.

Cody, whose car is new, will drive. Who's going to read the map?

your, you're ■ *Your* is a possessive pronoun. *You're* is the contraction for "you are."

Take your boots if you're going out in that snow.

Using the Right Word 10

waist, waste; wait, weight; **way, weigh;** who's, whose; **your, you're**

 Write the correct choice from those given in parentheses.

Example: Although Mariah and Sharlene have the same *(waist, waste)* measurement, they have very different body types.
waist

1. Ms. Hull, *(who's, whose)* dog ran away last week, is offering a reward for its safe return.

2. I have a friend who refuses to *(wait, weight)* for me if I am late.

3. Can you bring *(your, you're)* CD's to my party?

4. Some people gain *(wait, weight)* over the winter holidays.

5. The grocery store cashier must *(way, weigh)* fresh fruits and vegetables to get a price.

6. "Gee, *(your, you're)* swell," said Biff to Bunny.

7. The lost tourists asked if we knew the *(way, weigh)* to the beach.

8. Kirk Swenson, *(who's, whose)* a volunteer firefighter, was able to help when Dillon fainted.

9. Is throwing a clock in a landfill a *(waist, waste)* of time?

Model

Model the following sentences to practice using the words *your* and *you're* correctly.

> Skiing combines outdoor fun with knocking down trees with your face.
>
> —Dave Barry

> The trouble with the rat race is that even if you win, you're still a rat.
>
> —Lily Tomlin

Test Prep

Write the letter of the line in which an underlined word is used incorrectly. If all the words are correct, choose "D."

1. A I don't really enjoy my <u>biannual</u> visits to the dental hygienist.
B During my last visit, the dentist had <u>scene</u> a cavity.
C She said, "<u>It's</u> best that we fill it right away."
D All are used correctly.

2. A Dale always <u>seams</u> surprised at the yield from his garden.
B He harvests a huge <u>amount</u> of produce every year.
C It never goes to <u>waste</u>, though; he donates it to the food pantry.
D All are used correctly.

3. A Try to eat foods made from <u>whole</u> grains.
B They are better for you <u>than</u> processed foods are.
C Some people find that <u>they're</u> also tastier.
D All are used correctly.

4. A "Is it difficult to <u>teach</u> young adults how to drive?" Shayla asked.
B "It can be," the instructor said, "but I can <u>brake</u> if necessary."
C He pointed to an extra <u>petal</u> on the floor by the passenger seat.
D All are used correctly.

5. A Keiko asked Deepak to <u>borrow</u> her some of his DVD's.
B Deepak said he would <u>give his assent</u> on one condition.
C "You must let me use some of <u>your</u> CD's," he said.
D All are used correctly.

6. A We went to the humane society to <u>adopt</u> a kitten.
B It was hard to choose from <u>between</u> the nine or ten there.
C We ended up taking <u>two</u> kittens home with us.
D All are used correctly.

7. A Monique could <u>hear</u> her brothers fighting.
B "Please <u>quit</u> that!" she shouted.
C "I need <u>piece</u> right now!"
D All are used correctly.

8. A No one likes to have to <u>wait</u> in line.
B It's usually a <u>miner</u> inconvenience, but it still isn't fun.
C In fact, it can be <u>quite</u> aggravating.
D All are used correctly.

9. A The music teacher <u>passed</u> out the lyric sheets.
    B He said, "Let's try an initial read-through <u>all together</u>."
    C A <u>number</u> of students did not participate.
    D All are used correctly.

10. A Alyce took the team's loss <u>bad</u>.
    B She <u>threw</u> the volleyball up into the stands.
    C It hit some <u>poor</u> guy in the head.
    D All are used correctly.

11. A The man in the desert thought he would <u>die</u> of thirst.
    B The <u>scene</u> before him was unbelievable: water in the distance.
    C Fortunately, it was not just an <u>allusion</u> of water.
    D All are used correctly.

12. A When Francisco finished lunch, he asked, "<u>May</u> I be excused?"
    B "Wouldn't you like another <u>piece</u> of chicken?" Grandma asked.
    C "I couldn't <u>except</u> another bite," he said.
    D All are used correctly.

13. A I am working <u>fewer</u> hours now than I did over the summer.
    B It has had a definite <u>affect</u> on my spending.
    C Sometimes I don't have a <u>cent</u> to my name!
    D All are used correctly.

14. A Our neighbors often leave <u>their</u> dogs outside in a kennel.
    B They (the <u>latter</u>) will bark and bark and bark.
    C I think they must be <u>bored</u>.
    D All are used correctly.

15. A Alejandra knows how to play the <u>steel</u> drums.
    B She plays them very <u>good</u>.
    C Last spring, her band played at the <u>capitol</u> building.
    D All are used correctly.

16. A <u>Who's</u> supposed to take the garbage out?
    B We can't add anything <u>further</u> to this bag.
    C It must <u>way</u> a ton already.
    D All are used correctly.

Parts of Speech

Words in the English language are used in eight different ways. For this reason, there are eight parts of speech.

700.1 Noun

A word that names a person, a place, a thing, or an idea

Governor Smith-Jones   Oregon   hospital   religion

700.2 Pronoun

A word used in place of a noun

I   you   she   him   who   everyone   these   neither theirs   themselves   which

700.3 Verb

A word that expresses action or state of being

float   sniff   discover   seem   were   was

700.4 Adjective

A word that describes a noun or a pronoun

young   big   grim   Canadian   longer

700.5 Adverb

A word that describes a verb, an adjective, or another adverb

briefly   forward   regally   slowly   better

700.6 Preposition

The first word or words in a prepositional phrase (which functions as an adjective or an adverb)

away from   under   before   with   for   out of

700.7 Conjunction

A word that connects other words or groups of words

and   but   although   because   either, or   so

700.8 Interjection

A word that shows strong emotion or surprise

Oh no!   Yipes!   Good grief!   Well, . . .

Parts of Speech

Noun

A **noun** is a word that names something: a person, a place, a thing, or an idea.

    governor   **Oregon**   **hospital**   **Buddhism**   **love**

Classes of Nouns

The five classes of nouns are *proper, common, concrete, abstract,* and *collective.*

701.1   Proper Noun

A **proper noun** names a particular person, place, thing, or idea. Proper nouns are always capitalized.

Jackie Robinson	**Brooklyn**	**World Series**
Christianity	**Ebbets Field**	**Hinduism**

701.2   Common Noun

A **common noun** does not name a particular person, place, thing, or idea. Common nouns are not capitalized.

    person   **woman**   **president**   **park**   **baseball**   **government**

701.3   Concrete Noun

A **concrete noun** names a thing that is tangible (can be seen, touched, heard, smelled, or tasted). Concrete nouns are either proper or common.

    child   **Grand Canyon**   **music**   **aroma**   **fireworks**   **Becky**

701.4   Abstract Noun

An **abstract noun** names an idea, a condition, or a feeling—in other words, something that cannot be touched, smelled, tasted, seen, or heard.

    New Deal   **greed**   **poverty**   **progress**   **freedom**   **awe**

701.5   Collective Noun

A **collective noun** names a group or a unit.

    United States   **Portland Cementers**   **team**   **crowd**   **community**

Parts of Speech

Forms of Nouns

Nouns are grouped according to their *number, gender,* and *case.*

702.1 Number of a Noun

Number indicates whether the noun is singular or plural.

A **singular noun** refers to one person, place, thing, or idea.

actor   stadium   Canadian   bully   truth   child   person

A **plural noun** refers to more than one person, place, thing, or idea.

actors   stadiums   Canadians   bullies   truths   children   people

702.2 Gender of a Noun

Gender indicates whether a noun is masculine, feminine, neuter, or indefinite.

Masculine: uncle   brother   men   bull   rooster   stallion
Feminine: aunt   sister   women   cow   hen   filly
Neuter (without gender): tree   cobweb   flying fish   closet
Indefinite (masculine or feminine): president   plumber   doctor   parent

702.3 Case of a Noun

Case tells how nouns are related to other words used with them. There are three cases: *nominative, possessive,* and *objective.*

- A **nominative case** noun can be the subject of a clause.

   Patsy's heart was beating very wildly beneath his jacket. . . . That black horse there owed something to the orphan he had made.
                    —Paul Dunbar, "The Finish of Patsy Barnes"

   A nominative noun can also be a predicate noun (or predicate nominative), which follows a "be" verb *(am, is, are, was, were, be, being, been)* and renames the subject. In the sentence below, *type* renames *Mr. Cattanzara.*

   Mr. Cattanzara was a different type than those in the neighborhood.
                    —Bernard Malamud, "A Summer's Reading"

- A **possessive case** noun shows possession or ownership.

   Like the spider's claw, a part of him touches a world he will never enter.
                    —Loren Eiseley, "The Hidden Teacher"

- An **objective case** noun can be a direct object, an indirect object, or an object of the preposition.

   Marna always gives Mylo science-fiction books for his birthday.

   (*Mylo* is the indirect object and *books* is the direct object of the verb "gives." *Birthday* is the object of the preposition "for.")

Nouns

- Classes of Nouns
- Gender of Nouns

 For each underlined noun, write its class (there are at least two classes for each) and gender, as shown.

Example: When I was a child, my family vacationed at <u>Parker Lake</u>.
    class: proper, concrete   gender: neuter

1. I was one of nine children in my <u>family</u>.

2. All 11 of us took the three-hour trip in our <u>Country Squire</u>—a station wagon with "wood" panels on the sides.

3. You can imagine that the <u>time</u> passed rather slowly on that drive.

4. My littlest <u>sister</u> would sit in my mom's lap.

5. The front bench seat would also accommodate <u>Dad</u> and another sibling.

6. The three oldest kids—two <u>boys</u> and a girl, all teenagers—got the middle seat.

7. The back of the station wagon had a couple of seats that folded up from the middle, and four <u>kids</u> sat there.

8. What a <u>relief</u> to finally get out of the car!

9. We spent a <u>week</u> at the cabin before piling in again for the long ride home.

 ## Model

Model the following sentence to practice using proper, abstract nouns.

> Radical historians now tell the story of Thanksgiving from the point of view of the turkey.
>
> —Mason Cooley

Pronoun

A **pronoun** is a word used in place of a noun.

> I, you, she, it, which, that, themselves, whoever, me, he, they, mine, ours

The three types of pronouns are *simple, compound,* and *phrasal.*

> Simple: I, you, he, she, it, we, they, who, what
> Compound: myself, someone, anybody, everything, itself, whoever
> Phrasal: one another, each other

All pronouns have **antecedents**. An antecedent is the noun that the pronoun refers to or replaces.

> Ambrosch **was considered the important person in the family. Mrs. Shimerda and Ántonia always deferred to** him, **though** he **was often surly with them and contemptuous toward** his **father.**   —Willa Cather, *My Ántonia*

(*Ambrosch* is the antecedent of *him, he,* and *his.*)

NOTE: Each pronoun must agree with its antecedent. (See page **756**.)

704.1 Classes of Pronouns

The six classes of pronouns are *personal, reflexive and intensive, relative, indefinite, interrogative,* and *demonstrative.*

Personal

I, me, my, mine / we, us, our, ours
you, your, yours / they, them, their, theirs
he, him, his, she, her, hers, it, its

Reflexive and Intensive

myself, yourself, himself, herself, itself, ourselves, yourselves, themselves

Relative

what, who, whose, whom, which, that

Indefinite

all	both	everything	nobody	several
another	each	few	none	some
any	each one	many	no one	somebody
anybody	either	most	nothing	someone
anyone	everybody	much	one	something
anything	everyone	neither	other	such

Interrogative

who, whose, whom, which, what

Demonstrative

this, that, these, those

Pronouns 1

■ Antecedents

For the following paragraphs, write the antecedent of each underlined pronoun.

Example: 1. *Margaret Knight*

In the 1850s, it was not uncommon for children to work in factories. One of these children, Margaret Knight, was only 12 years old when **(1)** <u>she</u> saw a coworker suffer a serious injury from a machine that wouldn't stop. She invented a stop-motion device to prevent **(2)** <u>it</u> from happening again.

Margaret went on to invent a lot of other things, but she is probably best known for her 1868 invention, **(3)** <u>which</u> she thought of while working in a paper-bag factory. **(4)** <u>It</u> was an addition to the machines that made the paper bags. This new part automatically folded and glued the bags so **(5)** <u>they</u> had square bottoms. Workmen who were installing the part didn't want to listen to a woman's advice, but **(6)** <u>they</u> had no choice. Of course, the part worked, and this type of paper bag is still in use today.

Margaret Knight patented **(7)** <u>her</u> invention and eventually received patents for 25 other inventions. Among **(8)** <u>these</u> were a numbering machine and a window frame and sash. Upon her death in 1914, Margaret was remembered as "the female Edison."

Model

Model the following sentence to practice using a pronoun and an antecedent in the same sentence.

I never think of the future—it comes soon enough.

—Albert Einstein

706.1 Personal Pronoun

A **personal pronoun** can take the place of any noun.

> Our coach made her point loud and clear when she raised her voice.

- A **reflexive pronoun** is formed by adding *-self* or *-selves* to a personal pronoun. A reflexive pronoun can be a direct object, an indirect object, an object of the preposition, or a predicate nominative.

> Miss Sally Sunshine loves herself. (direct object of *loves*)
> Tomisha does not seem herself today. (predicate nominative)

- An **intensive pronoun** is a reflexive pronoun that intensifies, or emphasizes, the noun or pronoun it refers to.

> Leo himself taught his children to invest their lives in others.

706.2 Relative Pronoun

A **relative pronoun** relates or connects an adjective clause to the noun or pronoun it modifies.

> Students who study regularly get the best grades. Surprise!
> The dance, which we had looked forward to for weeks, was canceled.

(The relative pronoun *who* relates the adjective clause to *students; which* relates the adjective clause to *dance.*)

706.3 Indefinite Pronoun

An **indefinite pronoun** refers to unnamed or unknown people or things.

> I don't know if you've known anybody from that far back; if you've loved anybody that long, first as an infant, then as a child, then as a man. . . . (The antecedent of *anybody* is unknown.)
> —James Baldwin, "My Dungeon Shook: Letter to My Nephew"

706.4 Interrogative Pronoun

An **interrogative pronoun** asks a question.

> "Then, who are you? Who could you be? What do you want from my husband?"
> —Elie Wiesel, "The Scrolls, Too, Are Mortal"

706.5 Demonstrative Pronoun

A **demonstrative pronoun** points out people, places, or things without naming them.

> This shouldn't be too hard. That looks about right.
> These are the best ones. Those ought to be thrown out.

NOTE: When one of these words precedes a noun, it functions as an adjective, not a pronoun. (See **728.1**.)

> That movie bothers me. (*That* is an adjective.)

Pronouns 2

- Personal Pronouns (Reflexive and Intensive)
- Indefinite Pronouns
- Interrogative Pronouns

 Identify each underlined pronoun as *reflexive, intensive, indefinite,* or *interrogative*.

Example: <u>Who</u> was the comic chosen to host *Late Night* in 1993?
        interrogative

1. <u>Many</u> applied for the position, but Conan O'Brien was the one selected for the comedy-variety show.

2. O'Brien got his comedy career going for <u>himself</u> at Harvard, where he was president of the *Harvard Lampoon*.

3. Did <u>anyone</u> there realize he was headed for fame?

4. <u>What</u> did Conan <u>himself</u> see in his future?

5. In the late '80s and early '90s, <u>everybody</u> loved his work as a writer for *Saturday Night Live* and *The Simpsons*.

6. Then, in 1993, he found <u>himself</u> hosting a new late-night talk show.

7. I <u>myself</u> see a long, successful future for Conan.

 ## Model

Model the following sentences to practice using reflexive and intensive pronouns.

Never trust anything that can think for itself if you can't see where it keeps its brain.
      —J. K. Rowling, *Harry Potter and the Chamber of Secrets*

I was always looking outside myself for strength and confidence, but it comes from within.
      —Anna Freud

Forms of Personal Pronouns

The form of a personal pronoun indicates its *number* (singular or plural), its *person* (first, second, third), its *case* (nominative, possessive, or objective), and its *gender* (masculine, feminine, or neuter).

708.1 Number of a Pronoun

Personal pronouns are singular or plural. The singular personal pronouns include *my, him, he, she, it.* The plural personal pronouns include *we, you, them, our.* (*You* can be singular or plural.) Notice in the caption below that the first *you* is singular and the second *you* is plural.

"Larry, you need to keep all four tires on the road when turning.
Are you still with us back there?"

708.2 Person of a Pronoun

The **person** of a pronoun indicates whether the person, place, thing, or idea represented by the pronoun is speaking, is spoken to, or is spoken about.

- **First person** is used in place of the name of the speaker or speakers.

    "We don't do things like that," says Pa; "we're just and honest people.
    . . . I don't skip debts."

    —Jesse Stuart, "Split Cherry Tree"

- **Second person** pronouns name the person or persons spoken to.

    "If you hit your duck, you want me to go in after it?" Eugie said.

    —Gina Berriault, "The Stone Boy"

- **Third person** pronouns name the person or thing spoken about.

    She had hardly realized the news, further than to understand that she
    had been brought . . . face to face with something unexpected and final.
    It did not even occur to her to ask for any explanation.

    —Joseph Conrad, "The Idiots"

Pronouns 3

- Number of a Pronoun
- Person of a Pronoun

Identify the person and number of each underlined pronoun.

Example: "Rosa and Ruby, your bus is coming!" Mrs. Genara shouted.
   second person plural

1. They missed the bus.

2. The bus driver said he couldn't wait for them.

3. Mrs. Genara was mad that they'd missed it and she would have to drive Rosa and Ruby to school.

4. As they rode in the car, Rosa said, "It's not my fault."

5. "Well, I wasn't ready yet!" Ruby pouted.

6. "Why does it take you so long to get ready, Ruby?" Mrs. Genara asked.

7. "She never gets up on time," Rosa said.

8. "Don't be mad at us, Mom," Ruby said.

9. "Do me a favor," Mrs. Genara said, "and try to be on time from now on."

10. "We will," the girls said.

11. They grabbed their books and ran into the school.

Model

Write a few sentences using the following forms of personal pronouns: *first person plural, second person singular,* and *third person singular.* Identify each one.

710.1 Case of a Pronoun

The **case** of each pronoun tells how it is related to the other words used with it. There are three cases: *nominative, possessive,* and *objective.*

■ A **nominative case** pronoun can be the subject of a clause. The following are nominative forms: *I, you, he, she, it, we, they.*

> **I like life when things go well. You must live life in order to love life.**

A nominative pronoun is a *predicate nominative* if it follows a "be" verb (*am, is, are, was, were, be, being, been*) or another linking verb (*appear, become, feel,* etc.) and renames the subject.

> **"Oh, it's only she who scared me just now," said Mama to Papa, glancing over her shoulder.**
> **"Yes, it is I," said Mai in a superior tone.**

■ **Possessive case** pronouns show possession or ownership. Apostrophes, however, are not used with personal pronouns.

> **But as I placed my hand upon his shoulder, there came a strong shudder over his whole person.**
> —Edgar Allan Poe, "The Fall of the House of Usher"

■ An **objective case** pronoun can be a direct object, an indirect object, or an object of the preposition.

> **The kids loved it! We lit a campfire for them and told them old ghost stories.** (*It* is the direct object of the verb *loved. Them* is the object of the preposition *for* and the indirect object of the verb *told.*)

Number, Person, and Case of Personal Pronouns

	Nominative	Possessive	Objective
First Person Singular	I	my, mine	me
Second Person Singular	you	your, yours	you
Third Person Singular	he	his	him
	she	her, hers	her
	it	its	it

	Nominative	Possessive	Objective
First Person Plural	we	our, ours	us
Second Person Plural	you	your, yours	you
Third Person Plural	they	their, theirs	them

710.2 Gender of a Pronoun

Gender indicates whether a pronoun is masculine, feminine, or neuter.

Masculine: **he him his**   Feminine: **she her hers**
Neuter (without gender): **it its**

Pronouns 4

■ Case of a Pronoun

 Identify each underlined pronoun as *nominative, possessive,* or *objective.*

Example: 1. *possessive*

Colton, my sister's boyfriend, was eating food from **(1)** <u>our</u> refrigerator, and it was also **(2)** <u>he</u> who just walked in our front door without knocking. Maybe **(3)** <u>we</u> ought to start charging **(4)** <u>him</u> an entry fee.

"Make **(5)** <u>yourself</u> comfortable," **(6)** <u>my</u> brother, Gavin, said.

"Are **(7)** <u>you</u> being sarcastic?" Colton asked dully. He pulled **(8)** <u>his</u> head out of the fridge and closed **(9)** <u>it</u>.

"I am merely making a suggestion," Gavin said. "In fact, is there anything **(10)** <u>I</u> can get for **(11)** <u>you</u>?"

"No," he said, "**(12)** <u>your</u> sister is already getting **(13)** <u>me</u> a drink from the basement."

"How kind of **(14)** <u>her</u>," Gavin snickered.

"Yeah, **(15)** <u>she</u>'s great," Colton said.

Model

Use the following pronouns in a brief dialogue: *it, our, they,* and *you*. Identify the case of each one.

Test Prep

Read the following paragraphs. Write the letter of the part of speech of each underlined part from the choices given on the next page.

It took months to clear away the rubble remaining after the collapse of the <u>World Trade Center</u> in 2001. Once that was done, however, the
1
rebuilding could begin. <u>What</u> could possibly replace <u>it</u>? An international
2 **3**
contest to create a new design for the site resulted <u>in</u> the selection of
architect Daniel Libeskind's ambitious plan. <u>His</u> design for the 16-acre
4
site features a hanging garden and several new buildings.

The focal point of Libeskind's design is the <u>Freedom Tower</u>, topping
5
out at a symbolic 1,776 feet. As it emits light skyward, <u>it</u> will remind
people of the Statue of Liberty's torch—another beacon of freedom. With
assistance from architect <u>David Childs</u>, the building was redesigned
6
to use environmentally friendly <u>materials</u> and be a model of energy
7
efficiency. By 2010, the Freedom Tower will open <u>its</u> doors to the world.
8
<u>People</u> will be able to view key 9/11 artifacts at the Memorial
9
Museum. <u>It</u> will be adjacent to the World Trade Center Memorial.
10
"Reflecting <u>Absence</u>," as the memorial is known, was the winning entry
11
in the <u>World Trade Center Site Memorial Competition</u>. It consists of two
12
pools recessed in the footprints of the twin towers. Visitors will descend
from ground level into the memorial <u>itself</u> on ramps. <u>They</u> will enter
13 **14**
a cool, dark space where a thin curtain of water falls from above into
each pool. The names of the tragedy's <u>victims</u> will encircle the pools, and
15
<u>everyone</u> will recall the enormity of the disaster.
16

1. A proper abstract noun
   B proper concrete noun
   C common abstract noun
   D common concrete noun

2. A intensive pronoun
   B reflexive pronoun
   C interrogative pronoun
   D masculine pronoun

3. A reflexive pronoun
   B nominative pronoun
   C possessive pronoun
   D objective pronoun

4. A intensive pronoun
   B nominative pronoun
   C possessive pronoun
   D objective pronoun

5. A antecedent of "it" (in the next sentence)
   B objective pronoun
   C indefinite pronoun
   D common abstract noun

6. A feminine noun
   B masculine noun
   C neuter noun
   D indefinite noun

7. A feminine noun
   B masculine noun
   C neuter noun
   D indefinite noun

8. A plural objective pronoun
   B plural possessive pronoun
   C singular objective pronoun
   D singular possessive pronoun

9. A proper abstract noun
   B proper concrete noun
   C common abstract noun
   D common concrete noun

10. A antecedent of "artifacts"
    B nominative pronoun
    C possessive pronoun
    D objective pronoun

11. A proper abstract noun
    B proper concrete noun
    C common abstract noun
    D common concrete noun

12. A proper abstract noun
    B proper concrete noun
    C common abstract noun
    D common concrete noun

13. A intensive pronoun
    B reflexive pronoun
    C interrogative pronoun
    D feminine pronoun

14. A first person plural pronoun
    B third person plural pronoun
    C third person singular pronoun
    D second person plural pronoun

15. A proper abstract noun
    B proper concrete noun
    C common abstract noun
    D common concrete noun

16. A intensive pronoun
    B reflexive pronoun
    C interrogative pronoun
    D indefinite pronoun

Verb

A **verb** is a word that expresses action (*run, carried, declared*) or state of being (*is, are, seemed*).

Classes of Verbs

714.1 Linking Verbs

A **linking verb** links the subject to a noun or an adjective in the predicate.

In the outfield, the boy felt confident.
He was the best fielder around.

Common Linking Verbs

is	are	was	were	be	been	am

Additional Linking Verbs

smell	seem	grow	become	appear	sound
taste	feel	get	remain	stay	look	turn

714.2 Auxiliary Verbs

Auxiliary verbs, or helping verbs, are used to form some of the **tenses** (718.3), the **mood** (724.1), and the **voice** (722.2) of the main verb. (In the example below, the auxiliary verbs are in red; the main verbs are in blue.)

The long procession was led by white-robed priests, their faces streaked with red and yellow and white ash. By this time the flames had stopped spurting, and the pit consisted of a red-hot mass of burning wood, which attendants were leveling with long branches.

—Leonard Feinberg, "Fire Walking in Ceylon"

Common Auxiliary Verbs

is	was	being	did	have	would	shall	might
am	were	been	does	had	could	can	must
are	be	do	has	should	will	may	

Verbs 1

- Linking Verbs
- Auxiliary Verbs

 Write whether each underlined word is a linking verb or an auxiliary verb.

Example: Yvette <u>is</u> a woman who loves to garden.
           linking verb

1. She <u>can</u> get just about anything to grow.

2. Several of her friends <u>are</u> helping her tend a vegetable garden this summer.

3. They <u>seem</u> happy to do it—especially since they <u>will</u> reap what they sow!

4. It <u>was</u> so exciting to see the seedlings pop up out of the rich soil.

5. Before long, the plants <u>were</u> reaching for the sky.

6. Because it had <u>been</u> so hot and dry, Yvette <u>would</u> water the garden often.

7. Her friends have <u>been</u> weeding all along.

8. Yvette and her helpers <u>might</u> begin harvesting soon.

9. They <u>are</u> sure that everything will <u>taste</u> great!

 ## Model

Model the following sentence to practice using linking and auxiliary verbs.

It is true that I was born in Iowa, but I can't speak for my twin sister.
                                              —Abigail Van Buren

716.1 Action Verbs: Transitive and Intransitive

An **intransitive verb** communicates an action that is complete in itself. It does not need an object to receive the action.

> The boy flew on his skateboard. He jumped and flipped and twisted.

A **transitive verb** (red) is an action verb that needs an object (blue) to complete its meaning.

> The city council passed a strict noise ordinance.

While some action verbs are only transitive *or* intransitive, some can be either, depending on how they are used.

> He finally stopped to rest. (intransitive)
> He finally stopped the show. (transitive)

716.2 Objects with Transitive Verbs

- A **direct object** receives the action of a transitive verb directly from the subject. Without it, the transitive verb's meaning is incomplete.

  > The boy kicked his skateboard forward. (*Skateboard* is the direct object.)
  > Then he put one foot on it and rode like a pro.

- An **indirect object** also receives the action of a transitive verb, but indirectly. An indirect object names the person *to whom* or *for whom* something is done. (An indirect object can also name the thing *to what* or *for what* something is done.)

  > Ms. Oakfield showed us pictures of the solar system.
  > (*Us* is the indirect object.)
  > She gave Tony an A on his project.

  NOTE: When the word naming the indirect receiver of the action is in a prepositional phrase, it is no longer considered an indirect object.

  > Ms. Oakfield showed pictures of the solar system to us.
  > (*Us* is the object of the preposition *to*.)

Verbs 2

■ Transitive and Intransitive Verbs

 Write whether each underlined verb is transitive or intransitive. For a transitive verb, also write the direct object.

Example: Davonte <u>plays</u> the guitar as one of his hobbies.
transitive verb, guitar

1. Sometimes he <u>plays</u> with a bunch of friends in a band.

2. They really don't <u>sing</u> very well, if you ask me.

3. Despite that, they <u>auditioned</u> for the city talent show.

4. The judges <u>invited</u> the band back!

5. The band <u>bought</u> some funky clothes at a resale shop to wear at the show.

6. At the performance, they <u>sang</u> a song that one of them had written.

7. Simone <u>plucked</u> the strings of her bass.

8. The audience must have <u>liked</u> it, for they <u>called</u> for an encore.

9. Needless to say, that really <u>surprised</u> me.

10. Was I <u>missing</u> something that others <u>heard</u> in their music?

11. I had better <u>give</u> them another chance!

Model

Model the following sentences to practice using transitive and intransitive verbs.

He raised his head and gazed at me unblinking from beneath the rim of the dark hat.
　　　　　　　　　　—Chaim Potok, *The Gift of Asher Lev*

The hotel and its little outbuildings and the giraffe-like coconut palms hulked on shore, dark on darker.
　　　　　　　　　　—Scott Turow, *Pleading Guilty*

Forms of Verbs

A verb has different forms depending on its *number, person, tense, voice,* and *mood.*

718.1 Number of a Verb

Number indicates whether a verb is singular or plural. In a clause, the verb (in **blue** below) and its subject (in **red**) must both be singular or both be plural.

- **Singular**

   One large island floats off Italy's "toe."

   Italy's northern countryside includes the spectacular Alps.

- **Plural**

   Five small islands float inside Michigan's "thumb."

   The Porcupine Mountains rise above the shores of Lake Superior.

718.2 Person of a Verb

Person indicates whether the subject of the verb is first, second, or third person (is speaking, is spoken to, or is spoken about). The form of the verb usually changes only when a present-tense verb is used with a third-person singular pronoun.

	Singular	Plural
First Person	I sniff	we sniff
Second Person	you sniff	you sniff
Third Person	he/she/it sniffs	they sniff

718.3 Tense of a Verb

Tense indicates time. Each verb has three principal parts: the *present, past,* and *past participle.* All six tenses are formed from these principal parts. The past and past participle of regular verbs are formed by adding *ed* to the present form. For irregular verbs, the past and past participle are usually different words; however, a few have the same form in all three principal parts (see page **720.2**).

718.4 Simple Tenses

- **Present tense** expresses action that is happening at the present time, or action that happens continually, regularly.

   In September, sophomores smirk and joke about the "little freshies."

- **Past tense** expresses action that was completed at a particular time in the past.

   They forgot that just ninety days separated them from freshman status.

- **Future tense** expresses action that will take place in the future.

   They will recall this in three years when they will be freshmen again.

Verbs 3

- Number of a Verb
- Simple Tenses

 Write the verb or verbs in each sentence. Then identify each as *present, past,* or *future.* For present-tense verbs, write whether they are *singular* or *plural.*

Example: 1. is: *present, singular*

(1) The country of Taiwan, an island off the southeastern coast of China, is a bit smaller than the combined area of Maryland and Delaware. **(2)** Despite its size, its population will soon reach nearly 23 million. **(3)** Its capitalist economy thrives as a result of its exports—especially electronics and textiles—to other countries. **(4)** The exports go mainly to China, the United States, and Japan.

(5) Taiwan was settled by people from China in the seventh century. **(6)** In 1895, Japan acquired the island and began to modernize it. **(7)** Following World War II, it was returned to China as a province. **(8)** Though it never seceded from China, Taiwan has a separate government. **(9)** Will the island reunite with China? **(10)** This continues to be a major political issue, so only time will tell.

Model

Model the following sentence twice; use past-tense verbs in one and future-tense verbs in the other.

We make a living by what we get; we make a life by what we give.

—Sir Winston Churchill

Forms of Verbs (continued)

720.1 Perfect Tenses

■ **Present perfect tense** expresses action that began in the past but continues in the present or is completed in the present.

Our boat **has weathered** worse storms than this one.

■ **Past perfect tense** expresses an action in the past that occurred before another past action.

They reported, wrongly, that the hurricane **had missed** the island.

■ **Future perfect tense** expresses action that will begin in the future and be completed by a specific time in the future.

By this time tomorrow, the hurricane **will have smashed** into the coast.

720.2 Irregular Verbs

Common Irregular Verbs and Their Principal Parts

Present Tense	Past Tense	Past Participle	Present Tense	Past Tense	Past Participle	Present Tense	Past Tense	Past Participle
am, be	was, were	been	go	went	gone	shrink	shrank	shrunk
begin	began	begun	grow	grew	grown	sing	sang, sung	sung
bite	bit	bitten	hang	hanged	hanged	sink	sank, sunk	sunk
blow	blew	blown	(execute)			sit	sat	sat
break	broke	broken	hang	hung	hung	slay	slew	slain
bring	brought	brought	(suspend)			speak	spoke	spoken
buy	bought	bought	hide	hid	hidden, hid	spring	sprang,	sprung
catch	caught	caught	know	knew	known		sprung	
choose	chose	chosen	lay	laid	laid	steal	stole	stolen
come	came	come	lead	led	led	strive	strove	striven
dive	dove	dived	leave	left	left	swear	swore	sworn
do	did	done	lie	lay	lain	swim	swam	swum
draw	drew	drawn	(recline)			swing	swung	swung
drink	drank	drunk	lie	lied	lied	take	took	taken
drive	drove	driven	(deceive)			teach	taught	taught
eat	ate	eaten	lose	lost	lost	tear	tore	torn
fall	fell	fallen	make	made	made	throw	threw	thrown
fight	fought	fought	ride	rode	ridden	wake	waked,	waked,
flee	fled	fled	ring	rang	rung		woke	woken
fly	flew	flown	rise	rose	risen	wear	wore	worn
forsake	forsook	forsaken	run	ran	run	weave	weaved,	weaved,
freeze	froze	frozen	see	saw	seen		wove	woven
get	got	gotten	shake	shook	shaken	wring	wrung	wrung
give	gave	given	show	showed	shown	write	wrote	written

These verbs are the same in all principal parts: *burst, cost, cut, hurt, let, put, set,* and *spread.*

Verbs 4

- ### Irregular Verbs

Write the correct form (past tense or past participle) of the verb shown in parentheses to complete each sentence.

Example: The bread dough had _____ enough, so it was ready to bake. *(rise)*
     risen

1. Sarika treasured the pendant her father had _____ her. *(give)*

2. Mustafa _____ me to the mall in his dad's new car. *(drive)*

3. When I was in grade school, Mr. McCall _____ music to the whole student body. *(teach)*

4. My oldest sister has _____ a lawyer for three years. *(be)*

5. When Alemba _____ home from school, he grabbed the mail. *(get)*

6. He looked at each piece as he _____ it into the house. *(bring)*

7. Then he _____ it on the kitchen table for his mom. *(leave)*

8. This is my good friend Beryl, whom I have _____ since I was four years old. *(know)*

9. Once, our dog _____ a dead mouse behind the sofa. *(hide)*

10. Wade said, "That's one too many tests I've _____ today." *(take)*

11. She looks like she has _____ her best friend. *(lose)*

Model

Model the following sentences to practice using irregular verbs correctly.

> **We can't ask the middle class to pay more; their incomes went down and their taxes went up.**
> —Bill Clinton

> **Writers should be read, but neither seen nor heard.**
> —Daphne du Maurier

722.1 Continuous Tenses

■ A **present continuous tense** verb expresses action that is not completed at the time of stating it. The present continuous tense is formed by adding *am, is,* or *are* to the *-ing* form of the main verb.

Scientists are learning **a great deal from their study of the sky.**

■ A **past continuous tense** verb expresses action that was happening at a certain time in the past. This tense is formed by adding *was* or *were* to the *-ing* form of the main verb.

Astronomers were beginning **their quest for knowledge hundreds of years ago.**

■ A **future continuous tense** verb expresses action that will take place at a certain time in the future. This tense is formed by adding *will be* to the *-ing* form of the main verb.

Someday astronauts will be going **to Mars.**

This tense can also be formed by adding a phrase noting the future *(are going to)* plus *be* to the *-ing* form of the main verb.

They are going to be performing **many experiments.**

722.2 Voice of a Verb

Voice indicates whether the subject is acting or being acted upon.

■ **Active voice** indicates that the subject of the verb is, has been, or will be doing something.

For many years Lou Brock held **the base-stealing record.**

Active voice makes your writing more direct and lively.

■ **Passive voice** indicates that the subject of the verb is being, has been, or will be acted upon.

For many years the base-stealing record was held **by Lou Brock.**

NOTE: With a passive verb, the person or thing creating the action is not always stated.

The ordinance was overturned. (Who did the overturning?)

Tense	Active Voice Singular	Active Voice Plural	Passive Voice Singular	Passive Voice Plural
Present	I see you see he/she/it sees	we see you see they see	I am seen you are seen he/she/it is seen	we are seen you are seen they are seen
Past	I/he saw you saw	we/they saw you saw	I/it was seen you were seen	we/they were seen you were seen
Future	I/you/he will see	we/you/they will see	I/you/it will be seen	we/you/they will be seen

Verbs 5

■ Active and Passive Verbs

If any sentence or part of a sentence below is in the passive voice, rewrite it in the active voice. Write "active" if it's already in the active voice.

Example: 1. *active*

(1) In any election, young people have the most to gain by voting. **(2)** If the election isn't won by their favored candidate, these young people have to live with the consequences the longest. **(3)** Unfortunately, voting is done by only a low percentage of people from this age group (18 to 24).

(4) Although many young adults seem cynical about politics, some are taking action. **(5)** They are relying on more than just advertising to become informed. **(6)** Research is done to evaluate a candidate's record. **(7)** Personal connections are sought out. **(8)** A solid picture of each candidate—beyond sound bites and photo ops—is developed. **(9)** Then a decision on whom to vote for is made. **(10)** These young people are realizing the power they have to change things, and they are making a difference.

Model

Write the following sentences in the active voice.

The house was cleaned and dinner prepared by the young servant.

I like long walks, especially when they are taken by people who annoy me.

—Noel Coward

Parts of Speech

724.1 Mood of a Verb

The **mood** of a verb indicates the tone or attitude with which a statement is made.

- **Indicative mood** is used to state a fact or to ask a question.

  Sometimes I'd yell questions at the rocks and trees, and across gorges, or yodel, "What is the meaning of the void?" The answer was perfect silence, so I knew.

  —Jack Kerouac, "Alone on a Mountain Top"

- **Imperative mood** is used to give a command.

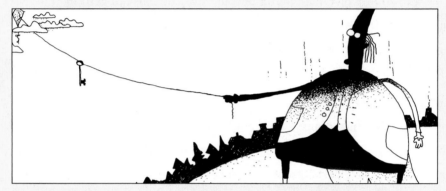

"Whatever you do, don't fly your kite during a storm."
—Mrs. Abiah Franklin

- **Subjunctive mood** is no longer commonly used; however, careful writers may choose to use it to express the exact manner in which their statements are meant.

  Use the subjunctive *were* to express a condition that is contrary to fact.

  If I were finished with my report, I could go to the movie.

  Use the subjunctive *were* after *as though* or *as if* to express an unreal condition.

  Mrs. Young acted as if she were sixteen again.

  Use the subjunctive *be* in "that" clauses to express necessity, legal decisions, or parliamentary motions.

  "It is moved and supported that no more than 6 million quad be used to explore the planet Earth."

  "Ridiculous! Knowing earthlings is bound to help us understand ourselves! Therefore, I move that the sum be amended to 12 million quad."

  "Stupidity! I move that all missions be postponed until we have living proof of life on Earth."

Verbs 6

- Mood of a Verb

Write whether each statement shows *indicative, imperative,* or *subjunctive* mood.

Example: Rhetta acts as though she were already selected prom queen.
     subjunctive

1. Mr. Martinez asked, "When is the prom, anyway?"

2. Stand in that line over there to renew your driver's license.

3. Then sit it the waiting area until your name is called.

4. Malcolm would attend Carson's party if he were not grounded.

5. The gentle, all-day rain was a welcome respite from the summer's long streak of sunny, 90-degree days.

6. Where are the Pyrenees Mountains?

7. Find out—look in an atlas!

8. The doctor recommended that Leticia's broken ribs be wrapped for at least three weeks.

9. Her friends visit her after school.

Model

Model the following sentence to practice using the subjunctive mood.

The studio thought it best that the odd movie first be distributed in a limited area.

Verbals

A **verbal** is a word that is derived from a verb but acts as another part of speech. There are three types of verbals: *gerunds, infinitives,* and *participles.* Each is often part of a verbal phrase.

726.1 Gerunds

A **gerund** is a verb form that ends in *ing* and is used as a noun.

Swimming **is my favorite pastime.** (subject)

I began swimming **at the age of six months.** (direct object)

Swimming in chlorinated pools **makes my eyes red.** (gerund phrase used as a subject)

726.2 Infinitives

An **infinitive** is a verb form that is usually introduced by *to;* the infinitive may be used as a noun, an adjective, or an adverb.

Most people find it easy to swim. (adverb modifying an adjective)

To swim the English Channel **must be a thrill.** (infinitive phrase as noun)

The urge to swim in tropical waters **is more common.** (infinitive phrase as adjective)

726.3 Participles

A **participle** is a verb form ending in *ing* or *ed* that acts as an adjective.

The workers raking leaves **are tired and hungry.** (participial phrase modifies *workers*)

The bags full of raked **leaves are evidence of their hard work.** (participle modifies *leaves*)

Verbs 7

- ### Verbals

Write whether each underlined word or phrase is a *gerund*, a *participle*, or an *infinitive*.

Example: 1. *gerund*

(1) <u>Eating</u> gelatin dessert is a childhood memory for many. It may be one of Baby's first solid foods because it is so easy (2) <u>to eat</u>. Toddlers and older children like the (3) <u>jiggling</u> food.

(4) <u>To make</u> gelatin, protein called collagen is obtained from (5) <u>cooked</u> animal skin, bones, and tissues. It is filtered and double purified. When collagen is heated, its molecules trap tiny particles of water, resulting in the familiar jellylike substance. (At this point, the Food and Drug Administration no longer considers it a meat product.) Then sugar and other flavorings are mixed in (6) <u>to create</u> the fun dessert.

Peter Cooper invented gelatin in 1845, and fruit flavors were first added in 1897. It became such a staple in America's kitchens that immigrants (7) <u>entering</u> Ellis Island were served gelatin as a welcome to America. (8) <u>Adding</u> vegetables and fruit to gelatin was a way (9) <u>to stretch</u> the family budget in the 1940s. Today people appreciate this sweet, (10) <u>satisfying</u> snack for its low-calorie goodness.

Model

Model the following sentences to practice using gerunds and participles.

Knowing that you know nothing makes you smartest of all.

—Aristotle

Failing to plan is planning to fail.

—Effie Jones

Parts of Speech

Adjective

An **adjective** describes or modifies a noun or a pronoun. The articles *a, an,* and *the* are also adjectives.

> The young **driver peeked through** the big **steering wheel.**
> (*The* and *young* modify *driver; the* and *big* modify *steering wheel.*)

728.1 Types of Adjectives

A **proper adjective** is created from a proper noun and is capitalized.

> In Canada (proper noun), **you will find many cultures and climates.**
> Canadian (proper adjective) **winters can be harsh.**

A **predicate adjective** follows a form of the "be" verb (or other linking verb) and describes the subject.

> **Late autumn seems** grim **to those who love summer.** (*Grim* modifies *autumn.*)

NOTE: Some words can be either adjectives or pronouns (*that, these, all, each, both, many, some,* and so on.). These words are adjectives when they come before the nouns they modify; they are pronouns when they stand alone.

> **Jiao made** both **goals.** (*Both* modifies *goals;* it is an adjective.)
> **Both** were scored in the final period. (*Both* stands alone; it is a pronoun.)

728.2 Forms of Adjectives

Adjectives have three forms: *positive, comparative,* and *superlative.*

- The **positive form** describes a noun or a pronoun without comparing it to anyone or anything else.
  > **The first game was** long and tiresome.

- The **comparative form** (*-er, more,* or *less*) compares two persons, places, things, or ideas.
  > **The second game was** longer and more tiresome **than the first.**

- The **superlative form** (*-est, most,* or *least*) compares three or more persons, places, things, or ideas.
  > **The third game was the** longest and most tiresome **of all.**

  NOTE: Use *more* and *most* (or *less* and *least*)—instead of adding a suffix—with many adjectives of two or more syllables.

Positive	Comparative	Superlative
big	bigger	biggest
helpful	more helpful	most helpful
painful	less painful	least painful

Adjectives

■ Types of Adjectives

Write the adjectives (not including articles or possessive pronouns) in each of the following sentences. Label predicate adjectives with a "P" (as shown).

Example: Many Caribbean countries are troubled.
  many, Caribbean, troubled (P)

1. Pale North Americans and Europeans enjoy these warm havens during their hemisphere's long, cold winters.

2. All residents of the Caribbean, however, must deal with this natural hazard: hurricanes.

3. In addition, individual islands have their own dilemmas.

4. One Caribbean island, Anguilla, has no arable land (so crops do not grow).

5. Its economic health depends heavily on the tourist industry.

6. The small island of Montserrat is highly subject to volcanic explosions.

7. Two-thirds of its population of 12,000 fled following the frightening eruption of the Soufriere Hills Volcano in 1995.

8. Continued eruptions have left half of the island uninhabitable.

9. The poorest country in the Western Hemisphere is Haiti.

10. Although a mere 29 percent of the land is arable, 65 percent of its people farm for a meager income.

11. Puerto Rico, a U.S. territory, has problems, too, including a high unemployment rate.

Model

Model the following sentence to practice using adjectives well.

He had broken thumbs and burnt fingers. He had thick, greasy fingernails he never cut and dusty hair.

—Sandra Cisneros, "One Holy Night"

Adverb

An **adverb** describes or modifies a verb, an adjective, or another adverb.

> She sneezed loudly. (*Loudly* modifies the verb *sneezed*.)
> Her sneezes are really dramatic. (*Really* modifies the adjective *dramatic*.)
> The sneeze exploded very noisily. (*Very* modifies the adverb *noisily*.)

An adverb usually tells *when, where, how,* or *how much*.

730.1 Types of Adverbs

Adverbs can be cataloged in four basic ways: *time, place, manner,* and *degree*.

TIME (These adverbs tell *when, how often,* and *how long.*)

> today, yesterday   daily, weekly   briefly, eternally

PLACE (These adverbs tell *where, to where,* and *from where.*)

> here, there   nearby, beyond   backward, forward

MANNER (These adverbs often end in *ly* and tell *how* something is done.)

> precisely   effectively   regally   smoothly   well

DEGREE (These adverbs tell *how much* or *how little.*)

> substantially   greatly   entirely   partly   too

NOTE: Some adverbs can be written with or without the *ly* ending. When in doubt, use the *ly* form.

> slow, slowly   loud, loudly   fair, fairly   tight, tightly   quick, quickly

730.2 Forms of Adverbs

Adverbs of manner have three forms: *positive, comparative,* and *superlative*.

- The **positive form** describes a verb, an adjective, or another adverb without comparing it to anyone or anything else.

  > Model X vacuum cleans well and runs quietly.

- The **comparative form** (*-er, more,* or *less*) compares how two things are done.

  > Model Y vacuum cleans better and runs more quietly than model X does.

- The **superlative form** (*-est, most,* or *least*) compares how three or more things are done.

  > Model Z vacuum cleans best and runs most quietly of all.

Positive	Comparative	Superlative
well	better	best
fast	faster	fastest
remorsefully	more remorsefully	most remorsefully

Adverbs

Number your paper from 1 to 12 and write down each adverb you find in the following paragraphs.

Example: 1. *carefully*

Carefully reading old science fiction stories sometimes leads scientists to experiment with the theories presented within them. For instance, powering spacecraft with something other than bulky fuel has long been a popular idea in science fiction. In 2005, a partnership between private investors in the United States and Russia effectively produced the world's first solar sail spacecraft.

A solar sail is powered by light. Photons (light particles) bounce off the surface of the craft's broad sails, thereby pushing it forward. The sails slowly turn to catch the sun, changing the angle of reflection to move the craft diagonally.

Unfortunately, the attempt to launch *Cosmos 1*, the first such vehicle, was unsuccessful. Scientists launched it from a Russian nuclear submarine in the Barents Sea, but the engine of the booster rocket failed 83 seconds later. Future (successful) missions may go to other planets and eventually even to the stars.

Model

Model the sentences below to practice using adverbs effectively.

> The thing that is really hard, and really amazing, is giving up on being perfect and beginning the work of becoming yourself.
>
> —Anna Quindlen

> I've always thought that a big laugh is a really loud noise from the soul saying, "Ain't that the truth."
>
> —Quincy Jones, *Victory of the Spirit*

Parts of Speech

Preposition

A **preposition** is the first word (or group of words) in a prepositional phrase. It shows the relationship between its object (a noun or a pronoun that follows the preposition) and another word in the sentence. The first noun or pronoun following a preposition is its object.

> **To make a mustache, Natasha placed the hairy caterpillar** under **her nose.**
> (*Under* shows the relationship between the verb, *placed*, and the object of the preposition, *nose*.)
> **The drowsy insect clung obediently** to the girl's upper lip.
> (The first noun following the preposition *to* is *lip; lip* is the object of the preposition.)

732.1 Prepositional Phrase

A **prepositional phrase** includes the preposition, the object of the preposition, and the modifiers of the object. A prepositional phrase functions as an adverb or as an adjective.

> **Some people** run away from caterpillars.
> (The phrase functions as an adverb and modifies the verb *run*.)
> **However, little** kids with inquisitive minds **enjoy their company.**
> (The phrase functions as an adjective and modifies the noun *kids*.)

NOTE: A preposition is always followed by an object; if there is no object, the word is an adverb, not a preposition.

> **Natasha never** played with caterpillars before. (The word *before* is not followed by an object; therefore, it functions as an adverb that modifies *played*, a verb.)

Common Prepositions

aboard	before	from	of	save
about	behind	from among	off	since
above	below	from between	on	subsequent to
according to	beneath	from under	on account of	together with
across	beside	in	on behalf of	through
across from	besides	in addition to	onto	throughout
after	between	in back of	on top of	till
against	beyond	in behalf of	opposite	to
along	by	in front of	out	toward
alongside	by means of	in place of	out of	under
along with	concerning	in regard to	outside of	underneath
amid	considering	inside	over	until
among	despite	inside of	over to	unto
apart from	down	in spite of	owing to	up
around	down from	instead of	past	up to
aside from	during	into	prior to	upon
at	except	like	regarding	with
away from	except for	near	round	within
because of	for	near to	round about	without

Prepositions

 Write the prepositions you find in each sentence.

Example: The Sears Tower, in Chicago, Illinois, remains one of the
world's tallest buildings since its completion on May 3, 1973.
in, of, since, on

1. At a height of 1,450 feet, it held the record as the tallest building for 25 years.

2. If spread across a single level, the building's 4.56 million square feet would cover 105 acres.

3. Miles of electrical wiring (1,500) and plumbing (25) run through the tower.

4. An elevator system with 104 cars services the 110 floors above three lower levels.

5. Each floor is divided into 75-square-foot column-free modules.

6. The building's base has nine modules, several of which terminate at different levels, leaving two at the top.

7. A restaurant on the 99th floor offers breathtaking views in all directions.

Model

As you scan the list of prepositions on the opposite page, you'll note that some of them can be used as other parts of speech as well. Model the following sentences, which use a word both as a preposition and as another part of speech.

Before our trip, we tied everything to the roof of the car, as we'd done many times before.

—Lisa Grossman

Time flies like an arrow. Fruit flies like a banana.

—Groucho Marx

Conjunction

A **conjunction** connects individual words or groups of words. There are three kinds of conjunctions: *coordinating, correlative,* and *subordinating.*

734.1 Coordinating Conjunctions

Coordinating conjunctions usually connect a word to a word, a phrase to a phrase, or a clause to a clause. The words, phrases, or clauses joined by a coordinating conjunction are equal in importance or are of the same type.

> I could tell by my old man's eyes that he *was nervous* and *wanted to smooth things over,* but Syl didn't give him a chance.
>
> —Albert Halper, "Prelude"

(*And* connects the two parts of a compound predicate; *but* connects two independent clauses that could stand on their own.)

734.2 Correlative Conjunctions

Correlative conjunctions are conjunctions used in pairs.

> They were not only exhausted by the day's journey but also sunburned.

734.3 Subordinating Conjunctions

Subordinating conjunctions connect two clauses that are *not* equally important, thereby showing the relationship between them. A subordinating conjunction connects a dependent clause to an independent clause in order to complete the meaning of the dependent clause.

> A brown trout will study the bait before he eats it. (The clause *before he eats it* is dependent. It depends on the rest of the sentence to complete its meaning.)

Kinds of Conjunctions

Coordinating: and, but, or, nor, for, yet, so

Correlative: either, or; neither, nor; not only, but also; both, and; whether, or

Subordinating: after, although, as, as if, as long as, as though, because, before, if, in order that, provided that, since, so that, that, though, till, unless, until, when, where, whereas, while

---

NOTE: Relative pronouns (page **706.2**) and conjunctive adverbs (page **618.2**) can also connect clauses.

Interjection

An **interjection** communicates strong emotion or surprise. Punctuation—a comma or an exclamation point—sets off an interjection from the rest of the sentence.

> Oh no! The TV broke. Good grief! I have nothing to do! Yipes, I'll go mad!

Conjunctions

Number your paper from 1 to 12. Write the conjunctions you find in the following paragraphs and label them *coordinating, subordinating,* **or** *correlative.* **(Write both correlative conjunctions as one answer.)**

Example: 1. *yet – coordinating*

Stem cells are cells whose functions are not specific, yet they have the potential to become any kind of body cell. They can be "trained" to become part of the surrounding tissue when they are injected into the body. Scientists hold great hope that stem cells will help cure not only organ diseases and various cancers but also neurological diseases such as Parkinson's, Alzheimer's, and multiple sclerosis. Provided that research continues, stem cells might also be coaxed to help repair damage from heart disease, strokes, and spinal cord injuries.

Stem cells from human embryos have generated controversy, but these amazing cells have also been found in liposuctioned fat. The fat stem cells have been programmed to work as muscle, bone, and cartilage cells. Since this source has been discovered only recently, it remains to be seen whether they will work or not in other areas of the body, too.

Model

Model the following sentences to practice using interjections effectively.

"Eureka!" shouted Gran. "This is what my recipe has been missing!"

Ahhh, a man with a sharp wit. Someone ought to take it away from him before he cuts himself.

—Peter da Silva

Test Prep

Read the following paragraphs. Write the letter of the answer that best describes each underlined part from the choices given on the next page.

Everyone thinks of Thomas Jefferson as a statesman—a <u>founding</u>
1
father who served as secretary of state, vice president, and president.
In addition, he <u>is remembered</u> as a writer, author of the Declaration of
2
Independence. But not everyone knows about the other sides of Thomas
Jefferson. He was a scientist, an architect, and a musician, as well.

Jefferson enjoyed all aspects of science, including astronomy,
anatomy, mathematics, physics, meteorology, and anthropology. As an
inventor, he <u>devised</u> machines such as the dumbwaiter, a machine for
3
<u>copying</u> handwriting, and the swivel chair. Jefferson <u>was</u> president of the
4   **5**
American Philosophical Society, the main scientific organization of the
time, and he wrote <u>scholarly</u> papers on paleontology. In botany, Jefferson
6
experimented with new varieties of vegetable seeds <u>from</u> Europe.
7

<u>Another</u> interest Jefferson explored was architecture. He designed
8
his own home, the magnificent Monticello, as well as the Virginia State
Capitol. <u>Although</u> his work <u>was influenced</u> by European design, he
9   **10**
helped develop the unique Federalist style of architecture that became
popular in America.

<u>Along with</u> his <u>more</u> technical interests, Thomas Jefferson was an
11   **12**
accomplished musician. He played the violin, practicing three hours a
day as a young man. His wife, Martha, played piano and guitar, and he
encouraged their children and grandchildren <u>to study</u> music as well. His
13

vast collection of music shows an eclectic taste that <u>included</u> chamber
                                                              14
pieces, historical works, orchestral music, song collections, and operas.

Scientist, architect, musician, <u>and</u> so much more: <u>truly</u>, Thomas
                                    15   **16**
Jefferson was the most versatile of American presidents.

1. A verb
   B verbal – gerund
   C verbal – infinitive
   D verbal – participle

2. A verb – active voice
   B verb – passive voice
   C verbal – participle
   D preposition

3. A action verb
   B linking verb
   C auxiliary verb
   D verbal – participle

4. A verb
   B verbal – gerund
   C verbal – infinitive
   D verbal – participle

5. A action verb
   B linking verb
   C auxiliary verb
   D verbal – gerund

6. A adverb
   B adjective
   C preposition
   D conjunction

7. A adverb
   B adjective
   C preposition
   D conjunction

8. A adverb
   B adjective
   C preposition
   D conjunction

9. A coordinating conjunction
   B subordinating conjunction
   C correlative conjunction
   D adverb

10. A verb – active voice
   B verb – passive voice
   C verbal – infinitive
   D verbal – gerund

11. A adverb
   B adjective
   C preposition
   D conjunction

12. A adverb
   B adjective
   C preposition
   D conjunction

13. A verb
   B verbal – gerund
   C verbal – infinitive
   D verbal – participle

14. A action verb
   B linking verb
   C auxiliary verb
   D verbal – participle

15. A coordinating conjunction
   B subordinating conjunction
   C correlative conjunction
   D preposition

16. A adverb
   B adjective
   C preposition
   D conjunction

Understanding Sentences

Constructing Sentences

A **sentence** is made up of one or more words that express a complete thought. Sentences begin with a capital letter; they end with a period, a question mark, or an exclamation point.

What should we do this afternoon? We could have a picnic. No, I hate the ants!

Using Subjects and Predicates

A sentence usually has a **subject** and a **predicate**. The subject is the part of the sentence about which something is said. The predicate, which contains the verb, is the part of the sentence that says something about the subject.

We write from aspiration and antagonism, as well as from experience.
—Ralph Waldo Emerson

738.1 The Subject

The **subject** is the part of the sentence about which something is said. The subject is always a noun; a pronoun; or a word, clause, or phrase that functions as a noun (such as a gerund or a gerund phrase or an infinitive).

> **Wolves howl.** (noun)
> **They howl for a variety of reasons.** (pronoun)
> **To establish their turf may be one reason.** (infinitive phrase)
> **Searching for "lost" pack members may be another.** (gerund phrase)
> **That wolves and dogs are similar animals seems obvious.** (noun clause)

- A **simple subject** is the subject without its modifiers.
  > **Most wildlife biologists disapprove of crossbreeding wolves and dogs.**

- A **complete subject** is the subject with all of its modifiers.
  > **Most wildlife biologists disapprove of crossbreeding wolves and dogs.**

- A **compound subject** is composed of two or more simple subjects.
  > **Wise breeders and owners know that wolf-dog puppies can display unexpected, destructive behaviors.**

738.2 Delayed Subject

In sentences that begin with *There* or *It* followed by a form of the "be" verb, the subject comes after the verb. The subject is also delayed in questions.

> **There was nothing in the refrigerator.** (The subject is *nothing*; the verb is *was*.)
> **Where is my sandwich?** (The subject is *sandwich*; the verb is *is*.)

Constructing Sentences 1

- Simple, Complete, and Compound Subjects
- Delayed Subjects

 Write the complete subject of each sentence. Circle the simple subject or subjects.

Example: There is always talk about alternative sources of energy.
(talk) about alternative sources of energy

1. Off the coast of Portugal, a truly unique power plant is starting to generate electricity.

2. Ocean waves are the source of the energy.

3. Giant sausage-shaped generators float on the water, using its wave motion to create electricity.

4. A Norwegian energy company and a Scottish manufacturer combined resources to build the generators.

5. The wave farm, consisting of about 30 generators, produces clean, renewable energy.

6. How much energy can the system generate?

7. Three generators can produce enough electricity to supply 1,500 homes.

8. For countries on oceans, renewable wave energy seems like the "wave" of the future.

 ## Model

Model the following sentences to practice using a delayed subject.

Why are our days numbered and not, say, lettered?

—Woody Allen

There is no cure for curiosity.

—Dorothy Parker

Sentences

740.1 The Predicate

The **predicate** is the part of the sentence that shows action or says something about the subject.

> Giant squid do exist.

- A **simple predicate** is the verb without its modifiers.

  > One giant squid measured nearly 60 feet long.

- A **complete predicate** is the simple predicate with all its modifiers.

  > One giant squid measured nearly 60 feet long.
  > (*Measured* is the simple predicate; *nearly 60 feet long* modifies *measured.*)

- A **compound predicate** is composed of two or more simple predicates.

  > A squid grasps its prey with tentacles and bites it with its beak.

  NOTE: A sentence can have a **compound subject** and a **compound predicate.**

  > Both sperm whales and giant squid live and occasionally clash in the deep waters off New Zealand's South Island.

- A **direct object** is part of the predicate and receives the action of the verb. (See **716.2.**)

  > Sperm whales sometimes eat giant squid.
  > (The direct object *giant squid* receives the action of the verb *eat* by answering the question *whales eat what?*)

  NOTE: The **direct object** may be compound.

  > In the past, whalers harvested oil, spermaceti, and ambergris from slain sperm whales.

740.2 Understood Subject and Predicate

Either the subject or the predicate may be "missing" from a sentence, but both must be clearly **understood.**

> Who is in the hot-air balloon?
> (*Who* is the subject; *is in the hot-air balloon* is the predicate.)
> No one.
> (*No one* is the subject; the predicate *is in the hot-air balloon* is understood.)
> Get out of the way!
> (The subject *you* is understood; *get out of the way* is the predicate.)

Constructing Sentences 2

■ Simple, Complete, and Compound Predicates

Write the complete predicate of each sentence. Circle the simple predicate or compound predicate.

Example: North America's greatest earthquake did not happen in California, Alaska, or Mexico.

(did) not (happen) in California, Alaska, or Mexico

1. A series of terrible earthquakes rattled the ground in the Mississippi River valley in the winter of 1811–1812.

2. The series of quakes are named after the town most affected by them, New Madrid, Missouri.

3. New Madrid lies on the Mississippi River at the confluence of southeastern Missouri, southern Illinois, western Kentucky, and northwest Tennessee.

4. Few structures within 250 miles of the town escaped damage that winter.

5. People as far away as Charleston, South Carolina, and Washington, D.C., felt the tremors.

6. The quakes disrupted the bed of the Mississippi and changed its course in two places.

7. The strongest three quakes of the series are estimated to have measured at least 8.0 on the Richter scale.

8. The area was sparsely settled and so suffered few fatalities.

9. Scientists warn, however, of another quake happening on the New Madrid fault within 35 years.

Model

Model the following sentence to practice using a compound predicate.

They come in once a week and weave up and down every aisle and arrive at the cash register, exhausted, with a tipsy heap of groceries.

—Susan Orlean, "All Mixed Up"

Sentences

Using Phrases

A **phrase** is a group of related words that function as a single part of speech. The sentence below contains a number of phrases.

Finishing the race will require running up some steep slopes.

finishing the race (This gerund phrase functions as a subject noun.)

will require (This phrase functions as a verb.)

running up some steep slopes (This gerund phrase acts as an object noun.)

742.1 Types of Phrases

- An **appositive phrase,** which follows a noun or a pronoun and renames it, consists of a noun and its modifiers. An appositive adds new information about the noun or pronoun it follows.

  The Trans-Siberian Railroad, the world's longest railway, stretches from Moscow to Vladivostok. (The appositive phrase renames *Trans-Siberian Railroad* and provides new information.)

- A **verbal phrase** is a phrase based on one of the three types of verbals: *gerund, infinitive,* or *participle.* (See **726.1, 726.2,** and **726.3.**)

  - A **gerund phrase** consists of a gerund and its modifiers. The whole phrase functions as a noun.

    Spotting the tiny mouse was easy for the hawk.
    (The gerund phrase is used as the subject of the sentence.)
    Dinner escaped by ducking under a rock.
    (The gerund phrase is the object of the preposition *by.*)

  - An **infinitive phrase** consists of an infinitive and its modifiers. The whole phrase functions either as a noun, an adjective, or an adverb.

    To shake every voter's hand was the candidate's goal.
    (The infinitive phrase functions as a noun used as the subject.)
    Your efforts to clean the chalkboard are appreciated.
    (The infinitive phrase is used as an adjective modifying *efforts.*)
    Please watch carefully to see the difference.
    (The infinitive phrase is used as an adverb modifying *watch.*)

  - A **participial phrase** consists of a past or present participle and its modifiers. The whole phrase functions as an adjective.

    Following his nose, the beagle took off like a jackrabbit.
    (The participial phrase modifies the noun *beagle.*)
    The raccoons, warned by the rustling, took cover.
    (The participial phrase modifies the noun *raccoons.*)

Constructing Sentences 3

- Appositive Phrases
- Verbal Phrases

 Identify each underlined phrase as an *appositive*, a *gerund*, an *infinitive*, or a *participial phrase.*

Example: More than 3,000 years ago, <u>making glass</u> out of sand became a reality.

gerund phrase

1. In Iraq and Syria, archaeologists have found pieces of glass <u>made in the third millennium B.C.E.</u>

2. The land was then known as Mesopotamia, <u>the land between the Tigris and Euphrates rivers</u>.

3. Glass was considered precious because it was difficult <u>to make</u> and, therefore, uncommon.

4. First silica, <u>the base material of glass</u>, had to be reduced to powder.

5. Then it was melted in a furnace, wrapped around a core <u>shaped from clay and dung</u>, and rolled on a smooth surface.

6. About 2,000 years ago, someone figured out how <u>to blow glass</u>.

7. At the same time, glassmakers started <u>adding lime and soda to the silica</u> prior to heating, making it softer and easier to mold.

8. Oddly enough, the addition of lead to the mixture, first <u>done in 1676</u>, makes the glass sparkle and shine even more.

9. Lead crystal, as it's called, is softer and easier <u>to cut</u> than other kinds of glass.

Model

Model the following sentence to practice using an appositive phrase.

My very existence, my life in the world, seemed like a hallucination.

—Haruki Murakami, "Sleep"

Sentences

Using Phrases *(continued)*

■ A **verb phrase** consists of a main verb preceded by one or more helping verbs.

> Snow has been falling for days. (*Has been falling* is a verb phrase.)

■ A **prepositional phrase** is a group of words beginning with a preposition and ending with a noun or a pronoun. Prepositional phrases function mainly as adjectives and adverbs.

> Reach for that catnip ball behind the couch. (The prepositional phrase *behind the couch* is used as an adjective modifying *catnip ball*.)
>
> Zach won the wheelchair race in record time. (*In record time* is used as an adverb modifying the verb *won*.)

■ An **absolute phrase** consists of a noun and a participle (plus the participle's object, if there is one, and any modifiers). An absolute phrase functions as an adjective that adds information to the entire sentence. Absolute phrases are always set off with commas.

> Its wheels clattering rhythmically over the rails, the train rolled into town. (The noun *wheels* is modified by the present participle *clattering*. The entire phrase modifies the rest of the sentence.)

Using Clauses

A **clause** is a group of related words that has both a subject and a predicate.

744.1 Independent and Dependent Clauses

An **independent clause** presents a complete thought and can stand alone as a sentence; a **dependent clause** (also called a *subordinate clause*) does not present a complete thought and cannot stand alone as a sentence.

> Sparrows make nests in cattle barns (independent clause) so that they can stay warm during the winter (dependent clause).

744.2 Types of Dependent Clauses

There are three basic types of dependent clauses: *adverb, noun,* and *adjective.*

■ An **adverb clause** is used like an adverb to modify a verb, an adjective, or an adverb. Adverb clauses begin with a subordinating conjunction. (See **734.3**.)

> If I study hard, I will pass this test. (The adverb clause modifies the verb *will pass*.)

■ A **noun clause** is used in place of a noun.

> However, the teacher said that the essay questions are based only on the last two chapters. (The noun clause functions as a direct object.)

■ An **adjective clause** modifies a noun or a pronoun.

> Tomorrow's test, which covers the entire book, is half essay and half short answers. (The adjective clause modifies the noun *test*.)

Constructing Sentences 4

■ Dependent Clauses

Write the first word of each dependent clause found in each sentence below, and then write its type: *adverb, adjective,* or *noun clause*. Note that some sentences have more than one dependent clause.

Example: Our language technically began when the Germanic tribes of Angles, Saxons, and Jutes began populating England around 400–500 C.E.

when—adverb clause

1. Their West Germanic dialects developed into a language that they could all understand.

2. When the Vikings invaded around 850 C.E., they added their North Germanic dialects to the mix that became known as Old English.

3. Middle English is generally dated back to the 1066 Norman invasion of England, which ended Anglo-Saxon rule there.

4. The Normans spoke a Germanic language that had been influenced by the Roman occupation and included Latin roots.

5. That modern English began around the time of Shakespeare shows his strong influence on the language; he added some 2,000 words to it.

6. As technology has grown, so has our language.

7. Most changes that have occurred since Shakespeare's time consist of the addition of names for things that did not exist when the language was new.

Model

Model the following sentences to practice using noun clauses effectively.

> I've found students shocked to learn that it can take me three years to finish a poem.
>
> —Carolyn Forche

> Suburbia is where the developer bulldozes out the trees and then names the streets after them.
>
> —Bill Vaughan

Sentences

Using Sentence Variety

A **sentence** may be classified according to the type of statement it makes, the way it is constructed, and its arrangement of words.

746.1 Kinds of Statements

Sentences can make five basic kinds of statements: *declarative, interrogative, imperative, exclamatory,* or *conditional.*

- **Declarative sentences** make statements. They tell us something about a person, a place, a thing, or an idea.

  The Statue of Liberty stands in New York Harbor.

  For over a century, it has greeted immigrants and visitors to America.

- **Interrogative sentences** ask questions.

  Did you know that the Statue of Liberty is made of copper and stands over 150 feet tall?

  Are we allowed to climb all the way to the top?

- **Imperative sentences** make commands. They often contain an understood subject *(you)* as in the examples below.

  Go see the Statue of Liberty.

  After a few weeks of physical conditioning, climb its 168 stairs.

- **Exclamatory sentences** communicate strong emotion or surprise.

  Climbing 168 stairs is not a dumb idea!

  Just muster some of that old pioneering spirit, that desire to try something new, that never-say-die attitude that made America great!

- **Conditional sentences** express wishes ("if . . . then" statements) or conditions contrary to fact.

  If I could design a country's flag, then I would use six colors behind a sun, a star, and a moon.

  I would feel as if I were representing many cultures in my design.

Kinds of Statements

■ **Sentence Variety**

 Write the kind of statement each sentence makes: declarative, interrogative, imperative, exclamatory, or conditional.

Example: Take a good look at your body.
            imperative

1. Did you know that you had 350 bones in your body when you were born?

2. Now 144 of them have fused together.

3. Your hands and feet contain more than half the bones in your body.

4. If your stomach did not produce a new lining every three days, it would digest itself in its own acid.

5. Over your lifetime, you will drink more than 16,000 gallons of water!

6. Has your brain stopped growing yet?

7. Most people's brains stop growing after the age of 15.

8. Move your little finger.

9. Your nervous system transmitted the messages enabling you to do that—at 180 miles per hour!

10. If your small intestine were not looped and folded inside you, it wouldn't fit in the abdomen.

11. It averages about 20 feet long.

 ## Model

Model the following exclamatory sentences.

> **What a blessing it would be if we could open and shut our ears as easily as we open and shut our eyes!**
> —Georg Christoph Lichtenberg

> **When I'm asked how to write, I answer—"Tell me a story!"**
> —Anne McCaffrey

Sentences

748.1 Types of Sentence Constructions

A sentence may be *simple, compound, complex,* or *compound-complex.* It all depends on the relationship between independent and dependent clauses.

- A **simple sentence** can have a single subject or a compound subject. It can have a single predicate or a compound predicate. However, a simple sentence has only one independent clause, and it has no dependent clauses.

  > **My** back aches.
  > (single subject; single predicate)
  > **My teeth and my** eyes hurt.
  > (compound subject; single predicate)
  > **My** throat and nose feel **sore and** look **red.**
  > (compound subject; compound predicate)
  > I must have caught the flu **from the sick kids in class.**
  > (independent clause with two phrases: *from the sick kids* and *in class*)

- A **compound sentence** consists of two independent clauses. The clauses must be joined by a comma and a coordinating conjunction or by a semicolon.

  > I usually don't mind missing school, but this is not fun.
  > I feel too sick to watch TV; I feel too sick to eat.

  NOTE: The comma can be omitted when the clauses are very short.
  > I wept and I wept.

- A **complex sentence** contains one independent clause (in black) and one or more dependent clauses (in red).

  > When I get back to school, I'm actually going to appreciate it.
  > (dependent clause; independent clause)
  > I won't even complain about math class, although I might be talking out of my head because I'm feverish.
  > (independent clause; two dependent clauses)

- A **compound-complex sentence** contains two or more independent clauses (in black) and one or more dependent clauses (in red).

  > Yes, I have a bad flu, and because I need to get well soon,
  > I won't think about school just yet.
  > (two independent clauses; one dependent clause)

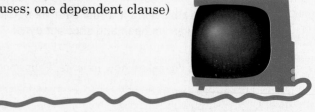

Types of Sentence Constructions

■ **Types of Sentences**

Identify each of the following sentences as a *simple, compound, complex,* or *compound-complex* sentence.

Example: How often do you grab a clear plastic bottle of water when you need a drink?

complex

1. If you are like the average U.S. citizen, you drink 61 liters of bottled water each year—and you pay more than 200 times the amount that you pay for a gallon of tap water.

2. You're paying for the convenience, not the safety.

3. Although there are federal standards for the safety of bottled water, rules for city tap water are stricter.

4. In addition, the standards do not even apply to bottled water that is not distributed across state lines.

5. State laws require little or no testing for impurities in bottled water.

6. Most city water is chlorinated to kill organisms, but bottlers seldom add it due to its taste.

7. Labels often do not indicate the source of the water; sometimes it is actually just bottled tap water.

8. Perhaps the bottler has added vitamins, herbs, flavoring, or sweeteners to the water to make it more appealing.

9. To be careful with your health, you may want to choose tap water over bottled, which would also save you money; and that's always a good thing.

Model

Model the following sentences to practice forming compound and complex sentences.

I slept, and dreamed that life was Beauty; I woke, and found that life was Duty.
—Ellen Sturgis Hooper

If fifty million people say a foolish thing, it is still a foolish thing.
—Anatole France

Sentences

750.1 Arrangements of Sentences

Depending on the arrangement of the words and the placement of emphasis, a sentence may also be classified as *loose, balanced, periodic,* or *cumulative.*

- A **loose sentence** expresses the main thought near the beginning and adds explanatory material as needed.

  > We hauled out the boxes of food and set up the camp stove, **all the time battling the hot wind that would not stop, even when we screamed into the sky.**

  > Memory performs the impossible for man—**holds together past and present, gives continuity and dignity to human life.**
  >
  > —Mark Van Doren, *Liberal Education*

- A **balanced sentence** is constructed so that it emphasizes a similarity or a contrast between two or more of its parts (words, phrases, or clauses).

  > **The wind in our ears** drove us crazy **and** pushed us on.
  > (The similar wording emphasizes the main idea in this sentence.)

  > **Experience is not** what happens to you; **it is what you do with** what happens to you.
  >
  > —Aldous Huxley

- A **periodic sentence** is one that postpones the crucial or most surprising idea until the end.

  > **Following my mother's repeated threats to ground me for life,** I decided it was time to propose a compromise.

  > **There is only one way to achieve happiness on this terrestrial ball—**and that is to have either a clear conscience or no conscience at all.
  >
  > —Ogden Nash, *I'm a Stranger Here Myself*

- A **cumulative sentence** places the general idea in the middle of the sentence with modifying clauses and phrases coming before and after.

  > **With careful thought and extra attention to detail,** I wrote out my plan for being a model teenager, **a teen who cared about neatness and reliability.**

  > **Not too long ago,** architects who planned college classrooms and dormitories were advised against making the furnishings too pleasant or comfortable **lest the students become distracted or fall asleep.**
  >
  > —Robert Sommer, "Hard Architecture"

Arrangements of Sentences

■ **Sentence Arrangements**

 Classify each of the following sentences as *loose, balanced, periodic,* or *cumulative.*

Example: Arturo is a good singer but not an exceptional one.
> *balanced*

1. Going through the motions of an audition for each school play, he usually got a starring role.

2. Until last spring, anyway, that was the case.

3. A new student auditioned—one who could sing quite well.

4. With unusual modesty, Victor belted out his own rendition of "If I Were a Rich Man," the same song that Arturo was going to use.

5. The drama teacher was impressed; Arturo was upset.

6. At that point, Arturo decided to sing a different song for his audition.

7. He remembered well a particular song from a play the school had presented two years ago.

8. Despite the blow to his self-esteem, Arturo did a credible job.

9. As it turned out, neither Arturo nor Victor got the lead role because it required someone who could dance like Fred Astaire.

 ## Model

Model the following balanced sentences.

> **Be sincere; be brief; be seated.**
>
> —Franklin D. Roosevelt

> **Men are mortal, but ideas are immortal.**
>
> —William Lippmann

Sentences

Getting Sentence Parts to Agree

Agreement of Subject and Verb

A verb must agree in number (singular or plural) with its subject.

> The student was proud of her quarter grades.

NOTE: Do not be confused by words that come between the subject and verb.

> The manager, as well as the players, is required to display good sportsmanship. (*Manager*, not *players*, is the subject.)

752.1 Compound Subjects

Compound subjects joined by *or* or *nor* take a singular verb.

> Neither Bev nor Kendra is going to the street dance.

NOTE: When one of the subjects joined by *or* or *nor* is singular and one is plural, the verb must agree with the subject nearer the verb.

> Neither Yoshi nor his friends are singing in the band anymore. (The plural subject *friends* is nearer the verb, so the plural verb *are* is correct.)

Compound subjects connected with *and* require a plural verb.

> Strength and balance are necessary for gymnastics.

752.2 Delayed Subjects

Delayed subjects occur when the verb comes before the subject in a sentence. In these inverted sentences, the delayed subject must agree with the verb.

> There are many hardworking students in our schools.
> There is present among many young people today a will to succeed.
> (*Students* and *will* are the true subjects of these sentences, not *there*.)

752.3 "Be" Verbs

When a sentence contains a form of the "be" verb—and a noun comes before and after that verb—the verb must agree with the subject, not the *complement* (the noun coming after the verb).

> The cause of his problem was the bad brakes.
> The bad brakes were the cause of his problem.

752.4 Special Cases

Some nouns that are **plural in form but singular in meaning** take a singular verb: *mumps, measles, news, mathematics, economics, gallows, shambles.*

> Measles is still considered a serious disease in many parts of the world.

Some nouns that are plural in form but singular in meaning take a plural verb: *scissors, trousers, tidings.*

> The scissors are missing again.

Agreement of Subject and Verb 1

■ **Subject-Verb Agreement**

For each sentence, write the correct verb from the choice given in parentheses.

Example: Marlon and his brothers *(plays, play)* instruments in the marching band.

play

1. The name of their school's team *(is, are)* the Bulldogs.

2. Tia or Eve *(works, work)* in the office a few hours a week.

3. Every morning in the school parking lot, there *(is, are)* seagulls looking for food.

4. Mahender thinks that most news *(is, are)* biased.

5. Neither the nectarines nor the watermelon *(is, are)* on sale this week.

6. All of the monkeys, in addition to the puma, *(was, were)* unusually noisy at the zoo today.

7. My pants *(has, have)* a big hole in the knee.

8. The ankle weights *(was, were)* the perfect gift for Marc.

9. Dad or my little sisters *(chooses, choose)* the bedtime book each night.

Model

Model the following sentences to practice subject-verb agreement.

Canada is a country whose main exports are hockey and cold fronts. Our main imports are baseball players and acid rain.
—Pierre Trudeau

The future belongs to those who believe in the beauty of their dreams.
—Eleanor Roosevelt

Sentences

Agreement of Subject and Verb *(continued)*

754.1 Collective Nouns

Collective nouns *(faculty, committee, team, congress, species, crowd, army, pair, squad)* take a singular verb when they refer to a group as a unit; collective nouns take a plural verb when they refer to the individuals within the group.

The favored team is losing, and the crowd is getting ugly. (Both *team* and *crowd* are considered units in this sentence, requiring the singular verb *is*.)

The pair were finally reunited after 20 years apart.

(Here, *pair* refers to two individuals, so the plural verb *were* is required.)

754.2 Indefinite Pronouns

Some **indefinite pronouns** are singular: *each, either, neither, one, everybody, another, anybody, everyone, nobody, everything, somebody,* and *someone.* They require a singular verb.

Everybody is invited to the cafeteria for refreshments.

Some **indefinite pronouns** are plural: *both, few, many,* and *several.*

Several like chocolate cake. Many ask for ice cream, too.

NOTE: Do not be confused by words or phrases that come between the indefinite pronoun and the verb.

One of the participants is (not *are*) going to have to stay late to clean up.

A Closer Look

Some **indefinite pronouns** can be either singular or plural: *all, any, most, none,* and *some.* These pronouns are singular if the number of the noun in the prepositional phrase is singular; they are plural if the noun is plural.

Most of the food complaints are coming from the seniors.
(*Complaints* is plural, so *most* is plural.)

Most of the tabletop is sticky with melted ice cream.
(*Tabletop* is singular, so *most* is singular.)

754.3 Relative Pronouns

When a **relative pronoun** *(who, which, that)* is used as the subject of a clause, the number of the verb is determined by the antecedent of the pronoun. (The antecedent is the word to which the pronoun refers.)

This is one of the books that are required for geography class.
(The relative pronoun *that* requires the plural verb *are* because its antecedent, *books,* is plural.)

NOTE: To test this type of sentence for agreement, read the "of" phrase first.

Of the books that are required for geography class, this is one.

Agreement of Subject and Verb 2

■ Subject-Verb Agreement

 For each underlined verb, state the reason it does not agree with its subject.

Example: 1. <u>Are</u> is plural, and its subject, <u>one</u>, is singular.

One of the themes Shakespeare presents in the play Romeo and Juliet <u>are</u> that the stars (representing fate) determine a person's life. During Shakespeare's time, people commonly believed that all of life <u>were</u> governed by the stars. The play carries this theme throughout, with frequent references to heavenly bodies.

In the play's prologue, the couple <u>is</u> referred to as "star-crossed lovers" whose lives are set by the fates. When Romeo thinks that Juliet is dead, he cries out, "I defy you, stars!" He is indicating that anyone who <u>use</u> free will can determine his own fate. Just before he kills himself, he comments that by dying he will "shake the yoke of inauspicious stars." He is suggesting that nobody <u>lose</u> the hold fate has on him or her until death.

Fate controlling us, represented by the skies, is one of the ideas that <u>is</u> present throughout Romeo and Juliet. From beginning to end, the lovers are doomed, yet everyone <u>continue</u> to love the story because it is as beautiful as the stars.

Model

Model the following sentences to practice subject-verb agreement with indefinite pronouns.

Everybody likes a kidder, but nobody lends him money.
—Arthur Miller

To create one's own world in any of the arts takes courage.
—Georgia O'Keeffe

Sentences

Agreement of Pronoun and Antecedent

A pronoun must agree in number, person, and gender with its *antecedent*. (The *antecedent* is the word to which the pronoun refers.)

> **Cal brought his gerbil to school.** (The antecedent of *his* is *Cal*. Both the pronoun and its antecedent are singular, third person, and masculine; therefore, the pronoun is said to "agree" with its antecedent.)

756.1 Agreement in Number

Use a **singular pronoun** to refer to such antecedents as *each, either, neither, one, anyone, anybody, everyone, everybody, somebody, another, nobody,* and *a person*.

> **Neither of the brothers likes his (not their) room.**

Two or more singular antecedents joined by *or* or *nor* are also referred to by a **singular pronoun.**

> **Either Connie or Sue left her headset in the library.**

If one of the antecedents joined by *or* or *nor* is singular and one is plural, the pronoun should agree with the nearer antecedent.

> **Neither the manager nor the players were crazy about their new uniforms.**

Use a **plural pronoun** to refer to plural antecedents as well as compound subjects joined by *and*.

> **Jared and Carlos are finishing their assignments.**

756.2 Agreement in Gender

Use a **masculine** or **feminine pronoun** depending upon the gender of the antecedent.

> **Is either Connor or Grace bringing her or his baseball glove?**

When *a person* or *everyone* is used to refer to both sexes or either sex, you will have to choose whether to offer optional pronouns or rewrite the sentence.

> **A person should be allowed to choose her or his own footwear.**
> (optional pronouns)
> **People should be allowed to choose their own footwear.**
> (rewritten in plural form)

Agreement of Pronoun and Antecedent

- **Pronoun-Antecedent Agreement**

 For each sentence below, first write the antecedent of the pronoun that appears later in the sentence. Then replace the incorrect pronoun with one that agrees with the antecedent. If the pronoun is correct as is, write "C."

Example: Should a driver always know the basic things about maintaining her car?
driver, his or her

1. Everyone should at least know how to take a flat tire off and put their spare tire on.

2. Neither Lasandra nor Renee knows how to change the oil in their car.

3. Phillip and Benito, on the other hand, know a lot about his cars.

4. Both of them work at tricking out their rides.

5. Benito or Phillip works at their brother's garage.

6. The mechanic or the lube techs were eating his lunch in the break room.

7. One of the lube techs was trying to clean their fingernails.

8. Lasandra's brakes were squealing, so a mechanic checked it for excessive wear.

9. The mechanic said that Lasandra was probably riding her brakes too much.

 ## Model

Model the following sentences to practice making a pronoun and its antecedent agree.

> Some people have so much respect for their superiors that they have none left for themselves.
>
> —Peter McArthur

> Never judge a book by its movie.
>
> —J. W. Eagan

Sentences

Test Prep

Read the following paragraphs. Write the letter of the best answer or answers for each underlined part from the choices given on the next page.

    Strong women have always helped make the United States great. Three <u>who made life better for women</u> were Elizabeth Cady Stanton, Susan B. Anthony, and Jane Addams.
1

    <u>The American Revolution began with the Boston Tea Party, and the women's rights movement began with a tea party of its own.</u> <u>Elizabeth Cady Stanton and four women friends</u> met for tea one day in 1848. They
2 **3**
discussed the importance of women gaining rights equal to men. This innocent tea party <u>led</u> to the formation of the Seneca Falls Convention. <u>Its
4 **5**
members drew up a declaration of women's rights that would serve as the foundation for the women's rights movement.</u>

    Susan B. Anthony's "radical" ideas included <u>paying women and men equally.</u> She also campaigned for women <u>to receive the same civil and
6 **7**
political rights</u> that African American males had. The <u>adoption</u> of the
8
nineteenth amendment, which gave women the right to vote, came about largely due to her efforts.

    <u>Jane Addams,</u> a tireless reformer, left a trail of accomplishments
9
<u>matched by few.</u> She founded Hull-House in Chicago, <u>a "settlement" house
10 **11**
that attracted well-educated people to poor areas.</u> Hull-House <u>provided services such as day care, libraries, an employment office, music and art
12
classes, and a little theater for the immigrants pouring into the country.</u> Addams pushed legislators for child labor laws and laws on education. <u>For these and other efforts, she was awarded the Nobel Peace Prize in 1931.</u>
13

The efforts of these three strong women—and many others like them—have advanced equal rights. <u>Although there is still much to do,</u>
14
American women <u>have made</u> great strides toward equality in the eyes of
15
men, the law, and the world.

1. **A** independent clause
    B dependent clause
    C verbal phrase
    D appositive phrase

2. **A** simple sentence
    B compound sentence
    C complex sentence
    D dependent clause

3. **A** complete predicate
    B simple predicate
    C simple subject
    D complete subject

4. **A** complete predicate
    B simple predicate
    C simple subject
    D complete subject

5. **A** simple sentence
    B compound sentence
    C complex sentence
    D dependent clause

6. **A** gerund phrase
    B infinitive phrase
    C participial phrase
    D appositive phrase

7. **A** gerund phrase
    B infinitive phrase
    C participial phrase
    D appositive phrase

8. **A** complete predicate
    B simple predicate
    C simple subject
    D complete subject

9. **A** complete predicate
    B simple predicate
    C simple subject
    D complete subject

10. **A** gerund phrase
    B infinitive phrase
    C participial phrase
    D appositive phrase

11. **A** gerund phrase
    B infinitive phrase
    C participial phrase
    D appositive phrase

12. **A** complete predicate
    B simple predicate
    C simple subject
    D complete subject

13. **A** simple sentence
    B compound sentence
    C complex sentence
    D dependent clause

14. **A** independent clause
    B dependent clause
    C verbal phrase
    D appositive phrase

15. **A** complete predicate
    B simple predicate
    C simple subject
    D complete subject

Sentences

Diagramming Sentences

A **graphic diagram** of a sentence is a picture of how the words in that sentence are related and how they fit together to form a complete thought.

760.1 Simple Sentence with One Subject and One Verb

Chris fishes.

Chris | fishes   subject | verb

760.2 Simple Sentence with a Predicate Adjective

Fish are delicious.

Fish | are \ delicious   subject | verb \ predicate adjective

760.3 Simple Sentence with a Predicate Noun and Adjectives

Fishing is my favorite hobby.

Fishing | is \ hobby   subject | verb \ predicate noun
my *favorite*   *adjective* *adjective*

NOTE: When possessive pronouns (*my, his, their,* etc.) are used as adjectives, they are placed on a diagonal line under the word they modify.

760.4 Simple Sentence with an Indirect and Direct Object

My grandpa gave us a trout.

grandpa | gave | trout   subject | verb | direct object
my   *us*   *a*   *adjective* *indirect object* *adjective*

NOTE: Articles (*a, an, the*) are adjectives and are placed on a diagonal line under the word they modify.

Sentence Diagramming 1

■ **Diagramming Sentences**

Diagram the following sentences.

Example: Jogging is a healthy activity.

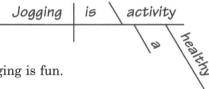

1. Jogging is fun.

2. Amanda jogs.

3. Thad's mom offered me a ride.

4. I gave her my new address.

5. Woodworking combines two different talents.

6. One is carpentry.

7. Jorge built a beautiful cabinet.

8. Ronald lent me his blue jacket.

9. His other jacket was dirty.

Sentences

Model

Model the following sentences to practice writing simple sentences with either a predicate noun or a predicate adjective.

The great omission in American life is solitude.

—Marya Mannes

People with courage and character always seem sinister to the rest.

—Hermann Hesse

Diagramming Sentences *(continued)*

762.1 Simple Sentence with a Prepositional Phrase

I like fishing by myself.

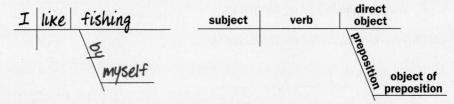

762.2 Simple Sentence with a Compound Subject and Verb

The team and fans clapped and cheered.

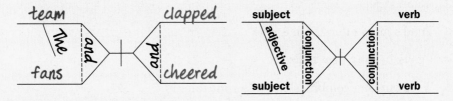

762.3 Compound Sentence

The team scored, and the crowd cheered wildly.

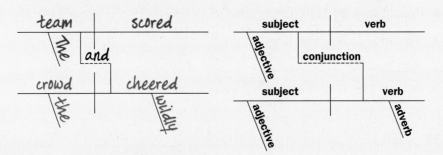

762.4 Complex Sentence with a Subordinate Clause

Before Erin scored, the crowd sat quietly.

Sentence Diagramming 2

■ **Diagramming Sentences**

Diagram the following sentences.

Example: The Rands enjoy rides in a hot-air balloon.

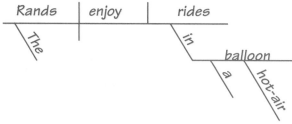

1. Kelli and Maria giggled and whispered.

2. The music started, but we could not stay for the dance.

3. As the ship pulled away, the passengers waved.

4. The cat disappeared into the night.

5. Grandpa shouted, and my brother stopped immediately.

6. I prefer bicycling on forest trails.

7. Although we rushed, we missed the bus.

Model

Model the following sentences to practice writing compound and complex sentences.

Don't become a mere recorder of facts, but try to penetrate the mystery of their origin.

—Isabel Allende

I used to think the phrase "burst into the room" was only for detective fiction until my son got his growth.

—Garrison Keillor, "Something from the Sixties"

Sentences

Credits

Page:

Page 353: Copyright © 2004 by Houghton Mifflin Company. Adapted and reproduced by permission from *The American Heritage College Dictionary*, Fourth Edition.

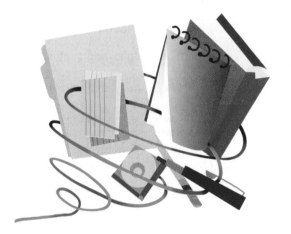

Photos:

Getty Images:
pages 81, 340 (jester)

www.jupiterimages.com:
pages 334, 338, 339, 340, 341

Acknowledgements

We're grateful to many people who helped bring *Write Source* to life. First, we must thank all the teachers and their students from across the country who contributed writing models and ideas.

In addition, we want to thank our Write Source/Great Source team for all their help:

Steven J. Augustyn, Laura Bachman, Ron Bachman, April Barrons, William Baughn, Heather Bazata, Colleen Belmont, Susan Boehm, Evelyn Curley, Chris Erickson, Mark Fairweather, Jean Fischer, Hillary Gammons, Mariellen Hanrahan, Tammy Hintz, Mary Anne Hoff, Judy Kerkhoff, Rob King, Lois Krenzke, Mark Lalumondier, Joyce Becker Lee, Ellen Leitheusser, Michele Order Litant, Dian Lynch, Colleen McCarthy, Pat Moore, Kevin Nelson, Doug Niles, Sue Paro, Linda Presto, Betsy Rassmussen, Pat Reigel, Jason C. Reynolds, Christine Rieker, Susan Rogalski, Steve Schend, Janae Sebranek, Lester Smith, Richard Spencer, Kathy Strom, Stephen D. Sullivan, Jean Varley, and Claire Ziffer.

Index

The index will help you find specific information in the handbook. Entries in italics are words from the "Using the Right Word" section. The colored boxes contain information you will use often.